Basic Bankruptcy Law for Paralegals

Basic Bankruptcy Law for Paralegals

Sixth Edition

David L. Buchbinder

Member, California, Pennsylvania,
and New Jersey Bars

ASPEN
PUBLISHERS

111 Eighth Avenue, New York, NY 10011
www.aspenpublishers.com

a Wolters Kluwer business
www.aspenpublishers.com

Printed in the United States of America.

1 2 3 4 5 6 7 8 9 0

ISBN 0-7355-5753-5

Library of Congress Cataloging-in-Publication Data

Buchbinder, David L.
Basic bankruptcy law for paralegals / David L. Buchbinder.—6th ed.
p. cm.
Includes index.
ISBN 0-7355-5753-5 (pbk. : alk. paper) 1. Bankruptcy—United States. 2. Legal assistants—United States—Handbooks, manuals, etc. I. Title.
KF1524.3.B758 2006
346.7307'8—dc22

2005030366

ISBN 0-536-34168-0

2006340076

EM/DS

This special edition published in cooperation with Pearson Custom Publishing.

About Aspen Publishers

Aspen Publishers, headquartered in New York City, is a leading information provider for attorneys, business professionals, and law students. Written by preeminent authorities, our products consist of analytical and practical information covering both U.S. and international topics. We publish in the full range of formats, including updated manuals, books, periodicals, CDs, and online products.

Our proprietary content is complemented by 2,500 legal databases, containing over 11 million documents, available through our Loislaw division. Aspen Publishers also offers a wide range of topical legal and business databases linked to Loislaw's primary material. Our mission is to provide accurate, timely, and authoritative content in easily accessible formats, supported by unmatched customer care.

To order any Aspen Publishers title, go to *www.aspenpublishers.com* or call 1-800-638-8437.

To reinstate your manual update service, call 1-800-638-8437.

For more information on Loislaw products, go to *www.loislaw.com* or call 1-800-364-2512.

For Customer Care issues, e-mail *CustomerCare@aspenpublishers.com;* call 1-800-234-1660; or fax 1-800-901-9075.

Aspen Publishers
a Wolters Kluwer business

To my beloved father, Ralph

Summary of Contents

Contents

Preface

This book has evolved from a need to develop a nuts-and-bolts description of the bankruptcy system written to be understood by nonlawyers.

My primary intent has been to design this text as a basic primer for legal assistants or paralegal students to help them grasp the practical aspects of representing debtors or creditors within the bankruptcy system. To meet this challenge, I have explained practice and theory together in as concise a format as possible. I have chosen this approach because practice is almost always dictated by the underlying theory, and it is easier to learn a practice when one has been provided with the basic theory behind it.

In the succeeding editions I have listened to the many thoughtful comments of paralegal instructors and students from all over the country, some of whom have gone to exceptional effort to hunt me down, to enhance the practical nature of the text, and to further simplify the subtleties and nuances of the Bankruptcy Code and system. Each new edition updates and revises the text to keep abreast of all statutory, case law, and rule changes that regularly take place.

Paralegals are invaluable in the bankruptcy system. Under proper legal supervision, paralegals can efficiently perform various tasks for clients at a substantial savings. Because much of bankruptcy practice is routine, presenting these routines and the reasons for them will help a paralegal be properly prepared to assist in a debtor or creditor bankruptcy practice. The introduction describes the role of paralegals in the bankruptcy system. The student should read the introduction twice, once at the beginning of the course and again at the end. In this way, the material will act as both an introduction and final review of the course.

It has not been my intent to analyze the complex subtleties of the Bankruptcy Code and its attendant case law interpretation, but rather to describe the routine events that occur in all bankruptcy proceedings, events that normally occur without dispute or litigation. These events account for a majority of bankruptcy practice, much of which is not problematic. Thus, law students and nonbankruptcy attorneys may also find this text a useful reference tool for finding the answers to common bankruptcy questions.

For example, by reading chapter 5 of the text, the forms accompanying chapter 5 in the forms manual, and appendix 1, any student or practitioner can quickly learn the basic principles of providing notices to creditors or parties in interest in bankruptcy proceedings, learn about the documents and timing involved, and receive some guidance as to the existence of applicable local rules in a given district.

My philosophical goal in undertaking this work has been to describe the Bankruptcy Code as a comprehensive system of debtor relief and debt collection, as well as the organization and practical functioning of this system. I am honored to have been given the opportunity to evolve the original work from the laboratory of actual use.

Upon completing this undertaking I have reached the inescapable conclusion that the Bankruptcy Code exists first and foremost as a tool of debt collection and not of debtor relief. Conversely, the debtor relief afforded by the Bankruptcy Code has been among the most liberal such relief ever provided in the evolution of bankruptcy laws in Western civilization. The 2005 legislation will be perceived by many to restrict debtor relief while enhancing the debt collection aspects of the Code.

This book has also been prepared with the secondary purpose of aiding creditor representatives in understanding how the bankruptcy system may be properly utilized as a debt collection device to increase overall recovery rates.

Finally, I am optimistic that having described the Bankruptcy Code in this manner I may aid, however slightly, in enhancing the efficiency of the system.

David L. Buchbinder

October 2005

Acknowledgments

Acknowledgments to the First Edition

In early 1987, my associate Lauren Austin made a wild suggestion that I taperecord my legal-assistant bankruptcy course at the University of San Diego and then transform the spoken word into a written text. After some thought, I decided to give it a whirl. My legal assistant at the time, Vicki Johnson, assisted me in the recording of my class during the spring of 1987.

Some 3,000 hours, 28 months, and five drafts later I take pleasure in gratefully acknowledging the encouragement and assistance of the many people who have aided me in this project.

My loyal long-distance typist, Joan Jackson, has been invaluable from the beginning of this project. She has been ably assisted by Lynn Williamson, Julie Rasmussen, and Mary Lou Staight, particularly in connection with the final manuscript draft. Numerous members of my staff have offered aid and sustenance with the footnotes and citation checking. Among them are Flora Calem, Beth Sandler, Adam Nach, and my friend and colleague, Mark R. Nims. Mr. Nims's comments were particularly instructive in helping me prepare a teacher's manual to accompany the text.

Susan Sullivan of the University of San Diego Legal Assistant Program has been a positive and encouraging force throughout. Indeed, but for her giving me an initial opportunity to teach, this book would never have been written.

Many of my colleagues, too numerous to mention individually, have also offered helpful advice and suggestions. I would particularly like to thank Kathryn Infante and Ted Simmons, Estate Administrators for the United States Bankruptcy Court for the Southern District of California, for their assistance. Ms. Infante provided me with the address of every Bankruptcy Court in the United States so the data resulting in the appendices could be obtained. Mr. Simmons regularly provided me with the statistical data contained in the footnotes regarding the numbers of annual bankruptcy filings nationwide. Mr. Larry Ramey of the United States Trustee Office provided me with this data for 1988.

The appendices turned out to be a project within a project. Ms. Austin rendered services above and beyond the call of duty in obtaining local rules from throughout the United States. Then she prepared preliminary tables from her own review of every set of rules. The effort involved has been considerable and the appendices would likely not exist but for her important contributions. Judge Keith M. Lundin of the Middle District of Tennessee gave me considerable encouragement when he caused an early draft of chapter 1, A Short History of Bankruptcy, to be published in the November 1988 issue of the Norton Bankruptcy Advisor.

The editorial staff at Little, Brown and Company has been most pleasant to work with. Richard Heuser, Elizabeth Kenny, Cathryn Capra, and Alistair Nevius have ably guided me through the actual publication preparation and process.

Finally, my thanks and love to my wife Deborah and my son Rafe for tolerating the many evening and weekend hours that have been devoted to this book

Acknowledgments to the Second, Third, Fourth, and Fifth Editions

I would like to thank those whose continuing support and encouragement have helped me bring to fruition the subsequent editions of Practical Guide, now known as Basic Bankruptcy Law for Paralegals.

Lynn Williamson, Julie Rasmussen, and Catherine Forrest provided many skillful services in the manuscript preparation and updating of the appendices for the second edition. Kristen DiPaolo was invaluable in helping me redraft the tutorial for the third edition.

Carolyn O'Sullivan, Betsy Kenny, Carol McGeehan, Jessica Barmack, Anne Starr, and Pat Wakeley of Little, Brown and Company have always been a pleasure to work with.

For the fourth edition, I would like to thank Betsy Kenny for her continuing supervision, and Curt Berkowitz and Barbara Rappaport for their time and care in bringing this edition to press on an expedited basis.

For the fifth edition, I have continued to be ably supervised by Betsy Kenny, Cathi Reinfelder, and Elsie Starbecker in the production process. I have also received invaluable editorial assistance from my wonderful friends Kathleen A. Cashman-Kramer, Mark Gallagher, and William Hanafee III.

I am also grateful for the many constructive comments from instructors and students throughout the country who have kindly taken time to provide me with their thoughts on improving the text. I have made my best efforts to incorporate your suggestions into these latter editions.

Finally, my thanks and love to Deborah and Rafe for their continuing patience for the time it takes to keep these materials up to date.

Acknowledgments to the Sixth Edition

The sixth edition has been daunting. Hard on the heels of the publication of the fifth edition in November 2004, Congress passed the Bankruptcy Abuse Prevention and Consumer Protection Act of 2005, the most radical and sweeping modifications to the Bankruptcy Code since its adoption in 1978. This has required the most thorough revision of this text in record time. I have been most ably assisted in this process through these many months by Betsy Kenny. In the final production, I have been further ably assisted in this rush process by Carmen Corral-Reid. Kathleen A. Cashman-Kramer provided invaluable editorial assistance and support throughout. Finally, my thanks and love to Rafe for putting up with me.

Basic Bankruptcy Law for Paralegals

Introduction

Paralegals and the Bankruptcy System

The use of paralegals to assist counsel engaged in bankruptcy practice has grown commensurate with the growth and acceptance of paralegals within the legal system in general. As in other areas of legal practice, bankruptcy paralegals can provide competent assistance to counsel in the areas of legal research, document preparation, fact investigation, and litigation support.

The Bankruptcy Courts that have examined the use of paralegals in bankruptcy practice overwhelmingly favor the concept. Many basic services can be provided to clients at a substantial cost savings because of the low hourly billing rates of paralegals compared to associate or partner attorneys. The services of paralegals can normally be compensated for under the bankruptcy system's fee application process described in chapter 7 infra. The Bankruptcy Courts' view of paralegal activity is best summed up in the following quotation:

> In effect, the goal of the paralegal is to perform a supervised legal function for a client at considerably less expense to the client. The concept is an efficient idea in today's legal market where attorney costs are escalating beyond the approach of clients in need of legal assistance.[1]

This is not to suggest, however, that a paralegal may operate independently of counsel in providing bankruptcy-related services to clients. The Bankruptcy Courts examining this issue have invariably and correctly found such independent activities to constitute the unauthorized practice of law.[2] In many states the unauthorized practice of law can be prosecuted as a misdemeanor. The paralegal must always tread cautiously in the face of clients who will invariably seek to pressure the paralegal to provide legal advice.

This text focuses on the theory, practice, and substantive law used by any member of the legal profession engaged in activity within the bankruptcy system, emphasizing the perspective of a paralegal working under the

1. In re Bonds Lucky Foods, Inc., No. 1, 76 Bankr. 664, 671 (E.D. Ark. 1986).
2. Geibank Indus. Bank v. Martin, 97 Bankr. 1013 (N.D. Ga. 1989). See chapters 7 and 9 infra.

supervision of counsel. This introduction will clarify the role and most useful functions that paralegals can provide to counsel in bankruptcy practice. The author suggests that students read this introduction at the beginning and end of the course. The second reading will act as a concise review of the course.

A. ROLE OF THE PARALEGAL

The role of paralegals in bankruptcy practice is similar to that of paralegals in other areas of legal practice. Research assistance, document preparation, and litigation support comprise the core of activity performed by paralegals in bankruptcy practice.

In the area of legal research, paralegals will be required to research specific legal issues based on counsel's factual analysis of a matter. The research activity may be as simple as verifying the existence and amount of a particular exemption, as described in chapter 9 of this text, or the research assignment may involve complex issues of adequate protection in relief from stay motions or cramdown issues in Chapter 11 proceedings as described, respectively, in chapters 12 and 26 of this text. Exemptions are items of property that individual debtors may keep after filing bankruptcy. Relief from stay motions typically concern an effort by a secured creditor to repossess or foreclose the debtor's property, such as a car or a home. Cramdown issues concern a reorganizing debtor's efforts to obtain court approval of a repayment plan over the objection of dissenting creditors. All of these issues are critical to the rights of debtors and creditors in bankruptcy proceedings. Paralegals can participate in many aspects of these activities. The course will illustrate and amplify these activities. Nonetheless, regardless of the simplicity or complexity of a research assignment, the basic research methodology presented in chapter 30 will allow many issues to be competently researched in minimal time.

In the area of document preparation, paralegals aiding in bankruptcy practice will often provide substantial assistance to counsel in preparing Statements and Schedules for a debtor or proofs of claim for a creditor. In these two areas, bankruptcy paralegals will likely render a majority of their services. Chapter 29 of this text is devoted solely as a tutorial for the preparation of a debtor's schedules.

In smaller firms paralegals may also be asked to prepare preliminary drafts of motions for relief from stay (see chapter 12 infra), complaints seeking to make use of a trustee's avoiding powers (see chapters 14-17 infra), complaints objecting to the dischargeability of a debt or the discharge of a debtor (see chapter 13 infra), and motions to sell property (see chapter 18 infra). In addition, paralegals will likely be asked to prepare preliminary drafts of all or a portion of briefs or memoranda in support of or in opposition to motions in any area of bankruptcy law.

In the realm of bankruptcy litigation, a paralegal will provide litigation support services similar to those performed in other areas of legal practice. Preparing digests of depositions, assembling and marking exhibits for a trial or evidentiary hearing, compiling factual data for counsel to prepare or respond to discovery requests, and making charts or other demonstrative aids are all activities that occur in bankruptcy practice.

B. COMMON ACTIVITIES

A summary of the activities most commonly performed by paralegals in bankruptcy practice will help the student to synthesize many of the materials found later in this text. This summary may also serve as a useful guide to practitioners, particularly those who do not regularly practice bankruptcy law.

When representing debtors, the most common activity performed by a paralegal is assisting counsel in the preparation of the basic documents required to be filed in a bankruptcy proceeding as described in chapters 4 and 7 of this text with regard to Chapter 7 proceedings, or as described in chapters 23 and 24 of this text with regard to Chapter 13 or Chapter 11 proceedings, respectively. The checklists and forms accompanying these text chapters will serve as useful practice aids for students in class and for practicing paralegals.

The most important basic documents in any proceeding, the Statements and Schedules, are very often prepared by paralegals in draft form from data provided by counsel. The tutorial contained in chapter 29 of this text concerning these basic pleadings has been designed to educate and assist students in the effective preparation and reading of these materials as well as to explain the reason or reasons for the required data and its organization.

In an asset case, a case in which the creditors will receive some repayment of their claims in the form of dividends, a paralegal will assist counsel and client in collecting and compiling various items described in chapter 11 of this text. This will help increase the dividend at minimal expense and effort by the estate. Paralegals may be required to learn the identity of and make the initial contact with the trustee, as described in chapter 11 of this text.

In Chapter 11 proceedings, business reorganizations (the most complex bankruptcies), a paralegal will assist counsel in monitoring and obtaining the debtor's compliance with the Chapter 11 operating rules described in chapter 24 infra. Paralegals will also render assistance with the confirmation procedure and balloting described in chapters 25 and 26 infra. The checklists and forms accompanying these chapters will serve as useful practice aids both in and out of the classroom environment.

When representing creditors, paralegals will perform a number of basic tasks. Preparing a proof of claim, as described in chapter 20 infra, is by far the most common. Providing support to counsel in the preparation and prosecution of a motion for relief from the automatic stay, as described in chapter 12 infra, is another common activity performed by paralegals for creditor clients.

Obtaining a copy and providing a preliminary report to counsel concerning the information contained in a debtor's Statements and Schedules is a task that is also regularly performed by paralegals for creditor clients. The analysis provided in chapter 29 of this text has been designed to assist paralegals in performing this preliminary review. Because this analysis will always help a creditor's counsel or a trustee to determine the initial likelihood of a recovery for the creditors, the importance of this review cannot be overemphasized. Any creditor client will need to know this information in order to determine how much effort to expend in attempting to recover a dividend from a bankruptcy estate.

For example, a first priority secured creditor will be able to make use of the data in pursuing a motion for relief from the automatic stay. On the other hand, a junior secured creditor may determine from a review of the schedules that a motion for relief from the automatic stay will not increase the likelihood of a recovery from the estate by a foreclosure of the property. When a client is a creditor in a Chapter 11 proceeding, the paralegal may be requested to review one or more operating reports so counsel can properly advise a client on the proceeding's progress (or lack thereof), the feasibility of a successful reorganization plan, and whether, in an appropriate case, the client should consider initiating a motion to dismiss or convert the proceeding. The description of a Chapter 11 operating report contained in chapter 24 infra and the discussion of the grounds for dismissal or conversion of a reorganization proceeding in chapter 23 infra will aid in performing this assignment.

When representing a trustee, a paralegal will assist in the claims review and objection procedures, in the classification of claims, and in preparing the many administrative reports a trustee is required to file with the United States Trustee. These procedures and many of the reports are identified in chapters 21 and 22 of this text.

Regardless of the party represented, a paralegal will always provide invaluable litigation support. This support may involve the performing of services in connection with any of the various motions or adversary proceedings described throughout this text. Other than legal issues involving specific application of the Bankruptcy Code or Federal Rules of Bankruptcy Procedure, the types of activity conducted will not vary from those in any other litigation: Facts and documents have to be investigated and organized, discovery may take place, depositions will have to be digested, briefs and motions may have to be written, and finally, the matter may have to be prepared for trial and actually tried. The value of paralegals to counsel in assisting with these services is well proven.

PART I

History and Introduction

1

A Short History of Bankruptcy

A. ORIGINS OF BANKRUPTCY SYSTEMS

Throughout history, financial crisis has affected the lives and relationships of individuals and businesses. Regardless of the era, unemployment, illness, unforeseen disaster, and technological advance have all caused financial failure. The methods developed by societies to resolve the effects of financial crisis are known as **bankruptcy systems**. Bankruptcy systems exist in any society where there are debtors (those who owe) and creditors (those who are owed). Bankruptcy systems have existed in some form from the first moment that a tribal chieftain or village elder ordered the seizure of a debtor's possessions and their distribution to multiple creditors in full or partial satisfaction of the creditors' claims.

Creditors have always sought to collect debts and debtors have always sought relief from debt. These contrasting concepts of debt collection and debtor relief are the foundation of any bankruptcy system. The primary focus of the **debt collection** features of bankruptcy systems has always been to formulate a body of rules ". . . to provide for the collection of assets of a debtor and the equitable distribution of the proceeds of those assets among . . . multiple creditors."[1] The primary focus of the **debtor relief** features of bankruptcy systems has vacillated throughout history from the extremes of punishment to forgiveness. Bankruptcy systems that have contained liberal debtor relief provisions have existed primarily in sophisticated economies where a continual reconciliation of accounts has been an economic necessity. Simpler economies have tended to contain more conservative debtor relief concepts, the mere sparing of life sometimes being considered revolutionary. The one

1. Merrick, A Thumbnail Sketch of Bankruptcy History, ABI Newsletter (July/Aug./Sept. 1987).

exception to this pattern appears to be ancient Israel, in which liberal debtor relief concepts prevailed in a simple agricultural economy.

While the historical trend of debtor relief has favored punishment rather than forgiveness, our present United States Bankruptcy Code departs from this trend in its liberal treatment of debtor relief. In many respects the U.S. Bankruptcy Code is perhaps the most liberal debtor relief bankruptcy system to come into existence since the jubilee year of the Old Testament.[2]

The jubilee year occurred every 50 years. (Every seventh year was a sabbatical year in which some limited form of debtor relief was afforded.[3]) The essence of the jubilee year is contained in the biblical verse: "And ye shall hallow the fiftieth year, and proclaim liberty throughout the land unto all inhabitants thereof; it shall be a jubilee unto you; and ye shall return every man unto his possession, and ye shall return every man unto his family."[4] In the jubilee year, all debts would be discharged, some mortgages released, and all indentured servants or slaves freed (the concept of **discharge**, legal relief from debt, is the basic element of debtor relief). During the intervening years any family member had the right to redeem, by payment, any property or persons that had been seized or given in satisfaction of a debt.[5]

The debtor relief provided for in the Old Testament most likely derived from even earlier regulations that existed in ancient Mesopotamia, from where the early Hebrews migrated to the region that became Israel. In the seventeenth century B.C., King Ammi-saduqa of Babylonia issued decrees releasing private debts in barley and silver and releasing people from debt slavery in an effort to resolve economic difficulties in his kingdom. This is the earliest recorded evidence of some form of debtor relief from which bankruptcy systems have evolved.[6]

Unlike ancient Israel, second chances were not generally given to debtors in the other ancient civilizations of the Mediterranean basin. Early Greek law did not seek to discharge debtors or reconcile accounts: A debt was always collectible. In the fifth century B.C., the Twelve Tables regulated only the procedures for selling an individual into slavery to satisfy a debt.[7]

2. 11 U.S.C The Bankruptcy Abuse Prevention and Consumer Protection Act of 2005 ("BAPA"), Pub. L. No. 109-8, 119 Stat. 23 (2005), limits and restricts the scope of debtor relief as it has existed in American Bankruptcy practice from 1979 through 2005. In this sense, BAPA demonstrates the pendulum-like nature in the treatment of debtor relief throughout history.
3. Leviticus 25:1-8.
4. Leviticus 25:10. If a portion of this verse seems familiar, it is because the phrase "proclaim liberty throughout the land unto all the inhabitants thereof" is the inscription on the Liberty Bell in Philadelphia.
5. Leviticus 25:11-55. The purpose of the jubilee year was to give debtors a second chance or fresh start. The "fresh start" concept is an essential feature of the United States Bankruptcy Code.
6. Leick, Gwendolyn, Mesopotamia-The Invention of the City, Penguin Books 2001, at page 187.
7. Countryman, Bankruptcy and the Individual Debtor — and a Modest Proposal to Return to the Seventeenth Century, 32 Cath. U. L. Rev. 809 (1983). Under the Twelve Tables a creditor had to provide a 60-day redemption period before a debtor could be sold into slavery. Payment of the debt within this period would prevent sale into slavery.

The commentators concur that death, slavery, mutilation, imprisonment, or exile were the lot of debtors in ancient Greece and also in republican Rome.[8]

Roman republican law also provided that multiple creditors could, upon exhibiting a debtor in the forum for three days, divide the debtor up into pieces in satisfaction of the debts. Evidence exists suggesting that multiple creditors could also seize a deceased debtor's corpse and hold it ransom from the debtor's heirs until the debts were satisfied.[9] This practice would make sense in Roman culture since the body had to remain whole if it were to commence a successful journey into the afterlife. The religious significance given to the satisfaction of debt thus acted as an incentive to repayment. This appears to have been the state of insolvency law, as such, during the Roman Republic.

As Rome became an empire, Roman debtor relief and collection law tended toward a greater liberality.[10] By approximately the second century A.D., debtor slavery had been abolished in the Empire. Debtor imprisonment continued to exist, but this was distinguishable from slavery in that creditors could not use the services of an imprisoned debtor. The debtor could be held for ransom only until friends or family of the debtor paid the debt.[11] (Debtor imprisonment has existed throughout history, including the twentieth century.)

The Roman Empire encompassed much of present-day Europe, North Africa, and the Middle East. This vast area, comparable in size to the United States, developed a sophisticated commercial economy permitting free trade throughout its territories. All this in a civilization without motor vehicles, aircraft, computers, or any form of instant long-distance communication. In this environment, Rome developed an insolvency system that permitted exemptions (an **exemption** is property that a debtor may protect from seizure by creditors) and restrained personal execution.[12] This restraint took the form of a debtor's ceding all assets for distribution to creditors. Although this act would not discharge the debts, it did act to prohibit creditors from killing, mutilating, or selling the debtor into bondage. This procedure was known as *cessio bonorum*.[13] The assets so surrendered were distributed according to statutory priorities similar to modern United States bankruptcy law.[14] To a modern American observer this procedure would appear similar to a Chapter 7 liquidation proceeding. A form of composition agreement in which a discharge could be

8. Id. See also Radin, Debt, 5 Ency. Soc. Sci. 33-34 (1931); Ford, Imprisonment for Debt, 25 Mich. L. Rev. 24 (1926).
9. Countryman, supra n.7; Radin, supra n.8; Ford, supra n.8.
10. Merrick, supra n.1; Radin, supra n.8; Ford, supra n.8.
11. Radin, supra n.8.
12. Radin, supra n.8 at 34, 37.
13. Merrick, supra n.1.
14. Riesenfeld, Evolution of Modern Bankruptcy Law, 31 Minn. L. Rev. 401, 432 (1947).

granted also came into use as the economy grew in sophistication.[15] A **composition agreement** is an agreement between a debtor and multiple creditors for the repayment of debt. These procedures would be recognizable today as the reorganization proceedings known as Chapter 11 and Chapter 13.

When the Western Roman Empire dissolved in the fifth century A.D., the then-existing economy of Western Europe also collapsed. Whereas for approximately five centuries it had been possible to trade between London and Constantinople (modern Istanbul) with identical currency, trade practices, laws, and language, this commonality ceased to exist. The rise of the Dark Ages caused a corresponding devolution of bankruptcy laws.

B. BANKRUPTCY IN THE MIDDLE AGES

During the Dark Ages the financial system of Western Europe receded as an important factor of daily life. Debtor imprisonment returned to vogue, prevailing throughout the period.[16] The Church proclaimed debt and insolvency sinful. Debtors were subject to excommunication while alive or denial of a Christian burial upon death.[17] As had been the case in early Rome, religious sanctions were once again utilized as an incentive to debt repayment.

The debtor punishments of the Dark Ages were not radically different from the earlier practices of the Roman Republic. They were consistent with a simpler society in which there once again existed few entities with multiple creditors. In the Dark Ages, a serf would generally be beholden to only two creditors: feudal lord and Church. Certainly neither could tolerate an unsatisfied debt from a subservient soul.

Punishment of debtors was necessary to assist the land-owning and religious ruling classes in maintaining their power. Forgiveness became a radical idea in this stratified economic structure. The lack of a commercial economy also eliminated any practical need for a reconciliation of accounts or balancing of books after an extended period of time.

15. Id. at 439, citing Code of Justinian VII.71.8. It should be noted that Justinian reigned as emperor of the Eastern Empire during the sixth century A.D. This was after the final collapse of the Western Empire, which most historians date at 476 A.D. The consensus appears to be that Justinian's Codes, therefore, do demonstrate the evolution of a bankruptcy law during the Empire.

    A *composition* is an agreement between a debtor and two or more creditors that satisfies the debts for less than payment in full. See chapters 3, 22-27 infra.

16. Ford, supra n.8 at 25; Radin, supra n.8 at 34.
17. Ford, supra n.8 at 25.

International commerce and trade began a resurgence in the tenth century. As trade recommenced, the credit system recommenced.[18] As the number of debtors with multiple creditors increased, the bankruptcy system began its Renaissance.

The first bankruptcy laws that arose in the late Middle Ages were to a large degree reenactments of the *cessio bonorum* of the Roman Empire.[19] The focus of such statutes was twofold: the prevention of fraud upon creditors stemming from an inequitable distribution of assets and the protection of the debtor from imprisonment. If all assets were surrendered for distribution to creditors there would be no imprisonment. A discharge was not given or contemplated. These statutes were limited to use by merchants only. Loss of a trading place or bench (*banca*) in the local market would befall a debtor who fraudulently concealed or transferred assets while not paying just debts. In Italy this was known as *banca rotta* and in France as *banquerotte*. This is the etymology of the English word *bankrupt*.[20]

The composition agreement began to reappear in Western European law as early as 1256 in Spain.[21] A composition agreement provided some form of debtor relief in that a debtor could be released from the debts due those creditors who agreed to the composition. By the seventeenth century, the composition agreement existed throughout Western Europe with the exception of England, where such statutes did not come into regular existence until after 1705.[22]

C. EARLY ENGLISH INSOLVENCY LAWS

The emphasis of early English insolvency law was on punishment. Forgiveness was rarely known to English debtors prior to 1705. This is an important point to recognize in any study of American bankruptcy law because the law of England as it existed in 1776 is the direct legal antecedent of American bankruptcy law.

Anglo-Saxon England practiced debtor imprisonment, although the sale of a debtor into slavery or debtor dissection was probably not permitted.[23] The first statute akin to a bankruptcy statute was enacted in 1283. The Statute of Acton Burnell authorized the seizure of a debtor's

18. Radin, supra n.8 at 34.
19. Merrick, supra n.1.
20. Countryman, supra n.7 at 810.
21. Riesenfeld, supra n.14 at 439-440.
22. Countryman, supra n.7 at 811-812. See infra this chapter.
23. Id. at 810-811. Ford, supra n.8 at 26.

assets to satisfy debt. If the assets seized were insufficient to satisfy the debt then imprisonment of the debtor would occur until the debt was paid.[24] We recognize at least part of this procedure today as a "writ of attachment," a common state law collection device.

From the thirteenth to fifteenth centuries, debtor imprisonment in England evolved under two related writs, *capias ad respondendum* and *capias ad satisfaciendum*. The former allowed a creditor to "attach" a debtor to ensure appearance at trial. The latter allowed a creditor to imprison a debtor in satisfaction of a judgment until the debt was actually paid.[25] Some form of debtor imprisonment existed in England until the twentieth century.[26]

The first true insolvency law in England was not enacted until 1543.[27] This delay, in contrast to the rest of Western Europe, is attributable to England's lack of substantial involvement in international trade until the sixteenth century.[28] The statute of 1543 permitted the seizure and distribution of a debtor's assets to creditors and imprisonment of the debtor if the debts remained unsatisfied. The proceeding applied only to merchants and was initiated by creditors. There was no discharge for the debtor.[29] To the extent that this proceeding was creditor initiated, it was similar to the present-day American involuntary petition.[30]

In 1571 the Statute of Elizabeth further refined the system of asset distribution to creditors. This statute defined fraudulent transfers as acts of bankruptcy. Transactions deemed fraudulent that occurred within a fixed time prior to the bankruptcy filing were considered void. For instance, concealing property from creditors would be one such act.[31] This statute is a likely basis of today's concept of an avoidable transfer, which is a major feature of our Bankruptcy Code.[32]

Composition agreements made their appearance in England rather late in comparison to the rest of Western Europe. When they did, compositions were permitted only in the Chancery Courts and only during a relatively short period of time (approximately 1583-1621). Another statute authorizing compositions existed for only one year, 1697-1698.[33] Because a discharge,

---

24. 11 Edw. (1283). Countryman, supra n.7 at 811.
25. Countryman, supra n.7 at 811; Ford, supra n.8 at 27-28. A writ of *capias ad satisfaciendum* was used in 1989 in New Jersey to place a debtor into custody. A bankruptcy court refused to abrogate the writ. See 76 A.B.A. J. 28 (Feb. 1990); In re Bona, 110 Bankr. 1012 (S.D.N.Y. 1990). A writ of *capias ad Satisfaciendum* was issued by the New Jersey state courts as recently as 2000 in Marshall v. Matthei, an unpublished opinion. See New Jersey Law Journal February 2, 2000.
26. Ford, supra n.8 at 31. Ford points out that in 1921, 424 contract debtors were held imprisoned in England.
27. 34 & 35 Henry VII, ch. 4 (1543).
28. Merrick, supra n.1 at 12.
29. Countryman, supra n.7 at 811-812; Merrick, supra n.1 at 13.
30. See chapter 4 infra.
31. 13 Eliz., ch. 7 (1571); Riesenfeld, supra n.14 at 422.
32. See chapters 15 to 17 infra.
33. Riesenfeld, supra n.14 at 442-443.

legal relief from debt, could occur only as a result of a composition, punishment prevailed over forgiveness in early English bankruptcy law.

In 1705 England enacted a statute in which a composition with creditors could effectuate a full discharge of all debt.[34] The Statute of Anne appears to be the first law to recognize a full discharge or legal relief of debt by a debtor since the jubilee year of the Old Testament. Otherwise, the Statute of Anne is remarkably similar in appearance to the bankruptcy system as it existed at the height of the Roman Empire.

Under the Statute of Anne a debtor would receive a full discharge and be able to retain exempt property provided that certain conditions were complied with. The conditions were that a minimum dividend of eight shillings per pound be paid to creditors and that no act in fraud of creditors had taken place prior to the bankruptcy. If a lesser dividend were to be paid, a commissioner would determine the debtor's exemptions.[35] In 1732, the Statute of George added the consent by four-fifths of the creditor body as a requirement of the debtor receiving a discharge.[36] These statutes compose the formal roots of American bankruptcy law.

D. BANKRUPTCY IN THE UNITED STATES

America is a nation of debtors: "it is stated that nearly half our total white immigration came over under indenture."[37] Indentured servitude acted as an alternative to debtor prison in some colonies.[38] Georgia was originally settled by indentured servants. In general, colonial bankruptcy law corresponded to that of England in the eighteenth century.[39]

One goal of the Constitutional Convention was to establish the free flow of trade and commerce between the various states. In the effort to achieve this goal, the framers reserved for Congress the power "to establish . . . uniform laws on the subject of Bankruptcies throughout the United States."[40] By virtue of the Supremacy Clause, which provides that federal law is the supreme law of the land, the enactment of a federal bankruptcy law preempts the states from so acting and acts as the supreme law of the land.[41]

34. 4 Anne, ch. 17 (1705).
35. Countryman, supra n.7 at 812.
36. 5 Geo. II, ch. 30 (1732); Countryman, supra n.7 at 812.
37. Countryman, supra n.7 at 813.
38. Countryman, supra n.7 at 813.
39. Ford, supra n.8 at 28.
40. U.S. Const., art. I, §8.
41. U.S. Const., art. VI.

The power granted Congress to enact federal law on the various subjects, including bankruptcy, that are described in Article I, Section 8, of the Constitution, does not however require congressional action within a described area. Thus, although Congress has the power to enact bankruptcy laws, it is not required to do so. Accordingly, there is no constitutional requirement that there be a federal bankruptcy law. Indeed, such laws were only in effect in the United States for short periods of time during the nineteenth century. A federal bankruptcy law has been continuously in effect since 1898.

Debtor imprisonment continued to be a prevalent practice in the United States until after 1830. After this date a movement toward debtor relief began and individual state constitutions began to abolish debtor imprisonment.[42] While debtor imprisonment lasted, however, there were periods of time during which substantially more debtors occupied prisons than convicted criminals.[43]

The first United States Bankruptcy Act was in effect from 1800 to 1803. This statute was virtually identical in its features to the law in England as it existed after 1732 as described above.[44]

The second United States Bankruptcy Act was enacted in 1841, effective in 1842, and repealed in 1843. This statute permitted voluntary proceedings and applied to nonmerchants as well as merchants. A voluntary proceeding was one initiated by a debtor seeking relief. Exemptions were expanded to include "necessaries of life" in addition to clothing. A discharge was granted with creditor consent. Certain transactions were void in fraud of creditors and some debts would not be affected by a discharge.[45]

The third Bankruptcy Act was in effect during the Reconstruction, 1867 to 1878.[46] This act expanded upon the scope of debtor relief provided for in the 1841 law by permitting state exemptions to be claimed by a debtor and by permitting, for the first time in a bankruptcy law since the Old Testament, a full discharge without creditor consent or payment of a dividend. Additionally, the 1867 Bankruptcy Act contained provisions permitting an "arrangement," or composition. Arrangements included elements similar to those of the present-day reorganization proceedings of Chapters 11 or 13.[47]

---

42. Ford, supra n.8 at 32-33.
43. Ford, supra n.8 at 29, reports that in Pennsylvania, New York, Massachusetts, and Maryland there were three to five times as many persons imprisoned for debt as for crime. Countryman, supra n.7 at 814, cites statistics indicating that debtors constituted approximately 20 percent of all prisoners in Boston during the 1820s.
44. 2 Stat. 19 (1800). Countryman, supra n.7 at 813; Riesenfeld, supra n.14 at 407. See also notes 34-36 supra.
45. 5 Stat. 440 (1841); 5 Stat. 614 (1843); Countryman, supra n.7 at 814-815; Riesenfeld, supra n.14 at 407, 423.
46. 14 Stat. 517 (1867); 20 Stat. 99 (1878).
47. Countryman, supra n.7 at 815-816; Riesenfeld, supra n.14 at 409, 423, 446-447.

A fourth Bankruptcy Act was enacted in 1898 and remained in effect, with amendments, until October 1, 1979, when the present Bankruptcy Code became law.[48] The 1898 Act contained all of the basic elements that are present in today's Bankruptcy Code. An amendment enacted in 1938 contained provisions creating Chapters XI and XIII, the reorganization proceedings that still exist under the Bankruptcy Code.[49] The Supreme Court described the Act's liberal debtor relief provisions as providing a "fresh start" to debtors in their financial affairs.[50]

In 1970 Congress authorized a commission to determine the desirability of reforming the Bankruptcy Act. In 1973 the Commission reported that modernization and recodification of the Bankruptcy Act was in order.[51] The report was accepted, and the Bankruptcy Code of 1978 was the result. An analysis of this Code in its present form, along with practical descriptions to aid in conducting many routine bankruptcy procedures, is the subject matter of this text.

Thus, the substantive foundations of our current United States Bankruptcy Code are rooted deep within the history of Western civilization. For individual debtors, the Bankruptcy Code emphasizes the discharge of debt and the allowance of exemptions, thus giving a fresh start to the debtor. Such liberal treatment of debtor relief has not existed since the jubilee and sabbatical years of ancient Israel. For creditors, the Bankruptcy Code emphasizes the orderly and consistent liquidation of assets and distribution of dividends. In various forms, this collection process has existed in sophisticated commercial economies since the Roman Empire.[52] Finally, the formal and stylistic aspects of the United States Bankruptcy Code began their evolution with the 1705 English Statute of Anne.

Summary

Bankruptcy systems exist in any society where there are debtors (those who owe) and creditors (those who are owed). The practice of the jubilee year in ancient Israel provided debtors a discharge or legal relief from debt.

48. 30 Stat. 541 (1898). See chapter 2 infra.
49. 52 Stat. 541 (1938). Countryman, supra n.7 at 817; Riesenfeld, supra n.14 at 408. See chapters 23-27 infra.
50. Local Loan Co. v. Hunt, 292 U.S. 234 (1934).
51. Countryman, supra n.7 at 818; Report of the Commission on the Bankruptcy Laws of the United States, H.R. Doc. No. 137, 82d Cong., 1st Sess., pt. I, ch. 17 (1973).
52. The growth of a highly interdependent global economy, globalization, has caused a corresponding growth of bankruptcy statutes throughout the world that bear many similarities to Chapter 11 of the United States Bankruptcy Code. China enacted a statute in 1986 that is similar to Chapter 11 but with special provisions unique to the nature of the communist state. See China's New Bankruptcy Law: A Translation and Brief Introduction, 61 Am. Bankr. L.J. 359 (1987).

In other ancient Mediterranean civilizations, debtors were punished and not legally forgiven from debt. During the latter Roman Empire, a bankruptcy system developed in a sophisticated commercial economy. In this system, debtors were allowed to protect property from creditors. This concept was and is known as exemptions.

Present American bankruptcy law, the United States Bankruptcy Code, has evolved from eighteenth-century English bankruptcy law. Our Bankruptcy Code provides for legal debtor relief in the form of a discharge and also permits debtors to protect exempt property. The Bankruptcy Code provides creditors with an orderly process to liquidate the debtor's nonexempt assets and distribute the proceeds as dividends. An analysis of the Code, in its present form, along with practical descriptions to aid in conducting many routine bankruptcy procedures is the subject matter of this text.

KEY TERMS

bankruptcy systems
composition agreement
debt collection
debtor relief
discharge
exemptions

DISCUSSION QUESTIONS

1. Why do individuals or businesses seek bankruptcy relief?
2. What distinguishes debtor relief from debt collection in a bankruptcy system?
3. How does the concept of debtor relief in modern American bankruptcy law compare with debtor relief found in England before the American Revolution? The Roman Empire? Medieval Europe?
4. Where does the term *bankruptcy* come from? What is the etymology of the term *bankruptcy*?

In 1991 Hungary became the first former Warsaw Pact country to enact a bankruptcy law. See ABI Newsletter (November/December, 1991). A law permitting business bankruptcies became effective in Russia in 1993. See ABI Journal, April 1993. Poland became the most recent country to update its bankruptcy laws with a statute similar to Chapter 11. See Bankruptcy Court Decisions Newsletter, June 10, 2003, LRP Publications: "Poland to enact new insolvency law to aid economy."

2

Introduction to the Bankruptcy Code

A. ORGANIZATION OF THE BANKRUPTCY CODE AND A NOTE ON THE TEXT

The Bankruptcy Code was enacted into law in 1978 and became effective on October 1, 1979.[1] It has since been significantly amended four times, in 1984, 1986, 1994 and 2005.[2] The first basic change from the Bankruptcy Act is the name of the law itself. The bankruptcy law is now properly known as the Bankruptcy Code. Any reference to the present law as the Bankruptcy Act is therefore incorrect. A second basic change from the Bankruptcy Act is that the various Chapters of the Bankruptcy Code are now identified by Arabic and not Roman numerals. Thus, a reference to a Chapter of the Bankruptcy Code by Roman numerals is also wrong. Although the Bankruptcy Act did use Roman numerals to identify its Chapters, the Bankruptcy Code uses Arabic numerals to identify all its Chapters.

1. Pub. L. No. 95-598, (92 Stat. 2549 1978).
2. The 1984 amendments are commonly known as BAFJA (the Bankruptcy Amendments and Federal Judgeship Act of 1984), Pub. L. No. 98-353 (July 10, 1984). The 1986 amendments are known as the Bankruptcy Judges, United States Trustees, and Family Farmer Bankruptcy Act of 1986, Pub. L. No. 99-554 (Oct. 27, 1986). The 1994 amendments are known as the Bankruptcy Reform Act of 1994, Pub. L. No. 103-394 (Oct. 26, 1994). Throughout this text these amendments shall be referred to as the Bankruptcy Reform Act.

The National Bankruptcy Review Commission, created in the 1994 amendments, delivered an 1100-page report to Congress in late 1997. The document made 170 recommendations for changes or additions to the Code. The Bankruptcy Abuse Prevention and Consumer Protection Act of 2005, Pub. L. 109-8, 119 Stat. 23 (April 20, 2005) has its genesis in pro-credit-industry legislation introduced in reaction to the Commission Report. Throughout this text these amendments shall be referred to as BAPA.

The Bankruptcy Code is divided into nine Chapters.[3] In its essence, it is primarily a self-contained system designed to resolve the financial affairs of a debtor. The Code's basic structure can be easily illustrated and briefly described in the form of a flow chart. This description also serves as a useful guide to understanding the organization of this text. Since the Bankruptcy Code is a system, it is best analyzed and described in a similar format, as in the nearby chart. I have attempted to use a "building block" approach, working from the simpler to the more complex concepts as the text progresses. This may necessitate some reference in earlier chapters of this text to concepts not discussed in detail until a later chapter. Where this occurs, an effort has been made to briefly define the concept described later. Reference back to the chart or to the glossary at the end of the text may help simplify this initial learning process. This same chart will also serve as an instant review of the entire text when it has been completed.

Code Chapters 1, 3, and 5 contain the rules that apply in all bankruptcy proceedings. These three Code Chapters contain the rules dealing with the fundamental debtor relief features of discharge, exemptions, and the automatic stay. These Chapters also contain the general rules regulating the debt collection features of claims and their priority of distribution.[4] These are the basic issues affecting debtors and creditors in a bankruptcy proceeding.

The remaining Code Chapters (7, 9, 11, 12, 13, and 15) comprise the specific types of bankruptcy proceedings that are available to debtors. The most common proceedings are Chapters 7, 11, and 13.[5] These three proceedings comprise in excess of 95 percent of all bankruptcies filed. Normally, the provisions contained in each of these Code Chapters will apply only to the specific Chapter proceeding that has actually been filed.[6]

B. OVERVIEW OF THE BANKRUPTCY CODE

Chapter 1 is the first Chapter of the Bankruptcy Code. It contains definitions and general procedural rules governing all bankruptcy proceedings.

3. All Chapters enacted in 1978 bore odd numbers (1, 3, 5, 7, 9, 11, and 13). Although apocryphal, it is believed Congress adopted this format so it could fill in other chapters later. In 1986 Congress did enact Chapter 12, the family farmer reorganization proceeding. A second reason for only enacting odd-numbered chapters may have been so that the various types of bankruptcy proceedings would still retain their common identities of Chapter 7 (VII), Chapter 11 (XI), and Chapter 13 (XIII). Chapter 15 was added to the Code in 2005 by BAPA.
4. See chapters 7, 9, 12, 13, 21, and 22 infra.
5. For the 12 months ending September 30, 2004, 1,618,987 bankruptcies were filed nationwide. 1,153,865 or 71 percent were Chapter 7; 454,412 or 28 percent were Chapter 13; 10,368 or 1 percent were Chapter 11. There were 238 Chapter 12 filings. American Bankruptcy Institute press release December 3, 2004, *www.abiworld.org*.
6. 11 U.S.C.§103.

BANKRUPTCY CODE FLOW CHART

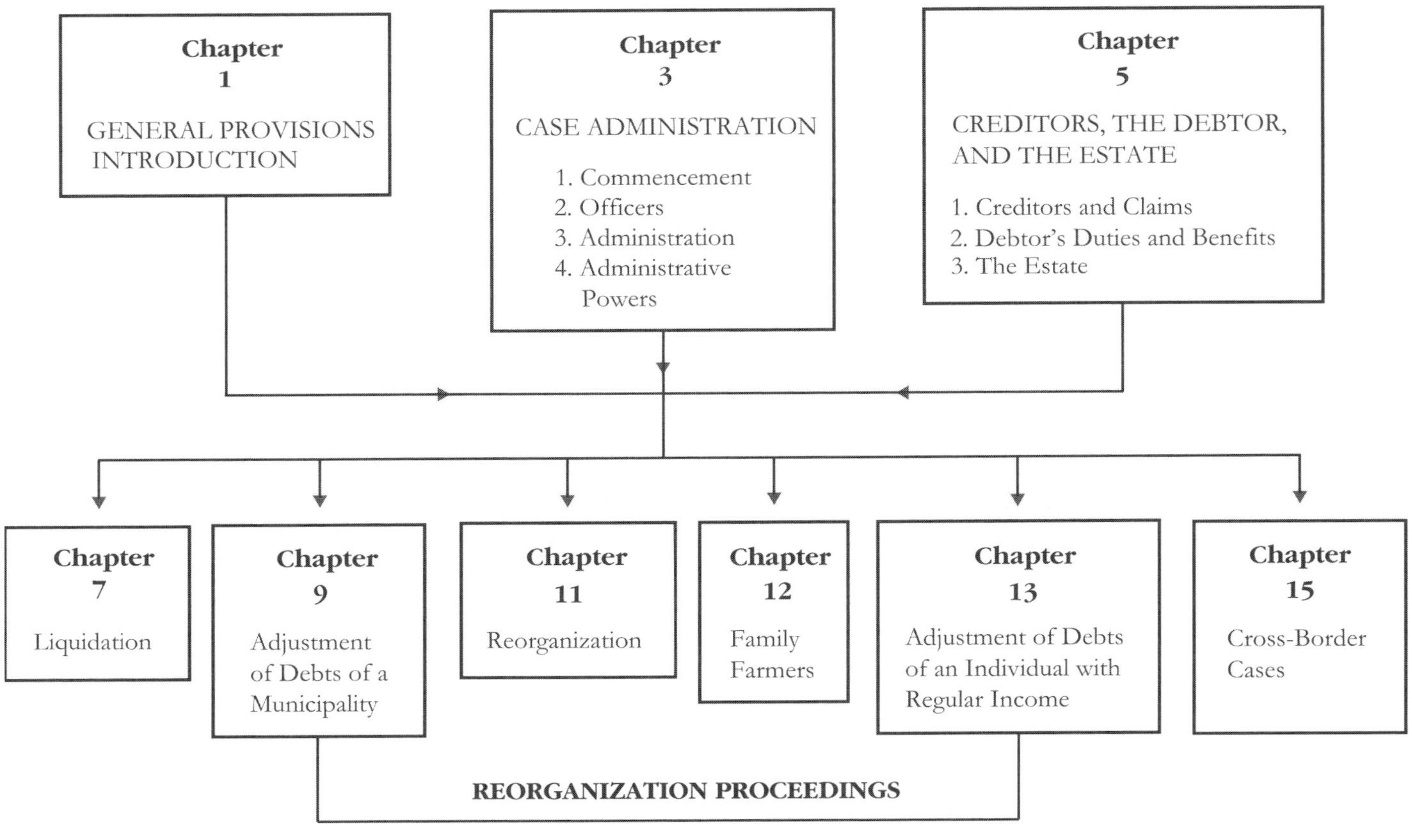

This Chapter can also be referred to as "Introduction." The provisions of Code Chapter 1 are described in chapters 5 and 6 of this text.

Code Chapter 3 contains various rules pertaining to the administration of bankruptcy estates, including rules relating to professionals and to such issues as the regulation of professional fees in bankruptcy proceedings.[7] This is part of the subject of chapter 7 of this text. Among the other rules of Chapter 3 are rules relating to the automatic stay and executory contracts.[8] These provisions are the subjects of chapters 12 and 19 of this text.

Code Chapter 5 contains rules governing creditors and claims, the debtor, and the estate. The core of the debtor relief and debt collection provisions is contained in this Code Chapter. The primary debtor relief features of exemptions and discharge are included here. These concepts are the subjects of chapters 9 and 13 infra. The debt collection features of claims and their priorities and the trustee's so-called avoiding powers are also contained in Code Chapter 5. These matters are the subject of chapters 14-17, 21, and 22 of this text.[9]

Chapters 1, 3, and 5 apply in any of the various Chapter proceedings that a debtor may file under the Bankruptcy Code, but the provisions of Chapters 7, 9, 11, 12, 13, or 15 will normally apply only to the Chapter in which the provision is contained, unless made specifically applicable by another Code section.[10] For example, a debtor files a Chapter 7 proceeding. Only the provisions of Chapters 1, 3, 5, and 7 will apply to the proceeding. The provisions of Chapter 11 (another "proceeding") will not.

Chapter 7 is the most common type of bankruptcy proceeding. It may be described in one word: liquidation. Over 70 percent of all bankruptcies filed are Chapter 7 proceedings.[11] In a **liquidation** proceeding, all the nonexempt assets of a debtor are sold. The proceeds are distributed to creditors according to their ranking. The basic details of Chapter 7 proceedings are the specific subjects of chapters 7, 8, 11, 20, and 22 of this text.

Chapter 13 is the second most common proceeding filed under the code. Chapter 13 is a reorganization proceeding for individuals with regular income where a qualified individual seeks expedited and summary approval of a repayment plan for a small consumer estate. Approximately 30 percent of all cases filed are Chapter 13 proceedings.[12] Chapter 13 is specifically analyzed in chapter 23 of this text.

A third type of proceeding is Chapter 11, which is commonly known as "Reorganization." Approximately 0.5 percent of all proceedings filed are

7. 11 U.S.C.§§326, 327, 330, 331. See chapter 7 infra.
8. 11 U.S.C.§§362, 365. See chapters 12 and 19 infra.
9. 11 U.S.C.§§501-510, 522, 523-524, 541-559. See chapters 9, 13-17, 21, and 22 infra.
10. 11 U.S.C.§103.
11. For the 12 months ending September 30, 2004, 71 percent of all proceedings filed were Chapter 7. American Bankruptcy Institute, supra n. 5.
12. For the fiscal year ending September 30, 2004, 28 percent of all proceedings filed were Chapter 13. American Bankruptcy Institute, supra n. 5.

Chapter 11.[13] Chapter 11 is the most complex, time-consuming, and expensive type of bankruptcy proceeding. In a **reorganization** proceeding a debtor seeks to avoid liquidation by proposing a viable plan of reorganization to the creditors that is successfully confirmed and performed. Chapter 11 is described in chapters 24 through 26 infra.

Both Chapter 11 and Chapter 13 are reorganization proceedings and, as a result, have many similarities. In a Chapter 11, a debtor seeks to reorganize its business and avoid liquidation. The business may be Joe's Donut Shop down at the corner or it may be Texaco, Inc. Similarly, in a Chapter 13, a qualified debtor proposes a plan to the court and creditors to repay debt over a period of time, thus reorganizing the individual's affairs. To this extent, the goals of a Chapter 11 or Chapter 13 are identical.

There are three other Chapter proceedings that some debtors may file. They are Chapter 9, Chapter 12, and Chapter 15. These three proceedings comprise the remaining available bankruptcy proceedings. Chapter 9 is a reorganization proceeding for a municipal corporation—a city. Municipal corporations seeking reorganization have been provided with a special reorganization proceeding because in addition to being business entities, a Chapter 9 debtor may also be a political entity. The provisions of Chapter 9 attempt to account for the special considerations that can arise when a political entity is also a debtor. Chapter 9 filings are rare. For example, in 1994, Orange County California filed a widely publicized Chapter 9 to avoid losses it incurred in speculative bond investments.

Chapter 12 was added to the Code in November 1986.[14] Chapter 12 is entitled the "Adjustment of Debts of a Family Farmer." It is a hybrid of Chapters 11 and 13. It has been enacted as an experiment to assist financially distressed family farmers who desire to reorganize their affairs. Chapter 12 has been enacted to give family farmers the essential benefits and cost savings of a Chapter 13 in what would otherwise have to be a Chapter 11 proceeding. Code Chapter 12 is described in chapter 27 of this text.

Chapter 15 was added to the Code in 2005. Entitled "Ancillary and Cross-Border Cases": "The purpose of the Chapter is to incorporate the Model Law on Cross-Border Insolvency so as to provide effective mechanisms for dealing with cases of cross-border insolvency . . ."[15] That is, Chapter 15 exists to help resolve insolvency issues arising from the advent of the so-called Global Economy in the 1990s, a current example of how insolvency systems evolve in sophisticated commercial economies.

---

13. For the 12 months ending September 30, 2004, six-tenths of 1 percent of all proceedings filed were Chapter 11. American Bankruptcy Institute, supra n. 5.
14. Pub. L. 99-554. Chapter 12 expired on July 1, 2000. However, its effectiveness was regularly extended at six-month intervals. Section 1001 of BAPA makes Chapter 12 a permanent addition to the Bankruptcy Code.
15. 11 U.S.C. §1501(a).

C. THE BANKRUPTCY SYSTEM

The Bankruptcy Code is designed to function as a system. This point cannot be overemphasized. It is the key to understanding how the Bankruptcy Code works to resolve the financial affairs of a debtor. This understanding will aid the paralegal in providing realistic and practical results for either debtor or creditor clients. For unlike many other areas of the law, a specific provision of the Bankruptcy Code is often best understood in the context of its role within the entire system and not as an isolated statute. When approached in this manner, many aspects of the Code that may at first appear illogical will become logical, rational, and understandable.

The system approach also helps in understanding the practical nature of the Code. In this context, the **Bankruptcy Code** is a largely self-contained legal, economic, and accounting system designed to reconcile all financial affairs of a debtor as they exist at the time of filing. All assets and liabilities are disclosed. Assets that are not exempt are available for liquidation and distribution to creditors according to a list of priorities designated by the Code. Most debts will also be subject to the debtor's discharge. This is the most basic description of a bankruptcy proceeding. The specific details of this basic process, the documents involved and how to prepare them, is the subject matter of chapters 7 and 29 of the text.

Bankruptcy proceedings appear and feel different than traditional litigation. For example, a Chapter filing of any type is best referred to as a proceeding. This distinguishes the bankruptcy proceeding itself from the various types of litigation or motions that may take place within the proceeding. For instance, a Chapter 7 proceeding may have activity occurring within it that constitutes independent litigation or other activity that will occur only by way of a motion. This semantic distinction will also help to understand bankruptcy jurisdiction in simple terms.[16] The text will describe some suggested methods for presenting issues to the Bankruptcy Court either by way of motion or litigation.

There are normally no plaintiffs or defendants in a bankruptcy proceeding. There is a debtor, a trustee, and creditors. Sometimes a debtor may have only one or two creditors, and sometimes a debtor may have several hundred or thousand creditors. But the major players will always be the debtor, a trustee, and the creditors. The **debtor** is the entity that is bankrupt and owes the debts. The **creditors** are the entities to whom the debts are owed. The **trustee** is an independent third party who liquidates the estate's assets and distributes dividends to the creditors. Trustees are described in chapter 10 of this text.

16. See chapter 28 infra.

The traditional adversarial approach is not necessarily the most practical way to approach a bankruptcy problem. The bankruptcy system generally functions most efficiently when the debtor, creditors, and trustee cooperate. All the major players, particularly in a reorganization proceeding, share a similar goal: satisfaction of debts while preserving the business. Litigation will not necessarily solve a debtor's problems or even define their solutions. In bankruptcy practice one must always be aware of the likely ultimate result and act on the basis of prudent economics. This philosophy will always aid in giving a reorganization proceeding the greatest chance for success. This philosophy also assists in the Chapter 7 effort to generate the greatest realistic dividend to unsecured creditors. This is the practical goal of Chapter 7, to "squeeze blood out of a turnip."

If there is any other area of law that is comparable to the bankruptcy system, it is the probate system.[17] In probate, an estate is liquidated and the proceeds distributed first to creditors and then to the beneficiaries of the estate according to distributive priorities set by state law. Similarly, in bankruptcy an estate is liquidated, the proceeds are distributed to creditors by statutory priorities, and then any remaining proceeds are returned to the debtor's shareholders or to the debtor.

Summary

The United States Bankruptcy Code is primarily a self-contained system designed to resolve the financial affairs of a debtor. The Bankruptcy Code is organized into Chapters. There are nine such Chapters at the present time. Three Chapters (1, 3, and 5) contain rules that apply in all of the various Chapter proceedings. The rules in these three Chapters include the basic features of debtor relief, discharge, exemptions, and the automatic stay, as well as the basic features of debt collection, claims, and their priority of distribution.

The remaining six Chapters of the Bankruptcy Code (7, 9, 11, 12, 13 and 15) comprise the various types of bankruptcy proceedings available to debtors. The different proceedings may be categorized as either "liquidation" or "reorganization" proceedings.

In a liquidation, a debtor's nonexempt assets are sold by a trustee and the proceeds are distributed to the creditors. In a reorganization, the debtor will seek approval of a repayment plan that will avoid liquidation.

17. At least one court has so observed. In In re Pacific Forest Industries, Inc., 95 Bankr. 740 (Bankr. C.D. Cal. 1989), the court said: "There is no other practice of law which is identical in nature to bankruptcy practice, but the Court believes that probate practice has some of the same elements. The attorney is dealing with a fiduciary, who he must advise. The decisions made by the Court may affect creditors who are not even yet known. There is a limited 'res' that will be dealt with and distributed."

Chapter 7 is a liquidation proceeding. Chapters 9, 11, 12, and 13 are reorganization proceedings that apply to specific types of debtors. Chapters 11 and 13 are the most common reorganization proceedings. A Chapter 11 is a business reorganization. A Chapter 13 is a consumer reorganization. Chapter 9 applies only to Municipal Corporations. Chapter 12 is a reorganization proceeding for family farmers.

Chapter 15 applies only to cross-border bankruptcies and may be either liquidations or reorganizations.

KEY TERMS

Bankruptcy Code	**liquidation**
creditors	**reorganization**
debtor	**trustee**

DISCUSSION QUESTIONS

1. What is the Bankruptcy Act? Bankruptcy Code?
2. What is a liquidation proceeding?
3. What is a reorganization proceeding?
4. Identify:
   a) Those Chapters of the Bankruptcy Code applicable to all bankruptcy proceedings;
   b) Those Chapters of the Bankruptcy Code applicable to liquidation proceedings;
   c) Those Chapters of the Bankruptcy Code applicable to reorganization proceedings.
5. Identify the major parties in a bankruptcy proceeding.

3

Alternatives to Bankruptcy Under State Law

Bankruptcy has alternative goals depending on one's perspective as a debtor or creditor. As a debtor, one primarily seeks a discharge from debt and a "fresh start." This is the major feature of debtor relief. As a creditor, one seeks to collect all or some of a debt. Understanding the role of bankruptcy as a tool in the debt collection process will help to increase the amount collected. This understanding commences with a description of the various alternatives to bankruptcy that are available under nonbankruptcy law to help resolve financial distress. These are **bankruptcy alternatives** that primarily seek a marshaling of assets for equitable distribution to the creditors and a full or partial release from the remaining debts of the debtor. These alternatives are bulk sales, described in Article 6, Uniform Commercial Code (in those jurisdictions that have not repealed Article 6), assignments for the benefit of creditors, and composition agreements. Sometimes, the effective use of these alternatives can accomplish the same results as a bankruptcy without ever having to file one.

When used effectively and efficiently, bankruptcy alternatives may provide a greater return to creditors at a fraction of the time and expense than is generally afforded by the bankruptcy system. Careful attention to the details of a particular state statute as well as to the ultimate result that would obtain within the bankruptcy system can sometimes avoid the time and expense of a bankruptcy proceeding with a greater return to creditors. In certain circumstances, the Bankruptcy Court may have the discretion to dismiss or abstain from hearing a bankruptcy proceeding if a nonbankruptcy alternative has been successfully implemented in accordance with prevailing nonbankruptcy law.[1]

1. 11 U.S.C. §305.

Filing a bankruptcy sometimes seems the easiest choice for a debtor in financial difficulty. It is easy for counsel to recommend a bankruptcy filing simply because the client desires it, without exploring the available nonbankruptcy alternatives. Although this recommendation may accommodate the client's wishes, it may not be in the client's best interest. Little or no thought is sometimes given to the basic issue of whether a client needs to go bankrupt as opposed to wanting to go bankrupt. Most debtors would prefer to *not* file bankruptcy. Most people do want to pay their bills, and many become very troubled about a decision to file a bankruptcy. If there is a reasonable way for a potential debtor to avoid a filing yet satisfy debt, the potential debtor will normally prefer that reasonable nonbankruptcy remedy. However, by the time many potential debtors seek legal advice, a filing is the only remedy. Nevertheless, it is always a recommended practice to explore a potential debtor's nonbankruptcy options. A debtor contemplating bankruptcy is analogous to a person who is ill. If the patient visits the doctor promptly, there may be a cure or treatment; if the financial difficulties of a potential debtor are diagnosed promptly, a debtor may be able to avoid bankruptcy.

A. ARTICLE 6 UCC BULK SALES

One nonbankruptcy alternative concerns business debtors and is known as **bulk sales**, the subject of UCC Article 6. The law of bulk sales was enacted around the turn of the century to deal with a merchant who sold the assets of a business and then absconded with the proceeds, leaving creditors unpaid. In a pretechnological time, it was nary impossible to trace the debtor and collect the debts due. In modern times, however, the proliferation of technology and the Uniform Enforcement of Foreign Judgments Act makes it possible to find a debtor in a distant locale and collect the debt. As a result, the National Conference of Commissioners on Uniform State Laws recommended the repeal of Article 6 in 1991. Simultaneously, the Commission recommended the adoption of a revised Article 6 for any state desiring to retain a law of bulk sales. As of 2002, 41 states have repealed Article 6.[2]

The statute is essentially a notice procedure that affords all claimants (creditors) a form of due process for the submittal of claims. Under Article 6, notice of the sale of more than half of all assets at one time or to one buyer is given to all of the claimants. Sales under the jurisdiction of a Court proceeding, however, and sales of less than $10,000 in assets or of more than

2. Article 6, Uniform Commercial Code (UCC). Prefatory Note to Article 6 and the Uniform Laws Annotated 2002 Electronic Pocket Part Update listing jurisdictions that have repealed Article 6.

$25,000,000 in assets are common exceptions.[3] Sales in the ordinary course of business do not fall within the statute. For example, the weekly trip to the supermarket does not require the grocer to comply with Article 6. If this were the case, it would be impossible for a business to conduct business.

Article 6 requires that when there are 200 or fewer claimants, all of them be mailed notice of the sale. When there are more than 200 claimaints, the notice may be published. The notice must describe all the pertinent data of the sale: the date of the sale; the date of distribution; the name and address of the seller; the name and address of the buyer; the type of assets being sold or an exact list of the items being sold.[4]

The notice must be given not less than 45 days prior to the sale and not more than 30 days after the buyer obtains a list of claimants from the seller.[5] The claimants have six months from the sale date to submit claims to the buyer.[6]

The notice should also contain a schedule of distribution, a description of the methodology that will be used to distribute proceeds to the claimants.[7] There are three general methods. The first, and the one that creditors prefer, is payment in full. This text's concern, however, is primarily with a debtor who is selling a business and is not going to be able to pay creditors in full. When this happens, the bulk sales notice should advise creditors that payment will be made on a pro rata basis, that is, "share and share alike." For instance, if there is enough money to pay 90 percent of the claims, pro rata means that all creditors will receive 90¢ on the dollar. Pro rata distribution is the general distribution rule of the bankruptcy system. A final distribution approach that an escrow holder may use is to advise creditors that if there are insufficient funds to pay claims in full, the funds will be interpleaded into state or federal court.

Interpleader is a civil proceeding where a stakeholder (someone who holds a fund of money or a piece of property for disputed claimants) deposits the property into court and the court determines the rights of the disputing parties to the fund or property. The stakeholder is relieved of former obligations once the disputed assets are controlled by the jurisdiction of the court.

For instance, in the context of a bulk sale, assume that you are the person in charge of paying creditor claims through a bulk sale. You have told creditors in the notice that they will not be paid in full and that you are going to distribute the proceeds on a pro rata basis. A tax claimant contacts you and says, "Your notice says you're paying everybody pro rata. Does that include

---

3. UCC §6-103.
4. UCC §6-105.
5. UCC §6-105(5).
6. UCC §6-104(1)(f).
7. UCC §6-106.

us?" You respond affirmatively. The claimant says, "Well, we're entitled to be paid in full because we have a priority." (In fact, under the Bankruptcy Code the tax creditor would most likely be entitled to payment in full before all or most of the other creditors.) If you then cannot amicably resolve the dispute, you can deposit the funds into court via interpleader, joining as defendants all of the claimants to the fund. The court would then determine the priorities between disputing claimants. You are now relieved of any potential liability.

The recommended method of distribution is to follow the distribution scheme of the Bankruptcy Code, effectuating a distribution exactly as it would occur in a Chapter 7 bankruptcy proceeding.[8] By proceeding in this manner, should a bankruptcy ensue, the prospect that creditors may have to return dividends to the estate due to the various avoiding powers of the trustee is minimized.[9]

To ensure compliance with the bulk sales statute, civil liabilities are imposed not only on the seller but also on the buyer or auctioneer.[10] Liability may occur if the notice is not given or is materially defective.

A buyer or auctioneer who fails to comply with the statute is liable to a claimant for an amount equal to the amount of the claim, less any amount that the claimant would not have received had the buyer complied with the statute. For example, if a claimant would have received a dividend of only 50 percent, the buyer is liable to a claimant for only 50 percent of the claim. Good faith compliance with the statute, or a good faith belief that Article 6 does not apply, are defenses in favor of the buyer or auctioneer.[11]

If a bulk sale is conducted by an auctioneer, the auctioneer is required to comply with the bulk sales statute. If the statute is not complied with, then the auctioneer can be held liable for the creditor's claims up to the reasonable value of the assets sold. Once again, the statute exists for the protection of the seller's creditors and not for the protection of the buyer. An auctioneer, however, is not penalized for any amounts owed creditors in excess of the reasonable value of the assets auctioned.[12]

If assets are sold by a bulk sale and creditors are not paid in full from the proceeds, creditors still retain all rights to pursue the debtor for the balance. Despite use of the alternative, bankruptcy may nonetheless be inevitable. Nevertheless, proper use of the bulk sales method of liquidation may pay appropriate dividends to creditors in less time or cost than a bankruptcy proceeding. If the creditors are paid according to the Bankruptcy Code's order of distribution but without the wait and cost of a bankruptcy

8. See chapters 21 and 22 infra for an analysis of the order of distribution in bankruptcy proceedings.
9. See chapters 15 through 17 infra.
10. UCC §6-106(1).
11. UCC §6-107.
12. UCC §6-108(4).

proceeding, this approach seems the more economically prudent option.[13] Sales taking place in the bankruptcy system are themselves exempt from the bulk sales law.[14] This is because the bankruptcy system uses its own notice procedures as described in chapters 5 and 18 of the text.

B. ASSIGNMENT FOR THE BENEFIT OF CREDITORS

A second alternative to filing a bankruptcy is called an assignment for the benefit of creditors. Some states have statutes regulating this practice. In those states with no statute, the practice is governed solely by the common law.

An **assignment for the benefit of creditors** takes place when a debtor, which may or may not be in financial distress, assigns its assets to a third party in trust to sell the assets and apply the proceeds to the payment of the creditors' claims. The third party is known as the assignee. The assignee assumes a role as both the liquidator and the distributor of the assets, similar to a bankruptcy trustee.[15] It is conceivable that the assignee may have to comply with the bulk sales law. Assignees should normally follow the distribution priorities set forth in the Bankruptcy Code to effect the most equitable distribution to creditors. Wholesale credit associations or other local entities may specialize as assignees. It is suggested that such a specialized entity be used in making an assignment for the benefit of creditors.

There are disadvantages to making an assignment for the benefit of creditors. First, if the creditors are not going to be paid in full and do not agree to discharge the debtor from the remainder of the debt, the creditors are free to pursue traditional collection methods for the balance. Thus, this alternative may only delay, not avoid, a bankruptcy filing.

Second, if a bankruptcy is subsequently filed within 90 days of any creditor distribution, that distribution may be a **preference** and any dividends paid creditors during this time may potentially be recovered by the bankruptcy trustee.[16] Preferences are the subject of chapter 16 of the text.

Third, the very act of making an assignment for the benefit of creditors constitutes grounds for entering an order for relief in an involuntary bankruptcy proceeding.[17]

13. See chapter 22 infra.
14. UCC §6-103(3)(i).
15. See chapter 10 infra. In Sherwood Partners, Inc. v. Lycos, Inc., 394 F.3d 1198 (9th Cir. 2005), the court acknowledged the "venerable common law pedigree" of assignments for the benefit of creditors.
16. See chapter 10 infra.
17. 11 U.S.C. §303(b)(2). See chapter 4 infra.

C. COMPOSITION AGREEMENTS

A third alternative to a bankruptcy proceeding is the common law concept of the composition agreement. Any transaction in which a debtor and creditor agree to a revision of their legal obligations to one another is a form of composition. Picking up the telephone and getting an extra month to pay a bill is a form of composition. Debt consolidations are a form of composition. A formal **composition agreement** comes into being when a debtor and multiple creditors agree to a revision of existing obligations.

When a debtor has a number of unpaid creditors, there is no prohibition against the debtor's entering into a joint repayment plan simultaneously with multiple creditors. A composition agreement is therefore an agreement between a debtor and two or more creditors to extend repayment terms or to accept less than full payment in discharge of debts. An accepted composition agreement becomes a new contract between the debtor and the consenting creditors. A written document, defining all the terms of repayment and signed by all the involved parties, is sufficient to be a valid composition agreement.

Composition agreements are not often entered into by individual consumer debtors, although there is no prohibition against it. Composition agreements are more often attempted by businesses in an effort to avoid a Chapter 11 proceeding. A composition agreement for a business should follow the same guidelines that would be followed in drafting a Chapter 11 plan as suggested in chapters 25 and 26 below. In this manner, the agreement can be utilized as a Chapter 11 plan should a Chapter 11 filing ultimately occur. This is permitted under Chapter 11 and can save substantial time and cost in any proceeding.[18] In the 1990s, this practice became popularly known as the "prepackaged Chapter 11." For example, Southland Corporation (the parent entity of 7-Eleven Stores) filed Chapter 11 with such a plan, which was approved by the Bankruptcy Court.

It is critical that a composition agreement attempt to comply with the provisions of Chapter 11 since the agreement binds only those creditors who consent to it. Any remaining creditors are still free to pursue traditional collection remedies, which often may result in a Chapter 11 filing. This is one drawback of composition agreements. For example, Volk Inc. enters into a composition agreement with most of its creditors, but Stasi, a hostile creditor, prefers to obtain a writ of attachment, thus forcing Volk Inc. to file a Chapter 11. If the provisions of Chapter 11 have been complied with in soliciting and obtaining approval of the composition agreement, there is

18. 11 U.S.C. §1126(b). In this circumstance, a composition agreement creditors Committee is also permitted to become a Chapter 11 Official Creditors Committee. See Federal Rule of Bankruptcy Procedure (FRBP) 2007. See also chapters 24 through 26 infra.

no reason why the composition agreement cannot be filed with the court as a Chapter 11 Plan of Reorganization upon filing. The Code in fact encourages this.[19] Acting in such a way may substantially reduce the length and expense of any subsequent Chapter 11 proceeding. A second drawback of composition agreements is the time factor. The extent of creditors' activity in the form of lawsuits or imminent foreclosure or repossession may simply make an effort at a composition impractical. Ultimately the reorganization proceedings of Chapters 9, 11, 12, and 13 are no more or less than judicially approved composition agreements.

BAPA adds two provisions to the Bankruptcy Code encouraging the use of composition agreements in consumer bankruptcy cases. First, a debtor can object to a creditor's claim and reduce it by 20 percent if a debtor can show by clear and convincing evidence that the debtor made, at least 60 days prior to the bankruptcy filing, an offer to repay at least 60 percent of a debt over a period "not to exceed the repayment period of the loan, or a reasonable extension thereof" and the debt is otherwise dischargeable.[20] Second, any creditor receiving payments pursuant to such a payment plan, so long as the plan is created by an approved credit counseling agency, will not be subject to having to return the payment to a bankruptcy trustee as a preference.[21]

These provisions are intended to encourage composition agreements in consumer cases. In the first instance, debtors are given an incentive to propose out of court 60 percent repayment plans, and creditors are subject to penalties in bankruptcy court for unreasonably refusing acceptance. The clear import of the provision is to encourage debtors to propose 60 percent or more composition agreements and for creditors to accept them. In the second instance, insulating approved composition agreement payments received by creditors from the trustee's preference powers acts as a further incentive for creditors to accept consumer compostion proposals.

Summary

It is always worthwhile to examine a potential debtor's alternatives to bankruptcy. There are three common alternatives used under state law. These are the bulk sale, assignment for the benefit of creditors, and the composition agreement.

Bulk sales are governed by Article 6 of the Uniform Commercial Code. Compliance with this law is necessary when a business is selling more than

19. In U.S.C. §1121(a); 11 U.S.C. §1126(b); 11 U.S.C. §1129(a)(1)(2). See chapters 24 through 26 infra.
20. 11 U.S.C. §502(k). See chapter 21 infra.
21. 11 U.S.C. §547(h). See chapter 16 infra.

50 percent of its assets at one time. It is basically a notice procedure so creditors can be paid their claims. To ensure compliance with this law, civil liabilities are imposed upon the buyer. Thus, the representative of a buyer in a transaction subject to a bulk sales notice will always want to be certain that the law is properly complied with.

Assignments for the benefit of creditors involve the transfer of a debtor's assets to a third party, in trust, to liquidate the assets and repay creditors. Specialized organizations exist in most localities, which act as assignees. It is suggested that these entities be used in any appropriate situation.

A composition agreement is an agreement between a debtor and multiple creditors for the repayment of existing debt. A composition agreement may be simple or complex. For example, a composition agreement for a business should be drafted and treated as if it were a Chapter 11 reorganization plan. Reorganization plans in the bankruptcy system are no more than judicially approved composition agreements.

KEY TERMS

assignment for the benefit of creditors
bankruptcy alternatives
bulk sales
composition agreement
preference

Chapter 3 Checklist

3.1 BULK SALES LAW (UCC ARTICLE 6)

3.1.1 Data to Obtain
1. Contract
2. Identity of parties
3. Identity of assets to be sold (such as: "all assets, inventory, equipment, fixtures, leasehold improvements and goodwill of Myron's Gourmet Carnitas Shoppe")
4. Purchase price
5. Address and deadline for the submittal of claims; and
6. Manner of repayment ("in full" or "pro rata" or "interpleader")

3.1.2 Publication
1. Prepare notice including all pertinent data from above

2. Submit to an approved publication (the advertising department of any newspaper can tell you if the paper is approved for this purpose); and
3. Publish at least the minimum number of times required by local statute (often, the newspaper will know this).

Note: In many jurisdictions, escrow companies or similar entities will handle the bulk sales compliance as part of the escrow transaction. It is recommended that these entities be used for this purpose.

DISCUSSION QUESTIONS

1. Identify a debtor's alternatives to a bankruptcy filing. Describe the advantages and disadvantages of each alternative in comparison to a bankruptcy proceeding for the same debtor.
2. How can a consumer debtor negotiate a composition agreement with creditors? What are the advantages of doing this? Should counsel for a consumer debtor attempt to negotiate the composition agreement?
3. Why has the bulk sales law contained in Article 6 of the Uniform Commercial Code been repealed by over 40 states?

4

Filing a Petition

The first step in initiating any bankruptcy proceeding is filing a petition. If filed by the debtor, the petition is called a **voluntary petition**.[1] A petition filed by creditors is known as an **involuntary petition**.[2] The debtor in an involuntary proceeding is known as an **alleged debtor** and is not generally considered bankrupt in a practical or legal sense until the court enters an order for relief.[3] A married couple of opposite sexes may be joint debtors in either a voluntary or involuntary proceeding.[4] Other related debtors must have separate petitions filed by or against them, although the Federal Rules of Bankruptcy Procedure permit procedural or substantive consolidation of proceedings in appropriate circumstances.[5]

A. GATEKEEPER PROVISIONS IN INDIVIDUAL BANKRUPTCIES: PREPETITION CREDIT COUNSELING

BAPA adds a number of provisions to the Bankruptcy Code that an individual debtor, or the debtor's legal representative, must actually comply with prior to filing a bankruptcy petition. These provisions may best be understood as gatekeeper provisions to individual bankruptcy because if they are not complied with, a filing may not take place, may be subject to dismissal, or a legal representative be subject to penalty.

1. 11 U.S.C. §301; Bankruptcy Rule 1002.
2. 11 U.S.C. §303.
3. 11 U.S.C. §303(f), (h).
4. 11 U.S.C. §302. 1 U.S.C. §7.
5. Bankruptcy Rule 1015. See infra this chapter for a more detailed description.

Section 109(h) of the Bankruptcy Code requires prepetition **credit counseling** as a prerequisite to an individual debtor seeking bankruptcy relief. Corporations and partnerships are not subject to these provisions. An individual seeking bankruptcy relief may not be a debtor and must participate in an individual or group credit counseling session from an approved credit counseling agency within 180 days prior to the filing of a petition.[6] Proof of participation is shown by filing with the court at the time a petition is filed, a certificate from the credit counseling agency that provided the services and a copy of any debt repayment plan developed by the agency.[7] Failure of a debtor to comply with these provisions may result in dismissal of the case.[8]

There are three exceptions to the prepetition credit counseling requirement. First, the United States Trustee may exempt a district from the requirement if the United States Trustee determines that approved credit counseling services in a district are not reasonably able to provide counseling services to individuals.[9] For example, large rural districts, such as Wyoming or Montana may be districts that might be found exempt.

Second, a debtor may file a certification with the court at the time of filing stating that "exigent circumstances" merit a waiver of the rule, provided that the debtor has made a request for counseling services and could not obtain them within five days of making a request from a counseling agency. A debtor seeeking a waiver for exigent circumstances must still obtain the required credit counseling within 30 days from filing the petition, except that the court, for cause, may order an additional 15 days.[10] Failure of a debtor to comply with the requirement to obtain prepetition counseling and file the certificate with the Bankruptcy Court will be grounds for dismissal of the case if the documents are not filed within the time periods provided for by the statute.

The third exception to the prepetition credit counseling requirement provides that if, after notice and hearing, the court finds that a debtor is not able to comply with the requirement due to mental incapacity, physical disability, or active military duty in a military combat zone the counseling requirement will be waived.[11]

Requiring individual debtors to obtain approved credit counseling as a prerequisite to file a petition is an entirely new concept in bankruptcy practice, raising questions and concerns that will have to be resolved by

---

6. 11 U.S.C. §109(h); 11 U.S.C. §111. The United States Trustee, a division of the Department of Justice, will designate approved credit counseling agencies. The role and function of the United States Trustee is discussed at Chapter 10 infra.
7. 11 U.S.C. §521(b).
8. 11 U.S.C. §109(h)(3)(B).
9. 11 U.S.C. §109 (h)(2)(A).
10. 11 U.S.C. §109 (h)(3)(B).
11. 11 U.S.C. §109(h)(4).

the courts. For example, what is an "exigent circumstance"? Is an imminent repossession, foreclosure, sheriff's sale, eviction, or termination of utility service an exigent circumstance? In any event, the five-day waiting period appears to be mandatory if the exigent circumstances exception is to apply. Since many debtors wait until the last minute to consult with a professional about their financial affairs, the five-day waiting period may increase foreclosures and repossessions, thereby depriving some debtors of the ability to save their homes or cars by seeking bankruptcy relief.

New Code Section 111 concerns approved budget and counseling agencies approved to provide prepetition credit counseling mandated by §109(h), or the financial management course now required as a condition to receive a Chapter 7 discharge (§727(a)(11)), or a Chapter 13 discharge (§1328(g)). (See chapters 7 and 23 infra.) The United States Trustee is charged with setting the requirements to approve these agencies and to evaluate them on a regular basis. Although agencies may charge a fee, services are required to be provided without ability to pay the fee. Prepetition credit counseling is likely to focus upon the ability to qualify for bankruptcy relief, the types of chapters available, and whether or not the debtor has the ability to propose a reasonable nonbankruptcy repayment plan to creditors. In this regard, if a debtor proposes to repay at least 60 percent over the loan repayment period, and the creditor unreasonably refuses, this may constitute ground to object to at least 20 percent of the claim in a bankruptcy case pursuant to new §502(k). Additionally, payments made to creditors pursuant to such a repayment plan will not be considered preferential pursuant to new §547(h).

Debt Relief Agency Provisions

A second group of gatekeeper provisions added to the Code by BAPA requires action, prior to the filing of a petition for relief, in individual cases by the debtor's **"debt relief agency"** providing **"bankruptcy assistance"** to an **"assisted person."** A debt relief agency, §101(12A), is any person, including a bankruptcy petition preparer, providing "bankruptcy assistance" (§101(4A), to an "assisted person" (§101(3)), a person whose debts are primarily consumer debts and whose nonexempt property has a value of less than $150,000.

New Section 527 requires a debt relief agency to provide a notice that all individual debtors must receive pursuant to 11 U.S.C. §342(b) describing the various chapters available to individual debtors along with a brief description of bankruptcy, on forms to be approved by the U.S. Trustee. Presumably, these forms will be similar to the informational handouts commonly distributed to individual debtors at meetings of creditors in Chapter 7 cases prior to enactment of the 2005 legislation. This notice is to be given within three days of offering to provide assistance to an assisted person, along with an additional notice itemizing the various duties that an assisted person will have in seeking bankruptcy relief, including the duty to be truthful, accurately disclose all assets and liabilities, and provide current monthly income, and the requirement that all petitions be subject to random audit. Section 527(b) requires that a statement be given to assisted persons about the obligations of the debt relief agency. The provision sets forth the terms of this statement.

New Section 528 requires written retainer agreements between debtors and all debt relief agencies within five days of first rendering services to an assisted person. The written retainer agreement must clearly and conspicuously explain the services to be rendered, the fees to be charged, and payment terms. Section 528 further requires that any advertising must make clear that any services being advertised are for bankruptcy services and clearly and conspicuously state: "We are a debt relief agency. We help people file for bankruptcy relief under the Bankruptcy Code," or a substantially similar statement. The purpose of these new provisions is that potential debtors will understand that they may be seeking bankruptcy relief and not debt counseling or some other form of debt relief.

New §526 enforces compliance with Sections 527 and 528. Section 526 requires a debt relief agency to perform all the services they promise to provide to an assisted person. These provisions of Sections 527 and 528 may not be waived. Failure to comply, or failure to comply with Sections 527 or 528 will make the debt relief agency liable for all damages and a refund of fees paid. Additionally, state attorneys general, the court, and the United States Trustee are given authority to enforce these provisions, including the authority to seek an injunction against a debt relief agency that repeatedly violates these provisions.

B. VOLUNTARY PETITIONS

A debtor initiates a voluntary proceeding simply by filing a petition conforming to Official Form 1.[12] The form itself is for the most part self-explanatory. The purpose of the various allegations contained in the petition is to establish for the court, creditors, and trustee that the debtor is qualified to be a debtor under the particular Chapter proceeding

12. 11 U.S.C. §301; Bankruptcy Rule 1002; Official Form No. 1. See forms disk, form 4.1.

commenced and that the proceeding has been filed in the district with proper venue.[13] The debtor's involvement in related or prior bankruptcy proceedings is also disclosed in the petition.

Venue pertains to the proper Bankruptcy Court (federal judicial district) in which a proceeding should be commenced. A proceeding may be commenced in any district meeting one of the following qualifications: (1) the district in which the petitioner is domiciled, resides, or has its principal place of business; (2) the district in which the debtor's principal United States assets are located; or (3) the district in which the debtor has complied with either of the above for the greatest portion of the 180 days preceding the petition's filing.[14] As a practical matter, this means that venue is appropriate if either requirement 1 or 2 is met for at least 91 days preceding the filing of the petition. If a debtor has been in existence for less than 91 days it would still qualify under either basic requirement because there will be no other location possible for establishing venue. Improper venue does not invalidate the effect of filing a petition.[15]

Venue may be changed upon a motion to the court if a proceeding is initiated in an improper district or if the transfer is for the convenience of the parties and witnesses and in the interest of justice. Alternatively, the court may dismiss a case that has been filed in an improper venue.[16] For instance, it may be more convenient for a business debtor's proceeding to take place in the district where the principal assets are located when this is different from the principal (or headquarters) business address. On the other hand, it may be more convenient and logical for the proceeding to take place in the district where the corporate headquarters is located when the debtor has multiple locations, such as the parent entity of a franchise business. Because most proceedings are initiated by consumers, venue is infrequently a problematic issue.

The Federal Rules of Bankruptcy Procedure require that a number of documents in addition to the petition be filed at the commencement of a voluntary proceeding or within certain limited time periods thereafter. Some of the required documents will vary depending upon the type of Chapter proceeding filed. Some of the documents may further vary according to the local rules of the district where the proceeding is filed.

In addition to the petition, a debtor must file certain other documents when a Chapter 7 petition is filed or the petition may *not* be accepted for filing by the court. In a situation where the debtor is filing to avoid an imminent foreclosure, repossession, or levy, a failure to file the minimum required

13. See chapters 5 and 7 infra.
14. 28 U.S.C. §1408, 11 U.S.C. §109(a).
15. 28 U.S.C. §1412.
16. 28 U.S.C. §1412; Bankruptcy Rule 1014.

documents necessary for the clerk to accept the petition for filing may be tantamount to legal malpractice. First, the filing fee must be paid at the time of filing. However, a debtor *in propria persona* (representing him or herself without an attorney) who has not paid any legal fees in connection with the proceeding may obtain approval to pay the filing fee in installments.[17] Second, every individual debtor must file a statement under penalty of perjury setting forth the Social Security Number or a statement that the debtor has no Social Security Number. This is because Federal Rule of Bankruptcy Procedure 1005 requires that all petitions contain only the last four digits of a debtor's Social Security Number to protect privacy.[18] A partnership petition must show all general partners' consent to the filing.[19] Third, a list containing the name and address of each creditor must be filed with the petition unless the schedules of Assets and Liabilities are filed at the same time.[20] Fourth, a debtor's attorney must also file a declaration that there has been a disclosure to the debtor of the various types of Chapter proceedings available.[21] This last item has been incorporated in the petition, Official Form 1. Finally, 11 U.S.C. §521(b) requires a consumer debtor to file a prepetition credit counseling certificate showing compliance with Bankruptcy Code Section 109(h) as discussed in Section A, supra, or a certification explaining the "exigent circumstances" to receive 30 days to comply with the requirement.

Within ten days of filing, a "bankruptcy petition preparer" shall file a declaration under penalty of perjury disclosing any fee received from or on behalf of the debtor within twelve months preceding the filing, and any unpaid fee charged to the debtor pursuant to Section 110 (see chapter 7 infra). An unsupervised paralegal may be a bankruptcy petition preparer as defined in the Code.

Filing all the above documents with the petition meets the minimum acceptable filing requirements. These minimum requirements will usually be used by regular bankruptcy practitioners only in an emergency, such as avoiding an immediate foreclosure, repossession, or attachment. Otherwise, it is recommended to file at the commencement of the case *all* documents described in this chapter that are required to be filed in connection with the proceeding. A filing that complies with only the minimum

17. Bankruptcy Rule 1006. 28 U.S.C. §1930(f), added by BAPA, permits qualified indigent debtors to apply for a waiver of filing fees. This will permit *in forma pauperis* petitions in appropriate circumstances. A qualified debtor is a debtor whose income is less than 150 percent of the official federal poverty line.
18. Bankruptcy Rule 1005; Bankruptcy Rule 1007(f).
19. Bankruptcy Rule 1004. Many Bankruptcy Court local rules require a corporate resolution authorizing a filing by a corporation.
20. Bankruptcy Rule 1007(a)(1).
21. 11 U.S.C. §342(b); Pub. L. No. 98-353 §322; 11 U.S.C. §521(a)(1); 11 U.S.C. §527; Bankruptcy Rule 2016(b). See Section A, supra.

requirements is sometimes colloquially referred to as a "quickie" or "short form" filing.

Within 15 days of filing a petition, a debtor must file a Statement of Financial Affairs, a Schedule of Assets and Liabilities, a Schedule of Current Income and Expenditures, and a Schedule of Executory Contracts and Unexpired Leases.[22] The Statement of Financial Affairs shall conform to Official Form 7. An individual debtor's required claim of exemptions must also be included in the schedules.[23] All of the documents described in this paragraph are commonly referred to by bankruptcy practitioners as **Statements and Schedules**.

BAPA imposes additional filing requirements. Debtors must file copies of all evidence of payments received by any employer of the debtor within 60 days of filing; a statement of the amount of net monthly income and disclosure of any change of income reasonably anticipated over the 12 months succeeding the filing of the petition; and the calculations necessary to determine compliance with Needs Based Bankruptcy (see chapter 5F and 5G infra); a statement of current monthly income and expenditures; and a record of interests in educational IRA accounts or similar programs. Failure to file a required document by the 45th day from the filing of the petition will result in automatic dismissal on day 46, although an extension of up to 45 days may be sought for "justification." The court may also decline to dismiss the case for failure to comply if the debtor has made a good faith effort to comply and the court finds that administration of the case would be in the best interests of the creditors.[24]

Not later than seven days prior to the meeting of creditors, individual debtors must provide to the trustee a copy of the debtor's federal income tax return for the tax year ending immediately prior to the filing of the petition. Failure to do so may result in dismissal of the case. Failure by a debtor to file any post-petition tax return can result in dismissal of the case if a taxing authority so requests.[25]

The **Statement of Affairs** is a questionnaire designed to elicit information sufficient to determine whether the debtor should receive a discharge or to reveal the existence of preferences or other avoidable transactions. The **Schedules** are an extended form of an accrual basis financial statement disclosing all liabilities and all assets of the debtor. The Schedule of Current Income and Expenditures discloses the existence or lack of surplus income after the payment of basic monthly expenses. It is relevant in Chapter 7 and Chapter 13 proceedings.[26] Chapter 29 infra is devoted solely to an analysis of

22. 11 U.S.C. §521(a)(1); Bankruptcy Rule 1007(b)(1).
23. Bankruptcy Rule 4003(a).
24. 11 U.S.C. §521(a)(1); 11 U.S.C. §521(f); 11 U.S.C. §521(i).
25. 11 U.S.C. §521(e).
26. 11 U.S.C. §521(a)(1); Bankruptcy Rule 1007(b). See chapter 23 infra.

these documents. These documents comprise the core matter from which the trustee or creditors may examine a debtor's financial affairs in any proceeding. They are the central "pleadings" of any bankruptcy. Whether the debtor is John Smith or K-Mart, the requirements are identical. The existence of nonexempt assets from which a distribution to creditors might occur is initially determined by analyzing the Statements and Schedules. The basic distributive rights of creditors to the assets can also be determined from a review of these documents.

Within 30 days of the filing, a consumer debtor must file a statement of intention with regard to the disposition of secured collateral.[27] At the behest of consumer credit organizations, this provision was added to the Code in 1984 to expedite notification to secured creditors regarding a debtor's intent to retain and pay for, or to surrender the collateral securing a secured debt. This requirement has helped to reduce relief from stay motions described in chapter 12 infra while assisting debtors and creditors alike in reducing the expenses and frustrations sometimes encountered in resolving a consumer's secured claim within the bankruptcy system. Chapters 12 and 21 of this text will describe in more detail the automatic stay, the rights of a secured creditor, and use of the statement of intention.

A debtor's counsel must also file a statement disclosing the compensation paid or to be paid in connection with the proceeding.[28] This document normally is to be filed within 15 days of the petition's filing.[29] The preparation and filing of the various documents described in the preceding pages comprise the essential core pleadings of any bankruptcy proceeding.

In a Chapter 13 proceeding a debtor must file the Chapter 13 plan within 15 days of the petition's filing.[30]

A number of additional basic documents must be filed in connection with a Chapter 11 or 12 proceeding. These materials are described in greater detail in chapters 24 and 27 infra.

Although it is permissible to file all of the required documents at various times, as noted above, it is generally more efficient and prudent to file them all when the petition is filed. This will ensure that all necessary actions have been taken to protect the debtor's rights from the proceeding's inception. This will also eliminate any need to remember what must be done next and within what time limit. These documents, although numerous, are not generally so extensive or complex that they cannot all be filed at the outset of a proceeding except in an emergency. Many districts, particularly those in urban areas, have approved forms available for use which helps make this

---

27. 11 U.S.C. §521(a)(2). See forms disk, form 21.3.
28. 11 U.S.C. §329.
29. Bankruptcy Rule 2016(b).
30. 11 U.S.C. §1321; Bankruptcy Rule 3015. See chapter 23 infra.

task even easier to perform. Samples of all of these forms appear in the forms disk accompanying this text.

In appropriate circumstances, such as a proceeding with numerous creditors, or a debtor with complex financial transactions to be described in the Statement of Affairs, the court has discretion to grant an extension of time for the filing of the Statements and Schedules.[31] Not filing the documents in a timely manner can result in a dismissal of the proceeding because the failure evidences a lack of prosecution.[32]

Section 302 of the Code permits the filing of joint cases. A **joint case** is filed by an individual and the individual's spouse, in other words, a husband and wife of different sexes. No other related entities may file a joint case.[33] However, there are provisions allowing the consolidation of two or more pending and related cases.[34] This is the only way two or more debtors who are not spouses may have a proceeding administered as one case.

For instance, if one spouse files a proceeding and then the other spouse files (assume they are separated so they each file a separate case), it is possible to obtain a court order consolidating the cases into one proceeding.

As another example, assume that a corporation files a bankruptcy proceeding and the owner of the corporation has guaranteed all of the corporation's debts and is subsequently forced to file an individual bankruptcy proceeding. Because many of the debts are identical (due to the guarantees), it is possible under the Bankruptcy Rules of Procedure to seek consolidation of the two proceedings into one.

As a third example, assume that a corporation and an individual file two separate and superficially distinct proceedings. Investigation discloses a distinct relationship between the debtors. Consolidation may also be appropriate in this instance.

Finally, assume that a group of related partnerships or corporations file proceedings. The partnerships may have a common general partner or partners. The corporations may be subsidiaries or affiliates of one another. (Subsidiaries and affiliates are described in more detail in chapter 6 infra.) Investigation may disclose substantial interrelationships between the various debtors that would make all proceedings more efficient and result in a more equitable distribution to all creditors if consolidation took place.

In each of the above examples consolidation may be appropriate, although only spouses may initiate a joint case. (A joint case could be

31. Bankruptcy Rule 1007(c).
32. 11 U.S.C. §707(a); Bankruptcy Rule 1017; 11 U.S.C. §521(1).
33. 11 U.S.C. §302(a). 1 U.S.C. §7 provides that: ". . . 'spouse' refers only to a person of the opposite sex who is a husband or a wife." In re Kandu, 315 Bankr. 123 (Bankr. W.D. Wash. 2004)
34. 11 U.S.C. §302(b); Bankruptcy Rule 1015.

commenced in the first example.) The court may consolidate two or more proceedings for all purposes. This is known as **substantive consolidation**. Substantively consolidated proceedings will proceed as one. Alternatively, the court may consolidate two or more proceedings for less than all purposes. This lesser form of consolidation is sometimes known as **administrative consolidation**.[35] Administrative consolidation may often save substantial time and expense in the administration of multiple related estates, although their assets and liabilities will remain segregated. It is a common occurrence in large corporate cases commonly filed in New York or Delaware that all the filing entities are administratively consolidated at the beginning of the case as a **first day order**. See chapter 24 infra.

C. INVOLUNTARY PETITIONS

An entity is placed into bankruptcy against its will by the filing of an involuntary petition against an alleged debtor. There are different instances in which creditors, shareholders, or partners may force an entity into bankruptcy. A petition filed by an entity other than the debtor is an involuntary petition. Section 303 of the Code contains the rules governing involuntary proceedings.[36] Section 303 is designed to equitably resolve the rights of an entity and its creditors while the issue of the involuntary bankruptcy is pending.

As discussed in chapter 1 supra, until the Bankruptcy Act of 1898, most bankruptcies were initiated as involuntary proceedings. That is, the proceedings were initiated by creditors against an alleged debtor. Until the Twentieth Century, involuntary bankruptcy was the traditional method of placing a debtor into bankruptcy. This is no longer the case in the United States. Almost all proceedings now filed are voluntary; involuntary proceedings are rare.

Under the Bankruptcy Act and its many predecessors, a debtor became legally bankrupt only when the court entered an order adjudicating the debtor bankrupt.[37] The Code has adopted the phrase "order for relief" to replace the prior language of "adjudicated as a bankrupt." Under the Bankruptcy Code, an order for relief is automatic when a voluntary petition is filed.[38] In an involuntary proceeding, an order for relief will only issue

35. Bankruptcy Rule 1015.
36. 11 U.S.C. §303.
37. 11 U.S.C. §41(f). This, of course, is a reference to 11 U.S.C. as it existed prior to October 1, 1978.
38. 11 U.S.C. §301.

upon a default by the debtor or upon the court's finding that cause exists to enter an order for relief in a contested proceeding.

The best way to consider the practical effect of an involuntary proceeding is to think of it in the terms of a traditional lawsuit. The creditors who initiate the proceeding are the equivalent of plaintiffs, although they are generally referred to as **petitioning creditors**. Until an order for relief is entered, the debtor is usually referred to as an alleged debtor. The alleged debtor is the equivalent of a defendant. The specific relief or judgment sought by the petitioning creditors is the entry of an **order for relief**.

An involuntary petition is filed and served in a manner identical to a summons and complaint in a traditional lawsuit. A debtor may or may not contest the petition. If there is no opposition the debtor will have an order for relief entered against it by default. If an alleged debtor contests the petition, the court will hold a trial to determine whether an order for relief should be entered. Discovery techniques and pretrial procedures may take place prior to the trial. The initiation of an involuntary petition thus constitutes the commencement of a lawsuit where the "plaintiffs" seek the entry of an "order for relief" as the judgment.[39]

The time period between the filing of an involuntary petition and the entry of an order for relief can perhaps best be described as the period of time during which the creditors believe an alleged debtor is bankrupt while the alleged debtor believes it is not bankrupt. This period of time is often referred to as the "gap" or "limbo" period. Other provisions of the Bankruptcy Code help to establish the distributive rights of any creditors whose claims arise during this period.[40] These provisions are described in detail in chapter 21 infra.

Creditors may initiate involuntary proceedings for a number of reasons. First, a proceeding may be initiated to prevent a debtor from continuing to commit known fraudulent transfers by wrongful dissipation of assets from the reach of creditors.

Second, there may occasionally arise a potential debtor who desperately needs to utilize the bankruptcy system, but who absolutely refuses to do so. Perhaps the debtor owns a piece of property with enough equity to pay all creditors in full, but the property is about to be foreclosed upon. The potential debtor insists that no bankruptcy will be filed. Creditors in this instance might initiate an involuntary bankruptcy to gain the benefits of the automatic stay thereby preventing the immediate foreclosure. This will protect any equity in the property for payment of the creditor claims.[41]

---

39. 11 U.S.C. §303(h); Bankruptcy Rule 1018.
40. 11 U.S.C. §502(f); 11 U.S.C. §507(a)(2). See chapter 21 infra.
41. 11 U.S.C. §362. See chapter 12 infra.

A third common reason for initiating an involuntary proceeding involves partnerships. As discussed above, a voluntary partnership filing must normally be accompanied by an authorization showing consent to the filing by all of the general partners or evidencing appropriate authority to file on behalf of all general partners.[42] Simply put, all general partners to a voluntary filing must sign the petition or the court must be provided with evidence that all general partners consent, such as a general management clause in favor of a managing partner or some other form of acceptable proxy. If one or more general partners refuse to consent to a voluntary filing, or if a debtor has a number of general partners and within the time limits for action it is not physically possible to obtain their written consent, the Code permits one general partner to initiate an involuntary proceeding.[43] Thus, one general partner may conceivably force a bankruptcy of the partnership over the objection of the remaining general partners.

An involuntary petition may only seek to place a debtor into Chapter 7 or Chapter 11 proceedings. An involuntary Chapter 12 or 13 proceeding cannot be initiated. Further, an involuntary proceeding may only be initiated against an entity that may be a debtor under Chapter 7 or Chapter 11.[44]

Three specific types of entities may not have involuntary proceedings initiated against them. Involuntary proceedings may not be initiated against certain charitable and nonprofit organizations, such as churches, schools, or charitable foundations. Farmers are exempt from involuntary proceedings because Congress has found essentially that one lean year should not permit a farmer to be forced into bankruptcy by its creditors. It is for this same reason that involuntary Chapter 12 proceedings may not be initiated, as they are proceedings for family farmers. Finally, because Chapter 13 is an effort by a consumer to repay debt, Congress has found that to permit involuntary Chapter 13 filings would be akin to creating a form of involuntary servitude, because it would force a debtor to repay debt.[45] Involuntary servitude is of course unconstitutional under the Thirteenth Amendment.[46]

The petitioning creditors are required to file a petition to initiate an involuntary proceeding. The format of an involuntary petition is contained in Official Form 5.[47] Because the filing of an involuntary petition initiates a lawsuit or assumes the status of a lawsuit, a summons must be issued and served on the alleged debtor. Once served with the summons, the alleged debtor has 20 days to respond to the petition.[48] If the alleged debtor does

---

42. Bankruptcy Rule 1004(a).
43. 11 U.S.C. §303(b)(3).
44. 11 U.S.C. §303(a). See also chapter 5 infra.
45. 11 U.S.C. §303(a). See also Historical and Revision Notes to Section 303.
46. U.S. Const. amend. XIII.
47. See forms disk, form 4.5.
48. Bankruptcy Rule 1010; Bankruptcy Rule 1011(b).

nothing, the creditors can have an order for relief entered by default. This activity is equivalent to obtaining a default judgment in traditional non-bankruptcy litigation.[49]

Section 303(b) identifies the creditors who may initiate an involuntary proceeding. Normally three unsecured creditors with undisputed aggregate claims of at least $12,300 are required to initiate a proceeding.[50] The three creditors join together and file the involuntary petition. If an alleged debtor has eleven or fewer undisputed unsecured creditors, then any one such creditor may initiate a petition as long as the petitioning creditor is owed at least $12,300.[51] For example, if a potential debtor has eleven unsecured creditors owed in the aggregate less than $12,300 it will be impossible for the creditors to initiate an involuntary proceeding against the debtor because there is less than $12,300 in total debt and no single creditor is owed at least $12,300.

If the alleged debtor is a partnership, an involuntary proceeding may be commenced by one or more of the general partners initiating the petition. This allows a partnership, where there is disagreement between the partners, to commence a proceeding without the consent of all general partners. If a general partner has filed a bankruptcy proceeding, the partner's bankruptcy trustee has the authority to initiate the involuntary proceeding against the partnership.[52]

For instance, assume a general partnership composed of three general partners, Moe, Curley, and Larry. The partnership owns a valuable piece of property that is about to be foreclosed upon. Moe and Larry want the partnership to file a bankruptcy immediately to gain the protections of the automatic stay. Curley opposes this. Moe and Larry file an involuntary petition against the partnership seeking the entry of an order for relief over the objection of Curley. If either Moe or Larry were themselves debtors in a bankruptcy proceeding, their bankruptcy trustee would also have a right to file the involuntary petition.

Once an involuntary petition is filed, additional qualified creditors may join in the filing of the petition simply by filing a onepage pleading with the court joining in the petition. This has the same effect as if the creditor had originally joined in the petition.[53] Significantly more than three creditors may therefore ultimately join in an involuntary petition.

---

49. 11 U.S.C. §303(b).
50. 11 U.S.C. §303(b)(1). The 1994 Amendments added §104(b) to the Code. This provision acts to tri-annually adjust a number of the amounts set forth in various provisions of the Bankruptcy Code, such as §303(b)(1). The first adjustment took place on April 1, 1998. The text reflects the 2004 adjustments.
51. 11 U.S.C. §303(b)(2).
52. 11 U.S.C. §303(b)(3).
53. 11 U.S.C. §303(c).

There are benefits to be gained by the petitioning creditors in seeking the joinder of as many creditors as possible to an involuntary proceeding. For instance, a debtor may be able to show that one or more of the three petitioning creditors does not really have a proper claim, or that the total of the three claims is less than $12,300, or that one or more of the claims is actually in dispute. In each of these circumstances a debtor may defeat an otherwise proper petition on this sort of technicality. The joinder of additional creditors provides for creditor unity and prevents a debtor from successfully contesting a petition on a procedural technicality. Joinder helps strengthen the case for the petitioning creditors.

An alleged debtor or nonpetitioning partner may contest the allegations of the petition.[54] The ability of an alleged debtor to do this makes the alleged debtor the functional equivalent of a defendant. If the allegations are contested, then the court will hold a trial to determine whether an order for relief should be entered. Due to the unique financial status that the initiation of an involuntary proceeding creates for an alleged debtor, the Federal Rules of Bankruptcy Procedure direct the court to give preference to the matter on its calendar.[55] The Federal Rules of Bankruptcy Procedure applicable to adversary proceedings, which are essentially the Federal Rules of Civil Procedure, apply in contested involuntary proceedings.[56]

The petitioning creditors must prove the existence of one of two circumstances to obtain an order for relief. The first circumstance is that the debtor is generally not paying its debts as they become due.[57] This is not the same as being insolvent. Ironically, the debtor's solvency is technically irrelevant to the determination of whether to enter an order for relief in an involuntary proceeding. A debtor who is not paying its bills on time may or may not be insolvent.

For example, a senior citizen with Alzheimer's disease may simply forget to pay bills or may throw them in the wastebasket. The person may be fabulously rich, but the person is not generally paying debts as they become due. An order for relief could be entered against this potential debtor. It is therefore important to recognize that the solvency of a debtor is not an issue to determine in connection with an involuntary proceeding except as insolvency may or may not relate to the debtor not generally paying its debts as they become due. Of course, presenting evidence of insolvency may be a relevant fact for the court to consider as evidence in making its determination.

---

54. Bankruptcy Rule 1011(a).
55. Bankruptcy Rule 1013(a).
56. Bankruptcy Rule 1018. See Part VII of the Federal Rules of Bankruptcy Procedure. See also chapter 12 infra describing adversary proceedings.
57. 11 U.S.C. §303(h)(1).

The second circumstance that can result in the entry of an order for relief in an involuntary proceeding is that within 120 days prior to the filing of the petition, a custodian took possession of some portion of the estate's assets. For instance, the appointment of a receiver or an assignment for benefit of creditors will cause this situation to arise.[58] The term *custodian* is discussed in more detail in chapter 6 infra.

If the court can find that one of the two circumstances described above exists, then an order for relief will be entered. Once an order for relief is entered, the petition will then proceed exactly as if it had been initiated by the filing of a voluntary petition. All the documents previously described in this chapter will have to be filed, but the time limits will be counted from the date of entry of the order for relief.[59] When the debtor is not available or does not file the required documents after the entry of an order for relief in an involuntary proceeding, it becomes the responsibility of the petitioning creditors to file the required documents to the best of their ability.[60]

The filing of an involuntary petition is a rather extreme creditor remedy. It has obvious and immediate adverse effects on an alleged debtor. For instance, a business may suffer immediate loss of business merely due to the announcement of the filing. Although the creditors require ample protection in appropriate cases, a debtor who may not be found bankrupt requires protection to preserve the estate without the burden or stigma of a pending Title 11 proceeding. An improperly filed petition or a contested petition that takes too long to resolve can sometimes be fatal to what may have previously been a successful individual or business and become a self-fulfilling prophecy. Because of the diametrically opposed concerns of the creditors and the alleged debtor in these circumstances, certain provisions contained in Section 303 protect an alleged debtor while the issue of the petition is pending. Other provisions are designed to protect the creditors during the "gap" or "limbo" period. Once again, this is the period of time between the initiation of the petition and either the entry of an order for relief or a dismissal of the petition. This limbo period can also be described as that period of time during which creditors consider the entity bankrupt, but the alleged debtor considers itself as not bankrupt.

When a debtor may be dissipating the assets of an estate in fraud of creditors while contesting a petition, the creditors can seek the immediate appointment of an interim trustee prior to the entry of an order for relief. The court has further discretion to enter any appropriate order necessary to preserve the estate.[61] This provision affords the creditors protection in an appropriate case.

58. 11 U.S.C. §303(h)(2).
59. Bankruptcy Rule 1007(c).
60. Bankruptcy Rule 1007(k).
61. 11 U.S.C. §303(g).

On the other hand, the court also has discretion to enter appropriate orders that protect the debtor. Under Section 303(e) the court can require petitioning creditors to post a bond to satisfy any damages that may be sustained by the debtor in the event the debtor is successful in contesting the petition.[62] The imposition of a significant bond acts as a deterrent to abusive creditors and a protection for debtors who do not properly belong in the bankruptcy system.

An alleged debtor may conduct business as usual. Consistent with the foregoing, however, the court may enter any appropriate order to protect the creditors or the alleged debtor.[63] This may sometimes result in the imposition of some controls and disclosure to the creditors regarding an alleged debtor's financial affairs while the involuntary petition remains pending.

If the court dismisses an involuntary petition, other than on agreement of the parties, the court has effectively rendered a judgment in favor of the alleged debtor. In this event, the court may order the petitioning creditors to pay the debtor's expenses, costs, attorneys' fees, and any actual damages caused by the petition. If the court further finds that the petitioners acted in bad faith, the court can also award a debtor punitive damages.[64] The bond referred to above should be based on an estimate of damages an alleged debtor may incur.[65] These burdens act as a deterrent to prevent creditors from abusing the system by wrongfully forcing entities into bankruptcy.

Summary

A bankruptcy proceeding is initiated by the filing of a petition. The petition may be filed voluntarily or involuntarily: When a debtor files the petition it is called a voluntary petition; when creditors file the petition it is called an involuntary petition. The voluntary petition is the most frequently used method of initiating a bankruptcy proceeding. Consumer debtors must obtain a credit counseling certificate from an approved credit counseling service within 180 days prior to filing, absent exigent circumstances. A debt relief-agency must provide disclosures to debtors and obtain written retainer agreements.

A debtor is not legally bankrupt until the court enters an order for relief. This order is automatic when a voluntary petition is filed and

62. 11 U.S.C. §303(e).
63. 11 U.S.C. §303(f).
64. 11 U.S.C. §303(i).
65. 11 U.S.C. §303(e).

is the judgment that the petitioning creditors seek in an involuntary petition.

A husband and wife may initiate a joint proceeding. No other combination of multiple debtors may initiate a proceeding together. However, two or more debtors may have their proceedings consolidated by motion for either substantive or administrative purposes.

The procedure of an involuntary petition can be compared to a nonbankruptcy lawsuit. The petitioning creditors are essentially plaintiffs who seek the entry of an order for relief against an alleged debtor who is essentially a defendant. An order for relief is entered upon either the debtor's default or after the court holds a trial upon a contested petition.

When an involuntary petition is contested, the court must be able to make one of two findings to enter an order for relief. The first of these is that the debtor is not generally paying its debts as they become due. The second is that within 120 days prior to the filing, a custodian has been appointed to administer assets of the debtor. A custodian could be an assignee for the benefit of creditors or a state court receiver.

The period of time between the filing of an involuntary petition and the entry of an order for relief or dismissal of the petition is known as the "limbo" or "gap" period. During this period the court may enter appropriate equitable orders to protect the rights of either the creditors or debtor. If the petition is dismissed, other than on agreement of the parties, the court may award the debtor costs, attorneys' fees, and actual damages. In an appropriate case, the court is empowered to award punitive damages.

When an order for relief is entered in an involuntary petition, the proceeding will thereafter continue as if it were a voluntary proceeding.

KEY TERMS

administrative consolidation
alleged debtor
assisted person
bankruptcy assistance
debt relief agency
involuntary petition
joint case
order for relief
petitioning creditors
prepetition credit counseling
Schedules
Statement of Affairs
Statements and Schedules
substantive consolidation
venue
voluntary petition

Chapter 4 Checklist

4.1 VOLUNTARY PETITION DOCUMENT CHECKLIST

	Authority
4.1.1 To Be Filed with Petition:	
1. Petition	Official Form 1
2. Filing fee filing fees as of October 17, 2005: Chapter 7—$274 Chapter 11—$1039 Chapter 12—$39 Chapter 13—$189 filing fees may be paid in installments or waived for indigent debtors	Bankruptcy Rule 1006
3. Statement of Social Security Number	Bankruptcy Rule 1007(f)
4. Corporate resolution or partnership consent	Bankruptcy Rule 1004; Local Rule
5. List of creditors	Bankruptcy Rule 1007(a)(1)
6. Prepetiton credit counseling certificate	§109(h)
4.1.2 To Be Filed within 10 Days of Petition — Bankruptcy Petition Preparer Statement of Compensation	§110 (h)
4.1.3 To Be Filed within 15 Days of Petition — Statements and Schedules:	
1. Schedules of Assets and Liabilities	11 U.S.C. §521(a)(1)(B)(i); Bankruptcy Rule 1007(b); Official Form 7
2. Schedule of Current Income and Expenditures; Schedule of Executory Contracts and Unexpired Leases	11 U.S.C. §521(a)(1)(B)(ii); Bankruptcy Rule 1007(b); Official Form 6

		Authority
	3. Statement of Financial Affairs	11 U.S.C. §521(a)(1)(B)(iii); Bankruptcy Rule 1007(b); Official Form 7
	4. Claims of exemptions	11 U.S.C. §522(1) Bankruptcy Rule 4003(a)
	5. Attorney statement of compensation paid or promised	11 U.S.C. §329; Bankruptcy Rule 2016(b)
4.1.4	To Be Filed within 30 Days of Petition: Statement of Intent re Secured Collateral	11 U.S.C. §521(a)(2)
4.1.5	To be filed within 45 days of Petition[66]	
	1. Attorney compliance with §342(b)	11 U.S.C.§521(a)(1)(B)(iii)
	2. Evidence of wages paid within 60 days of filing	11 U.S.C.§521(a)(1)(B)(iv)
	3. Calculation of current monthly income	11 U.S.C.§521(a)(1)(B)(v)
	4. Disclosure of any increases in income or expenses anticipated over the next 12 months	11 U.S.C.§521(a)(1)(B)(vi)
4.1.6	Within 7 days of creditor meeting provide trustee Tax return for year preceding the filing	11 U.S.C.§521(e)(2)(A)(i)
4.1.7.	Failure to file any required document within 45 days of filing results in automatic dismissal on 46th day. One 45-day extension may be obtained.	11 U.S.C.§521(i)

66. BAPA imposes these new requirements but does not state their deadline for filing except as set forth in 11 U.S.C. §521(i) requiring automatic dismissal on the 46th day if the required documents are not filed. The Bankruptcy Rules will undoubtedly be revised to account for these new requirements and should be consulted.

	Authority
4.2 SPECIAL CHAPTER 13 REQUIREMENTS	
4.2.1 Chapter 13 Plan (within 15 Days)	11 U.S.C. §1321; Bankruptcy Rule 3015
4.3 INVOLUNTARY PETITION CHECKLIST	
4.3.1 Summons and Involuntary Petition Official	11 U.S.C. §303; Form 5
4.3.2 Qualifying Creditors	
1. Three undisputed unsecured creditors owed at least $12,300 in aggregate	11 U.S.C. §303(b)(1)
2. One undisputed unsecured creditor owed at least $12,300 where there are eleven creditors or fewer	11 U.S.C. §303(b)(2)
3. One or more general partners where less than all consent to filing	11 U.S.C. §303(b)(3)
4.3.3 Obtaining an Order for Relief	
1. Default	11 U.S.C. §303(b)
2. Grounds for entering order in contested petition	
a. debtor is not generally paying debts as they become due	11 U.S.C. §303(h)(1)
b. appointment of custodian within 120 days of filing	11 U.S.C. §303(h)(2)

DISCUSSION QUESTIONS

1. How is a voluntary bankruptcy proceeding commenced?
2. What is a joint case?
3. How can multiple bankruptcy proceedings be consolidated? What is the difference between administrative and substantive consolidation?
4. Describe the basic documents filed by any debtor in a bankruptcy proceeding.

5. What are some of the reasons for initiating an involuntary bankruptcy against a debtor?
6. What are the grounds that petitioning creditors must prove to obtain an order for relief in an involuntary bankruptcy proceeding?
7. What provisions of the Bankruptcy Code protect the rights of creditors or the alleged debtor while an involuntary bankruptcy petition is pending?
8. What purposes might the prepetition credit counseling requirement serve? What drawbacks, if any, might the requirement have?

5

Chapter 1 — General Provisions

Chapter 1 of the Code contains a number of definitions and other general provisions. The provisions of Chapter 1 apply in all bankruptcy proceedings.[1] Many of the provisions of Chapter 1 are so broad and basic that their location and existence are sometimes forgotten when conducting bankruptcy research. Chapter 1 should not be overlooked. Substantial research time can be saved by seeking the meaning of a term or phrase within Chapter 1 rather than trying to find the answer by implication through use of another section or case law. Many items that are implicit in other Code sections or are not discussed in the case law are in fact explicitly set forth in Chapter 1.

Although not part of Chapter 1 of the Bankruptcy Code, the concept of "Needs Based Bankruptcy," 11 U.S.C. §707(b)(2), colloquially known as "means testing," determines who may be a debtor in Chapter 7. As a result, the material is covered in this chapter of the text. Needs Based Bankruptcy was introduced to the Bankruptcy Code by BAPA in 2005.

Section 102 contains several basic rules of construction. The phrases defined in Section 102 will always have the same meaning whenever used in another section of the Bankruptcy Code unless a specific provision states otherwise.

A. NOTICE AND A HEARING

The first provision of Section 102 describes the phrase **notice and hearing**. This phrase, wherever used, signifies that due process must be given to

1. 11 U.S.C. §103(a). See chapter 2 supra.

various parties involved in the proceeding before a court order authorizing the action that is sought to be performed can be obtained. In the context of the Bankruptcy Code, **due process** often means that the affected parties must merely be given notice and an *opportunity* to be heard. A hearing may not always be required.

When the phrase "after notice and a hearing" is used in a specific Code section there are two basic ways to proceed: a **noticed motion** or an **ex parte** application.[2] Many routine matters can be determined at a minimum of time and expense to all parties and prevent court calendars from becoming impossibly congested. Essentially, these are the general procedures governing motion practice in the Bankruptcy Courts.

The motion procedure set forth in Federal Rules of Bankruptcy Procedure (FRBP) Rule 9013 is the most common way of filing motions in the Bankruptcy Courts. Most matters coming through the Bankruptcy Court for decision will come before the court through this process.[3] The motion should state with particularity the relief sought, contain a proof of service, a notice of hearing, a proposed order for the relief requested, and be accompanied by one or more supporting affidavits unless the debtor is an individual consumer debtor.[4] When the value of an asset is in issue, as will commonly be the case in a motion for relief from the automatic stay (see chapter 12 infra), a valuation report must be filed with the motion.[5]

A motion typically must be "served at least 20 days prior to the hearing date," although local rules may vary this period in some situations.[6] Since FRBP 9006(f) requires that three additional days be added to any required notice period when the notice is given by mail, and since most notices are mailed in everyday practice, three days should be added to all notice periods. Notice periods, as described throughout the text, do *not* include this additional three-day period. A motion must be filed against any entity against whom relief is sought, the debtor, the debtor's attorney, the trustee, any creditor committee in the case (see chapter 10 infra), any entity having a lien on any property that may be affected by the motion's outcome, and

2. In 1999, amendments to the FRBP were proposed that would have standardized motion practice in bankruptcy courts throughout the country. The proposed rules revisions ultimately were not adopted. The Official Committee Note to the proposed rules stated: "These amendments provide more detailed procedural guidelines than provided in the past. This change is intended to increase uniformity in litigation practice among districts and to reduce the number of local rules." The text uses these proposed rules to discuss motion procedures because even though the rules were not adopted, they reflect motion procedures used in Bankruptcy Courts around the country (readers are advised to consult their own local rules).
3. FRBP 9013.
4. Proposed FRBP 9014(b). See also FRBP 9006(d); FRBP 9013.
5. Proposed FRBP 9014(b)(3)(B).
6. FRBP 2002(a). There are some exceptions to this general rule. For example, FRBP 2002(b) requires 25 days' notice of a Chapter 11 disclosure statement hearing (see chapter 26 infra). The exceptions are noted in the text and are summarized in the Appendix.

any other entity that may be entitled to notice, such as the United States Trustee.

Any response to a motion should be filed and served within any time periods set by local rules. Any party or entity served with the original motion must be served with any response filed by any party responding to the motion. It is possible that there may be multiple responses.[7] For example, a trustee seeks to sell a piece of real property subject to two mortgages, a tax lien, a judgment lien, and the debtor's claim of exemption. All five of these parties could conceivably file a response to the motion.

Unless the debtor is an individual consumer debtor, any response must be accompanied by a proof of service, a proposed order for the relief requested, one or more supporting affidavits if there is a factual dispute, and a report of value if the value of a property is an issue in the motion, such as in a motion for relief from the automatic stay (see chapter 12 infra).[8]

Section 342(c) provides that any notice to a creditor contain the last four digits of the debtor's taxpayer identification number. Notices are to be sent to the address specified by the creditor, which the creditor may designate in at least two notices sent to the debtor within 90 days prior to the filing pursuant to new §342(c)(2) (as a practical matter, this information will likely come to be found in monthly statements). Creditors will also be able to file notices with a bankruptcy court designating an address to which bankruptcy notices are to be sent in Chapter 7 and 13 cases. Notices sent to a different address will not be effective until brought to the creditor's attention, pursuant to new §342(g). This provision thus has a potentially dramatic effect upon the automatic stay, the consequences of which will be left for case law to evolve.

Sometimes a matter coming before the Bankruptcy Court by way of a motion may contain disputed issues of fact that require further hearing by the court before a ruling can be made. In these instances, the court may conduct one or more preliminary hearings, often known as status conferences; may permit the parties to conduct discovery as in a traditional lawsuit; and may ultimately conduct the equivalent of a trial, commonly known as an **evidentiary hearing**, when the trial arises from a motion.

For example, Fran Fine objects to the claim of a store, Looks Like Jewelry, in her Chapter 13 case. Fran claims that the creditor store defrauded her into believing that the cubic zirconia she bought was really a big diamond. To resolve the matter, the court permits the parties to conduct discovery and ultimately holds an evidentiary hearing to rule on the objection. If Fran were suing Looks Like Jewelry in a traditional lawsuit, the evidentiary hearing would be the trial.

---

7. FBP 9014.
8. FRBP 9014.

Some matters may be applied for without a noticed motion, on an ex parte basis (without notice in certain limited circumstances). A matter that comes before the court in this manner is generally called an *ex parte application*. Some examples of matters that may be brought before the court on an an ex parte application include conversion of a case (see chapter 8 infra), dismissal of a Chapter 13 case (see chapter 23 infra), and requests for Rule 2004 examinations (see chapter 7 infra).[9]

An ex parte application should set forth with particularity the relief sought and be accompanied by a proof of service and a proposed order.[10] Any ex parte application must be served on the debtor's attorney, the trustee, and a creditors committee in a case where there is a creditors committee and any other entity required by federal law or by the FRBP, including the United States Trustee. No response is required, and the court will generally enter the order requested if there is no response. The FRBPs do not set forth a response time. Typically, local rules require any response to be filed within five days.[11]

Sometimes emergencies arise that may require court orders in less time than the rules permit. For example, a trustee is appointed the interim trustee of a restaurant or store that sells perishable goods. The trustee cannot wait 20 days or more to obtain court approval to sell the inventory. The tomatoes will get soft. The milk and eggs will spoil. The rules contemplate this sort of emergency and permit an order to be entered on less than 20 days' notice. In local procedure, such a practice may also be known as an *order shortening time*. Section 102(1)(B)(ii) specifically permits this sort of relief in appropriate circumstances.

The appendix summarizes matters that may be filed as noticed motions and matters that may be filed as ex parte applications, along with a summary of the parties to be served in each instance.

In understanding the due process provisions of the Code described in Section 102, it is helpful to identify the types of activities requiring some form of due process. It is also helpful to explore the practical implications of the imposition of due process upon both the courts and parties involved with the bankruptcy system. Affording parties due process is one of the most important and overriding features of the Bankruptcy Code.

Because virtually all of a debtor's financial affairs are placed under the jurisdiction of the court in a bankruptcy proceeding, many of a debtor's financial activities will require prior court approval. For instance, in a Chapter 11 a debtor will require court approval to liquidate assets, to

9. FRBP 9013. See appendix 1 for a list of matters that may be the subject of an application for an order.
10. FRBP 9013.
11. See, e.g., Local Rule 9014-3(h) of the Eastern District of Pennsylvania and Local Rule 9013(d) of the District of New Jersey. Each of these rules permits the court to enter an order if no response is filed within the response period.

assume or reject existing leases, and even to approve the officer's salaries, among other things.[12] The trustee in a Chapter 7 will require court approval to liquidate or abandon assets, among other things.[13]

Most matters affecting the administration of an estate will require notice to all creditors by the party seeking permission to take a specific action. Matters affecting the rights of particular parties or assets, such as a motion for relief from the automatic stay, will require notice only to affected parties. Court orders in some ex parte matters may limit the notice period and may limit the number of parties who will actually receive the notice.[14]

Court action takes time. This "legal time" is often not consistent with the logic or pace of the business world. The time involved in making business decisions is often shorter than the bankruptcy system's decision-making process. Knowing how to use the system effectively can help to synchronize these two disparate and inconsistent decision-making processes as much as possible without requiring substantial compromise. Besides, the minimum legal notice requirements cannot be compromised; they must be complied with.

For instance, in many situations involving the operation of businesses in Chapter 11, the ability to properly assimilate the legal and business time systems can sometimes rescue an otherwise apparently hopeless situation. This may involve nothing more than advising a client how long it will realistically take to obtain a necessary court approval to perform a transaction so the client can plan accordingly. It may also involve prompt and immediate court action at the outset to define the basic rights between a debtor and hostile creditors. This prompt action, when required, can be the difference between the potential for success or the certainty of failure in a Chapter 11 proceeding.

B. RULES OF GRAMMATICAL CONSTRUCTION

The remainder of Section 102 deals with various statements of grammatic or semantic construction. Use of the singular includes the plural.[15] This is self-explanatory. The word "or" is not exclusive.[16] This means that when the word "or" appears, its use means that any listed choice available in

12. 11 U.S.C. §363; 11 U.S.C. §365; 11 U.S.C. §327; 11 U.S.C. §1107(b); Bankruptcy Rule 2014. See chapters 18, 19, and 24 infra.
13. 11 U.S.C. §363; 11 U.S.C. §554. See chapters 18 and 20 infra.
14. Bankruptcy Rule 2002.
15. 11 U.S.C. §102(7).
16. 11 U.S.C. §102(5).

the affected section may apply. Proof of one given alternative will normally result in the application of the appropriate Code section in issue. Often more than one alternative may apply. For example, Section 363(f) provides five alternative means of selling a property "free and clear of liens." The existence of at least one alternative must be found to exist with regard to each lien upon the property.[17]

The words "include" and "including" are deemed to not be limiting.[18] This means that if a given Code section makes use of the words "includes" or "including," any following list provides examples of actions that may be taken or proven to allow application of a particular section. If, however, actions or facts not within the given list are shown to be within the intent of the Code section involved, the additional action or facts may be considered by the court. For example, Section 1104(a)(1) provides a list of situations that justify the appointment of a trustee in a Chapter 11. The use of the word "including" in this section means that there may be other situations not specifically described that the court may also consider in determining to appoint a trustee.[19]

Conspicuously absent from Section 102 is a provision stating that the masculine includes the feminine. This is because the Bankruptcy Code has been written in a gender-neutral format.

C. POWERS OF THE COURT

Section 105 concerns the court's powers. The Bankruptcy Courts have traditionally been considered courts of equity. Recall from chapter 1 of the text that composition agreements in seventeenth-century England were within the jurisdiction of the Chancery, or equity courts. Courts of equity have always had much discretion to formulate rulings and orders to give practical effect to the matters before them. Section 105 specifically gives the Bankruptcy Court equitable authority to enact any orders that are necessary to carry out the provisions of the Bankruptcy Code.[20] Some would suggest that an argument to the court based upon Section 105 is weak, signifying no authority elsewhere in the Code to support a proposed action. In fact, a Section 105 issue may involve the court's being requested to rule against a specific provision in the Code where it does not make logical sense to apply it, such application not being in the best interests of the estate or creditors in

17. See chapter 18 infra.
18. 11 U.S.C. §102(3).
19. 11 U.S.C. §1104(a)(1). See chapter 10 infra.
20. 11 U.S.C. §105.

a unique situation. This section is specifically designed to deal with those unique circumstances that may arise from time to time where no Code provision governs the conduct of the parties in a particular transaction, or where the court's equitable powers are necessary to enable the bankruptcy system to properly perform its intended purpose as a debt collection device. Thus, when formulating an argument under Section 105, the most practical method of analysis is to apply the traditional nonbankruptcy concepts of equity balancing to the problem at hand. Reaching out to the court's inherent equitable powers is the essence of Section 105.

Section 105(d) authorizes the court, on its own motion and after notice to the parties in interest, to hold a status conference in any case and to issue any order deemed appropriate to ensure the expeditious and economic handling of a case. This provision was added to the Code in 1994 and simply codifies what had been the existing practice of many Bankruptcy Courts. Under this provision, for example, the court may monitor the status of an adversary proceeding (see chapter 12 section A infra) or the prosecution of a Chapter 11 proceeding to ensure that each matter is being pursued to a resolution.

D. STATUTES OF LIMITATIONS

Section 108 concerns the effect of a bankruptcy proceeding upon nonbankruptcy statutes of limitation for any rights exercisable by the debtor or estate. Section 108(a) effectively extends nonbankruptcy statutes of limitation for the protection of creditors and trustee. The reason for this is that the assets of a bankruptcy estate may include claims that a debtor has against third parties, such as personal injury claims or breach of contract claims. Sometimes, when a trustee is appointed in a proceeding, a debtor has not exercised its rights or a trustee does not immediately learn of the claim's existence. Section 108(a) therefore acts to extend any underlying nonbankruptcy statutes of limitation.

A trustee may select one of two defined limitations periods within which to proceed. The longer of the two periods may be utilized by the trustee to commence an action. Under Section 108(a), the limitations period will be the later of the original expiration date of the underlying statute of limitations, or two years after the entry of the order for relief.

For example, in California the statute of limitations to commence an action for breach of a written contract is four years.[21] Assume that a bankruptcy

21. Cal. Code Civ. Proc. §339.

is filed three years after a claim arises. The trustee would actually have a total of five years from the date the claim arose to bring an action on behalf of the estate, because the two-year extension provided for under Section 108(a) is later than the four-year period provided for under California law. If three years and 364 days had expired prior to the filing of the bankruptcy proceeding, the trustee would have two years and one day to bring the claim. On the other hand, if only one year has elapsed prior to the bankruptcy filing, the original four-year limitation period of nonbankruptcy law will apply because it is longer than two years after the entry of the order for relief. Finally, if the statute of limitations has expired prior to the bankruptcy filing, Section 108(a) does not revive the claim for the trustee.

E. WHO MAY BE A DEBTOR

Section 109 defines the entities that may be debtors in the various types of bankruptcy proceedings. Only *persons* may be debtors.[22] An individual is a person. A corporation can be a person. A partnership can also be a person.[23] A person has to reside or be domiciled in the United States or have a place of business or property in the United States. United States citizenship is not required to be a debtor in bankruptcy proceedings.[24]

Any person may file a Chapter 7 except railroads, insurance companies, banks, or savings and loan institutions.[25] The insurance company prohibition does not bar insurance agents from filing — only the companies actually writing the insurance policies. There are separate regulatory agencies that deal with insolvent insurance companies because there are myriad issues arising that are too complex and unusual to be considered within the purview of the bankruptcy system. For example, there are the rights of the policy holders, the rights of the claim holders, and the rights of the shareholders and other general creditors. Separate regulation pays more careful attention to these precise relationships. Similarly, banks and savings and loans are regulated when they become insolvent either by state agencies or, in the case of federally insured financial institutions, by either the Federal Savings and Loan Insurance Corporation (FSLIC), the Federal Deposit Insurance Corporation (FDIC), or their successor, the Resolution Trust

22. 11 U.S.C. §109(a). See chapter 6 infra.
23. 11 U.S.C. §101(41). See chapter 6 infra.
24. 11 U.S.C. §109(a).
25. 11 U.S.C. §109(b).

Corporation (RTC). When a financial institution is taken over by a regulatory agency it means that the institution is effectively bankrupt.

A Chapter 9 debtor may only be a municipality, if and only if state law permits the municipality to file a Chapter 9. States may bar municipalities from seeking Chapter 9 relief.[26]

Anyone who may be a debtor under Chapter 7 may be a debtor under Chapter 11 except stock brokers or commodity brokers.[27] A separate subchapter of Chapter 7 deals specifically with the issues arising when stock or commodity brokers file bankruptcy proceedings.[28] Filings of this type are most likely to occur only in those districts that are national financial centers, such as the Southern District of New York (New York City) and the Northern District of Illinois (Chicago). As a result, they are beyond the scope of this work. Railroads may file Chapter 11s. This is the only type of proceeding that railroads may file.[29]

In 1991, in Toibb v. Radloff, the U.S. Supreme Court examined whether or not an individual could qualify for Chapter 11 relief. In this case, an individual debtor not engaged in business sought Chapter 11 relief. The lower courts held that a nonbusiness debtor does not qualify for Chapter 11 relief. The Supreme Court applied the literal language of the Code and held that individuals may seek Chapter 11 relief, stating: "Under certain circumstances a consumer debtor's estate will be worth more if reorganized under Chapter 11 than if liquidated under Chapter 7."[30]

Recall that the 2005 BAPA legislation adds §109(h) to the Code. This provision requires individual debtors to obtain a credit counseling certificate as a prerequisite to filing, or to obtain a certificate within 30 days of filing when exigent circumstances are present. See Section 4A supra.

The definition of who may be a debtor under Chapter 12 is described in chapter 27 infra.

There are four requirements that must be met to qualify for Chapter 13 relief. First the debtor must be an individual. *Individual* means a human being, not a partnership or corporation. Second, the debtor must have regular income. Under the Bankruptcy Act, a debtor had to be a wage earner to qualify for Chapter XIII. Under the Bankruptcy Code, a debtor need only be an individual with regular income. The following sorts of individuals can qualify to be Chapter 13 debtors: wage earners, individuals whose regular income sources are Social Security, disability, or other sorts of pensions, and individuals whose source of regular income may be dividends from trusts or stocks. Regular income can be many things. Sooner or later there is certain to be a reported proceeding where a state lottery jackpot winner will file

26. 11 U.S.C. §109(c).
27. 11 U.S.C. §109(d).
28. 11 U.S.C. §§741-766.
29. 11 U.S.C. §109(d).
30. Toibb v. Radloff, 501 U.S. 157 (1991).

a Chapter 13. If the jackpot to the debtor is paid over a period of time, the payments should meet the regular income requirements of Section 109.

Regular income does not mean that the income must be the same amount whenever received. It means that the income should be received at regular intervals. Once a week, once a month, once in a while. A real estate agent receiving sporadic commissions will qualify as long as the amounts earned from the commissions can be predicted with some regularity.

Third, a Chapter 13 debtor must have unsecured debts of less than $307,675. Fourth, and finally, a Chapter 13 debtor must have secured debts of less than $922,975. If a Chapter 13 debtor has unsecured debts of $307,675 or more or secured debts of $922,975 or more, the individual may not file a Chapter 13 but instead will be required to file a Chapter 11 if repayment to creditors over time is desired. Further, Section 104(b) triannually adjusts the dollar limits contained in specified Code sections, including Section 109(e), to account for the effects of inflation. The limits stated in the text reflect the adjustment period, 2004–2007, which raised the respective limits from $290,525 to $307,675 and from $871,550 to $922,975 on April 1, 2004.[31]

Section 109(g), added to the Code in 1984, exists to prevent an abuse to the system most commonly known as serial filing. A **serial filing** exists when a debtor files a bankruptcy and has it dismissed by the court (usually when the real estate is about to be foreclosed or when the repossession is about to occur after the automatic stay has been relieved). The same debtor immediately files another bankruptcy proceeding, requiring the creditor to return to court and seek relief from the automatic stay a second time. In this instance, the debtor may be attempting to abuse the system. Under Section 109(g), if the court dismisses a case because a debtor has willfully failed to abide by court orders or if a debtor dismisses a case voluntarily after a creditor obtains relief from the automatic stay, then the debtor will not qualify to file a new proceeding for 180 days.[32] In some situations, a Chapter 13 filed after receiving a Chapter 7 discharge will be permissible. (See chapter 23 infra.)

F. NEEDS BASED BANKRUPTCY

"Needs Based Bankruptcy" or "means testing" is the most controversial aspect of the BAPA legislation, fundamentally altering practice in individual bankruptcy cases. The essence of this concept is that if an individual debtor can repay at least 25% of general unsecured debt over a 60-month period with minimum monthly payments of $100 ($6,000), or if a debtor can pay

31. 11 U.S.C. §109(e); 11 U.S.C. §101(30); 11 U.S.C. §104(b). See n.30 supra.
32. 11 U.S.C. §109(g).

$10,000 or more over 60 months without regard to the percentage repaid, then a Chapter 7 petition is subject to dismissal for abuse unless the debtor consents to or voluntarily converts the case to a Chapter 13.[33] Means testing may only apply if the debtor's current monthly income is less than the applicable state median income for a household of the debtor's size.[34] However, in such an event, the Court and United States trustee may nonetheless seek dismissal of a case for abuse under 11 U.S.C. §707(b)(1), which is procedurally identical to the law as it existed prior to the 2005 legislation.[35]

Because debtors and their attorneys are subject to penalties for improperly filing a Chapter 7 that should have been filed as a Chapter 13, the concept of needs based bankruptcy or means testing is a threshold issue. The nuances of this provision will determine a debtor's decision as to which Chapter to file and will greatly affect recommendations as to the course of action that a client should take.

To determine a debtor's ability to repay a portion of unsecured debt under Chapter 13, §707(b)(2) of the Code provides a formula. If a debtor falls within the formula's parameters, it will be presumed that the debtor's Chapter 7 filing is an abuse of Chapter 7, and a motion will be brought before the court to dismiss the petition as an abuse of Chapter 7. Prior to the 2005 legislation, a Chapter 7 petition was subject to dismissal pursuant to 11 U.S.C. §707(b) only for a "substantial abuse" of Chapter 7. Under the 2005 legislation, the word "substantial" has been eliminated from the statute's language in what is now 11 U.S.C. §707(b)(1), and the existence of the means testing formula makes one determinant of abuse a brightline test.

New §707(b)(2)(A) contains the formula that determines when a Chapter 7 debtor's filing will be presumed an abuse of Chapter 7. The first element in the formula is the debtor's **current monthly income** as defined by new §101(10A). This provision generally defines current monthly income as a debtor's average monthly income received from all sources in the 180 days prior to filing, without regard to whether or not the income is taxable. Current monthly income also includes amounts regularly paid by an entity other than the debtor for the household expenses of the debtor or a dependent of the debtor, but does not include Social Security benefits or payments to victims of terrorism.[36]

For example, June Cleaver earned $6,000 per month prior to being laid off three months prior to filing. She currently receives $1,200 every month in unemployment compensation and has received $2,400 since her

33. 11 U.S.C. §707(b)(2)(A). The amounts are subject to adjustment for inflation as per 11 U.S.C. §104(b).
34. 11 U.S.C. §707(b)(7).
35. See chapter 7 infra.
36. 11 U.S.C. §101(10A).

layoff. She is also entitled to receive $600 per month in spousal support, but has only received $1,200 in the past six months, and nothing in the past four months. Her father who lives in the household regularly contributes his $1,000 per month of Social Security benefits and his paycheck of $600 from Wal-Mart toward payment of the monthly household expenses. June's current monthly income is $4,200, consisting of a monthly average of $3,000 in compensation, $400.00 in unemployment, $200 in spousal support and $600 from her father's paycheck. Note, however, that her actual monthly income is only $2,800, consisting of her $1,200 unemployment compensation, her father's Social Security benefit of $1,000 and her father's $600 paycheck. The fact that June does not actually receive some of her "current monthly income" may or may not constitute "special circumstances" described below. Under needs based bankruptcy, "current monthly income" and actual income may not be identical.

June's current monthly income multiplied by 12 is $50,400. If this amount exceeds the median income of her state for a household of two, June must complete the means testing formula. If her current monthly income is equal to or less than the median income for her state, then her Chapter 7 is not subject to dismissal for abuse under needs based bankruptcy.[37]

"Median Family Income" is defined as income calculated by and reported by the Bureau of the Census for a family of similar size for the most recent year available, adjusted by the Consumer Price Index.[38]

The second step in the formula is to deduct three groups of sums from current monthly income. The first deduction is the debtor's monthly expenses as calculated according to Internal Revenue Service collection guidelines, excluding payments for debts. Some of these standards are national, and some are local. They include national standards for day-to-day expenses, local expenses for housing and utilities, local expenses for transportation, and other necessary expenses.[39] The current internet address is *http://www.irs.gov.* The Forms Disk includes additional links.

The following additional amounts are also included in this group of expenses: actual expenses paid for the care and support of an elderly or disabled household member or immediate family member; the amount of expenses that would be incurred to pay a Chapter 13 trustee in a Chapter 13, up to 10 percent of Plan payments; actual expense of a dependent child, up to $1,500 per year for private school tuition; and an allowance for housing and utilities or the actual expenses if documentation is provided.[40]

37. 11 U.S.C. §707(b)(7).
38. 11 U.S.C. §101 (39A).
39. 11 U.S.C. §707(b)(2)(A)(ii)(I).
40. 11 U.S.C. §707(b)(2)(A)(ii)(II)-(V).

Second, a debtor's average monthly payments contractually due to secured creditors for the 60 months following the petition are deducted from current monthly income. The payments to be made are totaled and then divided by 60. Thus, if a loan is to be paid off in the 24th month, the formula treats a portion of it being paid for 60 months. Additionally, cure payments that would be made in a Chapter 13 for loans secured by the debtor's primary residence, and vehicle loans are aggregated and divided by 60.[41]

Third, a debtor's expenses for payment of priority claims (claims payable pursuant to 11 U.S.C. §507(a)), such as priority taxes or unpaid support or alimony, are totaled and divided by 60 and the quotient deducted from current monthly income.[42]

If the amount of monthly income available to a debtor after subtracting the allowable deductions, when multiplied by 60, would permit general unsecured claimants to be paid the lesser of the greater of 25 percent of general unsecured claims or $6,000, or $10,000 over a 60-month period, then the Chapter 7 filing is presumed an abuse of Chapter 7. Stated another way, if a debtor can repay at least 25 percent of general unsecured debt over a 60-month period with minimum monthly payments of $100 ($6,000), or if a debtor can pay $10,000 or more over 60 months without regard to the percentage repaid, then abuse is presumed.[43] This means that if a motion is brought to dismiss the case as an abuse, once the court is shown facts permitting it to presume that the filing is an abuse, the burden of proof will shift to the debtor to show that the filing is not an abuse.

For example, assume in the above example that June Cleaver is a family of two (herself and her father) living in New Castle County, Delaware. She owes her unsecured creditors $20,000. Her monthly mortgage is $1,200. She is two payments behind. She has a $250 per month car payment. The loan has 36 payments remaining. She is two payments behind.

Based upon the IRS standards in effect at the time of writing, June is allowed a National Standards allowance of $794, a housing and utility allowance of $1,195, and a transportation allowance of $298, for a total of $2,287. Her monthly mortgage payment is $1,200. Her cure payment would be averaged over 60 months or be $40 per month. These amounts will supplant her IRS housing allowance because the court may consider the actual expense. Her monthly car payment is calculated as $150 (she owes $250 for 36 months but this is averaged over 60 months), and the cure payment of $500 is averaged over 60 at $8.33 per month. Her secured debt payments, less the IRS housing allowance, change her monthly expenses to a total of $2,490.33. If she proposed a Chapter 13 plan to cure the two

41. 11 U.S.C. §707(b)(2)(A)(iii).
42. 11 U.S.C. §707(b)(2)(A)(iv).
43. 11 U.S.C. §707(b)(2)(A)(i). The amounts are subject to adjustment for inflation as per 11 U.S.C. §104(b).

mortgage payments and the two car payments and to pay her unsecured creditors at least $100 per month for 60 months, her total payments would be $8,900 to which is added a hypothetical Chapter 13 trustee fee of 10 percent or $890, which divided by 60 is $14.83 per month. This last amount is added to her monthly expenses of $2,490.33 for a total of $2,505.16. Since her current monthly income calculated above is $4,200, she has surplus monthly income of $1,694.94 per month. This means that June can pay her general unsecured creditors $6,000 over 60 months, which is greater than 25 percent of $20,000 (which would be $5,000). According to the formula, June must either dismiss her case or convert it to a Chapter 13.

A debtor may rebut the presumption that a case is an abuse of Chapter 7 only by demonstrating the existence of "special circumstances" requiring an adjustment to current monthly income. To establish "special circumstances," a debtor must itemize each additional expense, provide documentation for each expense, and provide a detailed explanation of the special circumstances making the expense reasonable. A debtor might also show a change in income to also constitute special circumstances. In the example, for instance, if June's unemployment runs out and she does not have a job, she will not have sufficient income to fund a plan. The debtor must attest to the accuracy of the information provided. The presumption of abuse is only rebutted, if, after explaining and accounting for all the special circumstances, the debtor is unable to make the minimum payment required by the Needs Based Bankruptcy formula. If the ability to make the minimum payment still exists, the presumption is not rebutted.[44]

Even if a debtor successfully rebuts the presumption created by the Needs Based Bankruptcy formula, the statute still permits a creditor to seek dismissal as an abuse of Chapter 7 if, for example, the debtor has filed the petition in bad faith or, if under the totality of circumstances, the filing is an abuse of Chapter 7. The courts will have to create standards in the case law for bad faith filings or for filings that are an abuse of Chapter 7 under the totality of circumstances.[45]

The court, the United States Trustee, the trustee, or any party in interest may bring a motion to dismiss a case as an abuse of Chapter 7, if the debtor's current monthly income exceeds the applicable state median income for a particular debtor. If the debtor's income is less than the applicable state median, then no one will be able to bring a motion to dismiss under Needs Based Bankruptcy.[46] The United States Trustee is to review the debtor's schedules and file a statement within 10 days after the meeting of creditors as to whether or not the case should be presumed an abuse of Chapter 7 under

44. 11 U.S.C. §707(b)(2)(B).
45. 11 U.S.C. §707(b)(3). The courts will have to create standards in the case law for bad faith filings or for filings that are an abuse of Chapter 7 under the totality of circumstances.
46. 11 U.S.C. §707(b)(6)(7).

Needs Based Bankruptcy. The court is to provide a copy of the report to all creditors within five days. If the report indicates that the case is presumed to be an abuse of Chapter 7, then the United States Trustee must either file an appropriate motion within 30 days, or a further report indicating the reasons why such a motion would not be appropriate.[47]

If a trustee does bring a motion to dismiss for abuse of Chapter 7 and the court finds that the debtor was not substantially justified in filing Chapter 7, then the court may award the trustee attorneys fees and costs. The debtor's attorney is subject to FRBP 9011 and sanctions for failing to properly investigate a debtor's financial affairs and in not assessing the case as an abuse of Chapter 7.[48] Alternatively, the court may also award a debtor attorneys fees and costs if the court finds that a motion brought by a party in interest other than the United States Trustee or trustee was not substantially justified or brought the motion solely to coerce a debtor into waiving a right guaranteed by the Bankruptcy Code. This latter provision, however, will not apply to small businesses (businesses with 25 or fewer employees) with claims of less than $1000.[49]

Needs based bankruptcy or means testing, is an entirely new concept, and raises many issues. Whether or not or to what extent the provision is constitutional may be challenged. The scope of the inquiry that counsel must conduct to avoid sanctions will be subject to litigation. To the extent that the provision will require bankruptcy practitioners to resort, on a regular basis, to materials outside of the bankruptcy system (IRS regulations and census bureau data), the bankruptcy system is no longer entirely self-contained. The placement of burdens and penalties upon counsel for debtors may have a chilling effect upon bankruptcy attorneys.

G. NEEDS BASED BANKRUPTCY EXAMPLES

Example 1

Lemuel Gulliver, of Montgomery County, Pennsylvania, lost his $100,000 per year job at an engineering firm two months ago. He has since been collecting $2000 per month in unemployment. The unemployment runs out in two more months. His spouse does not work. They have two children, Bill and Ted, ages 10 and 12. When Gulliver was laid off, the Gullivers stopped making monthly payments of $1,600 on their mortgage

47. 11 U.S.C. §704(b).
48. 11 U.S.C. §707(b)(4).
49. 11 U.S.C. §707(b)(5).

in favor of the Lilliput Mortgage Co. Lilliput is threatening foreclosure of their home. The Bank of Laputa wants to repossess their car, a 2002 Chevrolet Blazer. They are two payments behind. They have 20 more payments of $500 to make. They owe the Internal Revenue Service $3,000 for unpaid 2004 taxes, which they could not pay after Lemuel was laid off. They have $20,000 in credit card debt.

The first step is to determine Gulliver's current monthly income as defined by §101(10A). Gulliver worked for four of the past six months receiving $8,333.33 per month, earning $33,333.33. He has collected two months of unemployment benefits at $2,000 per month, receiving $4,000. Since current monthly income is the average of income from all sources during the six-month period preceding the petition, both figures need to be added together and divided by 6, resulting in current monthly income pursuant to Needs Based Bankruptcy of $6,222.22. Assuming a median income of $68,578 for a household of four in Pennsylvania, since Gulliver's annual income of $74,666.64 exceeds the median allowable income, then Gulliver must complete the balance of the Needs Based Bankruptcy calculations.

The next step is to make the allowable deductions from Gulliver's current monthly income. Looking up the IRS national standards for living expenses permits Gulliver to deduct $1,564, $298 in operating expenses for one car, and an ownership expense of $475 for total deductions of $2,337 per month. Since the statute excludes payments for debts, Gulliver may not use the IRS housing figures because his mortgage payment is higher and to do otherwise would create duplication. Similarly, from the $475 ownership allowance, deduct the average monthly payment of $166.67. The total expenses in this group are $2,170.33. Gulliver may also deduct other necessary expenses, which minimally includes all of the taxes that were withheld from his paycheck. For purposes of this example, assume that this amount is $2,000 per month.

Pursuant to 11 U.S.C. §707(b)(2)(A)(iii), the Gullivers must average their secured debt repayments for the next 60 months. Their average mortgage payment is $1,600.00. Twenty payments of $500 remaining on the car total $10,000. Dividing this by 60 results in an average car payment of $166.67. The payments necessary to cure the defaults to the mortgage and car loan may also be accounted for, resulting in an additional monthly deduction of $70 ($4,200/60= $70).

Payments on any priority debt that Gulliver would have to repay in a Chapter 13 represent the final allowable deduction from current monthly income pursuant to 11 U.S.C. §707(b)(2)(A)(iv). The taxes due for 2004 are in this category. $3,000 divided by 60 is $50.

According to the formula then, Gulliver has current monthly income of $6,000, from which is deducted ($2,170.33 + $2,000 + $1,600 + $166.67 + $50 + 70), leaving a monthly surplus of $165.22 per month. From this amount,

Gulliver would be able to also deduct from the surplus up to 10 percent of his hypothetical Chapter 13 payment, of $165.22 per month, or $16.52, lowering the monthly surplus to $148.70.

Since Gulliver can pay his general unsecured creditors at least $100 per month for 60 months ($148.70×60=$8,922) and since he can repay his unsecured creditors at least 25 percent ($8,922÷20,000=.45), then a presumption of abuse exists pursuant to the means testing formula. The Court, United States Trustee, panel trustee or any party in interest could bring a motion to dismiss for abuse because Gulliver's current monthly income exceeds the state median for a household of four.

Gulliver may attempt to rebut the presumption of abuse by explaining to the court the special circumstances that his unemployment of $2,000 per month runs out in two months and his income will be nothing. If the court does not consider this a special circumstance, Gulliver must either dismiss his case or convert it to a Chapter 13.

Example 2

Yossarian earns $80,000 per year at Catch-22 Software in Santa Clara County, California. He recently had a personal injury judgement entered against him for $100,000. The judgement is not covered by any insurance. Yossarian also owes $50,000 in credit cards and $20,000 in unpaid child support. He has a spouse and one child, Milo. His mortgage is current. The payments are $4,000 per month. Car payments of $700 per month are current. There are 60 payments left. Yossarian wants to file Chapter 7 to discharge the judgement and the credit cards.

First, calculate Yossarian's current monthly income. $80,000 divided by 12 is $6666.67. Assume that $80,000 exceeds the median California income for a household of three, requiring completion of the Needs Based Bankruptcy formula.

Second, the Monthly National Standards for a family of three at Yossarian's income level is $1,439, plus a vehicle operating expense allowance of $373, and an ownership expense of zero because the average payment of $700 exceeds the ownership allowance of $475, for a living expense deduction of $2,287.

The average monthly payments for 60 months to secured creditors are $4,700 ($4,000 + $700).

The child support would be a priority claim in Chapter 13. $20,000 divided by 60 is $333.33.

Yossarian's allowable deductions total $7,320.33 exceeding his current monthly income of $6,666.67. Thus, no presumption of abuse will arise if Yossarian seeks Chapter 7 relief. Keep in mind also that there are additional deductions from current monthly income that have not been included in this example.

Summary

Chapter 1 of the Bankruptcy Code sets forth basic rules of construction and definitions that apply throughout the Code.

The most important provision of Chapter 1 pertains to the due process requirements in Code practice. Most actions that require court approval will require notice to creditors and an opportunity for them to be heard either by way of a notice of intent or a formal properly noticed motion. As a result of Bankruptcy Rule 9006, the effective by mail notice period is 23 days. In exceptional circumstances the court may approve an action without notice of a hearing or upon limited notice. An order obtained in such a manner is known as an ex parte order.

Section 105 provides Bankruptcy Courts with broad equitable powers to implement the purposes of the Bankruptcy Code.

Section 108 describes the effect of a bankruptcy proceeding on state statutes of limitation where the debtor is or may be a plaintiff.

Section 109 describes the entities that may be debtors in the various Chapter proceedings.

Section 707(b)(2) places further limitations upon the choice of Chapter filing that individual debtors may make by essentially requiring conversion a Chapter 13 or dismissal of the case if application of the needs based bankruptcy formula creates a presumption of abuse by the filing of a Chapter 7. Calculation of the formula applies if a debtor's current monthly income exceeds the state median family income for a household of similar size. Debtor's counsel is subject to potential sanctions if a motion is brought and granted, and counsel did not adequately confirm the debtor's representations. Alternatively, a moving party in interest that is a creditor is subject to sanctions for bringing an unsuccessful motion to dismiss or convert that is not well founded.

KEY TERMS

current monthly income
due process
ex parte
evidentiary hearing
means testing
motion for relief from automatic stay
needs based bankruptcy
notice and hearing
noticed motion
regular income
serial filing

Chapter 5 Checklist

5.1	MOTIONS	*Authority*
5.1.1	Notice and an Opportunity to Be Heard	11 U.S.C. §102(1)
5.1.2	Twenty-Three Day Notice Requirement	Bankruptcy Rules 2002(a), 9006(f)
5.1.2.1	Include debtor's name, address, and taxpayer identification number in any notice given.	§342(c)
5.1.3	Noticed Motions	FRBP 9013
5.1.3.1	State relief sought includes proof of service, proposed order, affidavits	FRBP 9013
5.1.3.2	Notice of hearing	Consult local rule
5.1.3.3	Valuation report if value in issue	Consult local rule
5.1.3.4	Serve any entity against whom relief sought or with interest in property, trustee, debtor, and U.S. Trustee where required	FRBP 9013
5.1.3.5	Response due no later than five days prior to hearing date and served on parties serving or served with motion	Consult local rule
5.1.3.6	Response to include proposed order, report of value if in issue, affidavits	Consult local rule
5.1.3.7	Court may enter order if no response filed	Consult local rule
5.1.4	Application for an Order	FRBP 9013
5.1.4.1	Set forth relief, proof of service, and proposed order	FRBP 9013
5.1.4.2	Order may be entered if no response filed.	Consult local rule

5.2 WHO MAY BE A DEBTOR

	Chapter	Permitted Debtor	Exceptions	Authority
5.2.1	7	Any person[50]	Railroads, insurance companies, federally insured financial institutions	11 U.S.C. §109(b)
5.2.2	9	Municipality		11 U.S.C. §109(c)
5.2.3	11	Any person qualified to be a Chapter 7 debtor	Stockbrokers, commodity brokers, railroads[51]	11 U.S.C. §109(d)
5.2.4	12	Family farmer with regular income		11 U.S.C. §101(18), §109(f)
5.2.5	13	Individual with regular income	Unsecured debts >$307,675, secured debts >$922,975	11 U.S.C. §101(30), §109(e)

5.3 NEEDS BASED BANKRUPTCY—11 U.S.C. §707(b)(2)

5.3.1.	Calculate debtor's current monthly income	§707(b)(2)(A)(i)
5.3.2.	Deduct IRS expense allowance	§707(b)(2)(A)(ii)
5.3.3.	Deduct average 60-month debt service	§707(b)(2)(A)(iii)
5.3.4.	Deduct priority claims paid over 60 months	§707(b)(2)(A)(iv)

50. A debtor must always be a *person*. Persons are individuals, partnerships, or corporations. 11 U.S.C. §§101(41), 109(a).
51. Stockbroker and commodity broker liquidations have special subchapters in Chapter 7. Subchapter III of Chapter 7 (§§741-752) applies to the former. Subchapter IV of Chapter 7 (§§761-766) applies to the latter. Subchapter IV of Chapter 11 (§§1161-1174) applies to railroad proceedings.

		Authority
5.3.5.	Abuse is presumed if disposable income permits repayment of 25% over 60 months with minimum payments of $100, or if debtor can repay $10,000 or more without regard to percent repaid	§707(b)(2)(A)(i)
5.3.6	Special circumstances may permit deviation	§707(b)(2)(B)

DISCUSSION QUESTIONS

1. Describe who may be a debtor in:
   a) Chapter 7,
   b) Chapter 11,
   c) Chapter 13.
2. Why are certain industries (banking, insurance, and railroads) not permitted to file Chapter 7 proceedings?
3. What are the procedures for filing or opposing a motion?
4. What distinguishes a noticed motion from an ex parte application?
5. When may a notice period be shortened?
6. What is meant by the phrase "needs based bankruptcy"? What purpose or purposes does the concept of needs based bankruptcy serve? Does needs based bankruptcy foster debtor relief or debt collection?

6

Useful Definitions — Section 101

Section 101 is often overlooked when conducting bankruptcy research. This is probably because many practitioners do not normally use Section 101 on a regular basis since it does not contain familiar substantive rules of bankruptcy law. Nevertheless, Section 101 is critical because it contains definitions of many terms that are used frequently throughout the Code. Reference to a Section 101 definition will sometimes save substantial research time and will help to explicitly resolve questions only answered implicitly by other Code provisions. This chapter is an analysis of the definitions used most frequently in all aspects of bankruptcy practice. This knowledge also helps in acquiring a basic understanding of the Bankruptcy Code and system.

A. AFFILIATES

Section 101(2) defines *affiliates*. Affiliates are (1) nondebtor entities that own or control a 20 percent or more interest in a debtor, (2) nondebtor entities in which a debtor owns or controls 20 percent or more of the ownership interest, and (3) nondebtor entities that control or operate substantially all of a debtor's assets.[1] Affiliates may or may not be debtors. Affiliates may or may not also be insiders of a debtor. The distinction between affiliates and insiders acquires significance in the area of a trustee's avoiding powers and in the Code's distributive provisions.[2]

1. 11 U.S.C. §101(2).
2. See chapters 15 through 17 and 21 infra.

For example, Engulf and Devour, Inc., is the owner of more than 20 percent each of ten smaller entities. If Engulf and Devour files a Chapter 11, all of the smaller entities are affiliates. If one of the smaller entities itself files a proceeding, Engulf and Devour would be a nondebtor affiliate.

B. CLAIM

Section 101(5) defines *claim*. Because a primary function of the bankruptcy system is to determine and pay dividends upon claims, it is germane to know when a transaction is considered to be a claim. Although the Code definition appears lengthy and complex, it may be translated into two simple sentences. First, a claim is a right to payment of any kind, whether or not the amount has been previously determined or liquidated. Second, a claim may also be a right to performance if the debtor's breach can be compensated by monetary damages, whether or not the amount has been previously determined.[3] A claim is considered liquidated when it has been reduced to a fixed sum.

C. COMMUNITY CLAIM

Section 101(7) defines *community claim*: a claim against community property that would be enforceable against community property under nonbankruptcy law.[4] This is of importance in those states utilizing community property law.[5] A debtor's discharge will normally effectuate a discharge on all the debtor's community property, even if one member of the community has not filed a proceeding.[6]

3. 11 U.S.C. §101(5).
4. 11 U.S.C. §101(7).
5. California, Arizona, New Mexico, Texas, Louisiana, Idaho, Nevada, and Washington.
6. See chapter 7 infra.

D. CORPORATION

Section 101(9) defines *corporation*. A corporation is a business organized and registered according to nonbankruptcy or state law. Corporations are also associations that have all the powers of corporations under state law but are not incorporated under state law, such as unincorporated associations or business trusts.[7] For example, an unincorporated labor union is considered a corporation under the Bankruptcy Code.

E. CREDITOR

Section 101(10) defines *creditor*. The definition of *creditor* is a corollary to the definition of *claim*. A creditor is normally an entity with a claim that arises before the petition is filed.[8] This is known, more simply, as a prepetition claim. Entities whose claims arise after filing are not generally considered creditors and are not affected by the bankruptcy proceeding except in several specific instances described elsewhere in this text.[9] A creditor not affected by a filing generally does not have its claim discharged and is generally not entitled to participate in any distribution of dividends.

F. CURRENT MONTHLY INCOME

An individual debtor's average monthly income, from all sources received, in the six months preceding the filing of a bankruptcy petition as set forth in 11 U.S.C. §101(10A). This includes any amount received on a regular basis from any household member for payment of household expenses excluding Social Security payments and payments to war crimes victims. Current monthly income is utilized to determine an individual debtor's qualifications for needs based bankruptcy. See Sections 5F and 5G supra.

For example, Robert Goodwin lives with his spouse and three children. Two of the children are his wife's children from a former marriage. Robert receives $700 per month in SSI income. His wife, Zephorah,

7. 11 U.S.C. §101(9).
8. 11 U.S.C. §101(10).
9. See chapters 8 and 21 infra. See also 11 U.S.C. §348(d); 11 U.S.C. §502(f), (g), (h), (i); 11 U.S.C. §503.

receives \$3,000 wages that started three months ago. The family received food stamp assistance in the amount of \$300 per month, but this ended two months ago. Zephorah is also entitled to receive \$250 per month in child support, but she hasn't received any payments in three months.

To determine Robert's current monthly income, each of the above amounts must be averaged for six months. Multiply each amount by the number of months actually received, divide by 6 and then total the results. In the example, the Goodwin's current monthly income is \$1,825, calculated as follows: $((\$3000 \times 3) + (300 \times 4) + (\$250 \times 3) = \$10{,}950) \div 6 = \$1{,}825$. Note that Robert's SSI income is not included.

G. CUSTODIAN

Section 101(11) defines *custodian*: a third party who has been appointed to administer assets of a debtor outside of the bankruptcy system. *Custodian* is a term of art used in the Bankruptcy Code to distinguish state court receivers, and others similarly situated, from bankruptcy trustees. A state court receiver appointed before the filing or an assignee for the benefit of creditors is the most common custodian encountered in bankruptcy practice. The trustees of a business trust are also custodians.[10]

H. DEBT

Section 101(12) defines *debt*: a liability on a claim.[11] That is, a debt is the inverse of a claim. A claim is what a creditor says it is owed; a debt is what a debtor says it owes. Ultimately, the two definitions are no more than two perspectives upon an identical transaction or event.

I. DEBT RELIEF AGENCY

A **debt relief agency**, 11 U.S.C. §101(12A), is essentially an individual consumer debtor's bankruptcy attorney or bankruptcy petition preparer

10. 11 U.S.C. §101(11).
11. 11 U.S.C. §101(12).

(see chapter 7 infra).[12] Debt relief agencies are required to provide individual consumer debtors with written retainer agreements and the various prepetition notices described at chapter 4A supra.

J. DOMESTIC SUPPORT OBLIGATIONS

A "**domestic support obligation**," 11 U.S.C. §101(14A), is an obligation owed for the payment of spousal support, child support or maintenance, whether or not the unpaid amount accrued before or after the filing of the bankruptcy petition.

K. EQUITY SECURITY HOLDER

Section 101(17) defines *equity security holder*: an entity owning an interest in a debtor.[13] The shareholders of a corporation are its equity security holders. The partners of a partnership are its equity security holders. Equity security holders normally receive dividends from a bankruptcy estate only after all other creditors are paid in full.[14]

L. INDIVIDUAL WITH REGULAR INCOME

Section 101(30) defines *individual with regular income*. The meaning of this phrase has been previously described in chapter 5 supra.

12. Additionally, §101(3A) defines most individual consumer debtors as "assisted persons." An assisted person is an individual consumer debtor with less than $150,000 in nonexempt assets. This definition includes most consumer debtors. The amount is subject to triannual adjustment pursuant to 11 U.S.C. §104(b). Section 101(4A) defines "bankruptcy assistance" as goods or services provided to an assisted person for the purpose of providing advice or representation with respect to a bankruptcy case.
13. 11 U.S.C. §101(16), (17).
14. See chapter 22 infra.

M. INSIDERS

Section 101(31) defines *insiders*. Insiders are generally those entities in control of a debtor, or the debtor's relatives. The exact definition of *insider* varies depending upon whether the debtor is an individual, a corporation, or a partnership. However, the basic principle is the same throughout. Those in control or who are related to a debtor (in a family or business sense) are normally considered insiders.[15] Thus, the officers and directors of a bankrupt corporation are insiders of the corporation. The corporation is also an insider of any officer or director who files a proceeding. Partners are insiders of one another. For example, David Addison and Madeleine Hayes are insiders to one another because they are partners of the Blue Moon Detective Agency. If they are married they would also be insiders because they would then be relatives.

An insider relationship between a debtor and creditor can affect the priority of dividend distribution to the insider creditor.[16] Insider status will also affect the time limits for certain transactions that may be avoidable by a trustee.[17]

It is erroneous to believe that insiders and equity security holders are synonymous. They are not. An insider may or may not be an equity security holder. An equity security holder may or may not be an insider. For example, Ma Kettle owns one share of IBM. She is an equity security holder of IBM but not an insider. On the other hand, President Smith of IBM owns no stock. He is considered an insider of IBM but not an equity security holder.

N. INSOLVENCY

Section 101(32) defines *insolvent*. An entity is normally insolvent when the entity's liabilities (debts) exceed the value of its assets (property). This is a common accountancy definition of *insolvent* and is also commonly known as "balance sheet insolvency." This definition will suffice for most bankruptcy purposes. However, the value of exempt and fraudulently transferred property is specifically excluded when performing this calculation.[18]

---

15. 11 U.S.C. §101(31).
16. See chapter 22 infra.
17. See chapters 15 through 17 infra.
18. 11 U.S.C. §101(32)(A).

A partnership is insolvent if its debts are greater than the value of the partnership assets, excluding any fraudulently transferred assets, plus the net worth of each general partner, determined exclusive of the partnership in issue.[19] This method of calculation is consistent with the common law principle that a general partner is personally liable for the partnership debts. For example, the Huey, Dewey, and Louie partnership has assets with a value of 25. The partnership has liabilities of 20. It is solvent. The partners fraudulently transfer assets with a value of 15 to Uncle Scrooge. The partnership is now insolvent, without considering the partners' net worth. Each partner, exclusive of the partnership, has a net worth of one. The total asset value is now 13 (the total value of the partnership assets and each partner's net worth). The value of the fraudulently transferred asset is not included in the computation. Because the debt owed is still 20, the partnership's liabilities (20) exceed its assets (13), and the partnership is deemed insolvent under the Code.

Historically, a debtor had to be insolvent to be bankrupt. However, the Code does not require that a debtor be insolvent to file a petition. Insolvency is absent from the Section 109 requirements of who may be a debtor.[20] Nor is insolvency an element of proof required to obtain the entry of an order for relief against a debtor in an involuntary proceeding. Proving that a debtor is not generally paying its debts as they become due does not necessarily imply that a debtor is insolvent. As described in chapter 5 supra, situations may arise where a solvent entity can have an order for relief entered against it in an involuntary proceeding. It is therefore erroneous to believe that a debtor must be insolvent to be bankrupt. Under the Code, the insolvency of a debtor is normally only a specific issue to determine in connection with the application of certain of the trustee's avoiding powers.[21]

O. JUDICIAL LIEN

Section 101(36) defines *judicial lien*: a lien obtained by virtue of a court order or judgment. It can be a judgment, a prejudgment writ of attachment, or a postjudgment writ of execution.[22]

---

19. 11 U.S.C. §101(32)(B).
20. See chapter 5 supra.
21. See chapters 15 through 17 infra.
22. 11 U.S.C. §101(36).

P. LIEN

Section 101(37) defines *lien*: a right to property to secure repayment of a debt or the performance of an obligation.[23] A lien in this sense may be either a judicial, consensual, or statutory lien. A trust deed or mortgage on real estate or a bank's security interest in a vehicle is a consensual lien. A mechanic's or landlord's lien is a statutory lien. A judicial lien has just been described above. The common factor of these various rights is that they all create liens, legally enforceable interests in property to secure repayment or performance of an obligation. The Code also contains some fine distinctions between the various types of liens.

Q. MEDIAN FAMILY INCOME

Section 101(39A) defines *median family income* as median income most recently calculated and reported by the Bureau of the Census, or if not currently calculated and reported, the most recently calculated and reported amount, adjusted upward by the Consumer Price Index.

R. PERSON

Section 101(41) defines *person*: any kind of entity, individual, partnership, or corporation, except a governmental unit.[24] However, a governmental unit is considered a person when it has acquired rights in connection with a loan guaranty agreement and seeks placement on a Chapter 11 Creditors Committee.[25] This definition, however, should not be construed to mean that governmental units are unaffected by operation of the Bankruptcy Code. Governmental units that are creditors are affected as much by

23. 11 U.S.C. §101(37).
24. 11 U.S.C. §101(41).
25. 11 U.S.C. §101(41); 11 U.S.C. §1102.

the Bankruptcy Code as private creditors. Section 106 specifically waives any sovereign immunity of a governmental unit when the governmental unit is a claimant.[26]

S. SECURITY

Section 101(49) defines *security*. Several definitions within the Bankruptcy Code use the word *security*. Each definition is separate. The definition of the word *security* in Section 101(49) includes the various commercial documents commonly used to evidence an ownership interest in an entity or in certain sorts of financial assets, such as bonds or certificates of deposit.[27] Use of the word *includes* in the definition means that the court has discretion to interpret a document not included on the list as also being a security.[28] For purposes of a basic understanding, any document that evidences an intangible financial right will generally be considered a security under the Code. However, currency, checks, and certain specialized options or commodities are specifically not considered security.[29] Although these items may evidence the existence of an asset or claim, they do not constitute security within the Code.

T. SECURITY AGREEMENT

Section 101(50) defines *security agreement*: an agreement that creates or provides for a security interest.[30] A security interest is an agreement that creates a consensual lien.[31] A bank loan to finance a new car purchase

26. 11 U.S.C. §106. In United States v. Nordic Village, Inc., 503 U.S. 30 (1992), the Supreme Court held that 11 U.S.C. §106 does not act to waive the sovereign immunity of the federal government to permit the recovery of money claims. A similar ruling was applied to the states in Hoffman v. Connecticut Dept. of Income Maint., 492 U.S. 96 (1989). Section 106 was completely rewritten in 1994 to overrule these holdings. The revised Section 106 constitutes, for all practical purposes, an effective waiver of sovereign immunity in bankruptcy cases. Pub. L. No. 103-394 §113 (1994). However, as a result of the Supreme Court's ruling in Seminole Tribe of Florida v. Florida, 517 U.S. 44 (1996) (a nonbankruptcy case), numerous courts have held that Section 106, even as rewritten, remains in violation of the Eleventh Amendment. See, e.g., Sacred Heart Hospital of Norristown v. Commonwealth of Pa. Dept. of Pub. Welfare, 133 F.3d 237 (1998). This area is highly unsettled.
27. 11 U.S.C. §101(49).
28. See chapter 5 supra.
29. 11 U.S.C. §101(49)(B).
30. 11 U.S.C. §101(50).
31. 11 U.S.C. §101(51).

usually creates a security interest in the car. A home loan is an agreement that usually creates a security interest in the real property by way of a mortgage or deed of trust. A security interest is generally considered perfected when the trust deed or mortgage is properly recorded or when a "UCC-1" is properly filed in a secured commercial transaction.

U. SINGLE ASSET REAL ESTATE

Section 101(51B) defines *single asset real estate*. Single asset real estate is real property that generates substantially all the gross income of a debtor who is not a family farmer and on which no substantial business is conducted other than the operation of the property and activities incidental thereto. Residential real property with three or fewer units is excluded from the definition. The purpose of this definition was to codify, for the sake of consistency, the many disparate conceptions of single asset real estate that had arisen in the case law.

For example, an apartment building with five units and secured debt of $500,000 (and whose only income is rental receipts) is single asset real estate. A golf course, restaurant, and subdivision project with secured debt of $20 million may or may not be a single asset real estate case. An office building with secured debt of $100 million is a single asset real estate case. Undeveloped land generating no income but with secured debt is single asset real estate.[32]

This provision is most relevant in connection with the automatic stay (see chapter 12 infra).

V. STATUTORY LIEN

Section 101(53) defines *statutory lien*: a lien created by operation of law and not by court order (a judicial lien) or agreement (consensual lien). A statutory lien cannot, however, include a judicial or consensual lien that may be created by statute. In this event, the lien would either be a judicial

32. 11 U.S.C. §101 (51B). See In re Oceanside Mission Assocs., 192 Bankr. 232, 234 (S.D. Cal. 1996), where the court stated: "If the debtor has no income, then substantially all of its income could be said to be generated by the property; i.e., substantially all of nothing is nothing."

or consensual lien but not a statutory lien.[33] Mechanic's liens or landlord's liens are common examples of liens that are created by statute or statutory liens.

W. TRANSFER

Section 101(54) defines *transfer*. The definition is intentionally broad. A transfer is any type of means that human beings might devise to dispose of property or interests in property. Additionally, the creation of a lien, the creation of a security interest and the foreclosure of a debtor's equity of redemption of property are all expressly noted as transfers.[34] This is an intentionally broad definition, because as technology develops there become more and more ways of creating means of transferring property or an interest in property.

Identifying precisely when a transaction takes place will determine the application of many substantive provisions of the Code, including determining when a preference or fraudulent transfer has occurred. Many of the following chapters will have occasion to discuss the effect of a transfer upon the operation of the Code section in issue.

Summary

Section 101 of the Code specifically defines many terms that are frequently used in other Code sections. This Section should not be overlooked when conducting bankruptcy research.

A claim is generally a right to payment or performance. A debt is the inverse of a claim.

Insiders are given special treatment in various Code sections. Whether the debtor is an individual, partnership, or corporation will determine who is an insider in relation to the debtor. Generally, family members or persons in control of a debtor's financial affairs will be insiders within the bankruptcy system.

The word *security* is contained within four different Section 101 definitions. Each of these definitions is different. This chart may assist in distinguishing between them:

---

33. 11 U.S.C. §101(53).
34. 11 U.S.C. §101(54).

Definition	*Description*	*Authority*
equity security holder	holder of an ownership interest in debtor (e.g., stock)	11 U.S.C. §101(17)
security	evidence of ownership (e.g., stock certificate)	11 U.S.C. §101(49)
security agreement	agreement creating a security interest	11 U.S.C. §101(50)
security interest	a consensual lien	11 U.S.C. §101(51)

Similarly, Section 101 contains four definitions of liens. These definitions are summarized as follows:

Definition	*Description*	*Authority*
lien	an interest in property to secure repayment or performance	11 U.S.C. §101(37)
judicial lien	a lien created by court order (e.g., writ of execution)	11 U.S.C. §101(36)
statutory lien	a lien created by statute	11 U.S.C. §101(53)
consensual lien	a lien created by a security agreement	11 U.S.C. §101(50), (51)

DISCUSSION QUESTIONS

1. What is the relationship between a claim and a debt?
2. What is an insider? Identify some possible reasons why the Bankruptcy Code may want to distinguish insiders from other parties to the proceeding?
3. What is a lien?
4. Identify the types of liens defined by the Bankruptcy Code.
5. What is the difference between *security* and *security agreement* as the Bankruptcy Code defines these terms?
6. Why is an equity security holder not defined as an insider by the Bankruptcy Code?

PART II

Debtor Relief

7

Overview of Chapter 7

A **consumer no asset** Chapter 7 proceeding is a proceeding filed by an individual debtor or joint debtors in which there will normally be no assets available for the trustee to administer for distribution of dividends to unsecured creditors. Any assets owned by the debtor will be either secured or exempt. Consumer no asset proceedings comprise a majority of all proceedings filed. However, the basic outline of a consumer no asset Chapter 7 proceeding applies equally to all other types of bankruptcy proceedings. This is because the practical process of a consumer no asset proceeding, including documents to be filed and appearances to make, forms the core of all activity occurring in any bankruptcy proceeding.

A no asset Chapter 7 proceeding is filed by an individual or by joint debtors. Husband and wife are joint debtors.[1] In a consumer no asset Chapter 7, the debtor seeks the basic goals of debtor relief. One goal is to be able to claim all or substantially all assets owned as **exempt** and therefore free from the reach of creditors or trustee.[2] In plain English, the debtor gets to keep exempt property. Second, debtors seek a discharge from the debt and claims subject to the proceeding. **Discharge** is the term used to describe the release from debt that a debtor receives in a bankruptcy proceeding.[3] A debtor achieving the two goals of exempting property and obtaining a discharge receives the fundamental debtor relief provided for by the Bankruptcy Code. The protections of the **automatic stay** comprise the final element of debtor relief. These elements of debtor relief permit a debtor to obtain a fresh start in the debtor's financial affairs.

The **fresh start** is the primary reason for a consumer debtor to seek bankruptcy relief. Describing how to accomplish this objective is the subject of the next three chapters of this text. The initiation of a proceeding, the entry of an order for relief, and the documents that must be filed in connection

1. 11 U.S.C. §§301, 302. See chapter 4 supra.
2. See chapter 9 infra.
3. 11 U.S.C. §524.

with a Chapter 7 proceeding have already been identified in chapter 4 supra. This chapter concerns the basic activities that occur after the filing in a typical proceeding. Focusing on a consumer no asset proceeding will provide a basic model of the essential activities that occur in all bankruptcies.

A. EMPLOYMENT AND COMPENSATION OF PROFESSIONALS

The Bankruptcy Code regulates the employment and compensation of professionals rendering services in any bankruptcy proceeding. Attorneys, accountants, appraisers, brokers, and the trustee are the most common such professionals. The provisions regulating professional employment and compensation are contained in Sections 326 through 331 of the Code.

Prior to filing a petition for an individual debtor, a debt relief agency (bankruptcy attorney or petition preparer—see chapters 4 and 6 supra) must provide the disclosures required by §527. These notices must be given within three business days of first rendering services to a debtor. Additionally, a bankruptcy attorney or petition preparer must enter into a written retainer agreement within five business days of first rendering services to a debtor pursuant to §528. Section 526 provides penalties for noncompliance with these provisions. See chapter 4A supra.

All attorneys representing debtors must file a Statement of Compensation with the Bankruptcy Court. This Statement describes the fee that an attorney has received or is going to receive in connection with the proceeding. This requirement is mandated by Section 329(a) and is implemented by Bankruptcy Rule 2016(b). All fees paid to attorneys by the debtor within a year prior to the filing are also subject to disclosure.[4] Section 110 imposes a similar requirement on nonattorneys who are considered bankruptcy petition preparers (paralegals, see section 7B infra).

Generally, a debtor or trustee may employ professionals. Attorneys, accountants, appraisers, and auctioneers are all professionals. A professional must be disinterested. The phrase **disinterested person** is defined at Bankruptcy Code Section 101(14). Most commonly, creditors, equity security holders, insiders, and persons who have an interest materially adverse to an estate are not disinterested. That is, the professional cannot normally have a potential or actual conflict of interest with the estate.[5] An attorney who is the debtor therefore cannot represent the trustee in the same proceeding. Their

4. 11 U.S.C. §329(a); Bankruptcy Rule 2016(b). See chapter 4 supra.
5. 11 U.S.C. §§101(14); 327(a).

interests are generally adverse to one another. Note, however, that the statute does not bar a nondisinterested person from representing a Chapter 7 debtor.[6] This is the one exception to the general rule. Thus, house counsel for a corporate debtor may represent the debtor in the corporation's Chapter 7 proceeding even if counsel is a creditor in the proceeding.

A professional is not disqualified from employment solely due to representation of a creditor, unless another creditor objects. If an objection is raised by another creditor, there will be no disqualification unless the court finds an actual conflict of interest.[7] This provision permits counsel for a single creditor to be approved as counsel for a creditors committee in a Chapter 11.[8] In such cases, counsel will normally be required to cease representing other parties in interest in connection with the bankruptcy proceeding.

A nondisinterested professional may also be employed for a special purpose provided that the professional is not adverse to the estate on the subject matter of the retention.[9] For instance, an attorney's knowledge and background of a debtor's activities may be so important that time and expense can be saved if the attorney/creditor continues to represent the debtor or trustee for limited purposes in the bankruptcy proceeding. Similarly, a debtor may have a personal injury claim as an asset and the trustee may wish to hire the debtor's personal injury attorney as special counsel for the estate to continue to prosecute the personal injury claim. The court will normally approve such applications to be retained for a special purpose.

In Chapter 11 proceedings, the debtor, known as a **debtor-in-possession**, assumes a status equivalent to a trustee and is thus subject to Section 327 in the retention of professionals. However, prefiling counsel for a Chapter 11 debtor-in-possession is not disqualified from employment for having previously represented a debtor.[10] This provision, along with Section 327(c), discussed above, allows a law firm to represent a regular client as a debtor-in-possession in a Chapter 11 proceeding even though the law firm itself may be a creditor.

To become properly retained by the estate or trustee, other than in a no asset proceeding, which merely involves the filing of the Statement of Compensation referred to above, a professional must file an application with the court and have the court approve the professional's retention by the estate or trustee.[11] This is the most important rule in connection with professional retention, namely that there be disclosure and prior court

6. 11 U.S.C. §327(a).
7. 11 U.S.C. §327(c).
8. 11 U.S.C. §327(c); 11 U.S.C. §1103(b).
9. 11 U.S.C. §327(e).
10. See chapter 10 infra. 11 U.S.C. §1107(b).
11. 11 U.S.C. §327(a); Bankruptcy Rule 2014.

approval. If the professional does not obtain court approval for the retention, the court may deny the award of any compensation to the unapproved professional, regardless of the quality or quantity of the services.[12] A law firm performing services in a bankruptcy estate must therefore be certain to obtain prompt court approval of its retention or counsel risks not being paid for the services rendered prior to approval of the retention.

A professional becomes approved to render services to a trustee, debtor-in-possession, or Official Creditor Committee by filing a motion for an order authorizing employment.[13] The motion must include facts showing the necessity of employment, the name of the person to be employed, and reasons for the selection. The motion must describe the services to be rendered, disclose compensation arrangements, state that the professional is qualified to be retained within the meaning of Section 327, and disclose any interest that may be adverse to the estate. The motion must also be accompanied by a statement of the professional that the professional is a disinterested person. Any issue reflecting upon disinterestedness must be disclosed, and this remains a continuing duty throughout the course of employment. The court may also approve the professional on an interim basis, for the period of time prior to the hearing, as an ex parte matter. Failure to proceed promptly to become properly retained can result in a denial of payment, as described above.[14]

Section 328 provides that professional fees are to be reasonable. This Section also provides for the payment of contingent fees in appropriate matters. Although contingent fee arrangements were not permitted in practice under the Bankruptcy Act, the Bankruptcy Code specifically allows them in appropriate instances.[15] A contingent fee agreement will not be used in representing a debtor for general purposes of the proceeding itself. A contingent fee arrangement might, however, be acceptable to collect accounts receivable or to continue to prosecute personal injury claims. These are areas of legal practice in which contingent fees are ordinary and customary.

In Chapter 7, 12, and 13 proceedings, prefiling retainers paid to counsel are acceptable although the reasonableness of the retainer may be examined by the court. Local custom should be ascertained to determine the generally accepted fees permitted for Chapter 7 or 13 proceedings in a given district. Although prefiling retainers are permitted in Chapter 9 and

12. See, e.g., In re Mahoney, Trocki & Assocs., 54 Bankr. 823 (S.D. Cal. 1985), disapproving retroactive approval of a professional in the context of an application for compensation except in certain limited and defined circumstances. The principles of this case have been widely followed.
13. 11 U.S.C. §327(a); 11 U.S.C. §1103(b); 11 U.S.C. §1107(b).
14. Bankruptcy Rule 2014; Bankruptcy Rule 2002; 11 U.S.C. §102. Representative forms are included in the forms disk accompanying this text. As to the duty of full disclosure and the risks of nondisclosure, see In re Leslie Fay Co., 175 Bankr. 525 (Bankr. S.D.N.Y. 1993).
15. 11 U.S.C. §328(a).

11 proceedings, local rule or practice may require compliance with the fee application process described below before any fees may be paid. Whether a retainer may be applied to the payment of fees prior to compliance with the fee application process is a matter of debate in the reported cases. See In re Printcrafters, Inc., 208 Bankr. 968 (Bankr. D. Colo. 1997), for a representative example.

Professionals approved to render services to a bankruptcy estate or trustee are not paid for their services every month. Most law firms and other businesses customarily send bills to clients or customers every month and there is an expectation of prompt payment. In bankruptcy practice this is not the case. The Bankruptcy Code does not allow professionals to apply for compensation more than once every 120 days. A fee application brought during the pendency of a proceeding is commonly known as an **interim fee application**. In an exceptionally large proceeding the court may approve more frequent periods for the bringing of interim fee applications, but this is a rare practice.[16] Frequently, a period of time significantly longer than 120 days will pass before an application for compensation is brought, for the simple reason that to pay compensation the estate has to have funds available. If there are no available means for paying, it will be pointless to bring an application for compensation. Applications for interim compensation should be brought only upon giving due consideration to the needs of the estate and the ability of the professional to render competent services with or without receiving compensation until the close of the case. An application to approve compensation is always required at either the close of the proceeding or when all services to be rendered are complete. Such an application is known as a **final fee application**.

Interim and final fee applications are brought before the bankruptcy court as noticed motions pursuant to FRBP 2016 and 9013. (See chapter 5 supra.) FRBP 2016(a) requires a fee application to detail all time and charges and describe the services rendered and expenses incurred. Any payments previously made must be disclosed. A description in summary form of all services rendered, broken down by amounts and percentage of time spent, should also be included and is required in many local rules.[17] A sample application is included in the forms disk accompanying this text.

In Lamie v. United States Trustee, 540 U.S. 526 (2004), the Supreme Court held that the precise wording of Bankruptcy Code Section 330(a)(1) does not permit a professional not employed by the estate to seek compensation therefrom. Thus, debtor's counsel in a case converted from Chapter 11 to Chapter 7 and in a Chapter 7 may not seek compensation from the bankruptcy estate.

---

16. 11 U.S.C. §331.
17. 11 U.S.C. §§330, 331; Bankruptcy Rule 2016(a).

The court will hold a hearing on an interim or final application for compensation. While a proceeding remains pending the court will typically award only a percentage of the current charges for which compensation is sought. A typical award is 70 percent of the current charges. This percentage may vary from district to district in accord with local practice. At the end of the proceeding there will be a final hearing to approve all compensation earned in the proceeding. At this time any withheld portions of prior applications may or may not be approved for payment.

The bankruptcy system makes a serious effort to control and limit the compensation paid to professionals. If counsel performs less than competently, the court has the discretion to "reward" such behavior when an application for compensation is brought. The "reward" may be a denial or reduction in the amount of compensation actually approved for payment. The Bankruptcy Courts scrutinize fee applications carefully. The United States Trustees have been specifically directed to review and comment upon applications for compensation brought in bankruptcy proceedings. The guidelines of a local United States Trustee will also need to be complied with. The Bankruptcy Court may, on its own motion, award less compensation than is requested. Among the factors the court will consider are the time spent, whether the services were necessary or beneficial to the estate, the complexity of the services, and the rates charged.[18]

A trustee's compensation is governed solely by Section 326. The trustee's maximum compensation is determined by an arithmetical formula based upon the percentage of an estate's assets that a trustee actually administers. The maximum compensation permitted a trustee is 3 percent of the value of the assets administered where the value of the assets administered is greater than $1 million. The percentage is higher for estates with a value of less than $1 million, but the maximum dollar compensation permitted at this level is $53,250.[19] This maximum compensation to a trustee is subject to review based on the same factors applicable to other professionals. Typically, a Bankruptcy Court will base a trustee's compensation on an equivalent hourly rate for legal or accounting services multiplied by the time a trustee has spent on a case, up to the maximum compensation permitted. In addition, a trustee is entitled to receive $60 from the debtor's initial filing fee.[20] Sometimes a trustee may put in ten minutes of work for the $60. Sometimes a trustee will work for many hours on a proceeding and still earn only the same $60. Further, a trustee does not receive compensation immediately, but

18. 11 U.S.C. §330, 28 U.S.C. §586(a)(3)(A). See chapter 10 infra.
19. 11 U.S.C. §326(a). 11 U.S.C. §330(a)(7) provides that a trustee's compensation awarded pursuant to Section §326 be considered as a commission.
20. 11 U.S.C. §330(b).

normally receives the statutory percentage compensation at the close of a proceeding. The fee from the debtor's filing fee is usually received some time after a proceeding is closed. In a large case with many assets and much work a trustee may apply for interim compensation, although the maximum compensation must remain within the limits permitted by Section 326.[21] A trustee's application for interim or final compensation is brought before the court as a noticed motion pursuant to FRBP 2016 and 9013. (See chapter 5 supra.)

All professional compensation is considered an expense of administration and does not normally create a claim as described in this chapter supra. Administrative expenses are further described in chapter 21 infra.

B. BANKRUPTCY PETITION PREPARERS

Section 110 of the Bankruptcy Code applies to bankruptcy petition preparers. Section 110(a) defines a **bankruptcy petition preparer** as a person other than an attorney or an attorney's employee under the attorney's direct supervision who prepares for compensation a document for filing with the Bankruptcy Court. An unsupervised paralegal may be a bankruptcy petition preparer. A *document for filing* is any document prepared for filing by a debtor in a bankruptcy case.

Section 110 is directed specifically at unsupervised paralegals preparing documents for filing by debtors with the Bankruptcy Court. This section does not, however, authorize unsupervised paralegals to prepare or file documents with the Bankruptcy Court unless applicable state law permits such activities by paralegals. Thus, Section 110 does not affect state laws concerning the unlawful practice of law. Such laws remain expressly in effect (§110(k); see chapter 9C infra and the cases cited therein). A paralegal must therefore ascertain local law before acting independently to prepare bankruptcy documents for filing with the Bankruptcy Court.

Section 110 sets forth eight basic requirements for bankruptcy petition preparers to comply with. They are as follows.

1. The preparer must sign the document and include the preparer's name and address (§110(b)).
2. Provide a notice to the debtor, prior to the prepartion of any document, stating that a petition preparer may not give legal advice (§110(b)(2)).

21. 11 U.S.C. §331.

3. The preparer shall include the preparer's Social Security number on the document (§110 (c)).
4. The preparer shall furnish the debtor with a copy of the document not later than the time the document is presented to the debtor for signature (§110(d)).
5. The preparer shall not execute any document on behalf of a debtor nor provide legal advice to the detor) (§110 (e)).
6. The preparer shall not use the word *legal* or any other similar term in advertisements or advertise under any "legal" category (§110(f)).
7. The preparer may not receive or collect payment for court fees (§110(g)).
8. The preparer shall, at the filing of the petition, file a declaration under penalty of perjury disclosing any fees paid or promised by or on behalf of the debtor (§110(h); FRBP 2016(c)).

Violations of any of the foregoing requirements are subject to a discretionary fine of $500 (§110(k)(1)(1)). Under §110(h), the court shall also disallow and order turned over to the trustee any fee found to be excessive. Acceptable fees will invariably vary from district to district; however, the 2005 legislation permits the adoption of rules that would set the fees bankruptcy petition preparers may charge.

Section 110(i) creates a civil remedy for damages against a bankruptcy petition preparer who violates Section 110 or commits any fraudulent, unfair, or deceptive act. The debtor, trustee, or United States Trustee may move and seek recovery of the debtor's actual damages, the greater of $2,000 or twice the amount paid by the debtor to the preparer, and reasonable costs and attorneys' fees for bringing the motion.

Section 110(j) provides yet a further check on a bankruptcy petition preparer's conduct by authorizing a party in interest, including the United States Trustee, to seek to enjoin a bankruptcy petition preparer from continuing to act as such where the preparer has engaged in fraudulent or deceptive conduct, has misrepresented the preparer's experience or education, or has violated Section 110 on a continuing basis. Like Section 110(i), Section 110(j) authorizes the court to award reasonable attorney's fees and costs to the successful moving party.[22]

A bankruptcy petition preparer also falls within the definition of a debt relief agency and is therefore also required to provide the notices set forth in §§342(b), 526, and 527 as described in chapter 4 and 7A supra.

---

22. See In re Rausch, 213 Bankr. 364 (D. Nev. 1997) (assessing damages for violations of Section 110). See In re Skobinsky, 167 Bankr. 45 (E.D. Pa. 1994) (permanently enjoining a petition preparer for violating Section 110). Section 110(k), added by BAPA, permits the court to triple the fines assessed against a bankruptcy petition preparer who advises a debtor to exclude assets, use a false social security number, fails to advise a debtor that the debtor is in fact filing a bankruptcy petition, or who files documents that do not disclose the bankruptcy petition preparer's identity.

The effect of Section 110 is to impose a heavy burden of compliance upon unsupervised paralegals who can prepare bankruptcy documents for debtors in a jurisdiction that has authorized such activities as not constituting the unlawful practice of law. However, although the requirements are numerous, any qualified and properly trained paralegal will not find compliance to be difficult.

C. THE CHAPTER 7 PROCESS

Although the Chapter 7 process is not set in motion in business cases until the debtor files a petition, in consumer cases, BAPA has created new requirements that effectively commence the Chapter 7 process before a petition is even filed. Recall that a consumer debtor must obtain a prepetition credit counseling certificate as a prerequisite to filing a petition absent a showing of exigent circumstances. Even if exigent circumstances are shown, the certificate must be obtained within 30 days of filing, or the case is subject to dismissal on the 46th day after filing. See chapter 4A supra. Also, recall that a debt relief agency must provide various notices to the debtor and enter into a written retainer agreement, within short intervals of time after first meeting a debtor. All of these provisions ought to be complied with at the initial conference with a client. See chapters 4A and 7A supra.

Once a debtor files a petition, a clear process is set in motion (see chart on page 103). The first event that occurs is the appointment of an interim trustee by the United States Trustee pursuant to Section 701. The **interim trustee** will serve as the trustee until the meeting of creditors.[23] In all districts there exist panels of private trustees. Private panel trustees are persons who act as trustees on a regular basis.

Under the United States Trustee system, which went into effect nationwide during 1988, the United States Trustee has been given the responsibility to appoint interim trustees.[24]

Next, the United States Trustee will send a notice to the creditors, to the debtor, and to the interim trustee advising all parties of the entry of an order for relief (the filing) and the appointment of the interim trustee.[25] This notice is usually given about five days after a proceeding is filed. Next, the United States Trustee will provide notice to the creditors advising them of the time and place of the **creditors meeting** to be held under Section

23. 11 U.S.C. §701.
24. 11 U.S.C. §701(a); 28 U.S.C. §586(a)(1). See chapter 10 infra.
25. 11 U.S.C. §342(a); Bankruptcy Rule 2002(a); Bankruptcy Rule 2008.

341.[26] The form of the notice shall be substantially in the manner of Official Form 16. A sample is included in the forms disk accompanying this text.

Section 342(c) of the Bankruptcy Code, added by BAPA, requires that a debtor include the last four digits of the debtor's social security number and provide notice to a creditor at the address specified by the creditor in either communications to the debtor or in a registry maintained by the court. Creditors are given an opportunity to advise the Bankruptcy Court of the address to send notices in Chapter 7 and 13 cases. Notices to creditors not given in compliance with this provision are not effective until brought to the creditor's attention. [27]

The creditors meeting is often erroneously called a "first meeting of creditors," although under the Code there is only one required meeting of creditors. This misnomer has arisen because under the Bankruptcy Act there was a first meeting of creditors and a last meeting of creditors. The word "first" is now superfluous. Federal Rule of Bankruptcy Procedure 2003 requires that the meeting of creditors take place not less than 20 (because 20 days' notice is required under Bankruptcy Rule 2002(a)) and not more than 40 days after the order for relief is entered.[28] Because this timing is based upon the entry of an order for relief, the same time limit applies in both voluntary and involuntary proceedings. Remember, once an order for relief is entered in an involuntary proceeding, the matter proceeds in a manner identical to a voluntary proceeding.[29]

The meeting of creditors is the most visible aspect of many bankruptcy proceedings. In a no asset proceeding it is normally the only appearance a debtor is required to make.[30] There is no judge present at the meeting of creditors, only a representative of the United States Trustee.[31] The representative administers the oath to the debtor and recites the debtor's duties under the Code as well as the discharge and reaffirmation process. The United States Trustee has been given the responsibility of conducting creditors meetings under the United States Trustee program.[32]

At the meeting of creditors, the creditors are given an opportunity to elect a trustee. Elections for a specific trustee are infrequent. Section 702 contains

26. 11 U.S.C. §§341, 342(a); Bankruptcy Rule 2002(a); Bankruptcy Rule 2003.
27. 11 U.S.C. §342(c); 11 U.S.C. §342(g). The author suspects that a directory of creditor addresses will find its way into publication so it will be easy for courts, debtor representatives, and creditors to comply with some aspects of this provision. What the consequences of non-compliance will be on debtors and creditors will have to evolve in the case law. For example, the automatic stay is generally effective without notice (see chapter 12 infra). How new §§342(c) and 342(g) will affect this rule will be unknown until the courts have been given the opportunity to explore these issues in the case law.
28. 11 U.S.C. §342(a); Bankruptcy Rule 2003. In a Chapter 13 case, the meeting of creditors may take place within 50 days of filing.
29. See chapter 4 supra.
30. 11 U.S.C. §343; Bankruptcy Rule 4002.
31. 11 U.S.C. §341(c); Bankruptcy Rule 2003(b).
32. 11 U.S.C. §341(a); 28 U.S.C. §586(a)(5); Bankruptcy Rule 2003.

CHAPTER 7
Debtor's View Timeline

Document	Authority
Petition	Official Form 1
Filing Fee	FRBP 1006
List of Creditors	FRBP 1007(a)(1) §521(a)(1)(A)
Statement of SSN	Official Form 21; FRBP 1007(f)
Credit counseling certificate	521(b)
List of 20 Largest Unsecured Claims — Chapter 11	FRBP 1007(d)
Corporate Debtor — Exhibit A	Official Form IX
Bankruptcy Petition Preparer/ Statement of Compensation	§110(h)

Document	Authority
Prepetition credit counseling	§109(h)
Debt relief agency disclosures/ signed contract	§§526-528

Document	Authority
Statement of Financial Affairs	§521(a)(1)(B), FRBP 1007(7)
Schedules of assets and liabilities	§521(a)(1)(B), FRBP 1007(b)
Schedule of current income and expenses	§707(b)(2)(c)
Certificate of debt relief disclosures and payments received within 60 days	§521(a) (1)
Statement of Compensation	§329; FRBP 2016
Plan Chapter 13	FRBP 3015

Document	Authority
Statement of Intention	§521(a)(2)
1st Plan Payment — Ch. 13	§1326(a)
DIP Bank Accounts — Ch. 11	§345
Retain Professionals. Pay Insiders — Ch. 11	§327
Commence Operating Reports — Ch. 11	FRBP 2015(a)

Time (Days) (approx.)	0	10	15	30	40	70	90	100	150
	A	B	C		D	E		F	G
Event	Petition Filed	Interim Trustee	Notice to Creditors		Creditor Meeting	Objections to Exemptions		Objection to Discharge/ Dischargeability	Discharge/ Reaffirmation
Authority	11 U.S.C. §301	11 U.S.C. §701	11 U.S.C. §341 FRBP 2002, 2003		11 U.S.C. §341(a)	FRBP 4003 (30 days after "D")		FRBP 4004, 4007 (60 days after "D")	11 U.S.C. §524 FRBP 4004 Personal Financial Management Course 11 U.S.C. §727(a)(11)

the procedure for conducting such an election. The interim trustee will become the permanent trustee unless the creditors elect another trustee.[33]

The trustee and creditors may examine the debtor or debtors at the creditors meeting. The trustee will ask questions based upon the trustee's review of the Statements and Schedules. In the typical no asset consumer proceeding, a trustee will normally ask ten basic questions. These questions are:

(1) State your name, Social Security Number, and current address for the record. The Trustee will also request proof of the same, such as a Social Security card and a driver's license or other similar document.[34]

(2) Have you read the Bankruptcy Information Sheet provided by the United States Trustee?[35]

(3) Did you sign the petition, schedules, statements, and related documents you filed with the court?

(4) Did you read the petition, schedules, statements, and related documents before you signed them?

(5) Are you personally familiar with the information contained in the petition, schedules, statements, and related documents?

(6) To the best of your knowledge, is the information contained in the petition, schedules, statements, and related documents true and correct?

(7) Are there any errors or omissions to bring to my, or the court's, attention at this time?

(8) Are all of your assets identified on the schedules?

(9) Have you listed all of your creditors on the schedules?

(10) Have you filed bankruptcy before? (If so, the trustee must obtain the case number and the discharge information to determine the debtor(s) discharge eligibility.)[36]

Many trustees will also ask the debtor: "What caused your financial difficulties?" The reason for this question is to comply with one of the requirements for a discharge — namely, that a debtor be able to describe satisfactorily a lack of assets to satisfy liabilities. See section 13E infra.

Section 341(d) to the Code requires the trustee to examine the debtor further to make sure the debtor is aware of:

1. the consequences of seeking a discharge, including the effects on credit history;
2. the debtor's right to file a petition under a different chapter of the Bankruptcy Code;

---

33. 11 U.S.C. §702(d).
34. 11 U.S.C. §521(h).
35. A sample Bankruptcy Information Sheet is contained at Form 7.7 in the forms disk. The information contained in the notice is similar to the notice required to be provided by a debt relief agency pursuant to 11 U.S.C. §342(b) within three days of providing bankruptcy assistance pursuant to 11 U.S.C. §527(a). See chapters 4A and 7A supra.
36. A debtor may only receive a discharge once every eight years. 11 U.S.C. §727(a)(8). See chapter 13 infra.

3. the effect of receiving a discharge of debts; and
4. the effect of reaffirmation (see Section 7E infra).

If there are specific assets in the estate or issues involving the estate that the trustee is concerned about, additional questions will likely be asked. For example, if the debtor owns a home, the trustee will probably ask a series of questions to determine whether there may be any equity in the home that may be used to pay a dividend to unsecured creditors. If the debtor owns a vehicle, the trustee may ask similar questions pertaining to it. If the debtor is a plaintiff in any lawsuit or if the debtor has previously been involved in a business, the trustee will ask questions about each of these activities. However, in a typical no asset consumer proceeding, the average debtor may not own real estate, and there is little or no realizable equity in vehicles in most instances. So the basic questions will be asked and no others. Because creditor meetings are usually scheduled in groups of ten or more, all to take place within an hour, there is not much time for extended examination. However, if the Statements and Schedules are complete and understandable and if the trustee is prepared, it is possible to successfully complete a series of examinations within a relatively short period of time.

After the trustee completes the examination, creditors are given an opportunity to further examine the debtor. A nonattorney may appear on behalf of creditors in consumer bankruptcy cases. For example, a paralegal working in the collection department of a department store could appear and question debtors.[37] Sometimes creditors or their counsel will advise the trustee and demonstrate that a debtor may not be disclosing all pertinent information. Sometimes creditors or their counsel waste everybody's time asking irrelevant questions unrelated to a debtor's financial affairs. Sometimes a representative of a bank or finance company simply wants to know where a secured asset is and if it is currently insured. Creditors do have a right to come to the creditors meeting and make inquiry of the debtor's assets and liabilities, but in actual practice, creditors rarely appear at these hearings.

D. RULE 2004 EXAMINATIONS

Sometimes, creditors or a trustee will want to examine a debtor for more time than is available at the creditors meeting. Alternatively, a trustee or creditor may desire to examine a third party, not the debtor, regarding the debtor's financial affairs. The Federal Rules of Bankruptcy Procedure

37. 11 U.S.C. §341(c). This provision was added by the 2005 legislation.

provide a method that allows any party in interest to take the examination of any person concerning a debtor's financial affairs. This method is called a **Rule 2004 Examination**.[38] Under the Bankruptcy Act this was known as a Rule 205 Examination. The prior and present rules are virtually identical. It has been stated of Rule 205, the predecessor to Rule 2004, that it is "in the nature of an inquisition."[39] Objections on grounds of relevancy are not normally acceptable during one of these examinations. In fact, most objections will not be appropriate in a Rule 2004 Examination. Any matter relevant to the proceeding is fair game in a Rule 2004 Examination.[40] Rule 2004 exists for the benefit of creditors or for the benefit of the trustee who desires to conduct an extensive examination of the debtor or a third party beyond the time limitations of the creditors meeting.

An order for a Rule 2004 Examination is obtained by the party seeking to conduct the examination's filing an application for an order with the court.[41] The order must be served personally, in a manner identical to service of a subpoena.[42] Nondebtor examinees and debtors, when required to travel more than 100 miles, one way, are entitled to compensation for mileage in reaching the place of examination.[43]

A Rule 2004 Examination, when appropriate, has several benefits in addition to the time factors described above. It is a form of discovery that permits a trustee or party in interest to determine the existence of assets or claims and the rights of the parties without incurring the additional expenses of commencing an adversary proceeding. In short, the Rule 2004 Examination is a method for conducting what are essentially depositions without having to file a lawsuit first. Rule 2004 Examinations are used extensively in motion practice under the Code. For example, a party may wish to take an appraiser's Rule 2004 Examination in connection with a motion for relief from the automatic stay. A creditors committee may take Rule 2004 Examinations in connection with a motion to appoint a trustee in a Chapter 11 proceeding.

E. DISCHARGE AND REAFFIRMATION

After the creditors meeting, the next and final event that occurs in a typical no asset consumer proceeding is that an individual debtor or joint debtors

38. Bankruptcy Rule 2004.
39. 12 Collier on Bankruptcy §705.15 at 2-93 (14th ed. 1973).
40. Bankruptcy Rule 2004(b).
41. Bankruptcy Rule 2004(a).
42. Bankruptcy Rule 2004(c).
43. Bankruptcy Rule 2004(e).

will receive a discharge.[44] Up until 1986 debtors were also required to appear in court, before a judge, to receive their discharge.[45] The discharge hearing was typically held between 60 and 90 days after the meeting of creditors. The 1986 amendments to the Code made the requirement of discharge hearings discretionary with the court unless there is a **reaffirmation agreement** to approve.[46] Under the 2005 amendments, there will be a hearing if the debtor does not have an attorney or if the reaffirmation agreement is presumed an undue hardship within the meaning of 11 U.S.C.§524(M)(1). Receipt of a discharge will be automatic unless an objection to the discharge itself is filed. Pursuant to the 2005 legislation, a debtor will not receive a Chapter 7 discharge unless the debtor completes a course in personal financial management approved by the United States Trustee.[47]

The discharge legally relieves a debtor of all dischargeable obligations.[48] Section 524 concerns the effect of a discharge. Generally, a discharge voids any existing judgment and permanently enjoins the collection of any debt subject to the discharge. Certain debts are specifically not dischargeable. These debts are analyzed in chapter 13 infra. Secured debts are effectively not dischargeable if the debtor wants to keep the collateral.[49] The right to receive a discharge may not be waived.[50] In community property states, the community property of a nonfiling spouse is entitled to a discharge unless the nonfiling spouse would not be entitled to receive a discharge in a proceeding under the Code.[51] This would be the case if the nonfiling spouse would be unable to receive a discharge for any of the reasons enumerated in Section 727 as described in chapter 13 infra.

Only a debtor's legal obligation to repay a discharged debt is relieved by a bankruptcy discharge; the underlying moral obligation to repay one's just debts is not affected by a bankruptcy discharge. Section 524(f) specifically states: "Nothing contained in . . . this section prevents a debtor from voluntarily repaying any debt."[52] So if a discharged debtor wants to voluntarily repay the neighborhood doctor, the law permits performance of the moral obligation. The reason for specific inclusion of this principle into the Code is historical.

Before the enactment of the Bankruptcy Code, the common law of many states held that a bankrupt debtor retained the moral obligation to repay debts after receiving a bankruptcy discharge. If a debtor performed

---

44. 11 U.S.C. §524; 11 U.S.C. §727. See chapter 13 infra.
45. See 11 U.S.C. §521(5) as it existed prior to November 1986.
46. 11 U.S.C. §524(d).
47. See chapter 13 infra; Bankruptcy Rule 4004. 11 U.S.C. §707(a)(11); 11 U.S.C. §111. See chapter 13 infra; Bankruptcy Rule 4004. A personal financial management course is also required to receive a Chapter 13 discharge. 11 U.S.C. §1328(g). See chapter 23 below.
48. 11 U.S.C. §524.
49. See chapter 21 infra.
50. 11 U.S.C. §524(a).
51. 11 U.S.C. §524(a)(3), (b).
52. 11 U.S.C. §524(f).

any part of the moral obligation by voluntarily repaying a portion of the debt, common law held that a new legal obligation to pay had been created by reaffirmation. Under this pre-Code law, creditors would try to convince a debtor who had received a bankruptcy discharge to "Come on, be a good guy and send in a payment." Many people who receive persistent phone calls like this tire of receiving them. Ultimately, a payment will be made simply to stop the phone from ringing. This one act could constitute reaffirmation under existing pre-Code state law and restore the previously discharged debtor's liability. The creditor could thus negate the effects of the bankruptcy and obtain a judgment for the balance of the "reaffirmed" debt.[53] While some reaffirmations were indeed proper, all were suspect under the Act because of the abuses committed by some creditors.

The various reaffirmation provisions contained in Section 524 are intended to curb creditor abuse. Thus, Section 524(f) is essential to explain the intent of Congress in enacting the specific reaffirmation provisions into the Code. The practical effect of this provision is that a debtor may voluntarily repay a discharged debt without creating a new legal obligation. The moral obligation is free to be performed by a debtor without risk. If the discharged debtor stops paying, the creditor has no enforceable claim. A new legal obligation is created only when the Code's reaffirmation provisions are complied with. A further practical effect of Section 524(f) is that a basic principle of contract law has been altered by enactment of the Bankruptcy Code.[54]

For example, Wimpy receives a discharge. Under Bankruptcy Act practice, if Brutus could convince Wimpy to repay any part of the discharged debt, and Wimpy performed, a new legal obligation had been created free of the effects of the prior bankruptcy discharge. Wimpy would again be legally obligated to pay his debt to Brutus. Under the Bankruptcy Code, no new legal obligation is created if Wimpy voluntarily makes a payment to Brutus unless the court has properly approved a reaffirmation agreement.

No discharged debt is considered to be legally reaffirmed unless the provisions of Sections 524(c), (d), and (k) are strictly complied with. Although the provisions are lengthy, their basic elements are not difficult to comprehend. First, there must be a written reaffirmation agreement entered into prior to entry of the debtor's discharge.[55] The agreement must contain a statement that it may be rescinded by the debtor at any time prior to receiving a discharge or 60 days from when the agreement is filed with the court, whichever comes later. The agreement must comply with the provisions of

53. A. Corbin, Corbin on Contracts, Chapter 9, §§222-230 (student ed. 1952), contains an excellent description of the moral obligation/reaffirmation law under common law.
54. 11 U.S.C. §524(c).
55. 11 U.S.C. §524(c)(1).

Section 524(k).[56] A debtor's attorney must file a declaration or affidavit representing that the agreement is fully informed and voluntary, that the agreement does not impose an undue hardship on the debtor, and that the attorney has fully advised the debtor of the effect and consequences of the reaffirmation and any default made under it.[57] If the debtor is not represented by an attorney, the court must also find that the agreement will not impose an undue hardship on and be in the best interests of the debtor.[58]

Section 524(k) specifies the documentation, contents of the documentation, and the procedures to follow to obtain approval of a reaffirmation agreement. The Amount Reaffirmed and Annual Percentage Rate must be the most conspicuously displayed terms, along with any introductory instructions to review the documents carefully.[59] A five-part document comprises the reaffirmation agreement. Part A contains numerous preliminary disclosures, primarily with respect to credit terms, repayment terms, whether or not there is any collateral, instructions about the approval procedure, and that the debtor has sixty days from the filing of the reaffirmation with the bankruptcy court to rescind the agreement.[60] Part B is the actual reaffirmation agreement and contains signature lines for the parties.[61] Part C is a certification of the debtor's attorney, if the debtor has an attorney, that the reaffirmation agreement is voluntary and will not create an undue hardship for the debtor.[62] Part D is the Debtor's Statement in Support of Reaffirmation Agreement, which acknowledges that the agreement is voluntary, that it will not impose an undue hardship, and that entering into the agreement is in the debtor's financial interest.[63] Part E is the Motion for Court Approval. This is used if the debtor is not represented by an attorney.[64]

The court may then hold a discharge and reaffirmation hearing that, if held, the debtor is required to attend.[65] The court must find that the elements of Section 524(c) have been strictly complied with and must further instruct the debtor that a reaffirmation agreement is not required for the debtor to voluntarily repay the debt, that approval of the agreement will create a new legally enforceable obligation of the debtor.[66] To reiterate, if a debtor decides

56. 11 U.S.C. §524(c)(2)(3).
57. 11 U.S.C. §524(c)(3).
58. 11 U.S.C. §524(c)(6).
59. 11 U.S.C. §524(k)(2). Annual Percentage Rate has the same meaning given it in the Federal Truth in Lending Act ("TILA"), 15 U.S.C. §1601 et seq.
60. 11 U.S.C. §524(k)(3). 11 U.S.C. §524(c)(4).
61. 11 U.S.C. §524(k)(4).
62. 11 U.S.C. §524(k)(5). In re Vargas, 257 Bankr. 157 (Bankr. N.J. 2001), discusses counsel's obligations to clients with respect to reaffirmation agreements.
63. 11 U.S.C. §524(k)(6).
64. 11 U.S.C. §524(k)(7). If the agreement creates a presumption of undue hardship by the debtor's expenses exceeding income, in the disclosures made in Part D, then the court must hold a hearing to determine if the debtor can make the proposed payments or disapprove the reaffirmation agreement. 11 U.S.C. §524(m).
65. 11 U.S.C. §524(d); 11 U.S.C. §524(k)(7); 11 U.S.C. §521(a)(5).
66. 11 U.S.C. §524(d)(1), (2), §524(k)(7), (m).

to pay $20 to Dr. Jones on a discharged debt because the debtor feels like she wants to pay the doctor, and the next month the debtor does not make a payment, Dr. Jones has no legal right to sue the debtor for any balance. There is no balance due because it has been discharged unless a reaffirmation agreement has been entered into and approved by the court. The courts are very strict about approving reaffirmation agreements and are reluctant to approve any except those concerning secured debts for the necessaries of life, such as car loans or certain purchase money security agreements. Very rarely will the court approve a reaffirmation agreement for an unsecured debt.

The case of In re Latanowich, 207 Bankr. 326 (Bankr. D. Mass. 1997), illustrates the proposition that the reaffirmation requirements must be strictly complied with to be enforceable. In this case, Sears Roebuck and Co. solicited a reaffirmation agreement from a debtor. Although the debtor entered into the agreement, Sears did not file the agreement with the court, rendering it unenforceable. The court not only found the agreement to be invalid, but sanctioned Sears for attempting to enforce it and enjoined Sears from seeking to enforce any reaffirmation agreement not filed with the court in compliance with the statute. The outcome in this case contributed to the substantial changes in reaffirmation agreement enacted in §524(k) in the 2005 legislation.

Section 524(i) provides that creditors who willfully misapply payments received under a confirmed plan are in violation of the discharge injunction provided for by §524. This requires, for example, mortgage lenders to properly credit payments made to them in Chapter 13 cases. Section 524(j), on the other hand, permits creditors to communicate with debtors about postpetition payments on home mortgages without the communications constituting a violation of the discharge injunction.

The above has been a synopsis of what takes place in a typical no asset consumer Chapter 7 proceeding. Objections to a debtor's discharge and the nondischargeability of specific debts is described in greater detail in chapter 13 infra.

Summary

The process that occurs in a no asset consumer Chapter 7 bankruptcy forms a basic model of the essential core activities that occur in all bankruptcy proceedings. Initiating the proceeding and identifying the documents required to be filed have been described in detail in chapter 4 supra.

All professionals rendering services to a bankruptcy estate, such as attorneys, accountants, and appraisers, must have their employment approved by the court at the commencement of the representation. In a Chapter 7, 12, or 13, this task is normally accomplished by filing the Statement of Compensation required by Bankruptcy Rule 2016(b). In

Chapter 9 or 11 proceedings, an application to be retained must be filed with and approved by the court. Additionally, a debt relief agency must also provide the various disclosures and enter into a written contract to provide services in a consumer bankruptcy case pursuant to Sections 526-528 as described in chapter 4, supra.

The fees of approved professionals rendering services to a bankruptcy estate may not be paid until the fees have been approved by the court. Court approval is obtained by filing an application for compensation, which is noticed to the creditors. A fee application brought while a case is pending is called an interim application. Generally, interim fee applications may not be brought in less than 120-day intervals. A fee application brought at the close of a proceeding or when all services have been rendered is called a *final application*.

Section 110 of the Code imposes eight requirements on bankruptcy petition preparers who prepare documents for filing by a debtor in the Bankruptcy Court. Paralegals not in the employ of an attorney are subject to this section. Fines, damages, and injunctive relief can be sought and obtained against a bankruptcy petition preparer found violating Section 110. However, while the section regulates the conduct of bankruptcy petition preparers, it expressly does not permit a bankruptcy petition preparer to perform services in a jurisdiction where the performance of such services will constitute the unauthorized practice of law.

When a Chapter 7 is filed, the United States Trustee will appoint an interim trustee. The interim trustee will normally become the permanent trustee, although creditors may elect a trustee. A creditors meeting will be held within 40 days of the filing. In a typical consumer no asset proceeding this will usually be the only appearance required by the debtor. At the meeting of creditors, the trustee and creditors may ask questions to the debtor concerning the debtor's financial affairs. If an extended examination is required, a party in interest (such as the trustee or a creditor) may take the equivalent of a deposition of the debtor pursuant to Bankruptcy Rule 2004.

Approximately 60 to 90 days after the meeting of creditors, a debtor will normally receive a discharge. Individual debtors are required to complete a course in personal financial management as a pre-requisite to receiving their discharge. The discharge relieves a debtor of all dischargeable legal obligations. Most debts are dischargeable. The discharge is the primary element of debtor relief provided for by the Bankruptcy Code. Exemptions (chapter 9 infra) and the automatic stay (chapter 12 infra) comprise the remaining elements of debtor relief.

Debtors may desire to reaffirm debts. When a debt or agrees to reaffirm a debt, the debt will not be subject to the discharge. The legal obligation to pay the debt will remain. To prevent abuse, a specific statutory procedure must be complied with for a debt to be considered legally reaffirmed.

KEY TERMS

automatic stay
bankruptcy petition preparer
consumer no asset
creditors meeting
debtor-in-possession
discharge
exempt
final fee application
fresh start
interim fee application
interim trustee
reaffirmation agreement
Rule 2004 Examination

Chapter 7 Checklist

7.1 COMPENSATION OF PROFESSIONALS

7.1.1 Retention of Counsel (Sections 327, 328, 329)

1. Chapter 7, 12, or 13 debtor counsel — compliance with Bankruptcy Rule 2016(b) statement
2. In all other situations, court approval required File:
    a. noticed motion for approval of retention,
    b. declaration of disinterest,
    c. order approving retention.

7.1.2 Applications for Compensation (Sections 327, 330, 331; Bankruptcy Rule 2016)

1. Not more than once every 120 days
2. Noticed motion
3. Application should include
    a. summary of services
    b. itemization of time and charges

7.2 REAFFIRMATION AGREEMENTS (Section 524(c)(k))

7.2.1 Elements

1. Written agreement prior to discharge (Section 524(c)(1))
2. Compliance with Section 524(k)
3. Affidavit of counsel that agreement is voluntary and informed (Section 524(c)(3))
4. Statement in agreement that debtor has 60 days to rescind (Section 524(c)(2))

7.2.2 Section 524(k) Requirements

Document	*Authority*
1. PART "A"— Preliminary Disclosures	11 U.S.C. §524(k)(3)
2. PART "B"— Reaffirmation Agreement	11 U.S.C. §524(k)(4)
3. PART "C"— Debtor's Attorney Certification	11 U.S.C. §524(k)(5)
4. PART "D"— Debtor's Statement in Support of Reaffirmation Agreement	11 U.S.C. §524(k)(6)(A)
5. Debtor Statement if attorney	11 U.S.C. §524(k)(6)(B)
6. PART "E"— Motion for Court Approval (No attorney)	11 U.S.C. §524(k)(7)
7. Court Order	11 U.S.C. §524(k)(8)

7.2.3 Hearings

1. If debtor has no attorney in connection with reaffirmation agreement 11 U.S.C. §524(d);
2. With or without an attorney if undue hardship is presumed, except where the debt is owed to a credit union pursuant to 11 U.S.C. §524(m).

7.3 BANKRUPTCY PETITION PREPARERS (Section 110)

7.3.1 Requirements

1. must sign document including name and address of preparer (Section 110(b));
2. provide Notice that preparer may not give legal advice (Section 110(b)(2))
3. must include preparer's Social Security number on document (Section 110(c));
4. must furnish debtor a copy of the document on or before its being presented to debtor for signature (Section 110(d));
5. may not execute a document on behalf of a debtor nor provide legal advice to a debtor (Section 110(e));

6. may not use the word *legal* or similar term in advertising and may not advertise under a "legal" category (Section 110(f));
7. may not receive or collect payment for court fees (Section 110(g));
8. Shall, at the filing of the petition, file a statement of compensation paid or promised (Section 110(h)).

7.3.2 Penalties

1. discretionary fine of $500 (11 U.S.C. §110(k));
2. disallowance of excessive fees (11 U.S.C. §110(h));
3. actual damages of $2,000 or twice amount paid by debtor (11 U.S.C. §110(i))
4. triple damages for disclosure failures (11 U.S.C. §110(k));
5. injunction against repeated conduct (11 U.S.C. §110(j));
6. attorney fees and costs (11 U.S.C. §110(i)(j)).

DISCUSSION QUESTIONS

1. When must the employment of a professional be approved by the court?
2. What is a fee application? Why might it be important to monitor professional fees in a bankruptcy proceeding?
3. Describe the basic Chapter 7 process.
4. What occurs at the creditors meeting?
5. What is a Rule 2004 Examination and when is such an examination commonly conducted?
6. What is the effect of a discharge?
7. What is reaffirmation? What are the legal requirements of a reaffirmation agreement?
8. May a paralegal receive fees from clients for the preparation of bankruptcy petitions and schedules if not authorized by state law? What are the potential consequences of preparing bankruptcy petitions for compensation without supervision when not authorized by state law?

8

Conversion and Dismissal

A party in interest, such as the debtor, may request the conversion of a proceeding from one Chapter to another. Conversion may occur more than once in the course of a single proceeding. **Conversion** means that a Chapter 7 is changed to a Chapter 11 or vice versa. Commonly, a Chapter 13 or Chapter 11 reorganization that has failed is converted to a Chapter 7 liquidation. A proceeding may also be dismissed upon motion by a party in interest under appropriate circumstances such as presumed abuse of Chapter 7 under the needs based bankruptcy formula (see chapter 5F supra). A **dismissal** will terminate a bankruptcy proceeding and render the proceeding ineffective.

Sections 348 and 349 contain provisions that apply to the conversion or dismissal of a proceeding. In addition, each Chapter proceeding has a specific conversion or dismissal provision that applies only to the Chapter proceeding involved.[1] All of these provisions, however, are somewhat interrelated. The basic principles contained in them are identical, particularly where conversion rather than dismissal is the issue. This chapter concerns the conversion procedure applicable in all proceedings, the effects of conversion in all proceedings, the effect of a dismissal in all proceedings, and the grounds for dismissal or conversion in Chapter 7 proceedings. The specific grounds for dismissal or conversion of Chapter 11, 12, and 13 reorganization proceedings are described in greater detail elsewhere in this text.[2]

A. CONVERSION

A debtor has one opportunity to freely convert a proceeding from one Chapter to another. A debtor may convert a Chapter 7 to another proceeding,

1. 11 U.S.C. §§706, 707, 1112, 1208, 1307.
2. See chapters 23, 24, and 27 infra.

unless the proceeding has been previously converted.[3] A debtor may convert a Chapter 11 to a Chapter 7, unless a trustee has been appointed, the proceeding was commenced as an involuntary proceeding, or the proceeding has been previously converted from one under another Chapter.[4] A debtor may convert from Chapter 12 to Chapter 7.[5] A Chapter 13 debtor may convert from Chapter 13 to Chapter 7.[6] A waiver of the right to convert is unenforceable.[7]

For example, Jed Clampett files a Chapter 7. One week later he discovers oil on his property. He may freely convert the Chapter 7 to a Chapter 11 or 13. Alternatively, Ponzi, Inc., files a Chapter 11. A trustee is appointed. Ponzi, Inc., may no longer freely convert the proceeding to a Chapter 7.

For a debtor to convert from one Chapter proceeding to another, the debtor must also be able to be a debtor under the particular Chapter to which conversion is desired. This is consistent with Section 109.[8]

To exercise the free option to convert, a debtor typically files an ex parte application simply stating that the debtor desires to convert to a specified Chapter and that the debtor is qualified to be a debtor under the Chapter proceeding to which conversion is sought. Theoretically, a statement as simple as, "I am a Chapter 13 debtor and desire to convert to Chapter 7. I am qualified to be a debtor under Chapter 7," will suffice in most instances. A sample form is included in the forms disk to this text. Although conversion is often effectuated by the filing of an ex parte application as noted above, technically, FRBP 1017(f) requires a noticed motion. Local Rules should be consulted for the acceptable procedure in a given court.

Other than the debtor's one free opportunity to convert from one Chapter proceeding to another, a proceeding may only be converted by obtaining court approval after proper notice to all parties in interest. Thus, a debtor desiring to convert from Chapter 7 to Chapter 11, when the proceeding has been previously converted, must first obtain court approval. Any other party in interest, the trustee, or any of the creditors may also move the court to convert a Chapter 7 to a Chapter 11.[9] Any party in interest may move the court to convert a proceeding from Chapter 11 to Chapter 7.[10] Any party in interest may move the court to convert a proceeding from Chapter 13 to Chapter 7 and may move to convert a Chapter 13 to a Chapter 11 or 12 prior

3. 11 U.S.C. §706(a).
4. 11 U.S.C. §1112(a). See chapter 24 infra.
5. 11 U.S.C. §1208(a). See chapter 27 infra.
6. 11 U.S.C. §1307(a). See chapter 23 infra.
7. 11 U.S.C. §706(a); 11 U.S.C. §1208(a); 11 U.S.C. §1307(a).
8. See chapter 5 supra. See also 11 U.S.C. §706(d); 11 U.S.C. §1112(f); 11 U.S.C. §1208(e); 11 U.S.C. §1307(f). The trend in the case law is that the debtor must seek conversion in good faith. See, e.g., In re Copper, 314 Bankr. 628 (BAP Cir. 6 2004).
9. 11 U.S.C. §706(b).
10. 11 U.S.C. §1112(b).

to confirmation of a Chapter 13 plan.[11] FRBP 1017(f) implements the various applicable provisions.

A nondebtor may not seek conversion of a proceeding from Chapter 7 to a Chapter 12 or 13 unless the debtor consents,[12] nor may a nondebtor seek conversion of a Chapter 11 to a Chapter 12 or 13.[13] A nondebtor may not seek conversion from Chapter 12 to Chapter 7 or 13.[14] A nondebtor may not seek conversion from Chapter 11 to Chapter 7 of those debtors who may not have an involuntary proceeding filed against them (charitable institutions, for instance),[15] nor may a nondebtor seek conversion of a Chapter 13 to a Chapter 7 if the debtor is a farmer.[16] The rationale of these various prohibitions on the ability of nondebtors to seek conversion of a proceeding from one Chapter to another is identical to the rationale described in chapter 4 supra regarding the exclusion of certain types of debtors from involuntary proceedings, and the prohibition against filing an involuntary Chapter 13.[17]

Section 348 describes the effects of conversion. For most purposes, the basic meaning of Section 348 is that if a case is converted from one Chapter to another, the proceeding is generally considered to have been filed under the converted-to Chapter as of the original petition date.[18] Although there are some exceptions, their normal effect is slight.[19] All claims, except the administrative claims of the converted proceeding, are considered to have arisen before the original filing date.[20] For example, a Chapter 7 is filed on May 28 and converted to a Chapter 11 on May 29. Under Section 348 the May 28 order for relief will generally be the effective date of the Chapter 11 filing. The major reason for this rule is that any other would hopelessly complicate and confuse the many accounting features contained in the bankruptcy system. Because one function of the bankruptcy system is to reconcile the financial affairs of a debtor as of a date certain, only one date should be used, not two or more.

When a Chapter 11 or 13 is converted to a Chapter 7, the debtor or superseded trustee is responsible for filing a final report and accounting with the court. Additionally, any necessary updating that may be required to make the Statements and Schedules accurately reflect changes in the debtor's financial condition occurring between the original filing date and the conversion date should also be prepared.[21]

11. 11 U.S.C. §1307(c); 11 U.S.C. §1307(d).
12. 11 U.S.C. §706(c).
13. 11 U.S.C. §1112(d).
14. 11 U.S.C. §1208.
15. 11 U.S.C. §1112(c). See chapter 4 supra.
16. 11 U.S.C. §1307(f).
17. See chapter 4 supra.
18. 11 U.S.C. §348(a).
19. 11 U.S.C. §348(b), (c).
20. 11 U.S.C. §348(d).
21. Bankruptcy Rule 1019.

B. DISMISSAL

A Chapter 7 may be dismissed upon order of the court. Unlike conversion, dismissal always requires a noticed motion, except that a Chapter 13 debtor may voluntarily dismiss a Chapter 13 case by filing an ex parte application if the case has not previously been converted.[22] Additionally, §521(i) requires automatic dismissal of a case on the 46th day after filing if a debtor has not filed all documents required by §521(a)(1).[23] Creditors, the trustee, or the United States Trustee may seek dismissal of a Chapter 7 for cause, including unreasonable delay or failure to pay filing fees.[24] The United States Trustee may seek dismissal if a debtor fails to file Statements and Schedules in a timely manner.[25]

The court, United States Trustee, trustee, or any party in interest may also seek a dismissal of a consumer proceeding pursuant to §707(b)(1) if allowing the proceeding would constitute an abuse of Chapter 7. This ground for dismissal creates a mechanism that, in appropriate circumstances, effectively forces a debtor to file a Chapter 11 or 13 if bankruptcy relief is to be obtained. Under "needs based bankruptcy," §707(b)(2) requires dismissal of a case where abuse is presumed pursuant to the formula described in chapter 5F supra. A motion brought pursuant to this provision must be brought within 60 days of the creditor meeting unless this deadline is extended by the court.[26]

A proceeding may also be dismissed upon a noticed motion if the court finds that dismissal is in the best interests of creditors.[27] For example, if a sale of the debtor's assets produces sufficient revenues to pay all creditors in full and provide a dividend to the debtor, dismissal may be a cost-effective remedy, as long as the order protects the creditors' rights to ensure prompt payment of the claims. Dismissal in such a manner may save substantial time and expense, result in payment to all creditors, and remove the bankruptcy as a stigma upon the debtor. The court's ruling on a motion to dismiss on this basis is not reviewable by appeal or otherwise.[28]

Section 349 describes the effects of a dismissal. Generally, a dismissal returns all parties to their rights and liabilities as they existed prior to the filing, as if nothing had ever happened.[29]

22. 11 U.S.C. §1307(b).
23. 11 U.S.C. §521(a)(1). See chapter 4B supra. The provision does permit a debtor to seek one 45-day extension.
24. 11 U.S.C. §707(a)(1)(2).
25. 11 U.S.C. §707(a)(3).
26. 11 U.S.C. §707(b)(1); FRBP 1017(e). See, e.g., In re Kornfeld, 164 F.3d 778 (2d Cir. 1999).
27. 11 U.S.C. §305(a).
28. 11 U.S.C. §305(c).
29. 11 U.S.C. §349.

Summary

A bankruptcy proceeding may be converted or dismissed. A conversion will switch a bankruptcy proceeding from one Chapter to another (such as from Chapter 11 to Chapter 7). A dismissal will terminate a bankruptcy proceeding and render the proceeding ineffective.

Normally, a debtor is given one free opportunity to convert a proceeding from one Chapter to another. This act is accomplished by filing an Application to Convert with the court.

Other than the debtor's one free opportunity to convert, conversion may only otherwise occur upon court order after a noticed motion. Thus, a creditor or United States Trustee seeking to convert a case must always do so by way of a noticed motion. If the proceeding has been previously converted (such as a debtor desiring to convert a second time) or if a trustee has been appointed in a Chapter 11 proceeding, without regard to any prior conversion, even the debtor must convert by way of a noticed motion.

The general effect of a conversion is that the proceeding is considered to have been filed under the converted-to Chapter as of the petition's original filing date. When a proceeding is converted, some additional reports will also be required to be filed with the court, primarily to update changes from the original filing.

Any Chapter proceeding may be dismissed for one of two reasons: for cause or when it is in the best interest of creditors. Each Chapter proceeding contains specific provisions defining the grounds for a dismissal for cause. Unreasonable delay that prejudices creditors or a failure to pay filing fees are two common reasons for dismissal for cause. A case may also be dismissed if the court finds that dismissal will be in the best interest of creditors. A consumer Chapter 7 case is subject to dismissal if allowing the proceeding would constitute an abuse of Chapter 7. The general effect of a dismissal is to essentially render the bankruptcy proceeding ineffective, as if it had never occurred.

KEY TERMS

conversion

dismissal

DISCUSSION QUESTIONS

1. What does it mean to convert a bankruptcy proceeding?
2. When may a debtor convert a case from one Chapter to another without a noticed motion?
3. When must a motion to convert be made?
4. What is the difference between conversion of a bankruptcy proceeding and a dismissal of a bankruptcy proceeding?
5. What sorts of conduct may be an abuse of Chapter 7 in addition to the presumption of abuse that may exist pursuant to "needs based bankruptcy"?

9

Exemptions

A. BACKGROUND

Individual debtors seek two primary goals in obtaining bankruptcy debtor relief: a discharge and the exemption of property. The achievement of these goals provides a debtor with a **fresh start** in the debtor's financial affairs. The fresh start concept is the basic foundation of congressional intent in permitting individual debtors to seek bankruptcy relief.[1]

Only individual debtors may claim **exemptions**.[2] Exemptions allow a debtor to protect property from the reach of creditors or trustee in a bankruptcy proceeding. Property for which an exemption is claimed and allowed is not subject to administration by a trustee and is not available for liquidation to pay a dividend to creditors.[3] A debtor may keep exempt property.

The concept of exemptions for individual debtors is a relatively recent one.[4] The Bankruptcy Act did not contain independent exemptions. Exemptions existed only as provided for under the state law of the debtor's domicile or residence. This led to the development of 50 bodies of law regarding exemptions in bankruptcy proceedings.

State exemption statutes have traditionally offered more protection to owners of real property than to owners of nonreal property. This occurs in the form of the **homestead exemption**. This exemption exists in spite of the practical reality that many individual debtors do not own real property. The rise of this exemption is a historical anachronism most likely rooted in

1. H.R. Rep. No. 595, 95th Cong., 1st Sess., 366-367 (1977); S. Rep. No. 989, 95th Cong., 2d Sess., 81 (1978).
2. 11 U.S.C. §522(b).
3. 11 U.S.C. §522(c).
4. See chapter 1 supra.

sixteenth- and seventeenth-century English bankruptcy law, which gave substantial protection to real property owners by preventing bankruptcy proceedings from being initiated against them.[5]

When Congress enacted the Bankruptcy Code, it decided to create a uniform set of federal exemptions. The **federal exemptions,** when properly utilized, eliminates the inherent economic discrimination that has existed between owners and nonowners of real property in that nonreal property owners may now have an opportunity to exempt property of a value equal to that of real property owners.[6] The federal exemption scheme also seeks to bring some national consistency to the concept of exempt property. In some states, exemption statutes reflect the style of early twenty-first century living, while other states have not significantly revised their exemption statutes in the past 100 years. There are still states in which church pews may be claimed exempt.[7] There are some states in which specific types of obsolete nineteenth-century farming implements may be claimed exempt.[8] And there are still other states with even more obscure exemptions that relate only to the nineteenth-century lifestyle.[9]

Section 522(b) provides that a debtor or joint debtors may elect to exempt property from one of two allowable sets of exemptions. A debtor may elect to utilize the exemptions that exist in the state where the debtor has been domiciled for at least 730 days (two years) prior to the filing of the petition, or the place where the debtor resided for a majority of the 180 days preceding the 730-day period, along with any other nonbankruptcy exemptions permitted by federal law, plus any property held by the debtor immediately preceding the filing as a tenant by the entirety, various individual retirement accounts and retirement funds that are exempt from federal income taxation, or a debtor may elect the exemptions provided for under the federal exemption scheme contained in 11 U.S.C. §522(d). If the time limits prevent a debtor from claiming any exemptions, then a debtor may select the federal exemptions. BAPA limits homestead exemptions under state law to $125,000 unless the property involved was acquired more than 1215 days prior to the filing of the petition, except for property acquired during the same period from a transfer of the debtor's principal residence in the same state.[10]

5. Leventhal, The Early History of English Bankruptcy, 67 U. Pa. L. Rev. 1 (1919).
6. See discussion concerning 11 U.S.C. §522(d)(5) infra.
7. Ala. Code §6-10-5.
8. See P.R. Laws Ann. tit. 32 §1130(3) permitting "one cart or wagon" to be exempt.
9. See N.H. Rev. Stat. Ann. §511-2(VII) (1983 and Supp. 1983) permitting exemption of "the uniform, arms and equipments of every officer and private in the militia."
10. 11 U.S.C. §522(b); 11 U.S.C. §522(p). The extended time periods and limitations on homestead amounts were added to the Bankruptcy Code by BAPA. Their intent is to discourage persons from moving to a state with high exemption limits and then declaring bankruptcy. These revisions will require the bankruptcy courts to become familiar with the exemption law of all jurisdictions.

For example, Tom Joad resides in Oklahoma. His employer, Rath Grapes, transfers Tom to California. If Tom files bankruptcy in California within 730 days of moving, his allowable state exemptions would be those of Oklahoma, and his homestead exemption would be limited to $125,000. On the other hand, if Tom lived in California in the first place and is transferred from northern to southern California, then his homestead exemption would be determined solely by California law since he has only moved within the state.

Although each individual debtor may claim a set of exemptions, joint debtors must each select the same set of exemptions.[11] That is, joint debtors must elect to utilize either the applicable state exemptions or the federal exemptions, but not both. If joint debtors cannot agree on which set to claim, or where none are claimed, the debtors are deemed to have selected the federal exemption scheme.[12] The now-prohibited practice of one debtor claiming exemptions under state law and one debtor claiming federal exemptions was known as **stacking**.

For example, John and Jane Smith wish to file a Chapter 7 proceeding. Each may select the allowable exemptions under the state law of their domicile (residence) or each may select the federal exemptions of 11 U.S.C. §522(d).[13] Both John and Jane will be able to claim a full set of exemptions under this election. If John and Jane forget to claim exemptions, or if they cannot agree on which set to claim, they will be deemed to have selected the federal exemptions. John, however, cannot claim exemptions under state law while Jane claims the federal exemptions.

There is, however, one provision of 11 U.S.C. §522(b) that complicates a debtor's election to claim exemptions. Section 522(b)(2) provides that debtors can claim property exempt under subsection (d) unless the state law applicable to the debtor does not so authorize. This means that Congress has provided the states an opportunity to withdraw from the federal exemption scheme of 11 U.S.C. §522(d). That is, state law may properly prevent a debtor or joint debtors from electing the federal exemptions. Thus, although the Bankruptcy Code gives a debtor an election to use state or federal exemptions, Congress has also given individual states the opportunity to "opt out" of the federal exemption scheme. In any state that has chosen to opt out of the federal exemptions, debtors are not given a choice of exemptions to elect. Debtors residing in such a state may only claim the exemptions provided for under the law of that particular state. In the above example, if Jane and John Smith resided in a state that has successfully

11. 11 U.S.C. §522(b)(1); 11 U.S.C. §522(m).
12. 11 U.S.C. §522(b).
13. The exemptions allowed under 11 U.S.C. §522(d) shall hereafter be referred to as the *federal exemptions*.

opted out of the federal exemptions, they would not be permitted an election. They could claim the exemptions of their state of domicile or could claim no exemptions. Thirty-four states had successfully opted out of the federal exemption scheme as of December 2003.[14] In those remaining states that have not opted out of the federal exemptions, a debtor will be able to elect state or federal exemptions pursuant to 11 U.S.C. §522(b).

B. SELECTING EXEMPTIONS

Other than the initial decision to file a bankruptcy petition in the first place, the decision to select appropriate exemptions is the most important decision to be made in the scope of a consumer no asset Chapter 7 proceeding and is also one of the most important decisions to make in any Chapter 12, 13, or individual Chapter 11 proceeding. Advice to a debtor concerning the proper exemptions to select is a legal decision and may only be made by a licensed attorney. Counseling a potential debtor regarding the choice of exemptions constitutes the practice of law. A nonattorney rendering this advice to a potential debtor may be guilty of the unauthorized practice of law, which is a criminal violation in many states.[15] In a state that has authorized paralegals to prepare bankruptcy petitions, the provisions of Code Section 110 will apply (see section 7B supra). This principle applies regardless of the apparent simplicity involved in counseling many potential debtors regarding the proper exemptions to select. This is not a work on the exemption law of individual states. Readers are left to their own devices to ascertain the specific exemption statutes of individual states. However, many of the items permitted to be claimed exempt under federal law are commonly permitted as exemptions under relevant state law.

Generally, a debtor should elect the exemptions that will allow the most property to be claimed exempt. Occasions may arise, however, in which a debtor for noneconomic reasons will want to not elect the exemptions that will exempt the most property. In these situations a professional must always remember that duty requires that the client always makes

14. As of December 2003 they are: Alabama, Arizona, California, Colorado, Delaware, Florida, Georgia, Idaho, Illinois, Indiana, Iowa, Kansas, Kentucky, Louisiana, Maine, Maryland, Mississippi, Missouri, Montana, Nebraska, Nevada, New York, North Carolina, North Dakota, Ohio, Oklahoma, Oregon, South Carolina, South Dakota, Tennessee, Utah, Virginia, West Virginia, and Wyoming. 4 Collier on Bankruptcy 522-513 (15th ed. rev. 2003).
15. In re Anderson, 79 Bankr. 482 (S.D. Cal. 1987). This case has been widely followed. See, e.g., In re Soulisak, 227 Bankr. 77 (E.D. Va. 1998).

the ultimate choice when alternatives are available. But, as a general rule, one should always recommend selection of the exemptions that will exempt the most possible property from administration by a trustee.

The debtor's ownership of real property subject to a homestead exemption under state law will normally determine which set of exemptions will be most appropriate for a debtor to select. In this instance counsel must make certain that the proper procedure to declare a homestead has been followed under applicable state law or the exemption may be lost and the property subject to administration by the trustee. Generally, a homestead declaration must be recorded prior to filing any bankruptcy petition or the exemption will be subject to invalidity under the trustee's avoiding powers.[16] However, where equity in the subject real property is limited or nonexistent, a debtor owning real property subject to a potential homestead exemption may, as a practical matter, gain greater ultimate benefits by claiming the federal rather than state exemptions.

A homestead exemption will normally allow an individual debtor to claim as exempt a defined amount of **equity** in the debtor's residence. Equity is the value of an asset over and above that of any liens or encumbrances. Of course, the equity must exist for the exemption to acquire any real value. Popular misconception to the contrary, a homestead exemption is not a guarantee to the property owner. For example, the Bunkers own a home with a value of $100,000. A mortgage in the amount of $80,000 encumbers the property. The Bunkers' equity in the home is thus $20,000. In a state with a homestead exemption of $20,000 or more, all of the equity may be claimed exempt. In a state with a homestead exemption of less than $20,000, only the maximum statutory amount would be subject to the exemption. BAPA limits a homestead exemption to $125,000 where a debtor has moved from one state to another in the 730 days preceding the filing of the petition, as discussed at 9A supra.

C. FEDERAL EXEMPTIONS

Section 522(d) contains the substantive federal exemptions. When reference is made to the federal exemptions, the reference is normally to the exemptions contained within Section 522(d). Consumer no asset Chapter 7 debtors not owning real estate with any significant equity will usually be

16. See chapter 15 infra.

able to exempt more property under these provisions than under any applicable state law, where the federal exemptions are available.

Bankruptcy Code Section 104(b), enacted in 1994, is designed to account for the effects of inflation on the Section 522(d) exemption amounts. Section 104(c) provides that the adjustments do not apply to cases filed before the date of a particular adjustment. For example, the $2,775 limit applicable to motor vehicles in §522(d)(2) before April 1, 2004, applies only to cases filed before this date.

Every third April, commencing in 1998, the exemption amounts are increased to reflect changes in the published Department of Labor consumer price index for all urban consumers for the most recent three-year period. The amounts are published in the Federal Register one month before they become effective. Thus, if total inflation for the period January 1, 1995, to December 31, 1997, is 10 percent, then all the Section 522(d) amounts will be raised accordingly, rounding off to the nearest $25. For example, the $15,000 limit in Section 522(d)(1) would become $16,500. The text reflects the changes effective as of April 1, 2004.

Section 522(d)(1) allows a debtor to exempt equity in the residence of the debtor, or real property owned by the debtor and resided in by a dependent, or in a burial plot owned by the debtor, up to $18,450. Joint debtors selecting the exemptions under 522(d) can conceivably exempt up to $36,900 of equity in real property of these types.[17] To claim this exemption under federal law it is not necessary to record a homestead or to take any action other than the procedures described below in this chapter. When claiming the federal exemptions, this exemption is automatically available.

Under Section 522(d)(2) each debtor may claim exempt $2,950 of equity in one motor vehicle.[18] Joint debtors may therefore claim a $2,950 exemption in equity in two vehicles if each debtor claims one vehicle exempt. However, joint debtors owning only one vehicle may only claim one exemption because the statute limits the exemption to only one vehicle.

Section 522(d)(3) permits a debtor to exempt household goods, household furniture, wearing apparel, books, animals, musical instruments, or crops held primarily for personal or household use. In other words, this exemption permits a debtor to exempt the so-called necessities of life. The Code eliminates the image of paupers wearing barrels with suspenders. The exemption is limited to an aggregate value of $9,850, while each item claimed exempt must have a value not exceeding $475.[19]

17. 11 U.S.C. §522(d)(1); §522(m).
18. 11 U.S.C. §522(d)(2).
19. 11 U.S.C. §522(d)(3).

Value is determined by looking at the realistic **market value** of the particular asset claimed exempt. This applies to all exemptions. BAPA requires that assets be valued in the Statements and Schedules at their **replacement value**, defined as "the price [a] retail merchant would charge for property of that kind considering the age and condition of that property."[20]

As a practical matter, the realistic market value of an asset is normally the asset's **liquidation value**, except in the case of real property. While personal property often has a depressed value in a bankruptcy, the fair market value of real property is usually affected less in the eyes of potential buyers. Liquidation value is normally the value that one would obtain in the context of a forced sale, such as a garage liquidation sale, public auction, or "going out of business" sale. This is a realistic perception, because if the same assets are liquidated by a bankruptcy trustee they will most likely be sold at a public auction to the highest bidders.[21]

The dollar limitations contained in 11 U.S.C. §522(d)(3) apply to each individual item of personal property claimed exempt. This proviso means exactly what it says: "any particular item." For example, if a debtor has an imported Chinese rosewood dining room table and eight accompanying rosewood chairs, the whole set together may be very valuable. However, "any particular item" means each individual chair and the table all as separate items. A living room set meets with the identical approach: Each end table is an individual item, each chair is an individual item, and so forth. The same applies to a bedroom set. The same analysis can apply to a home entertainment system: The television monitor is an individual item, the video cassette recorder is an individual item, the video game hardware is an individual item, the turntable is an individual item, the preamp is an individual item, the tuner is an individual item, the double-cassette tape deck is an individual item, the 20-band equalizer is an individual item, the compact disc player is an individual item, each speaker is an individual item. So long as the aggregate value is not greater than $9,850, and an individual item has a value not exceeding $475, all of the debtor's personal property may be properly claimed exempt under 11 U.S.C. §522(d)(3).

As a practical matter, it is not necessary to have a potential individual debtor provide a line-by-line itemization of all personal assets. Although there are occasions when a trustee will desire such data, it is generally not a necessity. A potential individual debtor need not normally provide an itemized list of wearing apparel, such as "twelve t-shirts, six Fruit-of-the-Looms" and so

---

20. 11 U.S.C. §506(a)(2); 11 U.S.C. §522(a)(2); 11 U.S.C. §527(a)(2)(B).
21. See chapters 10 and 18 infra. In the reorganization proceedings of Chapter 11 or 13, the retail value may need to be applied. See Associated Commercial Corp. v. Rash, 520 U.S. 953 (1997), discussed in chapter 21 infra. Case law will determine how "Rash" may be affected by BAPA and how "replacement value" is interpreted relative to liquidation value.

forth. Local practice may vary, however, and inquiry should always be made as to local custom, local rule, or any applicable guidelines of the United States Trustee.

For particular items that may have a value of more than $475, the exemption provided for under Section 522(d)(5), described below, may be an effective remedy for claiming such assets exempt. It is, however, prudent to itemize any items that may exceed the $475 per item limit.

Any unique collections should be itemized. If a debtor has potentially valuable furnishings or wardrobe, such as the rosewood dining room set mentioned above or a fur, obtaining a written appraisal prior to filing is helpful in preparing the debtor's schedules and in claiming exemptions. The appraisal will also be helpful in answering any questions of the trustee or creditors in connection with the asset's value. This one act can save time and expense, in the form of attorneys' fees, should the trustee wish to object to the exemption simply because no prior appraisal has been obtained. Debtors in this possible situation should reasonably be able to afford the nominal appraisal costs. Case law may very well determine that the duties imposed upon counsel under BAPA, to make "reasonable inquiry" to establish an asset's value, require written appraisals of unique assets. See Bankruptcy Code §527(a)(2)(B).

Section 522(d)(4) permits the exemption of $1,225 in jewelry held for personal use of the debtor or a dependent.[22] Most wedding rings can be safely exempted under this provision. Potentially valuable items of jewelry should be appraised beforehand as described above.

Section 522(d)(5) is perhaps the most important of the federal exemptions. It is the exemption that sets the federal exemptions apart from traditional state exemptions. In common parlance, Section 522(d)(5) is called the "omnibus," "catch-all," or "grubstake" exemption. The **catch-all exemption** consists of any unused portion of the federal homestead exemption (11 U.S.C. §522(d)(1) supra), up to the amount of $9,250, plus $975, for a total of $10,225 in any property of any kind.[23] "Any property" means all property, with one limited exception described below. Individual items of household goods worth more than $475 a piece may be claimed exempt under this provision. Jewelry not exempt under Section 522(d)(4) may be claimed exempt under this provision. Equity in a vehicle greater than $2,950 may be claimed exempt here. An otherwise nonexempt tax refund may be claimed exempt under this provision. Cash in the bank may be claimed exempt. A second vehicle owned by one debtor or a third vehicle owned by joint

22. 11 U.S.C. §522(d)(4).
23. 11 U.S.C. §522(d)(5).

debtors may be claimed exempt under this provision. Anything, absolutely, positively anything, may be claimed exempt under this provision.

Property recovered for the estate by the trustee's avoiding powers may conceivably be claimed exempt under Section 522(d)(5) as long as the transfer avoided by the trustee has been involuntary on the part of the debtor. Thus, property subject to an avoidable lien may be claimed exempt. However, if the debtor voluntarily made the avoidable transfer such as a preference or a fraudulent transfer to a relative, intending to conceal the property from creditors, or if the debtor fails to disclose the transfer in the Statements and Schedules, the transaction may not be claimed exempt under Section 522(d)(5). This is the one exception to the broad meaning of the phrase "any property." For example, creditor Snidely Whiplash obtains a judicial attachment on Debtor Nell's assets immediately prior to Nell filing her Chapter 7. Because the trustee can avoid this transaction, Nell may claim the assets exempt under Section 522(d)(5) or any other allowable exemption. If the trustee does not seek to set aside the avoidable transaction, Nell may take action herself to do so. However, if Nell proffered voluntary payment to Snidely as a preference, she likely could not claim the assets so transferred as exempt.[24]

The catch-all provision of Section §522(d)(5) attempts to eliminate the economic discrimination that existed prior to enactment of the Bankruptcy Code, when the existing exemptions available under state law favored homeowners substantially more than nonhomeowners. For individuals who did not own their homes, there generally existed no exemptions in state law beyond vehicle equity and the bare necessities of life. In enacting the Bankruptcy Code, Congress has concluded that it would be fair to create an exemption for nonhomeowners to afford them the same opportunities for a fresh start in their financial affairs that exists for homeowners able to take advantage of homestead exemptions. Hence, the catch-all exemption, which allows a debtor or debtors to claim exempt any property in existence up to the limits of the catch-all in lieu of a homestead exemption.

A debtor claiming real property exempt under the federal homestead provision (11 U.S.C. §522(d)(1)) may claim additional property exempt under the catch-all provision if there is an available balance after accounting for the real property equity. For example, Joe Debtor owns a house with $10,000 of equity. There is an unused balance of the Section 522(d)(1)

---

24. See the Legislative Notes to 11 U.S.C. §522(d). See also chapters 15 through 17 for a discussion of the trustee's avoiding powers. Although it may have been thought that voluntary preferences and even voluntary fraudulent transfers could be claimed exempt under §522(d)(5), recent case law has begun to disfavor use of §522(d)(5) to claim these transactions exempt. See, e.g., In re Roberts, 81 Bankr. 354 (W.D. Pa. 1987). See also 11 U.S.C. §522(g), (h), (j), which supports this view. 11 U.S.C. §522(o), added by BAPA, reduces the value of property by any amount attributable to fraudulent transfers.

exemption available for use under Section 522(d)(5) of $6,150 plus $975, for a total of $7,125. This amount may be used by Joe to claim any property in existence exempt.

Section 522(d)(6) allows a debtor to exempt $1,850 of value in tools of the trade or professional implements. For example, a word processor working as an independent contractor might be able to exempt a personal computer under this provision.[25]

Unmatured life insurance contracts are exempt under Section 522(d)(7).[26] Term insurance or policies with no cash value may also be claimed exempt under this provision.

Section 522(d)(8) allows a debtor to claim as exempt cash value in an insurance policy up to $9,850.[27] A whole life insurance policy bearing a cash value may therefore be fully or partially claimed exempt under this provision. Loans or other debts owed against the policy's cash value are specifically excluded from the total cash value claimed exempt when the insurance company has a right to set off the debt owed it against the policy's cash value.[28]

Professionally prescribed health aids of a debtor or a debtor's dependent such as glasses, contact lenses, or orthopedic shoes are exempt under Section 522(d)(9). There is no dollar limitation on this exemption.[29] Social Security benefits, welfare benefits, veterans benefits, alimony, qualified pension and profit sharing plans, and disability and unemployment benefits may all be claimed exempt under Section 522(d)(10).[30] In Rousey v. Jacoway, — U.S. —, —S. Ct. —, 73 U.S.L.W., 4277 (2005), the Supreme Court held that IRA accounts may be claimed exempt within the meaning of §522(d)(10), resolving a conflict amongst the circuits.

Under Section 522(d)(11) certain aspects of personal injury compensation may be claimed exempt. A right to receive compensation or property under a crime victim's reparation law may be claimed exempt without regard to amount.[31] Wrongful death recoveries for an individual of whom the debtor was a dependent, payment from a life insurance policy insuring the life of an individual of whom the debtor was a dependent, and compensation for lost future earnings of the debtor or of an individual of whom the debtor was or is a dependent may be claimed exempt "to the extent reasonably necessary for the support of the debtor or a dependent of the debtor."[32] The amount reasonably necessary for the support of a debtor or

---

25. 11 U.S.C. §522(d)(6).
26. 11 U.S.C. §522(d)(7).
27. 11 U.S.C. §522(d)(8).
28. 11 U.S.C. §542(d).
29. 11 U.S.C. §522(d)(9).
30. 11 U.S.C. §522(d)(10).
31. 11 U.S.C. §522(d)(11)(A).
32. 11 U.S.C. §522(d)(11)(B), (C), (E).

dependent of the debtor will be a question of fact in each individual case. Personal injury compensation may be claimed exempt up to $18,450. However, pain and suffering and actual damages are specifically not included in calculating the exemption amount.[33] For example, a debtor with a million dollar personal injury claim may conceivably claim all the recovery exempt. However, as a practical matter, since this debtor may be able to pay all creditors in full and leave a substantial balance for the debtor, if there is a recovery, a debtor in this situation might seek a dismissal of the bankruptcy proceeding under Section 305(a).[34]

11 U.S.C. §522(d)(12) expressly permits retirement funds exempt from taxation pursuant to the Internal Revenue Code to be claimed exempt. This includes 401 employer plans and IRA accounts. This exemption, added by BAPA and intended to resolve the case law debate upon whether or not IRA accounts could be claimed exempt, is consistent with the identical exemption also permitted to debtors not claiming the federal exemptions. See chapter 9A supra.

D. UNAFFECTED CLAIMS

Exemptions, contrary to popular opinion, do not protect a debtor's exempt property from the reach of all creditors. Exemptions do not protect otherwise exempt property from properly secured liens or properly filed tax liens. Nor do exemptions protect a debtor's otherwise exempt property from nondischargeable taxes, nondischargeable domestic support obligations or debts incurred by fraud in obtaining school financial aid.[35] For example, Mark Treasure has a mortgage debt and a tax lien recorded upon his home. His divorced spouse, Virginia, is owed support payments. Mark's homestead will not protect a foreclosure by the mortgage holder, a sale to the state for the nondischarged taxes, or a judicial seizure by Virginia for collection of the unpaid support.

It is not improper for a debtor to convert nonexempt to exempt property at any time prior to filing. The Legislative Notes to Section 522 specifically state: "... the debtor will be permitted to convert nonexempt property into exempt property before filing a bankruptcy petition. However, the excessive conversion of nonexempt to exempt property on the eve of

33. 11 U.S.C. §522(d)(11)(D). As to the pain and suffering calculation, see In re Scotti, 245 Bankr. 17 (Bankr. N.J. 2000).
34. See chapter 8 supra.
35. 11 U.S.C. §522(c).

a bankruptcy filing can result in the denial of a debtor's discharge."[36] Thus, Midas Touch could sell a piece of nonexempt antique jewelry prior to filing, buy a new refrigerator with the proceeds, and then claim the refrigerator exempt under Section 522(d)(3) or 522(d)(5). How the 2005 legislation may affect these practices will clarify itself in the case law.

E. LIEN AVOIDANCE TO PRESERVE EXEMPTION

An *unsecured* creditor cannot ask a debtor to agree to waive exemptions or any of a debtor's rights under Section 522. Any such waiver is unenforceable.[37] A debtor may avoid a judicial lien or a nonpossessory, **nonpurchase money security interest** in consumer, personal goods or household goods, tools of the trade, or professionally prescribed health aids to the extent that any such lien impairs an otherwise allowable exemption. Judicial liens attributable to domestic support obligations are not avoidable.[38] Generally, a secured creditor has a nonpurchase money security interest if the debt that created the security interest was not obtained for the purpose of purchasing the collateral subject to the security interest. Otherwise, the security interest is generally a **purchase money security interest**. For example, a debtor purchases a new living room set and obtains credit to do so. If the seller retains a security interest in the goods, it will likely be a purchase money security interest. However, if a debtor obtains a loan from the friendly neighborhood finance company for the purpose of going on vacation, any security interest the debtor grants the finance company in household furniture will be a nonpurchase money security interest. In this instance, if the debtor then files a bankruptcy petition, the latter security interest may be avoided if it impairs the debtor's ability to claim household furniture exempt.

Section 522(f)(1)(B) allows a debtor to avoid a nonpurchase money security interest to the extent that the collateral can be claimed exempt. So if all of the furniture given as collateral can be claimed exempt, the debtor can avoid the lien. Section 522(f)(4), added by BAPA, defines "household goods," solely for purposes of lien avoidance, as generally one TV, one VCR plus other specifically enumerated household goods. The same provision also excludes various items, such as works of art except by relatives, from

---

36. See Historical and Revision Notes to 11 U.S.C. §522. As to the possible denial of discharge, see Norwest Bank Nebraska v. Tveten, 848 F.2d 871 (8th Cir. 1988).
37. 11 U.S.C. §522(e).
38. 11 U.S.C. §522(f)(1)(A).

the definition of "household goods." Because the debt is discharged under Section 524, the finance company may not thereafter seek payment. Because the security interest is avoided, the debtor need not worry about the finance company repossessing the furniture. Section 522(f)(3) further limits the ability to avoid a nonpurchase money security interest in tools of the trade, farm animals, or crops if the value of the collateral exceeds $5,000.

A debtor must file a noticed motion to successfully avoid a lien subject to avoidance under Section 522(f). See chapter 5A supra.[39]

F. CLAIMING AND OBJECTING TO EXEMPTIONS

To properly claim exemptions a debtor must file a list of exemptions with the court. If a debtor fails to do so, a dependent of the debtor may file the list.[40] A debtor's claim of exemptions is to be filed at the same time as the Statements and Schedules, within 15 days of the date of filing.[41] The exemption schedule may be amended at any time prior to the close of the proceeding.[42]

The trustee or any creditor may object to a claim of exemption. An objection must be filed within 30 days of the conclusion of the Section 341(a) creditors meeting or within 30 days after any amendment is filed unless the court orders otherwise. Unless an objection is made, the property claimed exempt is exempt. The party raising an objection to a claim of exemption has the burden of proving the impropriety of the objection at any hearing held to resolve the objection.[43] An objection to a claim of exemption is filed as a noticed motion (see chapter 5A supra). A sample notice of objection is contained in the forms disk.

In Taylor v. Freeland & Kronz, the Supreme Court held that the 30-day deadline to object to a debtor's claim of exemption is to be strictly construed. In this case, a debtor claimed an exemption in the potential proceeds of an employment discrimination lawsuit against her former employer. She disclosed to the trustee at the creditors meeting that the suit might be worth $90,000. The trustee, however, did not object to

39. Bankruptcy Rule 4003(d), Bankruptcy Rule 9013.
40. 11 U.S.C. §522(l).
41. Bankruptcy Rule 4003(a). See chapter 4 supra and chapter 29 infra.
42. Bankruptcy Rule 1009(a).
43. 11 U.S.C. §522(l); Bankruptcy Rule 4003(b)(c).

the exemption because he did not believe the claim had any value. After the debtor obtained a $110,000 settlement, the trustee sought to recover the proceeds for the estate. The Supreme Court found a fatal flaw in the trustee's failure to object to the exemption in a timely manner. "Deadlines may lead to unwelcome results, but they prompt parties to act and they produce finality."[44]

Finally, if a debtor claims an exemption in property successfully recovered by the trustee's avoiding powers, the debtor's interest can be assessed its fair share of the costs incurred in recovering the asset.[45] For example, a trustee successfully avoids the transfer of an asset worth $10,000. The amount claimed exempt is $5,000. The cost of recovery is $2,000. One thousand dollars of the costs can be charged against the exemption (the debtor's fair share). The debtor will effectively realize $4,000 through use of the exemption in this example.

Summary

Exemptions are property that an individual debtor may protect from administration by a bankruptcy estate. Exempt property is not available for liquidation to pay a dividend to creditors. A debtor may keep exempt property. Exemptions are a primary element of debtor relief.

Section 522(b) of the Code permits individuals to claim exemptions either under applicable state law, generally where the debtor has been domiciled for the 730 days preceding the filing of the petition, or under §522(d) of the Code. These latter exemptions are commonly known as the federal exemptions. However, states have been afforded an opportunity to withdraw from the federal exemption scheme. Approximately 34 states have done so. Pursuant to 11 U.S.C. §522(p), homestead exemptions under State law are limited to $125,000 in certain circumstances.

The decision as to which set of or specific exemptions to select is one of the more important decisions to be made in any individual bankruptcy proceeding. The federal exemption list contains common exemptions, many of which are also normally permitted under state law.

Several specific types of debt are immune from a debtor's claim of exemptions. These types of debt are consensual liens and tax liens upon the property sought to be claimed exempt nondischargeable. These types of debt are consensual liens and tax liens upon the property sought to be

44. Taylor v. Freeland & Kronz, 503 U.S. 638 (1992).
45. 11 U.S.C. §522(k).

claimed exempt, domestic support obligations, and student financial aid obligations fraudulently obtained.

A debtor may, however, successfully avoid certain liens that may impair an allowable exemption. Judicial liens and nonpurchase money consensual liens are subject to this potential lien avoidance. A motion is normally required to avoid such a lien.

Exemptions are claimed by filing a list of exemptions with the court. This list comprises Schedule C of the schedules, Official Form 6.

A party in interest, such as a creditor or the trustee, wishing to object to a claim of exemption, must do so by way of a noticed motion. The motion must be brought within 30 days of the creditors meeting. If an amendment to a claim of exemption is filed, any objection to the amendment must be brought within 30 days of the amendment's being filed.

KEY TERMS

catch-all exemption
equity
exemptions
federal exemptions
fresh start
homestead exemption
liquidation value
market value
nonpurchase money security interest
purchase money security interest
replacement value
stacking

Chapter 9 Checklist

9.1 SUMMARY OF FEDERAL EXEMPTIONS

	Item	*Exemption Amount*	*Authority*
9.1.1	residence of debtor or dependent	$18,450	11 U.S.C. §522(d)(1)
9.1.2	motor vehicle	$2,950	11 U.S.C. §522(d)(2)
9.1.3	household goods, furniture, and wearing apparel	$475 per item up to $9,850 in aggregate	11 U.S.C. §522(d)(3)

	Item	*Exemption Amount*	*Authority*
9.1.4	personal jewelry	$1,225	11 U.S.C. §522(d)(4)
9.1.5	any property catch all	any unused portion of (d)(1) up to $9,250 plus $975 ($10,225 total)	11 U.S.C. §522(d)(5)
9.1.6	tools of trade	$1,850	11 U.S.C. §522(d)(6)
9.1.7	unmatured or term insurance	asset has no value	11 U.S.C. §522(d)(7)
9.1.8	cash value of insurance	$9,850	11 U.S.C. §522(d)(8)
9.1.9	professionally prescribed health aids	no limits	11 U.S.C. §522(d)(9)
9.1.10	Social Security, welfare, veterans, benefits, alimony, disability, or unemployment	varies	11 U.S.C. §522(d)(10)
9.1.11	certain personal injury claims	varies	11 U.S.C. §522(d)(11)
9.1.12	Retirement Accounts	varies	11 U.S.C. §522(d)(12)

9.2 RECORDING A DECLARATION OF HOMESTEAD[46]

9.2.1 Complete Appropriate Declaration

9.2.2 Have Debtors Sign Before a Notary Public

9.2.3 Record at Local Recorder or as Required by Local Law

46. This is a general procedure. Further reference to specifically applicable state law is recommended.

9.3 LIEN AVOIDANCE UNDER 11 U.S.C. §522(f)

9.3.1 Debtor Files a Noticed Motion to Avoid Before the Court

9.4 OBJECTING TO A CLAIM OF EXEMPTION

9.4.1 A Noticed Motion

9.4.2 Party Bringing Objection Bears Burden of Proof

9.4.3 Objection Must Be Filed Within 30 Days of Creditors Meeting or Within 30 Days of Any Amendment Filed by Debtor

DISCUSSION QUESTIONS

1. What are exemptions?
2. What is the purpose of exemptions?
3. What factors should be considered in selecting federal or state exemptions? Specific exemptions?
4. What is a homestead?
5. How does an individual debtor claim exemptions in a bankruptcy proceeding?
6. How are exemptions objected to in a bankruptcy proceeding?
7. How can a debtor avoid a lien that impairs an exemption?

10

Trustees, Examiners, and Creditors Committees

Chapter 7 of this text describes the general procedure for selecting and compensating trustees. This chapter focuses on the trustee's qualifications and duties. The related concepts of Chapter 11 Examiners and Official Creditors Committees are also discussed. The role and function of the **United States Trustee** is described. The 2005 BAPA legislation adds ombudsmen to the mix. These various entities collectively comprise the various fiduciaries peculiar to the bankruptcy system.

Trustees, examiners, creditor committees, and ombudsmen are unique players in the bankruptcy system, and these entities are of equal or greater importance than the debtor and individual creditors. Without these additional players, the bankruptcy system would simply not function because there would be no effective control oversight over a debtor or the debtor's assets. There would also be no effective personnel to effectuate a proper distribution of dividends to creditors.

A. TRUSTEES

Code Sections 321 to 325 concern the issues of who may be a **trustee**, how a trustee qualifies, and how a trustee is removed. Section 321 provides that a competent individual who has an office or resides in the district or in an adjacent district where the proceeding is pending may be a trustee in Chapter 7, 12, or 13. A competent individual is normally a disinterested person who has not previously served as examiner in the proceeding.[1]

1. 11 U.S.C. §321(a)(1), (b); 11 U.S.C. §701(a)(1).

A corporation that is authorized by its charter or bylaws to be a trustee and that has an office in the district where the proceeding is pending may also serve as a trustee.[2] The United States Trustee in the judicial district may also serve as trustee in a proceeding if necessary.[3]

To be appointed, the trustee must qualify to act as a trustee. In the case of private panel trustees described in chapter 7, these trustees need take no action if the court or United States Trustee has authorized a blanket bond that the trustee has previously obtained. This bond inures to the benefit of the creditors in all Chapter 7 estates in which the particular trustee has been appointed. To qualify as trustee, a nonpanel trustee or a trustee serving in a district that has not authorized a blanket bond for trustees will be required to post a bond with the court in each case that the trustee is appointed. The bond should be posted with the court within five days of the trustee's appointment.[4] These rules apply to trustees appointed in all proceedings, voluntary and involuntary.[5]

Prior to enactment and implementation of the United States Trustee system on a national basis in 1988, the court had the duty to set the amount of a trustee's bond.[6] Under the United States Trustee system, the United States Trustee has been given this responsibility.[7]

The amount of the trustee's bond is generally based upon a percentage of the estimated value of the assets subject to administration in a particular proceeding. The amount of a blanket bond is generally based on a percentage of the value of all funds on deposit by a panel trustee in all cases subject to the blanket bond. Local rule may require the bond amount to exceed 100 percent of all funds on hand to ensure maximum protection to the creditors of estates being administered by the trustee. Local rules will generally require a trustee to file a quarterly report of funds on deposit with the court or United States Trustee. The report may result in the bond being increased or decreased.[8]

The trustee is the official legal representative of the estate and in such capacity may sue as a plaintiff on behalf of the estate or be sued as a defendant on behalf of the estate.[9]

Sections 324 and 325 concern the removal of a trustee and appointment of a successor. A trustee may always be removed for cause. For example, cause will exist to remove a trustee who absconds with estate funds. However, it is unlikely that a trustee would be removed for exercising business

2. 11 U.S.C. §321(a)(2).
3. 11 U.S.C. §321(c).
4. 11 U.S.C. §322(a); Bankruptcy Rule 2010.
5. 11 U.S.C. §701; 11 U.S.C. §1104(d); 11 U.S.C. §1202(a); 11 U.S.C. §1302(a); Bankruptcy Rule 2001.
6. See 11 U.S.C. §322(b) as it existed prior to October 27, 1986.
7. 11 U.S.C. §322(b).
8. Bankruptcy Rule 2015.
9. 11 U.S.C. §323.

judgment that creditors disagree with, unless such judgment is tantamount to gross negligence or gross incompetence. The procedure for removing a trustee requires that a motion be made before the court. If a trustee dies or resigns during the administration of a proceeding, a successor will have to be appointed.[10]

A trustee will always be appointed in Chapter 7, 12, and 13 proceedings.[11] A trustee may or may not be appointed in a Chapter 11.[12] Although the United States Trustee has duties to perform in all proceedings, the United States Trustee will not generally perform the duties of an individual trustee in a specific proceeding unless it is necessary, required, or the United States Trustee has been directed to do so by the court. Further, although the United States Trustee is considered a party in interest for all purposes, the United States Trustee is specifically prohibited from filing a Plan of Reorganization in a Chapter 11 proceeding.[13]

B. THE UNITED STATES TRUSTEE

The United States Trustee program began as an experiment in selected districts when the Code became effective in 1979. In 1986 Congress decided to implement the program nationally. The 1986 Code amendments are entitled in part ". . . United States Trustees . . . Act of 1986."[14] The United States Trustee system operates as a division of the Department of Justice.

The United States Trustee's function is intended to be primarily administrative. Prior to enactment of the Code, Bankruptcy Judges performed many of the administrative acts that have now been delegated to the United States Trustee. This change has been initiated in an effort to redefine the Bankruptcy Judge in a more traditional judicial role. Under the Bankruptcy Act judges were known as referees until 1974. As referees, the judges played an active role in the administration of an estate while simultaneously determining the rights of all other parties in the proceeding. This created an inherent conflict within the system. The divestiture from the Bankruptcy Judges of their former administrative duties and the consequent delegation of these duties to the United States Trustee system is intended to resolve this conflict. Now, Bankruptcy Judges remain integral to, but independent from, the day-to-day administration of individual bankruptcy proceedings.

10. 11 U.S.C. §324, 325, 703; 11 U.S.C. §1105; Bankruptcy Rule 2012.
11. 11 U.S.C. §§701-703; 11 U.S.C. §1202; 11 U.S.C. §1302.
12. 11 U.S.C. §1104. See infra this chapter.
13. 11 U.S.C. §307, 28 U.S.C. §586(a)(1), (2).
14. Pub. L. No. 99-554, Title II §257(c), 100 Stat. 3114 (Oct. 27, 1986) (28 U.S.C. §§581-586).

In any Chapter proceeding filed, the United States Trustee is charged with monitoring the progress of all proceedings and is to act appropriately to "prevent undue delay."[15] The United States Trustee should be served with all notices, as described in chapter 5 supra. The United States Trustee is directed to act to ensure that a debtor pays all fees and files all required documents in connection with all proceedings.[16] The United States Trustee shall monitor applications for the retention of professionals and applications for professional compensation and is permitted to comment thereon to the court.[17] The local United States Trustee may have published guidelines. See a representative sample in the forms disk. The United States Trustee may also refer for investigation by the United States Attorney any matters that may constitute a bankruptcy crime.[18]

In Chapter 7 proceedings the United States Trustee maintains and supervises a panel of trustees.[19] In everyday practice the United States Trustee's performance of this duty includes appointing private panel Chapter 7 trustees and supervising and monitoring a private trustee's prompt administration of asset estates (see chapter 22 infra).

The 2005 BAPA legislation created new responsibilities for the United States Trustee. First, Bankruptcy Code Section 704(b) charges the United States Trustee to review the debtor's materials filed pursuant to Section 521 (see chapters 4 and 7, supra), and to file a statement within ten days of the meeting of creditors indicating whether or not the filing creates a presumed abuse of Chapter 7 under "needs based bankruptcy" (see chapter 5F, supra). If abuse is presumed, then within 30 days of the meeting of creditors, the United States trustee must file a motion to dismiss or convert or a statement setting forth the reasons why no motion is to be filed if abuse is presumed pursuant to "needs based bankruptcy."

Second, Section 603 of BAPA requires random audits of one out of 250 cases. Under BAPA, 28 U.S.C. §586(f) directs the United States Trustee to retain auditors and to file the audit reports with the Court.

Third, the United States Trustee is charged with the approval and oversight monitoring of nonprofit budget and credit counseling agencies providing pre-petition credit counseling pursuant to Section 109(h), or post-petition personal financial management courses as mandated by Sections 727(a)(11), and 1328(g) (see chapters 4 and 7, supra).

15. 25 U.S.C. §586(a)(3)(G).
16. 28 U.S.C. §586(a)(3)(D).
17. 28 U.S.C. §586(a)(3)(A), (H). See chapter 7 supra.
18. 28 U.S.C. §586(a)(3)(F). Bankruptcy crimes are defined in 18 U.S.C. §§151-157; 18 U.S.C. §1519. Generally, bankruptcy crimes include the fraudulent concealment of assets in connection with a pending proceeding or the commission of perjury or taking of a false oath may constitute a bankruptcy crime. The penalties are fines up to $5,000 and/or imprisonment for not more than five years.
19. 28 U.S.C. §586(a).

In Chapter 11 proceedings, the United States Trustee will function to a large degree as the "eyes and the ears" of the court. The United States Truste is directed to appoint and monitor Chapter 11 creditors committees.[20] The United States Trustee has also been charged with monitoring Chapter 11 Reorganization Plans and Disclosure Statements and is permitted to comment upon them.[21] This power is also granted to the United States Trustee in connection with Chapter 12 and 13 proceedings.[22]

In everyday practice the United States Trustee's involvement in a Chapter 11 proceeding can be extensive, particularly during the first 60 days of a Chapter 11. During this period, the United States Trustee will interact with a debtor-in-possession in several areas.

First, the United States Trustee will generally conduct an initial conference with the estate's representatives approximately two weeks after filing. At the initial conference, the United States Trustee will generally interview the parties present to obtain an overview of the case and to instruct counsel and the parties as to any local United States Trustee guidelines and as to the various administrative duties and responsibilities of a debtor-in-possession. In a small business Chapter 11 (see chapter 24, infra), 28 U.S.C. §586(a)(7) requires the United States Trustee to conduct an initial debtor interview. (See chapter 24 infra for a description of these duties.) The forms disk contains representative samples. The United States Trustee will follow up to monitor the debtor-in-possession's compliance with the rules and guidelines.

Second, the United States Trustee will preside at the meeting of the creditors held pursuant to 11 U.S.C. §341(a) and 11 U.S.C. §343.

Third, the United States Trustee will act to facilitate the organizing of an Official Creditors Committee. See infra this chapter.

The United States Trustee will collect quarterly fees from a debtor-in-possession pursuant to 28 U.S.C. §586(a)(3)(D) and 28 U.S.C. §1930(a)(6) (see chapter 24 infra).

Finally, the United States Trustee may bring motions to dismiss or convert Chapter 11 proceedings pursuant to 11 U.S.C. §586(a)(8) (see chapter 23, infra).

C. THE TRUSTEE'S DUTIES

Although there are separate provisions in each Chapter proceeding that specify the duties of a trustee appointed in a particular Chapter, the duties

20. 11 U.S.C. §1102; 28 U.S.C. §586(a)(3)(E). See infra this chapter.
21. 28 U.S.C. §586(a)(3)(B).
22. 28 U.S.C. §586(a)(3)(C).

remain essentially the same throughout the Code. Section 704(a) contains a list of twelve items that specify the duties of a Chapter 7 trustee. Section 1302 contains a list of items that specify the duties of a Chapter 13 trustee. A number of the duties described in Section 704(a) have been incorporated into this provision. Section 1106 specifies the duties of a Chapter 11 trustee. This section also incorporates many elements of Section 704(a). A similar situation pertains to the duties of a Chapter 12 trustee contained in Section 1202.[23] However, all of the duties of a trustee may be synthesized into four essential ones that can best be remembered by use of a mnemonic device the author refers to as the four *ates*. That is, the essential duties of a trustee can be described as follows: investig*ate*, liquid*ate*, litig*ate*, and administr*ate*.

Investigation is the initial duty performed by any trustee. A trustee must initially determine whether there are assets in an estate that can be liquidated to pay a dividend to creditors. In a consumer no asset or a small business proceeding, performance of this duty may involve little more than reviewing the Statements and Schedules and questioning the debtor at the meeting of creditors. In a larger proceeding, investigation may involve a review of significant records and documents and the taking of one or more Rule 2004 Examinations (see chapter 7 supra) before the trustee can logically proceed further in the administration of an estate.[24]

The liquidation duty is the most visible of a trustee's duties. Liquidation involves the trustee converting nonexempt assets into cash. This will always occur in a Chapter 7. Liquidation can be as simple as having a private sale or public auction of the inventory and equipment of a bankrupt business or can be as complex as selling the assets of a major business to one or more buyers in what may be complex and unrelated transactions. BAPA imposes the additional requirement for a trustee to make best efforts to transfer the patients of a health care business to another appropriate health care business.[25]

To fully liquidate an estate may require a trustee to sue third parties. Litigation is the third of the four *ates*. As the official representative of an estate, a trustee may pursue claims against third parties that would exist even if there had been no bankruptcy. For example, collecting accounts receivable that are due a debtor may require a trustee to initiate litigation. The trustee may be able to exercise one of the avoiding powers to recover assets of the estate for the benefit of creditors.[26] Presumably, when a trustee sues, the litigation will result in the obtaining of additional cash to pay the creditors of the estate. Thus, to a certain extent litigation is also a part of liquidation.

Finally, a trustee has to administer the assets that have been reduced to cash by liquidation or litigation. The trustee follows additional rules and

---

23. 11 U.S.C. §1302(b); 11 U.S.C. §704(a); 11 U.S.C. §1106(a); 11 U.S.C. §1202(b).
24. 11 U.S.C. §704(a)(4); 11 U.S.C. §1106(a)(3); 11 U.S.C. §1202(b)(2); 11 U.S.C. §1302(b)(1).
25. 11 U.S.C. §704(a)(1), (12).
26. See chapters 15 through 17 infra.

procedures for distributing the cash to creditors in the form of dividends. The accomplishment of this process is the major goal of unsecured creditors affected by the bankruptcy system and forms the essence of the debt collection aspects of the Bankruptcy Code. The process of maintaining and distributing the cash to creditors is known as administration. The specific details of this administrative process are described in chapter 22 infra.

BAPA imposes an additional administrative duty upon trustees to provide notices to the holders of claims for domestic support obligations that they may seek support assistance from a state agency, and to provide notice to the claim holder and state support agency when the discharge is granted, of the debtor's discharge and contact information. [27]

In a Chapter 12 or 13 proceeding, a trustee is not specifically directed to liquidate assets. A Chapter 12 trustee is required to ensure that the debtor commences to make timely payments under the debtor's plan.[28] A Chapter 13 trustee actually collects payments made under a Chapter 13 plan and distributes them to the creditors on a regular basis.[29]

D. DEBTOR-IN-POSSESSION

In Chapter 11 proceedings there may or may not be an active trustee. In the reorganization process that Chapter 11 represents, there is normally no trustee. Instead, the debtor functions as a **debtor-in-possession**.[30] The essence of this concept is that the debtor acts as its own trustee. Section 1107 describes the rights, powers, and duties of the Chapter 11 debtor-in-possession. These rights, powers, and duties are essentially the four *ates* described above. However, because the purpose of a Chapter 11 is to reorganize rather than to liquidate, it is more accurate to substitute the term *reorganize* in place of the term *liquidate*. How a debtor properly fulfills the duty to reorganize is described in chapters 24 through 26 infra.

E. OFFICIAL CREDITORS COMMITTEES

The Bankruptcy Code recognizes the practical reality that some debtors are not necessarily capable of acting as fiduciaries to their creditors as debtors-in-possession. In appropriate circumstances the creditors will not want the

27 11 U.S.C. §704(c); 11 U.S.C. §1106(c); 11 U.S.C. §1202(c); 11 U.S.C. §1302(d).
28. 11 U.S.C. §1202(b)(4). See chapter 27 infra.
29. 11 U.S.C. §1302(b)(3)(5). See chapter 23 infra.
30. 11 U.S.C. §1101(1); 11 U.S.C. §1107.

debtor to remain in full control of its financial affairs. A number of mechanisms have therefore been created to provide the creditors in a Chapter 11 proceeding with a substantial ability to monitor and control the proper performance by a debtor-in-possession of its statutory duties. These various mechanisms include providing the creditors an opportunity to seek the appointment of a trustee or examiner, the **Official Creditors Committee**, and the United States Trustee. The 2005 legislation creates ombudsmen to deal with privacy issues in the sale of customer lists, and the best interests of patients in health care bankruptcies.[31]

The Official Creditors Committee is the initial monitor of a debtor-inpossession's Chapter 11 financial affairs.[32] Keep in mind that a debtor experiencing financial difficulty will generally remain in full control of its activities. To the extent that a debtor can isolate one or more of its creditors and attempt to deal with each creditor independently, this is merely an application of the ancient Roman principle of "divide and conquer." The remedy to a debtor's use of this principle is another equally ancient principle: "In unity there is strength." The Official Creditors Committee is simply a mechanism that puts the latter principle into practice. The major purpose of the committee is to unite the unsecured creditors so they can deal with the debtor-in-possession collectively and not as individual isolated creditors.

The Official Creditors Committee is appointed by the United States Trustee from among the 20 largest unsecured creditors of a debtor-in-possession. At the initiation of a Chapter 11 proceeding, the debtor-in-possession files a list of its 20 largest unsecured creditors with the court along with all of the other documents required to be filed by a debtor upon initiating a proceeding. This list is to be filed within two days of filing a Chapter 11 petition.[33] From this list the United States Trustee will solicit creditors to serve on the committee.[34] When a sufficient number, in the United States Trustee's discretion, consent to appointment, the committee is officially appointed. The Official Creditors Committee is a **party in interest** to the proceeding. This means that the committee may file pleadings, initiate motions, or file plans of reorganization.[35]

Section 1102(a)(3), added to the Code in 1994, permits a small business Chapter 11 debtor to request the court not to appoint an Official Creditors Committee. (A **small business debtor** is defined in Chapter 11 as a debtor with less than $2 million of debt who elects treatment as a small business.) Upon a showing of cause, the request shall be granted. Since the concept of

31. 11 U.S.C. §332; 11 U.S.C. §333; 11 U.S.C. §1102-1103; 11 U.S.C. §1104. See chapter 24 infra.
32. 11 U.S.C. §§1102-1103.
33. Bankruptcy Rule 1007(d).
34. 11 U.S.C. §1102(a)(1).
35. 11 U.S.C. §1103.

the creditors committee is important to the Chapter 11 process, the case law will probably impose strict requirements on the granting of such motions.

The Official Creditors Committee has authority under the Code to hire its own professionals, such as counsel and accountants.[36] The expenses of the professionals employed by the Official Creditors Committee are an **administrative expense** of the estate. This means that any fees incurred are payable by the estate. Because many unsecured creditors do not necessarily have a right to recover attorneys' fees from a debtor when attempting to collect debts that are due, this is a powerful tool. These professionals are treated in the manner described in chapter 7 supra. Their employment must be approved by the court, and the committee's professionals are subject to the same fee application requirements discussed in chapter 7 supra. The membership of an Official Creditors Committee may also receive reimbursement of expenses incurred in the performance of duties for the estate, pursuant to Section 503(b)(3)(F).

Historically, creditors committees fail to become active in many Chapter 11 proceedings, usually to the ultimate detriment of the creditors. This failure may be directly attributed to the appointed committee members simply having no one explain to them the meaning and significance of the committee and membership upon it. This has been unfortunate because in many cases where the creditors committee organizes itself and retains professional assistance, the chances for a successful reorganization improve immeasurably. Alternatively, the committee can seek the prompt conversion of a Chapter 11 to a Chapter 7 if it appears reorganization will not succeed, thereby preserving any possible equity in the assets to pay dividends to the creditors. The committee can also assist the debtor in negotiating a feasible and confirmable plan of reorganization.[37] In an effort to increase the number of active committees, the Code has directed the United States Trustee to meet with the appointed committee promptly after its appointment so the committee can be educated as to its rights and purposes.[38] In an appropriate proceeding it may also be helpful for the debtor-in-possession to meet with a committee promptly after its appointment. This is not as incongruous as may appear at first glance to those used to thinking solely in adversarial terms. Because a successful Chapter 11 will result in payments to creditors and survival of the debtor, the best results are often achieved when the debtor and creditors find ways to work together to resolve the situation through a confirmable plan of reorganization. Input from the committee into the internal reorganization of a Chapter 11 debtor's affairs can also often provide an invaluable and essential service to an estate.[39]

36. 11 U.S.C. §1103(a).
37. 11 U.S.C. §1103(c)(3)(5).
38. 11 U.S.C. §1103(d).
39. 11 U.S.C. §1103(c)(1).

An Official Creditors Committee has the right to investigate the debtor's financial affairs, consult with the debtor or trustee (if one is appointed), request the appointment of a trustee or examiner, and, perhaps most important, assist in the formulation of a plan of reorganization on behalf of all unsecured creditors.[40] In the absence of the appointment of a trustee in a Chapter 11 proceeding, the court will often look to input from the committee to assist the court in making decisions that affect the estate. This is especially so where the committee has been organized and has independently investigated the debtor's financial affairs in a manner similar to that which would be conducted by a trustee.[41]

In an exceptionally large proceeding, the court may approve the appointment of multiple creditors committees. For example, there may be a committee of trade creditors and a committee of unsecured lenders.[42] On rare occasions, a creditors committee may be appointed in a Chapter 7.[43]

If a committee investigates a debtor and reasonably believes that the debtor or its insiders have committed fraud or are incompetent, the committee may seek the appointment of a trustee or examiner. Additionally, if a debtor-in-possession fails to follow the appropriate Chapter 11 operating rules (described in chapter 24 of this text), a committee, any creditor, or the United States Trustee may seek through motion a court order appointing a trustee or examiner in a Chapter 11 proceeding.[44]

F. CHAPTER 11 TRUSTEES AND EXAMINERS

Section 1104(a) provides three grounds for the appointment of a trustee or examiner in a Chapter 11 proceeding. The first ground is for cause, including fraud, dishonesty, incompetence, or gross mismanagement. For instance, the owner of a restaurant who is found to be misreporting sales while concealing cash is committing fraud against the creditors. The insiders of a business may simply be incapable of managing it properly. They may have no concept of budget, cash flow, or overhead costs, the inevitable results of which may be to operate the business unprofitably. Simple incompetence is probably the greatest single cause of a majority of all Chapter 11 proceedings filed by operating businesses.

---

40. 11 U.S.C. §1103(c).
41. 11 U.S.C. §1103(c)(2).
42. 11 U.S.C. §1102(a)(2).
43. 11 U.S.C. §705.
44. 11 U.S.C. §1104(a). As to the operating rules of a Chapter 11 debtor-in-possession, see chapter 24 infra.

For example, management may almost be presumed incompetent when it attempts to explain to unpaid creditors that a business is very profitable when there is no apparent extraneous reason to explain the business's debts, such as an unforeseen loss or a significant downturn in the general economy. Simply put, the basic problem of many Chapter 11 debtors is that they do not know how to count. If they can be taught arithmetic, their businesses stand a better chance to successfully reorganize.

Another example of gross mismanagement is a profitable business that has gotten into financial trouble because its insiders are spending all of the cash flow on personal luxury items such as late-model vehicles, expensive jewelry, weekend trips to Maui, and so forth, while the creditors remain unpaid.

A Chapter 11 debtor that unreasonably delays formulating a plan of reorganization may find itself the subject of a motion to appoint a trustee or examiner. In all three of these instances, a creditors committee, the United States Trustee, or any individual creditor may move the court for the appointment of a trustee or examiner. If the court finds cause the motion will be granted and a trustee or examiner appointed. A Chapter 11 trustee is appointed by the United States Trustee. Parties in interest may request that an election be held for the trustee. This election is conducted in a manner identical to that of electing Chapter 7 trustees. See Section 1104(b) and chapter 7C supra.[45]

The second ground for granting a motion to appoint a trustee or examiner is if the appointment is found to be in the best interests of the creditors.[46] This can be a rather nebulous concept. It usually comes into play when the creditors committee or a creditor or the United States Trustee moves for the appointment of a trustee or examiner, alleging any of the factual scenarios described above, but with insufficient proof to justify the appointment of a trustee or examiner for cause. Nevertheless, if it is clear to the court that the creditors have lost confidence in the debtor's management and that the appointment of an independent third party, a trustee, may help to restore confidence, then the appointment of a trustee or examiner may be found to be in the best interests of creditors. This situation can also arise in proceedings involving partnerships where the general partners are in constant dispute and can agree on no course of action in any matter. The impossibility of general partners' agreeing is a classic situation that justifies the appointment of a trustee in the best interests of creditors.

Third, under BAPA, if grounds exist to dismiss or convert the case from a Chapter 11, the court may instead appoint a trustee in the best interests of creditors.[47]

45. 11 U.S.C. §1104(a)(1).
46. 11 U.S.C. §1104(a)(2).
47. 11 U.S.C. §1104(a)(3).

A Chapter 11 trustee is very powerful. For example, a corporate debtor not in a bankruptcy proceeding is controlled by its board of directors and officers under applicable state law. However, a Chapter 11 trustee is superior to the officers and board in the chain of command, becoming, in a word, the boss. A Chapter 11 trustee is functionally a dictator. A Chapter 11 trustee has full power and authority under the Code to retain any insider in a management position or to relieve any or all insiders of their duties. To this extent, the appointment of a Chapter 11 trustee acts to supersede the charter or bylaws of a debtor corporation. Because the debtor has submitted itself to the court's jurisdiction, the appointment of a trustee is a burden it must accept.

A Chapter 11 trustee has the duties to investigate, litigate, and administrate as described above. Administration here includes following all Chapter 11 operating rules. A Chapter 11 trustee also has a duty to file a plan of reorganization or seek conversion of the proceeding to a Chapter 7.[48]

In many cases a trustee will retain current management. The decision to retain or relieve current management is, as a practical matter, the most important decision a Chapter 11 trustee makes. For instance, in a relatively small business the only people who really care enough about the business's survival and reorganization to operate it on a daily basis are the owners who are insiders. If such individuals are replaced by third parties, the new operators may not necessarily be concerned about the business's ultimate survival. The owners/insiders are usually the persons with the greatest incentive to save the business despite their actions being a cause of the filing.

A decision to change current management should not be made unless it is obvious that current management is either utterly incompetent, will not follow the trustee's instructions, or is demonstrably committing fraud. A Chapter 11 trustee fulfills the best role in a Chapter 11 by showing the debtor the correct path to an effective reorganization or by seeking conversion of the proceeding to a Chapter 7 if reorganization is not feasible.

Examiners are unique to Chapter 11 proceedings. Simply put, an **examiner** is someone who examines the debtor's affairs.[49] An examiner is usually appointed when a party has moved for the appointment of a trustee and the court determines that further independent investigation is required before a final decision can be made on the issue. An examiner may also be appointed to investigate a specific issue and to act as the "eyes and ears of the court in a fact-finding capacity.

An examiner is an independent third party who is usually given specific instructions by the court to investigate certain aspects of a debtor's

48. 11 U.S.C. §1106(a).
49. 11 U.S.C. §1106(b).

financial affairs. An examiner may be required to investigate all matters or simply a limited aspect of a debtor's financial affairs. The examiner will prepare a report for the benefit of the court and creditors. A Chapter 11 trustee also has a duty to prepare such a report regarding the debtor's financial affairs for the benefit of the court and creditors.[50]

An examiner's report may support the debtor or it may recommend the appointment of a trustee or conversion of the proceeding to a Chapter 7. The people who serve as examiners are usually the same people who are on a panel of trustees in a given district. The only qualification to serve as an examiner, however, is to be a disinterested person.

The court has discretion to expand the powers of the examiner without appointing a trustee, effectively making the examiner with expanded powers a quasi-trustee.[51] This may actually help to reduce expenses and expedite the administration of a large and complex case. However, a person who has served as examiner in a proceeding may not serve as trustee in the same proceeding.[52]

G. OMBUDSMEN

The 2005 legislation adds **ombudsmen** to the list of specialized entities that may perform services for a bankruptcy estate. An ombudsman may be appointed in two discrete situations. First, where an asset sale (see chapter 18) involves the sale of **personally identifiable information** (such as a customer list), then the court shall order the appointment of an ombudsman to review the seller's privacy policy and report on the potential losses or gains to consumers and the estate by the proposed sale.[53] Second, in a **health care business** bankruptcy, the court shall order an ombudsman to represent the interests of the patients where necessary and to regularly report to the court on the quality of patient care.[54]

Summary

The Bankruptcy Code has created several unique types of fiduciaries without which the bankruptcy system could not function. These fiduciaries

50. 11 U.S.C. §1106(a)(3)(4).
51. 11 U.S.C. §1106(b).
52. 11 U.S.C. §321(b).
53. 11 U.S.C. §332. "Personally identifiable information" is defined at 11 U.S.C. §101 (41A) and is generally a person's private information typically maintained in a customer list.
54. 11 U.S.C. §333. "Health care business" is defined at 11 U.S.C. §101 (27A) and generally includes hospitals, hospices, long-term care facilities and home health agencies.

are the trustee, United States Trustee, debtor-in-possession, Official Creditors Committee, examiners, and ombudsmen.

The trustee is appointed by the United States Trustee. The trustee administers the bankruptcy estate. Chapter 7, 12, and 13 proceedings will always have a trustee appointed. In a Chapter 11 proceeding, a trustee may only be appointed by way of a noticed motion. The grounds for granting such a motion are cause, such as fraud or gross incompetence, or because appointment of a trustee would be in the best interest of the creditors.

The United States Trustee program is a division of the Department of Justice responsible for monitoring the administration of bankruptcy estates. The United States Trustee also appoints private trustees in separate proceedings.

The debtor-in-possession is the entity created by a debtor filing a Chapter 11 reorganization proceeding. A debtor-in-possession is essentially a debtor acting as its own trustee.

The Official Creditors Committee is an entity created in a Chapter 11 to act on the collective behalf of unsecured creditors. The committee may retain professionals, appear as a party in interest, and propose a plan of reorganization.

An examiner is an individual appointed in a Chapter 11 proceeding to conduct an independent investigation of some or all of a debtor's financial affairs.

An ombudsman is appointed in connection with the sale of customer lists and in health care business bankruptcies to speak for the interests of the patients.

A trustee's duties can be summarized: investigate, liquidate, litigate, and administrate. A trustee's investigation will lead to the discovery of assets. The assets are reduced to cash by either liquidation or litigation. The process of collecting, maintaining, and distributing the cash to creditors is the administration of the estate.

KEY TERMS

administrative expense
debtor-in-possession
examiner
health care business
Official Creditors Committee
ombudsman
party in interest
personally identifiable information
small business debtor
trustee
United States Trustee

DISCUSSION QUESTIONS

1. What is the basic role of a bankruptcy trustee?
2. What are a bankruptcy trustee's basic duties? What is the difference between the duties of a Chapter 7 trustee and a trustee in a reorganization proceeding (Chapter 11, 12, or 13)?
3. What is the United States Trustee? What is its function?
4. What is a debtor-in-possession? What are a debtor-in-possession's duties?
5. What is an Official Creditor's Committee? What is the committee's role? May a committee retain its own professionals?
6. What are the grounds for the appointment of a trustee in a Chapter 11 proceeding?
7. What is an examiner?
8. What is an ombudsman? When is an ombudsman appointed?

11

Preparing a Proceeding for a Trustee

Private panel Chapter 7 trustees are busy people. In some districts a private panel trustee may be assigned 45 or more proceedings per month. Perhaps 10 to 15 percent of these proceedings will involve the trustee doing more than reviewing the file and asking the questions at the creditors meeting described in chapter 7 supra. If the trustee has been on a private panel for an extended period of time, the trustee will have an enormous case load. As a result, private panel trustees can be difficult to communicate with. However, there are some effective methods that can be used to promote effective communication with a trustee. Use of these methods will help to expedite efficient and prompt administration in consumer no asset proceedings and will also aid in the efficient and proper administration of small asset proceedings. In the latter type of proceeding, these methods will also increase, sometimes significantly, the recovery obtained for the payment of creditor dividends. This benefits a debtor as well as the creditors.

A. PREFILING ACTIONS

The primary rule is to properly prepare a proceeding for filing so that the Chapter 7 trustee's job will be made as easy as possible in order to achieve the greatest recovery and, hence, distribution. In a typical consumer no asset proceeding this will be relatively simple. In this instance all that is usually necessary is to prepare the Statements and Schedules thoroughly and clearly so that all the relevant data is easily analyzed. Chapter 29 of this text is a tutorial regarding the preparation of these documents in a clear and efficient manner. The general rule of preparation applies in all proceedings, but in a consumer no asset case the Statements and Schedules will constitute a majority of the effort involved. Their clarity will expedite administration and minimize the questioning that occurs at the creditors meeting under Section 342. For debtors that have little or no contact with the legal system, adequate preparation will also aid in minimizing any trauma caused by the bankruptcy filing.

In all consumer cases, BAPA imposes new requirements upon debtors, their counsel, and trustees, requiring more preparation. Counsel will need to prove that the prepetition disclosures required by §§527 and 528 have been given and that there is a prepetition retainer agreement as described in chapter 4 supra. The statement of current income will need to comply with the needs based bankruptcy formula described in chapter 5 supra; counsel will need to obtain all evidence of payments received by the debtor within 60 days of the filing date; and counsel will also need to obtain from the debtor the debtor's most recent tax return and for the three years preceding the filing if requested, as described in chapter 4 supra.

BAPA imposes the further requirement upon counsel to make "reasonable inquiry" as to the disclosures made by debtors in their Statements and Schedules, or risk the prospect of sanctions.[1] Case law will clarify the meaning of "reasonable inquiry," but at a minimum it is likely to include all the information otherwise required to be filed, credit reports, values of vehicles obtained from credible Internet sources, copies of documents of title, among other things.

Even in consumer no asset proceedings a situation may be present where it is likely the trustee will want to ask questions in addition to those described in chapter 7 supra. Perhaps there may be some form of inheritance as a potential asset, or a homestead. In these instances, the best thing to do is to obtain copies of any relevant documents from the debtor prior to filing. In any proceeding where it can be reasonably anticipated beforehand that the trustee will want to review documents in addition to the Statements and Schedules, it is always a good idea to have any such documents available so they can be delivered to the trustee promptly upon request.

In a small asset Chapter 7 business proceeding (and in *all* larger proceedings), effective preparation of the proceeding for the Chapter 7 trustee will require more effort. Although a larger proceeding will require more effort still, the type of effort will not vary. A typical small asset Chapter 7 liquidation, such as a small retail store or restaurant, will normally involve an inventory valued from a nominal amount to $50,000 or more and

1. 11 U.S.C. §527(a)(2)(B); 11 U.S.C. §707(b)(4). See chapters 4 and 5 supra.

equipment of similar value. There may also be accounts receivable to collect. In small asset business proceedings, one of the most common problems of debtors or their principals (whether the debtor is an individual, a corporation, or a partnership) is payroll or other nondischargeable taxes.[2] In proceedings of this sort, the debtor's or its insiders' primary concern will be to raise sufficient cash from the estate's liquidation to be able to satisfy a maximum amount of the nondischargeable obligations.

It is important to note that when a trustee is appointed, the trustee generally learns of the appointment only by receiving a copy of the bankruptcy petition and schedules in the mail, along with a stack of perhaps 15 or 20 other proceedings. If an estate contains assets that require prompt liquidation, unless the trustee reviews the files immediately (even if just to ascertain the existence of assets), the trustee may not know that any such assets exist until the meeting of creditors.

Recall that the creditors meeting may not occur until 40 days after the initial filing.[3] If nothing is done during this period, assets may be at a business premises without any type of security protection. The neighborhood kids can visit the place and help clean out the premises. Rent will continue to accrue. This rent will be an administrative expense payable before any tax creditors receive dividends. Gas and electric bills may continue to accrue and they will also receive administrative priority.[4] The longer assets go unattended the greater the likelihood they will dissipate to the detriment of all. As illustrated, this dissipation can occur by improper means or simply by the accrual of administrative expenses in the normal course of business. Both methods of dissipation can be substantially avoided by recognizing the practical difficulties encountered by trustees and by taking appropriate and simple common sense actions that will effectively minimize any unintentional dissipation of assets.

Prior to a filing, there are at least nine things that a debtor or counsel can do to properly prepare a proceeding for the trustee. The accomplishment of these tasks will expedite the liquidation at a minimum of time and expense. Because most of these tasks can be performed by the debtor, any additional time required to be spent by counsel is minimal. Generally, a debtor and counsel should take any action reasonably designed to achieve the mutually desirable goals of expediting liquidation at a minimum of expense. A paralegal will often participate in much of this activity. Every possible penny that can reasonably be saved or earned will only serve to increase the ultimate funds available for distribution to prepetition creditors.

---

2. See chapter 13 infra.
3. See chapter 7 supra.
4. See chapter 21 infra.

First, obtain the keys to the business premises before filing. The trustee will need them and this one step will allow the trustee to rapidly secure the premises without incurring the cost of a locksmith (on some occasions, a trustee will, however, want to change locks).

Second, all documents of title pertaining to the business's assets should be assembled. Ownership documents of vehicles are required in all states to transfer title to them. Having them in hand will save the trustee time and expense. All keys to any vehicles should also be assembled and properly identified.

Third, obtain the name, address, and telephone number of any landlords so the trustee will be able to make prompt arrangements to vacate the premises at a minimum of administrative expense.

Fourth, the debtor should provide as detailed an itemization as possible of all inventory and equipment of the business. If a valuation of these items is also included, this data will be invaluable to the trustee. This detailed information will not always be possible to have, but where it is, it should be provided to the trustee.

Fifth, the debtor should turn over to counsel all records and checks to all the business bank accounts. These should be promptly provided to the trustee. If the debtor is an individual, only the business accounts should be turned over promptly. Personal accounts should not be turned over unless requested by the trustee. Providing unrequested information only clutters the trustee and distracts attention from the prompt liquidation of those assets requiring it.

Sixth, the debtor should organize any accounts receivable records so that the trustee will have all relevant documentation necessary to properly collect the receivables. This includes any and all accounts receivable ledgers, other billing records, and any written contracts between the debtor and its customers. These records will provide the trustee with all necessary data to obtain a judgment if litigation is required to collect the account receivable. Where possible, the debtor should send a billing statement to all accounts receivable immediately prior to filing. Many otherwise collectable accounts receivable fail to be recovered by trustees simply because incomplete or inaccurate data are provided. If the billing records are computerized, a hard copy of the data and the software with programming should be provided. Following the above steps will expedite collection of a debtor's receivables and will reduce the possibility that the trustee will need to incur the further expense of retaining a collection agency or counsel to collect the receivables.

Seventh, any leased equipment not necessary for liquidation purposes should be returned to the lessor prior to filing. This includes leased vehicles where there is no residual equity for the estate, copy machines, postage meters, and so forth. Returning these items prefiling minimizes or eliminates any administrative rental claims that can be costly to resolve both in terms of attorneys' fees and the payment of such rent as an administrative expense.

Eighth, in some cases it may also be necessary to maintain any existing security system or guard service in place until the trustee can make a decision upon their continued use. This will obviously minimize the risk of loss of assets due to theft.

Finally, obtain the debtor's last three state and federal tax returns. The trustee will need this data to properly administer the estate. Any tax benefits contained in the prior returns will aid in reducing any taxes that may be incurred by a bankruptcy estate.

B. POSTFILING ACTIONS

Once a proceeding is filed, it is necessary to promptly communicate with the trustee to ensure that the physical aspects of a liquidation will proceed promptly. Trustees, like anyone else, cannot act if they do not know that action is necessary or required. There are four things that can be done promptly on filing to ensure rapid communication with a trustee. These items will help the liquidation process proceed without delay.

First, and most obvious, is for counsel to learn who the trustee will be. You cannot communicate with the trustee unless you know who the trustee is. Because the United States Trustee must promptly appoint an interim trustee, the United States Trustee's office will generally know who the interim trustee will be within 24 hours of filing.[5] Thus, if counsel contacts the United States Trustee and asks to know who the interim trustee is, prompt contact will become possible.

The second obvious action is to pick up the telephone and call the trustee. Because trustees do not necessarily return all phone calls, it is necessary to leave a message that will alert the trustee about the existence of the asset proceeding. The basic word to leave in the message is *assets*. Use of the word *assets* will normally result in the trustee responding within 24 hours. If more than 24 hours elapse without a reply from the trustee, then written correspondence is required. In a pressing matter, such as a restaurant bankruptcy, the correspondence should be hand-delivered immediately. It is a good idea to enclose a copy of the Statements and Schedules in the correspondence because the trustee may not receive a set

5. 11 U.S.C. §701. See chapter 7 supra.

from the United States Trustee for several days. Once the trustee has been communicated with, the trustee will normally move into action and commence the liquidation process.

The third action is for the debtor to close all bank accounts that will be turned over to the trustee and either write a check to the trustee for the balance or obtain a cashier's check from the bank for the amount of the account balance. This will eliminate any further charges by the bank for maintenance of the account.

Finally, the debtor or its insiders should cooperate fully with the trustee in the liquidation process. The trustee, or the trustee's representative, may want to meet the debtor at the business premises, for example. The trustee may need assistance in properly assembling accounts receivable data for collection purposes. The liquidation process will be easier and less expensive the greater the level of cooperation given the trustee by the debtor or its insiders.

All of the practical and common sense actions just described, both pre- and postfiling, will be useful in expediting the physical aspects of liquidation at a minimum of expense. This will ensure that a maximum amount of cash will be raised to distribute to the creditors as dividends. Where this results in payment in full of nondischargeable taxes, the debtor or its principals will be grateful.

Summary

It is important to make the trustee's job as simple as possible. Proper preparation of a proceeding before it is filed will often be sufficient to accomplish this task.

In all proceedings, proper preparation of the Statements and Schedules is critical. Chapter 29 of this text is a tutorial on this subject. Further, whenever it can be anticipated that the trustee may request additional documentation (such as a declaration of homestead, an escrow closing statement, or bank records), the practitioner should obtain the data from the client before the filing. Counsel must also maintain all documents required by BAPA together with any materials relied upon to satisfy the "reasonable inquiry" standard.

In business proceedings, there are nine simple steps that can be taken before a filing and four additional steps that can be taken immediately after a filing to rapidly commence the liquidation process. Generally, a debtor and counsel should take any action reasonably designed to achieve the mutually desirable goals of expediting liquidation at a minimum of expense.

Chapter 11 Checklist

11.1 PREFILING—ASSET CASE

- 11.1.1 Obtain Keys to Business for Delivery to Trustee
- 11.1.2 Obtain Documents of Title (Such as Vehicle Ownership Documents) and Keys to All Vehicles
- 11.1.3 Obtain Name and Address of Landlord(s)
- 11.1.4 Obtain Itemized Inventory and Equipment List, with Values, if Possible
- 11.1.5 Obtain Bank Records
- 11.1.6 Compile Accounts Receivable Data
- 11.1.7 Return Leased Equipment to Lessors
- 11.1.8 Maintain Security
- 11.1.9 Obtain Prior Years' Tax Returns

11.2 POSTFILING — ASSET CASE

- 11.2.1 Learn Identity of Trustee
- 11.2.2 Communicate with Trustee
- 11.2.3 Close Bank Accounts and Obtain Cashier's Check for Trustee
- 11.2.4 Encourage Insider Cooperation with Trustee

DISCUSSION QUESTIONS

1. What are the most important concerns of a debtor in a consumer no asset Chapter 7 proceeding?
2. What is a common primary concern in an asset proceeding?
3. What actions, before and after the filing of an asset case, should be taken by the debtor or counsel that can assist the trustee in maximizing a liquidation at a minimum of expense?

PART III

Bankruptcy Litigation

12

The Automatic Stay — 11 U.S.C. §362

A. INTRODUCTION TO BANKRUPTCY LITIGATION

Virtually all the issues previously discussed in this text that require a court decision are brought before the court through the various motion procedures described in chapter 5 supra. A second way in which issues are brought before the court for its decision is known as the **adversary proceeding**. Many of the subjects discussed in the next several chapters are commenced by the filing of an adversary proceeding in connection with the bankruptcy proceeding (case in chief). When an issue is brought before the court in the form of a motion and is opposed, it is considered a **contested matter**. A contested matter is treated as an adversary proceeding pursuant to Federal Rule of Bankruptcy Procedure 9014.

An adversary proceeding, except for its title, assumes the form of traditional nonbankruptcy litigation. That is, an adversary proceeding is an independent lawsuit taking place in the bankruptcy proceeding. Part VII of the Federal Rules of Bankruptcy Procedure contains the pertinent procedural rules applicable to adversary proceedings. With minor variations, these rules are essentially the Federal Rules of Civil Procedure, with which all practitioners should be familiar. The discovery and trial aspects of these rules may also apply in noticed motions.[1] For example, a contested involuntary petition will be governed by these rules, as would a contested motion to appoint a trustee or examiner in a Chapter 11. The practical equivalent of a trial in a contested matter is commonly known as an evidentiary hearing.

1. Bankruptcy Rule 9014.

Keeping these general concepts in mind will make it easy to understand how the issues described in the next several chapters are prosecuted and resolved in the bankruptcy system.

In remarking at how similar bankruptcy litigation is to other federal court litigation, at least one judge has commented: "In a routinized area, such as bankruptcy motion practice, one easily loses sight of some of such basics as the need to make out a prima facie case by competent evidence. Bankruptcy litigation is no different than any other federal litigation practice in this respect." (In re Roberts, 210 Bankr. 325 (Bankr. D. Iowa 1997).)

B. THE AUTOMATIC STAY

The final element of debtor relief is contained in Section 362 and is known as the **automatic stay**. (The other elements of debtor relief, discharge and exemptions, have been discussed in chapters 7 and 9 supra.) All readers have probably seen commercials on television or have read advertisements in newspapers that may advertise bankruptcy as follows: "Stop creditor harrassment. Stop foreclosure. Stop repossession." It is the automatic stay that allows these advertisements to make such bold and brazen claims. As shall be shown, these claims are not entirely accurate.

The essence of the automatic stay is that as of the moment a bankruptcy proceeding is filed, voluntarily or involuntarily, all creditor activity to collect debts, obtain judgments, or obtain property of a debtor to satisfy a debt is completely stopped. The automatic stay is effective the moment a petition is filed. The effectiveness or applicability of the automatic stay is not related to the entry of an order for relief.[2]

Once a proceeding has been commenced, creditors can take no further action to affect the assets or rights of the estate or debtor except in compliance with Section 362. Through this provision, creditors can attempt to be relieved of the stay's effect and may often be successful. The stay is automatic but is not permanent. Any implication to the contrary in any legal advertising is simply untrue.

A petition does not have to be filed within any particular time before an act is to occur to permit the automatic stay to become effective. For example, if a foreclosure sale is scheduled for 10:00 A.M. and a petition is filed at 9:59 A.M., the automatic stay prevents the foreclosure sale occurring or from being valid. However, if the bankruptcy filing occurs at 10:01 A.M., after the foreclosure sale, the automatic stay will not affect the foreclosure

2. 11 U.S.C. §362(a). See chapter 4 supra.

because it was not in effect when the foreclosure occurred. The automatic stay is effective with or without notice that a bankruptcy petition has been filed.[3] Nevertheless, it is certainly better practice to provide a creditor notice that a petition has been filed, even if only by telephone. The best approach is to transmit by facsimile or electronic means (e.g., e-mail) a file stamped copy of the first two pages of the petition to any specific creditor, or the creditor's attorney, to whom you want to provide immediate notice of the filing. This includes, for example, a creditor threatening to repossess a car, a creditor conducting an imminent foreclosure, or a utility company attempting to terminate the debtor's service for nonpayment.

C. ACTIVITY SUBJECT TO THE AUTOMATIC STAY

Section 362(a) itemizes the types of creditor activity that are affected by imposition of the automatic stay. Section 362(a)(1) prohibits the commencement or continuation of any judicial, administrative, or other proceeding against the debtor that was or could have been commenced before the filing of the petition to recover a prepetition claim.[4] In practical terms, the ABC Collection Company cannot file a lawsuit against the debtor once a petition has been filed. The XYZ Collection Agency cannot execute on the judgment that it obtained before the petition was filed. The LMN Collection Company cannot proceed with its motion for summary judgment in a case that was pending when the petition was filed. The QRS Collection Agency cannot obtain a default judgment on its prepetition claim. All legal actions against the debtor are stopped.

Section 362(a)(2) prohibits the enforcement of any prepetition judgment against the debtor or property of the estate.[5] A collection agency cannot execute upon its judgment or take a postjudgment debtor examination to ascertain the existence of assets. Recall, however, that all of this information will be disclosed in the bankruptcy, since it is contained in the Statements and Schedules.

Section 362(a)(3) stays any act to obtain possession of property of the estate or any act to exercise control over property of the estate.[6] This means

3. There is no requirement anywhere in the Code or Rules that requires prior notice of a filing to make the automatic stay effective. However, sanctions against a creditor without notice who violates the stay are likely to be minimal.
4. 11 U.S.C. §362(a)(1).
5. 11 U.S.C. §362(a)(2). As to property of the estate see chapter 14 infra.
6. 11 U.S.C. §362(a)(3).

that either by judicial process or otherwise, creditors cannot show up at the debtor's home or business and start repossessing unpaid-for merchandise. Thus, the automatic stay suspends any future attachments against the debtor or the estate. This also means that creditors cannot proceed outside of the bankruptcy system to seek the appointment of a receiver or other custodian to take control of a debtor's business or property.

Section 362(a)(4) stays any act to create, perfect, or enforce a lien against property of the estate.[7] This means that a creditor that has not perfected a security interest in collateral before the petition is filed can no longer do so; a creditor with an unperfected lien can no longer perfect it. There is one limited exception to this, which will be discussed in connection with Section 362(b)(3) below. A secured creditor is also stayed, under this subsection, from repossessing or foreclosing upon a perfected security interest.

Section 362(a)(5) stays any act to create, perfect, or enforce against property of the debtor any lien that secures a claim that arose before commencement of the case. This subsection extends the protections of Section 362(a)(4) to property of the debtor as opposed to property of the estate.[8] Thus, the exempt property of a debtor is also subject to the protections of the automatic stay.

Section 362(a)(6) stays any act to collect, assess, or recover a claim that arose before the filing of the petition.[9] This subsection includes within it the judicial activity referred to in Section 362(a)(1) or Section 362(a)(2) but also broadly extends to any form of creditor collection activity. Phone calls from a creditor seeking payment are stayed. A collection agency cannot continue to send the debtor collection notices in the mail. This subsection prevents creditor harrassment.

Section 362(a)(7) stays the making of setoffs without first obtaining relief from the automatic stay.[10] A setoff is the common law right of a creditor to balance mutual debts with a debtor. For example, Murat owes Ney $10 while Ney owes Murat $5. Ney can set off his debt to Murat and thus only have to collect $5 from Murat for both debts to be satisfied. Or Murat can offer Ney $5, set off the $5 Ney owes Murat, and both debts are extinguished.

Section 362(a)(8) stays the commencement or continuation of a proceeding before the United States Tax Court concerning the debtor.[11] This section is unusual because it does not stay an act against the debtor, but a proceeding concerning the debtor. This means that if the debtor has

7. 11 U.S.C. §362(a)(4).
8. 11 U.S.C. §362(a)(5).
9. 11 U.S.C. §362(a)(6).
10. 11 U.S.C. §362(a)(7).
11. 11 U.S.C. §362(a)(8).

initiated an action in the Tax Court, the action will still be stayed. The reason for this is that Section 505 of the Bankruptcy Code permits the Bankruptcy Court to determine tax issues in a bankruptcy proceeding.[12]

As is apparent from a review of the foregoing, only actions against the debtor or property of the estate or debtor are stayed. Actions by the debtor to collect debts or property from third parties are not. Creditors are not normally stayed from enforcing a debt against a nonbankruptcy debtor, guarantor, cosigner, or statutorily liable party (such as principal liability for payroll taxes).

D. ACTIVITY NOT SUBJECT TO THE AUTOMATIC STAY

Even though the automatic stay is a basic debtor relief protection of the bankruptcy system and even though it unquestionably applies to a very broad range of activities, there are also a number of actions that are not subject to the automatic stay. Actions that are not subject to the stay can proceed or continue without regard to the existence of the bankruptcy. These actions are the subject of Section 362(b).

The commencement or continuation of a criminal action or proceeding against the debtor is not stayed.[13] A debtor cannot avoid a murder trial by filing a bankruptcy petition. The reason for this exception to the automatic stay is obvious.

After enactment of the Bankruptcy Code an issue arose in those states where creditors could instigate criminal prosecutions against bad check writers. Was the prosecution an act to collect a debt and subject to the stay pursuant to 11 U.S.C. §362(a)(6) or was it a criminal prosecution and therefore not subject to the stay pursuant to 11 U.S.C. §362(b)(1)? The reported cases went both ways. Some Bankruptcy Courts held such prosecutions to be mere collection devices and therefore stayed, while other courts found them to be excepted criminal prosecutions.[14]

In 1986, in Kelly v. Robinson, the Supreme Court ruled that a criminal sentence to make restitution to creditors whose debts are subject to discharge in a bankruptcy proceeding is enforceable and therefore collection does not violate the automatic stay. The facts in this case were that in

12. 11 U.S.C. §505. See chapter 21 infra.
13. 11 U.S.C. §362(b)(1).
14. See, e.g., St. Joseph Wholesale Liquor Co. v. Butler, 45 Bankr. 46 (W.D. Mo. 1984), as an example of a case enforcing the stay.

November 1980 Carolyn Robinson pleaded guilty to larceny based on her wrongful receipt of $9,932.95 in welfare benefits from the State of Connecticut. She was placed on probation, one condition of which was the payment of $100 per month in restitution. In February 1981 Robinson filed a Chapter 7 bankruptcy. She listed the creditor in her schedules. The creditor did not oppose the dischargeability of the debt and Robinson received her discharge in May 1981. Subsequently, when the creditor sought to collect the debt, Robinson sought an order from the Bankruptcy Court that the debt, and hence the restitution order, had been discharged. The Supreme Court disagreed. Because criminal sentences and restitution orders were not dischargeable under either the Bankruptcy Act or the Bankruptcy Code, the Court reasoned, collection of the restitution order is not subject to the automatic stay. In addition, a further rationale to support this position is that society's interest in the criminal justice system outweighs its interest in the bankruptcy system.[15]

Section 362(b)(2) excepts from operation of the automatic stay the collection of "domestic support obligations" from property that is not property of the estate. The commencement or continuation of a paternity suit or the commencement or continuation of an action for a domestic support obligations is also excepted from the automatic stay. Custody disputes, domestic violence matters and the dissolution case itself, except to the extent it affects property of the estate (see chapter 14, infra) are not subject to the automatic stay.[16] As described in chapter 13 infra, domestic support obligations are not normally dischargeable. The collection of these nondischargeable debts other than from property of the estate does not violate the automatic stay. Property of the estate is described in greater detail in chapter 14 infra.

Property of the estate does not include a debtor's postpetition wages in a Chapter 7 or 11.[17] One practical meaning of Section 362(b)(2) is that a creditor with a prepetition claim for a domestic support obligations is not barred from proceeding in the proper forum to obtain any necessary orders to permit collection of domestic support obligations from a Chapter 7 or 11 debtor's wages. Because exemptions are also ineffective against these claims, Chapter 7 or 11 is essentially ineffective against them.[18] Thus, unless Mr. Smith files a Chapter 13, Mrs. Smith will retain many of her rights to collect alimony, support, or maintenance due, without regard to Mr. Smith's Chapter 7 petition.

15. Kelly v. Robinson, 479 U.S. 36 (1986). This holding was excluded from Chapter 13 proceedings in Pennsylvania Dept. of Public Welfare v. Davenport, 495 U.S. 552 (1990). However, this ruling was overruled by Congress in 1991 when it enacted 11 U.S.C. §1328(a)(3), which makes criminal restitution orders not dischargeable in Chapter 13 proceedings.

16. 11 U.S.C. §362(b)(2).

17. 11 U.S.C. §541(a)(6). See chapter 14 infra. This is not the case in a Chapter 13 proceeding, where a debtor's postpetition earnings are considered property of the estate. 11 U.S.C. §1306(a)(2). See chapters 14 and 23 infra.

18. 11 U.S.C. §522(c). See chapter 9 supra.

Section 362(b)(3) is a limited exception to the effect of the automatic stay regarding acts to perfect or to maintain or continue the perfection of an interest in property described in connection with Section 362(a)(4) above. Essentially, a secured creditor that has a nonbankruptcy law right to perfect an interest in property (such as by recording a Uniform Commercial Code [UCC] security interest in personal property by recording a mortgage or deed of trust upon real estate) within a statutory period of time may do so within the allowed time period or within 30 days of the underlying transaction otherwise subject to the automatic stay.[19] This situation will arise most commonly in secured transactions subject to the UCC. Generally, the UCC permits creditors in certain secured transactions grace periods to perfect security interests by properly filing any required documents with a County Recorder or Secretary of State for a particular state.[20] Thus, if a debtor files a bankruptcy proceeding within this time period, this exception to the automatic stay provides that it will not be violated if the creditor perfects its security interest within the nonbankruptcy statutory period or 30 days from the date of the bankruptcy filing. For example, if Sammy Connifer buys a new car on Thursday and files a Chapter 7 on Friday, as long as the bank perfects its lien upon the vehicle within any underlying statutory period, the act of perfection will not be a violation of the automatic stay under Section 362(b)(3). This provision may also permit the perfection of a state law mechanic's lien without such perfection being considered a violation of the automatic stay.

There is substantial case law in existence on this latter point. It is beyond the scope or purpose of this basic text to analyze this case law in detail. A creditor in this situation should carefully review the status of the case law on this point before proceeding so that no unintended violation of the stay is committed.

Section 362(b)(4) excepts from the stay the commencement or continuation of an action or proceeding by a governmental unit to enforce its police or regulatory power.[21] The rationale for this exception is identical to the exception for criminal actions or proceedings. For example, the EPA may still enjoin Polluters Inc. from violating the Environmental Protection Act. A zoning commission may still find a debtor in violation of zoning laws for having a restaurant in the middle of a residential neighborhood. These actions are not subject to the automatic stay.

Section 362(b)(4) also permits enforcement of any orders resulting from the enforcement of a governmental unit's police or regulatory powers

---

19. 11 U.S.C. §362(b)(3).
20. The time period for perfection may vary from state to state pursuant to U.C.C. §9-301(1).
21. 11 U.S.C. §362(b)(4).

other than the collection of a money judgment.[22] For instance, if the EPA issues an order against Polluters Inc. to pay a fine and clean up the mess, the monetary portion of the order is subject to the automatic stay, but the cleanup order is not.[23]

Sections 362(b)(6) and 362(b)(7) provide limited exceptions to the effect of the automatic stay upon setoffs as described above, but only in the context of proceedings involving stockbrokers or commodity brokers subject to the special subchapters of Chapter 7 applicable to these unique debtors.[24] Because these types of proceedings are very rare, these sections will usually not be relevant.

Section 362(b)(8) is also rarely used in practice. This provision permits the Department of Housing and Urban Development to commence foreclosure actions on properties subject to the National Housing Act. The exception is limited to commencing the foreclosure as opposed to completing it. The Department of Housing and Urban Development would still be required to obtain relief from the automatic stay in order to complete the foreclosure.[25]

Section 362(b)(9) provides that the issuance to the debtor of a notice of tax deficiency will not violate the automatic stay.[26] Although the Historical and Revision Notes explain that this provision is associated with a debtor's right to have the Bankruptcy Court or Tax Court determine the amount of the tax, a practical reason for this exception to the automatic stay is that the IRS computers will function regardless of what laws or human beings tell them. And even when human beings or laws tell them, the computers still function, often incorrectly. So Congress simply made the issuance of a tax deficiency an exception to the automatic stay to preclude taxing entities from being accused of always violating the stay by issuing notices of deficiency. The Bankruptcy Reform Act of 1994 expanded Section 362(b)(9) to include audits, demands for returns, and the assessment and issuance of a demand to pay a tax as additional exceptions to the automatic stay.

Section 362(b)(10) concerns an issue that may occasionally arise in business proceedings. If the debtor is a tenant of nonresidential real property and the lease has expired or otherwise terminated before the bankruptcy is filed, the landlord does not have to obtain relief from the automatic stay to properly evict the tenant.[27] This should be distinguished from the situation where the landlord thinks the lease has expired because a statutory notice to quit has been served on the tenant. The automatic stay would still likely apply in this latter instance. But

22. 11 U.S.C. §362(b)(4). The enforcement aspect of Section 362(b)(4) was contained in Section 362(b)(5) prior to 1994. In 1994, the two provisions were merged into the present form.
23. Midlantic Natl. Bank v. New Jersey Dept. of Envtl. Protection, 474 U.S. 494 (1986).
24. 11 U.S.C. §362(b)(6), (7).
25. 11 U.S.C. §362(b)(8). See also the Historical and Revision Notes to this provision.
26. 11 U.S.C. §362(b)(9).
27. 11 U.S.C. §362(b)(10).

where the nonresidential lease has been unequivocally terminated before the bankruptcy filing, the landlord does not have to obtain relief from the automatic stay to initiate unlawful detainer proceedings under applicable state law.

Sections 362(b)(11), (12), (13), and (17) involve unusual and limited commercial transactions involving the presentment and dishonor of negotiable instruments and certain foreclosures under the Federal Ship Mortgage Act. These transactions are rarely seen in bankruptcy proceedings. Sections 362(b)(12) and (13) do not apply to proceedings commenced after December 31, 1989.

Sections 362(b)(14), (15), and (16), added to the Code in 1990, except from the automatic stay actions to determine the accreditation, licensing, and eligibility of an educational institution to participate in federally guaranteed student loan programs. Thus, the College of Hard Knocks cannot file bankruptcy to prevent the loss of its accreditation or license. Nor will bankruptcy relief protect the college from losing the ability to participate in guaranteed student loan programs. Section 362(b)(18), added to the Code in 1994, excepts from the automatic stay the perfection of property tax liens for postpetition property taxes.[28]

Section 362(b)(19) permits the withholding of payment from a debtor's postpetition wages, repayments of a loans from retirement plans that are qualified as such pursuant to the Internal Revenue Code, such as 401(k) plans or loans from IRA accounts.

A number of provisions designed to curb the abuse of **serial bankruptcy** filings were added to the Code by BAPA. A **serial bankruptcy** filing takes place when a debtor files successive bankruptcies in an effort to delay creditor action, typically foreclosure of a home, eviction, or repossession. Each time a debtor files, the automatic stay stops the creditor and forces the creditor to seek relief from the stay. The debtor will then usually allow the case to be dismissed and then refile again just prior to the next scheduled foreclosure sale. In actual practice, it has not been uncommon to see debtors filing three or more consecutive bankruptcies.

Section 362(b)(20) is the first provision affecting serial bankruptcy filings. This provision excepts from the automatic stay actions to enforce liens against property for two years after the entry of an order by the court in a prior bankruptcy case that the prior filing was part of a scheme to delay, hinder, and defraud creditors involving multiple bankruptcy filings or a transfer of an interest in the property not consented to by the secured creditor. This sort of scheme is also now a separate and independent ground for seeking relief from the automatic stay pursuant to 11

28. 11 U.S.C. §362(b)(14), (15), (16), (18).

U.S.C. §362(d)(4). A debtor can seek to have the stay imposed in the subsequent case by filing a motion showing changed circumstances or good cause. [29]

Section 362(b)(21) excepts from the stay the enforcement of liens or security interests against real property if the debtor is not eligible to file because a bankruptcy has been filed within 180 days of dismissal of a prior case in violation of §109(g) (see chapter 5 supra), or if the bankruptcy court entered an order in a prior bankruptcy case prohibiting the debtor from being a debtor in another bankruptcy case.

Section 362(b)(22) permits an eviction to proceed if the landlord obtained a judgment for possession prior to the filing of the bankruptcy. Section 362(l) defers this for 30 days to provide the debtor an opportunity to cure and deposit all past due rent. Section 362(b)(23) permits evictions based upon endangerment to property or person or upon the use of illegal drugs, provided that the procedures of §362(m) are complied with.

Section 362(b)(24) excepts transfers that a trustee may not avoid pursuant to the trustee's powers as a super creditor (see chapter 15 infra) or the trustee's power to avoid postpetition transfers made without court approval (see chapter 17 infra).

New Section 362(b)(25) excepts investigations and action by a "securities self regulatory organization" to enforce the organization's regulatory power other than for monetary sanctions. This provision essentially extends the exception for a governmental unit's police or regulatory powers found in §362(b)(5) to stock exchanges and other private entities that regulate the issuance and sale of securities. Thus, a corporation found to have defrauded its investors by the entity and subject to sanctions therefrom cannot seek bankrtupcy protection in an effort to avoid the sanctions.

Section 362(b)(26) permits the setoff of prepetition tax refunds against prepetition tax claims. For example, a debtor is owed a tax refund for 2004, owes taxes for 2003, and files Chapter 7 in 2005. The Internal Revenue Service may use the 2004 refund and apply it to the 2003 tax liability without violating the automatic stay pursuant to this provision.

Section 362(b)(27) permits setoffs in certain financial transactions that will not be present in most cases. Section 262(b)(28) permits the

29. 11 U.S.C. §362(b)(20); 11 U.S.C. §362(d)(4). See Section 12F infra. As to the transfer of an interest in property to defraud creditors this is designed to prevent a person from transferring a partial interest in real property to a third person for the primary purpose of having the third person file a bankruptcy to gain the benefits of the automatic stay for the property.

Secretary of Health and Human Services to exclude a debtor from medicare participation.

E. DURATION OF THE AUTOMATIC STAY

The automatic stay, despite popular opinion and legal advertisements to the contrary, is not perpetual. The automatic stay may terminate by operation of law, it may be relieved on a motion by a creditor, it may effectively merge into the permanent injunction created by a debtor's discharge, or it may not exist at all in serial filing cases.[30] Section 362(c) concerns the duration of the automatic stay. Generally, the automatic stay remains in effect with regard to property of the estate until such time as the property is no longer property of the estate.[31] One way in which property might no longer be property of the estate would be if the trustee abandons it as burdensome.[32] Another way in which property will no longer be property of the estate is when the trustee files a Report of No Distribution in a no asset proceeding. This report effectively acts to abandon previously unadministered assets.

Any other acts affected by the automatic stay continue until the earliest of the time a proceeding is closed, the time a proceeding is dismissed, or, if a proceeding is an individual Chapter 7 or any Chapter 9, 11, 12, or 13, the time a discharge is granted or denied.[33] In practice, the earliest of these various dates in a Chapter 7 is usually when the discharge is granted, which, as described in chapter 7 supra, normally occurs about 90 days after the proceeding is filed. In a Chapter 11, a discharge is not received until a plan of reorganization is confirmed.[34] In Chapters 12 and 13, a discharge is not granted until the debtor's plan has been fully performed.[35] Thus, in non-Chapter 7 proceedings, events other than receipt of a discharge will often be the earlier of the possible dates.

BAPA adds two additional situations in which the stay is terminated by operation of law. Each situation is designed to curb serial filings, except when a debtor can demonstrate that the debtor is proceeding in good faith. Section 362(c)(3) relieves the stay 30 days after a filing in individual debtor cases who had a case pending in the preceding year that was dismissed, except for a case refiled under a reorganization Chapter if the

30. 11 U.S.C. §362(c), (d); 11 U.S.C. §524(a). See chapter 7 supra.
31. 11 U.S.C. §362(c)(1).
32. 11 U.S.C. §554. See chapter 20 infra.
33. 11 U.S.C. §362(c)(2).
34. 11 U.S.C. §1141(d). See chapter 26 infra.
35. 11 U.S.C. §1228(a); 11 U.S.C. §1328(a). See chapters 23 and 26 infra.

dismissal was under §707(b), discussed in chapter 5 supra. A party in interest, presumably the debtor in this situation, may file a motion to impose the stay if it can be demonstrated that the current petition has been filed in good faith. There is a presumption that the case is not in good faith if there have been two or more cases filed by the debtor within one year; a prior case within one year was dismissed for failure to file required documents; or the debtor failed to make adequate protection payments; or the debtor defaulted in performing a confirmed plan; or the debtor's financial or personal affairs are unchanged from the most recent previous case; or the previous case was dismissed after a creditor moved for or obtained relief from the automatic stay (see below this chapter).

Section 362(c)(4) provides that the stay does not go into effect for an individual debtor who has filed two or more cases within the preceding year that were dismissed, except for a case refiled under a reorganization Chapter if the dismissal was under §707(b), discussed in chapter 5 supra. A party in interest (presumably an affected creditor) can seek an application for an order that no stay is in effect. A party in interest, presumably the debtor, may file a motion seeking to impose the stay in a manner identical to that set forth in §362(c)(3), discussed in the preceding paragraph.

For example, Homer and Marge Simpson file Chapter 7. They fail to file schedules, and their case is dismissed. One month later they file a second Chapter 7. Pursuant to §362(c)(3), the automatic stay will be relieved as to their secured and leasehold creditors 30 days after the filing unless the Simpsons successfully move the court to impose the stay. If their second case is dismissed and they want to file a third, pursuant to §362(c)(4), there is no stay in effect at all unless the Simpsons successfully move the court to impose the stay. In this latter situation, the creditors may obtain an ex parte order that there is no stay in effect.

Although the automatic stay terminates when a debtor receives a discharge, creditors are not suddenly free to once again collect prepetition debts. Recall that the discharge is a permanent injunction with respect to all debts that are discharged.[36] In addition, exempt property is not liable for prepetition debts.[37] Technically, therefore, the automatic stay merges into the permanent injunction that results from the discharge order. Many people have an erroneous perception that the automatic stay is eternal. It is not. Rather, the automatic stay merges into a debtor's discharge. The discharge acts as an injunction against the collection of all discharged debts. This is an accurate representation of what occurs as a result of discharge.

BAPA adds two additional situations in which the stay is terminated by operation of law. First, §362(h) provides that if a debtor fails to timely file a

36. 11 U.S.C. §524(a). See chapter 7 supra.
37. 11 U.S.C. §522(c). See chapter 9 supra.

Statement of Intention and begin performance with respect to secured or leased personal property (see chapter 4 supra and chapter 21 infra), the property ceases to be property of the estate (see chapter 14 infra), which effectively terminates the stay. Second, §362(n) provides that the automatic stay does not apply to a second small business case filed within two years.

F. OBTAINING RELIEF FROM THE AUTOMATIC STAY

A creditor may seek an order of the court, in appropriate circumstances, relieving the automatic stay. This procedure is a noticed motion commonly known as a **motion for relief from the automatic stay**. A majority of bankruptcy litigation involves such motions. Relief from the automatic stay may involve termination or modification of the stay.[38] Four grounds are provided for a party seeking relief from the automatic stay. They are: (1) "for cause, including lack of adequate protection of an interest in property of such party in interest"; (2) with regard to acts against property of the estate (such as repossessions or foreclosures), if the debtor does not have any equity in the property and the property is not necessary to an effective reorganization; (3) in a single asset real estate case, failing within 90 days after the order for relief to file a plan that has a reasonable possibility of being confirmed within a reasonable time, or commencing monthly payments to all consensual secured lenders at the contract rate of interest; or, (4) real property that is part of a scheme to delay, hinder and defraud creditors involving multiple bankruptcy filings or a transfer of an interest in the property not consented to by the secured creditors.[39] The accompanying illustration (on page 178) describes the basic procedural steps that occur in motions for relief from the automatic stay.

Attempting to obtain relief from the automatic stay for cause introduces the concept of **adequate protection**. This concept is utilized frequently throughout the Bankruptcy Code. Adequate protection is defined in Section 361. In its essence, adequate protection simply means maintaining the status quo for an affected creditor during the pendency of the stay, to prevent the erosion of a creditor's interest in the property. Generally, only secured creditors will benefit from this provision. The most common form of adequate protection is requiring the trustee or debtor to

38. 11 U.S.C. §362(d). Bankruptcy Rule 4001(a)(1).
39. 11 U.S.C. §362(d)(1), (2), (3), (4). See chapter 6U supra for the definition of *single asset real estate*.

MOTIONS FOR RELIEF FROM STAY
(11 U.S.C. §362)

Creditor files motions and pleadings as per Checklist 12.3

Prior notice (Consult local rules)

OPPOSITION — TRUSTEE, DEBTORS, PARTY IN INTEREST

PRELIMINARY HEARING
11 U.S.C. §362(c)

Court Options (11 U.S.C. §362(d))

1. Grant motion:
    a) for cause, including lack of adequate protection;
    b) no equity;
    c) property not necessary for an effective reorganization
    d) single asset real estate
    e) multiple bankruptcy scheme
2. Deny motion
3. Schedule a final hearing within 30 days (11 U.S.C. §362(e)(1)).
4. Stay terminates 30 days after motion filed in individual case unless parties agree or court orders otherwise (11 U.S.C. §362(e)(2)).

FINAL HEARING
11 U.S.C. §362(c)

continue to make periodic payments on a debt subject to a secured claim.[40] Because the payments will act to minimize any increase in the creditor's claim occasioned by the stay, the payments will inhibit the erosion of the creditor's interest in the property. Providing additional or replacement collateral is also an acceptable method of providing adequate protection.[41] Finally, any other method that will serve the underlying purpose of providing adequate protection will also constitute adequate protection, except that a secured creditor cannot be given an administrative claim.[42] To do so would violate the distributive scheme of the Bankruptcy Code.[43]

For instance, if Chapter 7 debtors Jack and Jill Smith want to keep their home or vehicle, adequate protection simply means continuing to make normal payments to the secured creditor. If the Smiths are already in default (a common occurrence), adequate protection will also mean the ultimate curing of the default. Although Chapter 13 may provide a better remedy for the Smiths than Chapter 7 if they wish to save their home or car from foreclosure or repossession, any default will ultimately have to be cured. Typically, the ability to make current payments will permit the court to grant the Smiths some additional time to sell or refinance their home or car, thereby at least attempting to preserve any equity the Smiths may have in the home or car through any exemptions they have claimed.

In Chapter 11 proceedings, the issue of adequate protection will frequently arise when the debtor-in-possession is operating its business and is required to service its secured credit lines as a means of providing adequate protection. If inventory is sold and the credit line is not paid, the value of the creditor's interest in the property will erode because the collateral is being disposed of. This erosion will be even more significant if the collateral is not being replaced by new inventory. There are additional rights that a secured creditor may have in this instance. These are discussed in chapter 21 of this text.[44]

Cause for obtaining relief from the automatic stay may be other than lack of adequate protection. Recall that a Code section's use of the term including does not limit the statute's applicability to only those items specifically mentioned.[45] A common cause for relief from the stay, other than lack of adequate protection, arises in the case of the personal injury claimant where the debtor is a defendant. Many personal injury defendants have insurance coverage. The insurance company will normally pay the

40. 11 U.S.C. §361(1). These payments can be limited to interest on the secured portion of a debtor's debt. See United Savings Assn. of Texas v. Timbers of Inwood Forest Assocs., 484 U.S. 365 (1988). See also chapter 21 infra.
41. 11 U.S.C. §361(2). Also see chapter 21 infra.
42. 11 U.S.C. §361(3).
43. See chapters 21 and 22 infra.
44. See chapter 21 infra.
45. 11 U.S.C. §102(3). See chapter 5 supra.

claim up to the policy limits. It is traditional to grant relief from the stay to a creditor who can look to an insurance policy for recovery. The claimant may then proceed with litigation of the claim as long as the creditor agrees that it will not seek to enforce any judgment beyond the limits of the debtor's insurance coverage. Other creditors are not prejudiced because they have no right to payment of the claim covered by insurance. The trustee does not have any rights to collect the creditor's claim. The claim will only be paid to the one affected creditor, not all creditors.

The second ground for obtaining relief from the automatic stay, lack of equity in property, is the most frequent ground utilized by creditors seeking relief from the automatic stay. Simply put, a secured creditor will be entitled to some form of relief from the automatic stay if the debtor has no equity in the property. The example of a debtor with real estate subject to foreclosure illustrates the most common scenario. The methodology of the example, however, applies to any motion for relief from the automatic stay based on lack of equity.

Assume that debtor M. Krebs owns a home worth $100,000. Assume a first trust deed or mortgage debt encumbering the home in the amount of $75,000. Assume further that there are past due payments owed the trust deed or mortgage holder of $10,000. This means that the lender is actually owed $85,000. Next, the estimated costs of selling the property should be taken into account. This includes an estimate of commissions and closing costs, usually 8 to 10 percent of the selling price for a parcel of residential real property. In the example then, 10 percent of the sales price would be $10,000. The amount of any equity in the property is determined simply by subtracting the value of all liens, encumbrances, and the estimated costs of sale from the gross value of the property. Any remainder represents equity in the property. In the example, there would thus be $5,000 of realizable equity in M. Kreb's home. If the debtor has claimed this equity exempt, there are no grounds for relief from the stay because the debtor has equity in the property. So even if a sale of the property would provide no dividend to the unsecured creditors, if there is some equity available for the debtor to realize, the debtor may be able to maintain the automatic stay in effect.[46]

Generally, where the debtor's equity is less than 10 percent of the property's value, the courts are normally hesitant to maintain the stay for any length of time without requiring the debtor to provide some additional form of adequate protection as described above. The reason for this is that the value given is really only an estimate. If the actual sales price turns out to be lower than the estimate, the secured creditor's interest in the property may be impaired. Remember the concept of adequate protection exists for

46. 11 U.S.C. §362(d)(2).

the benefit of the creditor with an interest in the property, not for the benefit of the debtor.

Thus, in the situation where the equity is marginal, the court may not be inclined to grant relief from the stay, but will likely require the making of adequate protection payments as a condition of the automatic stay remaining in effect. The court will also probably set a deadline for the debtor to obtain a sale or refinancing of the property that will result in the cure of any prefiling arrearages. This deadline may be three months, two months, or six months. The court has discretion in structuring relief from automatic stay orders to try to do equity to the rights of both the creditor and the debtor.

Generally, if there is no equity in the property, the stay will be terminated. If the equity is marginal, as in the example, the stay may be maintained for a limited period of time conditioned upon the making of adequate protection payments. As the equity cushion increases above 10 percent of the property's estimated value, the court will become less inclined to require adequate protection payments or to set a deadline for the sale or refinance of the asset. Where there may be substantial equity for the unsecured creditors beyond any homestead exemption for the debtor, the court may decline to grant any relief, limited or otherwise, from the automatic stay. Such a denial of relief in this latter instance will normally be without prejudice to the creditor to renew its motion at a later date.

In a Chapter 7, because the proceeding is a liquidation, the property will never be necessary to an effective reorganization and this will not normally be an issue in a motion for relief from the automatic stay in a Chapter 7 proceeding. The necessity of the property to an effective reorganization does, however, become a critical issue in Chapters 11, 12, or 13 reorganization proceedings.[47] The principles illustrated above will also apply in these situations, but the intrinsic value of the asset to the debtor's business must also be taken into account. For instance, a print shop cannot do business without a printing press. Even if there is no equity in the press itself, because it is essential to the ability of the business to reorganize, relief from the stay may not necessarily be granted except after a period of time, so that all interested parties can ascertain whether the debtor has any realistic ability to reorganize. The courts must be creative in framing appropriate orders to protect the interests of all parties in these circumstances. On the one hand, the printing business in the example must effectively liquidate if the stay is terminated. On the other hand, the secured creditor is entitled to adequate protection of its interest in the property while the stay remains in effect.

47. 11 U.S.C. §362(d)(2)(B).

In single asset real estate cases, and recall that single asset real estate is real property generating substantially all income of a debtor (see chapter 6, supra). The purpose of this provision is to require a single asset real estate debtor to move the case along promptly by formulating a reorganization plan that the court finds has a reasonable possibility of being confirmed within a reasonable time — or by commencing to make adequate protection payments at the contract rate of interest. Failure to accomplish either alternative within the latter of 90 days from the entry of the order for relief (normally the filing date of the petition, see chapter 4 supra), or 30 days after the court determines that the provision applied constitutes grounds for relief from the stay. Whether a plan of reorganization has a reasonable possibility of being confirmed within a reasonable time will always be a question of fact for the court to determine.[48]

Section 362(d)(4) permits relief from the stay to be granted if the court finds that the bankruptcy filing was part of a scheme to delay, hinder, or defraud creditors involving a transfer of an interest in real estate not consented to by a secured creditor or without court approval, or multiple bankruptcy filings affecting the real property. For example, Spanky McFarland files an individual Chapter 7 case to stop the foreclosure of his home by Big Brutus Bank. The Bank obtains relief from the stay in Spanky's case, and just prior to the next scheduled foreclosure date, Spanky's wife Darla files Chapter 7 for the sole purpose of gaining the benefit of the automatic stay. Bank may obtain relief from the stay on the ground that Darla's filing was part of a scheme to defraud the Bank involving multiple filings affecting Spanky and Darla's home. If Spanky, alternatively, transfers a 10% interest in the real property to his best friend Alfalfa who then files bankruptcy to help prevent the home's foreclosure, Bank may seek relief from the stay on the ground that Spanky's transfer to Alfalfa was for the sole purpose of delaying Bank's foreclosure on the home.

In consumer cases, preparation of the motion documents, either in support of or in opposition to the motion, is relatively simple. Sample forms are contained in the forms disk accompanying this text. Commercial cases may involve parcels of property or equipment worth several million dollars where the equity may be substantial. In these situations resolution of the equity or reorganization issues may often require an extended evidentiary hearing. Appraisers will testify and may have their depositions taken, and even the underlying parties who participated in the original transaction may have their depositions taken to prepare for the hearing. (These depositions will be Rule 2004 Examinations. See chapter 7 supra.) Regardless of

48. The statutory language requiring a reorganization plan to have a "reasonable possibility of being confirmed within a reasonable time" comes directly from the Supreme Court case of United Savings Assn. of Texas v. Timbers of Inwood Forest Assocs., 484 U.S. 365 (1988). The meaning of the phrase has been the subject of much discussion in the case law. It is beyond the scope of this text to do more than introduce the issue.

what you call it, this is a piece of litigation and should be approached in a manner identical to any other litigation in the legal system.[49]

Section 362(e) deals with the length of time that the stay remains in effect once a motion for relief from the automatic stay is filed. This subsection effectively requires that a motion for relief from the automatic stay be resolved on an expedited basis.

First, the automatic stay terminates 30 days after a motion for relief is filed unless the court orders otherwise during the 30-day period.[50]

If a hearing is requested, the court will hold it within this 30-day period. This hearing is known as a preliminary hearing, but it may be considered a final hearing if the court so determines. The court will usually not accept oral testimony at a preliminary hearing. It will review any declarations submitted by the parties instead. If the court determines that it needs to hear further evidence, a final hearing will be scheduled. The final hearing must take place within 30 days of the preliminary hearing.[51]

Even if there is a preliminary hearing, the automatic stay will still terminate 30 days after the motion is filed unless the court maintains the automatic stay in effect pending the final hearing.[52] Often the court cannot schedule a final hearing within 30 days of the preliminary hearing, and the final hearing will take place more than 30 days after the motion is filed. When a debtor or trustee is in this situation, it is imperative to obtain an order from the court unequivocally maintaining the automatic stay in effect until the date of the final hearing. Unless this is done, the stay will be relieved pursuant to Section 362(e). The three different time periods explicit or implicit within Section 362(e) are sometimes referred to as the "30/30/30 rule."

Section 362(e)(2) applies in individual cases and terminates the stay 60 days after a motion for relief from stay is filed unless the court renders a final decision within the 60-day period, the parties agree otherwise or the court orders otherwise. For example, if the court denies the motion, the stay will remain in effect because the court has reached a final decision. If the parties reach an agreement to keep the stay in effect and reduce the agreement to an order approved by the court, the parties have agreed and the court has ordered otherwise

In an emergency, where irreparable harm may occur, it is possible to obtain ex parte relief from the automatic stay without a formal hearing.[53] This is extraordinary relief and as a result should not be taken lightly.

49. Bankruptcy Rule 4001(a)(1).
50. 11 U.S.C. §362(e)(1).
51. 11 U.S.C. §362(e)(1).
52. 11 U.S.C. §362(e)(1).
53. 11 U.S.C. §362(f); Bankruptcy Rule 4001(a)(3).

In any motion for relief from the automatic stay, the party bringing the motion bears the burden of proof on the issue of equity, while a party opposing the motion bears the burden of proof on all other issues.[54]

Finally, a party willfully violating the automatic stay can be sanctioned by the court. Sanctions may include actual damages, costs including attorneys' fees, and, in appropriate circumstances, punitive damages.[55]

Summary

Disputed issues will come before the Bankruptcy Court by way of noticed motions, ex parte applications, or adversary proceedings. An adversary proceeding exists when a separate lawsuit is filed in a bankruptcy proceeding. A motion for relief from the automatic stay is a noticed motion. An action to set aside a preference is an adversary proceeding. The prosecution of an adversary proceeding is governed by Part VII of the Federal Rules of Bankruptcy Procedure, which are essentially the Federal Rules of Civil Procedure. An opposed motion may be treated as an adversary proceeding pursuant to Bankruptcy Rule 9014.

The automatic stay is one of the three fundamental features of the debtor relief provided for by the Bankruptcy Code, the other two being discharge and exemptions, discussed respectively in chapters 7 and 9 supra. The automatic stay is the subject of Section 362 of the Bankruptcy Code. The automatic stay is a statutory bar to the conducting of collection activity by creditors after a bankruptcy petition has been filed. A summary of the most common actions subject or not subject to the automatic stay are contained in the checklist following this summary.

The automatic stay is not permanent. Pursuant to 11 U.S.C. §362(c), the stay will terminate upon the earlier of the time that the case is closed or dismissed, or, in an individual proceeding, when the debtor has received a discharge and the property is no longer property of the estate, or when the debtor has engaged in serial filings. In individual proceedings, the latter circumstances will normally trigger termination of the automatic stay. However, the effects of the automatic stay will merge into the permanent injunction contained in the debtor's discharge.

A creditor may bring a motion for relief from the automatic stay pursuant to 11 U.S.C. §362(d). Normally, secured creditors are the greatest beneficiaries of this provision. A sample motion is included in the forms disk accompanying this text. Relief from the automatic stay may be brought on

---

54. 11 U.S.C. §362(g).
55. 11 U.S.C. §362(k).

one of four basic grounds: cause, including lack of adequate protection; lack of equity in the property; or a single asset real estate case that fails to file a potentially confirmable plan or commence adequate protection payments within 90 days from the entry of the order for relief, or when the property has been subject to serial filings. A Bankruptcy Court may maintain the automatic stay in effect if the debtor or trustee can provide adequate protection. If adequate protection cannot be provided or if there is no equity in the property for the debtor or estate, the automatic stay will likely be relieved.

Adequate protection is described in Section 361 of the Code. Adequate protection involves various methods of protecting a secured creditor's interest in property of the debtor or estate during pendency of the automatic stay. The making of periodic payments and the providing of additional or replacement collateral are all methods of adequate protection.

A motion for relief from the automatic stay is to be given expedited treatment by the Bankruptcy Court as described in 11 U.S.C. §362(e). The automatic stay will terminate 30 days after it is filed unless the motion is opposed. If the motion is opposed, the court must hold a preliminary hearing within 30 days of the motion's filing. The automatic stay will also terminate 30 days after the motion is filed unless the court continues it in effect or unless the court requests or requires a final hearing. The final hearing must take place within 30 days of the preliminary hearing. The automatic stay will terminate 30 days after the preliminary hearing unless the court orders otherwise. In any scenario where any of these time limits will be exceeded, the party opposing the motion (debtor or trustee) must obtain a court order maintaining the automatic stay in effect until the later date. In individual cases, the stay will automatically terminate 60 days after the motion has been filed unless the parties agree or the court orders otherwise.

In any motion for relief from the automatic stay, the party bringing the motion bears the burden of proof on the issue of equity, while a party opposing the motion bears the burden of proof on all other issues.

KEY TERMS

adequate protection
adversary proceeding
automatic stay
contested matter
motion for relief from the automatic stay
serial bankruptcy

Chapter 12 Checklist

12.1	ACTIONS SUBJECT TO AUTOMATIC STAY		*Authority*
	12.1.1	Civil Actions or Administrative Legal Proceedings	11 U.S.C. §362(a)(1)
	12.1.2	Enforcement of Judgments	11 U.S.C. §362(a)(2)
	12.1.3	Acts to Obtain Possession or Control of Property of the Estate	11 U.S.C. §362(a)(3)
	12.1.4	Acts to Perfect Liens upon Property of the Estate	11 U.S.C. §362(a)(4)
	12.1.5	Acts to Perfect Liens upon Property of the Debtor	11 U.S.C. §362(a)(5)
	12.1.6	Any Act to Collect a Prepetition Claim	11 U.S.C. §362(a)(6)
	12.1.7	The Making of Setoffs	11 U.S.C. §362(a)(7)
	12.1.8	Proceedings before the United States Tax Court	11 U.S.C. §362(a)(8)
12.2	COMMON ACTIONS EXCEPTED FROM THE AUTOMATIC STAY		
	12.2.1	Criminal Prosecutions	11 U.S.C. §362(b)(1)
	12.2.2	Collection of Domestic Support Obligations	11 U.S.C. §362(b)(2)
	12.2.3	Lien Perfection within Statutory Grace Period	11 U.S.C. §362(b)(3)
	12.2.4	Governmental Proceedings to Enforce Police or Regulatory Powers Other than Enforcement of Money Judgments	11 U.S.C. §362(b)(4)
	12.2.5	Limited Setoffs in Commodity Broker or Stockbroker Proceedings	11 U.S.C. §362(b)(6), (7)
	12.2.6	HUD Foreclosures Subject to National Housing Act	11 U.S.C. §362(b)(8)
	12.2.7	Issuance of a Notice of Tax Deficiency, Audit, Demand for Returns or Assessment	11 U.S.C. §362(b)(9)

		Authority
12.2.8	Expired Nonresidential Real Property Lease	11 U.S.C. §362(b)(10)
12.2.9	Retirement Loan Repayments	11 U.S.C. §362(b)(19)
12.2.10	Residential Evictions	11 U.S.C. §362(b)(22)

12.3 MOTION FOR RELIEF FROM AUTOMATIC STAY[56]

12.3.1 Moving Party

1. Notice of motion
2. Motion
3. Declaration of provable value
4. Exhibits
   a. promissory note
   b. document evidencing security interest (UCC-1, mortgage, or trust deed)
   c. appraisal
5. Any other document required by local rule

12.3.2 Opposing Party

1. Request for hearing
2. Declaration or affidavits in opposition
3. Points and authorities
4. Exhibit: appraisals
5. Any other document required by local rule

12.3.3 Motion to Impose Stay for Cause Shown

1. Serial filings	11 U.S.C. §362(c)(3), (4)
2. Statement of Intention	11 U.S.C. §362(h)
3. Small Business Cases	11 U.S.C. §362 (n)
4. Residential evictions	11 U.S.C. §362(b)(22), (l)

12.4 MOTION TIME LIMITS (11 U.S.C. §362(e))

12.4.1 Hearing Dates

1. Preliminary hearing within 30 days of filing motion
2. Final hearing within 30 days preliminary hearing

12.4.2 Length of Stay (30/30/30 Rule)

1. Terminates 30 days after motion filed, if unopposed
2. Terminates 30 days after preliminary hearing, unless court orders otherwise

56. See chapter 5A supra.

3. Terminates 30 days after final hearing, unless court orders otherwise
4. Terminates 60 days from filing of motion in individual cases unless the parties or court orders otherwise.

DISCUSSION QUESTIONS

1. What is a contested matter? Adversary proceeding?
2. Can more than one motion or adversary proceeding be pending within a bankruptcy proceeding at the same time?
3. What is the purpose of the automatic stay?
4. What activities are subject to the automatic stay?
5. What activities are not subject to the automatic stay?
6. How long does the automatic stay remain in effect? What is the effect of a discharge on the automatic stay?
7. Describe the procedure used for obtaining relief from the automatic stay.
8. What is adequate protection? Why is a secured creditor entitled to adequate protection?
9. Describe the situations in which a debtor may want to file a motion to impose the automatic stay. Why would a debtor want to do so?

13

Objections to Discharge and Dischargeability of Debts

A. DISTINGUISHING DISCHARGE AND DISCHARGEABILITY OF DEBTS

Most debts are relieved when a debtor receives a discharge. However, some debts are not dischargeable. **Nondischargeable debts** are described in Section 523 of the Code. Within Section 523, specific types of debts will be excepted from the debtor's discharge. That is, the bankruptcy will not relieve the debtor of legal liability on such a claim. The creditor's right to collect the debt will be unaffected by the bankruptcy. In addition, a debtor's exempt property will not be exempt from some nondischargeable debts.[1]

A corollary to Section 523 is the objection to discharge described in Section 727, and thereby applicable only in Chapter 7 proceedings.[2] Under Section 727, a debtor may be denied a discharge completely. That is, notwithstanding the bankruptcy, a denial of discharge will prevent a debtor from obtaining legal relief from **any** debt. This is the critical distinction between sections 523 and 727. Section 523 concerns the dischargeability of specific debts while Section 727 is concerned with the discharge in its entirety. When the debtor's discharge is denied, the debtor will remain legally obligated to pay all prepetition debt.

Section 523 contains 19 specific types of debt that are not dischargeable. Three types of debt will require an affected creditor to initiate an adversary

1. 11 U.S.C. §522(c). See chapter 9 supra.
2. 11 U.S.C. §103. See chapter 2 supra.

proceeding commonly known as a Complaint to Determine the Dischargeability of Debt and to thereafter obtain a judgment that the debt is nondischargeable.[3] For any such affected debts a creditor must file the complaint within a specific deadline or the debt will be discharged.[4] All remaining debts described by Section 523(a) will automatically not be dischargeable. In these latter instances, an affected creditor will not be required to take any action for the debt to be deemed not dischargeable by operation of law. Nondischargeable debts not requiring a judgment of nondischargeability shall be analyzed first. Nondischargeable debts that require a judgment of nondischargeability by the filing of a complaint shall be analyzed second.

B. DEBTS NONDISCHARGEABLE WITHOUT CREDITOR ACTION

Section 523(a)(1) provides that obligations accorded priority status under Section 507(a)(8), or gap claims incurred during the pendency of an involuntary proceeding will not be discharged.[5] These types of debts comprise 507(a)(8) most tax obligations. As a practical matter, this will commonly mean that all payroll taxes, sales taxes, and most income taxes are not dischargeable. The exceptions to this general rule are extremely limited and their analysis is beyond the scope of this basic text. The tax claims that most frequently appear in bankruptcy proceedings will be of the variety that more likely than not will be nondischargeable. Exemptions will not protect otherwise exempt property from a nondischargeable tax claim.[6]

The second type of debt that is automatically nondischargeable is the so-called **unlisted debt**, the subject of Section 523(a)(3). Under this provision, if a debtor fails to list a creditor in the schedules so that the creditor does not receive notice of the filing, then the claim will be nondischargeable if the creditor cannot file a timely proof of claim or otherwise object to dischargeability where there would be ground to do so. Thus, if no claims bar date is set, such as in a no asset proceeding, the claim will still be discharged because there has been no deadline set for creditors to file claims. Actual knowledge of the bankruptcy by a creditor, despite lack of notice, will cause an unlisted debt to be discharged.[7] The rationale behind this provision is that if a creditor is prevented from receiving a dividend due to a lack of notice to permit filing of

3. Bankruptcy Rule 4004; 4007.
4. Bankruptcy Rule 4007.
5. 11 U.S.C. §523(a)(1). See chapter 4, supra and chapter 21 infra.
6. 11 U.S.C. §522(c). See chapter 9 supra.
7. 11 U.S.C. §523(a)(3)(A), (B). See Judd v. Wolfe, 78 F.3d 110 (3d Cir. 1996).

a claim, then the claim should not be discharged. On the other hand, if there has been no prejudice to the creditor, the discharge should be unaffected. For example, Matt Memory files a Chapter 7 and fails to list Barney's Beanery as a creditor. If the proceeding has a claims bar date set and Barney has no actual knowledge of the case so that a timely claim can be filed, the debt will be nondischargeable. In addition, if Barney would have had a claim against Matt for fraud, the unlisted claim might also be nondischargeable. Otherwise, the debt will be discharged.

As a practical matter, it may occasionally become necessary for a creditor to initiate an adversary proceeding to seek a judgment from the Bankruptcy Court that an unlisted debt is nondischargeable so that a state court judge will then believe the creditor in any subsequent action initiated to collect the debt. Conversely, the debtor may seek to initiate a complaint to determine that the debt has indeed been discharged so as to convince a state court that the debt may not be collected. A debtor may always initiate a complaint to determine the dischargeability of a debt.[8]

Similarly, if a creditor's claim is one that would be nondischargeable only if a timely complaint is filed as described above, and the creditor cannot do so due to lack of actual knowledge of the proceeding, the debt will also be nondischargeable.[9] A creditor in this position has been prejudiced because it has been deprived of the ability to file a timely complaint to determine the dischargeability of the debt.

A third type of debt that is nondischargeable without requiring affirmative action by a creditor is a debt for a domestic support obligation, unless the debt has been assigned to another entity except for collection purposes. Domestic support obligations are also accorded a priority status in the payment of claims.[10] For example, suppose a spouse who is meant to receive child support does not receive it and is required to go on temporary aid to needy families (TANF, formerly AFDC) so the children can eat. When the spouse obtains TANF, the spouse is normally required to assign any child support rights to the TANF agency for purposes of seeking collection from the nonpaying spouse. Once the obligation has been assigned, it becomes generally dischargeable. If the support right has not been assigned to a third entity, then the obligation remains nondischargeable and the unpaid spouse may still collect any arrears. Exemptions will not protect otherwise exempt property from a nondischargeable support obligation.[11] Debts incurred in connection with divorce or separation made in accordance with nonbankruptcy law or approved by a governmental unit, that are not domestic support obligations, are also nondischargeable pursuant to Section

8. Bankruptcy Rule 4007(a).
9. 11 U.S.C. §523(a)(3)(B).
10. 11 U.S.C. §523(a)(5). 11 U.S.C. §507(a)(1). See chapter 21 infra.
11. 11 U.S.C. §522(c). See chapter 9 supra.

523(a)(15).This means that separation agreements, property settlements, and decrees of equitable distribution are all automatically nondischargeable. This provision, added by BAPA, radically alters the former law, which held, through case law and the predecessor provision of Section 523(a)(15), that property settlement agreements and similar documents were only nondischargeable if found to be in the nature of support or, for cases filed from October 22, 1994, through the effective date of BAPA, October 17, 2005, if the nonfiling debtor challenged the discharge of the debt as a hardship. The ensuing discussion retains its vitality because the prior law will continue to apply to cases pending before BAPA's effective date.

Prior to October 22, 1994, property settlements were fully dischargeable, although whether or not an obligation was alimony, support, or otherwise was left to the sole discretion of the bankruptcy courts.[12] The courts looked to a number of factors to determine whether a domestic obligation was nondischargeable support or otherwise, including the length of the marriage, interpretation of the document, whether or not the payments were intended for dependents, and so forth.[13]

Under the Bankruptcy Reform Act of 1994, Section 523(a)(15) rendered nondischargeable obligations for other than alimony or support unless the debtor could show sufficient hardship such that discharge of the debt would result in a benefit to the debtor that outweighs the detrimental consequences to a former spouse or child of the debtor. Further, debts subject to this provision were not automatically nondischargeable, but required the nonfiling spouse to affirmatively challenge the discharge. The 2005 amendment to this Code Section makes the debt automatically nondischargeable.

For example, Tom and Kitty Kaat enter into a dissolution agreement which provides that Kitty gets the house, Tom gets the car, and Tom is to pay all family bills and is to pay Kitty a monthly support allowance equal to the monthly mortgage payment on the home. For a case filed under BAPA, all of these debts are likely nondischargeable domestic support obligations in Tom's Chapter 7. Under the prior law, in Tom's Chapter 7, the obligation to pay the family bills is probably dischargeable while the obligation to pay the monthly support allowance is not. Under pre-BAPA Section 523(a)(15), Kitty may object to the dischargeability of Tom's obligation to pay the family bills and the mortgage. If Tom is discharged from the family bills, Kitty may remain liable to the creditors without recourse against Tom, which may also result in a bankruptcy filing by Kitty as well. Also remember that if Tom is in arrears on his support payments when he files his petition, Kitty is unaffected by the automatic stay in her ability to collect the arrears from Tom's postpetition

12. 11 U.S.C. §523(a)(5)(B) as it existed prior to October 17, 2005.
13. In re Nelson, 16 Bankr. 658 (M.D. Tenn. 1981); Shaver v. Shaver, 736 F.2d 1314 (9th Cir. 1984).

wages.[14] Nor will Tom's claimed exemptions protect his property from Kitty's efforts to collect any arrears.[15]

The next type of debt that is automatically nondischargeable is a fine or penalty to a governmental unit other than compensation for actual pecuniary loss. Nevertheless, a penalty relating to a nondischargeable tax will remain nondischargeable. In addition, a fine or penalty assessed more than three years before a Bankruptcy filing will be dischargeable.[16] For example, Tom Toxic is fined $50,000 for the cost of a toxic waste cleanup and is penalized another $25,000 for the violation. Toxic then files a Chapter 7 proceeding. The $50,000 fine is dischargeable because it represents a fine for actual pecuniary loss. The $25,000 penalty fine is not dischargeable.

Student loans are automatically nondischargeable. However, for a student loan to be nondischargeable, the student loan must be made, insured, or guaranteed by a governmental unit or made under a program funded by a governmental unit or a nonprofit institution. The loan will only be dischargeable if the debtor can show that the loan's nondischargeability would impose an undue hardship upon the debtor and the debtor's dependents.[17] As a practical matter, a debtor will normally file any complaint to determine the dischargeability of a student loan obligation because, as has been noted, the debtor may desire to initiate a complaint to determine that an otherwise nondischargeable debt is indeed dischargeable.[18]

The judicial test that has gained the widest acceptance in determining when a student loan is dischargeable on the grounds of undue hardship is known as the *Brunner* test (for Brunner v. New York State Higher Education Services Corp., 831 F.2d 395 (2d Cir. 1987)). Under this approach, a student loan may be discharged if the debtor can pass a three-part test:

1. Based on current income and expenses, the debtor cannot maintain a "minimal" standard of living for the debtor and dependents, if the educational loan is repaid as scheduled;
2. The debtor's present situation is likely to continue for a significant portion of the repayment period; and
3. The debtor has made good faith efforts to repay the educational loans.

---

14. 11 U.S.C. §362(b)(2). See chapter 12 supra.
15. 11 U.S.C. §522(c). 11 U.S.C. §522(f). See chapter 9 supra.
16. 11 U.S.C. §523(a)(7). The pendency of a prior bankruptcy proceeding during this period may act to extend it. Young v. United States, 535 U.S. 43 (2002). See chapter 21 infra.
17. 11 U.S.C. §523(a)(8). Failure to pay an invoice for unpaid tuition may be dischargeable because no loan has been made. See, e.g., In re Mehta, 310 F.3d 308 (3d Cir. 2002).
18. Bankruptcy Rule 4007(a).

The *Brunner* test has been adopted by the Third (In re Faish, 72 F.3d 298 (1995)); Fourth (In re Kasey, 1999 U.S. App. LEXIS 15909, *vacated and remanded*, 187 F.3d 630 (1999)); Fifth (In re Gerhardt, 348 F.3d 89 (2003)); Sixth (In re Hornsby, 144 F.3d 433 (1998)); Seventh (In re Roberson, 999 F.2d 1132 (1993)); Ninth (In re Pena, 155 F.3d 1108 (1998)); and Eleventh (In re Cox 338 F.3d 1238 (2003)) Circuits. The Tenth Circuit has left the matter to individual Bankruptcy Courts (In re Woodcock, 45 F.3d 363 (1995)). In Tennessee Student Assistance Corp. v. Hood, 541 U.S. 440 (2004), the Supreme Court held that the sovereign immunity provided for by the Eleventh Amendment does not prevent debtors from bringing complaints to determine the dischargeability of student loan debts (see page 67, supra, at footnote 25).

For example, Jeff Speccoli obtains a guaranteed student loan, graduates, and then defaults in the loan repayment. Jeff majored in physical education with a specialty in surf instruction. Jeff files a Chapter 7 to discharge the loan. Jeff initiates a complaint to determine the debt's dischargeability on the grounds of undue hardship, citing an inability to earn sufficient income as a surf instructor to repay the debt. Unfortunately for Jeff, this will probably not act to discharge the debt. The inability to earn sufficient income from one's education will not render a student loan dischargeable. On the other hand, if Jeff were involved in an accident and thereby rendered incapable of being a surf instructor, under the *Brunner* test the debt might be held dischargeable only if the court could find that the injury would render him incapable of repaying the loan for a significant portion of the repayment period. The court has broad discretion in this area, but it is generally very difficult for a debtor to obtain discharge of a guaranteed student loan on the grounds of undue hardship.

A mere bank loan obtained by a student for educational purposes, but not subject to a governmental student loan insurance or guarantee program, will be discharged. For instance, Suzie Creamcheese obtains a loan from the XYZ bank and uses it to go to the Zappa School of Composition. Because the loan is not insured or guaranteed, if Suzie subsequently commences a Chapter 7 proceeding, the debt will be discharged.

Section 523(a)(9) makes debts arising as a result of the debtor driving or operating a vessel or aircraft while intoxicated or under the influence of other substances nondischargeable.[19] Prior to enactment of this provision into the Code, it was a common practice for uninsured drivers who had caused damages while driving under the influence to simply file a bankruptcy to discharge any liability to the damaged or injured party. Some case law prior to 1984 attempted to hold that damages caused while driving while intoxi-

19. 11 U.S.C. §523(a)(9).

cated were willful and malicious and denied a discharge of the debt on this ground.[20] This, however, required the damaged party to initiate a complaint objecting to the debt's dischargeability. The enactment of Section 523(a)(9) obviates a party damaged in such circumstances from having to file a separate action to determine the debt's dischargeability.

Section 523(a)(10) provides that any debt or debts nondischargeable in a prior bankruptcy proceeding will remain nondischargeable and no new determination of the debt's dischargeability will have to be made.[21] Section 523(b) further provides that any debt not discharged in a proceeding under the former Bankruptcy Act will remain automatically not discharged in a proceeding filed by the same debtor under the Bankruptcy Code.[22]

Sections 523(a)(11) and (12) make automatically nondischargeable debts due to a federal depository institution where the debtor was in a fiduciary relationship with the financial institution.

Section 523(a)(13) makes nondischargeable restitution awards in criminal cases.

Section 523(a)(14) excepts from discharge debts incurred to pay federal taxes that would otherwise be nondischargeable. For example, Jack Zoran owes $1,000 in federal income taxes. He gets a cash advance on a credit card, pays the taxes, and files Chapter 7 four months later. Under §523(a)(14), because the taxes were not dischargeable, the cash advance becomes nondischargeable. One problem that creditors may have with this provision is the level of proof necessary to show that the loan was obtained to pay a nondischargeable tax claim. Section 523(14A), added in 2005, extends this approach to all other taxing authorities.

Section 523(a)(16) makes nondischargeable any postpetition condominium or cooperative housing assessments that are incurred while the debtor or trustee has an interest in the unit. This provision eliminates a substantial amount of inconsistency and uncertainty that had arisen in the case law regarding this issue before enactment of this provision in 1994.

Section 523(a)(17) makes nondischargeable debts incurred by prisoners for court fees. Section 523(a)(18) makes nondischargeable debts owed to pension or retirement plans, such as a loan from a 401(k) Plan.

Section 523(a)(19) makes nondischargeable debts arising under violations of Federal or State securities laws or regulations. This provision was added to the Code by the Sarbanes-Oxley Act of 2002 (Pub. L. No. 107-204, 116 Stat. 745) in the wake of accounting scandals that occurred in well-publicized bankruptcies such as Enron Corporation and Global Crossing.

---

20. See the discussion concerning §523(a)(6) infra in this chapter.
21. 11 U.S.C. §523(a)(10).
22. 11 U.S.C. §523(b).

C. DEBTS NONDISCHARGEABLE WITH CREDITOR ACTION

Three remaining types of debt that are nondischargeable under Section 523(a) all require a creditor to initiate an adversary proceeding and obtain a judgment denying dischargeability of the debt in question. If no complaint is initiated in a timely manner or the debtor obtains a judgment in its favor, the debt involved will be discharged.[23]

The first and most frequently utilized of these provisions is Section 523(a)(2), which concerns various forms of fraud. Under this provision there are three forms of fraud that may not be dischargeable. The simplest of these is the form of fraud that makes nondischargeable any debt obtained by the use of a materially false written financial statement concerning the debtor or its insider upon which the creditor relies in extending credit and that the debtor has made with the intent to deceive.[24] Simply put, a debt may be held nondischargeable if the debt was incurred by use of an intentionally false written financial statement.

For example, Fred and Wilma go visit their friendly neighborhood finance company to obtain a vacation loan. In completing their financial statement, they omit a $10,000 debt owed to Wilma's parents. Subsequently, Fred and Wilma file a Chapter 7 listing the debt owed to Wilma's parents. The finance company may seek to have the vacation loan debt ruled nondischargeable based on the omission of the $10,000 debt to Wilma's parents in the original loan application.

In situations where a debtor obtains a renewal of credit or borrows additional funds from a creditor, if a new financial statement is obtained that is materially false, then only that portion of the debt representing the new funds borrowed in reliance upon the false written financial statement will be subject to nondischargeability. This is known as the **fresh cash rule.**[25] Using the above example, Fred and Wilma are already indebted to the finance company when they seek the vacation loan. The finance company rewrites the loan, adding in the new funds borrowed. Because the financial statement obtained in connection with the new funds borrowed is false, the original debt will be discharged, but the additional funds borrowed will not be if the creditor timely objects. The creditor's damages from the fraud are only the additional monies borrowed.

A second form of fraud that may be nondischargeable is actual fraud, false pretenses, or a false representation, other than a statement concerning

23. 11 U.S.C. §523(c).
24. 11 U.S.C. §523(a)(2)(B).
25. In re Duncan, 123 Bankr. 383 (C.D. Cal. 1991).

the debtor's or an insider's financial condition.[26] Note that false statements concerning a debtor's financial condition are excluded from this definition. This means that any oral misrepresentation regarding the debtor's financial condition will not by itself constitute grounds for an objection to the discharge of a debt based on fraud. A false written financial statement is covered as described above.

In practice, the sort of actual fraud that seems to be held nondischargeable is fraud so egregious that it would be an injustice to permit a debtor to be relieved from the liability. The necessary elements to prove this form of fraud nondischargeable are the traditional tort elements of fraud: that the debtor has made a knowingly false representation with intent to deceive the creditor, that the creditor has relied on the misrepresentation and has sustained damages as a result.[27] For example, debtor Dimmesdale visits Mr. LaFata, a custom tailor recently emigrated from Italy to the United States. Mr. LaFata makes Dimmesdale a couple of custom suits, and Dimmesdale pays for them. In the process, he convinces Mr. LaFata that he is part owner of a trucking company. However, in reality and unknown to LaFata, Dimmesdale is actually a minister. After paying for the first two suits, Mr. LaFata gives debtor Dimmesdale a charge account. In the space of the next six months, Dimmesdale incurs a debt to Mr. LaFata in excess of $30,000. Meanwhile, Reverend Dimmesdale is continually complimented by his congregants about his beautiful new suits. He tells his congregants that he has met a new tailor who is a real nice guy and that he is being provided the suits for free. Because he is up on the pulpit where many people see him, it is a good promotion for the tailor. Reverend Dimmesdale then files bankruptcy, and LaFata objects to the discharge of the debt due him. The debt is nondischargeable.[28]

In Field v. Mans 516 U.S. 59 (1995), the Supreme Court examined the form of reliance that a plaintiff must prove in a nondischargeability fraud claim brought under 11 U.S.C. §523(a)(2). The Court ruled that a creditor need only prove that reliance was justifiable as opposed to reasonable: ". . . The difference between justifiable and reasonable reliance is that the former is a subjective standard, whereas the latter is an objective standard of conduct." In *Field*, Mans transferred property in violation of a due-upontransfer clause and then sought the lender's consent, which was not given. At a later date, the debtor filed for bankruptcy. Only then did the lender learn that the property had been improperly transferred, wiping out the lender's position in the collateral. The lender had never reviewed the relevant real estate records to determine whether the unconsented-to transfer had taken place. In reversing

26. 11 U.S.C. §523(a)(2)(A).
27. In re Britton, 950 F.2d 602 (9th Cir. 1991).
28. See LaFata v. Burklow, 60 Bankr. 728 (S.D. Cal. 1986).

the lower courts, which had ruled in Mans's favor, and in ruling that Field's reliance upon the debtor's representations need only be justifiable, the Supreme Court rejected the notion that a lender must always investigate the veracity of a debtor's representations.

All damages resulting from the debtor's fraud are nondischargeable. In Cohen v. De La Cruz, 523 U.S. 213 (1998), a debtor landlord had been found liable for willfully and intentionally violating a rent control ordinance. The damages awarded by the trial court included treble damages for violation of the New Jersey Consumer Fraud Act. The Supreme Court held that once it is established that specific money or property has been obtained by fraud, "any debt" arising therefrom is excepted from discharge.

In Archer v. Warner, 538 U.S. 314 (2003), the Archers sued the Warners for fraud in connection with the sale of a business. The parties entered into a settlement and release agreement. After performing most of the settlement agreement, the Warners filed bankruptcy. The Archers, as creditors, contended that the remaining claim was nondischargeable as a result of fraud. The Warners, as debtors, contended that the settlement agreement created an entirely new debt that was not obtained fraudulently. The Supreme Court held that the prebankruptcy settlement did not prevent the creditor from seeking a determination of dischargeability in the debtor's subsequent bankruptcy.

A third form of fraud concerns debtors who have a problem sometimes colloquially referred to as "credit carditis." This problem is also known as the prepetition "shopping spree." The essence of the problem pertains to debtors who, on the eve of bankruptcy, purchase luxury goods on credit or make credit purchases up to maximum credit limits and then file a Chapter 7 claiming all the goods purchased as exempt. A similar situation arises where a debtor obtains cash advances on credit cards immediately prior to filing, spends the money, and then files a Chapter proceeding. In each instance, either the goods are exempt or the money is gone but the debt has been discharged. This was the situation prior to 1984.

Section 523(a)(2)(C) was enacted in an effort to help resolve this perceived abuse of the bankruptcy system by debtors. Under this provision, consumer debts owed to a single creditor totalling more than $500 for luxury goods or services incurred within 90 days prior to filing are presumed nondischargeable. This means that if a creditor can demonstrate transactions falling within the description, the objection to dischargeability is considered to have been proven and the burden of proof will then shift to the debtor to prove that the debt is dischargeable. Additionally, cash advances totalling more than $750 and incurred within 70 days prior to filing are also presumed nondischargeable. Thus, a debt incurred by obtaining a large cash advance from an automatic teller immediately prior to filing a bankruptcy may be presumed to be nondischargeable.

This subsection defines *luxury goods or services* as goods or services not reasonably necessary to support or maintain the debtor or a dependent of the debtor. Thus, a cash advance obtained by the debtor at the racetrack is probably nondischargeable, but if the debtor can show that the money has been used to purchase food, medicine, or other necessaries, the debt may be dischargeable. Alternatively, if $500 or more is spent on a 48-inch stereo video monitor, the debt is probably nondischargeable, but if the purchases are for summer clothes for the kids, for blue jeans and shorts and socks, the debt may be dischargeable.[29]

The text, however, reflects amounts provided for by BAPA rather than the adjustments that otherwise became effective on April 1, 2004. These amounts, applicable to cases filed before October 17, 2005, are $1,225 and $750, respectively. The time period, in theses instances, is 60 days.

The second type of debt that is nondischargeable only upon the obtaining of a judgment of nondischargeability is for fraud or defalcation while acting in a fiduciary capacity, embezzlement, or larceny. For instance, a trustee who takes trust money, goes to Tahiti, and then files a bankruptcy will find that the debt thus created is nondischargeable. A state court receiver who absconds to another state with receivership property and then files a bankruptcy will find the debt created to be nondischargeable. An employee who falsifies business records while embezzling funds from the business and who then goes bankrupt will also find that this debt is nondischargeable.[30]

Finally, willful and malicious injury by the debtor to another or another's property may also be nondischargeable, but the creditor must file a complaint in order to determine the issue.[31] In Kawaauhau v. Geiger, 523 U.S. 57 (1998), the Supreme Court held that "willfull and malicious" means that the actor must act with the intent to cause injury to become nondischargeable. In this case, Geiger had been found liable for medical malpractice and reckless conduct, but not for a malicious act. The Court found that gross negligence or recklessness does not satisfy the statutory standard.

Many intentional torts will not be dischargeable. However, just as in the instance of actual fraud discussed above, the willful and malicious injury has to be such that it would be an injustice to permit the debtor to be

29. 11 U.S.C. §523(a)(2)(C). Section 104(b), added in 1994, accounts for the effects of inflation on these amounts at three-year intervals. The first adjustment took place in April 1998.
30. 11 U.S.C. §523(a)(4).
31. 11 U.S.C. §523(a)(6).

freely relieved of liability for the wrong committed. Keep in mind that issues of nondischargeability are not as concerned with the underlying issue of liability so much as they are concerned with whether, despite the bankruptcy filing, the debt created should be relieved through the bankruptcy system. Certainly, though, if there is no underlying liability, then there is no debt for which to determine the dischargeability.

D. COMPLAINTS TO DETERMINE DISCHARGEABILITY OF A DEBT

Federal Rule of Bankruptcy Procedure 4007 contains rules regarding who may file and the time limits for initiating a **complaint to determine the dischargeability of a debt**. As already noted, the debtor or any affected creditor may initiate such a complaint.[32] A debtor may desire to initiate a complaint to seek a judgment that a debt that may be automatically nondischargeable is in fact discharged. For example, a debtor may file an adversary proceeding to seek a judgment that a student loan is dischargeable on the grounds of undue hardship. A complaint to determine the dischargeability of a debt that is normally considered automatically nondischargeable may be filed at any time, and a bankruptcy proceeding may be reopened to allow for this determination to be made.[33]

On the other hand, where the determination involves the type of debt that requires the creditor to initiate a complaint, the rules contain strict time limits on the initiation of such complaints. If no complaint is timely initiated, the debt will be discharged.[34] In a Chapter 7 or 11, the complaint must be filed within 60 days of the date first set for the meeting of creditors held pursuant to Section 341.[35] In a Chapter 13, the deadline is set when the debtor applies for a discharge upon completion of a Chapter 13 plan.[36] In either situation, the time period may be extended by motion or voluntary agreement, provided that the motion or agreement is made before the expiration of the deadline set for the filing of the complaint.[37]

If a creditor objects to the discharge of a consumer debt on the grounds of fraud and if the debt is found dischargeable, the court may award costs and attorneys' fees to the debtor if the court finds that the creditor's position

32. Bankruptcy Rule 4007(a).
33. 11 U.S.C. §350; Bankruptcy Rule 4007(b).
34. 11 U.S.C. §523(c).
35. Bankruptcy Rule 4007(c).
36. Bankruptcy Rule 4007(d).
37. Bankruptcy Rule 4007(c); 4007(d).

was not substantially justified.[38] The purpose of this provision is to deter creditors from initiating unfounded objections to dischargeability solely in order to gain an undue economic advantage over a debtor.

In Grogan v. Garner, 498 U.S. 279 (1991), the Supreme Court ruled that in complaints objecting to the dischargeability of debts, the burden of proof is by a preponderance of the evidence. This ruling reversed the law of many circuits that had required a plaintiff to prove its case by clear and convincing evidence to prevail.

In *Grogan*, supra, the creditor had obtained a jury verdict for fraud, which was affirmed on appeal. After the debtor filed Chapter 11, the creditor filed a timely complaint objecting to the debt's dischargeability pursuant to 11 U.S.C. §523(a)(2)(A), actual fraud. The Bankruptcy Court, relying on the jury verdict, held the debt to be nondischargeable. The Eighth Circuit Court of Appeals reversed, but the Supreme Court reinstated the trial court's holding. The Court noted that the Code does not specify a burden of proof standard in dischargeability complaints. The Court also rejected the argument that the higher level of proof required by a "clear and convincing" standard is necessary to aid in a debtor's fresh start.

E. OBJECTING TO DISCHARGE

While Section 523 affects only the dischargeability of certain specific debts, under Section 727 a debtor may have a discharge completely denied. A debtor whose discharge is denied under Section 727(a) will not receive the debtor relief of legal release from any debt. Although Section 727 appears only in Chapter 7, it is also applicable in Chapter 11 proceedings, but not in Chapter 12 or 13 proceedings.[39]

Only individual debtors receive Chapter 7 discharges. Corporations and partnerships do not.[40] A Chapter 7 discharge may be obtained only once every eight years, and may not be obtained within six years of receiving a Chapter 12 or Chapter 13 discharge unless the Plan provided for payment of at least 70 percent of unsecured claims.[41]

So, if a debtor files a bankruptcy petition and has received a discharge within the past six years, the debtor is not entitled to a discharge in the second proceeding. A debtor may also waive a discharge if the waiver is in

38. 11 U.S.C. §523(d).
39. 11 U.S.C. §103; 11 U.S.C. §1141(d)(3)(c). See chapter 2 supra and chapters 25-26 infra.
40. 11 U.S.C. §727(a)(1).
41. 11 U.S.C. §727(a)(8); 11 U.S.C. §727(a)(9).

writing executed after the bankruptcy filing and is approved by the court.[42]

Most of the remaining provisions of Section 727(a) deny debtors a discharge due to activities that can be most succinctly described as inequitable conduct. That is, these provisions will deny a discharge if the debtor's conduct is such that it would be unjust to grant the debtor a discharge. A discharge may be denied if the debtor has concealed, transferred, or destroyed records or property of the estate with the intent to hinder, delay, or defraud creditors within one year prior to filing.[43]

A discharge may be denied if the debtor knowingly and fraudulently makes a false oath or withholds records relating to the debtor's financial condition from the trustee.[44] A discharge may be denied if the debtor refuses to obey court orders in connection with the case or fails to testify unless immunity has been granted.[45] The denial of a discharge on the grounds set forth in this paragraph may also result in criminal violations under federal law.[46]

A discharge may be denied if the debtor fails to satisfactorily explain any loss or deficiency of assets to meet the debtor's liabilities.[47] For instance, Mac MacHeath files a set of Statements and Schedules describing no assets and no prior businesses but listing claims of $10 million, and he fails to explain how he acquired $10 million of debt while retaining no assets and not being engaged in business. Someone does not normally acquire substantial debt without being engaged in business or retaining any assets without explanation. In this circumstance, the discharge may be denied.

BAPA adds Section 727(a)(11), which requires individual debtors to complete a postpetition financial management course in order to receive a discharge. Thus, coupled with the requirement to undergo credit counseling as a prerequisite to filing a petition (see chapter 4 supra), individual bankruptcy debtors must now undergo each of pre- and postpetition financial counseling, the former as a prerequisite to filing, and the latter as a prerequisite to receiving a discharge.

A discharge may be denied to a debtor who destroys, conceals, mutilates, falsifies, or fails to keep books and records from which the debtor's financial condition may be ascertained, unless such acts are justified under the circumstances of the case.[48] For instance, most individual consumer

42. 11 U.S.C. §727(a)(10).
43. 11 U.S.C. §727(a)(2).
44. 11 U.S.C. §727(a)(4).
45. 11 U.S.C. §727(a)(6).
46. 18 U.S.C. §152.
47. 11 U.S.C. §727(a)(5).
48. 11 U.S.C. §727(a)(3).

debtors do not keep many financial records. There is no law requiring individuals to maintain checkbooks. Low-income debtors may not have earned sufficient income to require the filing of income tax returns. But most individual debtors do have some files at home with perhaps some bills, checkbook registers, and prior year income tax returns. An individual ordinary consumer debtor cannot be expected or required to have many more records than this. Many individuals do have substantially more personal financial records in their possession, but at a minimum, recent bills, checkbook registers, and tax returns are all that can or should be expected.

The rule is that a debtor should be able to produce the minimum amount of records necessary or required by nonbankruptcy law to support the type of financial activity in which the debtor has been engaged prior to the bankruptcy filing.[49] Thus, if the debtor is Grandma Smith, who subsists solely on Social Security and pays all of her expenses by cash or money order, she should not be denied a discharge because she does not keep books and records. She is keeping the books and records necessary to support the activities in which she is engaged, which in this case is virtually none. However, if Grandma Smith has $10 million of debts and makes the same representations, her discharge may be denied.

On the other hand, if a debtor is engaged in business, there are certain minimum records that the debtor will be required to maintain under nonbankruptcy law. Payroll and payroll tax records are required by both federal and local law. Sales tax records and sales records will be required to be maintained where there are local sales taxes to pay. If the debtor has not maintained these records or cannot adequately justify their lack of existence, the discharge may be denied.

A discharge may be denied a debtor who has committed any of the above described acts within a year prior to filing, during the pendency of the debtor's bankruptcy proceeding, or in connection with another bankruptcy proceeding concerning an insider.[50] For example, Mac MacHeath files a Chapter 7 for his corporation Mac's Knives, Inc. The corporation has no records whatsoever. MacHeath then files his own personal Chapter 7. His personal discharge may be denied due to his failure to have kept records for his bankrupt insider corporation.

49. In re Underhill, 82 F.2d 258 (2d Cir. 1936); Stewart Enterprises v. Morton, 621 F.2d 968 (9th Cir. 1980). See also, In re Costello, 299 Bankr. 882 (Bankr. N.D. Ill. 2003) where the debtor's discharge was denied because his only explanation as to the unavailability of records was that mice ate them.

50. 11 U.S.C. §727(a)(7).

F. COMPLAINTS OBJECTING TO DISCHARGE

Any creditor, the trustee, or the United States Trustee may file a **complaint objecting to a discharge** under Section 727(a).[51] The objection is made by filing an adversary proceeding objecting to the discharge within 60 days of the date first set for the creditors meeting under Section 341(a) in a Chapter 7, or no later than the date first set for the confirmation hearing on the debtor's plan of reorganization in a Chapter 11 proceeding.[52] An extension of this time period can be obtained for cause if a motion for the extension is made before expiration of the time periods permitted by the rules.[53] Unless a timely complaint is filed, the debtor will receive a discharge.[54]

In Kontrick v. Ryan, 540 U.S. 443 (2004), the Supreme Court examined whether the sixty-day time limit is jurisdictional or subject to waiver if not raised until after a trial on the merits. In this case, Ryan obtained a judgment against Kontrick. Kontrick intentionally concealed his assets from Ryan and admitted as much. Although Ryan filed his complaint objecting to discharge in a timely manner, he amended the complaint to add an additional claim after expiration of the sixty-day time limit. After losing at trial, Kontrick moved the court to dismiss the added claim because it had not been filed in a timely manner. Ryan contended that Kontrick's earlier failure to have raised the issue acted to waive the defense. The Supreme Court held that the sixty-day time limit to file the complaint objecting to discharge is not jurisdictional and is waived if not raised until after the matter has been litigated. Although involving an objection to discharge, the scope of this holding will likely apply to complaints objecting to the dischargeability of debts subject to FRBP 4007, since the operative language in the applicable rules is identical.

A discharge may be revoked if fraudulently obtained and the fraud is not known until after the discharge has been granted, if the debtor fails to turn over property of the estate subsequent to receiving a discharge, or if the debtor fails to cooperate in a random audit (see chapter 7, supra). The trustee, a creditor, or the United States Trustee may file a complaint to revoke the discharge within one year of the original discharge date where the ground of revocation is fraud. Where the ground for revocation is a failure to turn over estate property, the same parties may initiate a complaint before the later of one year after the discharge is received or one year after

51. 11 U.S.C. §727(c).
52. Bankruptcy Rule 4004(a).
53. Bankruptcy Rule 4004(b).
54. Bankruptcy Rule 4004(c).

the proceeding is closed.[55] Normally, the later date will be one year after the proceeding is closed.

Summary

Certain debts will not be affected by a debtor's discharge. These debts are known as nondischargeable debts. Occasionally, a debtor may be denied a discharge. When a debt is nondischargeable or a debtor is denied a discharge, the bankruptcy will not provide the debtor with legal relief from a specific debt in the former instance and from all debt in the latter.

The following debts are nondischargeable without an affected creditor being required to take any affirmative action.

Debt	*Code Section*
priority tax claims	523(a)(1)
unlisted debts	523(a)(3)
domestic support obligations	523(a)(5), (15)
certain fines and penalties	523(a)(7)
guaranteed student loans	523(a)(8)
damages from DWI conviction	523(a)(9)
debt nondischarged in prior bankruptcy	523(a)(10)
financial institution fraud	523(a)(11), (12)
restitution award	523(a)(13)
loans obtained to pay nondischargeable taxes	523(a)(14), (14A)
postpetition homeowner's assessments	523(a)(16)
prisoner court costs	523(a)(17)
pension plan loans	523(a)(18)
debts arising from federal or state securities law violations	523(a)(19)

A creditor may object to the discharge of the following debts:

Debt	*Code Section*
fraud	523(a)(2)
intentional fraud	523(a)(2)(A)
false written financial statement	523(a)(2)(B)
limited prepetition credit transactions	523(a)(2)(C)
defalcation, larceny, embezzlement	523(a)(4)
willful and malicious injury	523(a)(6)

55. 11 U.S.C. §727(d)(e).

A creditor objects to the dischargeability of a debt by filing a complaint to determine the dischargeability of the debt. The creditor's object is to obtain a judgment that the debt is not dischargeable. The complaint must be filed within 60 days of the date first set for the meeting of creditors pursuant to Section 341(a) or the debt will be discharged.

A debtor may also initiate a complaint to determine dischargeability of a debt and may do so at any time. A debtor might want to initiate such a complaint to obtain a judgment that an automatically nondischargeable debt is, in fact, dischargeable.

Only individuals are entitled to a Chapter 7 discharge; corporations and partnerships are not. A Chapter 7 discharge may only be obtained once every eight years. A discharge can be denied if a debtor has engaged in various sorts of inequitable conduct, including a failure to maintain proper books and records or for concealing assets. Individual debtors will be denied a discharge if they fail to complete a postpetition financial management course.

KEY TERMS

complaint objecting to a discharge

complaint to determine dischargeability of a debts

fresh cash rule

nondischargeable debts

unlisted debt

DISCUSSION QUESTIONS

1. What is the difference between an objection to a debtor's discharge and an objection to the dischargeability of a debt?

2. Why are certain debts nondischargeable without an affected creditor being required to initiate an adversary proceeding? Identify these debts.

3. What debts become nondischargeable only by a creditor commencing a complaint objecting to dischargeability of the debt?

4. What are the deadlines for initiating a complaint to determine dischargeability of a debt or an objection to the debtor's discharge?

5. Why would a debtor desire to initiate a complaint to determine dischargeability of a debt?

6. Under what circumstances can a debtor be denied a discharge?

14

Property of the Estate and Turnover Complaints

A. PROPERTY OF THE ESTATE

The concept of **property of the estate** has been mentioned frequently but has not been previously discussed. Just as exemptions and discharge are fundamental to debtor relief, the concept of property of the estate is fundamental to a trustee's administration of an estate and is fundamental to the rights of creditors affected by a bankruptcy filing. Property of the estate not claimed exempt is subject to administration by a trustee by way of liquidation or abandonment of the property. With regard to secured creditors, the automatic stay protects property of the estate from foreclosure or repossession. With regard to unsecured creditors, the proceeds obtained from any liquidation of estate property by the trustee represent the funds that will ultimately be available for a distribution of dividends to the creditors. The basic right of a trustee to recover property of the estate is known as a turnover complaint. Additional rights, commonly known as **avoiding powers**, have been provided to the trustee to permit the further recovery of property of the estate.[1]

Section 541 defines and describes *property of the estate*. The commencement of a proceeding creates an estate. This occurs whether the proceeding is voluntary or involuntary and irrespective of the Chapter proceeding filed.[2] The basic concept is that all property in which the estate has an interest, wherever located and by whomever held, constitutes property of the estate as defined by Section 541.[3] In short, property commonly

1. See chapters 15 through 17 infra with regard to the trustee's avoiding powers.
2. 11 U.S.C. §541(a).
3. 11 U.S.C. §541(a)(1). For example, prepetition lottery winnings are property of the estate. See In re Pizzi, 153 Bankr. 357 (S.D. Fla. 1993).

known as the assets of an estate is synonymous with property of the estate. Even exempt property constitutes property of the estate, although such property is not available for the payment of creditor dividends.[4] The balance of Section 541 makes an effort to clarify and create specific exclusions to the rather broad definition of *estate property* provided for by the Bankruptcy Code.

In a community property jurisdiction, all interests of the debtor and debtor's spouse in community property as of the commencement of the proceeding that is under the sole, equal, or joint management and control of the debtor or that is liable for an allowable claim against the debtor or both the debtor and the debtor's spouse constitutes property of the estate.[5] More simply put, property of the estate generally includes the community property interests of a nonfiling debtor spouse. For example, if a debtor in a community property jurisdiction files a bankruptcy proceeding but the debtor's spouse does not, all community property is still normally considered to be property of the estate.

The above rule as to community property is consistent with the treatment of community debt and the debtor's discharge. It should be recalled that community debts will normally be discharged as to the community property of both spouses.[6] It is possible to file a Chapter 7 proceeding for one spouse in a community property jurisdiction and effectively gain a discharge for both spouses as to all community debts for which any community property may be liable. However, the separate property of the nonfiling spouse will remain liable for the otherwise discharged community debts and the automatic stay will be ineffective as to the nonfiling spouse, who may still potentially be the subject of creditor action to collect the debts. Nevertheless, any judgment obtained against the nonfiling spouse will not be enforceable against community property that has been property of the bankruptcy estate.

Property of the estate also includes any property recovered by the trustee through use of the avoiding powers or by operation of any other Code Section.[7] For instance, if the court finds that counsel has received excessive compensation under Section 329(b), any portion of the fee ordered to be refunded by counsel becomes property of the estate.

Section 541(a)(5) concerns certain limited interests in property acquired by a debtor within 180 days after filing a bankruptcy so long as the property in question would have been property of the estate had the interest existed on

4. See Historical and Revision Note to Section 541. See also 11 U.S.C. §522(b) and chapter 9 supra.
5. 11 U.S.C. §541(a)(2).
6. 11 U.S.C. §524(a)(3). See chapter 7 supra.
7. 11 U.S.C. §541(a)(3)(4).

PROPERTY OF THE ESTATE

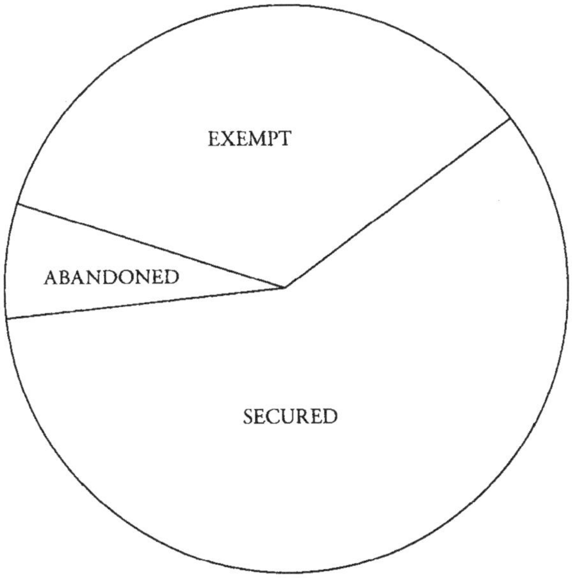

All property in which the debtor has a legal or equitable interest at the commencement of a case is property of the estate (11 U.S.C. §541(a)). During the course of the case, the trustee must "administer" all the property. The figure illustrates a typical consumer no-asset Chapter 7 where all property is either collateral for one or more secured creditors (see chapter 21 infra), exempt (see chapter 9 supra), or abandoned by the trustee as burdensome or of inconsequential value to the estate (see chapter 20 infra).

the date of filing. These limited interests are property a debtor becomes entitled to receive by bequest, devise, or inheritance; property that a debtor becomes entitled to receive by way of a property settlement, agreement, or interlocutory or final divorce decree with the debtor's spouse; and property that the debtor becomes entitled to receive as a beneficiary of a life insurance policy or a death benefit plan.[8] By virtue of this subsection, Congress has expressed a policy that potential windfalls to the debtor received within 180

8. 11 U.S.C. §541(a)(5).

days of filing shall be made available to pay a dividend to the creditors. Note, however, the irony that true windfalls, such as a lottery jackpot, are not subject to this provision. Thus, a lottery jackpot won by the debtor ten days after a bankruptcy filing from a lottery ticket purchased postpetition will not be available to satisfy the claims of prepetition creditors unless the debtor desires it. Of course, if the debtor purchased the winning lottery ticket prepetition, the winnings would be property of the estate.[9] On the other hand, if the debtor's grandmother dies 175 days after the bankruptcy filing, any inheritance will be property of the bankruptcy estate.

An important clarification to the concept of property of the estate is that items that may best be called "the fruit of the tree" are also property of the estate. Proceeds, product, offspring, or rent from property of the estate will also be property of the estate.[10] More simply put, property generated from property of the estate will itself be property of the estate. For example, the proceeds earned by an operating business after a Chapter 11 filing are property of the estate. If a fruit orchard is part of an estate, the fruit growing on the trees is part of the estate. If the debtor owns a sheep ranch, the lambs born after the filing are property of the estate. Property produced from estate property will itself be estate property.

Earnings from personal services performed by an individual debtor after the bankruptcy filing are not property of the estate in a Chapter 7. This exception applies in individual Chapter 11, 12 and 13 proceedings. Simply put, an individual debtor's postpetition wages are not property of the estate.[11] This rule applies to self-employment earnings for personal services as well as to a wage earner's paycheck. For example, a doctor's postpetition fees earned for providing services to patients are not property of the estate in the doctor's Chapter 7. If the debtor is a real estate agent, a commission earned postfiling is not property of the estate. If the debtor is a movie star or professional athlete bound to a prefiling long-term contract, the fee earned for personal services rendered after the bankruptcy filing is not property of the estate.[12]

There is one major exception to the rule that postpetition earnings for personal services are not property of the estate. This exception applies in individual Chapter 11, 12 and 13 proceedings. In these Chapters, postpetition earnings *are* considered to be property of the estate.[13] The reason for this rule is that the debtor's postfiling earnings generally comprise the source of distributions to creditors in individual reorganization cases. It is

---

9. See In re Pizzi, note 3 supra.
10. 11 U.S.C. §541(a)(6).
11. 11 U.S.C. §541(a)(6).
12. In re Tia Carrere, 64 Bankr. 156 (C.D. Cal. 1986).
13. 11 U.S.C. §1115; 11 U.S.C. §1207(a)(2); 11 U.S.C. §1306(a)(2). See chapters 23 and 27 infra.

logical that the source of creditor repayment itself be considered estate property.

Property of the estate does *not* include any power that the debtor may exercise solely for the benefit of another entity.[14] For example, if a debtor possesses a power of attorney exercisable for a third party, the power of attorney is not property of the estate.

Any interest that a debtor may claim to have in a nonresidential lease of real property the term of which has expired prior to filing or during the proceeding is not property of the estate or ceases to be property of the estate in the latter event.[15] Thus, the landlord of an expired nonresidential lease need not seek relief from the automatic stay to be able to remove the lessee from the premises subject to the expired lease. In the first place, the landlord's action is excepted from the automatic stay. In the second place, the automatic stay is relieved as to an act against property when the property ceases to be property of the estate.[16] A nonresidential lease would normally be considered a commercial lease in a nonbankruptcy environment. BAPA provides additional exclusions from property of the estate, including certain educational IRA or TAP funds, some retirement funds, and property that has been pledged as collateral for a loan. This latter category comprises pawned property.[17]

Sometimes a trust or other transactional document contains **ipso facto clauses** that restrict a transfer of or purport to forfeit an interest in property upon the holder of the interest becoming insolvent or commencing a bankruptcy proceeding. These ipso facto clauses are not enforceable in a bankruptcy proceeding to defeat the holder's property interest. A debtor's interest in such a transaction will remain property of the estate.[18] For example, Thurston Howell III gives his nephew Gilligan title to an island. The deed contains language that renders Gilligan's title to the island forfeited if Gilligan becomes insolvent or files a bankruptcy proceeding. If Gilligan then files a bankruptcy, the forfeiture clause will be unenforceable. Gilligan's trustee may be able to sell the island to pay a dividend to Gilligan's creditors.

On the other hand, **spendthrift trusts** are enforceable in bankruptcy proceedings, and the principal property of a valid spendthrift trust will not be considered property of a bankruptcy estate.[19] A spendthrift trust exists when the trust instrument contains provisions restricting the transfer of a beneficial

14. 11 U.S.C. §541(b)(1).
15. 11 U.S.C. §541(b)(2).
16. 11 U.S.C. §362(b)(10); 11 U.S.C. §362(c). See chapter 12 supra.
17. 11 U.S.C. §541(b)(5), (6), (7), (8).
18. 11 U.S.C. §541(c)(1).
19. 11 U.S.C. §541(c)(2).

interest in the trust. Spendthrift trusts are trusts that are created to prevent creditors of the trust beneficiaries from seizing the trust's principal assets to pay the beneficiaries' debts. One form of spendthrift trust is created to preserve a family fortune from the financial indiscretions of the family members who are its beneficiaries. For example, Richie Rich has a very bad day in Las Vegas and is left with no choice but to file a Chapter 7 to discharge the legal gambling debts owed to his casino creditors. He is the beneficiary of a valid spendthrift trust. Neither the trustee nor the creditors can invade the trust principal to satisfy Richie's debts. However, the income that Richie receives from the trust for at least 180 days after filing may become property of the estate because the income is not earnings from personal services and is likely an interest from bequest, devise, or inheritance.[20]

A second form of spendthrift trust may come into existence through a qualified pension plan containing so-called spendthrift provisions. In 1992, in Patterson v. Shumate, 504 U.S. 753, the Supreme Court held that a debtor's beneficial interest in an Employment Retirement Income Security Act (ERISA) qualified pension plan is excluded from property of the estate.

Mr. Shumate was one of 400 participants in the Coleman Furniture Corporation pension plan. The plan qualified as an ERISA plan and contained spendthrift provisions. In 1984 Shumate became a Chapter 7 debtor. Shumate's trustee attempted to recover Shumate's interest in the pension plan as estate property. The district court ruled in the trustee's favor. Its decision was based on its interpretation that the phrase "applicable nonbankruptcy law" used in section 541(c)(2) meant only state law, not federal law. The Supreme Court reversed the district court, holding that the phrase "applicable nonbankruptcy law" includes federal nonbankruptcy law such as ERISA. Accordingly, a valid spendthrift provision in an ERISA plan will exclude the debtor's beneficial interest from being considered property of the estate.

Finally, property in which the debtor holds bare legal title only is property of the estate only to the extent of the debtor's interest in it.[21] For example, if the debtor is a real estate trust deed or mortgage company servicing loans for third parties, the debtor's interest will extend only to any fees the debtor may be entitled to receive in connection with the loan servicing agreements. Any interest in the proceeds of the notes payable to nondebtor third parties would not be property of the estate.

---

20. 11 U.S.C. §541(a)(5). See above discussion.
21. 11 U.S.C. §541(d).

B. TURNOVER COMPLAINTS

Having defined *property of the estate*, the next task is to describe how a trustee or debtor-in-possession acquires the property for purposes of liquidation or other administration. Recall that recovery of estate property for purposes of liquidation and administration is an important aspect of the trustee's duties.[22] When a bankruptcy is filed, estate property will be in one of two places: either in the possession or control of the debtor or in the possession or control of third parties. The Code provides the trustee with various rights that allow the trustee to recover all estate property for purposes of administration. Property of the estate is recoverable by a trustee through the use of a **turnover complaint** or through exercise of the trustee's various avoiding powers.

The concept of turnover is simple. Someone has property of the estate: It may be the debtor, it may be a third party, it could be anyone. If the third party refuses to voluntarily turn the property over to the trustee, the court can order the third party to turn it over. The concept is this simple. The trustee has an almost absolute right to recover property of the estate for the benefit of creditors.[23] The exceptions to this rule are quite limited. An entity without actual knowledge or notice of the bankruptcy that transfers property of the estate to an entity other than the trustee does not later have to turn the property over to the trustee.[24] For instance, XYZ, Inc., files a Chapter 7. XYZ's customers continue to send in their payments to XYZ instead of to the trustee. Whether or not the trustee ultimately receives the payments as property of the estate the payments are considered to have been made. An insurance company with automatic premium payment requirements may pay itself from property of the estate to the extent the payment is required to pay a premium or carry out a nonforfeiture option.[25] Any applicable setoff right may also limit a trustee's turnover rights.[26]

Attorneys or accountants in possession of the books or records of an estate can be directed to turn over such records to the trustee. Although, in limited instances, traditional privileges may be utilized to protect the materials from turnover, in cases involving entities other than individuals, the trustee normally becomes the holder of any applicable privilege.[27]

---

22. See chapter 10 supra.
23. 11 U.S.C. §542(a).
24. 11 U.S.C. §542(c).
25. 11 U.S.C. §542(d).
26. 11 U.S.C. §542(b). See chapter 17 infra.
27. 11 U.S.C. §542(e); 11 U.S.C. §521(4); Commodity Futures Trading Commn. v. Weintraub, 471 U.S. 343 (1985).

Special rules govern the turnover of estate property in the hands of a **custodian**.[28] In this instance, the custodian is a third party with custody of the property prior to the bankruptcy filing, such as an assignee for the benefit of creditors, or a state court receiver, or a nonbankruptcy trustee.[29] Although a custodian with knowledge of the commencement of a bankruptcy proceeding is supposed to turn over property of the estate to the bankruptcy trustee, Section 543 gives consideration to the custodian's rights.[30] The custodian may file an accounting of the custodian's activities, seek payment of any compensation that may be due, and generally be permitted to take all actions that would be required to fulfill and relieve the custodian's duties under nonbankruptcy law.[31] In an exceptional instance, the court, notwithstanding the appointment of a bankruptcy trustee, may permit the custodian to remain in possession of the property if the estate is solvent and if the custodian's continued presence would be in the best interest of the owners of the debtor.[32] For instance, perhaps the debtor owns a large apartment project and the custodian is better suited than the trustee to continue management of the property on behalf of the estate. The custodian ought to stay put. This is an instance where logic and common sense should prevail.

A turnover order is normally sought by filing an adversary proceeding known as a turnover complaint and joining as defendants those parties against whom the turnover is sought. However, a turnover proceeding may be brought before the court by way of a noticed motion rather than a complaint when the sole purpose of the motion is to seek a turnover of property held only by the debtor.[33]

Summary

The filing of a bankruptcy proceeding creates an estate. All property in which the debtor has an interest becomes property of the estate. Property of the estate is subject to administration by the bankruptcy trustee for the distribution of dividends to the creditors. Property of the estate is the subject of Code Section 541.

There are a number of clarifications contained in Section 541 including or excluding certain interests as property of the estate. The following list identifies these special inclusions or exclusions:

---

28. 11 U.S.C. §543.
29. 11 U.S.C. §101(11). See chapter 6 supra.
30. 11 U.S.C. §543(b).
31. 11 U.S.C. §543(b)(2), (c)(2); Bankruptcy Rule 6002.
32. 11 U.S.C. §543(d).
33. Bankruptcy Rule 7001(1).

1. Included as Property of the Estate:

	Item	*Statute*
a.	Community property	11 U.S.C. §541(a)(2)
b.	Property recovered by the trustee	11 U.S.C. §541(a)(3)(4)
c.	Property acquired within 180 days of filing by bequest, inheritance, or devise, domestic property settlement, life insurance proceeds	11 U.S.C. §541(a)(5)
d.	Proceeds, product, or offspring from property of the estate	11 U.S.C. §541(a)(6)
e.	Property subject to an ipso facto clause	11 U.S.C. §541(c)(1)

2. Excluded as Property of the Estate:

	Item	*Statute*
a.	Personal postfiling earnings of an individual Chapter 7 or 11 debtor	11 U.S.C. §541(a)(6)
b.	Powers exercisable for the benefit of another (e.g., power of attorney)	11 U.S.C. §541(b)(1)
c.	Interest in an expired nonresidential lease	11 U.S.C. §541(b)(2)
d.	Principal assets of a spendthrift trust	11 U.S.C. §541(c)(2)
e.	Property in which the debtor holds bare legal title	11 U.S.C. §541(d)

The trustee may recover property of the estate by initiating an adversary proceeding known as a turnover complaint. This right is provided the trustee by Section 542 of the Code. Where the turnover is sought from the debtor, the trustee may proceed by way of a noticed motion.

KEY TERMS

avoiding powers
custodian
ipso facto clauses
property of the estate
spendthrift trusts
turnover complaint

DISCUSSION QUESTIONS

1. What is meant by the phrase "property of the estate"?
2. Why is the general definition of *estate property* contained in 11 U.S.C. §541(a) intentionally broad?
3. Why are postpetition wages of a debtor not considered property of the estate in Chapter 7? Why are postpetition wages of an individual debtor property of the estate in Chapters 11, 12 or 13?
4. Why is the product or proceeds of estate property also considered estate property?
5. What is an ipso facto clause?
6. What is a turnover complaint?

15

Avoiding Powers — Introduction

A. FUNCTION OF THE TRUSTEE'S AVOIDING POWERS

In addition to the turnover right, the Bankruptcy Code has given the trustee rights to recover as estate property property transferred in fraud of creditors or property distributed inequitably to the creditors during certain defined periods prior to a bankruptcy filing. Unauthorized postpetition transfers may also be recoverable. Collectively, these rights are commonly known as the trustee's avoiding powers. An **avoiding power** is the ability of a trustee to avoid certain pre- or postpetition transactions that would otherwise be valid under nonbankruptcy law. The purpose of the avoiding powers is to effectuate the Bankruptcy Code's function as a debt collection tool. This is often described as the orderly and consistent liquidation of a debtor's assets and their distribution to creditors. The successful use by a trustee of an avoiding power will recover as estate property assets that would no longer be considered property of the debtor in a nonbankruptcy environment.

The avoiding powers are designed to provide consistency and uniformity to the liquidation of bankruptcy estates and the distribution of dividends to creditors. The existence of the trustee's avoiding powers acts to prevent creditors from racing to the courthouse on the eve of a debtor's bankruptcy filing to seek unfair advantage relative to the overall creditor body. The avoiding powers also act to prohibit the enactment of conflicting nonbankruptcy nonfederal laws that might otherwise tend to defeat operation of the bankruptcy system.

The avoiding powers are contained in multiple sections of the Bankruptcy Code. The most commonly used avoiding powers are the strong arm clause, preferences, fraudulent transfers, and unauthorized postpetition transfers. The next three text chapters will focus on these avoiding powers.

B. STRONG ARM CLAUSE

Section 544 gives the trustee various powers collectively and commonly known as the strong arm powers, or the **strong arm clause.** These are the first most basic of the avoiding powers. This provision existed under the Bankruptcy Act as Section 70(c).[1] Because much prior case law concerning this provision remains effective under the Code, it is a useful reference for those requiring additional research. In its essence, Section 544 transforms a trustee into a "super-creditor" as of the commencement of a bankruptcy proceeding.

First, the trustee is given the power of a creditor who at the time of filing obtains a judicial lien on all of the debtor's property subject to a judicial lien, whether or not such a creditor exists.[2] Thus, the trustee has the status of a perfected and secured judgment creditor. This power gives the trustee priority over all other creditors who do not possess any superior lien rights upon property of the estate. This provision gives the trustee a superior right to all assets of the estate for the protection of all creditors.

Second, Section 544 gives the trustee the power of a creditor who at the time of filing has an execution of judgment returned unsatisfied, whether or not such a creditor actually exists.[3] This provision, in conjunction with the first, provides a trustee with blanket protection to avoid any other creditor's efforts to gain a superior right in estate property subsequent to the commencement of the bankruptcy proceeding.

Third, the trustee is given the status of a bona fide purchaser of real property from the debtor, whether or not such a purchaser actually exists.[4] Thus, no entity can obtain an interest superior to the trustee's in a debtor's real estate subsequent to the bankruptcy filing. For example, a debtor's transfer of real estate one day after a petition is filed is in violation of the trustee's strong arm rights.

The strong arm rights collectively place the trustee in full command of all a debtor's assets affected by the bankruptcy proceeding. It is the trustee, through proper use of the Bankruptcy Code, who initially determines the rights of the creditors to the various assets and the proper order of distribution of any funds received from a liquidation of the assets. The trustee can of course be aided by the court in making these determinations.

1. See Historical and Revision Notes to 11 U.S.C. §544.
2. 11 U.S.C. §544(a)(1).
3. 11 U.S.C. §544(a)(2).
4. 11 U.S.C. §544(a)(3).

C. LIMITATIONS ON AVOIDING POWERS

Section 546 contains several limitations on the exercise of the trustee's avoiding powers. Actions on the avoiding powers must be commenced within one year of the trustee's appointment or two years after the entry of the order for relief, whichever is later, but any action must be commenced before the close or dismissal of the case.[5] This provision is essentially a statute of limitations upon the exercise of the trustee's avoiding powers.

Please note that this limitations period is measured from the entry of the order for relief or the date of the trustee's appointment, whichever is later. For example, a Chapter 11 may have been pending for 23 months prior to the trustee's appointment. Nonetheless, the trustee has one year from the date of appointment to exercise the avoiding powers. The logic of this rule is to prevent Chapter 11 debtors from filing a proceeding and then refraining from exercising an avoiding power to the detriment of all creditors. For example, John Smith fraudulently transfers real estate to his children on the eve of a Chapter 11 filing. He then files the Chapter 11 and plans to delay action for two years so that the fraudulent transfer cannot be avoided because of the Section 546 time limits. Twenty-three months later, a trustee is appointed. Unfortunately for John Smith, the trustee will have one year to commence action rather than one month.

A second limitation on the exercise of the trustee's avoiding powers concerns the limited rights of certain creditors to perfect or to continue the perfection of a security interest in property notwithstanding the commencement of a bankruptcy proceeding.[6] This is a corollary to and is consistent with the identical exception to the automatic stay.[7] The limitation is that if nonbankruptcy law permits the perfection of an interest in property to relate back to a time prior to actual perfection, the fortuitous intervention of a bankruptcy filing will not defeat the creditor's nonbankruptcy rights to perfect the interest in accordance with nonbankruptcy law. The most common scenario that arises is the perfection of a security interest under the Uniform Commercial Code. Under the Uniform Commercial Code a creditor normally has a ten-day statutory grace period to perfect a security interest.[8] If a bankruptcy intervenes during any applicable time period, Section 546(b) permits the creditor to complete perfection of its security interest within the statutory time period. In this event the validity and priority of the security interest will be honored in the bankruptcy proceeding. Similarly, if a state mechanic's lien law permits perfection of the lien to relate back to a prior

---

5. 11 U.S.C. §546(a).
6. 11 U.S.C. §546(b).
7. 11 U.S.C. §362(b)(3). See chapter 12 supra.
8. UCC §9-301(1).

date, then a mechanic's lien may be perfected by an affected creditor subsequent to a bankruptcy filing.

One purpose that this provision serves is to prevent a debtor from buying an asset on credit and then filing a bankruptcy before the creditor can perfect its security interest. If this could be done, then a debtor could claim the asset exempt, and the creditor would be unsecured. Such a rule would undoubtedly increase the cost of consumer credit and decrease its availability. Giving the creditor the benefit of any statutory grace period is simply fair. The Historical and Revision Notes to Section 546(b) state:

> The purpose of the subsection is to protect, in spite of the surprise intervention of a bankruptcy petition, those whom State law protects by allowing them to perfect their liens or interests as of an effective date that is earlier than the date of perfection.[9]

A third limitation on exercise of the trustee's avoiding powers concerns the rights of creditors to reclaim goods under either common law or the Uniform Commercial Code.[10] A right of reclamation is a creditor's right, in certain defined circumstances, to repossess goods previously sold to the debtor on an unsecured basis. Under this provision, a seller with a reclamation right may actually reacquire the merchandise from the buyer/debtor despite the filing of the bankruptcy if the debtor has received the goods in the ordinary course of business while insolvent within 45 days before the bankruptcy filing, and if the seller makes written demand to reclaim the goods not later than 45 days after the debtor receives the goods or 20 days after the case is filed if the 45 days expires after commencement of the case. For example, the owner of an insolvent store buys $10,000 of inventory on Thursday and files a bankruptcy on the following Monday. If the creditor gives a written reclamation notice to the debtor within 45 days after delivery, the seller may be able to recover the goods despite the intervening bankruptcy filing. The Bankruptcy Court may deny the reclamation demand, but only if the court gives the seller an administrative claim.[11] This section arises infrequently in actual practice.

Section 546(d) was added to the Bankruptcy Code in 1984 in reaction to a well-publicized matter that gave bankruptcy law some momentary notoriety. A grain elevator cooperative in Arkansas filed a bankruptcy. The farmers who had stored their grain in the grain elevator showed up with shotguns to reclaim their grain, and federal marshals were required to prevent the vigilante repossession. The Bankruptcy Court had held that the grain stored in the bankrupt grain elevator by the farmers was no longer their property but was property of the estate. The farmers were mere unse-

9. Historical and Revision Notes to Section 546.
10. 11 U.S.C. §546(c).
11. 11 U.S.C. §546(c)(2). As to administrative claims, see chapter 21, infra.

cured creditors.[12] Congress thought that this was an unfair predicament to put farmers in, so Section 546(d) was enacted to deal with the rights of farmers or fishermen who sell their products to a grain storage facility or fish processing plant. Under Section 546(d), a farmer or fisherman is given the right to reclaim products from an insolvent grain storage facility or fish-processing plant if a written demand for reclamation is made within ten days after the product is delivered. The court may deny the reclamation request but must give the farmer or fisherman, like the seller of goods, an administrative claim or a lien on other assets of the estate.[13]

In stockbroker Chapter 7 proceedings, margin payments are normally not avoidable.[14] The Bankruptcy Reform Act of 1994 added a new Section 546(h) to the Code. This provision allows a trustee to return to a seller of goods any goods sold to the debtor prepetition, if such return is in the best interests of the estate. Warehouseman's liens are not avoidable by a trustee pursuant to 11 U.S.C. §546(i) enacted in 2005.

D. STATUTORY LIEN AVOIDANCE

Section 545 allows a trustee to avoid certain types of statutory liens. Recall that a **statutory lien** is a lien created by operation of law, not by court order (a judicial lien) or agreement (a consensual lien).[15] The first type of statutory lien that is avoidable is a lien that purports to become effective only upon the debtor's insolvency, the filing of a bankruptcy proceeding, or having a financial condition that fails to meet a defined standard.[16] Such statutes are the legislative equivalent of ipso facto clauses, which are disfavored by the Code.[17] The purpose of this provision is to prevent states from enacting liens that would give certain creditors priority only in the event of a debtor's bankruptcy filing.

Second, a statutory lien may be avoided if it cannot be enforced against a bona fide purchaser of the debtor's property at the commencement of the bankruptcy proceeding, whether or not such a purchaser exists except for a purchaser at a government tax lien sale.[18] For example, if a state mechanic's lien law requires recordation of the lien prior to the lien being deemed perfected, alien recorded subsequent to a bankruptcy filing may be avoidable. Finally, statutory rent liens or liens for distress of rent are avoidable.[19]

12. Missouri v. United States Bankr. Ct. for E.D. of Ark., 647 F.2d 768 (8th Cir. 1981).
13. 11 U.S.C. §546(d).
14. 11 U.S.C. §546(e)(f)(g).
15. 11 U.S.C. §101(53). See chapter 6 supra.
16. 11 U.S.C. §545(1).
17. See chapter 14 supra.
18. 11 U.S.C. §545(2).
19. 11 U.S.C. §545(3), (4).

Summary

The abilities given a trustee to avoid certain pre- or postfiling transactions that would otherwise be valid under nonbankruptcy law are known as the avoiding powers. Preferences, fraudulent transfers, and the ability to set aside unauthorized postpetition transfers are the most common avoiding powers.

The underlying purpose of the avoiding powers is often described as the orderly and consistent liquidation of a debtor's assets and their distribution to creditors. This philosophy is the foundation of the debt collection features of the bankruptcy system. The avoiding powers attempt to eliminate the effects of creditors racing to the courthouse to improve their position on the eve of a bankruptcy filing.

The initial avoiding power provides a trustee rights that make the trustee a "super-creditor" with priority to estate assets over the claims of most creditors. This permits the trustee to properly collect the assets for liquidation. This provision is known as the strong arm clause. Statutory liens, liens created by statute, will be avoidable in some situations, most notably where the lien comes into existence only if a debtor files a bankruptcy proceeding.

A trustee is given a period two years from the date of appointment to initiate an adversary proceeding to exercise an avoiding power.

Not all transactions or creditors will be subject to the avoiding powers. Limited creditors may be permitted to perfect liens in property for a limited period of time after a bankruptcy is filed. Limited unsecured creditors may also possess a right of reclamation, the right to repossess goods or crops.

KEY TERMS

avoiding power
strong arm clause
statutory lien

DISCUSSION QUESTIONS

1. What is the concept underlying the trustee's avoiding powers?
2. Why is a trustee considered a "super-creditor"?
3. When may a secured creditor perfect a claim after a bankruptcy filing?
4. How long does a trustee have to exercise the avoiding powers?
5. How are a trustee's avoiding powers exercised?

16

Avoidable Preferences — 11 U.S.C. §547

A. INTRODUCTION AND DEFINITIONS

The most common of the trustee's avoiding powers are known as **preferences**. Preferences permit a trustee to recover assets transferred to a creditor on the eve of the bankruptcy filing so that the assets may be distributed fairly to all creditors. The reason for preferences is to facilitate an orderly distribution to all creditors. A secondary function of preference avoidability is to stop creditors from racing to the courthouse on the eve of bankruptcy to unfairly improve their chances of receiving payment.

A preference generally occurs when a debtor, on the eve of bankruptcy, transfers property or interest in property to one or more creditors in full or partial satisfaction of debt to the exclusion of all other creditors. The avoidable transfer may be voluntary or involuntary. Creditors receiving a preference have their claims wholly or partially satisfied while the remaining creditors receive nothing. Permitting a trustee to avoid these transactions and to recover property transferred for the estate so that it may be liquidated and the proceeds distributed fairly to all creditors is the goal of this avoiding power.

To illustrate, U.S. Grant owns an insolvent dry goods store. One month before filing a Chapter 7, Grant voluntarily pays in full the claims of creditors Sherman, Sheridan, and Meade. Creditors Lee, Jackson, and Longstreet receive no payments. Utilizing preference powers, Grant's Chapter 7 trustee, Lincoln, may recover the payments made to the first group of creditors so that equal dividends may ultimately be paid to all of Grant's creditors. If Lee, Jackson, and Longstreet obtain a writ of attachment, outflanking Grant with this involuntary transfer, Lincoln would also be able to avoid this transaction as a preference.

The concept of avoidable preferences does not exist outside of the bankruptcy system. When a consumer or business pays its debts in a nonbankruptcy environment, they may be paid in any order desired. For instance, in a month where cash flow is insufficient to pay all debts on a current basis, a consumer decides to postpone payment of the dentist's bill until next month. Other creditors have been "preferred" over the dentist. A debtor that is not bankrupt may normally "prefer" or pay creditors in any order desired.

Culpability or the intent of the entity receiving or giving the preference is not an issue in determining the avoidability of a preference. The only concern is the overriding philosophy of the bankruptcy system that all creditors with the same distributive priority under the Bankruptcy Code should be treated equally in the receipt of dividends. Intent or culpability is irrelevant to this consideration.

Keep in mind that the avoiding powers are also possessed by a Chapter 11 debtor-in-possession.[1] So even though a debtor-in-possession may in fact be the very entity that committed the preference in the first place, the debtorin-possession still has an opportunity to avoid the preference for the benefit of all creditors.

Section 547 of the Bankruptcy Code regulates the avoidance of preferences. The most practical way to attempt an understanding of this Section and its various subdivisions is to conceive of an avoidable preference as a cause of action or claim upon which relief may be granted. In this sense, the determination of the existence of or defenses to an avoidable preference can most easily be described in the format of a traditional lawsuit. That is, to successfully avoid a preference, there are various elements that the trustee must prove. Similarly, the party or parties against whom a preference is sought to be avoided may raise issues that in traditional litigation would be considered affirmative defenses. Actions to avoid preferences are always commenced as adversary proceedings when the trustee seeks affirmative relief.[2] The trustee is the plaintiff; the party or parties who received the preference are the defendants.

Section 547 is one of the few Bankruptcy Code sections containing definitions that are unique to it. These definitions are contained in Section 547(a). The first of these is **inventory**: any form of personal property that a debtor uses to produce revenue. Thus, inventory for preference purposes may be raw material, finished product, merchandise on shelves, or cars available for rental.[3]

The second unique definition and the most critical, is **new value**. *New value*, in simple and practical terms, means new consideration for the debt. **Consideration** is normally the element of exchange in any contract. New value is not created when a new obligation is substituted for an exisiting obligation.[4] A preference may arise by the payment of money, a transfer of property, or the granting of a security interest in property of the debtor. For

1. 11 U.S.C. §1107. See chapter 10 supra.
2. Bankruptcy Rule 7001.
3. 11 U.S.C. §547(a)(1).
4. 11 U.S.C. §547(a)(2).

example, George owes Brad $10,000. George offers Brad a lien in his Sherman tank to secure repayment of the debt. To the extent that Brad is not loaning more money to George in exchange for the lien, there is no new value. The lien in the tank will be an avoidable preference. A preference is therefore any transaction that places one creditor in a preferred position over other otherwise similar creditors, such as an unsecured creditor's becoming secured on the eve of a bankruptcy filing. Much of the preference litigation taking place before the Bankruptcy Court does not usually involve a creditor that has been paid money but rather a creditor that has received a security interest in property on the eve of bankruptcy. The definition of *new value* helps in determining whether the granting of such a security interest is or is not a transfer that may be deemed an avoidable preference.

Receivable is a third unique definition in Section 547. A *receivable* is a right to payment, whether or not such right has been earned by performance.[5]

A fourth and final definition is not a definition at all but a necessary rule that helps create a consistent national scheme regarding tax preferences, because the Internal Revenue Code and each individual state has its independent definitions concerning when a tax debt is incurred. Section 547(a)(4) provides that a tax debt is incurred on the date it is last payable without penalty, including any extensions.[6] This means that for purposes of income taxes, for example, a tax debt is incurred on April 15 for a prior year's taxes.

B. ELEMENTS OF A PREFERENCE

Section 547(b) describes the six elements that a trustee must prove to successfully avoid a preference. Each element must be proven for the trustee to prevail. Failure to prove any element will result in a failure to avoid the preference. These six elements constitute the cause of action or claim for relief.

The first element is that there be a "transfer of an interest of the debtor in property."[7] Any sort of **transfer** of a debtor's interest in an asset may be avoidable. Recall that the Code defines *transfer* as any method that human beings may devise to transfer property or an interest in it.[8] This definition of *transfer* is intentionally broad. Thus, outright payment of cash or the transfer of a physical asset, such as real estate or inventory, to a creditor by a debtor will constitute a transfer. The grant or attempted granting of a security interest in real or personal property to a creditor by a debtor will also constitute a transfer.

5. 11 U.S.C. §547(a)(3).
6. 11 U.S.C. §547(a)(4).
7. 11 U.S.C. §547(b).
8. 11 U.S.C. §101(54). See chapter 6 supra.

The second element of an avoidable preference is that the transfer be "to or for the benefit of a creditor."[9] The "to a creditor" portion is fairly simple: The money, property, or security interest is transferred directly to the creditor by the debtor.

A transfer is made "for the benefit of a creditor" if it is to a creditor of a creditor. In this instance, even though the original creditor has received no direct transfer, the transfer has still been made for that creditor's benefit. For example, Huey owes Louie, and Louie owes Dewey. Louie tells Huey that if Huey pays Dewey for Louie, then Huey will no longer owe Louie, and Louie will no longer owe Dewey. Huey's payment of Louie's debt to Dewey is a transfer for the benefit of a creditor, namely Louie. Huey's financial books may not show that the payment to Dewey is for Louie, but Louie's claim against Huey has still been satisfied.

The third element is that the transfer be "for or on account of an antecedent debt owed by the debtor before the transfer was made."[10] **Antecedent debt** means that the debt was incurred or existed before the transfer was made. The most common form of antecedent debt is a past-due bill. In the George and Brad example, supra, the $10,000 debt due Brad is an antecedent debt when the lien is offered by George.

The fourth element of an avoidable preference is that the transfer be made "while the debtor was insolvent."[11] As noted earlier in this chapter, if the debtor is not insolvent, the order of debt repayment is of no concern to anyone. A debtor is generally **insolvent** when liabilities exceed assets.[12]

The fifth element is time. One of two time periods is considered in determining the existence of an avoidable preference. The first of these is the period 90 days prior to filing of a bankruptcy. An otherwise preferential transfer occurring before this time period will not constitute an avoidable preference.[13] However, when insiders are the subject of a preference action, the relevant time period is extended to one year prior to the filing of the bankruptcy petition.[14] For example, Elle Woods owes $10,000 to a grandparent for money loaned to attend law school. The grandparent is repaid from Woods' first paycheck. Woods files a bankruptcy proceeding six months later. The payment will be an avoidable preference since it was made to an insider within one year prior to filing of the petition.

The sixth and final element of an avoidable preference is that the creditor must "receive more than such creditor would receive" in a Chapter 7 if the transfer had not been made.[15] Simply put, the transfer must result in the

9. 11 U.S.C. §547(b)(1).
10. 11 U.S.C. §547(b)(2).
11. 11 U.S.C. §547(b)(3).
12. 11 U.S.C. §101(32). See chapter 6 supra.
13. 11 U.S.C. §547(b)(4)(A).
14. 11 U.S.C. §547(b)(4)(B).
15. 11 U.S.C. §547(b)(5).

creditor having a greater percentage of its debt repaid by the transfer than the creditor would receive as a Chapter 7 dividend if the transfer had not been made. For example, a creditor receiving payment in full, when a Chapter 7 dividend would pay only 50 percent, has received a preference payment equal to 50 percent of the debt. Similarly, a creditor that improves its position from unsecured to secured by the transfer of a security interest in property receives more than it would otherwise receive as a Chapter 7 dividend because it receives the collateral rather than a speculative right to a portion of the proceeds from a sale of the collateral.

Carefully focusing on the final element of an avoidable preference may aid in facilitating the settlement of preference disputes. In any situation where the parties can reasonably estimate the potential dividend to an affected class of creditor in a Chapter 7 proceeding, it is necessary only to calculate any excess received by the creditor and to then have the creditor return this excess to the estate and waive any further claim against the estate. The creditor will have received its dividend while the remaining creditors will have had their "fair share" returned at a minimum of expense in attorneys' fees or litigation expenses, not to mention a substantial savings in time. All this will further increase the total ultimate return to the estate's creditors, of whom the creditor receiving the preference is one.

A trustee must prove the existence of each element in order for the preference to be avoided. If one element remains unproven, a preference may exist, but it will not be an avoidable preference.[16]

Under Section 547(f) a debtor is presumed insolvent during the 90 days immediately prior to the filing of the bankruptcy petition.[17] This means that the trustee does not have to affirmatively prove the debtor's insolvency when the preferential transfer occurs within 90 days prior to a bankruptcy filing. In this instance, the entity against whom the claim is brought will bear the burden of proving that the debtor was solvent during the 90-day period. As a corollary, this also means that if the subject of the avoidable preference is an insider transaction occurring more than 90 days prior to filing but within one year of the bankruptcy filing, the trustee will now have the burden of proving the debtor's insolvency during the period of time more than 90 days prior to the bankruptcy filing.

In the most common preference cases, many of the elements are generally not difficult to prove. For instance, payment of a long-overdue loan owed to a relative or payment of a long-overdue bank loan is easily identified as a transfer to a creditor on account of an antecedent debt. If the payment was made within 90 days of filing, the debtor is presumed insolvent. Because most proceedings have no assets, most avoidable

16. 11 U.S.C. §547(g).
17. 11 U.S.C. §547(f).

preferences should generally be fully recoverable. Documents evidencing the debt, the transfer, and the transfer's timing should generally be sufficient to prove all the basic elements of an avoidable preference.

The final element of a preference, that the creditor has received more than the creditor would otherwise receive in a Chapter 7 proceeding, is often easy to prove, as noted above. Full analysis of the ultimate effect on the creditor body can result in settlement of many preference claims asserted by a trustee. This usually requires some educated guesswork but is not overly difficult. Because the most common proceeding is a no asset Chapter 7, any creditor receiving a preference is receiving more than it otherwise would in a Chapter 7 proceeding. If a creditor owed $1,000 receives a preference of $1,000, does the creditor receive more than it otherwise would in the Chapter 7? Obviously, yes. But, the more difficult question is, how much more? For example, assume that the creditor receiving $1,000 is one of ten creditors. Assume also that the aggregate total of debts is $10,000. If $1,000 is available to distribute to creditors, the amount of dividend that each of these creditors will receive is 10 percent, because 1,000 is 10 percent of 10,000. The creditor in the example therefore received $900 more than it would in the Chapter 7. Thus, $900 is the actual amount of the avoidable preference. The creditor should be permitted to settle the dispute by returning $900 to the estate and waiving further claims against the estate.

In a large proceeding these calculations can become complex and uncertain. Nevertheless, agreement as to an estimated amount of dividend often may lead to swift and economical settlement of avoidable preference disputes. This approach is more practical than incurring significant attorneys' fees in avoiding the preference, because the fees act to erode the ultimate dividend payable to all creditors. The suggested approach should result in greater overall distributions to the creditor body, primarily due to the reduced attorneys' fee burden.

C. AFFIRMATIVE DEFENSES

The elements of an avoidable preference thus constitute a cause of action or claim upon which relief may be granted that is unique to a bankruptcy proceeding. To complement the cause of action or claim, there also exists the functional equivalent of affirmative defenses to an avoidable preference claim. These "affirmative defenses" are described in Section 547(c) and (i) and can be easily grasped if conceived of as affirmative defenses to the avoidable preference claim. Most of these defenses exist to legitimize transactions occurring in the normal course of business, transactions that the fortuity of a bankruptcy filing should not invalidate.

The first affirmative defense is that the transfer is intended to be a **contemporaneous transfer for new value** and is in fact a substantially contemporaneous exchange.[18] That is, if there is new consideration present from both parties, the transfer will not be an avoidable preference. For example, in the usual preference transaction, a debtor in default to a creditor pays the creditor all or a portion of the debt due. The creditor does not give the debtor any new consideration in return for the payment. Recall the example earlier in this chapter of the debt owed by George to Brad. There is no new value between the parties in the example, and the payment therefore is an avoidable preference. New value generally involves an exchange of present or new consideration between the debtor and creditor. For instance, when Opie Taylor goes to the Ziffle Finance Company to refinance an existing loan and borrows an additional $500, the $500 is new value. It was not owed or previously loaned to Opie. Conversely, the preexisting loan amount would be an antecedent debt.

Substantially contemporaneous generally means an exchange taking place in the normal course of business. If a transfer is perfected within any nonbankruptcy grace periods, as described in chapter 14 supra, the transfer will normally be considered substantially contemporaneous. For example, if the bank loans a debtor money to purchase a new car but the bank fails to perfect its lien in the vehicle for one week, the transaction will still be considered substantially contemporaneous because the lien date will likely fall within any applicable nonbankruptcy grace period. The reason for this flexibility is that if such a rule did not exist, it would be possible for trustees or debtors to avoid recently obtained valid liens on a debtor's assets by successfully claiming that the security interest is a preference. If this were the case, the credit industry would be in chaos and the availability of credit in American society would be reduced significantly. The statute therefore tries to reconcile this necessary fact of economic existence with the orderly distribution of assets to all creditors in the event of financial failure.

The second affirmative defense to a preference action involves an ordinary business practice, the payment of accounts payable on a regular basis. Some businesses pay them once every 30 days, or once every 40 days, or perhaps only once every 90 days, but they pay them on a regular basis. If a creditor can show that the debt was incurred in the ordinary course of the debtor's and creditor's financial affairs and was paid in the ordinary course of the debtor's and creditor's financial affairs or according to ordinary business terms, then the transfer will not constitute an avoidable preference.[19] Simply put, if a creditor can show that the transfer was generally made in the ordinary course of business, the transfer will not

18. 11 U.S.C. §547(c)(1).
19. 11 U.S.C. §547(c)(2).

constitute an avoidable preference. The logic and rationale here is that if a debtor is in the habit of paying its bills every 60 days and a creditor's bill is paid within such a period after being incurred, the transfer should not be considered an avoidable preference because the debt has been paid in the ordinary course of business. This provision attempts to accept the reality of the marketplace and does not attempt to alter it due to the happenstance of a bankruptcy filing.

A difficult situation arises when a debtor makes a customary monthly payment on a long-term unsecured obligation, such as the outstanding balance owed on a line of credit or unsecured promissory note obligation. Does the antecedent nature of the debt render payments made within any applicable preference period avoidable, or, because the payments are made in the ordinary course of business, are they defensible? The Supreme Court faced this issue in the Union Bank v. Wolas, 502 U.S. 151 (1991).

On December 17, 1986, the debtor ZZZZ Best Co., Inc. borrowed $7 million from Union Bank. On July 8, 1987, the debtor filed a Chapter 7 petition. In the 90 days preceding the bankruptcy, the debtor paid Union Bank $100,000 in interest payments and a $2,500 loan commitment fee. The Bankruptcy Court and district courts found for the bank creditor. The Ninth Circuit reversed. Because of a conflicting ruling from the Sixth Circuit, the Supreme Court granted certiorari to review the matter.[20]

The Supreme Court held that a payment in the ordinary course will qualify for the preference exception irrespective of whether the underlying nature of the debt is long-term or short-term. Thus, the payments to the bank fell within the ordinary course of business exception.

The third affirmative defense to an avoidable preference is that, so long as the security interest secures new value, perfection of a security interest within 30 days of a debtor acquiring the property will not be an avoidable preference.[21] For example, Alfred Newman borrows $10,000 from the Last National Bank and gives the bank a security interest in an obsolete stereo system. If the bank perfects its security interest within 30 days, the perfection will not constitute an avoidable preference. Recall that even if Newman files a bankruptcy proceeding within the 30-day period, under Section 546 the bank might still be able to perfect its interest within the 30-day period.[22]

The fourth affirmative defense will normally arise only in proceedings involving business debtors. Essentially, a transfer will not be avoidable as

20. The conflicting Sixth Circuit ruling was In re Finn, 909 F.2d 968 (1990).
21. 11 U.S.C. §547(c)(3).
22. 11 U.S.C. §546(b). See chapter 15 supra. Recall also that the bank may perfect its interest within any applicable postfiling period as an exception to the automatic stay. 11 U.S.C. §362(b)(3). See chapter 12 supra.

a preference if, after the transfer, the creditor gives new value to the debtor that is unsecured.[23] For example, a payment in advance will not be an avoidable preference.

The fifth affirmative defense concerns a business financing arrangement commonly known as a **floating lien**. A *floating lien* is generally a line of credit from a bank or other financial institution secured by the inventory, equipment, or proceeds of the debtor's business. In the normal course of business, a debtor constantly sells existing inventory and replaces it with more inventory. Because the security interest attaches to the new inventory that the debtor purchases in place of the sold merchandise, the lien is said to "float." The test of this defense to avoidable preferences is identical to the test described in Section 553 involving setoffs.[24] This test is commonly referred to as the "improvement of position" test. Generally, a floating lien will not constitute a preference to the extent that the creditor does not "improve its position" in the 90 days prior to a bankruptcy filing.[25] To determine whether a creditor has improved its position, the amount of the debt and the value of the collateral as of a date 90 days prior to the bankruptcy filing are compared with the amount of the debt and the value of the collateral on the date of the bankruptcy filing. To the extent that the creditor improves its secured position during the 90-day period, the improvement will be an avoidable preference, but maintenance of the creditor's position at the level held 90 days prior to the bankruptcy filing will not be.

For example, 90 days prior to filing a Chapter 11, Total Roto, Inc., owes the Bank of Plunger $200,000 secured by $100,000 in collateral. At this time, $100,000 of the debt is unsecured. On the date of filing the debt has been decreased to $100,000 and remains secured by $100,000 of collateral. There is no longer an unsecured portion of the debt. The $100,000 in payments will be considered a preference because they have reduced the amount by which the debt exceeded the value of the security interest from $100,000 to zero. Stated another way, payments made to an undercollateralized secured creditor within 90 days of a bankruptcy filing (one year if the creditor is an insider) are preferential to the extent that the unsecured portion of the debt is decreased. The reduction of the unsecured portion of a secured claim is the portion of the debt measured. In the example, this decrease is $100,000. On the other hand, if payments of $100,000 are made during the preference period but the amount of debt and value of the collateral remain respectively at $200,000 and $100,000 on the date of filing, then the $100,000 in payments would not constitute an avoidable preference because the unsecured portion of the debt has not been reduced.

23. 11 U.S.C. §547(c)(4).
24. See chapter 17 infra.
25. 11 U.S.C. §547(c)(5).

The example may be illustrated by the following diagram and formula:

	d	si	(d – si)	
1. 90 days prior*	$200,000	$100,000	$100,000	or $(d_1 - si_1)$
2. filing date	$100,000	$100,000	-0-	$> (d_2 - si_2)$

d = amount of debt; si = value at collateral; (d = si) = unsecured portion of claim

*One year if insider.

To the extent that the unsecured portion of the debt is greater on the earlier date than on the later date, the difference will constitute an avoidable preference. To the extent there is no change or an increase in the undersecured portion of the debt, there is no avoidable preference. In the example, the creditor has eliminated all of its unsecured debt during the preference period: The entire amount may be preferential. The same statement can be stated mathematically: If $(d_1 - si_1) > (d_2 - si_2)$, then the difference is an improvement in position and thus preferential. The first sum is a computation as of the commencement of the preference period, 90 days or one year prior to the filing, respectively. The second sum is computed as of the filing date.

This formula can be described in a third and perhaps even simpler way: A secured creditor is only considered secured up to the value of its collateral.[26] Any additional amount due the creditor is considered an unsecured debt. Thus, determine the amount of the unsecured debt due the creditor at the beginning of the preference period and compare it to the amount of the unsecured debt due the creditor on the filing. To the extent that the amount of the unsecured debt has decreased, the decrease may be an avoidable preference. On the other hand, unfortunately for the creditor, to the extent that the amount of unsecured debt increases, the creditor bears the consequences.

A statutory lien that the trustee cannot avoid under Section 545 is also not avoidable as a preference.[27]

Transfers made in the payment of domestic support obligations are not avoidable as preferences.[28]

The eighth affirmative defense to an avoidable preference concerns consumer debtors. An individual consumer debtor may make aggregate transfers of less than $600 and the transfers will not constitute avoidable preferences.[29] This defense reflects a common occurrence in consumer

26. See chapter 21 infra. 11 U.S.C. §506.
27. 11 U.S.C. §547(c)(6). See also chapter 15 supra.
28. 11 U.S.C. §547(c)(7).
29. 11 U.S.C. §547(c)(8).

situations. A potential no asset consumer debtor may have two or three creditors who the debtor really wants to pay and not include as creditors in the bankruptcy filing. The creditors might be a credit card or medical bill, a phone bill, or perhaps a gas and electric bill. Without this defense to the trustee's avoidable preference powers, payment of all of these small debts would be avoidable. However, because an individual consumer debtor is permitted to make preferences of less than $600 in aggregate, a consumer debtor may pay small debts that they prefer to not include in the bankruptcy filing. The only limitation is that the grand total not exceed $600.

A final affirmative defense exists in business bankruptcies where the value of the transfer is less than $5,000. As a practical matter, this will eliminate many transactions that would otherwise be avoidable preferences.[30]

D. MISCELLANEOUS PROVISIONS

Section 547(d) permits a trustee to avoid a transfer to a surety furnishing a bond to dissolve a judicial lien if the underlying lien is also avoidable by the trustee.[31] For example, Snidely Whiplash attaches Nell's assets by a court order. Nell obtains a bond, giving the bond company a lien on her home to release the attachment. In Nell's subsequent Chapter 7 filing, the trustee may avoid the bonding company's lien if Snidely's judicial lien can also be avoided.

Section 547(e) further clarifies the timing of when a transfer occurs for purposes of determining whether the transfer is an avoidable preference. A transfer of real property is completed when the trust deed or grant deed or other deed is recorded or when the transferee acquires an interest in property that is superior to that of a bona fide purchaser.[32] Similarly, the transfer of an interest in personal property is considered perfected when the creditor files its UCC documents, or when the creditor cannot acquire a judicial lien superior to the rights of the transferee.[33]

In Barnhill v. Johnson, 503 U.S. 393 (1992), the Supreme Court ruled that a transfer by check is not complete until the check has cleared the payor's bank. In this case the debtor delivered a check to Barnhill on November 18. The check was dated November 19 and was honored by the bank on November 20. After the debtor filed Chapter 11, it was agreed that November 20 was the 90th day prior to the bankruptcy filing.

30. 11 U.S.C. §547(c)(9).
31. 11 U.S.C. §547(d).
32. 11 U.S.C. §547(e)(1)(A).
33. 11 U.S.C. §547(e)(1)(B).

In holding that the check's date of honor by the debtor's bank is the relevant date of transfer, the Supreme Court reasoned that because under the Uniform Commercial Code the debtor could dishonor the check until it cleared, the debtor therefore retained rights in the funds and that the transfer was not complete within the meaning of 11 U.S.C. §547(e)(1)(B).

This decision may lead to some uncertainty in practice on the part of creditors because the date that a check is honored by debtor's bank will generally be known only to the debtor because this date will appear only on the canceled check. This information will not be readily available to a creditor unless the debtor discloses it.

The second portion of Section 547(e) makes it unequivocal that creditors have at least thirty days to perfect security interests before a transfer will be considered a preference. Thus, a creditor will usually have at least thirty days to perfect a security interest, even if a bankruptcy intervenes during the thirty-day period.[34]

Finally, Section 547(g) allocates the burden of proof in preference actions. The trustee bears the burden of proving the elements of an avoidable preference as itemized by Section 547(b). Conversely, the creditor or other defendant has the burden of proof regarding any of the defenses provided for in Section 547(c).[35] This rule is consistent with the prior observation that the elements of a preference constitute a traditional cause of action or claim peculiar to the bankruptcy system, while the defenses are the equivalent of affirmative defenses available to defendants in traditional nonbankruptcy litigation.

Section 547(h), added by BAPA, exempts from preference liability any payments made to creditors pursuant to a repayment plan created for an individual debtor by a prepetition repayment plan. This provision encourages composition agreements in individual cases. See chapter 3 supra.

Section 547(i), also added by BAPA, creates the equivalent of another affirmative defense in preference actions. This provision provides that when the trustee can avoid a security interest preference because the transfer benefitted an insider, the trustee may only recover against the insider to the extent that the transfer took place between 90 days and one year prior to the bankruptcy. For example, DePrizio guarantees the debt of DePrizio, Inc. Six months prior to filing bankruptcy, DePrizio, Inc., gives creditor Crystal a security interest in business assets to secure repayment of an overdue loan. After DePrizio, Inc., files bankruptcy, its trustee may avoid the preference only as to De Prizio, but not as to Crystal.

34. 11 U.S.C. §547(e)(2). See chapters 12 and 15 supra.
35. 11 U.S.C. §547(g).

Summary

A transfer of property or an interest in property to a creditor, on the eve of bankruptcy, in full or partial satisfaction of debt to the exclusion of other creditors, is a preference. A preference meeting the elements of Code Section 547 will be avoidable by a trustee. When a preference is avoided, a trustee will recover the property transferred so that it may be liquidated and the proceeds distributed fairly to all creditors. An avoidable preference is determined by the trustee initiating an adversary proceeding.

A trustee must prove six elements to prove the existence of an avoidable preference. The defendant in the adversary proceeding may be able to show the existence of one or more of several available defenses to defeat the trustee's preference claim. The elements of the claim and the potential defenses are summarized in the checklist below.

KEY TERMS

antecedent debt
consideration
contemporaneous transfer for new value
floating lien
insolvents
inventory
new value
preferences
receivable
substantially contemporaneous
transfer

Chapter 16 Checklist

16.1 ELEMENTS OF A PREFERENCE (ALL MUST BE PROVEN)

		Authority
16.1.1	Transfer of Property or an Interest in Property	11 U.S.C. §547(b)
16.1.2	To or for the Benefit of a Creditor	11 U.S.C. §547(b)(1)
16.1.3	On or for Account of an Antecedent or Preexisting Debt	11 U.S.C. §547(b)(2)

		Authority
16.1.4	Made While the Debtor Is Insolvent	11 U.S.C. §547(b)(3)
	(Insolvency Is Presumed within 90 Days of Filing)	11 U.S.C. §547(f)
16.1.5	Made	
	1. Within 90 days of filing, or	11 U.S.C. §547(b)(4)(A)
	2. Within one year if the transferee is an insider	11 U.S.C. §547(b)(4)(B)
16.1.6	That Enables the Creditor to Receive a Greater Chapter 7 Dividend than It Would Otherwise Receive	11 U.S.C. §547(b)(5)

16.2 PREFERENCE DEFENSES (ONE MUST BE SHOWN)

16.2.1	A Contemporaneous Exchange for New Value	11 U.S.C. §547(c)(1)
16.2.2	A Debt Incurred and Paid in the Ordinary Course of Business	11 U.S.C. §547(c)(2)
16.2.3	Within Any Nonbankruptcy Perfection Periods or Within 20 Days of Debtor Receiving Possession	11 U.S.C. §547(c)(3)
16.2.4	Unsecured Debt Incurred for New Value	11 U.S.C. §547(c)(4)
16.2.5	Floating Liens, Except for Improvement of Position	11 U.S.C. §547(c)(5)
16.2.6	Unavoidable Statutory Liens	11 U.S.C. §547(c)(6)
16.2.7	Domestic Support Obligations	11 U.S.C. §547(c)(7)
16.2.8	A Consumer Debtor's Consumer Debtsof up to $600 (Permits Preferential Payment of Nominal Debts)	11 U.S.C. §547(c)(8)
16.2.9	Business Transfers less than $5,000	11 U.S.C. §547(c)(9)
16.2.10	Consumer Approved Repayment Plan	11 U.S.C. §547(h)

16.2.11 Noninsider Security Interests for the Benefit of Insider — 11 U.S.C. §547(i)

16.3 PLAINTIFF/TRUSTEE PLEADINGS

16.3.1 Summons and Complaint

16.3.2 Cover Sheet, as Required by Local Rule

16.3.3 Evidence Proving Preference
1. Checks
2. Contracts
3. Recorded documents
4. Documents of title

16.4 DEFENDANT/TRANSFEREE PLEADINGS

16.4.1 Answer

16.4.2 Evidence Proving Defense
1. Checks
2. Contracts
3. Recorded documents
4. Documents of title

DISCUSSION QUESTIONS

1. What is the concept underlying avoidable preferences in the bankruptcy system?
2. What are the elements of an avoidable preference?
3. What affirmative defenses exist to defeat an otherwise avoidable preference?
4. What presumption exists to assist a trustee in proving the existence of an avoidable preference?
5. When is a transfer considered complete for purposes of an avoidable preference?

17

Fraudulent and Postpetition Transfers

A. FRAUDULENT TRANSFERS

Section 548 permits a trustee to avoid a **fraudulent transfer**. In addition, many states have adopted the Uniform Fraudulent Transfer Act. This Act creates independent rights, under state law, for creditors to attempt to set aside fraudulent transfers.[1] The concept of fraudulent transfers is relatively simple. Generally, *fraudulent transfers* are transfers made by a debtor with actual intent to hinder, delay, or defraud creditors. A transfer without reasonable or fair consideration may also be a fraudulent transfer. The most common example of a fraudulent transfer occurs when a debtor transfers $10,000 to a close friend or relative saying, "hold onto this for me until things get a little better." The debtor then files bankruptcy expecting to "reclaim" the asset transferred when the bankruptcy is over. Similarly, the debtor's conveying a quitclaim deed to a grandparent saying, "hold onto this, Grandma, until things get a little better," is also a fraudulent transfer. In each instance the critical action is that the debtor has attempted to conceal property from the creditors. These sorts of transactions have been traditionally disfavored in the law. The earliest forms of "insolvency" debt collection laws and those prevalent in the Middle Ages involved the avoidance of fraudulent transfers as described in chapter 1 supra.

There are two basic ways in which a fraudulent transfer may be proven under the Bankruptcy Code. The first is to prove that the transfer was made with actual intent to hinder, delay, or defraud creditors.[2] Each of the above examples probably meets this standard.

1. Uniform Fraudulent Transfer Act, 7A U.L.A. 7 (West Supp. 1985).
2. 11 U.S.C. §548(a)(1)(A).

The second manner of proving the existence of a fraudulent transfer is to show that the transfer has been made for less than a reasonably equivalent value in exchange and that the debtor was insolvent either prior to or as a result of the transfer.[3] Simply put, the transfer must essentially be for less than fair consideration. For instance, if Dr. Smith sells Will Robinson a robot for $10 when the robot has been appraised for $1 million, the transfer is likely to be deemed for less than a reasonably equivalent value in exchange. If a debtor transfers a boat to the debtor's best friend for $500 when the boat is worth $30,000, this transfer is likely to be deemed for less than a reasonably equivalent value in exchange. However, the "less than reasonably equivalent exchange" standard should not be interpreted necessarily to imply that the consideration should or must be at the fair market value of the asset that is subject to transfer. For example, a liquidation sale may be a "reasonably equivalent exchange."[4]

In BFP v. RTC, 511 U.S. 531 (1994), BFP contended that the price obtained at a regularly conducted foreclosure sale constituted a fraudulent transfer because the property was sold at the foreclosure sale for $433,000, whereas the alleged fair market value of the property was $725,000 at the time of foreclosure. In holding that the price obtained in a noncollusive real estate mortgage foreclosure sale, held in compliance with applicable state law, does not constitute a fraudulent transfer, Justice Scalia wrote: ". . . the only legitimate evidence of the property's value at the time it is sold is the foreclosure sale price itself."

In addition to the transfer being for less than a reasonably equivalent value in exchange, the transfer must have either been made while the debtor is insolvent or as a result of the transfer the debtor has been rendered insolvent or undercapitalized (without sufficient remaining assets to conduct ordinary business).[5] Thus, a transfer for less than a reasonably equivalent exchange must be made while the debtor is insolvent or must render the debtor insolvent or the transfer will not be considered fraudulent. A solvent multi-millionaire may transfer assets to charity on a regular basis without fear of reprisal from creditors. On the other hand, if the multi-millionaire is rendered insolvent as a result of the charitable giving, the gift becomes an avoidable fraudulent transfer.

Additionally, BAPA modifies Section 548(a) to expressly render transfer made to insiders under employment contracts and not in the ordinary course of business to be fraudulent transfers where the debtor is insolvent or rendered insolvent as a result of the transfer, or if the purpose of the transfer is to hinder, delay, or defraud creditors. The purpose of this provision is

3. 11 U.S.C. §548(a)(1)(B).
4. In re BFP, 974 F.2d 1144 (9th Cir. 1992); *affirmed*, BFP v. RTC 511 U.S. 531 (1994).
5. 11 U.S.C. §548(a)(1)(B)(ii).

to eliminate large bonuses given to corporate executives shortly prior to the corporations they manage filing for bankruptcy relief. These practices became widely publicized in cases like Enron, Worldcom, and Adelphia Communications.

Section 548(a)(2) limits the recovery by a trustee of charitable contributions as fraudulent transfers. A charitable contribution can be a fraudulent transfer because it is a gift and is therefore made without consideration. However, Section 548(a)(2) provides that charitable contributions of up to 15 percent of a debtor's gross annual income for the year in which the contribution is made, or is consistent with the debtor's practices in making the contribution, shall not be avoidable by the trustee. For example, a debtor earns $40,000 per year. Payment of a church tithe by the debtor of up to $6,000, 15 percent of the debtor's income, will not be avoidable as a fraudulent transfer by the debtor's bankruptcy trustee.

Section 548(b) concerns a special problem relating to partnership debtors. Any transfer of partnership property or an interest therein to a general partner within one year prior to a bankruptcy filing by the partnership is avoidable by a trustee if the transfer is made when the partnership is insolvent or if the partnership has been rendered insolvent as a result of the transfer.[6] The rationale behind this provision is that a general partner is an insider of the partnership. The general partner cannot "take the money and run."

Section 548(c) contains some protection for the transferee, the entity receiving the fraudulent transfer. If the transferee obtained the transferred property for value and in good faith and if the transfer is not avoidable by any other avoiding power, then the transferee is granted a lien on the transfer to the extent of any value given by the transferee.[7] For instance, a purchaser of real estate who has a purchase set aside as a fraudulent transfer obtains a lien upon the property to the extent of the purchase price paid as long as the purchase was in good faith and not avoidable under any other avoiding power of the trustee. Thus, if the transfer is also a preference, Section 548(c) will not apply.

A transfer is deemed complete for the purpose of determining the existence of a fraudulent transfer when the transfer is perfected so that a good-faith purchaser cannot acquire an interest in the property superior to that of the transferee.[8] That is, a transfer is complete when the deed is recorded or the transferee acquires rights to the property that would be superior to those of third parties in a nonbankruptcy environment.

The major difference between Bankruptcy Code Section 548 and nonbankruptcy fraudulent transfer law is that under nonbankruptcy law the statute of limitations is normally longer than that provided for by Section 548.

6. 11 U.S.C. §548(b).
7. 11 U.S.C. §548(c).
8. 11 U.S.C. §548(d)(1).

Recall that pursuant to Section 546(a) a trustee has only two years from the date of appointment to assert the claim. Further, Section 548 limits bankruptcy fraudulent transfers to those transfers occurring within two years prior to the bankruptcy filing.[9] Nonbankruptcy fraudulent transfer statutes under state law may provide longer time periods both for commencing the action and for determining what transfers are subject to challenge. Recall further that under Section 108 a trustee may have as long as two years added to a nonbankruptcy statute of limitations.[10] Thus, a trustee may seek to avoid as a fraudulent transfer under nonbankruptcy law a transfer that would not necessarily be avoidable under the Bankruptcy Code.

An action to avoid a fraudulent transfer is always initiated by filing an adversary complaint. When initiating such a complaint, it is always a recommended practice to allege the trustee's rights under both the Bankruptcy Code and any applicable nonbankruptcy law for the reasons described in the preceding paragraph.

B. POSTPETITION TRANSFERS

The trustee's final avoiding power permits the avoidance of certain **postpetition transfers**. Transfers of estate property taking place after a bankruptcy proceeding is filed may be avoidable by the trustee. For instance, in an involuntary proceeding, a debtor may transfer property of the estate before an order for relief is entered. Whether or not a subsequently appointed trustee may set aside this transfer is the subject matter of Section 549. From another perspective, a debtor filing a bankruptcy proceeding may, in violation of the Bankruptcy Code, transfer property of the estate to a third party after the filing but before the trustee can acquire custody of the property. Or a Chapter 11 debtor pays prepetition debt postpetition without proper court approval. Although these various transactions may have been avoidable as fraudulent transfers or preferences had they occurred before the bankruptcy filing, when they occur after a filing they are avoidable as improper postpetition transactions.

Essentially, a trustee may avoid any postpetition transaction that has not been authorized by the Bankruptcy Court or otherwise permitted by the Bankruptcy Code.[11] Section 549(a) acts to assist the trustee in performing

9. 11 U.S.C. §548(a).
10. See chapter 5 supra.
11. 11 U.S.C. §549(a). Postpetition transactions occurring in the normal course of business in a Chapter 11 proceeding will not necessarily require prior court approval. See chapter 18 infra.

the duty to liquidate the property of the estate. Many sales, uses, or leases of property of an estate require prior court approval.[12] A sale of property of the estate without obtaining prior court approval is avoidable.

Transactions for present consideration occurring during the gap period in an involuntary proceeding are not normally avoidable.[13] This is consistent with Section 303(f), which allows an alleged debtor in an involuntary proceeding to conduct business as usual prior to the entry of an order for relief unless the court orders otherwise.[14]

Under Section 549(c), a trustee cannot avoid a postpetition transfer of real property to a bona fide purchaser unless a copy of the petition has been filed in the place where the transfer of property may be perfected to complete the transaction.[15] This provides notice to all that the property is subject to the jurisdiction of the Bankruptcy Court. As long as the property remains property of the estate, it cannot be sold without court approval. This is similar to the concept of the lis pendens in nonbankruptcy proceedings affecting real estate. The effect of the recording is to prevent an unauthorized transfer of the real property.

A complaint to avoid a postpetition transaction may only be commenced within the earlier of two years after the transfer or the time the bankruptcy proceeding is closed or dismissed.[16] An action to avoid a postpetition transaction is always commenced as an adversary proceeding.

C. LIABILITY OF TRANSFEREES

Section 550 concerns the liability of the transferee of an avoided transfer: what the recipient of the avoidable preference must return or pay to the estate, what the transferee of a fraudulent transfer must return or pay to the estate, or what the transferee of an improper postpetition transaction must return or pay to the estate. This Section also concerns any rights retained by the transferees of avoided transactions.

A trustee may recover from a transferee the property transferred or the value of the property transferred.[17] The recovery may be obtained not only from the actual transferee but from a transferee of the transferee who does not acquire the property in good faith.[18] Thus, in successfully avoiding a

12. See chapter 18 infra.
13. 11 U.S.C. §549(b).
14. 11 U.S.C. §303(f). See chapter 4 supra.
15. 11 U.S.C. §549(c).
16. 11 U.S.C. §549(d).
17. 11 U.S.C. §550(a).
18. 11 U.S.C. §550(a)(2), (b).

fraudulent transfer, the trustee may recover either the value of the property or the property itself from the transferee or from a transferee of the transferee who has knowledge that the transaction is fraudulent. For example, if Jethro Clampett fraudulently transfers real estate to his Granny and then she transfers the property to Miss Hathaway, the trustee can recover the value of the property from Granny or may recover the property from Miss Hathaway if Miss Hathaway had knowledge that the transfer was fraudulent. On the other hand, if the third party has acted in good faith, the trustee may not recover from the third party.

Similarly, if a trustee is avoiding a preference, the recovery is limited to the property transferred or the value of the property. Thus, if a security interest in property of the estate is successfully avoided, invalidation of the security interest will be the trustee's recovery. If the successfully avoided preference is a cash payment or other outright transfer of property, the trustee is entitled to a recovery of the property to the extent the transfer exceeds the Chapter 7 dividend that the transferee would otherwise receive. For example, a creditor receiving full payment where the total dividend is to be 50 percent will only have to return 50 percent of the property transferred.

Regardless of how many potential entities a trustee may be entitled to recover from in a successful avoidance action (such as a transferee and then a transferee of the transferee), the trustee is only entitled to one satisfaction.[19] Thus, in the first of the above examples, the trustee could recover either the value of the property from Granny or the property itself from Miss Hathaway, but not both.

If a trustee recovers property from a good-faith transferee, then the good-faith transferee is given a right to reimbursement from the estate for any improvements made to the property. Improvements are considered to be physical additions to the property, or repair or maintenance costs expended in preserving the asset, or the cost of servicing any debt existing on the property. This right to reimbursement assumes the status of a lien upon the property.[20] This rule is equitable in nature. An estate should not receive a windfall in recovering property subject to a successful avoidance action. For instance, a debtor makes an unauthorized postpetition transfer of a motor home to a prepetition creditor in repayment of a prepetition debt. The creditor is unaware of the bankruptcy filing at the time of the transfer. While the creditor has possession of the motor home, the creditor makes payments on a loan secured by the motor home, replaces the tires, and insures and maintains the vehicle. Then a trustee learns of the transfer and commences an avoiding action. Because the creditor was unaware of the bankruptcy filing and has therefore presumably acted in good faith, the creditor is entitled to

19. 11 U.S.C. §550(d).
20. 11 U.S.C. §550(e).

reimbursement for the costs of maintaining the vehicle, the new tires, insurance payments, and any payments made on the underlying loan.

Section 551 preserves for the benefit of the estate any avoided transfer. That is, any right obtained by an estate from the avoidance of a transfer is a right of the estate, not of any other creditor.[21] The practical effect of this Section is that if, for example, a trustee avoids a second priority security interest in an asset, the estate becomes, in essence, the second priority holder of an interest in the asset. Any junior lienholders of the asset do not benefit from the avoidance by improving their position in the property. Their position is unaffected. Stated another way, the estate steps into the shoes of the transferee of an avoided transfer. This is similar to an insurance company's right of subrogation in tort law.

Section 552 concerns the postpetition effect of a security interest. The applicability of this Section will normally arise only in business Chapter 11 proceedings. Recall that the **floating lien** is a common financing arrangement of a retail or manufacturing business;[22] a financing entity has given the debtor a line of credit secured by all of the debtor's existing or after-acquired physical assets. This is why the lien is called a floating lien: because it "floats" upon the proceeds and products acquired by the debtor from the original collateral. If the debtor defaults upon a loan subject to a floating lien, the financing entity may repossess all the assets subject to the lien.

Under Section 552, any property that a debtor acquires after the filing of a bankruptcy proceeding is not subject to a prepetition lien resulting from a security agreement.[23] That is, after-acquired property is not generally subject to a prepetition consensual lien, except for floating liens. Floating liens do retain their hold on postpetition property, to the extent that the afteracquired property is traceable to the collateral subject to the lien, unless the court orders otherwise. A perfected security interest in the rents and revenues of a hotel, motel, or public facility therein also extends to the postpetition rents and revenues unless the court orders otherwise.[24] For example, Chat'N Chew Restaurant files Chapter 11 owing its secured creditor bank $100,000. Among the bank's collateral are inventory and the cash generated from sale of the inventory. As long as Chat'N Chew uses the cash subject to the bank's lien to purchase more inventory, the bank's lien will remain intact subject to Section 552(b). On the other hand, if Chat'N Chew sequesters the proceeds received from the sale of the inventory and uses other cash to make new purchases, the bank's lien will not extend to this new inventory not purchased from the bank's cash collateral.[25]

---

21. 11 U.S.C. §551.
22. See chapter 16 supra in connection with 11 U.S.C. §547(c)(5).
23. 11 U.S.C. §552(a).
24. 11 U.S.C. §552(b).
25. As to a secured creditor's rights in cash collateral, see chapter 18 infra.

Section 552 should not be construed to imply that a secured creditor loses its rights upon the filing by a debtor of a bankruptcy proceeding. Quite the contrary is true. As has already been seen, a secured creditor is entitled to adequate protection of its security interest, and a secured creditor may seek relief from the automatic stay to enforce its rights as a secured creditor.[26] Other provisions restrict a debtor's right to utilize a secured creditor's cash collateral.[27] Section 552 concerns only the effect of a prepetition security agreement on property acquired by a debtor or the estate after filing, not the validity of the security agreement itself.

D. SETOFFS

Section 553 concerns the treatment of setoffs under the Bankruptcy Code. A **setoff** is the common law right of a creditor to balance mutual debts with a debtor.[28] In bookkeeping terms setoffs are also known as reconciliations. To determine a setoff, simply subtract the smaller debt from the larger. Any balance remaining due either of the parties is still owed, but the remainder of the mutual debts have been set off. For example, Stan owes Laurel $10 and Laurel owes Stan $5. To set off these debts, the debt owed from Laurel to Stan is deemed satisfied ($5) and Stan now owes Laurel $5 instead of $10.

Section 553 permits the setoff of mutual prepetition debts.[29] Court approval is theoretically required because the automatic stay applies to the making of setoffs.[30] A creditor may not use a disallowed claim to make a setoff.[31] A creditor may not utilize as a setoff a claim assigned to it by another entity within 90 days of the bankruptcy filing.[32] Nor may a creditor utilize, for purposes of setoff, a debt owed to the debtor and incurred within 90 days prior to filing for the purpose of obtaining a setoff right.[33] As is the case with preferences, the debtor is presumed insolvent 90 days prior to the bankruptcy filing.[34] These provisions effectively preclude the obtaining of a preference by setoff.

Section 553(b) is a repetition of the improvement of position test described previously in connection with avoidable preferences.[35] Essentially,

26. See chapter 12 supra.
27. See chapter 18 infra.
28. See chapter 12 supra.
29. 11 U.S.C. §553(a).
30. 11 U.S.C. §362(a)(7). See chapter 12 supra.
31. 11 U.S.C. §553(a)(1). See chapter 21 infra.
32. 11 U.S.C. §553(a)(2).
33. 11 U.S.C. §553(a)(3).
34. 11 U.S.C. §553(c).
35. See chapter 16 supra.

the trustee may recover from a creditor who has made a setoff within 90 days prior to the bankruptcy filing the amount of the setoff to the extent that the setoff constitutes an improvement of the creditor's position in relation to other creditors. Or, more plainly, the trustee may avoid a setoff to the extent that it constitutes an avoidable preference. In this context, the setoff is the equivalent of a transfer. To the extent the transfer creates a preference, the setoff is avoidable. Simply consider a creditor's ability to make a setoff as identical to having a security interest in one of the debtor's assets, namely the debt owed to the debtor by the creditor. In this context, the same formula described in chapter 16 supra can be applied with no actual change: $(d_1 - si_1) > (d_2 - si_2)$, where *d* is the debt due the creditor by the debtor and *s* is the debt due by the creditor to the debtor. The numerals *1* and *2* pertain respectively to the dates 90 days prior to the bankruptcy filing (*1*) and the filing date (*2*). To the extent that the sum on date *2* is less than the sum on date *1*, the creditor cannot make the setoff. This difference is the extent of the "improved position."

As a practical matter, most creditors do not bring relief from stay motions to obtain permission to make setoffs. Most debtors and trustees do not seek sanctions against creditors for doing so. Setoff issues will most commonly arise by way of noticed motions. The issue may arise in connection with relief from stay motions or in the context of claims objections, to name but two instances.

Summary

A transfer made by a debtor with intent to hinder, delay, or defraud creditors is a fraudulent transfer. A transfer without fair or reasonable consideration made while a debtor is insolvent or that renders a debtor insolvent is also fraudulent. Transfers to corporate executives not in the ordinary course of business, such as the payment of large bonuses on the eve of bankruptcy, may also be avoidable as a fraudulent transfer.

Section 548 of the Bankruptcy Code permits a trustee to avoid fraudulent transfers occurring within two years prior to the bankruptcy filing. Nonbank-ruptcy or state law may also permit creditors to avoid fraudulent transfers. A trustee may also be able to utilize the state law of fraudulent transfers. This may permit a trustee to avoid fraudulent transfers occurring more than one year before the bankruptcy filing. An action to avoid a fraudulent transfer is commenced by filing an adversary proceeding.

A transfer of estate property after a bankruptcy filing that is made without court approval or is not otherwise authorized by the Bankruptcy Code is an unauthorized postpetition transaction that may be avoided by the trustee. Actions to avoid postpetition transactions are initiated by filing an adversary proceeding. Avoidable postpetition transactions are the subject of Bankruptcy Code Section 549.

Section 550 determines the liability of a transferee of an avoided transfer. Conversely, Section 550 also defines the recovery that each party may receive. Generally, the trustee is entitled to either a recovery of the property or the value of the property. A good-faith transferee will be allowed a claim for reimbursement from the estate for any improvements or repairs made to the asset or maintenance costs expended in preserving the asset. This claim will assume the status of a lien upon the property.

Section 551 provides a right of subrogation to a trustee successfully avoiding an avoidable transfer. That is, the trustee takes the place of the former transferee. This preserves the status of the transferred assets in relation to the rights of all other creditors.

Section 552 defines the postpetition effect of a security interest. Normally, a prepetition lien will not attach to property acquired by an estate after filing except for floating liens.

Section 553 retains for creditors the common law right of a creditor to set off mutual debts with a debtor. However, in certain defined circumstances, a setoff will be avoidable to the extent that it constitutes the equivalent of a preference. Properly, the making of a setoff by a creditor requires obtaining relief from the automatic stay. Setoff issues will normally arise within the context of a motion.

KEY TERMS

floating lien
fraudulent transfer
postpetition transfers
setoff

DISCUSSION QUESTIONS

1. What is a fraudulent transfer?
2. How is applicable state law concerning fraudulent transfers useful to a trustee seeking to set aside a fraudulent transfer?
3. What is an improper postpetition transfer?
4. What may a trustee recover in the successful exercise of an avoiding power?
5. What is a setoff?

PART IV

Liquidation and Claims

18

Use, Sale, or Lease of Property

A. LIQUIDATING ESTATE ASSETS

The next five chapters describe the basic concepts regarding the liquidation and distribution of estate assets or, in the case of reorganization proceedings, the preservation of assets for the benefit of creditors. The process of liquidation, allowance and classification of claims, and ultimate distribution of dividends to creditors is the core of the Code's debt collection features.

The first subject concerns the use, sale, or lease of property of the estate. Related to this subject are the issues of an estate incurring credit or exercising or terminating the benefits or burdens of a lease or franchise type agreement.[1] Preservation of an estate's cash after its physical assets have been liquidated and how property may be abandoned by a trustee complete the liquidation provisions of the Code.[2] Collectively, these matters comprise the methods by which the property of an estate is liquidated and cash preserved for the payment of dividends to creditors through the bankruptcy system.

Section 363 concerns the use, sale, or lease of estate property. The liquidation of any asset in a bankruptcy estate is subject to this section.

B. GENERAL RULES

The basic rule is that a trustee may use, sell, or lease property of the estate, other than in the ordinary course of business, only after notice and a

1. 11 U.S.C. §364; 11 U.S.C. §365. See chapters 19 and 20 infra.
2. See chapter 20 infra.

hearing.[3] This means that in a Chapter 7 liquidation, *any* use, sale, or lease of estate property will require notice and a hearing because a liquidation is *not* conducted in the ordinary course of business. On the other hand, in a Chapter 11, 12, or 13 proceeding, only transactions *not* in the ordinary course of business will require prior court approval.[4]

Recall that the phrase "notice and hearing" is specifically defined in Section 102.[5] Bankruptcy Rule 6004 sets forth the procedure used to obtain court approval for a sale of estate property. The rule requires at least 20 days' prior notice of the sale and notice of a hearing date if a party objects. Only if a party objects to the sale within five days of any deadline set forth in the notice does the matter then receive treatment as a noticed motion.[6] The rule is structured in this manner so that a sale or auction can go forward with certainty in most cases. In actual practice, objections to sales are rare except in the largest cases. A sale may take place by private sale or public auction. A private sale is a sale to a single buyer at an agreed-upon price. A public auction may be conducted by either a professional auctioneer or in open court where, essentially, a private sale is held subject to overbid in a court-supervised bidding procedure.[7]

The phrase **ordinary course of business** generally means normal, everyday business transactions. If a trustee is authorized to conduct the business of the debtor or if the debtor is a debtor-in-possession, normal, everyday business transactions do not require prior court approval. Transactions that are not normal, everyday transactions do require prior court approval. A practical test is to determine if the assets to be sold are capital or not. A sale involving capital assets must always have prior court approval before proceeding. If the transaction does not involve sale of a capital asset, prior court approval will probably not be required. A **capital asset** is one that is used to operate the business, such as equipment or fixtures. A **noncapital asset** is, for example, the inventory of an operating business.

For instance, assume that the debtor-in-possession owns a restaurant. It is not necessary for the debtor to obtain a court order every time the debtor wants to buy supplies or inventory so the restaurant can operate. It is also unnecessary to obtain a court order before serving a meal to a customer. (It is doubtful that customers would be patient enough to wait for such an order.) However, if the debtor wants to buy a new stove or

3. 11 U.S.C. §363(b)(1).When the asset for sale is a customer list with private data, the trustee must comply with the privacy policy of the seller. The court will order the United States Trustee to appoint an ombudsman pursuant to 11 U.S.C. §332. The ombudsman's purpose is to ensure that the privacy policy is followed. See chapter 10, supra.
4. 11 U.S.C. §363(c)(1). See infra this chapter.
5. 11 U.S.C. §102(1). See chapter 5 supra.
6. Bankruptcy Rule 6004(a). A sale of property with a value of $2,500 or less requires objection within 15 days of notice, or the sale may proceed. Bankruptcy Rule 6004(d).
7. Bankruptcy Rule 6004(f)(1).

wants to sell the restaurant, court approval will be required because these latter activities are not in the ordinary course of the restaurant business.

Conducting normal business operations does not require prior court approval in a Chapter 11. In a Chapter 7, because the business is being liquidated, nothing that a trustee does is in the ordinary course of business. Any sale of assets that a Chapter 7 trustee undertakes requires prior notice to creditors.

Section 721 does, however, give a Chapter 7 trustee an opportunity to operate a business for a limited time with court approval.[8] When such approval is obtained, the Chapter 7 trustee will be able to conduct normal business operations of the debtor for the order's duration.[9] A Chapter 7 trustee may seek such approval when it is in the best interests of creditors. For instance, if the debtor's primary asset is a bakery, keeping the facility open to sell all produced inventory at full value may be a good idea. If a sale of the business is pending when the Chapter 7 is filed, the buyer may want the business to continue operations prior to court approval of the sale. In these instances, the best interest of creditors will involve a prudent business judgment by the trustee — namely, taking the course of action that will most likely provide the creditors with the greatest ultimate dividend.

Normally, a Chapter 7 trustee will hold a public auction of an estate's assets. A trustee may seek ex parte approval to liquidate estate assets where the liquidation must be conducted immediately if the assets are to retain any value. For example, if the estate's primary asset is a restaurant and there is unused inventory, the trustee might obtain an ex parte order to sell the inventory without delay because a 20-day notice will only result in stale eggs, lettuce, tomatoes, and milk that are not likely to fetch a worthwhile price.

Section 363(c)(1) is the converse of Section 363(b)(1). If the debtor is authorized to operate a business, ordinary business operations may be conducted without prior court approval.[10] The difference between the two sections is that Section 363(b)(1) requires a trustee to give notice if property is being used, sold, or leased other than in the ordinary course of business, while Section 363(c)(1) affirmatively states that a trustee or debtor-in-possession does not need to obtain prior court approval to conduct ordinary business transactions of the estate. Section 363(c)(1) makes explicit what Section 363(b)(1) only implies.

The forms disk contains a number of sample forms used in conducting bankruptcy sales. Generally, any notice should contain enough description so a creditor or party in interest can determine whether to oppose the sale. Identification of the asset or assets being sold, the buyer, and the purchase price should be adequate in a private sale. The treatment to be afforded any

8. 11 U.S.C. §721.
9. 11 U.S.C. §363(c)(1).
10. 11 U.S.C. §363(c)(1).

claim secured by the property being sold should be disclosed. In the case of a public auction or sale subject to overbid in court, the notice should additionally disclose the location of the auction or sale and any requirements to qualify for overbidding.

C. USE OF CASH COLLATERAL

Section 363(c)(2) restricts a trustee's use of a secured creditor's **cash collateral** unless one of two conditions can be satisfied. *Cash collateral* is defined, for purposes of this provision, as cash or cash equivalents in which an entity other than the estate may have an interest. Cash collateral also includes hotel or motel revenues.[11] For example, a secured creditor with a security interest in accounts receivable, the proceeds of sales, or a floating lien as described in chapter 17 supra, has a security interest in cash collateral.

The first condition that will permit a debtor's use of cash collateral is the secured creditor's consent.[12] Use of this method should always be tried first. If consent cannot be obtained, use of the cash collateral will require court approval by filing a noticed motion.[13] To obtain court approval, a debtor or trustee will be required to provide adequate protection to any affected secured creditor.[14]

Obtaining the use of cash collateral can be a critical issue in the early stages of a Chapter 11 proceeding. If a secured creditor does not consent to the debtor's use of the cash collateral, it can become impossible to conduct business operations because a debtor is selling products and the secured creditor is receiving the proceeds, but the day-to-day expenses have no source of repayment. It becomes difficult to meet payroll and other basic expenses in this situation. As a result, the Code directs the court to give calendar priority to a motion to use cash collateral. The motion is to be scheduled "in accordance with the needs of the debtor" and the court is to act promptly on any request to use cash collateral.[15]

It is improper to use a secured creditor's cash collateral without the secured creditor's consent or prior court order. A secured creditor whose cash collateral is used without consent will obtain a first priority adminis-

11. 11 U.S.C. §363(a).
12. 11 U.S.C. §363(c)(2)(A).
13. 11 U.S.C. §363(c)(2)(B). Bankruptcy Rule 4001(b).
14. 11 U.S.C. §363(c)(3); 11 U.S.C. §363(e). See chapter 12 for a discussion of adequate protection.
15. 11 U.S.C. §363(c)(3); Bankruptcy Rule 4001(b).

trative claim upon the assets of the estate up to the amount of the improperly used cash collateral.[16] In Chapter 11 cases involving large corporations such as U.S. Air or K-Mart, consensual cash collateral orders generally containing these priority protections are typically approved by the court as a *first-day order*.

A motion to use cash collateral bears many similarities to a motion for relief from the automatic stay. Adequate protection for a creditor in these circumstances may require more than a monthly cash payment. A debtor may have to show the court that a creditor's equity in the collateral will not be impaired. This may very well require additional or replacement collateral. The court may also be required to make a preliminary determination as to the debtor's prospects of achieving a successful reorganization. Like a motion for relief from the automatic stay, there may also be both a preliminary and final hearing in connection with a motion to use cash collateral.[17]

A debtor-in-possession or trustee is required to keep cash collateral sequestered in a separate identified bank account.[18] This means that a debtor cannot commingle a creditor's cash collateral with other estate funds that are not cash collateral, unless the use of such funds has been permitted. Presumably, the segregation requirement acts as a further form of adequate protection to a secured creditor.

D. EFFECT OF THE AUTOMATIC STAY

Subsection 363(d) concerns the interaction between Section 363 and Section 362, the automatic stay. If the court has entered any order modifying or relieving the stay, then any sale, use, or lease of estate property has to be consistent with any order modifying or granting relief from the stay that has already been entered.[19] This means, in practical terms, that if the court grants a creditor relief from the automatic stay to foreclose upon estate property, any sale by the trustee must occur before the foreclosure sale unless the court orders otherwise. Additionally, the property must also be sold in accordance with applicable nonbankruptcy law. For example, if there is a local law requirement that there be title insurance, then the requirement must be followed.

16. 11 U.S.C. §507(b).
17. 11 U.S.C. §363(c)(3).
18. 11 U.S.C. §363(c)(4).
19. 11 U.S.C. §363(d).

E. SALES FREE AND CLEAR OF LIENS

While the above provisions pay careful heed to the rights of secured creditors, Section 363(f) acts to protect an estate's rights to sell estate property over the objection of a recalcitrant or hostile secured creditor. For example, Snidely Whiplash obtains a second deed of trust or mortgage on Nell's home as security for a loan. Nell defaults and then files a Chapter 7 proceeding to prevent the foreclosure sale.[20] Nell's trustee, Dudley Doright, obtains a buyer for the property that will pay all secured claims in full, Nell's homestead, and a dividend to unsecured creditors. Snidely plans to object because if he can foreclose and resell, he will receive a big profit for himself instead of Nell and her other creditors. Snidely would prefer to obtain relief from the automatic stay and foreclose. Preventing this tactic by a secured creditor is a major underlying premise of Section 363(f). Section 363(f) is a frequently litigated provision of Section 363. It allows a trustee to sell property free and clear of liens or interests.[21] The essence of this provision is that the bankruptcy court may order a sale of property over the objection and free of the interest of a recalcitrant or hostile secured creditor. Use of this procedure will be effective to pass clear title to the property over the objection of any lienholders. Use of this provision requires a noticed motion. A motion to sell property free and clear of liens must be brought as a noticed motion, not by way of the abbreviated notice procedures discussed earlier in this chapter.[22]

A property may be sold free and clear of liens or interests if one of five conditions described in the provision is satisfied as to each lienholder. These conditions are exclusive. Only one condition must be found applicable to each lien for the section to be effective, although compliance with more than one condition will often be possible.

First, the sale may occur if nonbankruptcy law will permit a sale of the property free and clear of the interests or liens.[23] For instance, a property may be sold free and clear of a trust deed or mortgage interest but not sold free and clear of a public utility easement or a government lien for real property taxes. Although nonbankruptcy law will permit a sale free of the interest in the first instance, nonbankruptcy law will not generally permit a sale free of the interest in the latter two instances.

Second, if an affected creditor consents to the sale, the property may be sold free of the consenting creditor's interest.[24] If an affected creditor

---

20. See chapter 12 supra.
21. 11 U.S.C. §363(f).
22. Bankruptcy Rule 6004(c). See also chapter 5 supra.
23. 11 U.S.C. §363(f)(1).
24. 11 U.S.C. §363(f)(2).

agrees to allow an act that it might otherwise prohibit or object to, the Bankruptcy Code will normally recognize such consent. This is simply common sense. Undisputed secured creditors who are going to be paid in full from the sale's proceeds will normally consent.

Third, if the property is being sold for an amount greater than the value of all liens owed upon it, then the sale will be permitted.[25] For example, if a house is worth $100,000 while the bank is owed $50,000 and the Whiplash Finance Company another $15,000, a sale for $100,000 will be for more than the two creditors are owed and the sale will be permitted to take place over the objection of either creditor. Because the two creditors will receive what they are entitled to — namely, payment in full of their claims — they will not be permitted to prevent the sale. It is this specific provision that most frequently prevents a recalcitrant or hostile lien creditor from wrongfully preventing liquidation of estate property. The creditor is paid its claim from the sale proceeds. In the event of a dispute the lien will attach to the proceeds, and their distribution will occur only upon further court order. Permitting the lien to attach to the proceeds is a form of adequate protection for the affected lienholder.[26]

Fourth, the sale will be permitted if the interest is in bona fide dispute.[27] This is unrelated to the issue of whether the property is being sold for more than the amount of the liens upon it. In this instance, the sale price might even be for less than the amount of the liens upon the property. For example, property encumbered by $65,000 of liens is being sold for $60,000. However, the trustee asserts that one lien is a preference, and the court believes that this assertion may be meritorious. Because the creditor's interest is in bona fide dispute, the sale may be permitted to take place free of the creditor's disputed interest. This provision permits a sale free of the alleged interest of a creditor who may be ultimately found to have no interest in the property. Normally, however, the court will allow the interest to attach to any available proceeds pending resolution of the dispute. The creditor is entitled to this protection.

Finally, the entity, usually the secured creditor, could be compelled to accept money rather than an interest in the property.[28] That is, if the lien holder could be ordered to receive payment in a nonbankruptcy legal proceeding in exchange for a release of the lien, the sale may be permitted.

As noted above, if at least one of the above five circumstances exists as to each lien or interest, a property may be sold free and clear of the liens or interests. Often, especially when dealing with a piece of property that may have multiple lien or interest holders upon it (such as three trust deeds or mortgages), one or more of the conditions will have to be satisfied to allow

---

25. 11 U.S.C. §363(f)(3).
26. See legislative history to 11 U.S.C. §363(f)(3).
27. 11 U.S.C. §363(f)(4).
28. 11 U.S.C. §363(f)(5).

the sale to proceed. For example, a tax lien for real property taxes will require full payment (Section 363(f)(1)). A secured creditor may consent to the sale (Section 363(f)(2)). A junior disputed lien may not be paid in full (Section 363(f)(4)). In this latter instance, the lien may attach to the proceeds of sale. Many situations will arise in which compliance with multiple provisions of Section 363(f) will be necessary to permit a sale of property free and clear of all liens and interests.

F. OTHER PROPERTY INTERESTS

Section 363(g) permits a trustee to sell property of an estate free and clear of any right of dower or curtesy. This provision applies only in those states where dower and curtesy exist. Hence, this provision has no applicability in a community property jurisdiction. Sections 363(i) and (j) act to protect the rights of a co-owner with a dower or curtesy right by either permitting the interest holder to match the sale price of the property or requiring the trustee to pay to the interest holder any share of the proceeds to which the interest holder may be entitled.[29]

In a community property jurisdiction, a nondebtor community property interest holder in estate property may match the purchase bid of a proposed sale and thus preserve the property for the nondebtor. However, a nondebtor community property interest holder is not entitled to a separate distribution of the sale proceeds when a sale does occur. This is because all community property of a debtor constitutes property of the estate and all community debt is discharged to the extent of the community property.[30]

Section 363(h) concerns the sale of property that is subject to joint ownership interests such as joint tenancy, tenancy in common, or tenancy by the entirety. For example, a husband and wife own a home in joint tenancy. One spouse files bankruptcy and the other does not. The couple is also involved in a divorce. A property settlement agreement has been entered into, which provides that each spouse retains a joint tenancy interest in the home while one spouse retains rights to reside in the home until the children reach the age of 18. When the children reach 18, the home will be sold and the spouses will realize the value of their respective interests. The spouse not residing in the home then files a bankruptcy proceeding. The trustee determines that there is equity in the home to pay unsecured creditors a dividend and the trustee decides to sell the house. The spouse residing in the house would rather that this not happen and opposes the sale. Section 363(h)

29. 11 U.S.C. §363(g), (i), (j).
30. 11 U.S.C. §363(i); 11 U.S.C. §541(a)(2); 11 U.S.C. §524(a)(3). See also chapters 7 and 14 supra.

allows the trustee to sell the property over the objection of the nondebtor joint or cotenant if four conditions can be complied with. Unlike a sale free and clear of liens where compliance with but one statutory condition may be satisfactory to permit a sale, all four conditions of Section 363(h) must be shown to apply before the court will approve the sale. Bankruptcy Rule 7001(3) requires the filing of an adversary proceeding to obtain approval of a sale subject to Section 363(h). In this instance, the motion procedures will be inappropriate.

The first condition that the trustee must show is that it would not be practicable to partition the property.[31] For example, it is not likely that a single family residence can be legally partitioned, such as splitting the lot in two and giving half to the filing spouse and half to the nonfiling spouse. The lot split might be illegal under the applicable nonbankruptcy law of many jurisdictions and the market value of the property divided is likely to be significantly less than if the property remained undivided.

Second, the trustee must show that a sale of only the estate's interest in the property will realize significantly less for the estate than a sale of the whole.[32] For instance, it is not likely that someone would want to purchase a half-interest in a home as a tenant in common or joint tenant with an unknown third party, particularly when the buyer might not be able to reside in the premises. A sale of the whole property is therefore likely to generate more proceeds than a sale of the debtor's interest alone.

Third, the trustee must show that the benefit to the estate of a sale of the property outweighs any detriment to the co-owners.[33] Generally, this comparison is based solely on economic factors. If the sale will provide an economic benefit to an estate's creditors and the co-owner is paid the value of the co-owner's interest in the property, there will usually be no detriment found to the nondebtor co-owner. Frankly, in the case of a nondebtor spouse with a right of occupancy, a check for the net equity in the property may have substantially less ultimate monetary value than the right to live in the premises for a fixed period of time, not to mention the potential adverse effects on a family's quality of life from being dispossessed from one residence to another.

Fourth, the trustee must show that the property is not used in the production, transmission, distribution, or sale of electric energy, natural or synthetic gas, or light and power.[34] If the debtor owns a windmill and sells energy to a third party, the trustee cannot sell the property over the objection of the co-owner. The intent of this provision is to protect a public utility

31. 11 U.S.C. §363(h)(1).
32. 11 U.S.C. §363(h)(2).
33. 11 U.S.C. §363(h)(3).
34. 11 U.S.C. §363(h)(4).

from the potential effects of a bankruptcy filing by a joint owner of the property.[35] This provision is rarely problematic.

If the trustee demonstrates all four of the above conditions, the court may approve a sale of the property including the interest of the nondebtor co-owner. The nondebtor does have a right to match the proposed purchase price and thus purchase the estate's interest in the asset.[36] If the property is sold, the trustee must distribute the net proceeds to the estate and co-owners according to their respective interests.[37] That is, the nonfiling spouse will receive payment of his or her interest in the property. For example, if a sale generates $30,000 in net proceeds to two equal co-owners, the estate will receive $15,000 for distribution to the creditors and the nondebtor co-owner will receive the remaining $15,000.

Thus, the best remedy for a nonfiling spouse who lives in a property and wants to continue to live there is to find a way to purchase the bankrupt spouse's interest in the property and pay the trustee pursuant to 11 U.S.C. §363(i). This right exists in both community property and nonco munity property jurisdictions. Although this may not be a feasible approach in some cases, it is usually the path of least resistance.

G. MISCELLANEOUS PROVISIONS

A secured creditor, like a co-owner, may bid on a sale of the property subject to the secured claim and, if the successful bidder, may offset against the bid price the amount of the secured claim.[38]

Section 363(l) concerns ipso facto clauses.[39] Recall that a bankruptcy **ipso facto clause** is a clause in a contract or deed or other document that makes insolvency, financial condition, or a bankruptcy filing an act of default. Such clauses are generally disfavored by the Bankruptcy Code and are unenforceable. So if a party asserts that an ipso facto clause prevents the sale or use of property of the estate, the ipso facto clause will be unenforceable.

Section 363(n) prevents collusive bidding in a bankruptcy sale.[40] For example, a group of potential bidders at a bankruptcy auction conspire together beforehand by agreeing to not bid against one another for certain assets. Each conspirator is thus assured of purchasing certain assets at a predetermined price. If the trustee discovers that this sort of activity has occurred, the trustee may avoid the sale and recover either the property or

35. See Historical and Revision Notes to Section 363(h).
36. 11 U.S.C. §363(i).
37. 11 U.S.C. §363(j).
38. 11 U.S.C. §363(k).
39. 11 U.S.C. §363(l). See chapter 14 supra.
40. 11 U.S.C. §363(n).

the difference between the actual price and the fair value price of the assets, including costs and attorneys' fees.

Section 363(o) protects consumers to the extent that the sale of commercial paper in consumer credit transactions retains all of the protections provided for by consumer law, such as the Federal Truth in Lending Act (15 U.S.C. §1601 et seq.).

It is difficult to successfully appeal a Bankruptcy Court order approving a sale, lease, or use of property under Section 363. The primary reason for this is that unless the transaction is stayed pending appeal, the reversal or modification upon appeal will not affect the validity of the sale to a goodfaith purchaser. Knowledge of the appeal's existence will not deprive the purchaser of good faith.[41] In short, unless the sale is stayed pending appeal, any appeal will likely be moot once the transaction closes. This is a strict and arbitrary provision. It exists to protect estates from frivolous appeals designed solely to delay or frustrate the effective administration of the bankruptcy system.

In any hearing under Section 363, the trustee has the burden of proof on any issue of adequate protection. A party asserting an interest in estate property bears the burden of proof on any issue regarding the validity, priority, or extent of the interest in the property.[42]

Summary

Section 363 of the Bankruptcy Code is the basic Code provision regulating the liquidation of estate assets by the use, sale, or lease of estate property. This section, along with the material in chapters 19 through 22 infra, comprises the core of the Code's debt-collection features.

Many sales, leases, or uses of estate property will require prior Bankruptcy Court approval. Some will not. The checklist categorizes the general types of activities that will require prior court approval and those that will not. When prior court approval is necessary, notice and a hearing will also be required. Bankruptcy Rule 6004 requires prior notice of a sale. If an objection is filed, the matter is then treated as a noticed motion.

A sale requiring court approval may take place by way of either a private sale or public auction. A private sale is a sale to a specific buyer identified in advance (such as a buyer of real estate). A public auction is a sale to the highest bidder bidding at the auction. Sometimes a private sale will be subject to overbid in open court. This is a form of auction.

Where an estate's cash is part of a secured creditor's lien, the cash collateral may not be used by the estate unless the creditor consents or the

41. 11 U.S.C. §363(m).
42. 11 U.S.C. §363(p).

court approves use of the cash collateral. A creditor with cash collateral rights is entitled to adequate protection to permit use of the cash collateral by the estate. The Code requires the Bankruptcy Court to give expedited treatment to a motion for the use of cash collateral.

Any use, sale, or lease of estate property must be consistent with any existing orders relieving or modifying the automatic stay pursuant to 11 U.S.C. §363(d).

Section 363(f) permits property of an estate to be sold free and clear of liens or interests. This provision permits the court to approve a sale over the objection or recalcitrance of lienholders. The provision contains five conditions, at least one of which must be found applicable to each lien or interest holder for the sale to be approved. The checklist summarizes these conditions.

Sections 363(g) and (i) account for the marital property interests of dower, curtesy, and community property.

Section 363(h) permits a sale of property subject to co-ownership by a nondebtor only if four conditions can be shown. The three most relevant conditions are that a partition of the property is impracticable, that a sale of only the estate's interest would realize significantly less than a sale of the whole, and that any benefit to the estate outweighs any detriment to the coowner.

KEY TERMS

capital asset
cash collateral
ipso facto clause
noncapital asset
ordinary course of business

Chapter 18 Checklist

18.1	SALES REQUIRING PRIOR COURT APPROVAL		*Authority*
	18.1.1	Prior Court Approval Required	11 U.S.C. §363(b)(1)
		1. All Chapter 7 sales, except as in 18.1.2 ¶2	11 U.S.C. §363(b)(1)
		2. Sales not in the ordinary course of business	11 U.S.C. §363(b)(1)

		Authority
18.1.2	Court Approval Not Required	
	1. Chapter 9, 11, 12, or 13 sales in the ordinary course of business	11 U.S.C. §363(b)(1), (c)(1)
	2. Chapter 7 sales in the ordinary course of business when a Chapter 7 trustee is authorized to operate	11 U.S.C. §363(c)(1)
18.2	SALES FREE AND CLEAR OF LIENS — CONDITIONS	
18.2.1	Nonbankruptcy Law Permits	11 U.S.C. §363(f)(1)
18.2.2	Lienholders Consent	11 U.S.C. §363(f)(2)
18.2.3	All Liens Will Be Paid in Full	11 U.S.C. §363(f)(3)
18.2.4	Lien Is in Good-Faith Dispute	11 U.S.C. §363(f)(4)
18.2.5	Lienholder Could Be Legally Compelled to Accept Money Satisfaction	11 U.S.C. §363(f)(5)

DISCUSSION QUESTIONS

1. Describe the common methods by which a bankruptcy trustee liquidates an estate's assets. When does a sale of estate property require court approval?
2. What is cash collateral? What actions must a trustee take to be authorized to use cash collateral?
3. How can property be sold over the objection of a lienholder?
4. Under what conditions may a trustee sell a nondebtor's interest in property owned as a cotenant or joint tenant with the debtor?
5. Why is it necessary to protect private information in the sale of customer lists?

19

Executory Contracts and Leases

A. EXECUTORY CONTRACTS

Executory contracts are contracts for which performance remains due to some extent on both sides.[1] This is the most widely accepted definition. For example, an unexpired lease is an executory contract. The landlord has a continuing obligation to provide the premises to the tenant while the tenant has a continuing obligation to pay rent to the landlord and abide by the remaining lease provisions. Performance remains due to some extent on both sides.

Many other business activities are also executory contracts. Such a contract can constitute the most important asset of a bankruptcy estate. A franchise agreement to operate a business is usually an executory contract. **License** agreements to operate a business or to market a product line are executory contracts. Thus, a golf shop's license to use a specific name, such as "MacDuffer," in exchange for royalty payments is an executory contract. The entity issuing the license, the **licensor** (the owner of the name "MacDuffer"), has a continuing obligation to allow the license holder to use the name and sell products with the "MacDuffer" name. The holder of the license, the **licensee**, has a continuing obligation to provide accountings to the licensor and to pay regular royalties, called license fees, to the licensor. Substantial performance remains due on both sides, and hence the transaction is an executory contract. Without the license, the golf shop's value or ability to succeed may be seriously or fatally impaired. A Burger King

1. See Historical and Revision Notes to 11 U.S.C. §365. This is also known as the "Countryman" definition in honor of Professor Vernon Countryman, who described it in two articles titled Executory Contracts in Bankruptcy, 57 Minn. L. Rev. 439 (1973); 58 Minn. L. Rev. 479 (1974).

restaurant franchise is an executory contract. Certainly the value of the franchise is lower if the franchisee loses the right to operate the hamburger stand as a Burger King restaurant.[2] An uncompleted contract to manufacture products or to construct a building is an executory contract.

In each of the above instances, if a trustee or debtor-in-possession is the holder of the franchise or the manufacturer of the product, the value of the franchise or value of the contract may be critical to the ability of the debtor to successfully reorganize or to provide creditors with a dividend in the event of a Chapter 7 proceeding. In such a situation, the executory contract is a benefit. Assigning the executory contract to a third party or retaining the contract and continuing to perform according to its terms is a right a debtor or trustee may seek to preserve. On the other hand, if the contract is burdensome and is itself a major cause of the bankruptcy filing, the debtor or trustee may desire to abandon or reject the contract.[3]

Conversely, in each of the above instances, the nondebtor party to the contract is a creditor. This is obvious in instances where the debtor owes payments to the nondebtor party at the commencement of a proceeding, but this is also true where any payments may be current at the commencement of a proceeding but where future performance remains due. If monies are due or performance is not forthcoming, the creditor may seek to preserve its right to collect payment or terminate the contract. Yet recall that the automatic stay prevents collection or termination of the contract unless there is no equity in the property or the property is not necessary to an effective reorganization (not likely where the debtor is a franchise).

Section 365 of the Bankruptcy Code concerns executory contracts and unexpired leases. Were it not for this provision, executory contracts and unexpired leases would be treated in a manner identical to all other property of the estate and be subject to the same rules. The reason for this special treatment is that an executory contract or unexpired lease is a specialized interest in property, which often may be sold, used, or leased. However, the parties to an executory contract or lease, debtor or nondebtor, may have rights or interests to protect that are different from or additional to a simple right to receive payment or performance. Accordingly, Section 365 has been created to account for the special conditions existing between the parties to an executory contract or unexpired lease.

Section 365 reconciles the competing desires of a debtor or creditor to retain or terminate an executory contract. In its essence, Section 365 treats a nondebtor party to an executory contract as the functional equivalent of a secured creditor, the contract rights constituting the creditor's security for the debtor's performance of the contract. Because the court must approve

---

2. In re Rovine Corp., 6 Bankr. 661 (W.D. Tenn. 1980).
3. As to abandonment, see chapter 20 infra.

a decision to assume or reject the contract when called upon to do so, the matter is also similar to a motion for relief from stay.

One of two actions may be taken with an executory contract in a bankruptcy. A trustee or debtor-in-possession may assume or reject an executory contract or unexpired lease. In individual Chapter 7 cases, the debtor may assume a lease of personal property if not assumed by the trustee.[4] This is accomplished either by way of a noticed motion procedure to assume or reject the contract or by operation of the various time periods contained in Section 365.[5] The remainder of Section 365 describes the conditions and time periods under which an executory contract or unexpired lease may be assumed or rejected.

B. ASSUMING A CONTRACT

For an executory contract to be assumed, the trustee must meet certain conditions. Section 365(b) states these conditions. Every condition must be complied with for the assumption to occur. The first condition the trustee must meet is to cure or provide **adequate assurance** that any existing default will be promptly cured. Nonmonetary defaults that are impossible for a trustee to cure need not be cured except from and after the time of assumption.[6] The term *adequate assurance* has essentially the same meaning as adequate protection.[7] Thus, six months of past-due rent must either be paid, an agreement must be made with the landlord to cure the arrearage over a period of time, or the trustee must prove to the court that the default can be cured within a prompt period of time. A trustee or debtor-in-possession who wants the contract's benefits must also accept the burdens and perform the contract.[8]

Second, the trustee must provide compensation or adequate assurance that the nondebtor party will be compensated for any actual damages arising from any default. This compensation may include attorneys' fees and costs incurred.[9]

Third, and perhaps most important, a trustee or debtor-in-possession must provide adequate assurance of future performance under the

4. 11 U.S.C. §365(a), (p). The phrase *executory contract* will also mean *unexpired lease* for the duration of this chapter except where otherwise stated.
5. Bankruptcy Rule 6006. See chapter 5 supra and part C of this chapter infra.
6. 11 U.S.C. §365(b)(1)(A).
7. 11 U.S.C. §361. See chapter 12 supra.
8. 11 U.S.C. §365(b)(1).
9. 11 U.S.C. §365(b)(1)(B).

contract.[10] This may be as simple as the court's reviewing a future financial projection and concluding that the trustee will likely be able to pay the rent on time or as complex as a debtor-in-possession's being required to convince the court and the creditor that the debtor-in-possession has sufficient financial and physical resources to provide adequate assurance that performance will be rendered and the contract completed.

All of these conditions are consistent with the discussion in chapter 12 supra concerning the concept of adequate protection in connection with the automatic stay. Recall that adequate protection involves making payments or providing additional or replacement collateral. Curing a default and providing assurances of future performance under the term "adequate assurances" is virtually identical.[11] Further, although Section 365(b) is phrased so as to apply only to defaulted executory contracts, the Bankruptcy Courts generally require compliance with Section 365(b)(1) by a trustee or debtor-in-possession in any motion to assume an executory contract.[12]

The 2005 legislation adds Section 365(p) to the Bankruptcy Code. This provision permits an individual Chapter 7 debtor to assume a personal property lease if the trustee does not do so. In such an event, the creditor may condition the assumption on cure of any outstanding default set by the contract. Further, a creditor contacting an individual debtor to assume a personal property lease will not violate the automatic stay. Unless the trustee or debtor assumes the lease, rejection of the lease terminates the automatic stay as to the leased property. This means that the creditor may then seek repossession of its property without having to formally seek relief from the stay pursuant to the procedures described in chapter 12, supra.

A default created by an alleged *ipso facto clause* is not enforceable by the nondebtor party. Any clause in a contract placing a debtor in default solely because a bankruptcy proceeding has been filed or because the debtor may be insolvent is not enforceable. A debtor is not required to provide adequate assurances that it will not be bankrupt. Additionally, penalty rates imposed by virtue of nonmonetary defaults cannot be enforced by the nondebtor party.[13]

Subsection 365(b)(3) concerns shopping center leases and the meaning of adequate assurance of performance of a shopping center lease. A unique concern in shopping center leases is provisions regarding the tenant mix and the necessary fact that a shopping center contains multiple

10. 11 U.S.C. §365(b)(1)(C).
11. See chapter 12 supra.
12. See also 11 U.S.C. §365(f)(2).
13. 11 U.S.C. §365(b)(2). See discussion of ipso facto clauses generally in chapter 14 supra.

leases often with interrelated provisions. In these instances, adequate assurance of future performance will mean that the lease will be used for its intended purpose only and will not violate any other lease agreement concerning the shopping center.[14] A lease provision limiting a premise's use to a boutique and a provision barring other boutique tenants are examples of tenant mix provisions.

Finally, where a lease requires a lessor to provide services or amenities to a debtor, the lessor may refuse to provide the services or amenities prior to assumption unless the trustee can pay for the services.[15]

Section 365(c) contains further limitations on a trustee's ability to assume an executory contract, even if adequate assurance and a cure of any defaults can be made. First, if nonbankruptcy law excuses a party from accepting performance from an assignee of the trustee, then nonbankruptcy law will be honored unless the nondebtor party to the contract consents to the assignment.[16] That is, if a nonbankruptcy statute permits a party to a contract to prohibit assignment of an executory contract, then this statute will be honored. For example, federal law generally prohibits the assignment of a government contract unless the federal government consents. This is known as the **Anti-Assignment Act**.[17] If a trustee proposes to assume and assign a government contract to a third party, the Anti-Assignment Act will be given effect and the executory contract may not be assigned unless the federal government consents. On the other hand, an anti-assignment clause in a contract may not be an effective bar to a Section 365 assignment because the contract clause is not a statute.

If a nonresidential lease of real property has been terminated prior to the entry of an order for relief, the lease may not be assumed.[18] This is a rational rule because in this event there is nothing for a trustee to assume.

As a practical matter, if there is a risk that an executory contract will be terminated prior to a bankruptcy filing, the filing should take place promptly to avoid the contract's termination. Imposition of the automatic stay accomplishes this goal. This rule of thumb applies to all executory contracts. In most situations, if a nondebtor party properly terminates an executory contract prior to commencement of the bankruptcy proceeding, then there is no executory contract in existence to assume. Whether or not the contract exists to assume can sometimes mean the difference between a successful or unsuccessful result for the estate and its creditors.

If an executory contract is to make a loan or other financial commitment, then the contract may not be assumed. A debtor or trustee cannot force a

14. 11 U.S.C. §365(b)(3).
15. 11 U.S.C. §365(b)(4).
16. 11 U.S.C. §365(c)(1).
17. 41 U.S.C. §15.
18. 11 U.S.C. §365(c)(3).

lender to perform a loan commitment if the borrower files a bankruptcy.[19] This does not imply that a bankruptcy estate may not obtain credit. The question of an estate obtaining credit is governed solely by Section 364, not Section 365.[20] Thus, a debtor with a prepetition loan commitment will have to proceed by Section 364 if postpetition approval of the loan is sought. This is described in chapter 20 infra.

C. TIME LIMITS FOR ASSUMPTION

Section 365(d) concerns the time limits within which executory contracts may or must be assumed. Different rules will apply depending on the type of Chapter proceeding involved and whether the subject matter of assumption is a lease of real or personal property. Real property is further distinguished by its characterization as residential or nonresidential real property. A lease is of **residential** real property most commonly when the debtor resides in the premises subject to the lease. A lease is **nonresidential** in virtually all other situations. This chapter's checklist summarizes these time limits.

First, in a Chapter 7, if a trustee does not act affirmatively to assume or reject any executory contract or lease of real or personal property within 60 days after the order for relief is entered, then the contract or lease is deemed rejected. No court action is required to effectuate the rejection.[21] To translate, a Chapter 7 trustee has 60 days to assume or reject any executory contract or unexpired lease of real property or personal property. If the trustee takes no action within the 60-day period, then the contract or lease is deemed to be automatically rejected and terminated. For example, if a franchise store is permanently closed, no action need be taken by the franchisor to revoke the franchise in a Chapter 7. If a copy machine is returned to the lessor, no other action needs to be taken to reject the lease. The burden is therefore on the Chapter 7 trustee to obtain a court order if assumption is desired. A trustee who has a buyer for a franchise will proceed by Section 365 to assume and assign the contract.

As a practical matter, in consumer Chapter 7 proceedings trustees do not usually act to assume residential real property leases, nor do debtors proceed to obtain court approval to assume them. Also, as a practical matter, lessors do not proceed to court on day 61 seeking to evict the

19. 11 U.S.C. §365(c)(2).
20. See chapter 20 infra.
21. 11 U.S.C. §365(d)(1); §365(d)(4).

debtor tenant. A lessor is generally satisfied if a tenant is continuing to pay rent. On the other hand, if the rent is in default upon the entry of an order for relief, the automatic stay may bar an eviction of the tenant debtor from the premises in some circumstances (see chapter 12 supra). A lessor may move the court for rejection of the lease or relief from the stay to terminate the lease. Alternatively, if the lessor waits until the sixty-first day after the entry of an order for relief, the lease will be deemed rejected and the lessor may be able to obtain a writ of possession directly from the Bankruptcy Court.

In an individual Chapter 7, if a trustee does not assume a lease of personal property, the debtor may assume the lease by notifying the creditor and curing the lease pursuant to the terms of the contract as set forth in Section 365(p), discussed above. This may or may not mean that an individual debtor may assume the lease more than 60 days after a filing, because the provision also provides that the automatic stay is automatically terminated if the lease is not assumed. Since Section 362(h) (see chapter 12 supra) relieves the stay with respect to personal property leases if the lease is not assumed within the "Statement of Intention" period (see chapter 21 infra), this may mean that a debtor must effectively act to assume a lease of personal property within the first 30 days of the case irrespective of the Section 365 time limits. Since Section 365(p) is an entirely new provision, this is one of the issues that the courts will have to determine.

In proceedings other than a Chapter 7, such as a Chapter 11 reorganization, a trustee or debtor-in-possession may assume or reject an executory contract or lease of personal property or an unexpired residential lease at any time prior to court confirmation of a plan proposed under the particular Chapter.[22] Thus, a franchise does not terminate 60 days after filing if a debtorin-possession does not assume the franchise prior to this date. Conversely, because there is no definite time limit to assume an executory contract in a non-Chapter 7 proceeding, any party may bring the matter before the court and request that a date certain be set for the debtor to assume or reject the contract.

A motion to assume or reject may or may not be combined with a motion for relief from stay. The latter is not necessary in this instance. In the case of a personal property lease, a motion may take the form of a motion for relief from stay, as opposed to a motion to assume or reject.

In the case of a real estate lease, a lessor will bring a motion to assume or reject the lease before the court, so that any defaults can be ordered promptly cured or the lease rejected without undue delay.

---

22. 11 U.S.C. §365(d)(2). However, in Chapter 13, personal property lease payments must be paid current during pendency of the case. 11 U.S.C. §1326(a)(1). See chapter 23 infra.

A nonresidential real estate lessor may take this approach when the lessor desires to act promptly after the lessee's bankruptcy filing rather than wait 120 days (see infra this chapter). Any motion will also ask the court to order appropriate adequate protection in the form of adequate assurances of future performance.

Recall that a lessor of residential real property may continue prosecution of an unlawful detainer or eviction proceeding as an exception to the automatic stay if the debtor does not pay postpetition rent on a timely basis, if the lease has already been terminated pursuant to the lease or State law, or if the debtor has filed a bankruptcy petition within the past year and failed to pay postpetition rent. See chapter 12 supra. The effect of all these provisions is to minimize the effect of bankruptcy upon landlords of residential real estate.

In the case of other types of executory contracts, such as a manufacturing contract, a trustee or debtor-in-possession may want to bring a motion to assume the contract if the nondebtor party refuses to perform after the debtor's bankruptcy filing. This will force the nondebtor to abide by the contract's terms. A nondebtor party may wish to bring a motion to have the contract rejected if there are prepetition defaults that require cure before the contract's performance can be completed.

If a trustee or debtor-in-possession does choose to assume an executory contract, the contract's terms must be abided by, although the court may defer performance for up to 60 days.[23] A trustee or debtor-in-possession must accept the burdens as well as the benefits in assuming an executory contract.[24]

In any Chapter proceeding, a nonresidential lease of real property must be assumed within 120 days after an order for relief is entered or the lease will be deemed rejected. A nonresidential lease that is rejected requires the trustee or debtor-in-possession to surrender the premises to the lessor and thus, conversely, entitles the lessor to obtain immediate court approval for an eviction order. The court may extend this 120-day period only upon a motion of the lessor or trustee for cause and only for 90 days, unless the lessor consents to further extensions.[25] This 120-day time limit is strictly enforced by most Bankruptcy Courts.

The 120-day rule is of critical importance where the debtor is a party to a nonresidential real property lease. If the debtor is a restaurant or retail store, a failure to properly act to assume the lease within 120 days after filing will probably result in the debtor's liquidation.

---

23. 11 U.S.C. §365(d)(3).
24. 11 U.S.C. §365(f)(2).
25. 11 U.S.C. §365(d)(4).

D. MISCELLANEOUS PROVISIONS

Section 365(e) concerns ipso facto clauses where a trustee wants to assume an executory contract that is not otherwise in default at the time of assumption. Ipso facto clauses are unenforceable. However, if nonbankruptcy law permits termination upon bankruptcy or insolvency unless the nondebtor party consents, such nonbankruptcy law will be honored. Further, a contract to extend credit may not be enforceable postpetition. The rationale for this is the same as described in connection with Section 365(c) supra.[26]

Often when a trustee or debtor-in-possession wants to assume an executory contract, it is for the primary purpose of assigning the contract to a third party. For example, the debtor who owns the Burger King franchise desires to sell it. Section 365(f) concerns the issues that arise in the effort to assign the contract.

Section 365(f) generally permits the assignment of an executory contract.[27] However, the assignment will only be permitted if any defaults are cured, and only if the nondebtor party is provided with adequate assurance of future performance.[28] In other words, a contract must be assumed in order to be assigned. The general policy of the Bankruptcy Code is to permit the assignment of executory contracts.[29]

If an executory contract is rejected, a determination must be made as to the type of claim against the estate the nondebtor party will have. The claim can become either a prepetition unsecured claim or an administrative claim. The status of the claim will have a dramatic effect upon the distributive priority accorded to it.[30] Generally, the rejection of an executory contract is considered a breach of the contract.[31] Where a contract is rejected without ever having been assumed, rejection is considered to have occurred immediately prior to the bankruptcy filing.[32] This means that the nondebtor party will normally stand in the status of a prepetition unsecured creditor.

On the other hand, if a trustee does assume an executory contract but then later rejects it, or if the executory contract is assumed and the proceeding is then converted to a Chapter 7, the breach is considered to have occurred at the time of rejection or, if the proceeding has been converted,

26. 11 U.S.C. §365(e).
27. 11 U.S.C. §365(f)(1).
28. 11 U.S.C. §365(f)(2).
29. See Historical and Revision Notes to Section 365(f).
30. See chapter 21 infra.
31. 11 U.S.C. §365(g); 11 U.S.C. §365(h)(1).
32. 11 U.S.C. §365(g)(1).

immediately prior to conversion.[33] Thus, the assumption of an executory contract will have the practical effect of making any subsequent claim of the nondebtor party an administrative claim. Administrative claims have a higher distributive priority than general unsecured claims.[34]

Section 365(h)(2) concerns the rights of a nondebtor lessee where the trustee or debtor-in-possession is the lessor or seller of timeshare interests and rejects, rather than assumes, the executory contract.[35] The lessee or timeshare purchaser may elect either to treat the contract as terminated or to remain in possession for the term of the lease or timeshare interest.[36] In the former situation, the nondebtor's rights are limited to a claim for damages, which will likely be a general unsecured claim. In the latter instance, the nondebtor's claim is limited to a setoff against the lease or timeshare price to the extent of any actual damages sustained as a result of the trustee's rejection of the contract.[37]

E. REAL ESTATE CONTRACTS

A contract for a sale of real estate that is pending when a bankruptcy proceeding commences is an executory contract. Because the seller still has an obligation to convey title to the property and the purchaser still has an obligation to pay the price, performance remains due to some extent on both sides. Sections 365(i) and (j) concern the issues raised by this scenario. If a trustee rejects an executory contract in which the debtor is the seller, the purchaser's rights will vary depending upon whether the buyer is in possession of the real property. If the purchaser is not in possession, the purchaser is unaffected by Section 365(i) and its rights will be determined elsewhere in the Code. If the purchaser is in possession, the purchaser may elect to treat the contract as terminated or may remain in possession of the property. If the purchaser remains in possession of the property, the purchaser may complete the purchase and force the debtor or trustee to convey title. The purchase price may be offset by the amount of the purchaser's damages but the purchaser acquires no further claim.[38] To summarize, a purchaser in possession may elect either to terminate the transaction or to enforce the contract.

If the purchaser of real estate in a rejected sale of real estate treats the contract as terminated, the purchaser acquires a lien on the debtor's interest

33. 11 U.S.C. §365(g)(2).
34. See chapter 21 infra.
35. The provision relating to timeshare interests was added to the Code in 1984.
36. 11 U.S.C. §365(h)(1).
37. 11 U.S.C. §365(h)(2).

in the property to recover any part of the purchase price paid prior to rejection. A purchaser not in possession of real estate that is the subject of a rejected executory contract has a similar lien right.[39] This lien right will make the rejected purchaser the equivalent of a secured creditor.

The assignment of an executory contract under Section 365 relieves the trustee and estate of any liability arising after the assignment.[40]

F. INTELLECTUAL PROPERTY

Section 365(n) was enacted in 1988.[41] The provisions of Section 365(n) give special treatment to executory contracts involving **intellectual property**. Patents, copyrights, and trademarks are common forms of intellectual property. Prior to enactment of these provisions, an executory contract involving intellectual property was governed by the rules described above.

The most common form of intellectual property contract is known as a license. The owner of the patent or copyright is known as the licensor. The manufacturer or publisher is known as the licensee.

If a trustee rejects an intellectual property executory contract and the debtor is the licensor, the licensee has an option to either retain its rights and keep the contract in effect or to terminate the contract. If the licensee keeps the contract in effect, performance proceeds. The only effect of the bankruptcy is that the trustee is directed to cooperate with the licensee.[42] Of course, to the extent that royalties are not exempt, they will normally constitute property of the estate.

Summary

Executory contracts are contracts for which performance remains due to some extent on both sides. Franchise or license agreements are common executory contracts. Real estate leases, whether of residential or nonresidential property, are specialized types of executory contracts. The effects of a bankruptcy upon executory contracts and unexpired leases is the subject of Bankruptcy Code Section 365.

---

38. 11 U.S.C. §365(i).
39. 11 U.S.C. §365(j).
40. 11 U.S.C. §365(k).
41. Pub. L. No. 100-56, 102 Stat. 2538 (October 18, 1988).
42. 11 U.S.C. §365(n).

An executory contract may either be assumed or rejected by a bankruptcy estate. In an individual Chapter 7, if the trustee does not assume a lease of personal property, the debtor may do so. At some point in time in any bankruptcy proceeding, all executory contracts will have to be assumed or rejected. In many situations, assumption will have to occur within a fixed time period, normally 60 days after the bankruptcy filing, or the contract will be deemed rejected. The checklist accompanying this chapter describes the time limits involved in the assumption of executory contracts. Assumption of an executory contract will always require a court order or be contained within the provisions of a confirmed reorganization plan.

When an estate wants to assume an executory contract, the estate must promptly cure any existing monetary defaults, compensate the nondebtor party for any actual damages, and provide adequate assurance of future performance. This latter requirement is very similar to the concept of adequate protection that has been previously discussed in connection with automatic stay and cash collateral issues in chapters 12 and 18 supra.

A trustee may not assume or assign an executory contract if a nonbankruptcy statute prohibits assignment absent the consent of the nondebtor party to the contract. Executory contracts to extend credit or make loans to a debtor may not be assumed or assigned. These transactions are more properly characterized as loans to the estate. These transactions are described in chapter 20 infra.

The effect given to a rejected executory contract differs depending upon whether the contract has been previously assumed. Claims arising from a contract rejected by operation of the time limits set forth in the Code or that are never assumed are treated as prepetition unsecured claims. When an executory contract is assumed, however, claims arising from it will thereafter receive treatment as an administrative expense and be entitled to a higher distributive priority in the event of liquidation. That is, an executory contract assumed in a Chapter 11 proceeding is treated as an administrative claim of the Chapter 11 in the event the proceeding is converted to a Chapter 7.

Section 365 contains several other features pertaining to specific types of contracts. Contracts for timeshare ownership are given special treatment in Section 365(h). Sections 365(i) and (j) regard contracts for the sale of real estate. Generally, a nondebtor buyer in possession will have greater rights to force assumption of the contract than a nondebtor buyer not in possession. Section 365(n), added to the Code in 1988, clarifies the effect of bankruptcy upon an executory contract involving intellectual property, such as patents or copyrights.

KEY TERMS

adequate assurance
Anti-Assignment Act
executory contracts
intellectual property license
license
licensor
nonresidential
residential

Chapter 19 Checklist

19.1 TIME LIMITS FOR ASSUMPTION OR REJECTION OF EXECUTORY CONTRACTS OR UNEXPIRED LEASES

	Chapter	*Nonresidential Leases*	*Executory Contracts/ Residential Leases*	*Statute*
19.1.1	7	120 days	60 days	11 U.S.C. §365(d)(1), (4)
19.1.2	9	120 days	before confirmation or prior court order after motion	11 U.S.C. §365(d)(2), (4)
19.1.3	11	120 days	before confirmation or prior court order after motion	11 U.S.C. §365(d)(2), (4)
19.1.4	12	120 days	before confirmation or prior court order after motion	11 U.S.C. §365(d)(2), (4)

	Chapter	Nonresidential Leases	Executory Contracts/ Residential Leases	Statute
19.1.5	13	120 days	before confirmation or prior court order after motion	11 U.S.C. §365(d)(2), (4)

DISCUSSION QUESTIONS

1. What is an executory contract? Can the following be executory contracts: license agreement? royalty contract? franchise agreement? unexpired lease? pending contract for the sale of real estate? installment loan contract?
2. What is adequate assurance of performance?
3. What must a trustee or debtor-in-possession do to assume an unexpired lease or executory contract?
4. What are the time limits within which an executory contract must or may be assumed in the various Chapter proceedings? Unexpired nonresidential lease? Residential lease?
5. What is the difference between assumption and assignment?
6. What is the effect of assumption or rejection of an executory contract or lease upon any claims of the nondebtor party to the contract?
7. What are the rights of a purchaser of an executory contract for the purchase of real estate?

20

Miscellaneous Provisions Regarding Property of the Estate

A. PRESERVATION OF CASH

The ultimate asset that a trustee will administer in any estate is cash. This is implicit in the trustee's primary duty to liquidate the assets of an estate.[1] Cash in the custody of a Chapter 11 debtor-in-possession is an estate asset. Section 345 regulates the preservation and use of cash assets in bankruptcy estates.

Section 345 illustrates the major difference between a bankruptcy and a nonbankruptcy trustee. Under nonbankruptcy law, nonbankruptcy trustees are generally permitted to invest trust funds in any prudent business manner. For example, a nonbankruptcy trustee may invest trust funds in making secured loans (secured by adequate collateral), stocks, bonds, or other investments designed to yield the greatest return at a minimum of risk. In fact, a nonbankruptcy trustee who invests trust funds only in savings accounts could possibly be held in violation of the trustee's duties to prudently maximize returns on the assets.

On the other hand, a bankruptcy trustee is not given broad discretion to invest estate assets. A bankruptcy trustee is quite restricted in the uses that may be made of an estate's cash. One fear is that because the bankruptcy system is designed to protect the assets of an estate for its creditors, no risks should be taken to cause further losses to the estate funds. Further,

1. See chapter 10 supra.

giving bankruptcy trustees discretion to invest estate funds would likely result in substantial litigation by debtors and creditors alike, constantly challenging a trustee's business judgment as either too liberal or too conservative. Under these circumstances, no reasonable person would want to be a bankruptcy trustee. Thus, rather than creating a complex set of rules about what might or might not be a prudent investment of estate funds and permitting second guessing or Monday morning quarterbacking, the Bankruptcy Code limits a bankruptcy trustee's use of funds to deposits in a federally insured bank or savings and loan institution unless the court orders otherwise.[2]

A trustee may do one of two things with estate funds. They may be placed on deposit in an interest bearing account or they may be placed into insured certificates of deposit.[3]

In addition to being limited to investing estate funds as described, a trustee must also keep the money in approved depositories. An approved Bankruptcy Court depository is a federally insured bank or savings and loan that is willing to guarantee payment of estate funds in excess of $100,000 on deposit.[4] At all federally insured banks or savings and loan institutions, individual accounts are normally guaranteed only up to $100,000. This means that if the institution is itself declared insolvent, the insurance will only pay up to $100,000 per account. As a result, a financial institution wanting to act as a depository for bankruptcy funds must guarantee payment of deposits in excess of $100,000 per account.[5] This is a great irony of the Bankruptcy Code.

Local bankruptcy rules will often further amplify the above rules and relate them to the amount of the trustee's bond, as discussed in chapter 10 of this text. Many Bankruptcy Courts or United States Trustees will maintain lists of approved depositories for bankruptcy funds in a given area. An approved depository is one that has posted the requisite guaranty of funds on deposit of more than $100,000.

Many financial institutions are willing to comply with these provisions of the Bankruptcy Code or Rules. A major reason is that the funds are likely to be on deposit with the bank for a significantly longer time than ordinary nonbankruptcy accounts. The financial institution will thereby have use of the funds for exceptional periods of time at relatively low rates of interest. As a result, the handling of bankruptcy deposits is profitable for many financial institutions, despite the above rules.

2. 11 U.S.C. §345(a).
3. 11 U.S.C. §345(a). See also the Historical and Revision Notes to Section 345(a). The notes imply that government bonds may also be appropriate investments. However, as a practical matter, the administration of most bankruptcy estates can be completed in substantially less time than the longevity rates of most government bonds. This makes them impractical as useful investments by a bankruptcy trustee.
4. 11 U.S.C. §345(b).
5. 11 U.S.C. §345(b).

B. UTILITY SERVICE/DISCRIMINATION

Section 366 concerns the rights of public utility companies to discontinue or provide service to debtors or bankruptcy estates. This provision eliminates a practice that existed under the former Bankruptcy Act. Under the Bankruptcy Act, if a debtor listed a public utility company as a creditor, the public utility would promptly cut off the debtor's service. To restore service, the utility would charge the debtor an excessive deposit, the practical effect of which was to make utility debts nondischargeable. Section 366 has been enacted into the Code to give a debtor protection from discrimination by a public utility because a bankruptcy proceeding has been filed and the utility has been listed as a creditor.[6] Simply put, a public utility may not refuse or discontinue service because a debtor initiates a bankruptcy proceeding and lists the utility as a creditor.

However, the public utility may request a reasonable deposit or security from the debtor or trustee to provide adequate assurance of future performance. This phrase generally means the same as "adequate protection" in other than Chapter 11 cases. If the deposit is not made, then the utility can discontinue service. The method of determining the reasonableness of the deposit may vary from district to district. Amounts equal to three months of service will not necessarily be unreasonable. If either a debtor, trustee, or debtor-in-possession believes that the deposit request is unreasonable, the Bankruptcy Court has authority to rule on its reasonableness. In Chapter 11 cases, "adequate assurance" means a cash deposit or other similar security. Further, the court may not consider the lack of security prepetition or the fact that the debtor may be current to a particular utility in reviewing the reasonableness of a security deposit request. Additionally, as an exception to the rule that setoffs are subject to the automatic stay (see chapter 12 supra), a utility company of a Chapter 11 debtor may setoff a prepetition security deposit against a prepetition debt without a court order.[7]

Similar to Section 366, Section 525 prevents governmental and private discrimination against debtors under the Bankruptcy Code. In addition, a government entity or business that makes government-insured or guaranteed student loans may not deny such a loan to a person who is or has been a debtor in a bankruptcy case.[8]

In FCC v. Nextwave Personal Communications, Inc., 537 U.S. 293 (2003), the Supreme Court examined Section 525(a) which prevents

6. 11 U.S.C. §366(a).
7. 11 U.S.C. §366(b)(c)
8. 11 U.S.C. §525.

governmental discrimination or action against an entity that files bankruptcy owing dischargeable debts to the government. In this case, Nextwave owned a number of valuable licenses that had been issued by the FCC. When Nextwave sought Chapter 11 relief, it owed the government substantial unpaid obligations for the purchase of the licenses. When Nextwave attempted to treat the licenses as estate property, the FCC asserted that the licenses had been revoked due to the defaulted payments. The Supreme Court affirmed the ruling of the Court of Appeals, finding that by revoking the licenses for nonpayment, the FCC had violated Section 525(a): "We think that Congress meant what it said: The government is not to revoke a bankruptcy debtor's license solely because of a failure to pay his debts."

C. ABANDONMENT

Sometimes an asset subject to administration is of no value or is of burdensome value to an estate. The asset may be a burdensome executory contract, a worthless piece of equipment, or a parcel of real property with no equity, for example. Section 554 allows a trustee to **abandon** property of the estate that is burdensome or of inconsequential value. Federal Rule of Bankruptcy Procedure 6007 contains the technical procedure for the formal abandonment of an asset. Local rules may add further details. An abandonment procedure is initiated by way of the notice procedures described in chapter 5 supra. Form 20.1 in the forms disk is a sample report of abandonment.

Under Section 554, a trustee may abandon property of the estate that is burdensome or of no value to the estate, or a creditor or party in interest may move the court to compel the trustee to abandon an asset.[9] The term *burdensome* generally means that the trustee cannot afford to maintain the property. The term *inconsequential value to the estate* generally means either that the property has no equity or the property has no realizable value for the creditors.

The question of what will be burdensome will vary from case to case. Burdensome may mean that a trustee will incur substantial expenses to maintain the property and has no source of money to accomplish the task. In this instance, a trustee will have to abandon the property. A common example is a parcel of real property with no equity. It is a waste of estate

9. 11 U.S.C. §554(a), (b).

assets to incur maintenance expenses on such property. The asset will therefore be abandoned so the trustee can avoid the expense.

Another common example of burdensome property is the uncollected accounts receivable of a business. On paper, the amount of uncollected accounts receivable may be substantial, but after investigation, the trustee may determine that the costs of collection will exceed any likely recovery. The trustee can then abandon the assets. Perhaps a debtor lists a tort claim as an asset in the Schedules and the trustee determines, after investigation, that the claim is meritless. The trustee abandons the claim because it is burdensome or of no value to the estate.

A trustee must abandon assets because a trustee has to administer *all* property of the estate before a case may be properly closed. A trustee may abandon assets by providing notice to the creditors pursuant to Bankruptcy Rule 6007. If the notice is opposed, the matter is treated as a noticed motion.[10]

A secured creditor may sometimes be able to make use of abandonment as a potentially less expensive alternative to a motion for relief from stay. Any party in interest may seek an abandonment order.[11] Recall that the automatic stay is relieved by statute as to an act against property when a debtor has been discharged and the property is no longer property of the estate.[12] Thus, when a debtor is discharged, if a secured creditor obtains an abandonment of its collateral by the trustee, the automatic stay is then relieved without further action since the property is no longer property of the estate.

However, a trustee may not necessarily abandon an asset as burdensome simply because the asset is subject to an environmental cleanup order of a governmental unit. In this instance, the Supreme Court has placed the public policy of environmental concerns above that of the Bankruptcy Code.[13]

D. OBTAINING CREDIT

Section 364 of the Bankruptcy Code concerns the subject of an estate obtaining credit during a bankruptcy proceeding. This is not as ludicrous as may appear at first glance. To the uninitiated, the question is certain to arise as to why a debtor would want to obtain credit in bankruptcy proceeding, or,

10. 11 U.S.C. §554(c), (d); Bankruptcy Rule 5009. See chapter 22 infra.
11. 11 U.S.C. §554(b). A motion to compel abandonment requires a $150 filing fee.
12. 11 U.S.C. §362(c). See chapter 12 supra.
13. Midlantic Natl. Bank v. New Jersey Dept. of Envtl. Protection, 474 U.S. 494 (1986).

perhaps more importantly or practically, why anyone would give credit to a trustee or debtor-in-possession in a bankruptcy proceeding. Obtaining credit does not usually occur in a Chapter 7 proceeding except in very extraordinary circumstances. For instance, a trustee with permission to operate the debtor's business for a limited period of time under Section 721 might require credit to do so.

In a Chapter 11 proceeding, obtaining postpetition credit is sometimes a very important aspect of the proceeding. Sometimes the obtaining of new credit is the only way in which a Chapter 11 debtor-in-possession will acquire a realistic opportunity to survive and rehabilitate. Remember that a Chapter 11 debtor can be a very large entity. Whether the debtor-in-possession is a car dealership, a chain of retail stores, a chain of restaurants, or a manufacturer, it will usually require some form of credit to function efficiently. These debtors generally have large credit lines from banks or other financial institutions. Whether or not the loans are in default at the time of filing, the debtor-in-possession will require the consent of the lender banks or financial institutions to continue a credit relationship, or the debtor will probably not survive for very long in the Chapter 11. Many times in Chapter 11 proceedings, the debtor finds, and the creditors will concur, that if the debtor receives an infusion of cash in the form of credit or otherwise, the debtor will gain the opportunity it needs to restore viability, which may result in a successful plan of reorganization and repayment to creditors.

Sometimes credit will come from entities that are already creditors of the estate who merely extend additional credit to the debtor in exchange for additional collateral and adequate protection. A lender may also improve its priority position by extending postpetition credit, as shall be described below. In this event, a motion to incur postpetition credit may be combined with a motion to use cash collateral under Section 363(c).[14] Sometimes the lender is an entirely new third party. Some investment banks have insolvency departments, which specialize in financing Chapter 11 or other distressed debtors.[15]

There are different forms of credit that may be incurred by a trustee or debtor-in-possession. The simplest is unsecured credit. If a trustee or debtorin-possession is operating a business under any Chapter proceeding, the estate will incur debt in the ordinary course of business. When office supplies are ordered and billed, this is unsecured credit. Any other ordinary trade payable is unsecured debt. A debtor-in-possession or trustee operating a business may obtain unsecured credit in the ordinary course of

---

14. See chapter 18 supra.
15. For example, Credit Suisse First Boston. Most major banks also have specialized departments for the type of debtor-in-possession financing seen in larger cases of the variety that are frequently filed in the Southern District of New York or the District of Delaware.

business without having to obtain court approval.[16] Thus, every time a restaurant in a Chapter 11 buys 100 pounds of hamburger on a 30-day invoice, a court order is not required to permit the purchase. This is a transaction in the **ordinary course of business.**

On the other hand, if an estate wants to obtain unsecured credit not in the ordinary course of business, then the estate must obtain prior court approval by making a noticed motion.[17] A loan is not in the ordinary course of business when it is obtained for other than the day-to-day operations of the estate. An unsecured loan for purposes of meeting payroll is not in the ordinary course of business.[18] If prior court approval is obtained, then the debt will be accorded administrative priority for purposes of repayment.[19] If prior court approval is not obtained, then the creditor may find itself subordinated to the status of a general unsecured prepetition creditor.[20] This may seem a harsh result, but the purpose of the rule is to attempt to protect the prepetition creditor body from any further erosion or impairment of their ultimate ability to receive a dividend. Allowing a creditor to obtain an administrative priority will create such an impairment. Thus, the Code requires prior court approval so a determination can be made that the incurring of new debt not in the ordinary course of business will be in the ultimate best interests of the prepetition creditors.

If a trustee or debtor-in-possession cannot obtain unsecured credit outside the ordinary course of business, it may be able to obtain the credit on a secured basis. This always requires court approval by making a noticed motion.[21] The reasons for this are identical to the reasons just given for obtaining unsecured credit outside the ordinary course of business. The loan will become an administrative expense and be payable before any dividends to the prepetition creditors. Because approval of the loan may decrease the prepetition creditors' likelihood of receiving a dividend, the court has to weigh this risk against the positive effects the loan will have upon the estate's ultimate ability to successfully reorganize. If the court's perception is that the loan will do nothing but prolong an inevitable liquidation, then the court may not approve the loan.

Under Subsection 364(c), the court has a number of options to exercise in granting secured priority administrative credit. The court may give the loan priority over all other expenses of the bankruptcy, including all other administrative expenses. That is, the loan may be given priority over

16. 11 U.S.C. §364(a).
17. 11 U.S.C. §364(b). Bankruptcy Rule 4001(c).
18. See In re Lockwood Enters., Inc., 52 Bankr. 871 (S.D.N.Y. 1985). But see In re Gloria Mfg. Corp., 65 Bankr. 341 (E.D. Va. 1985).
19. See chapter 21 infra.
20. In re Lockwood Enters., Inc., 52 Bankr. 871 (S.D.N.Y. 1985); In re Alafia Land Dev. Corp., 40 Bankr. 1 (M.D. Fla. 1984).
21. 11 U.S.C. §364(c). Bankruptcy Rule 4001(c).

even the professional fees incurred in the bankruptcy. Or the court may permit the lender to obtain a security interest in any assets of the debtor not already subject to a secured interest. Or the court may give the creditor a junior lien on property that is already secured, such as a second deed of trust or mortgage upon a parcel of real estate.[22]

Sometimes when a Chapter 11 debtor-in-possession seeks to obtain approval of a secured administrative debt, all of the estate property is already subject to liens by prepetition secured creditors. In this situation, the court may also permit the incurring of secured administrative debt. The court must find, however, that the credit is not otherwise obtainable and any existing secured creditor whose position may be affected by the new debt must be given adequate protection. The trustee has the burden of proving that such adequate protection exists.[23]

As in the case of the sale of estate property, the approval of a postpetition loan transaction is unaffected by any appeal unless the order has been stayed pending appeal.[24]

The approval of postpetition credit under Section 364 is governed by the motion procedures described in chapter 5 supra. Notice of the hearing is limited to the Official Creditors Committee or the 20 largest unsecured creditors of the estate and any other parties the court directs. This permits a debtor to act promptly in the early stages of a proceeding.[25]

E. HEALTH CARE BANKRUPTCIES

The 2005 BAPA legislation adds provisions designed to account for the dispostion of patient records and the transfer of patients from a closing facility in a **health care business** bankruptcy. The primary purpose of these provisions is to protect the privacy of the records and the safety of the patients. A health care business is generally any business that provides services to patients.[26] The court will appoint an ombudsman to represent the interests of patients unless the court finds that the appointment is not necessary.[27] If a trustee has insufficient funds to preserve and store patient records, Section 351 specifies the procedure to follow to make the records

22. 11 U.S.C. §364(c)(1), (2), (3).
23. 11 U.S.C. §364(d).
24. 11 U.S.C. §364(e).
25. Bankruptcy Rule 4001(c).
26. 11 U.S.C. §101(27A).
27. 11 U.S.C. §333. See chapter 10 supra.

available to patients or to abandon the records. Section 704(12) imposes upon a Chapter 7 trustee the obligation to transfer patients to other appropriate facilities. Sections 1106 and 1107 impose a similar obligation upon a Chapter 11 Debtor-in-Possession.

F. SYSTEM EXAMPLE

A major premise of the Bankruptcy Code is that it is designed to function as a self-contained system.[28] An example utilizing many of the issues raised in this and the preceding two chapters illustrates this theory. Gizmos Inc. manufactures gizmos and whatchamacallits for Engulf & Devour. Gizmos has a credit line with the Yours Is Ours Bank. All assets of Gizmos are secured in favor of the bank. Gizmos falls behind in its payments to its suppliers, who cease shipping it parts to produce its products. As a result, Gizmos falls behind in its production schedule. Engulf & Devour want to terminate the contract. The bank wants to call the credit line due. Gizmos files a Chapter 11 to prevent the contract from being terminated and to prevent the bank from seizing assets due to the automatic stay (Section 362). An investor, Alex Keaton, comes forward. He agrees to loan monies to Gizmos on a superpriority secured basis and further agrees that the loan will be converted from debt to equity if Gizmos can reorganize. Gizmos then files a motion to incur superpriority secured debt under Section 364(d), a motion to assume the Engulf & Devour contract under Section 365(a), and a motion to use the bank's cash collateral under Section 363(c). Both Engulf & Devour and the bank are entitled to adequate protection as defined in Section 361. All of these provisions working together will be required to accomplish the goals sought by Gizmos and to properly protect the rights of all creditors.

Summary

Section 345 of the Bankruptcy Code restricts the investment of an estate's cash assets. Generally, cash assets must be placed on deposit in interest bearing accounts or certificates of deposit in federally insured financial institutions. An estate's funds may also be invested in government bonds, but, as a practical matter, the longevity of the bonds exceeds the effective

28. See chapter 2 supra.

length of most bankruptcy proceedings. A financial institution accepting the deposit of bankruptcy funds must guarantee the amount on deposit greater than the normal government limits of $100,000.

A utility may not refuse to continue or to provide service to a bankruptcy estate or debtor simply because of a bankruptcy filing. A utility may, however, request a reasonable deposit as a condition of providing future service.

A government or private entity may not discriminate against a debtor solely as a result of a bankruptcy filing.

A trustee may abandon assets that are burdensome to or of inconsequential value to the estate. All assets must be administered by the trustee before the bankruptcy proceeding may be closed. An asset is generally burdensome if the trustee cannot afford to maintain it. An asset with unserviceable secured debt is an example. An asset is generally of inconsequential value to an estate if it is valueless or if the likely costs of collection would exceed any likely recovery. A meritless personal injury suit is an example. Abandonment will require a court order obtained through the motion procedure. A secured creditor may sometimes be able to make effective use of the abandonment procedure as an alternative to a motion for relief from the automatic stay.

Section 364 regulates the obtaining of credit by a bankruptcy estate. A Chapter 7 estate will only make use of this provision if a trustee is authorized to operate a business or in extraordinary circumstances. A reorganization debtor will frequently make reference to or use of this provision.

The obtaining of unsecured credit in the ordinary course of business does not require court approval. Any postpetition secured loan or loan not incurred in the ordinary course of business will always require court approval. If court approval is obtained, the loan will have priority as an administrative expense.

On the other hand, if the loan is obtained without court approval, it will be relegated to the status of a prepetition unsecured claim.

An administrative secured loan may be given priority over all other expenses of the estate, including other administrative expenses. However, the court will not permit a secured loan or priority secured loan unless it can be shown that there is no other form of loan available to the debtor.

In health care business bankruptcies, special provisions protect the privacy and disposition of patient records, and facilitate the safe transfer of patients from a closing facility. The court will appoint an ombudsman to represent the interests of the patients.

KEY TERMS

abandon
health care business
ordinary course of business

DISCUSSION QUESTIONS

1. Why does the Bankruptcy Code restrict the use of an estate's cash by a trustee?
2. How must a trustee maintain a bankruptcy estate's cash assets?
3. What are the purposes of abandonment?
4. How does a trustee abandon estate property?
5. When may a secured creditor benefit from the abandonment procedure?
6. Under what circumstances may an estate incur unsecured credit without court approval?
7. Under what circumstances must an estate obtain court approval to incur credit?
8. Identify reasons why special provisions exist to protect patients and their records in health care bankruptcies.

21

Claims

A. CLAIM DETERMINATION

Three of the trustee's four basic duties have been described elsewhere in this text: investigation (chapters 8, 10, 11, 12, 14), liquidation (chapters 18-20), and litigation (chapters 10, 12-18). The process of completing these duties and distributing dividends to the creditors is a function of the fourth of the trustee's basic duties: administration. This process is the least discussed and least visible of the trustee's duties unless it is being performed inefficiently, usually in terms of undue delay. Once all assets have been liquidated, the determination of "who gets what and in what order" and doing so promptly is the goal of efficient bankruptcy administration. This chapter shall describe the general rules and procedures for determining claims and their priority. The next chapter shall describe the entire process of dividend distribution.

An easy way to comprehend the claim determination process is to compare it to the posture of a debtor and creditor in a nonbankruptcy action to collect the debt. The creditor is the plaintiff. The creditor wants its bill paid. The debtor is the defendant. The debtor may or may not have defenses to the claim. These same defenses may be raised in the bankruptcy.[1]

A claim entitled to receive a dividend from the bankruptcy estate (i.e., that the claimant would have been entitled to a judgment in a nonbankruptcy environment), is an **allowed claim**.[2]

Whether a claim is allowed or disallowed and the order in which the claim is paid should not be confused with the concept of dischargeability. These two concepts are often confused by practitioners who do not

1. 11 U.S.C. §§502(b)(1), 558.
2. 11 U.S.C. §§502(a), 507, 724, 726, 1111, 1123, 1222, 1322.

properly perceive the difference between them. Whether a claim is dischargeable has no effect on its allowability. A claim that is nondischargeable may be allowable, in which case the creditor will receive a dividend from the bankruptcy estate if a dividend becomes payable. This means that if a debt is nondischargeable, the creditor's receipt of a dividend will reduce the debtor's remaining nondischargeable liability. The creditor with a nondischargeable claim will therefore retain two sources of recovery, the estate and the debtor. The fact that a debt is not dischargeable does not normally affect the creditor's right to receive a dividend from the estate.

Sections 501 through 510 concern the filing and allowance of claims. Recall that a debtor in any proceeding is required to file a list of creditors in its Schedules and is also required to state whether the claim is disputed, contingent, or unliquidated.[3] These labels place the creditors and trustee on notice as to the debtor's position regarding each claim.

B. FILING A PROOF OF CLAIM

For a claim to be allowed and entitled to a dividend, a **proof of claim** must always be filed in a Chapter 7.[4] In Chapter 11, however, a creditor whose claim is listed as undisputed by the debtor is not required to file a claim in order for the claim to be deemed allowed. A claim scheduled as undisputed in a Chapter 11 is deemed allowed without a proof of claim being filed.[5]

It is always wise to file a proof of claim. Even when a notice from the court or United States Trustee recommends against the filing of a claim until further notice, a proof of claim should always be filed as promptly as possible if it is known that there will most likely be a distribution of dividends. There is one very good reason for following this approach.

The original notice to creditors from the United States Trustee requesting that claims not be filed is the standard procedure in most districts. See the sample notice at Form 7.6 on the forms disk. Note how the form requests creditors not to file claims. The customary no asset notice is disseminated without regard to whether there will in fact be funds available to distribute as dividends. If a subsequent notice is distributed six or twelve months later requesting creditors to file claims, the creditors may forget to do so or may have to locate closed records before the amount of the claim can be properly calculated. On the other hand, if a claim is

3. See chapter 7 supra; 11 U.S.C. §521(a)(1); Bankruptcy Rule 1007. See also chapter 29 infra.
4. 11 U.S.C. §502(a); Bankruptcy Rules 3002, 3003(c).
5. 11 U.S.C. §1111(a).

promptly filed at the inception of the bankruptcy, it usually takes little time to complete the proof of claim form attaching any relevant documents as exhibits. Once this is done, the creditor's right to receive a dividend from the estate is fully protected and there is nothing else to be done except wait for any dividend that may result from the simple effort of having filed the claim.

A creditor or codebtor of the debtor may file a proof of claim. The debtor or trustee may file a proof of claim for a particular creditor. This does not frequently occur in actual practice. An equity security holder may also file a proof of claim.[6] Because definite deadlines are set for the filing of proofs of claim, codebtors, the debtor, or the trustee may file a claim to preserve a creditor's rights to receive a dividend. For example, if a debtor owes substantial tax liabilities, the debtor may want to file a proof of claim on behalf of any tax creditors to ensure that the tax claims will be entitled to receive any dividend that may become payable by the estate.

Once a claim is filed, if a creditor changes address after filing the proof of claim, the creditor must advise the court of the address change. If this is not done, the trustee will not know where to send a dividend check, or the check will be returned and the dividend will be forfeited.[7]

In a Chapter 7 proceeding, the deadline for filing a proof of claim is 90 days after the date first set for the Section 341 creditors meeting, unless the creditor is a governmental entity, in which case the bar date is 180 days after the entry of the order for relief (normally the filing of the bankruptcy petition). This deadline is known as the **claims bar date** in all bankruptcy proceedings. There are several important exceptions to this general rule. Two of them affect most proceedings. The first important exception is if the United States Trustee initially notifies creditors to not file claims, as noted in the sample notice included on the forms disk. If a bar date is set at a later date, the creditors are given 90 days' notice from the time of the later notice to file proofs of claim. The second exception permits a nondebtor party to a rejected executory contract to file a proof of claim within such time as the court may direct.[8] In a Chapter 11 proceeding, claims listed as undisputed are deemed allowed. Other claimants must file a proof of claim within any deadline that is set by the court upon application by the debtor-in-possession and provision of notice to creditors of the claims bar date.[9]

6. 11 U.S.C. §501; Bankruptcy Rule 3001.
7. 11 U.S.C. §347; Bankruptcy Rule 3009. In a Chapter 7, this forfeiture is to the United States (28 U.S.C. Chapter 129). In other proceedings the forfeiture is to the debtor or entity acquiring the debtor's assets under the plan.
8. Bankruptcy Rule 3002(c).
9. Bankruptcy Rule 3003(c).

A proof of claim may be filed by using a standard form that replicates Official Bankruptcy Form 10. A sample form is included on the forms disk accompanying this text. The form will be self-explanatory once this present chapter has been completed by the reader. In addition to the form, it is recommended that evidence of the claim be attached to the form, such as a promissory note, the invoice, and so forth. Evidence of a security interest, such as a recorded mortgage or UCC Financing Statement, should also be attached. This data is summarized in checklist 21.1 accompanying this chapter. The proof of claim should be served on the trustee.[10]

C. CLAIMS OBJECTIONS — PROCEDURE

Section 502 contains the basic rules for determining the allowance or disallowance of a claim. Administratively, once the claims bar date expires, the trustee will review the claims and may or may not object to them. Unless a claim is objected to, it is deemed allowed.[11] An allowed claim is entitled to receive a dividend.

A claim is objected to by the trustee or debtor filing and noticing a motion objecting to the claim. A sample notice of claim objection for use by a Chapter 7 trustee is included on the forms disk accompanying this text. A hearing on an objection to a claim requires 30 days' notice to the creditor. An opposed objection will assume the status of a contested matter that will treat the objection as an adversary proceeding as described in chapter 12 supra.[12]

A trustee may object to a claim on either procedural or substantive grounds. There are three typical procedural grounds for objecting to claims. First, that the claim was filed tardily (after expiration of the claims bar date). The Supreme Court has ruled that a standard of excusable neglect may, in appropriate circumstances, obviate the harsh effects on a late-filed claim. In Pioneer Investment Services v. Brunswick, 507 U.S. 380 (1993), the creditors received the customary Notice to Creditors. However, the notice actually contained a claims bar date. Experienced bankruptcy counsel, assuming that the notice did not contain a claims bar date, advised the creditor that it would not be necessary to file a claim until a bar date was set. The Supreme Court set aside rulings of the lower courts, which disallowed the creditor's late-filed claim, stating:

10. Bankruptcy Rule 3001.
11. 11 U.S.C. §502(a).
12. Bankruptcy Rule 3007.

> We do, however, consider significant that the notice of bar date provided by the Bankruptcy Court in this case was outside the ordinary course in bankruptcy cases. . . . We conclude that the unusual form of notice employed in this case requires a finding that the neglect of respondents' counsel was, under all the circumstances, "excusable." 507 U.S. 398-399.

Section 502(b)(9) of the Bankruptcy Code provides that a late-filed claim is not allowed except for priority claims (see Section 21K infra), which, pursuant to 11 U.S.C. §726(a)(1), may now be filed up to the date the trustee commences final distribution of the estate.

A second procedural claims objection is that the claim is a duplicate of a claim previously filed. It is only necessary to file a proof of claim once. The trustee must object to a duplicate claim since each claim filed must be reconciled before any distribution can occur. A third common procedural objection to a proof of claim is that the claim lacks adequate supporting documentation. Generally, a claim should contain documentation that would be sufficient to support a default judgment in a nonbankruptcy debt collection case. Nevertheless, a proof of claim properly signed and filed constitutes prima facie evidence of the claim's allowability. That is, a properly filed claim creates a presumption of the claim's validity.[13]

D. CLAIMS OBJECTIONS—SUBSTANCE

Substantive claims objections are more complex than procedural objections. There are two groups of substantive objections. The first is any defense the debtor would have had to the claim outside of the bankruptcy system. Any such defense is also a defense to the claim in a bankruptcy proceeding.[14] This is common sense. If a debt would be defensible outside the bankruptcy system, the fortuity of the bankruptcy should not eliminate the defense. For example, Mutt owes Jeff $10,000. However, the statute of limitations for collection has expired. If Mutt files a bankruptcy, Jeff's claim is not revived. The prior expiration of the statute of limitations will still be a defense to the claim in the bankruptcy.

The second group of substantive claim objections exists because of, rather than in spite of, the bankruptcy. These objections exist primarily because of the accounting peculiarities of the bankruptcy system, which

---

13. Bankruptcy Rule 3001(f).
14. 11 U.S.C. §502(b)(1); 11 U.S.C. §558.

attempts to account for the collective rights of all creditors. Secondarily, these objections limit certain claims from receiving potential windfalls as a result of the bankruptcy. These various grounds of objection are contained in Section 502(b).

A claim for unmatured interest is not allowable. That is, an unsecured creditor may only claim interest accrued up to the date of the bankruptcy filing. Postpetition interest on an unsecured claim is generally not allowable. An unsecured creditor cannot file a claim six months after a filing, adding any finance charges that have accrued between the date of the bankruptcy filing and the date the proof of claim is filed.[15] Postpetition interest on unsecured claims only becomes payable if all unsecured claims are paid in full and assets still remain available for distribution, as described in chapter 22 infra.

A claim for a property tax that exceeds the value of the estate's interest in the property is disallowed to the extent of the excess.[16] Do not confuse this limitation on allowability of the claim with the claim's dischargeability. The objection to a property tax claim is not related to the claim's dischargeability. To repeat, the concept of claim allowance should not be confused with the claim's dischargeability. A claim objection concerns the amount of a debt that will be entitled to receive a dividend from the bankruptcy estate. If the debt is also nondischargeable, the debtor will remain liable for any portion of the debt not paid by the estate.

Next, if the claimant is an insider or an attorney of the debtor, the claim will be disallowable to the extent it exceeds the reasonable value of the attorney's or insider's services. This prevents attorneys or insiders from filing excessive claims on the supposition that if a small dividend is distributed, the actual debt will be paid in full. This provision also aids a trustee in fully investigating the financial relationships between a debtor, its insiders, and attorneys.[17]

An unmatured and nondischargeable claim for alimony, support, or maintenance is not allowable.[18] For example, Mrs. Kramer is owed $1,000 in child support when Mr. Kramer files a Chapter 7. A proof of claim may be filed for the past due amount, even though the debt is nondischargeable. Any dividend will reduce the unpaid portion of the nondischargeable claim as described above. However, if Mr. Kramer continues to not pay the support after the bankruptcy filing, Mrs. Kramer may not file a claim for the additional support because it was not matured when the Chapter 7 was filed.

15. 11 U.S.C. §502(b)(2).
16. 11 U.S.C. §502(b)(3).
17. 11 U.S.C. §502(b)(4).
18. 11 U.S.C. §502(b)(5).

Also remember that the collection of alimony, maintenance, or support from property that is not property of the estate is excepted from the automatic stay.[19] As a result, a creditor spouse may continue to exercise all available nonbankruptcy remedies to collect nondischargeable or newly accruing alimony, maintenance, or support as long as the source of payment is not property of the estate.

Section 502(b)(6) limits a landlord's claim for future rent caused by the rejection of an unexpired real property lease. In many states a landlord may obtain judgment from a tenant for the entire amount of rent remaining due under the term of a lease. In a multi-year commercial lease this amount can be substantial. The Bankruptcy Code places limitations upon the future rent that a landlord may seek in determining the amount of an allowed claim. A claim based upon a real property lease is limited to the amount of unpaid rent due on the earlier of the date prior to filing of the petition or the amount of unpaid rent due on the date the landlord regains possession of the premises. The landlord's claim for future rent is limited to the greater of one year's rent reserved under the lease or 15 percent of the total rent remaining under the lease, not to exceed three years. It is thus necessary to calculate the total rent under the lease for one year and then 15 percent of the total rent for three years. The greater of these two amounts is the maximum amount of a real property lessor's future rent claim.[20]

For example, assume that Felix's Cat Shoppe has a five-year lease. The first year's rent is $1,000 per month. The lease provides that the monthly rent will rise $500 in each subsequent year. Thus, the rent in year five will be $3,000 per month. The Shoppe stops paying rent at the end of ten months and files a Chapter 7 proceeding at the end of year one of the lease. Under Section 502(b)(6), the landlord's claim will be $20,000. The claim for unpaid rent on the date of filing is $2,000, and the second year's rent is $18,000 ($1,500×12). Fifteen percent of three years' rent is $10,800. (The total rent for year two is $18,000, year three, $24,000, and year four, $30,000. Fifteen percent of this total is $10,800.) One year's rent is therefore greater than 15 percent of three years' rent.

A future rent claim is determined without regard to acceleration. This means that any clause in a lease that accelerates the rent due upon termination of the lease will not serve to increase the amount of allowable claim.[21]

A claim for a terminated employment contract is limited to one year's compensation dated from the earlier of the date of the petition's filing or the date when the contract is terminated, plus any compensation actually

19. 11 U.S.C. §362(b)(2). See chapter 12 supra.
20. 11 U.S.C. §502(b)(6).
21. 11 U.S.C. §502(b)(6)(B).

unpaid at the time of the bankruptcy filing.[22] For example, a professional track team, The Snails, files a Chapter 7. The athletes with multi-year contracts have their claim limited to one year's compensation and any compensation unpaid at the time of filing.

Sometimes, claims are filed that cannot be readily computed. For instance, a personal injury claim filed against an estate, which has not proceeded to judgment, may have an unknown value. Section 502(c) allows a trustee to have the court estimate the claim. This procedure is an expedient that allows a trustee to administer a bankruptcy estate in a reasonable period of time. Sometimes estimation is the only practical solution, and the Code permits this practice.[23]

Section 502(d) permits a trustee to utilize the avoiding powers as the basis for an objection to a claim. In this context, the avoiding power is used defensively as opposed to offensively. Here, the trustee does not seek an affirmative judgment but attempts to defeat a claim filed by a creditor that is the transferee of an avoidable transfer or other unreturned property of the estate.[24]

Section 502(e) concerns a creditor that files a claim for contribution or for reimbursement in some form from the debtor. For example, one of two general partners pays all the partnership debt while the other general partner files a Chapter 7. The general partner who has paid all the partnership debt files a proof of claim for contribution in the bankrupt partner's bankruptcy proceeding. The claim for contribution will be allowable only if there is no nonbankruptcy defense to the bankrupt partner's contribution.[25]

Claims arising in the ordinary course of business in an involuntary proceeding are deemed prepetition claims for the purpose of allowance to the extent they arise between the commencement of the bankruptcy and the earlier of the appointment of a trustee or the entry of an order for relief.[26] A claim arising from the rejection of an executory contract is considered to have arisen immediately prior to the date of filing of the petition.[27] A claim arising from the disallowance of a setoff, of a returned avoided transfer, or avoidance of a lien under Section 522 will also be considered to have arisen immediately prior to the filing of the original petition.[28] In each of these instances this means that the amount of claim to allow will be determined as if the claim had been incurred prepetition. However, the distributive priority accorded the claim may vary, as described infra this chapter.

22. 11 U.S.C. §502(b)(7).
23. 11 U.S.C. §502(c).
24. 11 U.S.C. §502(d).
25. 11 U.S.C. §502(e).
26. 11 U.S.C. §502(f). See chapter 4 supra.
27. 11 U.S.C. §502(g). See chapter 19 supra.
28. 11 U.S.C. §502(h). See chapter 9 supra.

A priority tax claim that does not arise or is not assessed until after the filing, but that is for a prefiling tax period, is considered to arise immediately before the bankruptcy filing. This makes the claim a prepetition priority claim as opposed to a potential administrative expense claim.[29]

Section 502(j) permits the court to reconsider for cause any claim that has been disallowed. An affected creditor may bring a motion before the court to reconsider an order disallowing the claim.[30]

Section 502(k), added by BAPA, permits a debtor to bring a motion to reduce a consumer claim by up to 20% if the debtor can prove by clear and convincing evidence that the creditor unreasonably refused to negotiate, within 60 days of the bankruptcy filing, an alternative repayment schedule to repay at least 60% of the debt within a reasonable period. Any payment made pursuant to such a proposal is also protected from the trustee's preference powers. The purpose of these provisions is to encourage composition agreements in consumer cases (see chapter 3, supra).

E. ADMINISTRATIVE EXPENSES

Section 503 concerns **administrative expenses**. Generally, administrative expenses are all claims incurred by an estate after an order for relief has been entered as well as any approved professional expenses incurred after commencement of the bankruptcy. Administrative expenses are normally accorded the highest distributive priority under the Bankruptcy Code except perhaps for superpriority secured claims approved by the court under Sections 364 or 507(b).[31] In a Chapter 7 proceeding, administrative expenses will normally include the trustee's fees pursuant to Section 326 and all costs the trustee incurs in administering and liquidating the estate, such as auctioneer's fees, postpetition rent, and attorneys' fees. In a Chapter 11, all expenses incurred in operating the estate's business will be administrative expenses, including postpetition taxes, rent, payroll, and accounts payable. Generally, any expense incurred by an estate after the commencement of a bankruptcy will be an administrative expense.[32] Regardless of the type of claim incurred as an administrative expense, administrative expenses are all considered to be one class of claim for purposes of

29. 11 U.S.C. §502(i).
30. 11 U.S.C. §502(j); Bankruptcy Rule 3008.
31. See chapters 18 and 20 supra and infra this chapter. In individual bankruptcies, domestic support obligations may have priority over most administrative expenses. See infra this chapter.
32. 11 U.S.C. §503(b)(1).

ultimate distribution. If an estate cannot pay all of its administrative expenses in full, all of the administrative claims will be placed into one class and will share the estate proceeds on a pro rata basis. In this instance, administrative tax claims would share an estate's proceeds pro rata with other administrative claims.[33]

Administrative expenses also include attorneys' or professionals' fees approved by the court after notice and hearing.[34] These fees are subject to the notice and hearing requirements of Sections 330 and 331 prior to payment being made.[35] The expenses incurred by a creditor in successfully prosecuting an involuntary petition, the recovery of property for the estate or the rendition of a substantial contribution to a proceeding, including attorneys' and accountants' fees, may also be given administrative priority. Expenses incurred by members of Official Creditors Committees in the performance of their duties are also payable as an administrative expense after court approval.[36] The theory here is that a creditor rendering a substantial benefit to an estate and to all its creditors should be rewarded by receiving reimbursement for any reasonable expenses incurred.

If a lease is assumed during the course of a case, presumably a Chapter 11, and is later rejected, the landlord is entitled to an administrative claim equal to any unpaid postpetition obligations and two years of unpaid rent under the lease. The balance of any claim is computed as per Section 502(b)(6) discussed in Section 21D above. [37]

The costs of closing a health care facility and disposing of patient records are allowed administrative expenses.[38] Finally, the value of goods sold within 20 days prior to the filing in the ordinary course of business are given administrative priority. [39]

F. FEE SHARING PROHIBITION

Section 504 prohibits fee sharing, a practice that is common in some areas of the legal profession outside of the bankruptcy system. Section 504 prohibits referral fees in bankruptcy proceedings. A professional performing services in a bankruptcy proceeding may not share a fee or agree to share a fee except with members of that person's own firm or a public

33. 11 U.S.C. §507(a)(1); 11 U.S.C. §726(b). See chapter 22 infra.
34. 11 U.S.C. §503(b)(2).
35. See chapter 7 supra.
36. 11 U.S.C. §503(b)(3), (4), (5).
37. 11 U.S.C. §503(b)(7).
38. 11 U.S.C. §503(b)(8). See chapter 20 supra.
39. 11 U.S.C. §503(b)(9). See chapter 15 supra.

service attorney referral program.[40] For example, if Joe Lawyer refers a bankruptcy to Mary Attorney and requests a one-third referral fee, he may not receive the referral fee. If a fee sharing agreement is made and is discovered by the trustee, Joe Lawyer will be required to reimburse to the estate the amount of the fee paid to him as the referral fee.

G. TAX CLAIMS DETERMINATION

Section 505 permits the Bankruptcy Court to determine previously undetermined tax claims.[41] This provision specifically states that the Bankruptcy Court has jurisdiction to rule on the validity of tax claims affecting an estate. This is important for maintaining uniformity and consistency in the administration of tax claims in bankruptcy estates.

One activity trustees must complete in many asset estates before an estate may be closed is filing a final tax return for the estate and paying any taxes owed by the estate. However, just because a return has been filed and any taxes paid does not mean that the trustee is released from potential liability. The taxing entity might audit the return or find additional taxes due after the return is filed. Any prudent trustee will therefore not close an estate until the tax return filed is no longer subject to audit or redetermination. This wait could delay the final administration of any estate by several years! Section 505(b) attempts to solve this problem; without this provision, no prudent bankruptcy trustee would ever close an estate.

Under Section 505(b), a trustee may submit a tax return to a taxing entity, complying with any applicable regulation for the filing of tax returns by bankruptcy estates, paying any taxes that are due, and requesting that the taxing entity determine within 60 days whether it wants to examine the tax return. If the taxing entity does not request an examination or other review within 60 days, the taxing entity can no longer object to the trustee's return, and both the estate and trustee are released from further liability. If the taxing entity does request a review or audit, the review or audit must be completed within 180 days after the return is filed or the estate and trustee are relieved from any further liability.[42] The trustee may then conclude administration of the estate without the risk of incurring further liability for any additional or unknown taxes by the estate.

---

40. 11 U.S.C. §504.
41. 11 U.S.C. §505(a)(1).
42. 11 U.S.C. §505(b)(2). Section 505(b)(1) directs the court to maintain an address register for providing governmental entities notices pursuant to Section 505.

H. SECURED CLAIMS

The problem of determining the extent of a secured creditor's secured claim is the subject of Section 506. A **secured creditor** is a creditor with a lien upon property in which the estate has an interest. The lien may be consensual, judicial, or statutory.[43] A creditor with a right of setoff is also considered a secured creditor for purposes of this provision. The significance of the value of a secured creditor's collateral has been previously described in connection with Sections 362 and 361, relief from the automatic stay and adequate protection.[44]

The focal point of Section 506 lies in determining the value of the collateral securing a secured claim. A secured creditor will often argue that its collateral is worth less than the amount of its claim. A debtor or trustee, on the other hand, will often argue that the collateral is worth more than the amount of the secured claim upon it. A creditor who successfully argues that the value of its collateral is less than the amount of its claim may have grounds for relief from the automatic stay due to lack of equity in the property securing the claim. This may also affect the amount of any adequate protection payments ordered by the court. For example, in United Savings Association of Texas v. Timbers of Inwood Forest Associates, 485 U.S. 195 (1988), the Supreme Court held that an **undersecured creditor**, a creditor whose collateral is worth less than the amount of its claim, is not entitled to adequate protection payments on the undersecured portion of its claim. In *Timbers* the debtor owed the creditor over $4.3 million, while the value of the collateral was not more than $4.25 million. Because the value of the collateral was worth less than the amount of the debt, the creditor was undersecured. Because Section 506(b) of the Code limits the allowance of postpetition interest only up to the value of the collateral, the Supreme Court reasoned that the undersecured creditor is not entitled to interest as adequate protection.[45]

Conversely, a debtor or trustee will want to show that the value of a secured creditor's collateral is more than that suggested by the creditor, because then there may be equity in the property that may result in the automatic stay's remaining in effect. If the debtor or trustee can show that the collateral has significant equity, then it is possible the court will not order interim adequate protection payments. This frequently happens in consumer proceedings involving residences. If the court feels that there is a significant **equity cushion**, the difference between the amount of the claim

43. See chapter 6 supra.
44. See chapter 12 supra.
45. United Savings Assn. of Tex. v. Timbers of Inwood Forest Assocs., 485 U.S. 195 (1988). 11 U.S.C. §506(b).

and the actual value of the collateral, in the debtor's residence, the court may keep the automatic stay in effect indefinitely and not require any adequate protection payments. Recall the more extensive discussion of this issue in chapter 12 supra.

In Associates Commercial Corporation v. Rash, 520 U.S. 953 (1997), the Supreme Court confronted the valuation issue head on. In this case, a Chapter 13 debtor attempted to have a tractor truck valued at its wholesale value of $28,500, while the secured lender argued that the value should be the vehicle's retail value of $41,000. The creditor argued that the higher retail value should be used because the debtor was intending to retain and use the vehicle. In agreeing with the creditor, the Supreme Court adopted a replacement value approach, stating:

> The "disposition or use" of the collateral thus turns on the alternative the debtor chooses — in one case the collateral will be surrendered to the creditor, and in the other, the collateral will be retained and used by the debtor. Applying a foreclosure value standard when the cram down option is invoked attributes no significance to the different consequences of the debtor's choice to surrender the property or retain it. A replacement-value standard, on the other hand, distinguishes retention from surrender and renders meaningful the key words "disposition or use." (520 U.S. 953, 962 (1997)).

The 2005 legislation codifies the result in *Rash* at 11 U.S.C. §506(a)(2), applicable in individual Chapter 7 and 13 cases.

Regardless of the type of lien involved, a claim is secured only to the extent of the value of the creditor's interest in the property. To this extent, the creditor must look to the collateral for satisfaction of its claim. A creditor who is undersecured, whose collateral is not worth the amount of its claim, becomes an unsecured creditor for any deficiency and is entitled to receive a dividend as an unsecured creditor for the unsecured portion of the claim. However, if the property is not disposed of in the bankruptcy, the lien "passes through bankruptcy unaffected." This was the ruling of the Supreme Court in Dewsnup v. Timm, a case in which the debtor owed the creditor $120,000, while the value of the collateral was only $39,000. The debtor contended that the amount of debt that exceeded the value of the collateral should be considered discharged as an unsecured claim, thus reducing the creditor's secured obligation to $39,000. Relying on precedent established in case law under the Bankruptcy Act, the Court disagreed with the debtor's position, stating: "[W]e are not convinced that Congress intended to depart from the pre-Code rule that liens pass through bankruptcy unaffected." The secured creditor will thus bear the burden of any postbankruptcy depreciation or, conversely, gain the benefit of any postbankruptcy appreciation in the value of the collateral, up to the amount of the claim.[46]

To the extent that the value of the collateral is greater than the amount of a secured claim, the lienholder is entitled to payment of interest, attorneys' fees, and other reasonable charges provided for under any agreement that is the source of the claim.[47] A trustee incurring expenses in preserving the collateral of a secured creditor may seek to have such costs surcharged against the secured claim.[48] A secured creditor is not required to file a proof of claim for the secured portion of its claim to be allowed.[49] The reason for this latter provision is that a secured creditor's interest in collateral is proprietary in nature. However, a prudent secured creditor should file a contingent unsecured claim so that any potential deficiency can be properly preserved as an unsecured claim.

In Chapter 13 cases, when personal property collateral is worth less than the amount of the claim, debtors have sought to **strip down** the loan and pay the creditor the value of the collateral only. The stripped down portion is treated as an unsecured claim. For example, Douglas Frasier owns a 1991 Whatzit worth $5,000. The Bank of Ours is owed $7,000 and has the car as collateral. In a Chapter 13 case, Doug can strip down the $2,000 unsecured portion of the debt by proposing to pay Bank $5,000, the value of the collateral. See, for example, In re Yi, 219 Bankr. 394 (E.D. Va. 1998). See chapter 23 infra.

BAPA places limits on the practice of stripping down purchase money loans on motor vehicles in Chapter 13 cases. Recall that a purchase money loan is the loan obtained for the purpose of purchasing the car. Section 1325(a) effectively provides that strip down may not take place where the debt was incurred to purchase a motor vehicle within 910 days preceding the bankruptcy filing, or one year preceding the bankruptcy filing for any other personal property. If the debtor files a second case within two years of the first case, then the value of the security in the second case is treated the same as in the first case. In the above example, if Doug bought the car within 910 days of his filing, Bank's secured claim would be the entire $7,000 debt. However, if Doug did not give the car as collateral to finance its purchase, then he may still be permitted to strip down the loan under BAPA.

A noticed motion to determine the value of a secured creditor's collateral is commonly known as a **valuation hearing**. This is begun as a noticed motion and will become a contested matter if opposed. A valuation hearing may be sought by any party in interest and will most

46. Dewsnup v. Timm, 502 U.S. 410, 417 (1992), 11 U.S.C. §506(a).
47. 11 U.S.C. §506(b).
48. 11 U.S.C. §506(c). Only the trustee may assert this right. Individual creditors may not. See Hartford Underwriters Ins. Co. v. Union Planters Bank, N.A., 530 U.S. 1 (2000).
49. 11 U.S.C. §506(d)(2).

commonly arise in connection with a relief from stay motion or a reorganization proceeding confirmation hearing.[50]

I. STATEMENT OF INTENTION

A debtor of consumer debt secured by estate property is required to advise secured creditors as to the debtor's intention regarding disposition of the creditor's collateral during the bankruptcy proceeding. Section 521(a)(2) requires an individual debtor to advise secured creditors with secured consumer debt of the debtor's intended disposition of the secured claim. This notice must be given within 30 days of filing and is known as a **Statement of Intention**. A sample form is included in the forms manual accompanying this text. Essentially, the debtor must advise each secured creditor that the debtor intends either to return the collateral, to reaffirm the obligation, or to redeem the collateral. The debtor must perform the intention within 30 days of the date first set for the meeting of creditors. If the debtor fails to reaffirm or redeem within the time period, the automatic stay is relieved by operation of law, and the property is no longer considered property of the estate, unless the trustee brings a motion that the property will benefit the estate.[51] The rationale behind this provision is that the notice will allow a secured creditor to determine whether a motion for relief from the automatic stay or other relief is necessary, and under the 2005 legislation, allow a creditor to determine when the automatic stay is terminated by operation of law pursuant to Section 362(h).

Many secured creditors are satisfied if a debtor's intent is merely to continue making payments, and the debtor may advise the creditor of this intention in the statement.[52] Debtors should welcome the apathy of secured creditors who will accept the simple continuation of payments. The reason for this is that if a debtor continues making payments but does not formally reaffirm the debt, the creditor's only remedy upon a subsequent default will be repossession of the collateral. Any deficiency will have been discharged in the bankruptcy proceeding as an unsecured claim. Secured creditors should always insist on reaffirmation agreements as a condition of allowing a debtor to retain collateral where the debtor has

50. Bankruptcy Rule 3012. See chapter 12 supra and chapters 23, 26, and 27 infra.
51. 11 U.S.C. §362(h); 11 U.S.C. §521(a)(2), (6).
52. This is the majority judicial view. See, e.g., In re Laubacher, 150 Bankr. 200 (N.D. Ohio 1992). Continuing to make installment payments as they become due is also known as the "fourth option," the other three being redemption, surrender, or reaffirmation as discussed in the text. The 2005 BAPA legislation, however, may be found by the courts to eliminate the "fourth option."

recourse to a deficiency after a repossession. An approved reaffirmation agreement will preserve the creditor's deficiency rights in the event of a subsequent default.[53]

J. REDEMPTION

Redemption involves the right of a Chapter 7 consumer debtor to pay a secured creditor the fair market value of the collateral, thereby obtaining a release of the lien. If consumer property is exempt or abandoned, a debtor may pay to the secured creditor, in a lump sum, the amount of its secured claim. This means, in essence, paying to the secured creditor the collateral's value.[54] For example, the Nortons are Chapter 7 consumer debtors. They owe $2,000 to Cramden's Used Cars, which has a lien in a 1973 Ford Pinto as collateral. The vehicle is worth $500. If the Nortons pay Cramden a lump sum of $500 and claim the vehicle exempt, the lien will be released from the vehicle and the balance of Cramden's claim will be discharged as an unsecured debt. A valuation hearing may be held to determine the amount necessary for the debtor to pay to redeem the collateral.

K. PRIORITY CLAIMS

Certain claims are categorized as unsecured priority claims. **Priority claims** are required to be satisfied prior to other general unsecured claims in all proceedings unless an affected creditor agrees to a lesser treatment. Priority claims are themselves prioritized in the order described in Section 507(a). Each higher numbered class of claim described in Section 507(a) has priority over each of the lesser numbered claims. Thus, all claims under Section 507(a)(1) will be paid in full before any claims under Section 507(a)(2) and so forth. Contrary to popular belief, there are actually a number of claims that have priority over tax claims.

The first category of priority claims are claims for domestic support obligations. However, the expenses of the Chapter 7 trustee, including professional fees, shall be paid ahead of the domestic support obligations.

53. See chapter 7 supra.
54. 11 U.S.C. §722.

This ensures that the trustee and the trustee's professionals will be compensated for collecting the funds that pay the domestic support obligation.[55]

The second category of priority claims is administrative expenses under Section 503, including any filing fees incurred in connection with the bankruptcy.[56] The third category of priority claims is unsecured gap claims incurred under Section 502. Note, however, that although the claim is allowed as if it were incurred prepetition, as described supra in this chapter, the claim has a distribution priority over virtually all other unsecured claims. A **gap period claim** is a claim incurred during that period of time between the filing of an involuntary petition and prior to the entry of an order for relief.[57]

The fourth category of priority claims concerns unpaid wages. Wage claims, including vacation, severance, or sick leave pay, are accorded a priority of up to $10,000 per individual for wages earned within 180 days prior to the commencement of the proceeding or the date on which the debtor's business ceased operating, whichever occurs first. Priority wage claimants include independent contractors who earned at least 75 percent of their independent contractor income from the debtor in the twelve months prior to the bankruptcy filing or cessation of the business.[58] These alternative dates account for the close of a business several months or more prior to an actual Bankruptcy filing. A wage claim of greater than $10,000 becomes a general unsecured claim to the extent of any excess. For example, Wimpy is owed $11,000 from Brutus Burgers. The wages were all incurred within 180 days prior to Brutus Burgers' bankruptcy filing. Ten thousand dollars of the claim will be a priority claim under Section 507(a)(4). The remaining $1,000 will be a general unsecured claim.

Section 507(a)(5) is for unpaid contributions to an employee benefit plan, up to $10,000 per employee for unpaid contributions earned within 180 days prior to the date of the bankruptcy filing or the close of the debtor's business, whichever occurs first.[59] Any excess is treated as a general unsecured claim as described above in connection with priority wage claims.

The sixth priority claim was added to the Bankruptcy Code in 1984. This priority concerns the unsecured claims of grain producers or fishermen for their produce or catch in the possession of a storage facility as previously described in the context of Section 546.[60] Recall that under

55. 11 U.S.C. §507(a)(1). See chapter 13 supra.
56. 11 U.S.C. §507(a)(2).
57. 11 U.S.C. §507(a)(3). See chapter 4 supra.
58. 11 U.S.C. §507(a)(4).
59. 11 U.S.C. §507(a)(5).
60. See chapter 15 supra.

Section 546(d) farmers or fishermen have a right to reclaim their products within ten days after delivery to an insolvent storage facility. These same creditors are also granted a priority claim of up to $4,000 per claimant.[61] Once again, similar to wage claims, to the extent the claim exceeds $4,000, the excess becomes a general unsecured claim.

The seventh category of priority claim deals with a situation that will often arise when a retail business files a bankruptcy proceeding. This situation involves consumers who have made deposits for consumer goods or services, such as furniture or appliances. The business files a bankruptcy before the furniture or appliance is delivered. In such a situation, the individual consumer is given a priority claim of up to $1,800 for the goods or services not provided.[62] Once again, any excess amount of the claim will become a general unsecured claim.

The eighth priority claim is priority tax claims. Congress has determined, in enacting the Bankruptcy Code, that all the preceding categories of priority claims will be paid in full *before* satisfaction of unsecured prepetition tax claims. Suffice it to say that the most common (income, sales, and payroll taxes) are all given priority status. Priority tax claims include income taxes incurred within three years prior to the bankruptcy filing, withholding taxes of any kind (this will include all payroll and most sales taxes), any employer taxes due on any priority wage claims, excise taxes, customs duties, and any penalties on any of the above where the penalty is compensation for actual loss.[63] Priority tax claims are those taxes that are deemed nondischargeable.[64] This is the only claim provision in the Code that relates directly to the issue of the claim's dischargeability. Section 507(a)(9) makes a commitment by a financial institution to meet minimum capital requirements to an appropriate regulatory agency as a ninth priority unsecured claim.

Section 507(a)(10), added by the 2005 legislation, grants priority status to death or personal injury resulting from the operation of a motor vehicle or vessel because the debtor was intoxicated on alcohol or drugs.

Section 507(b) provides a secured creditor a priority claim superior to all other administrative expenses where the creditor's collateral has been sold, used, or leased without consent or court approval.[65]

---

61. 11 U.S.C. §507(a)(6).
62. 11 U.S.C. §507(a)(7).
63. 11 U.S.C. §507(a)(8). The three-year period is tolled during any period in which a prior bankruptcy is pending. Thus, where debtor filed Chapter 7 during the three-year period, received a discharge, and then filed Chapter 13, the Supreme Court held that the three-year period would be extended to include the time period of the first bankruptcy. Young v. U.S., 535 U.S. 43 (2002).
64. See chapter 13 supra.
65. 11 U.S.C. §507(b). See the discussion of cash collateral in chapter 18 supra.

Section 104(b) of the Code increases all the dollar limits in Sections 507(a)(4), (5), (6) and (7) to account for the effects of inflation (see Section 5E supra). The next adjustment date is April, 2007.

L. PARTNERSHIP CLAIMS

Section 508 requires that a creditor of a partnership who receives a dividend from a non-debtor general partner may not receive further dividends from the partnership's bankruptcy proceeding in which the identical claim has been filed until all other creditors have received a distribution equal to that received from the general partner.[66] For example, a creditor of The Three Musketeers receives a payment from Porthos, a general partner, equal to 50 percent of the claim. The creditor, Richelieu, may not receive a dividend from the bankruptcy estate until all the other Musketeer creditors have received payment of 50 percent of their claims. This provision is intended to facilitate the fundamental debt collection concept of bankruptcy proceedings that creditors in an equal class should share the assets of the debtor estate on an equal basis.

M. CODEBTOR CLAIMS

Section 509 concerns the claims of a codebtor of a debtor. The cosigner of a loan is a codebtor. A general partner of a partnership personally liable for the partnership debts is a codebtor. A junior lienholder that satisfies a senior lienholder is considered a codebtor for these purposes.

Generally, if a codebtor pays the debts of a debtor, then the codebtor acquires the rights of the satisfied creditor.[67] For example, if a general partner pays a partnership debt, the general partner will acquire the claim of the satisfied creditor and will essentially become that creditor. A codebtor asserting a claim in such circumstances should provide proof of payment of the claim in any proof of claim filed by the codebtor in the debtor's bankruptcy proceeding.[68] However, the codebtor will not acquire the rights of the paid creditor to the extent that the claim is disallowed or subordinated under Section 510.[69]

66. 11 U.S.C. §508.
67. 11 U.S.C. §509(a).
68. Bankruptcy Rule 3001(e).
69. 11 U.S.C. §509(b).

N. SUBORDINATION

The final concept to be dealt with in the area of claims is that of **subordination**. A claim that is subordinated is given a lesser priority than it is otherwise entitled to under the Bankruptcy Code. A creditor may be subordinated for two reasons.

The first and most logical reason is if a creditor consents to subordinate itself to a lesser priority claim.[70] Frequently, in Chapter 11 proceedings, for example, creditors may request insiders to subordinate any claims to those of the noninsiders as a condition to the noninsiders' approval of a reorganization plan. In large reorganizations where there may be multiple issues of bonds, each issue typically contains consensual provisions that rank a particular bond issue in order of priority with any predecessor issues. A creditor may agree to subordination. It is a guiding principle of the Bankruptcy Code that a creditor may always agree to accept lesser treatment than the law may otherwise entitle it to.

A second common manner in which a creditor may be subordinated is under the doctrine of *equitable subordination*. A claim may be equitably subordinated by motion.[71] There are logical and equitable reasons why the claim of a creditor might be equitably subordinated. The most common reason for subordination of a claim under this theory is because the creditor involved has been guilty of "bad acts." The creditor has done something that in all fairness requires the creditor to be paid after other creditors instead of along with them.

For instance, insiders receive excessive salaries from a debtor corporation and then loan a portion of the salary back to the company, becoming among the company's largest creditors in the process. If the excessive salaries have damaged a company at the expense of the company's creditors, perhaps the insider claims should be subordinated and paid after other claims. Perhaps a major factor for the company's predicament is the excessive salaries.

Perhaps an insider overreaches, obtaining a preference for the payment of claims by obtaining a security interest in all assets of the debtor company. The philanthropic insider creditor opines, "My God, my company is losing money but it owes me $200,000. I'll give myself a security interest in my company and wait 90 days: Then I'll file a bankruptcy and foreclose. I'll get my company back free of any creditor

70. 11 U.S.C. §510(a).
71. 11 U.S.C. §510(c).

claims." This creditor may become the subject of an equitable subordination motion. By deviously trying to improve its position, the insider may find itself on the receiving end of a motion for equitable subordination.

Summary

The determination of claims and the distribution of dividends to allowed claim holders is a basic function of the trustee's duty to administrate a bankruptcy estate. This and the next chapter describe this process. Sections 501 to 510 of the Bankruptcy Code govern the determination of claims against a Bankruptcy estate.

A creditor, other than a secured creditor not entitled to a deficiency, must always file a proof of claim to be entitled to receive a dividend from a Chapter 7 estate. A proof of claim must be filed before the expiration of any claims bar date set by the United States Trustee or court to receive proper treatment. A late claim, other than a priority claim, is subordinated to all other claims. As a practical matter this means no dividend in most cases. A Chapter 11 claim scheduled as undisputed by the debtor-in-possession need not file a proof of claim.

It is recommended to always file a proof of claim. A sample proof of claim is included in the forms manual accompanying this text. A proof of claim should always attach documentary evidence verifying the claim.

A trustee or debtor-in-possession may object to a claim. A hearing on an objection to a claim requires 30-day notice. A claims objection is a noticed motion, and it is treated as a contested matter, as described in chapter 12 supra, if it is opposed. A sample notice of objection for use by a Chapter 7 trustee is included in the forms manual.

Objections to a claim may be procedural or substantive in nature. Examples of procedural objections include duplicate claims, claims not containing supporting evidence, and late filed claims.

Substantive objections to a claim fall into two groups and are primarily the subject of Code Section 502(b). The first group includes any defense existing to the claim under nonbankruptcy law. A defense based upon expiration of an appropriate statute of limitation is an example. The second group consists of a number of objections to specific types of claims specifically provided for in the Bankruptcy Code. These various objections are outlined in the checklist accompanying this chapter.

Administrative expenses are claims incurred by a bankruptcy estate. In a typical Chapter 7, administrative expenses will consist primarily of the costs of liquidation. In a Chapter 11, all expenses incurred in operating the debtor-in-possession are administrative expenses. The professional fees of trustees, attorneys, or other professionals and the expenses of Official Creditors Committee members are also administrative expenses.

Bankruptcy Code Section 504 prohibits referral fees in bankruptcy proceedings except to public service attorney referral programs. The recipient of a referral fee must reimburse the referral fee to the estate.

Section 505 provides the Bankruptcy Court with jurisdiction to hear and determine tax claims affecting an estate. The provision also contains a procedure providing for expedited release of a bankruptcy estate and trustee from liability for taxes due by a bankruptcy estate for which returns have been filed and all taxes paid.

Section 506 contains provisions relating to the determination of a secured claim. The provisions will also have relevance in relief from stay and adequate protection matters. A claim is generally secured only to the value of any collateral. In Chapter 13 proceedings, the value of the collateral will be the amount of the debt due for purchase money loans on motor vehicles acquired within 910 days of the bankruptcy filing, or one year prior to the filing in the case of personal property contracts.

To the extent that the collateral is worth less than the claim, the deficiency is an unsecured claim. To the extent that the collateral is worth more than the claim, a secured creditor is entitled to have postpetition interest and all charges allowed under the security agreement added to the claim. The value of collateral is determined by a valuation hearing. A secured claim may also be charged with the costs incurred by the estate in maintaining or preserving the collateral. If the collateral is not disposed of in the bankruptcy, the lien will survive the bankruptcy unaffected.

A debtor is required to advise a secured creditor of consumer debt of the debtor's intent as to disposition of the creditor's collateral after the bankruptcy filing. A debtor may reaffirm the debt, return, or redeem the collateral. Redemption permits an individual consumer debtor to pay a lump sum to a secured creditor equal to the value of the collateral. A valuation hearing may be necessary to determine the adequacy of the redemption amount. A valuation hearing is a noticed motion. If a debtor fails to file a Statement of Intention, or fails to perform a stated intention, within 45 days after the meeting of creditors, the automatic stay will be terminated by operation of law pursuant to Section 362(h).

Section 507 identifies priority claims. The listed claims are given priority over all other claims in the specific order set forth by Section 507(a). Priority claims are summarized in the checklist to this chapter.

Section 508 regards the effect on partnership cases of distributions by nondebtor partners.

Section 509 permits a codebtor of a debtor to acquire the claims of any claim paid by the codebtor. A payment by a nondebtor guarantor to a creditor is an example.

Section 510 allows a claim to be subordinated. When a claim is subordinated, it is accorded a lesser status than the claim is otherwise entitled to by the Bankruptcy Code. For example, an insider may subordinate its claims to that of noninsiders. A claim may be subordinated by agreement or by court order.

KEY TERMS

administrative expenses
allowed claim
claims bar date
equity cushion
gap period claim
priority claims
proof of claim
redemption
secured creditor
Statement of Intention
strip down
subordination
undersecured creditor
valuation hearing

Chapter 21 Checklist

		Authority
21.1	FILING A PROOF OF CLAIM	
21.1.1	Deadline: By Claims Bar Date Set by Court or United States Trustee	Bankruptcy Rule 3002(c)
21.1.2	Documents	
	1. Proof of claim — Official Form 10	Bankruptcy Rule 3001(a)
	2. Evidence of claim (such as promissory note; invoice)	Bankruptcy Rule 3001(c)
	3. Evidence of perfection of security interest (such as recorded mortgage or UCC financing statement)	Bankruptcy Rule 3001(d)
21.2	OBJECTION TO PROOF OF CLAIM	
21.2.1	Objection Documents	
	1. Notice of objection — 30-day notice required	Bankruptcy Rule 3007
	2. Declarations, where necessary	

			Authority
		3. Points and authorities, where necessary	
21.3	PROCEDURAL CLAIMS OBJECTIONS		
	21.3.1	Late Filed Claims	11 U.S.C. §502(b)(9) Bankruptcy Rules 3002, 3003
	21.3.2	Duplicate Claims	
	21.3.3	Claim Lacks Adequate Supporting Documentation	Bankruptcy Rule 3001(c),(d),(f)
21.4	SUBSTANTIVE CLAIM OBJECTIONS		
	21.4.1	A Defense to the Claim Applicable Under Nonbankruptcy Law (Such as Statute of Limitations)	11 U.S.C. §502(b)(1)
	21.4.2	Postpetition Interest	11 U.S.C. §502(b)(2)
	21.4.3	A Property Tax Claim Exceeding the Property's Value	11 U.S.C. §502(b)(3)
	21.4.4	Excessive or Unreasonable Insider Attorneys' Fee Claims	11 U.S.C. §502(b)(4)
	21.4.5	Postpetition Alimony, Support, or Maintenance Payments	11 U.S.C. §502(b)(5)
	21.4.6	Future Rent on a Rejected Lease Limited to Greater of One Year's Rent or 15 Percent of Three Years' Rent Remaining under Lease, Plus Actual Unpaid Rent	11 U.S.C. §502(b)(6)
	21.4.7	One Year's Compensation, Plus Any Actual Unpaid Compensation Due Under a Long-Term Employment Contract	11 U.S.C. §502(b)(7)
	21.4.8	Claim Is Subject to the Trustee's Avoiding Powers	11 U.S.C. §502(d)

		Authority
21.4.9	Unreasonable Refusal to Accept Composition in Consumer Case	11 U.S.C. §502(k)

21.5 PRIORITY CLAIMS

21.5.1	Domestic Support Obligations	11 U.S.C. §507(a)(2)[72]
21.5.2	Administrative Claims	11 U.S.C. §§503, 507(a)(2)
21.5.3	"Gap Claims" Incurred in Involuntary Proceeding	11 U.S.C. §507(a)(3)
21.5.4	Unpaid Wages and Benefits Incurred within 90 Days up to $10,000 per Individual	11 U.S.C. §507(a)(4)
21.5.5	Pension Plan Contributions Incurred within 180 days up to $10,000 per Employee	11 U.S.C. §507(a)(5)
21.5.6	Farmers or Fishermen with Crops or Catch in Storage Facility	11 U.S.C. §507(a)(6)
21.5.7	Deposits for Consumer Goods or Services of up to $1,800	11 U.S.C. §507(a)(7)
21.5.8	Most Tax Claims	11 U.S.C. §507(a)(8)
21.5.9	Financial Institution Minimum Capital	11 U.S.C. §507(a)(9)
21.5.10	Death or Personal Injury Caused by Substance Abuse	11 U.S.C. §507(a)(10)
21.5.11	Secured Administrative Claim Where Collateral Used without Consent or Prior Court Orde	11 U.S.C. §507(b)

72. The expenses incurred by the trustee in administering assets resulting in payment of the domestic support obligations are paid first. 11 U.S.C. §507(a)(1)(C).

21.6 STATEMENT OF INTENTION (11 U.S.C. §521(2))

21.6.1 Contents

1. Notice required to be given secured creditors of consumer debt, advising of intended disposition of collateral after a Chapter 7 filing
2. Methods of disposition
   a. reaffirm
   b. return collateral
   c. redeem collateral

21.6.2 Time Limits

1. Notice must be given within 30 days of filing
2. Intention must be performed within 30 days of date first set for meeting of creditors
3. Stay relieved by operation of law at end of time period (11 U.S.C. §362(h)).

DISCUSSION QUESTIONS

1. How and when should a creditor file a proof of claim in a bankruptcy proceeding?
2. How does the trustee object to a proof of claim? What are the various grounds for objection to a proof of claim that the trustee may raise?
3. What is an administrative claim?
4. How is the amount of a secured claim determined? Does a secured claim survive the bankruptcy?
5. What is the Statement of Intention procedure? What are its purposes? Should a debtor be permitted to continue payments unless the creditor objects?
6. What are the various priority unsecured claims?
7. What does it mean to subordinate a creditor's claim? How may a creditor's claim be subordinated in a bankruptcy proceeding?

22

Administration

A. ORDER OF DISTRIBUTION

When the assets of an estate have been fully liquidated and all allowable claims have been determined as to priority and amount, the proceeds will be distributed to the creditors. This is the ultimate goal of creditors in any bankruptcy proceeding: the receipt of a dividend. Success in any bankruptcy proceeding is based not upon the traditional adversary notions of winning or losing but upon the percentage of dividend that the unsecured creditors ultimately receive. This simple concept is the forest; everything else is trees. This very basic, simple, and fundamental goal is often overlooked or forgotten by bench, bar, debtors, and creditors, all of whom are mired in the seemingly infinite details of bankruptcy litigation and administration. Unlike many other areas of the law, a bankruptcy proceeding has no winners or losers in the conventional sense of these terms. A bankruptcy proceeding is most successful when the creditors are paid in full and the debtor retains assets. This can happen in reorganization proceedings and even, on rare occasions, in Chapter 7 proceedings. Certainly when *all* parties receive precisely what they are entitled to, no one should be considered a loser because everyone is a winner.

The order of claims distribution for nonsecured creditors is precise and is contained in Section 726. Although described only in Chapter 7, these distributive provisions apply by implication in all other Chapter proceedings. This is because all reorganization plans must be consistent with the provisions of Chapter 7 and must provide unsecured creditors with at least the same treatment they would receive in a Chapter 7.[1]

The first category of claims that receives payment is priority claims, including administrative claims, so long as the priority claims are filed

1. 11 U.S.C. §§1129(a)(7), 1225(a)(4), 1325(a)(4). See chapters 23, 26, and 27 infra.

before the distribution is made.[2] If a Chapter 11, 12, or 13 is converted to a Chapter 7, the Chapter 7 administrative expenses will have priority over the prior Chapter's administrative expenses and the administrative expenses of the superseded Chapter will drop into a second priority.[3] For example, a Chapter 11 is converted to a Chapter 7. The administrative expenses of the Chapter 7 will have priority over the administrative expenses of the Chapter 11. Collectively, the administrative expenses will have priority over other nonsecured claims.

Next, priority claims allowed under Section 507 are paid. Each subclass of priority claim is to be satisfied in full before the next subclass may receive a dividend.[4]

Although not entirely accurate, the next category of claims to logically place on a list of priorities is secured claims. This is not entirely accurate because a secured creditor is entitled to receive its collateral or the value thereof. This may be done by the creditor obtaining relief from the automatic stay and subsequent foreclosure or repossession of the collateral, abandonment, or return of the collateral by the debtor. Alternatively, if the trustee sells the collateral, a secured creditor is entitled to payment from the sales proceeds up to the amount of the secured claim.[5] If the secured creditor's collateral has a value of less than the amount of the allowed claim, then any deficiency becomes an unsecured claim and is treated like any other unsecured claim.

General unsecured creditors comprise the next category of creditor entitled to receive dividends from a bankruptcy estate. Unsecured creditors who file their claims in a timely manner will receive dividends first. A claim is filed in a timely manner if it is filed before the expiration of the claims bar date, as described in chapter 21 supra.[6] Unsecured creditors filing proofs of claim after expiration of a claims bar date will have their dividends subordinated to timely filed unsecured claims.[7] Penalties that are not compensation for actual damages or claims for punitive or exemplary damages are payable only after payment in full to all other unsecured creditors.[8]

After all unsecured creditors are paid in full, any creditors subordinated under Section 510(c) will then receive dividends.

If all creditors are paid in full and there are still assets available for distribution, then the creditors are entitled to payment of interest on their claims from after the date of the petition.[9] If interest is paid and there are still

2. 11 U.S.C. §726(a)(1); 11 U.S.C. §507. See chapter 21 supra.
3. 11 U.S.C. §726(b).
4. 11 U.S.C. §726(b). See chapter 21 supra.
5. 11 U.S.C. §506. See chapters 18 and 21 supra.
6. 11 U.S.C. §726(a)(2); 11 U.S.C. §501; Bankruptcy Rules 3001-3003. See chapter 21 supra.
7. 11 U.S.C. §726(a)(3).
8. 11 U.S.C. §726(a)(4).
9. 11 U.S.C. §726(a)(5).

assets remaining, any remainder is distributed to the debtor.[10] In the latter instance it is said that the estate is *solvent* because its assets exceed its liabilities. The chart below sets forth the general order of distribution in the bankruptcy system. The checklist accompanying this chapter is a more complete list.

GENERAL PRIORITY OF CLAIMS	
	1. Administrative (503)
	2. Priority (507)
	3. Secured (506)
	4. Unsecured (726)
	5. Subordinated (510(c))
	6. Interest (726)
Solvent Estate	7. Debtor (726)

When a Chapter 7 trustee knows that there will be a distribution to the creditors, the trustee will request the court or United States Trustee to set a claims bar date. This is because, as a practical matter, a claims bar date is generally only set after a trustee requests one.[11] When a claims bar date is set, all creditors will receive a notice advising them to file claims within the claims bar date.

B. METHOD OF DISTRIBUTION

When assets are distributed, they are distributed on a **pro rata** basis to each category or class of claim until the class has been paid in full.[12] *Pro rata* means that if there are insufficient assets to pay the claims of a class in full, then the claimants within the class are paid an equal percentage of their claims. In essence, pro rata means share and share alike. This concept is the principle underlying the trustee's avoiding powers, that creditors of the same class shall share the assets available for distribution equally. For example, if there is only enough to pay half of the unsecured claims, each claim will receive a dividend of 50 percent. Once a class of claims is paid in

10. 11 U.S.C. §726(a)(6).
11. Bankruptcy Rule 3002(c)(5). See chapter 21 supra.
12. 11 U.S.C. §726(b).

full, the immediately junior class of claims will receive a dividend, and so forth until that class is reached to which only a pro rata distribution can be made. In a typical Chapter 7 small asset case, the administrative and priority claims are often paid in full, secured creditors will obtain their collateral, and there is a pro rata distribution to unsecured creditors. Of course, secured creditors are always paid according to their rights in secured collateral. This is the one exception to the rule of pro rata distribution.

C. BANKRUPTCY ADMINISTRATION TIMELINE

The schematic below illustrates the *minimum* period of time it should reasonably take to administer most small asset Chapter 7 proceedings through the bankruptcy system. This minimum period is in excess of one year. Typically, the length of time it takes to fully administer an estate is longer than the minimum shown. The actions identified attempt to itemize the most important events that take place during the process, from the petition's filing to the close of the case.

The act of filing is obvious. The Section 341(a) creditors meeting is required to take place within 40 days of the date of filing.[13] A discharge is usually received about 90 days after the Section 341(a) meeting. The discharge is to be issued forthwith after expiration of the deadline to object to the discharge, 60 days after the date first set for the meeting of creditors.[14]

In consumer debtor no asset proceedings, virtually all involvement by the debtor and counsel with the proceeding will terminate when the discharge is received or about four months after the case is filed. As a practical matter, this is the end of the bankruptcy for the debtor. But note that if there are assets in the estate, the proceeding has just begun. The trustee may be liquidating or litigating over the assets for an indefinite period of time. That is why liquidation and litigation are shown as indicated on the illustration. The length of time these functions take can vary considerably.

The next items on the time line are the actual steps that a trustee must take to fully administer a proceeding within the bankruptcy system. First, the trustee in an asset proceeding has to request a claims bar date unless such a date was set in the original notice to creditors, which, as noted in chapter 21 supra, rarely occurs. Creditors are required to be given 90 days' notice to file claims in a Chapter 7 or 13 proceeding, except that a governmental unit may file a claim within 180 days from the filing date.[15]

13. Bankruptcy Rule 2003. See chapter 7 supra.
14. Bankruptcy Rule 4004.
15. 11 U.S.C. §502(b)(9); Bankruptcy Rule 3002(c).

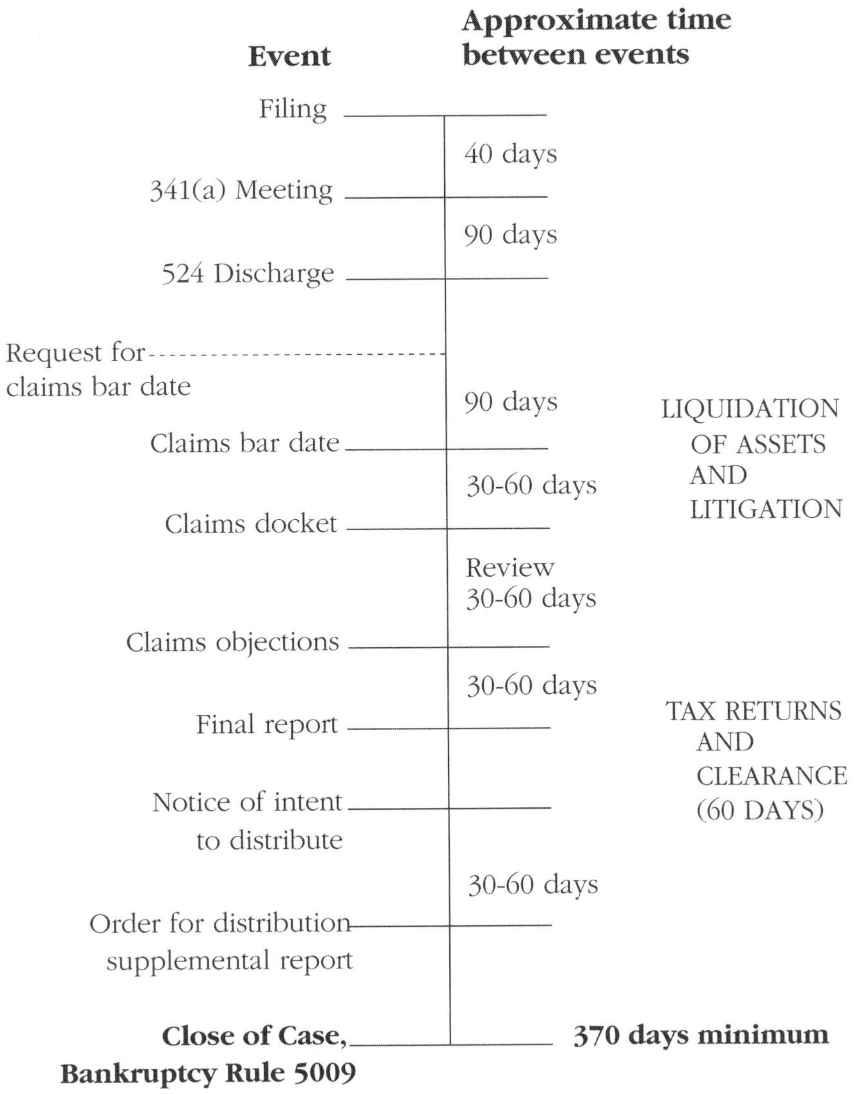

When the bar date expires, the court will prepare a **claims docket** for the trustee. The *claims docket* is an itemized summary of the filed claims, including the name and address of the creditor, the general classification of the claim (secured, unsecured, priority), and the amount of the claim. This information is compiled from the proof of claims forms.

The trustee will then review the docket and inspect actual filed claims where necessary. If a purpose would be served, the trustee must then bring objections to any objectionable claims and have them determined by the court.[16] A purpose is served if claims objections will increase the ultimate

16. 11 U.S.C. §704(5).

dividends payable to creditors. A trustee is not required to bring objections that will provide no benefit to an estate. For example, a trustee anticipates a 5 percent distribution to unsecured creditors in a proceeding. Several creditors have included postpetition interest in their claims. The amounts of included interest are less than $100. Although the postpetition interest claims are objectionable, the only result to be achieved is having $5 more to distribute (5 percent of $100), hardly worth the time and effort of a claims objection.

Creditors are required to receive 30 days' notice of any hearing on an objection to a claim. If the objection is to the claim's substance, the court may treat the objection as a contested matter or adversary proceeding. The objection may then take an indefinite period of time to resolve because it has now entered the realm of litigation.[17]

Once all liquidation, litigation, and claims objections have been resolved, the trustee will finally know which creditors are entitled to receive a dividend. The trustee will also know what funds are available to pay a dividend with. The trustee will then prepare and file a final report with the court and United States Trustee.[18] When the final report is approved, the distribution will occur. The creditors will be given notice of the trustee's intent to distribute the estate and, of course, they may object to the proposed distribution. Any court hearing held to determine any such objection will result in further delay.

Another act that must be taken in tandem with all of the court process and administration is that the trustee may have to file tax returns and wait for 60 days to elapse before obtaining clearance from various taxing entities pursuant to Section 505. A trustee who has had to file tax returns in a proceeding should not act to close the estate until clearance has been obtained from any taxing entities pursuant to Section 505.[19]

Federal Rule of Bankruptcy Procedure 5009 provides that if a trustee has filed a final report and certified that the estate has been fully administered, then there is a presumption that an estate has been fully administered.[20] That is, the case is closed.

If all the above time limits are totaled, in the smallest and simplest type of asset proceeding, the fastest administration will be approximately 12 to 15 months. In a no asset proceeding, administration is usually completed in about six months. The trustee will file a report of no assets in the matter and the proceeding will then be closed by the court in the normal course of business.

---

17. Bankruptcy Rule 3007. See chapter 21 supra.
18. 11 U.S.C. §704(9); Bankruptcy Rule 2015.
19. See chapter 21 supra.
20. Bankruptcy Rule 5009. See also 11 U.S.C. §350(a).

Summary

The ultimate goal of creditors in any bankruptcy proceeding is to receive a dividend. The percentage of dividend returned to the creditor body determines the success of any proceeding. Adversarial notions of winning or losing are not part of this final equation. Often, cooperation of the creditor body toward the ultimate common goal will achieve a greater return to all classes of creditors.

Dividends are distributed to claims by classes. Each class must be paid in full before the next immediate junior class receives a dividend. When there are insufficient assets to pay a class in full, the creditors within the class receive a pro rata or percentage distribution of their claims. No lesser classes will receive a dividend. When all classes are paid in full and assets remain available to return to the debtor, an estate is considered solvent. The general order of classification is: administrative, priority, secured, unsecured, subordinated, interest, and finally debtor. The checklist accompanying this chapter is a more thorough list.

It takes approximately 12 to 15 months to administer even the simplest asset estate. Estates with substantial assets or litigation, or both, will take years to fully administer. A no-asset proceeding will take about six months to fully administer. The administration timeline contained in this chapter itemizes the steps taken to fully administer an estate.

KEY TERMS

claims docket **pro rata**

Chapter 22 Checklist

			Authority
22.1	ORDER OF CLAIMS DISTRIBUTION		
	22.1.1	Priority Secured Administrative Claims	11 U.S.C. §§503, 507(a)(1), 507(b), 726(a)(1)
	22.1.2	Administrative Claims	11 U.S.C. §§503, 507(a)(1), 726(a)(1)
	22.1.3	Priority Claims	11 U.S.C. §§507(a)(2)-(10), 726(a)(2)

		Authority
22.1.4	Secured Claims[21]	11 U.S.C. §506
22.1.5	Timely Filed Unsecured Claims	11 U.S.C. §726(a)(2)
22.1.6	Late Filed Unsecured Claims	11 U.S.C. §726(a)(3)
22.1.7	Fines or Penalties Not Compensation for Actual Damages; Punitive Damages	11 U.S.C. §726(a)(4)
22.1.8	Subordinated Claims	11 U.S.C. §510(c)
22.1.9	Postpetition Interest	11 U.S.C. §726(a)(5)
22.1.10	Debtor—Solvent Estate	11 U.S.C. §726(a)(6)

DISCUSSION QUESTIONS

1. What is the order of claims distribution in a bankruptcy proceeding? How does a class of claims receive a distribution when the trustee has insufficient funds to pay the class members in full?
2. What basic events must occur before a Chapter 7 bankruptcy asset estate may be closed?

21. This is the logical placement for secured claims in a table of this nature. However, as the text indicates, this placement is not entirely accurate, because the secured creditor has a property interest in its collateral.

PART V

Reorganization Proceedings

23

Chapter 13: Reorganization Proceedings

A. INTRODUCTION — REORGANIZATION PROCEEDINGS

There are two basic types of proceedings available to debtors in the bankruptcy system: **liquidations** and **reorganizations**.[1] A Chapter 7 is a liquidation proceeding. In a liquidation, nonexempt assets are sold, dividends may or may not be distributed to the creditors, and the debtor is relieved of further liability by receiving a discharge.[2] In reorganization proceedings, on the other hand, a debtor will attempt to repay debt and retain nonexempt assets or continue to operate the business. Reorganization proceedings are, in their essence, no more or less than judicially approved composition agreements, the approval of which is binding upon all creditors of a debtor.[3]

The next five chapters of this text describe the most common reorganization proceedings, Chapters 13, 11, and 12. Chapter 9, applicable to municipal corporations, is rarely filed. Chapter 13 is a reorganization proceeding for individuals with regular income. Chapter 12 is a reorganization

1. See chapter 2 supra.
2. See chapter 7 supra.
3. See chapter 3 supra.

proceeding for family farmers or fishermen with regular income. Chapter 11 is a reorganization proceeding for all other debtors.[4]

Chapter 13 is a program for individuals (and their spouses) with regular income who have unsecured debts of less than $307,675 and secured debts of less than $922,975.[5] A qualified individual may attempt to repay debts over a period of time not to exceed five years.[6] If the plan is successfully performed, a Chapter 13 debtor will be able to retain nonexempt assets and will receive a discharge.[7] Some reasons for filing a Chapter 13 include protecting homes from foreclosure or cars from repossession by the opportunity to cure defaults on secured debt, compliance with needs based bankruptcy (see chapter 5 supra) a sincere desire to repay debt, and a potentially less onerous effect on the ability to obtain new credit.

B. SPECIAL CHAPTER 13 PROVISIONS

Chapter 13 has its own trustee system. This is the subject of Section 1302. A district may have a standing Chapter 13 trustee, one individual who will act as trustee in all Chapter 13 proceedings filed within the district, or Chapter 13 trustees may be appointed in a manner similar to Chapter 7 trustees. Most districts have one or more standing trustees. The United States Trustee appoints all Chapter 13 trustees.[8] The major difference between a Chapter 13 trustee and a Chapter 7 trustee is that the Chapter 13 trustee is responsible for administering monthly plan payments from Chapter 13 debtors and distributing the payments to the creditors on a regular basis.[9]

A Chapter 13 has the added benefit of making the automatic stay applicable to a codebtor of a consumer debtor who has not also filed a bankruptcy proceeding.[10] For example, a debtor files a Chapter 13 but the debtor's spouse does not. Under Section 1301, the automatic stay will apply to the debtor and the spouse of the nonfiling debtor. Thus, for example, there will be instances in which only one spouse will need to file a Chapter 13 while the remaining spouse will gain the benefit but avoid the burden of having filed a bankruptcy proceeding.

4. See chapter 5 supra.
5. 11 U.S.C. §109(e). 11 U.S.C. §104(b). This provision triannually adjusts the dollar limits contained in §109(e). The amounts shown reflect the amounts that became effective April 1, 2004. See chapter 5 supra.
6. 11 U.S.C. §1322(d).
7. 11 U.S.C. §1328(a).
8. 11 U.S.C. §1302(a).
9. 11 U.S.C. §1326(c).
10. 11 U.S.C. §1301.

Chapter 13 debtors have rights and powers that are slightly different from those of Chapter 7 or Chapter 11 debtors. Generally, Chapter 13 trustees will not go out into the community and attempt to operate a small business owned by a Chapter 13 debtor. If a Chapter 13 debtor is engaged in business, the debtor is permitted to continue to operate the business and is given the right to use, sell, and lease property of the estate pursuant to Section 363 or to incur credit pursuant to Section 364.[11] Thus, a sole proprietorship business meeting the Chapter 13 filing requirements may be a Chapter 13 debtor and is permitted to continue operating the business after the filing. The income from operating the proprietorship will constitute the regular income required to perform the Chapter 13 plan.

Section 1306 concerns **property of the estate** in a Chapter 13. In Chapter 13, or Chapter 11 for an individual, a debtor's postpetition earnings from services are considered property of the estate, unlike Chapter 7. The reason for this is that the regular income that is the source of the plan payments will come from the postpetition earnings received for services performed by the debtor. As a result, postpetition income is considered property of the estate. Also, a Chapter 13 debtor will normally remain in possession of all its property. Nonexempt property will not normally be turned over to the trustee's custody.[12]

A Chapter 13 debtor must comply with the requirement to file a prepetition credit counseling certificate as a prerequisite to filing the case (see chapter 4 supra). A Chapter 13 debtor files a Statement of Financial Affairs and Schedules and a statement of current income and current expenditures as debtors filing other Chapter proceedings will. These documents must be filed within 15 days of filing the petition unless the court orders otherwise.[13] A Chapter 13 plan must also be filed within 15 days of filing the petition, unless the court orders otherwise.[14]

Section 1326(a) requires Chapter 13 debtors to make adequate protection payments to creditors holding security interests in personal property, and to provide evidence of the payment to the trustee. A debtor must also provide proof of any required insurance coverage to the creditor within 60 days after filing the case.

Section 1308 requires that a debtor must have filed all tax returns for the period four years prior to the filing. The meeting of creditors may be continued for up to 120 days to permit the debtor to file the returns. Failure to file the returns can be grounds for dismissal of the case or conversion to Chapter 7 (see Section C infra).

---

11. 11 U.S.C. §§1303, 1304. See chapters 18 and 20 supra.
12. 11 U.S.C. §1306. See chapter 14 supra. 11 U.S.C. §1115. See chapter 24 infra.
13. 11 U.S.C. §109(h) (see chapter 4 supra). Bankruptcy Rule 1007(b)(1), (c).
14. Bankruptcy Rule 3015.

C. DISMISSAL OR CONVERSION — REORGANIZATION PROVISIONS

Section 1307 concerns the **dismissal** of a Chapter 13 or the **conversion** of a Chapter 13 to another proceeding.[15] Section 1112, applicable in Chapter 11 proceedings, is very similar. Accordingly, this discussion will summarize both provisions. Each section provides the grounds for a proceeding to be dismissed or converted to another Chapter under the Code. The typical situation is conversion from a Chapter 13 or 11 to a Chapter 7 proceeding — that is, from a reorganization to a liquidation.

Consistent with the principles described in chapter 8 supra, Sections 1112 and 1307 permit a debtor one opportunity to convert a proceeding from one Chapter to another. In a Chapter 13, this right may not be waived. If a debtor wishes to convert from a Chapter 11 to a Chapter 13, the debtor must, however, meet the Chapter 13 filing qualifications. In a Chapter 11 proceeding, if the debtor is no longer a debtor-in-possession (for example, if a trustee has been appointed), or the proceeding has been commenced as an involuntary proceeding or has been previously converted, the debtor will not be able to freely convert the proceeding to another Chapter. In these circumstances, the debtor will have to obtain a court order to permit conversion. The ability to freely convert a proceeding from one Chapter to another takes place by filing a one-page application with the court stating that the Chapter 13 (or other reorganization) debtor is qualified to be a Chapter 7 debtor and wants to be a Chapter 7 debtor.[16]

Conversely, if a debtor has previously converted from one Chapter to another and conversion is desired for a second time, court approval will be required. A motion procedure is required to accomplish this task. The court will not permit debtors to convert from Chapter to Chapter repeatedly.

Subsections 1112(b) and 1307(c) provide a number of grounds for obtaining the dismissal or conversion of a reorganization proceeding to another Chapter for cause upon a noticed motion. The common situation that arises is where a trustee or creditors seek conversion of a proceeding from a reorganization to a Chapter 7 liquidation because the reorganization has failed. Each provision uses the term *including* before listing the grounds that can result in dismissal or conversion. Recall that use of the term *including* means that the list is not exhaustive.[17] The court may find additional causes that may also constitute grounds for dismissal or conversion. However, the items identified cover the most common causes for

15. See chapter 8 supra.
16. 11 U.S.C. §1112(a); 11 U.S.C. §1307(a). See chapter 8 supra.
17. 11 U.S.C. §102(3). See chapter 5 supra.

converting a Chapter 11 or 13 to a Chapter 7 or why the proceeding should be dismissed. In a Chapter 11 case, if it is shown that a plan may be confirmed within the exclusivity periods of Section 1121 (see chapter 24 infra) or a reasonable time or if there is reasonable justification for the debtor's actions or lack thereof, the court may deny a motion to convert or dismiss. Unless the moving parties agree, a motion to convert or dismiss a Chapter 11 must be decided within 45 days of its filing.

The first cause under 1112(b)(4) is a continuing *loss or diminution* of the estate and the absence of a reasonable likelihood of rehabilitation.[18] This means that when a Chapter 11 estate is continuing to lose substantial amounts of money in operating under Chapter 11, or when it becomes apparent to the court and creditors that the reorganization has failed, conversion or dismissal will be in the best interest of the creditors and should occur. For example, Grandma Takeda's Instant Kosher Chicken Soup, Inc., a Chapter 11 debtor-in-possession, files operating reports that show that over an extended period of time the debtor is profitable. However, no plan has been proposed and the debtor intends to operate for as long as possible without filing a plan. Some debtors will take this approach because they incorrectly believe that Chapter 11 is a comfortable security blanket and it may appear possible to remain a Chapter 11 debtor indefinitely. This perception is an illusion. If the debtor persists, such behavior will return to haunt the debtor because it will ultimately constitute cause for a conversion or dismissal of the proceeding. The United States Trustee regularly files motions to dismiss or convert based on a debtor's unreasonable delay. The purpose of this subsection is to prevent debtors from abusing the system by indefinitely postponing a resolution of their financial difficulties. In Chapter 11 cases, failure to comply with the administrative rules of Chapter 11 (see Chapter 24 infra), gross mismanagement of the estate, unauthorized use of a secured claimant's cash collateral (see chapter 18 supra), failure to maintain insurance in force, failure to pay post-petition taxes or to file tax returns can all constitute cause for conversion or dismissal of the case.[19]

Unreasonable delay prejudicial to the creditors is a cause for dismissal or conversion of a Chapter 13 case[20]. Unreasonable delay takes place when a debtor fails to file a plan for no apparent purpose.

A fourth cause for conversion or dismissal of a reorganization proceeding is the *failure to propose a plan* within any deadline set by the court. This time period may be flexible in Chapter 11. However, as noted above, a Chapter 13 plan must be filed 15 days after a petition is filed.[21]

18. 11 U.S.C. §1112(b)(4)(A).
19. 11 U.S.C. §1112(b)(4)(B)(C)(D), (F), (H), (I).
20. 11 U.S.C. §1307(c)(1).
21. 11 U.S.C. §1112(b)(4)(J); 11 U.S.C. §1307(c)(3); 11 U.S.C. §1321; Bankruptcy Rule 3015.

A fifth cause for dismissal or conversion of a reorganization proceeding is *failure to obtain confirmation* by the court of every plan proposed.[22] Usually, if the court denies confirmation of a first attempt at a plan, the debtor may make a second attempt to get a plan confirmed. If the second plan cannot be confirmed, the debtor can theoretically try again and again and again. Ultimately, the creditors will tire of this. When they do, the repeated failure to obtain confirmation will constitute cause for conversion or dismissal of the reorganization proceeding.

A sixth cause for dismissal or conversion of a reorganization is if the *confirmation of a plan is revoked.*[23] In all reorganization proceedings, a confirmed plan may be revoked, primarily on the grounds of fraud. A confirmation's revocation may be grounds for conversion or dismissal of the proceeding.

A seventh cause for dismissal or conversion is an *inability to effectuate consummation* of a confirmed plan, or failure to commence making timely Chapter 13 payments.[24] This means that if a plan is confirmed but performance does not commence, this failure may constitute cause for dismissal or conversion. This cause is to be distinguished from the eighth cause, which permits dismissal or conversion due to a *material default with regard to a confirmed plan.*[25] In this latter event, performance has begun, but then stops or defaults.

A ninth cause for conversion or dismissal of a reorganization proceeding is the *termination of the plan because of some condition* specified in the plan other than the completion of payments.[26] For example, a plan provides that unless an escrow closes by a date certain, the proceeding will automatically be converted to a Chapter 7. If the condition occurs, the proceeding will be converted.

Failure to pay any required court fees will constitute cause for dismissal or conversion.[27] In a Chapter 13, the United States Trustee may seek dismissal or conversion if the debtor *fails to timely file required pleadings*, such as the Statement of Financial Affairs, Schedules, Schedule of Current Income and Expenditures, or tax returns for the four years prior to the filing of the Chapter 13 petition. In a Chapter 11, failure to provide information reasonably requested by the United States Trustee will produce a similar result.[28]

---

22. 11 U.S.C. §1307(c)(5).
23. 11 U.S.C. §1112(b)(4)(L); 11 U.S.C. §1307(c)(7).
24. 11 U.S.C. §1112(b)(4)(M); 11 U.S.C. §1307(c)(4).
25. 11 U.S.C. §1112(b)(4)(N); 11 U.S.C. §1307(c)(6).
26. 11 U.S.C. §1112(b)(4)(O); 11 U.S.C. §1307(c)(8).
27. 11 U.S.C. §1112(b)(4)(K); 11 U.S.C. §1307(c)(2).
28. 11 U.S.C. §1112(b)(4)(H); 11 U.S.C. §1307(c)(9)(10); 11 U.S.C. §1308.

Finally, in a Chapter 13, failure to pay a postpetition domestic support obligation is grounds for dismissal or conversion.[29]

When a reorganization proceeding is converted to a Chapter 7, the debtor is required to file a final report and to update the Statement of Affairs and Schedule of Assets and Liabilities to account for the estate's activities during the reorganization proceeding. When a Chapter 13 is converted to another Chapter under the Bankruptcy Code, the property of the estate consists of all the property under the possession or control of the debtor on the conversion date, and the value of any secured claim shall continue to be considered fully secured unless the claim has been paid in full prior to conversion of the case.[30]

D. CHAPTER 13 PLAN PROVISIONS

The main component of a Chapter 13 proceeding is, of course, the **plan**. Sections 1321 through 1330 contain the provisions regarding the contents of and the procedure for obtaining **confirmation** (approval), and performance of the plan. The plan is, in its essence, a new contract between the debtor and all the creditors. A confirmed plan is nothing more than a composition agreement that has obtained court approval. The forms manual contains a sample Chapter 13 plan.

A Chapter 13 debtor shall file a plan.[31] The Federal Rules of Bankruptcy Procedure require that a Chapter 13 plan be filed within 15 days of the petition's filing. A failure to do so, as noted above, will constitute cause for dismissal or conversion.[32] A Chapter 13 debtor must file the plan promptly because the entire procedure is intended to be expeditious.

Section 1322 prescribes the contents of a Chapter 13 Plan. There are **mandatory provisions** that are required to be in any plan. There are also permissive provisions that may be included in a plan.

The mandatory elements of a Chapter 13 plan are described in Section 1322(a). These provisions must be included in a Chapter 13 plan. The first mandatory provision is that the debtor will pay sufficient sums into the plan that it will be performed.[33] Courts interpreting the 2005 legislation may find

---

29. 11 U.S.C. §1307(c)(11).
30. Bankruptcy Rule 1019; 11 U.S.C. §348(f).
31. 11 U.S.C. §1321.
32. Bankruptcy Rule 3015. 11 U.S.C. §1307(c)(3).
33. 11 U.S.C. §1322(a)(1).

that this provision mandates the minimum needs based bankruptcy dividend to unsecured claimants of at least $6,000 over 60 months ($100 per month), when applicable (see chapter 4 supra). The second requirement is that all priority claims must be paid in full unless the holder of any such claim agrees otherwise.[34] As has been noted elsewhere in this text, a creditor may always voluntarily agree to a lesser treatment than may be mandated by the Code. For example, a priority wage claimant may agree to accept repayment as a general unsecured creditor.

The 2005 legislation created a fourth mandatory Chapter 13 plan provision. Section 1322(a)(4) provides that if there is a domestic support obligation owed to a governmental entity, then the plan may provide for less than payment in full of this claim if the debtor pays all disposable income into the plan for a five-year period.

The third mandatory element of a Chapter 13 plan is that if the plan classifies claims, each claim holder within a given class must be treated identically, unless a creditor agrees to a lesser treatment.[35] In other words, a debtor cannot propose to pay some unsecured creditors a 20 percent dividend and other unsecured creditors a 50 percent dividend. All creditors in a given class must be treated equally unless a specific creditor consents to a lesser treatment. This is consistent with the repayment philosophy of the bankruptcy system described in chapters 21 and 22 supra.

Section 1322(b) describes the **permissive provisions** that may be included in a Chapter 13 plan. A *permissive provision* is a provision that may be included in the plan but is not required to be in the plan. A permissive plan provision may also involve facts that, if present, will make inclusion of the permissive plan provision mandatory. For example, a Chapter 13 debtor has an executory contract. It must be assumed or rejected in the plan. Section 365(p), added to the Code in 2005, requires that an executory contract be assumed prior to confirmation of a Chapter 13 plan, or be deemed rejected and the automatic stay terminated by operation of law (see chapter 19 supra).

First, a debtor may designate more than one class of unsecured claims, so long as there is no discrimination between creditors.[36] (There will not usually be more than one class of unsecured claims in a Chapter 13, but this happens frequently in Chapter 11 proceedings.[37]) For example, a Chapter 13 debtor has several claims for which there is also a codebtor who is not a debtor in the bankruptcy proceeding. These creditors could theoretically be placed into a separate class to account for the codebtor's liability.

34. 11 U.S.C. §1322(a)(2). As to priority claims, see chapter 21 supra.
35. 11 U.S.C. §1322(a)(3).
36. 11 U.S.C. §1322(b)(1).
37. See chapter 25 infra.

However, a debtor may not create two classes of unsecured claims and pay one class a 10 percent dividend and the other class a 50 percent dividend. This latter activity will constitute unfair discrimination against the affected creditors receiving the lesser dividend.

Second, a Chapter 13 plan may modify the rights of secured creditors other than those creditors whose only security is real property that is the debtor's principal residence.[38] Stated another way, a Chapter 13 plan may seek to modify the rights of secured creditors whose collateral is other than the debtor's residence. For instance, a Chapter 13 plan may propose to reduce the amount of monthly payments and extend the loan repayment period on a secured car loan so the debtor will be able to afford to complete the contract and keep the car. However, the debtor cannot propose to modify the terms of secured home loans, except to cure any prepetition default, unless any affected secured creditors agree.

In Nobelman v. American Sav. Bank, 508 U.S. 324 (1993), the Supreme Court prohibited a practice that had been approved in some circuits, permitting the bifurcation of a secured claim into secured and unsecured portions. Under this practice, a claim secured by a lien upon a Chapter 13 debtor's residence was considered secured only up to the value of the collateral; the undersecured portion of the debt became an unsecured debt and subject to a Chapter 13 discharge. For example, in *Nobelman*, supra, the debtor sought to value the creditor's residential collateral at $23,500, although the total amount of the debt was $71,335 at the time of the petition. The Supreme Court held that Section 1322(b)(2) prevents modification of the creditor's rights and thus precludes bifurcation. That is, the debtor would be required to account for the full amount of the creditor's claim ($71,335) rather than the lesser value ($23,500) of the collateral. In short, the statutory language of Section 1322(b)(2) means what it says.

BAPA places limits on this practice of bifurcating or "stripping down" secured claims, at least where the collateral is personal property. First, if the debtor has purchased personal property collateral within one year from the filing date, or if the claim is for a purchase money security interest in a motor vehicle purchased within 910 days (2.5 years) prior to the filing, Section 1325(a) effectively provides that the allowed amount of the secured claim be the amount due under the contract. Second, Section 506(a) requires that the collateral be valued at the price a retail merchant would charge for similar collateral (see chapter 21 supra). The practical effect of these provisions is to effectively eliminate the ability to bifurcate or strip down a secured claim into secured and unsecured portions, since many purchase money contracts are of short duration.

---

38. 11 U.S.C. §1322(b)(2).

When the collateral is the debtor's home, there is a debate in the case law as to whether a claim secured by real property or a combination of real and personal property may be "stripped off" or eliminated in a Chapter 13 case. The majority view holds that if there is no value at all in the real property for the benefit of the secured claimant, then the claim is fully unsecured. The minority view holds that any secured claim secured by an interest in the debtor's home must be paid. For example, Mr. Truman owns real estate worth $50,000. He owes Dome Mortgage Company a senior mortgage of $55,000 and the Control Finance Company a junior mortgage of $10,000. Under one view, the Control debt may be stripped off because there is no value in the property to support it. Under the contrary view, the debt may not be stripped off because the collateral is Truman's home. If the debt is stripped off, it is treated as an unsecured claim and is subject to Truman's Chapter 13 discharge. See chapter 21H, supra. BAPA may limit this practice to the extent that the debtor must either pay the claim or receive a Chapter 13 discharge for the secured claim subject to strip down or strip off to be so treated. If the case is dismissed or converted to a Chapter 7, the strip off or strip down will not apply.[39]

A related issue concerns the debtor who seeks Chapter 13 relief to pay secured debt after receiving a Chapter 7 discharge. The Supreme Court examined this issue in Johnson v. Home State Bank, 501 U.S. 78 (1991). In this case the Johnsons owed the bank $470,000 secured by a mortgage upon real estate. During the pendency of a state court judicial foreclosure action the Johnsons filed a Chapter 7 and received a discharge. The bank's right to proceed against the collateral survived the bankruptcy.[40] After obtaining relief from the stay, the bank obtained a foreclosure judgment of $200,000. The Johnsons then filed a Chapter 13 and proposed to pay the claim in five annual payments. The Supreme Court held that notwithstanding the prior Chapter 7 discharge, the bank still possessed a claim against the property, so the Johnsons could file Chapter 13 to satisfy it.

Section 1322(c) of the Code limits a debtor's ability to cure a default on an obligation secured by the debtor's principal residence by requiring the cure to be made before a foreclosure sale can be properly conducted. The provision therefore overrules Johnson v. Home State Bank because the facts of the case involved a cure of the default after the foreclosure sale had

39. "'Stripping off' a lien occurs when the entire lien is avoided, whereas 'stripping down' occurs when an undersecured lien is bifurcated and the unsecured portion is avoided." In re Yi, 219 Bankr. 394 (E.D. Va. 1998). Every Circuit that has ruled on this issue to date has followed the majority rule. In re McDonald, 205 F.3d 606 (3d Cir. 2000); In re Bartee, 212 F.3d 277 (5th Cir. 2000); In re Pond, 252 F.3d 122 (2d Cir. 2000); In re Tanner, 217 F.3d 1357 (11th Cir. 2000); and In re Lam, 211 Bankr. 36 (BAP 9th Cir. 1997). In re Bauler, 215 Bankr. 628 (Bankr. N.M. 1997) represents the minority view. 11 U.S.C. §1325(a)(5)(B)(i) is the provision limiting the effect of a strip off or strip down in a dismissed or converted case.

40. See discussion of Dewsnup v. Timm, 502 U.S. 410 (1992), chapter 21 supra.

been conducted. However, Section 1322(c) also permits a Chapter 13 debtor to modify, within the plan, an obligation secured by the debtor's principal residence that becomes due during performance of the plan so long as the obligation is paid in full by completion of the plan.

The filing of a Chapter 13 after receiving a Chapter 7 discharge is colloquially known as a "Chapter 20" and is not uncommon. In *Johnson*, supra, for example, the Johnsons did not originally qualify for Chapter 13 because the secured debt owed the bank, $470,000, exceeded the then-Chapter 13 secured debt limit of $350,000. After they received their Chapter 7 discharge and the bank obtained its foreclosure judgment, the $200,000 secured claim fell within the Chapter 13 debt limit, permitting the Johnsons to seek Chapter 13 relief.

BAPA places limits upon the Chapter 20 concept. Section 362(c)(3) relieves the automatic stay 30 days after the filing of the case if the debtor was the debtor in another case that was dismissed in the previous year, unless the dismissal was dismissal for abuse of Chapter 7 pursuant to Section 707(b)(2) (see chapter 4 supra), or unless the court imposes the stay after a motion and finds that the filing of the later case is in good faith. Section 362(c)(4) provides that if a debtor had two or more cases dismissed within the previous year, the stay will not go into effect at all unless the court so orders after a motion (see chapter 12 supra). The net effect of these provisions is to prevent repeat or serial filings. However, since the provisions are only triggered by prior dismissals, receipt of a Chapter 7 discharge followed by a Chapter 13 filing may not be affected.

Third, a Chapter 13 plan may provide for the cure or waiver of any default.[41] This is precisely what most Chapter 13 plans attempt. There are five different classes of creditors that are generally paid through a Chapter 13 plan. They are administrative claims, priority claims, defaults on car loans, defaults on home loans, and general unsecured creditors. A common Chapter 13 plan will cure the defaults on the home loan or the car loan or both and pay a dividend to the unsecured creditors. Most Chapter 13 debtors' major purpose in filing a Chapter 13 is to protect a home or car from foreclosure or repossession rather than to satisfy unsecured debt.

A fourth permissive element that a Chapter 13 plan may include is that payments to unsecured creditors may be made at the same time as payments to secured creditors.[42] In other words, a Chapter 13 plan is not required to provide that all payments made will first satisfy secured creditor defaults and then unsecured creditors will receive dividends. A Chapter 13 plan may allocate its payments toward secured claim defaults and unsecured creditors at the same time.

---

41. 11 U.S.C. §1322(b)(3).
42. 11 U.S.C. §1322(b)(4).

Fifth, a Chapter 13 plan frequently may provide for a cure of defaults on any claim, priority, secured, or unsecured, even though the final payment on the claim is not due until after the plan is completed.[43] For example, John Smith is three payments behind on his car loan. He files a Chapter 13 to cure the default, thereby preventing repossession. The plan proposes to repay the three payments over twelve months. There are three years of payments left under the contract. This plan will cure the default on a secured claim for which the last payment is due after the plan is performed. This is permissible and is what many debtors are seeking with a Chapter 13, a mechanism to cure existing defaults.

This same provision also requires that any current payments coming due on any underlying long term debts be maintained during pendency of the Chapter 13.[44] Some Chapter 13 debtors form an improper impression that if the Chapter 13 plan payments are made, other ongoing payments do not have to be made. This is absolutely untrue. All that the Chapter 13 payment will do is to cure any default owed prior to the filing date. A debtor still has the obligation to continue to make current payments on home or car loans and any other debt for which the date of final payment falls after completion of the plan. The inevitable result of a failure to maintain current payments by the debtor will be a motion for relief from stay brought by a secured creditor or a motion for dismissal or conversion.

Next, a Chapter 13 plan may assume or reject executory contracts or unexpired leases. Section 365(p), added by the 2005 legislation, relieves the automatic stay as to leased property if the lease is not assumed in the plan.[45] The plan may also provide for the payment of certain limited postpetition tax claims or consumer debts necessary for a debtor's performance of the plan.[46] The plan may provide for payment of a claim from property of the estate. For example, the debtor may propose to sell a nonexempt asset and to apply the proceeds toward performance of the plan.[47] The plan may provide that property of the estate will vest in the debtor upon confirmation.[48] If all claims are paid in full, and if there are nondischargeable claims, then postpetition interest becomes payable on the claims.[49] The plan may contain any other provision that is not inconsistent with the Bankruptcy Code.[50]

Section 1322(e) permits a lender to obtain interest on the cure of a default if the underlying agreement or nonbankruptcy law permits the same.

43. 11 U.S.C. §1322(b)(5).
44. 11 U.S.C. §1322(b)(5).
45. 11 U.S.C. §1322(b)(7); 11 U.S.C. §365(p)(3). See chapter 19 supra.
46. 11 U.S.C. §1322(b)(6); 11 U.S.C. §1305.
47. 11 U.S.C. §1322(b)(8).
48. 11 U.S.C. §1322(b)(9).
49. 11 U.S.C. §1322(b)(10).
50. 11 U.S.C. §1322(b)(11).

If the debtor and the debtor's spouse's income are equal to or greater than the median national family income for a family of equal or lesser size, then the plan must be five years in duration. If the debtor and the debtor's spouse's income are less than the median national family income for a family of equal or lesser size, then the plan must be a minimum of three years in duration, and the court may approve a plan of up to five years in length. National median family income is determined as last reported by the Bureau of the Census. For example, the Census Bureau provides that for a family of four in the year 2003, median family income in California is $67,814. A family earning more than this would be required to have a five-year Chapter 13 plan. A family earning less than this would be required to have a minimum three-year Chapter 13 plan. Recall that median family income is also a threshold amount of income for application of needs based bankruptcy in Chapter 7 cases (see chapter 5, supra).[51]

A Chapter 13 plan may be modified at any time before confirmation. Of course, any such modification must comply with Section 1322. A debtor might discover that the plan is in error and amend it. This is analogous to amending a complaint before an answer is filed in traditional nonbankruptcy litigation.[52]

E. CONFIRMATION HEARINGS

Unlike Chapter 11, which is far more complex, the procedures for obtaining confirmation of a Chapter 13 plan are expedited and somewhat summary.[53] A Chapter 13 plan is confirmed at a confirmation hearing. Creditors do not have an opportunity to vote on acceptance of a Chapter 13 plan, although they may object.[54] However, unlike the creditors meeting, the confirmation hearing is held before a judge. This entire process is very expeditious. The confirmation hearing is to be held within 45 days of the meeting of creditors. The debtor will have filed Statements and Schedules along with a plan. Notice of the creditor meeting and confirmation hearing will have been given to all parties in interest. A sample Chapter 13 notice to creditors is included in the forms manual.

A debtor must commence making payments under the plan within 30 days of filing the plan. If the plan has not yet been confirmed, then the debtor is supposed to tender the first plan payment to the trustee, who will

51. 11 U.S.C. §1322(d). Census Bureau National median family income data may be accessed at http://www.census.gov/hhes/income and www.usdoj.gov/ust.
52. 11 U.S.C. §1323.
53. As to the Chapter 11 confirmation procedures, see generally chapter 26 infra.
54. 11 U.S.C. §1324.

then tender the payment or payments to the trustee when the plan has been confirmed. Recall that adequate protection payments to personal property secured claimants or lessors must be made until distributions under the plan begin. This acts as additional incentive to expedite the payment and confirmation process.[55] The above procedures make it relatively inexpensive and speedy for a debtor to pursue a Chapter 13 alternative as a solution for financial distress. In addition, these rapid procedures prevent debtors from abusing Chapter 13 as a haven to avoid debt repayment.

F. CONFIRMATION CONDITIONS

At the confirmation hearing, the court will confirm the plan, but only if the court finds that the plan meets all the conditions of Section 1325(a). Under Section 1325(a), the court must make nine findings to approve the plan. If any of the nine items are missing, the plan cannot be confirmed.

The first finding that the court must make is that the plan complies with the provisions of Chapter 13 and the Bankruptcy Code.[56] This will not generally be a problematic issue. Second, the court must find that any filing fees required to be paid for initiating the Chapter 13 have been paid.[57] Third, the court must find that the plan has been proposed in good faith and not for any means forbidden by law.[58] For example, if the debtor is seeking to utilize Chapter 13 to accomplish an improper motive or to commit an act that would otherwise be illegal, the plan will not be confirmable.

Fourth, the court must find that unsecured creditors will receive a dividend not less than that they would have received if the proceeding were a Chapter 7.[59] This requirement is commonly known as the "best interests of creditors" test. For example, if there is $10,000 of nonexempt property in the debtor's Chapter 13 estate, the Chapter 13 priority and unsecured creditors must receive a total dividend of at least $10,000, because this is what they would receive in a Chapter 7. Because most Chapter 13 proceedings would be no asset Chapter 7 proceedings, this finding is rarely a problematic issue.

The fifth finding relates to secured claims. Three alternatives are provided. The existence of at least one alternative must be found as to each

55. 11 U.S.C. §1326(a)(3). See Section 23B, supra.
56. 11 U.S.C. §1325(a)(1).
57. 11 U.S.C. §1325(a)(2).
58. 11 U.S.C. §1325(a)(3).
59. 11 U.S.C. §1325(a)(4).

secured claim for the plan to be confirmed. These requirements, in their essence, comprise alternative methods of adequate protection and preservation of the secured creditor's rights during performance of the plan. First, a secured creditor may accept the plan. If a secured claimant accepts the plan, the acceptance will aid in obtaining confirmation. The remaining alternatives concern what happens if a secured claimant does not accept the plan. If the plan provides that the holder of the claim will retain its lien until the earliest of payment in full of the debt or receipt of a Chapter 13 discharge then confirmation may occur over the secured creditor's objection. The lien is also retained if the case is converted or dismissed. The concept of approving a plan under these circumstances over a creditor's objection is commonly known as **cramdown**. A creditor will not be heard to object to confirmation if the creditor will receive all it would have received in a nonbankruptcy environment. This is the underlying principle of the cramdown concept in reorganization proceedings. Finally, a debtor may propose to surrender the collateral to the secured creditor. To summarize, as to each secured claim the court must find that each creditor either agrees to the plan, is paid the full amount of the secured claim, or will receive a return of its collateral.[60]

BAPA adds three new confirmation requirements. First, that the petition has been filed in good faith. This provision will likely be used in reconciling needs based bankruptcy issues with Chapter 13, and in dealing with the continuing problems raised by serial bankruptcy filings (see chapter 12 supra); second, that all postpetition domestic support obligations have been paid; third, that all postpetition tax returns have been timely filed pursuant to Section 1308.[61]

In Till v. SCS Credit Corp., 541 U.S. 465, the Supreme Court held that secured creditors, for cramdown purposes, are entitled to interest on their claims based upon the prime interest rate plus a premium for risk that can be proven by the creditor, and not on the underlying rate provided for by the contract. In this case, the debtors owed $4,894.89 to the creditor when they filed their Chapter 13. They proposed to pay the secured portion of the claim, $4,000, over installments at an interest rate of 9.5 percent, or the prime rate plus 1.5 percent. The creditor insisted upon receiving its contract rate of 21 percent. A likely effect of this ruling will make it easier for Chapter 13 creditors to reduce interest rates on collateral not secured solely by their primary residence.

60. 11 U.S.C. §1325(a)(5).
61. 11 U.S.C. §1325(a)(7), (8) and (9).

G. FEASIBILITY ANALYSIS

The final finding that the court must make to permit confirmation of a Chapter 13 plan is that the debtor will be able to make all payments under and comply with the plan.[62] The court must find that the plan is feasible. This determination is the most critical and problematic in a Chapter 13. If a plan is not feasible, the debtor will likely need to proceed with Chapter 7 if the bankruptcy system is to be of use in resolving the debtor's financial problems. Determining whether a feasible plan can be proposed will most likely decide the type of proceeding filed by the debtor in the first place. The following analysis reflects the state of the law before BAPA. The text will attempt to point out some of BAPA's potential effects.

To determine a plan's feasibility some calculation is required. First, determine the amount necessary to pay in full all administrative expenses and priority claims and to cure any defaults on secured debts. Second, determine the minimum amount necessary to pay unsecured creditors at least as much as they would receive in a Chapter 7. This total will be the *minimum* amount necessary to pay through the plan over its proposed length. Nonetheless, some courts do not generally favor zero percent or nominal unsecured dividends over objection even if the debtor's Chapter 7 would be a no asset proceeding. This is an area where local practice and custom should be ascertained.[63]

The third step used in determining the feasibility of a Chapter 13 plan is to determine the debtor's monthly budget. Schedules I and J comprise an estimated monthly family budget. This budget shows the income the family receives every month and what it will cost this family to meet its basic expenses *before* making its Chapter 13 plan payments. The expenses are subtracted from the income. If there is a surplus left after meeting the monthly living expenses, the surplus represents the amount available to pay into the plan on a monthly basis. If there is no surplus or if there is a deficit, the plan is not feasible. The debtor should file a Chapter 7 if the debtor wants to use the bankruptcy system.

If the budget shows a surplus of available income with which to make plan payments, the fourth step of the feasibility calculation can be

62. 11 U.S.C. §1325(a)(6).

63. See discussion above regarding 11 U.S.C. §§1322(a), 1325(a)(5), 1325(a)(4). Whether or not this amount must include the minimum calculated needs based payment under Section 707(b)(2), or whether or not needs based bankruptcy will eliminate the zero percent or nominal plan in cases that would fall under the needs based formula (see chapter 5, supra) are issues that the courts will need to explore.

performed. Divide the total minimum amount that must be paid into the plan by the available monthly surplus. The quotient will be the number of months it will take to perform the plan. If the quotient is equal to or less than 60, the plan is likely feasible. The smaller the available surplus or the closer the plan approaches to 60 months in duration, the more doubtful it will be that the plan will be found feasible by the court. Under BAPA, if the debtor's median family income is less than the national family median income for a family of similar size (see Section 23D supra), then the plan may not exceed three years in duration unless the court orders otherwise, but in no event may the plan exceed five years in duration. If the debtor's median family income is equal to or greater than the national family median income for a family of similar size, then the plan must be five years in duration. If the minimum available payment would make the plan exceed five years, it is not feasible.[64] Checklist 23.2 infra summarizes the above in a formula format.

A greater understanding of the feasibility issue can be gained through use of an extended example. Robinson Crusoe files a Chapter 13. He owes $1,000 in income taxes and $600 as a priority wage claim to his servant Friday. Bank of Defoe holds a mortgage on Crusoe's island that is six payments in default, totalling $2,500. Crusoe's unsecured creditors are owed $5,000. All Crusoe's assets are exempt. Thus, Crusoe's unsecured creditors would receive no dividend in a Chapter 7. The minimum amount that Crusoe *must* pay back is therefore $4,100 (income tax, wage claim, and past due mortgage payments).

Crusoe's Chapter 13 statement shows that he will have surplus income of $150 per month with which to make payments under the plan. Performing the final calculation, dividing $4,100 by $150, yields a result of 27.33. It will take approximately 28 months for Crusoe to pay the minimum possible Chapter 13 plan he might propose. This plan could be found feasible, but note that it does not provide any dividend to unsecured creditors. This can affect feasibility and will not permit a cramdown in the event of objections by unsecured creditors.

Under BAPA, Crusoe's current monthly income would need to be known. If Crusoe's income is less than the national family median income for a family of similar size, then he must propose at least a 3-year (36-month plan) if he wants to effectuate a cramdown. This would pay his unsecured creditors a dividend of approximately 25% (36 – 27.33 = 8.67 × $150 = $1,300.50). If Crusoe's income is equal to or greater than the national family median income for a family of similar size, then he must propose a 5-year (60-month) plan to effectuate a cramdown. This would pay his unsecured creditors substantially in full (60 – 27.33 = 32.67 × $150 = $4,900.50). Whether

64. 11 U.S.C. §1322(d).

or not either of these scenarios would be confirmable and subject to cramdown over the objection of unsecured creditors is the subject of 11 U.S.C. §1325(b).

H. CRAMDOWN

Secured or unsecured creditors may object to the plan. Unlike Chapter 11, there is no voting procedure in Chapter 13. Unless a creditor objects to the plan, the creditor's acceptance is presumed. If a creditor or creditors do object to the plan, confirmation can still be obtained through a procedure commonly known as cramdown. This procedure has already been identified with regard to the secured creditors of a Chapter 13 debtor. Section 1325(b) describes the cramdown procedure when unsecured creditors object to a Chapter 13 plan.

Under Section 1325(b) there are two methods in which the debtor may effectuate a Chapter 13 cramdown upon unsecured creditors. The first method is that if the creditors are going to be paid in full, then the plan will be confirmed over their objection.[65] Creditors who will be paid in full through the plan will not be heard to object. Payment in full is, after all, the ultimate creditor goal in a bankruptcy proceeding.

Most of the time, however, creditors are not proposed to be paid in full. In this instance, the second method of cramdown is necessary. If the unsecured creditors cannot be paid in full, a cramdown may still occur if the debtor proposes to place all disposable income into the plan for the *"applicable commitment period."*[66] **Disposable income** invokes application of the needs based bankruptcy formula discussed in chapter 5 supra. The Debtor's current monthly income and expenses are determined in a manner identical to Chapter 7, except that postpetition domestic support obligations, charitable religious contributions of up to 15% of gross income, and business expenses if the debtor is engaged in the operation of a business. If the debtor's current monthly income is less than the state median income for the debtor's household size, then the plan must be no less than three years in duration to effectuate a cramdown. If the debtor's current monthly income is equal to or greater than the state median income for the debtor's household size, then the plan must be of five years duration to effectuate a cramdown. When the creditors are paid in full, the plan may be less than these time periods.[67]

65. 11 U.S.C. §1325(b)(1)(A).
66. 11 U.S.C. §1325(b)(1)(B).
67. 11 U.S.C. §1325(b)(2), (3), (4).

Thus, if Robinson Crusoe's unsecured creditors in the above example object to the plan, Crusoe must either pay them in full or propose a three- or five-year plan, depending upon his current monthly income as illustrated above. If Crusoe proposes to pay all disposable income into the plan for the appropriate three- or five-year period, the plan can be confirmed over the objection of unsecured creditors.

I. EFFECT OF CONFIRMATION AND CHAPTER 13 DISCHARGE

A confirmed Chapter 13 plan is a judicially approved composition agreement. When a Chapter 13 plan is confirmed, it acts as a new contract between the debtor and all creditors. All creditors are bound by the Chapter 13 plan.[68] This is the big difference between a Chapter 13 and a nonbankruptcy composition agreement. In the latter case, any objecting creditors are not bound to the agreement.

Once performance of a Chapter 13 plan has been completed, and the debtor certifies that any postpetition domestic support obligations have been paid, a Chapter 13 debtor becomes entitled to a Chapter 13 discharge. A Chapter 13 discharge is similar to a Chapter 7 discharge. A Chapter 13 Debtor must also complete a postpetition personal financial management course identical to Chapter 7.[69]

An obligation for which final payment is due after the plan is completed is not dischargeable in Chapter 13.[70] For example, in the fifth year of a 30-year mortgage the debtor files a Chapter 13. The Chapter 13 plan cures the default and the debtor receives a discharge. The mortgage itself is not discharged because the last payment is due after the last payment under the plan. Taxes are not dischargeable to the same extent that they are not dischargeable in Chapter 7 cases (but since all priority taxes must be paid in full through the plan, this is a moot point). Domestic, support obligations are not discharged by a Chapter 13. Next, student loans remain nondischargeable to the same extent that they are not dischargeable in Chapter 7 proceedings. Debts incurred fraudulently, unlisted debts, and fiduciary defalcations are not dischargeable in Chapter 13. Damages resulting from

68. 11 U.S.C. §1327.
69. 11 U.S.C. §1328(a)(g).
70. 11 U.S.C. §1328(a)(1).

substance abuse are nondischargeable to the same extent that they are not dischargeable in Chapter 7 proceedings.[71] Criminal restitution orders or criminal fines are not dischargeable.[72] Finally, restitution orders or civil damage awards resulting from wilful or malicious injury, or wrongful death, are not dischargeable.[73]

A Chapter 13 debtor who has not fully completed a plan may still apply for and receive a discharge if the court finds that a failure to complete the plan is due to circumstances for which the debtor should not justly be held accountable and if unsecured creditors have received at least the amount of dividend they would have received in a Chapter 7 proceeding.[74] A death of one of two joint debtors is such a circumstance. If the court can make such findings for a debtor that has not completed a Chapter 13 plan, the debtor will receive a discharge that is identical to a Chapter 7 discharge.[75] That is, debts that are nondischargeable through a Chapter 7 are also nondischargeable through a Chapter 13 discharge obtained under these circumstances.

Prior to the 2005 BAPA legislation, many debts that were not dischargeable in Chapter 7 were in fact dischargeable in Chapter 13. The theory was that since a debtor was making an effort to repay debt, the scope of the discharge should be broader. However, as the 2005 reforms suggest a strong swing of the pendulum in favor of debt collection as opposed to debtor relief, the net effect of the reforms makes Chapter 13 more significant as a debt collection tool as opposed to providing honest but unfortunate debtors with a fresh start in their financial affairs.

If the debtor has received a discharge in a Chapter 7, 11, or 12 filed within four years from the filing of the Chapter 13, then no debts are dischargeable. If the debtor received a Chapter 13 discharge within two years prior to the filing, then no debts are dischargeable. These provisions, added by BAPA, are an important departure from prior law and will seriously limit the concept of the Chapter 20 described above in Section 23D supra.[76]

A Chapter 13 discharge may be revoked if the court finds that the discharge was fraudulently obtained. Revocation must be sought within one year of the discharge's being granted.[77] Confirmation of a Chapter 13 plan that has been fraudulently obtained may also be revoked.[78]

---

71. 11 U.S.C. §1328(a)(2).
72. 11 U.S.C. §1328(a)(4).
73. See chapter 13 supra.
74. 11 U.S.C. §1328(b).
75. 11 U.S.C. §1328(c).
76. 11 U.S.C. §1328(f).
77. 11 U.S.C. §1328(e).
78. 11 U.S.C. §1330.

One of three things can happen during the life of a confirmed plan. The debtor may perform and complete the plan in a timely manner. This is the goal of the system. Or the debtor may receive a windfall during the life of the plan and wish to accelerate performance. Under Section 1329 the debtor may ask the court for permission to modify the plan to accelerate its performance. Or, third, the debtor may become unable to make payments under a confirmed plan. In this instance the debtor may ask the court to modify the plan to lower the payments or to extend the plan's duration. This is permissible as long as the modified plan still complies with the provisions of Chapter 13 and as long as final performance of the plan is still no longer than five years from the original commencement of the plan.[79] If the plan cannot be successfully modified, then conversion of the proceeding to a Chapter 7 may become necessary.

Summary

This and the next four text chapters describe the reorganization proceedings of Chapter 13, Chapter 11, and Chapter 12. In a reorganization proceeding, a debtor will attempt to repay debt and retain nonexempt assets or continue to operate a business. Reorganization proceedings are, in their essence, no more or less than judicially approved composition agreements.

Chapter 13 is a program for individuals with regular income who have unsecured debts of less than $307,675 and secured debts of less than $922,975. A qualified individual may attempt repayment of debt over a period not to exceed five years.

The Chapter 13 procedure is expedited. The checklist accompanying this chapter itemizes the important deadlines, documents to file, and the hearing dates involved in a Chapter 13 proceeding.

A trustee will always be appointed in a Chapter 13. The most important function of the Chapter 13 trustee is to collect the plan payments and distribute dividends to creditors.

A Chapter 13 plan must contain four mandatory elements. A Chapter 13 plan may contain various permissive elements. The mandatory requirements are that the plan provide for payments, that priority claims be paid in full, that all claims within a given class be treated equally, and that domestic support obligations owed to a governmental entity may only be paid less then in full if the debtor proposes a five-year plan.

The permissive elements of a Chapter 13 plan include the debtor's providing for more than one class of unsecured claims, modifying the

79. 11 U.S.C. §1329.

rights of certain secured creditors, the cure or waiver of defaults, and simultaneous payments to secured and unsecured creditors.

A Chapter 13 plan is confirmed at a confirmation hearing. The court must make nine findings to confirm a plan. If one of the findings cannot be made, the plan may not be confirmed. The plan must comply with the provisions of the Bankruptcy Code. Any filing fees must be paid. The plan must be proposed in good faith. The creditors must receive a dividend not less than the dividend that they would receive in a Chapter 7 proceeding. These issues are not generally problematic. With regard to secured creditors, the court must find either that the creditor consents, the creditor will be paid the full value of its secured claim, or that any collateral will be returned to the creditor. The petition must have been filed in good faith. All post-petition domestic support obligations must be current. All postpetition tax returns must be filed.

Finally, the court must find that the plan is feasible. This requires a determination that the debtor can afford to make the plan payments. The checklist accompanying this chapter describes a simple formula to use in making this calculation.

If creditors object to a Chapter 13 plan, the plan may still be approved over their objections through use of a procedure commonly known as cramdown. A cramdown of unsecured creditors will occur in a Chapter 13 if the plan will pay the creditors in full or if all the debtor's disposable income is paid into the plan for a period of time from three to five years, depending upon whether or not the debtor's family income is less or more than the national median family income for a family of similar size. Disposable income is determined in accordance with needs based bankruptcy (see chapter 5, supra).

A Chapter 13 plan may be modified after confirmation to accelerate or reduce performance. The modified plan must still meet the confirmation requirements.

A debtor completing performance of a Chapter 13 plan, completing a financial management course and remaining current on postpetition domestic support obligations receives a discharge. Under BAPA, a Chapter 13 discharge is virtually identical to a Chapter 7 discharge. Additionally, debts for which the last payment is due after performance of the plan (such as a 30-year home loan) are not dischargeable. In special circumstances, a debtor may receive a hardship discharge in Chapter 13, which has the same effect as a Chapter 7 discharge. A discharge will not issue if the debtor received a Chapter 7, 11, or 12 discharge within four years from the filing of the Chapter 13, or has received a Chapter 13 discharge in another case within two years of the filing.

Confirmation of a Chapter 13 plan may be revoked if the court finds that confirmation was fraudulently obtained.

A reorganization proceeding may be dismissed or converted to a Chapter 7 liquidation for cause. The causes identified by the Code are delineated in the checklist accompanying this chapter.

KEY TERMS

Applicable Commitment Period	**mandatory provisions**
confirmation	**permissive provisions**
conversion	**plan**
cramdown	**property of the estate**
dismissal	**reorganization**
disposable income	**strip down**
liquidation	**strip off**

Chapter 23 Checklist

23.1 DOCUMENTS AND DEADLINES IN CHAPTER 13

		Deadline	*Statute*
23.1.1	Petition	at filing	Bankruptcy Rule 1002
23.1.2	Credit Counseling Certificate at filing		11.U.S.C. §109(h)
23.1.3	Statement of Financial Affairs, Schedules	15 days	Bankruptcy Rule 1007(b)(2), (c)
23.1.4	Chapter 13 Plan	15 days	Bankruptcy Rule 3015
23.1.5	Attorneys' Fee Statement	creditors meeting	Bankruptcy Rule 2016
23.1.6	First Plan Payment	30 days	11 U.S.C. §1326
23.1.7	Adequate Protection Payments	30 days	11 U.S.C. §1326(a)

23.1.8	Plan Performance:		
	1. Family Income < SMFI[80]	3 years	11 U.S.C. §1322(d)
	2. Family Income => SMFI[81]	5 years	11 U.S.C. §1322(d)
23.1.9	File tax returns for last 4 years	creditor meeting	11 U.S.C. §1308

23.2 CHAPTER 13 FEASIBILITY FORMULA

23.2.1 Add (A)dministrative Claims, (P)riority Claims, and (M)inimum Chapter 7 Dividend (A + P + M)

23.2.2 Determine Existence of Surplus or Deficit in Monthly Budget (Deficit Means Plan Is Not Feasible) (B)

23.2.3 Divide the Total Reached in 23.2.1 by Any Budget Surplus $(A + P + M) \div B$

23.2.4 If Answer Obtained in 23.2.3 Is 36 or Less, the Plan Is Likely Feasible. If Answer Obtained in 23.2.3 Is 36-60, the Plan May Be Feasible. $(A + P + M) \div (B) \leq 60$

23.2.5 Plan must be 3-5 years duration depending upon current monthly income. Add amounts necessary to comply with mandatory length to 23.2.4.

23.3 CAUSES FOR CONVERSION OR DISMISSAL

		Statute
23.3.1	Loss or Diminution — Reorganization Unlikely	11 U.S.C. §1112(b)(4)(A)
23.3.2	Failure to follow operating rules	11 U.S.C. §1112 (b)(4)(B)(C)(C) (F)(H)(I)
23.3.3	Unreasonable Delay Prejudicial to Creditors	11 U.S.C. §1307(c)(1)
23.3.4	Failure to Propose a Plan within Court Deadlines	11 U.S.C. §§1112(b)(4)(J), 1307(c)(3)

80. "SMFI" means state family median income for a family of similar size.
81. Ibid.

		Statute
23.3.5	Failure to Obtain Confirmation of Any Plan	11 U.S.C. §1307(c)(5)
23.3.6	Revocation of Confirmation	11 U.S.C. §§1112(b)(4)(L), 1307(c)(7)
23.3.7	Inability to Commence Plan	11 U.S.C. §§1112(b)(4)(M), 1307(c)(4)
23.3.8	Material Default in Plan	11 U.S.C. §§1112(b)(4)(N), 1307(c)(6)
23.3.9	Occurrence of a Condition Stated in Plan	11 U.S.C. §§1112(b)(4)(Q), 1307(c)(2)
23.3.10	Failure to Pay Court Fees	11 U.S.C. §§1112(b)(4)(K), 1307(c)(2)
23.3.11	Failure to File Chapter 13 Statement	11 U.S.C. §1307(c)(9), (10)
23.3.12	Failure to pay postpetition domestic support obligations	11 U.S.C. §1307(c)(11)
23.3.13	Failure to file tax returns	11 U.S.C. §1308

DISCUSSION QUESTIONS

1. What is the purpose of a reorganization proceeding?
2. What are the grounds for dismissal or conversion of a reorganization proceeding?
3. What documents must a Chapter 13 debtor file with the court? What are the deadlines for filing each document? What is the effect of a failure to file a required document?
4. What is the permissible length of a Chapter 13 plan?

5. What elements must be included in a Chapter 13 plan?
6. What elements may be included in a Chapter 13 plan?
7. What findings must the court make to confirm a Chapter 13 plan? How is a plan's feasibility determined?
8. How does a creditor object to confirmation of a Chapter 13 plan?
9. What is meant by the term *cramdown*? How can a Chapter 13 debtor cramdown a plan over the objection of an unsecured creditor?
10. How and when may a Chapter 13 plan be modified?
11. What is the effect of a Chapter 13 discharge? How, if at all, does a Chapter 13 discharge differ from a Chapter 7 discharge? What is a "hardship" discharge?
12. What is a "Chapter 20"?

24

Chapter 11: Introduction and Administration

A. INTRODUCTION TO CHAPTER 11

Chapter 11 is the most complex, time-consuming, and expensive of all bankruptcy proceedings to prosecute. Although Chapter 11s constitute less than 1 percent of all bankruptcies filed, perhaps as much as 90 percent of all time expended by the Bankruptcy Court involves Chapter 11 proceedings.[1] The various topics described elsewhere in this text, relief from stay motions, the assumption or rejection of executory contracts, the use or sale of property including the use of cash collateral, and the obtaining of credit by a bankruptcy estate, are all recurring issues in Chapter 11 proceedings. Each issue must be dealt with independently, but the resolution of each issue may involve one or more evidentiary hearings. Further, and most critically, the resolution of one or more of these issues may often be essential in determining whether the proceeding will be given an opportunity for a successful outcome or if conversion to Chapter 7 will be the likely final result.

Often, a resolution of any or all of the above issues may be required at the inception of a Chapter 11 proceeding. For example, a manufacturing debtor-in-possession may need to obtain a cash collateral order, obtain postpetition secured credit, and assume existing manufacturing contracts within a relatively short period of time after the Chapter 11 filing. These activities will involve motions under Sections 363, 364, and 365, respectively.[2] Simultaneously, a debtor-in-possession may be required to defend

1. According to figures available from the American Bankruptcy Institute, Chapter 11 proceedings comprised 0.6 percent of all filings for the calendar year ending December 31, 2004, or 10,368 out of 1,618,883 total filings.
2. See chapters 18, 19, and 20 supra.

motions to appoint a trustee or examiner under Section 1104 or motions for relief from stay or adequate protection under Sections 362 and 361.[3] All of these activities may occur and be determined before a debtor-in-possession can even begin to consider proposing a plan of reorganization. It is in Chapter 11 practice that the Bankruptcy Code most frequently and visibly operates as a complete system affecting all of a debtor's financial affairs. In large reorganizations typical of the Southern District of New York or the District of Delaware, any or all of those matters may be the subject of one or more **first-day orders** sought at the beginning of the case.

Like Chapter 13, the goal of Chapter 11 is for a debtor to successfully reorganize its affairs so it may repay debt, retain assets, and remain in business. Like Chapter 13, this is accomplished by a debtor-in-possession proposing a plan of reorganization and obtaining its confirmation. Unlike Chapter 13, the Chapter 11 plan confirmation process is complex and lengthy. At least two court hearings are required to obtain confirmation. A further important difference is that the creditors in a Chapter 11 are afforded an opportunity to vote for or against the plan. It normally takes a minimum of four to six months to obtain confirmation of a typical Chapter 11 plan.[4] Like a Chapter 13, a confirmed Chapter 11 plan is nothing more or less than a judicially approved composition agreement.

A number of actions, many of which have been described elsewhere in this text, virtually all of which must be taken by a Chapter 11 debtor within 120 days of filing to ensure that all provisions of the Bankruptcy Code and Federal Rules of Bankruptcy Procedure are properly complied with in the prosecution of the Chapter 11 proceeding. Further, because a Chapter 11 may remain pending for an indefinite period of time prior to confirmation of a plan and because the debtor acts as its own trustee as a debtor-inpossession, a number of operating rules have been created to monitor a debtor-in-possession's compliance with the Bankruptcy Code and Rules. These operating rules are generally implemented by guidelines published by the local United States Trustee. A sample set of guidelines is contained in the forms manual accompanying this text. This chapter concerns the initial actions and ongoing operating procedures that a debtor-in-possession must follow prior to confirmation of a plan. The following two chapters will describe the procedure and requirements for proposing and obtaining confirmation of a Chapter 11 plan.

Chapter 11 has no initial qualifying requirements in terms of the amount of debt that a debtor must owe or the type of entity that the debtor must be. Essentially, any entity that may file a Chapter 7 may file a Chapter 11.[5] Chapter 11 is intentionally designed in this way. A corporation as large

3. See chapters 10 and 12 supra.
4. See chapter 26 infra.
5. 11 U.S.C. §109. See chapter 5 supra.

as Enron or an individual debtor owing just slightly in excess of the Chapter 13 debt limits may each file a Chapter 11.[6] This is a unique feature of Chapter 11. It is designed to work for small debtors as well as large debtors. When a large corporation files, the filing is undoubtedly reported in the media. For example, Enron, Worldcom, United Airlines, Continental Airlines, U.S. Air, and K-Mart have all been involved in widely publicized Chapter 11 cases in recent years. In remarks before the American Bankruptcy Institute, Chief Justice William H. Rehnquist stated: "Chapter 11 has become a major tool for restructuring corporate America, with broad implications for employees, retirees, business competitors, and the economy as a whole."[7]

The Bankruptcy Reform Act of 1994 created a new subcategory of Chapter 11 debtor, the **small business debtor**. A *small business debtor* is defined as a debtor with liquidated debts not in excess of $2 million and who elects treatment as a small business. A small business, however, may not be a debtor whose primary activity is owning and operating real estate.[8] A small business may have no creditor committee if the court so orders and must expedite the formulation of a reorganization plan (see chapter 10 supra and chapter 25 infra).

Chapter 11 is more than a legal program for the reorganization of a debtor. It is incorrect to think of Chapter 11 reorganization as solely a legal process. A debtor often may have one or more serious problems that may precipitate the Chapter 11 filing. Sometimes, as in the case of Texaco, the problem is related to one event, such as a large judgment that the debtor cannot satisfy without imposition of a repayment plan over the objection of the judgment creditor.

Sometimes a debtor's problems are related to fraud, mismanagement, or the gross incompetence of its insiders. In these situations, more than a legal reorganization will be required to solve the debtor's problems. As a practical matter, the entire business may have to be internally reorganized in addition to the external reorganization represented by the plan. Internal reorganization may be as simple as teaching a debtor how to count and manage a budget over an extended period of time. This single problem is a major cause of many Chapter 11 filings. Sometimes, internal reorganization can be quite complex and involve a change of insider management, plant closings, layoffs, and so forth.

Sometimes a Chapter 11 will involve a partnership with one piece of real property that is in foreclosure. This sort of proceeding has relatively

6. Texaco, Inc. and a number of its subsidiaries filed a Chapter 11 proceeding in the Southern District of New York. Texaco successfully reorganized in 1988. As to individuals, see Toibb v. Radloff, 501 U.S. 157 (1991), discussed in section 5E supra.

7. Remarks of Chief Justice William H. Rehnquist, Annual Spring Meeting of the American Bankruptcy Institute, May 18, 1992.

8. 11 U.S.C. §101(51C).

few problematic issues because all the debtor seeks is to refinance or sell the property so as to avoid the foreclosure and realize a profit. Not much may happen in the proceeding until a secured creditor moves for relief from the stay or the debtor can propose a plan.

Most Chapter 11 debtors-in-possession are operating businesses. The filing of the proceeding makes the debtor a debtor-in-possession.[9] A debtor-in-possession is the functional equivalent of a trustee.[10] As illustrated elsewhere, the debtor-in-possession is authorized to conduct ordinary business affairs without court approval except as required by Sections 363, 364, or 365.[11]

The United States Trustee has been charged with monitoring a Chapter 11 debtor-in-possession's postpetition operations to ensure compliance with the provisions of the Bankruptcy Code and Rules.[12] Additionally, one role of the Official Creditors Committee is to be active in monitoring the debtor's affairs during the proceeding.[13]

There are definite benefits that a debtor gains from a Chapter 11 filing. A business in serious financial condition may continue to operate without danger of immediate closure by any of its creditors. This breathing spell theoretically provides the debtor with an opportunity to attempt the successful reorganization of its financial affairs.

However, there are burdens that a debtor must accept along with the benefits of a Chapter 11 proceeding. The largest burden is that a debtor will be required to comply with many court rules. The true meaning of these rules is that by filing a Chapter 11, the debtor-in-possession effectively becomes an involuntary partner with its creditors. The debtor's financial affairs will no longer be private. They will be subject to constant monitoring and criticism by the creditors committee, individual creditors, or the United States Trustee.[14] All of these entities have the opportunity to intrude into and attempt to control the debtor's financial affairs in manners not normally possible in a nonbankruptcy environment. The debtor-in-possession owes a duty to its creditors and the court to follow all applicable Chapter 11 operating rules.

If a debtor-in-possession fails to comply with the operating rules, the Official Creditors Committee or the United States Trustee or any creditor may move the court for the appointment of a trustee or an examiner, thus removing the debtor from possession.[15] Alternatively, if the proceeding

9. 11 U.S.C. §1101(1).
10. 11 U.S.C. §1107. See chapter 10 supra.
11. See chapters 18, 19, and 20 supra.
12. 28 U.S.C. §586(a)(3). See chapter 10 supra.
13. 11 U.S.C. §1103. See chapter 10 supra.
14. See chapter 10 supra.
15. See chapter 10 supra.

fails as a Chapter 11 or if the debtor fails to comply with the operating rules, a Chapter 11 proceeding may be converted to a Chapter 7 or dismissed pursuant to the conditions previously outlined in connection with Section 1112.[16]

B. ACTIONS TO TAKE WITHIN 120 DAYS OF FILING

At the moment of filing a Chapter 11, a debtor must file the following documents with the court:

1. petition, along with payment of an $1039 filing fee;
2. a corporate resolution or partnership consent authorizing the filing;
3. a list containing the names and addresses of each creditor unless the Schedules are filed with the petition;
4. a list of the 20 largest unsecured claimants including the amount of the claims; and
5. a corporate debtor must file Exhibit A to Voluntary Petition.
6. an individual debtor must file a credit counseling certificate (11 U.S.C. §109(h); 11 U.S.C. §521(b). See chapter 4 supra).
7. a small business debtor must file, within three days, its most recent balance sheet, statement of operations, cash-flow statement, federal income tax return or a statement under penalty of perjury as to which of the items has not been prepared or filed (11 U.S.C. §1116(1)).

Some of these time periods may be extended upon application to the court or United States Trustee.[17]

Within 15 days of filing the petition, a Chapter 11 debtor must file the following additional documents with the court:

8. a list of all equity security holders of the debtor;
9. the Statement of Financial Affairs;
10. Schedules of Assets and Liabilities; and
11. a Statement of Executory Contracts.

16. 11 U.S.C. §1112. See chapter 23 supra for a more detailed description of §1112.
17. 11 U.S.C. §302; Bankruptcy Rules 1002, 1004, 1006, 1007(a), (d). See chapter 4 supra.

These time periods may be extended upon application to the court or United States Trustee.[18] The United States Trustee will conduct an informal conference known as an Initial Debtor Interview with representatives of the debtor to discuss the operating requirements and to implement compliance with the rules and guidelines applicable within a given district. In a small business case, Section 1116(2) mandates an Initial Debtor Interview. Form 10.1 is a sample of a local United States Trustee guidelines.

Within 30 days of filing, the debtor must also file an inventory, if ordered to do so by the United States Trustee, and commence to file operating reports.[19] Local rules may also supplement these basic requirements. Any applications to retain professionals, such as attorneys or accountants, must also be filed during the same initial 30-day period or within 30 days of the professional's retention.

Finally, a debtor-in-possession must act within 120 days to assume any lease of nonresidential real property or the lease is deemed rejected.[20]

C. DEBTOR-IN-POSSESSION BANK ACCOUNTS

Local rules or United States Trustee guidelines may add other actions that must be performed by a Chapter 11 debtor-in-possession promptly after the filing or on an ongoing basis. First, a debtor-in-possession will be required to deposit all funds in an approved depository pursuant to Section 345. Recall that an approved depository is a bank or savings and loan that guarantees bankruptcy deposits of greater than $100,000.[21]

Next, local rules will require a debtor-in-possession to close its old bank accounts and open new ones. Because part of the theory behind the debtor-in-possession concept is that it is a new entity separate and distinct from the prepetition debtor, the requirement of establishing new bank accounts helps implement the theory. This requirement also serves as a useful accounting mechanism for the debtor because it closes the prepetition books and opens new ones.

Local rules or United States Trustee guidelines may require that at least three accounts be established. They are normally a general account, a payroll account, and a tax account. These new accounts will be required to identify the debtor as a debtor-in-possession. For example, it will not

18. Bankruptcy Rules 1007(a)(3)(4), 1007(b)(1).
19. Bankruptcy Rule 2015. As to small business debtors, 11 U.S.C. §1116 codifies these requirements.
20. 11 U.S.C. §365(d)(4). See chapter 19 supra.
21. 11 U.S.C. §345. See chapter 20 supra.

D.I.P. Account/Cash Flow

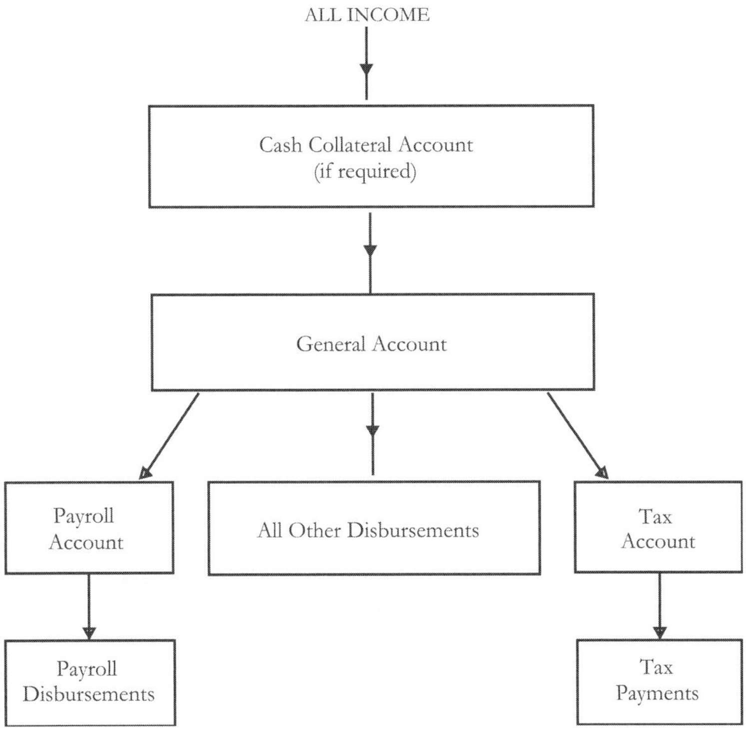

generally be acceptable for ABC Inc. to identify itself as such on its checks. The checks must now state "ABC Inc., Debtor-in-Possession," along with the case number. Local rules or United States Trustee guidelines should be consulted to identify the acceptable legend required in a given district.

The requirement of multiple bank accounts is designed to assist debtors in efficiently managing their cash flow, ensuring to the greatest extent possible that payroll and tax obligations will be satisfied properly and promptly and that any party in interest who desires may easily trace a debtor's cash flow during the Chapter 11. All income that a debtor receives is to be deposited into the general account. From the general account all disbursements are made to the debtor. For example, there will be disbursements from the general account into the payroll account to meet payroll. There will be disbursements from the general account into the tax account as the taxes are incurred. All other postpetition debts of the estate will be paid from the general account.

A large debtor may actually have more than three bank accounts. For example, a debtor-in-possession accumulating cash surpluses should open a savings account so the surplus funds can earn interest. In addition, any secured creditor's cash collateral will be required to be deposited into a cash collateral account before disbursement into other accounts. If use of the cash collateral is allowed, disbursements from the cash collateral account will be directed as the parties and court agree. The accompanying diagram indicates the general flow of cash through debtor-in-possession accounts.

D. INSIDER COMPENSATION

Local rules may require that a debtorin-possession obtain an order from the court approving any compensation to be paid the debtor's insiders. In districts utilizing a rule of this nature, a Chapter 11 debtor will subject the salary of its insiders to the scrutiny of creditors and approval by the court. The basic theory behind this rule is that any affected insiders should not be permitted to abuse the bankruptcy system by paying themselves excessive salaries at the expense of creditors. Approval of insider salaries will generally require a noticed motion.[22] The court may approve compensation on an interim basis while this process is pending. The United States Trustee normally monitors applications for insider compensation and may challenge the amount sought.

It is in the court's discretion to decide what will constitute reasonable compensation to an insider. The practitioner should be prepared to demonstrate two sets of facts to the court. First, the court should be shown what duties the insider performs for the debtor, such as the number of hours per week worked, a job description, and, if available, a comparison of salaries for similar positions in the debtor's industry. Second, there should be disclosure of the insider's basic monthly living expenses. A budget statement similar to those used in Chapter 7 and Chapter 13 proceedings should suffice in most situations. The insider employees of a debtorin-possession will necessarily be entitled to salaries, because it will be difficult or impossible for the debtor to reorganize if its key employees are prohibited from receiving a paycheck at least sufficient to meet basic monthly living expenses, especially in small business debtor cases. This is common sense.

Once all of the foregoing acts have been accomplished, the Chapter 11 proceeding has been properly organized to function in compliance with all Federal Rules of Bankruptcy Procedure save two, the continuing duty to file operating reports and the obligation to pay quarterly fees to the United States Trustee pursuant to 28 U.S.C. §1930(a)(6). The amount of this fee

22. See chapter 5 supra.

depends on the total disbursements made by the debtor-in-possession until dismissal or conversion of a case.[23] Checklist 24.3 infra is a table of United States Trustee quarterly fees.

E. OPERATING REPORTS

The most important ongoing duty of a Chapter 11 debtor-in-possession is to file operating reports. This is required by both the Code and the Rules.[24] Local rules or United States Trustee guidelines will generally require the reports to be filed on a monthly basis. Oddly enough, there is no official form of an operating report and many local rules do not specify a particular format. Section 308 mandates the basic items to be included in operating reports in small business cases. A format approved by the United States Trustee is included in the forms manual accompanying this text.

The operating report serves a number of critical functions in the administration of a Chapter 11 proceeding. It is a regular report of a debtor's ongoing postpetition business operations. It will advise the creditors, Official Creditors Committee, and the United States Trustee if the debtor is generating profits or losses during the proceeding. If the debtor is incurring debts that it is not timely paying, if any improper disbursements are being made (avoidable postpetition transactions, for example), or if any transactions have taken place without the requisite prior court approval (such as administrative loans or unauthorized use of cash collateral), this information will be disclosed in the report.[25] Undue delay in the formulation of a plan to the creditors' prejudice can be ascertained from review of a series of operating reports. Examination of the report will allow a creditor, the Official Creditors Committee, or the United States Trustee to determine whether a proceeding should continue, be converted or dismissed, or have a trustee appointed to oversee the debtor's operations even more closely. From the results contained in operating reports, the parties will be able to evaluate the feasibility of any proposed plan that relies on operating revenues for performance.

For example, if Linus's Security Blankets, Inc., has been in a Chapter 11 for four years while accumulating cash profits sufficient to pay all claims in

23. On January 26, 1996, 28 U.S.C. §1930(a)(6), which is the operative statute for the assessment and collection of quarterly fees, was amended into its present form. Prior to this date, quarterly fees ended upon confirmation of the plan. Now collection will continue until the case is dismissed, converted, or the plan is fully performed and the case closed. Pub. L. No. 104-99, 110 Stat. 26 (1996).
24. 11 U.S.C. §308; 11 U.S.C. §1106(a)(1); 11 U.S.C. §704(8); 11 U.S.C. §1116(4); Bankruptcy Rule 2015(a)(3).
25. 11 U.S.C. §§364, 549, 363(c). See chapters 17, 18, and 20 supra.

full, the creditors might propose their own plan or seek dismissal or conversion of the proceeding. On the other hand, if a proceeding appears interminable and a series of reports indicates that adequate profits cannot be generated to repay creditors, then the creditors may use this data to seek conversion of the proceeding to a Chapter 7. In short, the operating reports comprise an official record of a debtor-in-possession's postpetition financial activities. This record will demonstrate whether a proceeding is destined for success or failure.

Ideally, an accurate operating report will contain elements of the two basic accounting methods, cash or accrual. Each accounting method will disclose certain aspects of the debtor's postpetition financial status that may be germane to a continuation of the proceeding as a Chapter 11.

The **cash method** of accounting is the accounting method that virtually all individuals use every day of their lives. The cash method of accounting accounts for cash at the time it is received or spent. The **accrual method** of accounting, on the other hand, identifies as income any right to receive payment for goods delivered or services performed. For example, an account receivable is considered income under the accrual method of accounting, while it would not be so considered in the cash method of accounting until the receivable is actually paid. In addition, the accrual method of accounting identifies as an expense any debt that has been incurred even though it has not yet been paid. Most businesses that have inventory are required, for tax purposes, to use the accrual method of accounting on a regular basis. Manufacturing entities are also required to use the accrual method of accounting. The Schedules of Assets and Liabilities that a debtor must file in any bankruptcy proceeding are really not much more than a form of accrual basis financial statements. The accrual method describes all obligations that have been accrued but not paid by a debtor while itemizing all of a debtor's assets. This is the essence of the accrual method of accounting. The cash method of accounting identifies whether the debtor-in-possession has more or less cash on hand at the beginning or end of a reporting period as time passes. The accrual method of accounting identifies, over a period of time, whether the receivables are increasing or decreasing or if outstanding accounts payable are increasing or decreasing.

An operating report must contain an itemization of all receipts and disbursements made by a debtor-in-possession.[26] This is a cash basis representation of the debtor-in-possession's activities. Each bank account maintained by a debtor-in-possession should have its own itemized disbursement schedule included in the monthly operating report. Each

26. 11 U.S.C. §308 mandates these items in small business operating reports. See also Bankruptcy Rule 2015(2)(3).

disbursement must be identified. It may be sufficient in many cases simply to attach a copy of the debtor-in-possession's check register as an exhibit to the report. The check register will identify the check number, the amount, and the identity of the payee.

A debtor-in-possession should avoid making cash disbursements. If, however, cash disbursements are made, the debtor-in-possession should maintain detailed records of them. The invoices paid or payment receipts should be maintained and itemized in the report so that all transactions conducted by a debtor are accounted for. Otherwise, an examiner, a trustee, a creditor, or the United States Trustee will assume that the cash disbursement was improper.

The report should reconcile, or balance, a debtor-in-possession's bank accounts. This part of the report will disclose the amount on deposit in each account at the beginning and end of a reporting period. Each account should be identified by name, address, and account number.

The accrual portion of an operating report, where required, will identify whether the debtor is or is not generally paying its postpetition debts as they become due. The debtor should disclose debts that are accrued but unpaid and the length of time such debts have been unpaid. Similarly, an aging report of accounts receivable should also be provided.

F. REVIEWING OPERATING REPORTS

As noted above, an **operating report** serves as an official record of the debtor-in-possession's postpetition financial affairs. It discloses whether the reorganization is succeeding or failing. Having generally described the contents of an operating report, practical uses of them can now be further illustrated.

A compilation of data from one or more operating reports can provide admissible evidence as to positive or negative trends in a Chapter 11 proceeding. First, total up all receipts for any number of months during the procee-ding for which data are desired. Observe whether receipts are increasing or decreasing every month. A calculation might also be made as to the average monthly receipts. Observe the trend. Is it increasing or decreasing? If receipts are rising, the time may have arrived to propose a plan. On the other hand, if receipts are decreasing every month, it might be time to file a motion to convert, especially if the accrued but unpaid expenses are accumulating rapidly.

Second, examine the disbursements. Verify that any insider compensation has been approved by the court, where required, and that the amount paid does not exceed the court-approved amount. If the report discloses that an insider has suddenly received a substantial raise, this may be brought to the attention of the court. If there are substantial cash disbursements, without any verification, this should be considered evidence of improper management.

Next, review the bank account balances. If the balances at the end of each reporting period are increasing, this may be evidence that the proceeding is succeeding. On the other hand, if the balance is consistently negative or is decreasing from one reporting period to the next, this may be evidence that the proceeding is failing.

The list of accrued but unpaid expenses can be very revealing. Many businesses usually pay their bills 30 to 40 days after receiving them. It is not uncommon to have an entire month of accounts payable to be accrued and unpaid at any given point in time in the normal operation of any business. This should not be considered a sign of financial difficulty. Thus, if a list of accrued but unpaid expenses is roughly equivalent to a debtor's monthly cash expenses (by reviewing a series of reports these averages can be computed), this should not be construed as a sign of failure. Sometimes, even two months of arrears do not necessarily signify danger. But once a debtor shows three months or more of unpaid postpetition debt, it is time to reconsider the continuance of the proceeding as a Chapter 11. A debtor's representative should recommend that the matter be converted to a Chapter 7. A creditor's representative may move the court for conversion or the appointment of a trustee or examiner to investigate the status of the proceeding in greater detail. Remember, all unpaid postpetition debts are administrative expenses.[27] The greater they are, the less will be available for payment of dividends to the prepetition unsecured creditors if the proceeding is converted to a Chapter 7.

In a large proceeding sometimes even one or two months of accrued and unpaid expenses can be fatal. In some situations, the delay of even a week in filing a report can result in accrual of additional substantial unpaid expenses without knowledge to the creditors. The best way to prevent this in a large proceeding is to make sure that the Official Creditors Committee is organized immediately and demand that a debtor provide informal weekly or biweekly reports of operations to the committee. In an appropriate matter, the United States Trustee might undertake such intervention.

The burden of being a Chapter 11 debtor-in-possession is that the debtor becomes an involuntary partner with its creditors. Any effort to conceal the truth from the creditors will ultimately work to the debtor's detriment. Full cooperation and disclosure should be the norm, particularly because the most successful Chapter 11 proceedings are more a

27. See chapter 21 supra.

process of reconciliation between debtor and creditors than a process of continual adversarial dispute. Full compliance by a debtor-in-possession of all operating rules will only help to increase the chance for a successful outcome to the proceeding.

Summary

Chapter 11 is the most complex, time-consuming, and expensive of all bankruptcy proceedings to prosecute. Chapter 11 is available to any debtor qualified to be a Chapter 7 debtor. A major corporation or the corner store may each file Chapter 11 proceedings.

As is the case with Chapter 13, the goal of a Chapter 11 debtor-in-possession is to obtain court confirmation of a repayment plan. In Chapter 11, the plan is called a plan of reorganization. However, this is where the similarity ends. The process for obtaining confirmation of a Chapter 11 reorganization plan is complex and time-consuming. Further, a Chapter 11 debtor-in-possession is subject to substantially more administrative requirements than a Chapter 13 debtor. The checklist accompanying this chapter outlines these requirements.

The most important administrative requirement placed upon a debtorin-possession is to file regular operating reports with the court. The checklist accompanying this chapter outlines the critical elements of an operating report. The forms manual accompanying this text contains a sample operating report approved by the United States Trustee.

The practical effect of the Chapter 11 debtor-in-possession rules is to make the debtor an involuntary partner with its creditors. Cooperation and disclosure are required to be the norm. Full compliance by a debtor-in-possession of all operating rules will only help to increase the chance for a successful outcome to the proceeding.

KEY TERMS

accrual method
cash method
first-day order
operating report
small business debtor

Chapter 24 Checklist

24.1 CHAPTER 11 ADMINISTRATION— DOCUMENTS AND DEADLINES

		Authority
24.1.1	**Deadline—At Filing**	
	1. Petition and $1039 filing fee	Bankruptcy Rules 1002, 1006
	2. Corporate resolution of 1004 partnership authorization	Bankruptcy Rule
	3. List of creditors, unless schedules filed at filing	Bankruptcy Rule 1007(a)(1)
	4. List of 20 largest unsecured claims	Bankruptcy Rule 1007(d)
	5. Corporate debtor—Exhibit A to Voluntary Petition	Bankruptcy Rule Official Form 1x
	6. Individual debtor credit counseling certificate	11 U.S.C. §109(h); 11 U.S.C. §521(b)
	7. Small business debtor financial statements; tax returns	11 U.S.C. §1116(1)
24.1.2	**Deadline—Within 15 Days of Filing**	
	1. List of equity security holders	Bankruptcy Rule 1007(a)(3)
	2. Statement of Financial Affairs	11 U.S.C. §521(1), Bankruptcy Rule 1007(b)
	3. Schedules of Assets and Liabilities	11 U.S.C. §521(1), Bankruptcy Rule 1007(b)
	4. Statement of Executory Contracts	Bankruptcy Rule 1007(b)
	5. Debtor-in-possession bank accounts	11 U.S.C. §345, consult local rules
	6. Attorney statement of compensation	11 U.S.C. §329, Bankruptcy Rule 2016(b)

		Authority
24.1.3	Deadline—Within 30 Days of Filing	
	1. Applications to retain professionals	11 U.S.C. §327, Bankruptcy Rule 2014, consult local rules
	2. Applications for insider compensation	consult local rules
	3. Commence operating reports	Bankruptcy Rule 2015(a)(2), (3); 11 U.S.C. §1116(4)
	4. File inventory if United States Trustee requires	Bankruptcy Rule 2015(a)(1)
24.1.4	Deadline—Within 120 Days of Filing Assume nonresidential property leases	11 U.S.C. §365(d)(4)

24.2 OPERATING REPORT—MAJOR FEATURES

24.2.1 Summary of Receipts

24.2.2 Itemization of Disbursements

24.2.3 Identification of Bank Accounts

24.2.4 Reconciliation of Bank Balances

24.2.5 List of Accrued and Unpaid Postpetition Debt

24.2.6 List of Accrued and Uncollected Postpetition Accounts Receivable

24.3 UNITED STATES TRUSTEE QUARTERLY FEES

Disbursements/Quarter	*Fee*
less than $15,000	$ 250
$15,000 to $75,000	$ 500
$75,000 to $150,000	$ 750
$150,000 to $225,000	$ 1,250
$225,000 to $300,000	$ 1,500
$300,000 to $1,000,000	$ 3,750
$1,000,000 to $2,000,000	$ 5,000
$2,000,000 to $3,000,000	$ 7,500
$3,000,000 to $5,000,000	$ 8,000
$5,000,000 or more	$10,000

DISCUSSION QUESTIONS

1. What distinguishes a Chapter 11 bankruptcy from other bankruptcy proceedings?
2. What documents must a Chapter 11 debtor file with the court? What are the deadlines for filing each document? What is the effect of a failure to file a required document?
3. What rules must a debtor-in-possession comply with regarding the administration of a Chapter 11 estate?
4. What is an operating report? Describe the major features of an operating report.
5. What is the role of the United States Trustee in the supervision of a debtor-in-possession?

25

Chapter 11: Elements of a Plan

A. CONFIRMATION PROCESS — OVERVIEW

The process of formulating and obtaining confirmation of a Chapter 11 reorganization plan is the most complex process in the Bankruptcy Code. A Chapter 11 reorganization plan is known as a **Plan of Reorganization**. There are a number of steps that must be carefully followed and many rules to apply to achieve confirmation. In typical situations, this process will take from four to six months. This chapter analyzes the elements of a plan. Chapter 26 infra describes the details of the confirmation process.

The goal of a Chapter 11 proceeding is to obtain confirmation of a Chapter 11 reorganization plan that will satisfy creditors while retaining assets or continuing the debtor's business. An overview of the entire process will be helpful.

The first step is to file a reorganization plan. Along with the plan, the **plan proponent** (entity filing the plan) must also file a document known as a **disclosure statement**.[1] A disclosure statement is similar to a disclosure document used in stock transactions. The purpose of a disclosure statement is to tell the creditors anything about the plan and debtor that may affect the creditors' decision to vote for or against the plan.

Once the plan and disclosure statement have been filed, a hearing will be held to approve the disclosure statement.[2] Creditors must receive 25 days' notice of a hearing on approval of the disclosure statement.[3] This is an exception

1. 11 U.S.C. §1121; Bankruptcy Rule 3016(b).
2. 11 U.S.C. §1125(b); Bankruptcy Rule 3017(a).
3. Bankruptcy Rules 2002(b), 3017(a).

to the general rule contained in Federal Rule of Bankruptcy Procedure 2002, which requires 20 days' notice to creditors in most instances.[4]

A small business debtor may have a disclosure statement conditionally approved and then combine the disclosure and confirmation hearings. Theoretically, this procedure will shorten the time it takes to confirm a small business Chapter 11 plan (11 U.S.C. §1125(f); see chapter 26 infra).

Once the court approves the disclosure statement as containing "adequate information," the plan proponent may solicit acceptances or rejections (votes) of the plan in attempting to seek confirmation.[5] The plan proponent must send all creditors a copy of the plan, a copy of the disclosure statement, a copy of the order approving the disclosure statement, a notice of the hearing on confirmation of the plan, and a ballot. Twenty-five days' notice of the confirmation hearing is required.[6] Creditors return their ballots to the plan proponent, who must file a report with the court summarizing the results of the balloting. This report, along with all original ballots, is filed before the hearing.[7] Samples of these various documents are included in the forms manual accompanying this text. The checklist for this chapter summarizes these documents. Collectively, this group of documents is called a **confirmation packet**.

Finally, the court will hold a confirmation hearing. At this hearing, the court will either confirm or deny confirmation of the plan.[8] The entire confirmation process is summarized in the nearby flowchart. The forms manual contains a sample plan and disclosure statement. Reference to them will greatly aid in illustrating the concepts introduced in the next two chapters.

B. TIME TO FILE A PLAN

Section 1121 regulates when a plan may be filed and who may file one. Unless a trustee has been appointed, only the debtor may file a plan during the 120-day period following the entry of an order for relief.[9] This **exclusivity period** is intended to provide a debtor with breathing room to permit an attempt at reorganization free from the interference that would be caused by a competing plan.

4. See chapter 5 supra.
5. 11 U.S.C. §1126; Bankruptcy Rule 3017(c). See chapter 26 infra.
6. Bankruptcy Rule 3017(d); 2002(b).
7. Bankruptcy Rule 3018.
8. 11 U.S.C. §1128. See chapter 26 infra.
9. 11 U.S.C. §1121(b). Recall that the order for relief is entered upon filing a voluntary petition and is the judgment sought by the petitioners in an involuntary proceeding. See chapter 4 supra.

CHAPTER 11 PLAN CONFIRMATION PROCESS

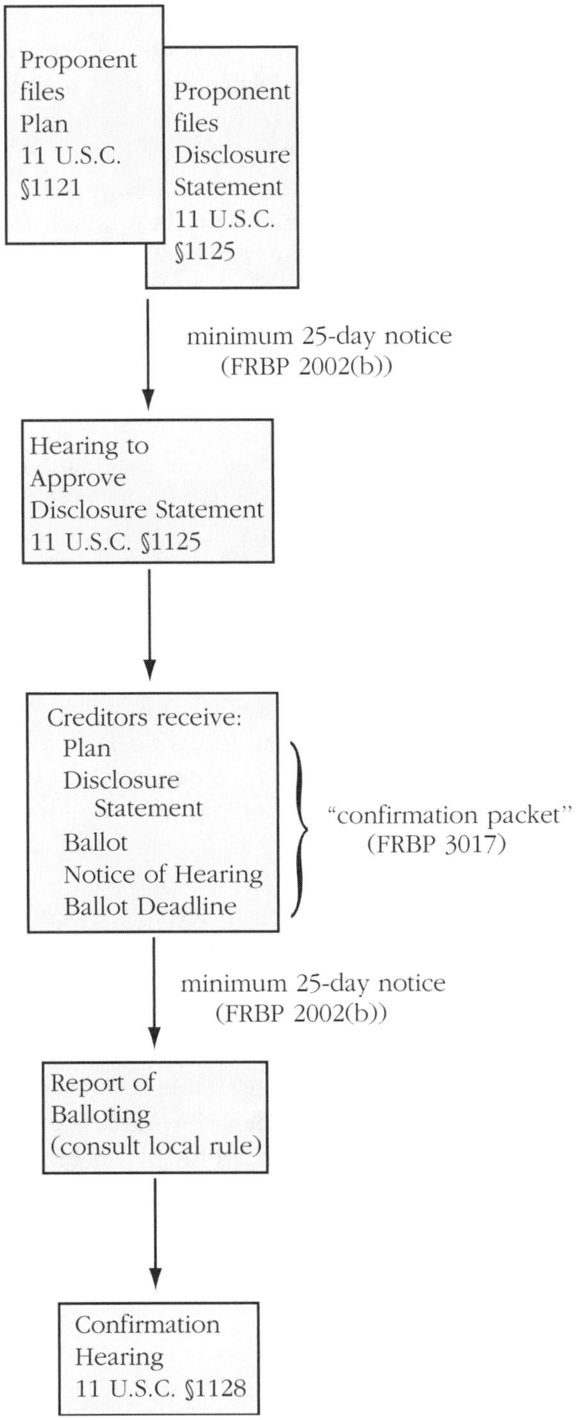

If a debtor does file a plan within the 120-day exclusivity period, the period is extended to a date 180 days from the entry of the order for relief. The reason for the extension of the exclusivity period to 180 days is to provide the debtor an opportunity to obtain confirmation of a plan without having to defend against a competing plan at the same time.[10]

For example, Flora and Fauna, Inc., files a Chapter 11 on February 13. Flora and Fauna, Inc., has an exclusive right until June 13 (120 days) to file a plan. If a plan is filed by Flora and Fauna, Inc., during this period, whether on day 1 or day 120, the period of exclusivity is now extended to August 12 (180 days). During this entire period of time no other party may file a plan. This time period provides Flora and Fauna, Inc., with an opportunity to reorganize its affairs without interference from competing plans of reorganization filed by creditors. On the other hand, if Flora and Fauna, Inc.'s, creditors obtain the appointment of a trustee, the exclusivity period will automatically end.

It is also possible for a debtor to obtain an extension of either of the time periods described above, pursuant to 11 U.S.C. §1121(d). However, such a request must be made within the exclusivity period. The 120-day exclusivity period may not, however, be extended to a date more than 18 months after the order for relief. The 180-day period to obtain confirmation may not, however, be extended to a date more than 20 months after the order for relief. These rules prevent debtors from obtaining indefinite extensions of exclusivity.[11]

There are three events that terminate a debtor-in-possession's period of exclusivity to file a plan. They are the appointment of a trustee, as noted above, the lapse of 120 days after the entry of an order for relief if no plan has been filed, and the lapse of 180 days after the entry of an order for relief if a plan that has been filed has not yet been confirmed.[12]

Small business debtors have been provided with independent exclusivity rules in 11 U.S.C. §1121(e). For a small business, the exclusivity period is 180 days, and in all events, the plan must be filed within 300 days from the order for relief. The court may reduce the time period. The 180-day exclusivity period may be extended upon a showing that it is more likely than not that the court will confirm a plan within a reasonable period of time. Additional extensions may be granted upon a further showing of these elements. The plan must be confirmed within 45 days after the plan is filed, pursuant to 11 U.S.C. §1129(e), unless the court extends exclusivity upon the same showing described above. Failure to make this showing within the time periods is cause for dismissal or conversion pursuant to 11 U.S.C. §1112(b)(2).

---

10. 11 U.S.C. §1121(c)(3).
11. 11 U.S.C. §1121(d).
12. 11 U.S.C. §1121(c).

Once the exclusivity period expires, any party in interest except the United States Trustee may file a reorganization plan.[13] A private trustee may file a plan, the debtor may file a plan, the Official Creditors Committee may file a plan, or an individual creditor may file a plan. It is for this reason that the party filing a plan is known as the plan proponent. More often than not this will be the debtor.

C. PLAN CHARACTERISTICS

As a practical matter, the confirmation process takes a minimum of four to six months to complete. Because 25 days' notice is required to be given for the disclosure statement and confirmation hearings, respectively, and because a debtor must set a deadline to receive ballots, tabulate them, and then file a report with the court, it is better practice to separate the disclosure statement and confirmation hearings by at least 60 days so that ample time will exist for compilation of the ballots and filing of the necessary reports prior to the confirmation hearing. If this will result in the effort at confirmation exceeding the statutory 180-day exclusivity period, the court may extend the period of exclusivity for cause because the debtor is in the process of seeking confirmation of its timely filed plan.

A confirmed Chapter 11 reorganization plan is nothing more than a judicially approved composition agreement. When confirmed, the plan constitutes a new contract between the debtor and its creditors. As a result, Chapter 11 is an area of the law where practitioners may exercise some creativity and imagination in the formulation of plans and disclosure statements.

Any reasonable and lawful method of repaying debt can conceivably form the basis of a Chapter 11 plan. The plan may consist of simple repayment to creditors over a period of time from surplus revenues in a manner similar to a Chapter 13 plan, the plan may be a refinancing of the debtor's business, the plan may call for a sale of the business, the plan may involve infusion of investment capital, or the plan may be any combination of all these ideas. The larger a proceeding the more complex the financial concepts will become, but the basic premise is that any reasonable and lawful business method for reorganizing a debtor's financial affairs that can meet with creditor acceptance is a proper foundation for a Chapter 11 plan. Thus, paradoxically, the rules can be highly flexible despite their apparent rigidity.

---

13. 11 U.S.C. §1121(c); 11 U.S.C. §307.

D. CLASSIFICATION OF CLAIMS

Section 1122 concerns the classification of claims within a plan. All creditors must be placed within classes. All creditors in a given class must have claims that are substantially similar.[14] For example, a secured creditor and an unsecured creditor may not be included in the same class because these claims are not substantially similar. A priority tax claim may not be merged with unsecured claims. Multiple unsecured claims may be included within the same class. More than one secured claim may also be included in the same class, but it is a better and recommended practice to separately classify each secured claim. The reason for this is that different secured creditors will have different collateral or differing rights regarding the same collateral. As a result each secured claim should be separately classified.

Section 1122 does not require that all creditors of the same type be placed within the same class. Thus, it is possible to divide substantially similar claims into separate classes. For example, federal tax claims may comprise one class of claims and nonfederal tax claims another class of claims. Similarly, a business may subclassify its unsecured claims into separate classes for suppliers of goods or services, unsecured noteholders, and so on. However, claims may not be classified so as to gerrymander affirmative votes on a plan.[15]

It is specifically possible to create what is called a **convenience class** of creditors.[16] In many Chapter 11 proceedings there are typically a number of small unsecured creditors who have only become so because the debtor's Chapter 11 filing fortuitously occurred when their monthly invoices had not been paid. These creditors are usually owed such relatively small sums that the cost of administering their claims through a plan is likely to be more costly than the claim or dividend. Accordingly, a debtor may create a class of convenience claims and give the class a treatment that would be otherwise impermissible over creditor objection. A debtor may propose that all unsecured claims of less than a fixed amount, such as $500, will be classified as the convenience class and will receive a one-time dividend in discharge of their debts. This dividend may be greater or lesser than that offered to other unsecured creditors. The plan may also provide that any claimant reducing its claim to qualify for convenience treatment may voluntarily elect to become a member of the convenience class.

For example, Chen's Hofbrau House, Inc., has ten unsecured creditors who are owed $100 or less each. Chen's total debt is $150,000. Because it

14. 11 U.S.C. §1122(a).
15. In re Greystone III Joint Venture, 948 F.2d 134 (5th Cir. 1991).
16. 11 U.S.C. §1122(b).

would be uneconomical to write each small creditor a check every three months for four or five years, creation of a convenience class is permitted and its members are paid a one-time dividend on confirmation of the plan in full discharge of the claims included within the class.

In its essence then, Section 1122 merely requires that a Chapter 11 reorganization plan must create classes of claims. This may be as simple as organizing the claims into classes paralleling the distribution scheme described in chapters 21 and 22 supra. Or class creation can be highly complex, involving the creation of separate classes for multiple secured creditors, several categories of unsecured claims, and several classes of shareholders or bondholders. A Chapter 11 plan for a major corporation can be hundreds of pages long.

It is good practice to create a separate class for each secured claim. The reason for this is that each secured claimholder usually has either different collateral or different rights with respect to the same collateral than other secured creditors. To the extent that there is different collateral or different rights in the same collateral, the rights of each claimholder may be different in degree and kind.[17] As a result, classification of each secured claim into separate classes will properly account for any differences in the claims. With respect to unsecured claims, it is not uncommon to see three classes of unsecured claims within a plan in the form of a convenience class, a trade creditor class, and a class of unsecured noteholders. Insider claims often form a fourth class of unsecured claim. A final class or classes will be the interests of the equity security holders, the owners of the debtor.

A reorganization plan is not created in a vacuum. Recall that one function of the Official Creditors Committee is to negotiate a plan with the debtor so that the committee can recommend acceptance or rejection of the plan to the unsecured creditors.[18] All parties in interest will save time and money when a debtor negotiates a plan with the Official Creditors Committee in the first place. The debtor will know what the Official Creditors Committee will require to recommend acceptance of the plan to the unsecured creditors. On the other hand, the Official Creditors Committee should be realistic in recognizing just how much "blood" can be squeezed out of the "turnip." Negotiation can result in a less expensive and more prompt confirmation process. Every penny saved in administrative expenses is another penny in the pockets of the unsecured creditors. A failure to attempt negotiation of a plan's terms can result in substantial time-consuming and expensive litigation at any step in the confirmation process. The time and expense consumed in litigating these issues can sometimes, ironically, make the reorganization impossible.

---

17. 11 U.S.C. §506. See chapter 21 supra.
18. See chapter 10 supra.

E. MANDATORY PLAN PROVISIONS

Section 1123 is similar to Section 1322 in Chapter 13.[19] Like Section 1322, Section 1123 prescribes the **mandatory** and **permissive elements** of a Chapter 11 plan. The provisions of Section 1123(a) are mandatory and must be included in any Chapter 11 plan. On the other hand, the elements of Section 1123(b) are permissive.

First, the plan must designate classes of claims and interests. The classes should be organized consistent with Section 1122, as described above. A class of interests represents the interests of the debtor's equity security holders, such as shareholders, partners, or an individual debtor.[20]

Second, the plan must specify which of the classes are impaired or not impaired under the plan.[21] The concept of impairment is the subject of Section 1124 and is discussed below in this chapter.

Third, the treatment accorded to impaired claims or interests must be described.[22] This is usually the heart of any plan.

Fourth, each creditor in the same class must be treated the same, unless a particular creditor agrees to a lesser treatment.[23] In other words, in the negotiation of a plan, a creditor may agree to accept less than the Code entitles it to. This is a practical application of the principle of voluntary subordination, described in chapter 21 supra. The rules are designed for a debtor to propose a minimum performance plan that the court may be required to approve over the objections of virtually all claims by way of the Chapter 11 cramdown procedures discussed in chapter 26 infra.[24] A creditor can always voluntarily agree to a lesser treatment of its claim than the Code requires or provides.

Fifth, a plan must provide adequate means for its implementation.[25] That is, the plan must advise all parties how the plan will be performed. It is not sufficient to merely promise that creditors are going to be repaid. The plan must describe "who, what, when, where, and how" the plan will be performed. Section 1123(a)(5) provides a list of ten methods but is not allinclusive. The list merely provides examples of methods that may be used to perform a plan. Any other reasonable and lawful method of performance devised by a plan's proponent will also be acceptable. Refinancing, sale, periodic repayments, or new investment capital are all acceptable repayment methods, as described earlier in this chapter. Combinations of some or all of these methods can be included in the plan. These are the most common

19. See chapter 23 supra.
20. 11 U.S.C. §1123(a)(1).
21. 11 U.S.C. §1123(a)(2).
22. 11 U.S.C. §1123(a)(3).
23. 11 U.S.C. §1123(a)(4).
24. 11 U.S.C. §1129(b).
25. 11 U.S.C. §1123(a)(5).

methods proposed for performance of a Chapter 11 reorganization plan. The Code mandates that a method of repayment be provided for, but not what the repayment method must be.

A debtor can propose to liquidate assets as a Chapter 11 plan performance method.[26] A debtor may choose to liquidate through a Chapter 11 rather than a Chapter 7 for a number of reasons. First, a Chapter 11 may protect the reputation of the debtor's insiders more than a Chapter 7 would. Second, a Chapter 11 debtor remains in control of the business as a debtor-in-possession, rather than a trustee's being appointed to assume control of the estate. There may be situations when this will increase the prospects for creditor dividends. Finally, the Chapter 11 process may sometimes involve less time and expense to liquidate an estate and pay creditors dividends than a Chapter 7 proceeding. For example, if the debtor is in a small specialized industry, management will likely have contacts unavailable to a Chapter 7 trustee that will aid in maximizing the price obtained from a liquidation of assets. Further, if the debtor is in a Chapter 11, the debtor does not have to deal with all the timetables described in chapter 22 supra. The debtor may sell the assets, propose a plan, obtain confirmation, and pay creditors in a fraction of the time that a Chapter 7 proceeding would take, but with exactly the same or better results.

Sixth, a plan involving a corporate debtor must provide that the corporation's charter will provide appropriate representation on its board of directors to various classes of shareholders.[27] In most proceedings, compliance with this provision will not be problematic.

Seventh, the plan must be in the interests of the creditors and equity security holders and be consistent with public policy respecting the selection of a debtor's insiders.[28] This means that the plan must identify the post-confirmation insiders of the debtor.

Finally, in Chapter 11 cases for individual debtors, the debtor must commit postpetition earnings for personal services as is necessary for performance of the plan. To aid in implementing this provision, Section 1115 makes the postpetition earnings for personal services property of the estate in a manner similar to Chapter 13.[29]

F. PERMISSIVE PLAN PROVISIONS

Subsection 1123(b) describes the permissive elements of a Chapter 11 plan. Permissive elements are elements that may be included but are not

26. 11 U.S.C. §1123(a)(5)(D).
27. 11 U.S.C. §1123(a)(6).
28. 11 U.S.C. §1123(a)(7).
29. 11 U.S.C. §1123(a)(8); 11 U.S.C. §1115; 11 U.S.C. §1306. As to Chapter 13, see chapter 23 supra.

required to be in a Chapter 11 plan. It is nevertheless recommended to include these items within a plan. Further, and identical to Chapter 13 plans, if facts exist requiring the need for a permissive plan provision, the provision becomes mandatory. For example, the existence of an unexpired lease or executory contract is a common occurrence.

First, a plan may impair or leave unimpaired a class of claims or interests.[30] Once again, impairment is described below in connection with Section 1124.

Second, a plan may provide for the assumption or rejection of any executory contracts that have not been previously assumed or rejected during the Chapter 11 proceeding.[31] As a practical matter, it is good practice to specifically provide for the assumption or rejection of all executory contracts within a reorganization plan. This may be as simple as a short paragraph assuming all executory contracts not previously assumed or rejected, or exactly the converse. This sort of simple provision appears in the sample plan included in the forms manual. Such a clause may be as complex as separately identifying and assuming or rejecting each individual executory contract. Further, it is important for the nondebtor party to an executory contract to know the debtor's intent with regard to assumption or rejection because this will affect the nondebtor party's status as a creditor in the proceeding and thus ultimately the nondebtor party's decision to vote for or against the plan.

The plan may provide for the settlement or enforcement of any claims that the estate may have.[32] In other words, the plan may act as a settlement agreement of any dispute involving the estate should the plan be confirmed. The plan may also provide for the sale of all or substantially all assets and distribution of the proceeds to claimholders.[33] This is another indication that liquidation is an acceptable method for performance of a Chapter 11 plan.

Section 1123(b)(5) prohibits modification of a security interest in real property that is the debtor's principal residence, but otherwise it permits modification of creditor rights. This provision is identical to that of Section 1322(b)(2) (see section 23D supra).

The final permissive provision of Section 1123 is that a Chapter 11 reorganization plan may contain any provision not inconsistent with the Bankruptcy Code.[34] However, when a creditor classifies claims, the classifications should follow the scheme and order described in chapters 21 and

30. 11 U.S.C. §1123(b)(1).
31. 11 U.S.C. §1123(b)(2). See also chapter 19 supra.
32. 11 U.S.C. §1123(b)(3).
33. 11 U.S.C. §1123(b)(4).
34. 11 U.S.C. §1123(b)(6).

22 supra. To act otherwise, absent the consent of any affected creditor, would not be consistent with the provisions of the Bankruptcy Code.

If the Chapter 11 debtor is an individual, the individual's exempt property may not be included in the plan unless the debtor consents.[35] In other words, an individual debtor's exemptions are preserved in a Chapter 11 reorganization plan. If a debtor wants to voluntarily make exempt property available to perform a plan, this is acceptable. However, the creditors may not force an individual debtor to give up any claimed exemptions in a Chapter 11 plan.

Section 1123(d) permits the charging of interest upon interest if applicable nonbankruptcy law allows it.

G. IMPAIRED CLAIMS

Section 1124 creates a distinction between impaired and unimpaired claims or interests. This concept is peculiar to Chapter 11. Generally, an **unimpaired claim** is a claim that is being paid according to its terms on the effective date of the plan. Conversely, a claim not being paid according to its terms on the effective date of the plan is an **impaired claim**. For example, when a class of unsecured claims is scheduled to be paid in full on the effective date of a plan, the class is unimpaired. Unless a class is unimpaired, the class is impaired. The **effective date of the plan** is that date defined in the plan as the plan's commencement date. This date may be the date on which the court approves confirmation, or it may be a date on which a specific event is scheduled to occur, such as the close of an escrow in a sale or the funding of a refinancing loan. Although it is not a requirement of §1123, a plan should always define its effective date.

There is an important difference in treatment accorded to unimpaired versus impaired classes of claims. An unimpaired class of claims is deemed to have accepted a plan whether or not the class votes to accept or reject the plan.[36] This is a major reason why Section 1123 mandates that a plan designate classes of impaired claims.[37] Only impaired creditors are entitled to vote for or against confirmation of the plan. This is consistent with the identical concept appearing in Chapter 13 that a creditor receiving payment or performance of all it would be entitled to under nonbankruptcy law will not be permitted to object to the debtor's performance. Impaired classes, on the other hand, will get a chance to vote to accept or reject a plan.

---

35. 11 U.S.C. §1123(c).
36. 11 U.S.C. §1126(f). See chapter 26 infra.
37. 11 U.S.C. §1123(a)(3). See discussion supra.

Section 1124 describes three conditions under which a class of claims or interests will be considered unimpaired. Unless a class meets one of the three conditions for unimpairment, the class will be impaired. First, a class of claims is unimpaired if the plan provides that the class will be paid in full on the effective date of the plan or that the rights of the class members will be left unaltered by the plan.[38] That is, an unsecured claim paid in full or according to its terms on the effective date of the plan is unimpaired. Second, if a plan proposes to continue to pay a creditor its regular installment payments as they become due and there are no defaults, or any defaults are cured on the effective date of the plan, the creditor will be considered unimpaired.[39] This is virtually identical in its effect with the similar concept appearing in Chapter 13 that permits a cure of defaults on debts not fully due until after the plan is performed.

Third, a class of claims will be considered unimpaired notwithstanding any contractual provision allowing a creditor to accelerate payment after a default if the plan cures the default, reinstates the obligation according to its terms, pays to the holder of the claim any consequential damages, and does not otherwise alter the rights of the affected claimholders.[40] This is an extremely important provision because it dramatically affects the rights of debtor and creditors alike. In plain English, this provision effectively allows a debtor to reinstate any defaulted obligation so long as the creditor is otherwise paid according to the underlying terms of its contract. Not only will the obligation be reinstated, but because the claim or class will be considered unimpaired, the claimant will be deemed to have accepted the plan.

For example, a debtor may reinstate a defaulted trust deed or mortgage obligation through a Chapter 11 plan even if any underlying state law reinstatement period has expired. If the formula of Section 1124(2) is followed by the debtor, the claim will be considered unimpaired and the creditor's acceptance of the plan presumed.

An unsecured obligation may also be affected by Section 1124(2). For example, Marian's Maids, Inc., owes an unsecured loan to the Bank of Nottingham. The due date of the unsecured loan is five years. Three payments are in default and the bank has accelerated the obligation. As long as the Chapter 11 reorganization plan proposes to pay the three defaulted payments and otherwise reinstate the obligation, the claim will not be impaired and will not accelerate. Because the creditor is receiving what it bargained for it is unimpaired. Conversely, if a creditor or class of creditors is not receiving what it or they have bargained for, the claim or class of claims is impaired. Needless to say, most plans will impair one or more class of claims or interests.

38. 11 U.S.C. §1124(1).
39. 11 U.S.C. §1124(2)(A)(B).
40. 11 U.S.C. §1124(2).

Summary

The process of formulating and obtaining confirmation of a Chapter 11 reorganization plan, known as a Plan of Reorganization, is the most complex and time-consuming process in the Bankruptcy Code. The entire process will average four to six months, at a minimum.

The process involves filing a plan and a disclosure statement with the court. The disclosure statement is a history of the debtor-in-possession, an analysis of the proposed plan, and a description of the debtor's ability to perform the plan. The disclosure statement is approved by the court at a disclosure statement hearing. This hearing requires a 25-day notice to creditors. When the disclosure statement has been approved, the proponent of the plan may solicit the votes of those creditors entitled to vote. The results of the balloting are filed with the court. The court will hold a confirmation hearing to determine if the plan may be confirmed. The confirmation hearing also requires 25-day notice to the creditors. A checklist of this process is contained in the checklist to this chapter.

A debtor-in-possession is given the exclusive right to file a reorganization plan for 120 days following the entry of an order for relief. This exclusivity period can be extended to 180 days if a plan is filed during the initial 120-day period or if a motion for an extension of time is filed during the initial 120-day period. In no event can the exclusivity period extend past 20 months. The exclusivity period terminates if a trustee is appointed. A small business debtor has a 180-day exclusivity period and must have a plan filed within 300 days after the entry of the order for relief, unless the court extends the time period.

Any Chapter 11 reorganization plan must classify the claims of creditors and the interests of the equity security holders (owners of the debtor). All claims within a given class must be similar, such as administrative or priority claims. A convenience class of claims may also be created. Generally, the classification scheme should follow the priorities outlined in chapters 21 and 22 supra.

A Chapter 11 reorganization plan must contain various mandatory provisions. A Chapter 11 plan may also contain various permissive provisions. An outline of the mandatory and permissive plan provisions is contained in the checklist accompanying this chapter. The forms manual accompanying this text contains a sample reorganization plan, along with all other basic documents necessary to confirmation.

One of the most important mandatory plan provisions requires designation of impaired classes of claims. Classes of claims that are impaired are entitled to vote for acceptance or rejection of the plan. Classes of claims that are unimpaired are deemed to accept the plan. Generally, a class of claims is unimpaired if it is paid in full when the plan is confirmed or if the class is paid according to the terms of the obligation as it existed before the Chapter 11 was filed.

KEY TERMS

confirmation packet
convenience class
disclosure statement
effective date of the plan
exclusivity period
impaired claim
mandatory elements
permissive elements
Plan of Reorganization
plan proponent
unimpaired claim

Chapter 25 Checklist

25.1 CHAPTER 11 CONFIRMATION PROCESS

		Prior Notice Required	*Authority*
25.1.1	File a Reorganization Plan	—	11 U.S.C. §1121, Bankruptcy Rule 3016(a)
25.1.2	File a Disclosure Statement	—	11 U.S.C. §1125, Bankruptcy Rule 3016(b)
25.1.3	Disclosure Statement Hearing	25 days	11 U.S.C. §1125(b), Bankruptcy Rules 2002(b), 3017(a)
25.1.4	Voting Deadline Set	at disclosure statement hearing	Bankruptcy Rule 3017(c)
25.1.5	Confirmation Hearing	25 days	11 U.S.C. §1128, Bankruptcy Rule 2002(b)
25.1.6	Report of Balloting	prior to confirmation hearing	Bankruptcy Rule 3018, consult local rule

25.2	**DOCUMENTS SUBMITTED TO CREDITORS FOR CONFIRMATION HEARING (CONFIRMATION PACKET)**	*Rule*
25.2.1	Plan or Court-Approved Summary	Bankruptcy Rule 3017(d)(1)
25.2.2	Disclosure Statement and Order Approving Same	Bankruptcy Rule 3017(d)(2)
25.2.3	Notice of the Balloting Deadline	Bankruptcy Rule 3017(d)(3)
25.2.4	Notice of the Confirmation Hearing	Bankruptcy Rule 3017(d)
25.2.5	Ballot—Official Form 30	Bankruptcy Rule 3018(c)
25.3	**MANDATORY CHAPTER 11 PLAN PROVISIONS**	*Statute*
25.3.1	Designate Classes of Claims and Interests	11 U.S.C. §§1122, 1123(a)(1)
25.3.2	Specify Unimpaired Classes	11 U.S.C. §1123(a)(2)
25.3.3	Specify Treatment of Impaired Classes	11 U.S.C. §1123(a)(3)
25.3.4	Provide Equal Treatment of Claims in a Given Class	11 U.S.C. §1123(a)(4)
25.3.5	Provide Adequate Means for the Plan's Performance	11 U.S.C. §1123(a)(5)
25.3.6	Corporate Charter Provision	11 U.S.C. §1123(a)(6)
25.3.7	Disclose Postconfirmation Insiders	11 U.S.C. §1123(a)(7)
25.3.8	Individual Debtor Earnings	11 U.S.C. §1123(a)(8); 11 U.S.C. §1115
25.4	**PERMISSIVE CHAPTER 11 PLAN PROVISIONS**	
25.4.1	Impair Classes	11 U.S.C. §1123(b)(1)
25.4.2	Assume or Reject Executory Contracts Not Previously Acted Upon	11 U.S.C. §1123(b)(2)

		Statute
25.4.3	Provide for Settlement of Disputes	11 U.S.C. §1123(b)(3)
25.4.4	Provide for Liquidation of Assets	11 U.S.C. §1123(b)(4)
25.4.5	Modify Creditor Rights Unless Secured by Principal Residence	11 U.S.C. §1123(b)(5)
25.4.6	Include Any Provision Consistent with Bankruptcy Code	11 U.S.C. §1123(b)(6)

DISCUSSION QUESTIONS

1. Describe the procedure that a plan proponent must follow to obtain confirmation of a Chapter 11 reorganization plan. Identify the essential documents that must be filed with the court during the confirmation process.
2. When may a Chapter 11 reorganization plan be filed? What is the "exclusivity period"?
3. How are claims classified in a Chapter 11 reorganization plan?
4. What elements must be included in a Chapter 11 reorganization plan?
5. What elements may be included in a Chapter 11 reorganization plan?
6. What is an impaired claim? An unimpaired claim? What are the important differences between the two?

26

Chapter 11: Plan Confirmation

A. DISCLOSURE STATEMENT

Once a debtor-in-possession has formulated and filed a plan, the debtor must embark upon the confirmation process. Any proponent of a plan must follow the same process. A synopsis of this process was described at the beginning of chapter 25 supra. This chapter analyzes the process in greater detail.

When a plan is filed, it generally must be accompanied by a disclosure statement. Votes may not be solicited from creditors until the court approves the disclosure statement's contents.[1] The disclosure statement hearing is the first step in the Chapter 11 reorganization plan confirmation process. Creditors and other parties in interest are entitled to 25 days' notice of the hearing (an exception to the 20-day notice period generally used throughout the bankruptcy system). A small business debtor may obtain conditional approval of a disclosure statement. Votes can be solicited therefrom and the court may combine the disclosure and confirmation hearings. Theoretically, this procedure will expedite the confirmation process for a small business estate.[2]

A **disclosure statement** must contain information sufficient to enable a creditor or interest holder to determine whether to vote for acceptance or rejection of the plan. The Code defines this as providing all parties with "adequate information."[3] The disclosure statement should be written in

1. 11 U.S.C. §1125(b); Bankruptcy Rule 3017(d); Bankruptcy Rule 3017.1 applies to small businesses.
2. Bankruptcy Rule 2002(b); Bankruptcy Rule 3017(a). See chapter 5 supra. 11 U.S.C. §1125(f) applies to small business debtors, as does Bankruptcy Rule 3017.1.
3. 11 U.S.C. §1125(a)(1).

plain English so that anyone can understand its contents. This will be difficult, especially in complex cases, but it is not impossible.

A disclosure statement should follow the basic principles of journalism: "Who, what, where, when, why, and how." A history of the debtor should be provided, identifying the causes of the Chapter 11 filing and disclosing all relevant factors that may have contributed to the debtor's financial difficulties.

The disclosure statement should summarize the debtor's progress during the Chapter 11 proceeding. A summary of the most important information from the operating reports can be helpful, particularly as a means of comparing the debtor's actual postpetition results with any projections of future performance provided elsewhere in the disclosure statement. Comparing a debtor's actual Chapter 11 performance with the proposed plan will permit the plan's feasibility to be more rapidly and efficiently assessed by the court and creditors.

The disclosure statement should contain an easily understood summary of the plan. The summary should describe the practical effect of the plan rather than its technical terms. For example, a disclosure statement for Bonehead Burgers states that: "Class 7 creditors will receive dividends equalling 50 percent of the total allowed claims in monthly installments not exceeding 48 months." Without reference to other portions of the plan or disclosure statement this is a confusing statement. The statement would be better stated in the disclosure statement as: "Unsecured creditors will receive payments equal to 50 percent of their claims in monthly payments over four years."

A disclosure statement should contain a description of how the plan will be performed. For example, if the plan involves a sale of assets or refinancing, describe the terms of the sale or refinancing. In a workout situation where the claims will be paid dividends over a period of time from the debtor's surplus revenues, the disclosure statement should have a **pro forma** attached to it. A *pro forma* is a financial projection of revenues and profits that a debtor expects to generate over the life of the plan. Any pro forma should be based upon actual past performance or be able to account in detail for variations from past performance. For instance, it would be imprudent for a debtor that has been in a Chapter 11 proceeding for two years posting annual sales increases of 10 percent to suddenly project annual increases of 25 percent in a plan pro forma without any explanation.

The disclosure statement should compare the plan to the likely results if the matter were a Chapter 7 proceeding. This is commonly known as a **liquidation analysis**. The reason for this is that for a plan to be confirmed, one finding that the court must make is that creditors will receive a dividend at least equal to any dividend that would be received in a Chapter 7 proceeding.[4] This point should be demonstrated in the disclosure statement so creditors will be able to utilize the liquidation analysis in determining whether to vote to accept or reject the plan.

The disclosure statement should describe the balloting procedure for voting on the plan and how parties in interest may file objections to the plan's confirmation. Some courts also require a description of the cramdown procedures, the use of which may allow court approval of the plan over the creditors' objection.

BAPA makes it mandatory to include a discussion of the potential material federal tax consequences of a Chapter 11 plan. Presumably, this includes a statement that there are no tax consequences to the plan.

A disclosure statement may contain other items as well. The foregoing covers just the basic elements. Any factor relating to a finding the court must make in connection with Section 1129 that may be problematic should also be described in the disclosure statement. A brief summary of the important items that should be included in a disclosure statement appears in the checklist accompanying this chapter. In small business cases, the court may find that the plan provides adequate disclosure and so order. BAPA further authorizes the formulation of a standard form disclosure statement to be used in all small business cases. The purpose of developing a standard form is to meet the needs of creditors, the courts and the United States Trustee in acquiring adequate information while at the same time providing economy and simplicity for small business debtors.[5]

Chapter 11 disclosure statements are somewhat similar to stock offerings or other types of documents that are regulated by federal or state securities laws. However, a Chapter 11 disclosure statement is specifically exempt from federal or state securities laws regulating the adequacy of such documents. Nevertheless, any governmental official or agency charged with the administration of securities laws may be heard by the Bankruptcy Court on the adequacy of a Chapter 11 disclosure statement. Such an entity does not have a right of appeal or review from the Bankruptcy Court's decision. Thus, parties engaged in seeking approval of a Chapter 11 plan are given a "safe harbor" from federal or state securities disclosure laws in connection with the confirmation process.[6]

---

4. 11 U.S.C. §1129(a)(7). See infra this chapter.
5. See In re Scioto Valley Mortg. Co., 88 Bankr. 168 (S.D. Ohio 1988). This case includes a detailed list of items that should be included in any Chapter 11 disclosure statement. 11 U.S.C. §1125(f) authorizes the standard form in small business cases, or permits a finding that no disclosure statement will be required where the plan itself provides adequate information.
6. 11 U.S.C. §§1125(c), (d), (e); 11 U.S.C. §1145.

B. PLAN CONFIRMATION PACKET

When the court approves the disclosure statement, the plan's proponent must next send to all parties in interest a notice of the confirmation hearing, the plan, the disclosure statement, a ballot, and a notice of the deadline to file acceptances or rejections to the plan.[7] All creditors and equity security holders are now given an opportunity to vote for or against the plan.[8] The results of the voting are compiled into a report, which is filed with the court prior to the confirmation hearing.[9] Section 1126 contains the provisions governing acceptance of the plan and the balloting procedures. In large reorganizations common to the Southern District of New York or the District of Delaware, plan proponents will also file a separate motion to approve solicitation and balloting procedures.

C. VOTING RULES

Impaired creditors with allowed claims are entitled to vote for or against a plan. A class of claims accepts a plan if, among those voting, a majority of creditors in number and two-thirds in dollar amount vote to accept the plan.[10] This is a dual requirement. If either less than a majority of creditors in number or less than two-thirds in dollar amount vote to accept a plan, among those voting, then the class has rejected the plan and a cramdown procedure will be necessary to confirm the plan over the class rejection.[11] To determine class acceptance, simply total the number of voting creditors in a class and the amount of their claims. For example, twelve creditors collectively owed $12,000 vote on a plan. The class accepts the plan if seven creditors owed $8,000 or more vote to accept. If only six vote for acceptance, the class will have rejected the plan (less than a majority). If less than $8,000 in total dollar amount votes to accept, the class will have rejected the plan, even if eleven creditors voted to accept the plan (less than two-thirds in amount). Both a majority in number and two-thirds in dollar amount are required for class acceptance of a plan.

7. Bankruptcy Rule 3017(d).
8. 11 U.S.C. §1126(a); Bankruptcy Rules 3017(c), 3017.1(a); Bankruptcy Rule 3018(a).
9. Bankruptcy Rule 3018.
10. 11 U.S.C. §§1126(a), (c).
11. 11 U.S.C. §1129(b). See this chapter infra for discussion of cramdown.

A class of interests, such as shareholders, will accept a plan if two-thirds in dollar amount of the class of interests accepts the plan.[12] Simply put, a class of interests accepts a plan if two-thirds of the ownership percentage votes to accept. The raw number of voters is not relevant in this instance. This would not be an accurate measure of acceptance by a class of shareholders in a corporation or partnership. One entity may own 50 percent of all shares. The only relevant element here is the percentage of shares that have voted to accept the plan.

The Bankruptcy Code contemplates that an unsuccessful attempt at a composition agreement will sometimes lead to a Chapter 11 filing. This is the subject of Section 1126(b). For example, Metternich Consulting, Inc., attempts a composition agreement before a Chapter 11 filing. If Metternich follows procedures similar to the Chapter 11 confirmation process, presenting the equivalent of a disclosure statement, plan, and ballot to the creditors in a manner consistent with the Chapter 11 plan process, then any acceptances to the composition that are obtained from creditors prior to the Chapter 11 filing may be acceptable as proper ballots.[13] If the debtor can thus show to the court that the composition process was treated in a manner similar to a Chapter 11 proceeding, then prepetition acceptances to the composition can be used as acceptances to an identical Chapter 11 plan. This recognizes the fact that debtors attempting to negotiate composition agreements with their creditors are still subject to any legal action taken by nonconsenting creditors, thus sometimes forcing the Chapter 11 filing. Section 1126(b) creates a mechanism that allows and encourages composition agreements by giving them the potential to be confirmable as Chapter 11 plans. An effort at a composition agreement that nonetheless ends up in Bankruptcy Court is also commonly referred to as a "**prepackaged bankruptcy**."

For example, National Wagonworks attempts to negotiate a composition agreement with its creditors. The proposed agreement, and its accompanying "disclosure statement" are identical to a Chapter 11 plan and disclosure statement. Enough creditors consent to the plan to make it confirmable as a Chapter 11 plan. One creditor, Hupmobile Inc., does not consent and seeks to enforce a writ of execution to seize the assets of National Wagonworks. The seizure would make performance of the composition impossible. Because a nonbankruptcy composition agreement cannot be legally enforced against a nonconsenting creditor, National Wagonworks must file a Chapter 11 if it is to prevent the seizure by Hupmobile so the plan can proceed. Section 1126(b) will permit the prompt confirmation of the composition as a Chapter 11 plan that will also

12. 11 U.S.C. §1126(d).
13. 11 U.S.C. §1126(b).

bind Hupmobile over its objection. This is a further illustration of the fundamental principle that a reorganization plan is no more or less than a court-approved composition agreement.

A vote obtained in bad faith or that has been solicited in violation of the Chapter 11 rules may be disallowed. In a prepackaged bankruptcy, a vote solicited before the filing of a petition is not in bad faith if solicited in compliance with applicable nonbankruptcy law. It is better practice, however, to mirror the Bankruptcy Code requirements as closely as possible.[14]

A class of unimpaired claims is conclusively presumed to have accepted a plan.[15] Thus, if a debtor proposes to pay all creditors in full on the effective date of the plan, all creditors are unimpaired. The votes of creditors will not be a problematic issue at the confirmation hearing. Conversely, a class that will receive no dividend under the plan is deemed to have rejected it.[16]

D. MODIFICATION OF THE PLAN

A plan may be modified at any time before confirmation, as long as the disclosure statement requirements are complied with.[17] After confirmation, modification may be sought for reasons similar to the reasons for seeking modification of a Chapter 13 plan.[18] Either a debtor will acquire the ability to accelerate a plan's performance, or, conversely, the payments will have to be reduced or the performance period extended. A plan proponent may bring a motion before the court to modify a plan. The court will not permit modification of a confirmed plan if the plan has been **substantially consummated**, except in cases involving individuals.[19] Generally, this means the taking of an irrevocable act in performance of a plan, such as closing an escrow for a sale of the business, completing a refinancing, or repaying a substantial percentage of a promised dividend.[20] A postconfirmation motion to modify a plan must also comply with Section 1125 and

14. 11 U.S.C. §1126(e), (g). Additionally, in a prepackaged bankruptcy, 11 U.S.C. §341(e) provides that the meeting of creditors may not be held if excused by the court upon a showing of cause.
15. 11 U.S.C. §1126(f).
16. 11 U.S.C. §1126(g).
17. 11 U.S.C. §1127(a).
18. 11 U.S.C. §1127(b). See chapter 23 supra.
19. 11 U.S.C. §1127(b); 11 U.S.C. §1101(2); 11 U.S.C. §1127(e).
20. 11 U.S.C. §1101(2).

provide adequate disclosure. Creditors may modify a prior ballot (that is, change their votes) due to the modified plan.[21]

E. BALLOTING REPORT

After the balloting is complete and the Rule 3018 report is filed with the court, the confirmation hearing takes place.[22] At the confirmation hearing the court will determine whether the requirements for confirmation have been complied with. The standards for confirmation are delineated in Section 1129. This is perhaps the most complex and most litigated provision of Chapter 11.

F. CONFIRMATION CONDITIONS

At the confirmation hearing, the court will confirm the plan only if it finds that the plan meets each and every requirement of Section 1129(a). This general principle is identical to that of Section 1325 in Chapter 13, as described in chapter 23 supra. Under Section 1129(a), the court must make 16 findings. If any item is missing, the plan may not be confirmed. Many of the findings that the court must make will not be problematic in most proceedings.

First, the court must find that the plan complies with all provisions of the Bankruptcy Code.[23] A plan that follows the guidelines described in chapter 25 supra will likely be in compliance with the Code. Second, the proponent of the plan must comply with any applicable provisions of the Bankruptcy Code.[24] This means that the proponent of the plan must be an entity that may file a plan pursuant to Section 1121. Third, the plan must be proposed in good faith and not by any means forbidden by law.[25] A plan designed to accomplish an improper motive or that would be illegal under applicable nonbankruptcy law is probably not a plan that has been proposed in good faith. Fourth, any fees to be paid to an issuer of securities or for acquiring property under the plan must be approved by the court as

21. 11 U.S.C. §§1127(c), (d).
22. 11 U.S.C. §1128. A Chapter 11 confirmation hearing is treated as a noticed motion. Bankruptcy Rules 3020, 9014.
23. 11 U.S.C. §1129(a)(1).
24. 11 U.S.C. §1129(a)(2).
25. 11 U.S.C. §1129(a)(3).

reasonable.[26] Fifth, the court must approve the debtor's postconfirmation management. This will include disclosure of all insiders to be employed by the debtor during the life of the plan, including their approximate duties, compensation, and manner of election. In this connection, the court must also find that the continuance of such individuals in the employ of the debtor is in the interests of the creditors, equity security holders, and public policy.[27] Sixth, if the debtor's rates are subject to governmental regulation, the Bankruptcy Court must find that any applicable regulatory agency has approved any rate changes provided for in the Chapter 11 plan.[28] Because most debtors do not fall into this category, this provision will rarely apply. Disputes regarding any of the six foregoing confirmation requirements arise infrequently. The final four elements present a somewhat different state of affairs.

Seventh, the court must find that as to each impaired class of claims, the individual claimholders have either accepted the plan or will be receiving, on the effective date of the plan, an amount not less than the class would receive in the event the debtor were liquidated under Chapter 7.[29] This is also known as the "best interests of creditors" test. This provision means that unless an impaired class is to receive dividends in amounts at least equal to a hypothetical Chapter 7 dividend paid on the effective date of the plan, the plan cannot be confirmed because it is not in the best interests of creditors. This is why a comparison of the Chapter 11 plan to the results that would be achieved if the proceeding were a Chapter 7 (liquidation analysis) should be included in a disclosure statement. Further, the hypothetical Chapter 7 dividend is the minimum amount that an objecting creditor within a given accepting class must receive for the plan to be confirmable. The mere fact that creditors are assured a minimum dividend, however, does not act to approve the plan over rejection of the plan by a class. Approval of a plan over class rejection will require use of the Chapter 11 cramdown procedures.[30]

For example, Brutus is an unsecured creditor of Wimpy. Wimpy proposes a Chapter 11 plan that will pay unsecured creditors less than they would receive in a Chapter 7 proceeding. Out of sympathy, the unsecured creditors accept the plan as a class. Brutus objects on the ground that he is not receiving a dividend greater than he would receive in a Chapter 7. The plan is not confirmable over Brutus's objection, despite overall acceptance by the class.

---

26. 11 U.S.C. §1129(a)(4).
27. 11 U.S.C. §1129(a)(5).
28. 11 U.S.C. §1129(a)(6).
29. 11 U.S.C. §1129(a)(7)(A).
30. See infra this chapter.

Eighth, the court must find that each class either accepts the plan or is unimpaired.[31] Because unimpaired classes are conclusively presumed to have accepted a plan, their votes are unnecessary and the plan can be confirmed even if they object. Simply put, a creditor receiving either payment in full or the performance it would be entitled to under nonbankruptcy law will not be heard to object to the plan's confirmation. A class accepts a plan in accordance with the voting rules described above.

If an impaired class of claims or interests does not accept a plan, the plan will only be confirmable if the debtor can successfully comply with the Chapter 11 cramdown provisions.[32] For example, the plan of Green Acres, Inc., proposes to pay a secured claim holder by returning acreage to the creditor equal to the value of the claim, while Green Acres, Inc., will keep the rest. The secured creditor rejects the plan. Because the creditor is allegedly receiving what it would receive in a Chapter 7, the plan complies with Section 1129(a)(7). However, because the creditor has not accepted the plan and is not unimpaired, the plan cannot be confirmed absent a successful cramdown.

Ninth, the court must find that the plan will pay all administrative expenses in full on the effective date of the plan and all other nontax priority claims in cash on the effective date of the plan, unless any affected class of priority claim agrees to deferred payments.[33] For example, the priority wage claimants of the Poughkeepsie Polos, a reorganizing professional polo team, do not agree to receive payment of their priority wage claims on a future date. The Polos must either pay the priority wage claims in full on the effective date of the plan or the plan cannot be confirmed.

Priority tax claims may be paid over a period not exceeding five years from the date of the Order for Relief, so long as all penalties and interest are paid over the period. Secured tax claims may also be paid on this basis.[34] Secured tax claims may also be paid on this basis. This means that if a debtor is willing to pay a tax claim in full, including all penalties and interest, payment of the claim may be deferred. Alternatively, a debtor that can afford to do so and pays an unsecured priority tax claim in full on the effective date of the plan will only need to satisfy the amount of the claim as it existed on the original Chapter 11 filing date. This approach, when feasible, can save payment of substantial penalties and interest. The Supreme Court has held that a plan proponent may, in appropriate circumstances, allocate the application of dividends to tax claims. For example, the plan proponent

31. 11 U.S.C. §1129(a)(8).
32. 11 U.S.C. §1129(b)(1). See infra this chapter.
33. 11 U.S.C. §§1129(a)(9)(A), (B).
34. 11 U.S.C. §1129(a)(9)(C). See also 11 U.S.C. §511, added by BAPA, codifying the rate of interest to pay on tax claims.

may propose to allocate a tax dividend first to any portion of the claim to which a nondebtor may also be liable. This may aid such individuals in avoiding personal liability for the taxes.[35]

Tenth, the court must find that at least one impaired noninsider class has accepted the plan.[36] Thus, if a plan contains only one impaired class and this class rejects the plan, the plan may not be confirmed. In this instance, cramdown will not provide the debtor with a remedy because only class rejections under the eighth finding described above may be overcome by a cramdown.[37] Although one class of rejecting impaired claims may be subject to a cramdown, if it is the *only* impaired class, the plan will not be confirmable. Or, stated in another way, there must be at least two impaired classes in a plan, one of which accepts the plan, before the court can consider application of the cramdown provisions to the rejecting impaired class.

Eleventh, the court must find that the reorganization is not likely to be followed by further reorganization or liquidation unless the plan so provides.[38] This is commonly known as a **feasibility requirement**. This determination will involve careful analysis of any pro forma or other financial data presented in the disclosure statement to determine the likelihood of the debtor successfully performing the promises contained in the plan. This may also involve a determination of the likelihood of a proposed sale or refinancing occurring within a specified period of time. The formula described in chapter 23 supra for analyzing Chapter 13 plans will also apply in Chapter 11 proceedings, albeit on a more complex level.

Twelfth, the court must find that any fees due the court will be paid in full on the effective date of the plan.[39] Thirteenth, plans involving certain types of employee retirement or benefit plans must comply with the provisions of Section 1114. This provision is not likely to be problematic in most cases.[40]

BAPA imposes three new confirmation conditions. First, in a Chapter 11 case for an individual, all postpetition domestic support obligations are current at the time of confirmation. Second, again applicable in Chapter 11 cases for individuals, if the holder of an unsecured claim objects, then the debtor must submit all disposable income for a five-year period into the plan unless all creditors can be paid in full sooner. Third, applicable in all cases, all transfers of property are to be made in accordance with local law.[41]

35. United States v. Energy Resources Co., 495 U.S. 545 (1990).
36. 11 U.S.C. §1129(a)(10).
37. 11 U.S.C. §1129(b)(1). Only Section 1129(a)(8) may be overridden by a cramdown procedure by the specific terms of the statute.
38. 11 U.S.C. §1129(a)(11).
39. 11 U.S.C. §1129(a)(12).
40. 11 U.S.C. §1114; 11 U.S.C. §1129(a)(13).
41. 11 U.S.C. §1129(a)(14), (15), (16).

G. CHAPTER 11 CRAMDOWN

When there is an impaired class of claims that has not accepted the plan, the Chapter 11 cramdown procedure is available as long as at least one other impaired class has accepted the plan. Similar to Chapter 13, when a plan is successfully "crammed down," a Chapter 11 plan is approved over the dissenting class or classes that led to the cramdown procedure. Any good Chapter 11 plan will be constructed so as to be able to achieve a successful cramdown upon dissenting classes. Ultimately, the ability to achieve a successful cramdown is the acid test of a quality Chapter 11 plan. Cramdown litigation is among the most intense in the bankruptcy system.

Cramdown battles can be expensive and time-consuming. As a result, they can be very counterproductive to the reorganization's successful outcome. The costs of the litigation will increase administrative expenses. This increase may affect the plan's feasibility. If a cramdown dispute occurs over a lengthy period of time, the underlying facts and circumstances can change. These changes may also impact upon a plan's feasibility. Although cramdown disputes are unavoidable in many instances, the parties should always endeavor to resolve the dispute by negotiation and not litigation, lest the "victor" be left standing alone in the rubble of the debtor.

For the court to proceed with a cramdown, it must first find that all other elements of Section 1129(a) have been complied with except those in Section 1129(a)(8). That is, the court must find the plan in compliance with all other elements of Section 1129(a), except the plan's acceptance by one or more impaired classes, in order to begin a cramdown analysis. To achieve a successful cramdown, the court must find that the plan does not discriminate unfairly and that the plan is fair and equitable with regard to each class of rejecting impaired claims or interests against whom cramdown is sought.[42] The issue of unfair discrimination is often raised but is rarely found. More frequently, it is the "fair and equitable" standard that creates dispute. Fortunately, Section 1129(b)(2) defines the meaning of "fair and equitable" depending upon whether the class of claim to be crammed down is secured, unsecured, or is a class of interest holders.

A plan may be confirmed over rejection by a class of secured claims in any of three situations. First, the plan may be confirmed over rejection by the class if the secured class retains any collateral and will, in addition, receive payments equal to the allowed amount of the secured claim over the life of the plan.[43] Second, a Chapter 11 plan may be confirmed over the objection of a class of secured claims if the collateral is to be sold free

42. 11 U.S.C. §1129(b)(1).
43. 11 U.S.C. §1129(b)(2)(A)(i).

and clear of liens and the claim is to be paid in full from the proceeds.[44] Third, a plan may be approved over the objection of a class of secured claims if the debtor provides the claimant with the "indubitable equivalent" of its claims.[45] This final method means that if a class of secured claims is given property or cash equal to the full value of the secured claim, the plan may be approved over objection of the secured class of claim. A substantial body of case law has developed in this area, the analysis of which is beyond the scope of this text. Suffice it to say that as a practical matter many courts view payment in full in cash as the only form of indubitable equivalent for payment of a secured creditor's claim. Any other proposal is likely to result in substantial and expensive litigation.

In summary, the concept of cramdown with regard to a class of secured claims is simple. If the class is going to be paid the full value of its claims in some manner, including a return of its collateral, the plan will be confirmable over the claimant's objection. This is the common thread contained in each of the three alternative methods of secured creditor Chapter 11 cramdown.

There are two methods of obtaining confirmation over rejection of a plan by a class of unsecured claims. The first method is very simple. If the plan proposes to pay an affected unsecured class in full on either the effective date of the plan or over time, the plan will be confirmable.[46] Once again, a class that will receive all that it is entitled to will not be heard to complain. Second, if a class of unsecured claims is not going to be paid in full, the court must find that no junior class of claims or interests will retain any interest in any property of the estate.[47] This is commonly known as the **absolute priority rule**. In its essence, this rule means that if the shareholders are proposing to retain an interest in a reorganized debtor they will not be able to do so unless any rejecting class of unsecured claims is paid in full.

A complex issue arises when an operating business proposes to pay its unsecured claimants an amount equal to or greater than the class would receive in a Chapter 7 proceeding, but where the interest holders will be retaining an interest in the reorganized debtor. Some cases have permitted this practice, holding that the debtor has in essence "repurchased" the value of the business from the creditors.[48] Other cases do not permit this practice and require payment in full to a rejecting impaired class if any junior class retains any interest in the debtor.[49] Still other cases have

44. 11 U.S.C. §1129(b)(2)(A)(ii).
45. 11 U.S.C. §1129(b)(2)(A)(iii).
46. 11 U.S.C. §1129(b)(2)(B)(i).
47. 11 U.S.C. §1129(b)(2)(B)(ii). See also the Historical and Revision Notes to this subsection.
48. In re Star City Rebuilders, Inc., 62 Bankr. 983 (W.D. Va. 1986).
49. In re Genesee Cement, Inc., 31 Bankr. 442 (E.D. Mich. 1983).

adopted a rule that permits a junior class to retain an interest if present and substantial consideration is paid into the plan for the retention of such interest. This is known as the "infusion of new capital" exception to the absolute priority rule.[50] In 1988, the United States Supreme Court held that the performance of services by an insider to a reorganized debtor (known as sweat equity) will not constitute "new capital" that will permit confirmation by way of cramdown. The Supreme Court in this decision even questioned the continued viability of the "infusion of new capital" rule referred to above.[51]

In Bank of America v. 203 North La Salle Street Partnership, 526 U.S. 434 (1999), the Supreme Court expressly declined to definitively rule on the existence of the new value exception to the absolute priority rule, but did rule that it is insufficient to offer shares in a reorganized debtor solely to the old equity interests. In *La Salle*, the debtor was a limited partnership that owned 15 floors of a high-rise building in Chicago's Loop. The bank was owed approximately $93 million, of which $38.5 million was considered to be unsecured. *La Salle*'s plan proposed to pay the bank the full value of its secured claim but a dividend of only about 16 percent on its unsecured claim and a discharge as to the balance. The source of funding for the plan was to be a $6.125 million infusion of new capital into the partnership. However, only old partners could become partners in the reorganized debtor. As the largest unsecured creditor, the bank objected to the plan, initiating the cramdown dispute. The Supreme Court found on these facts: "[A]ssuming a new value corollary, that plans providing junior interest holders with exclusive opportunities free from competition and without benefit of market valuation fall within the prohibition of §1129(b)(2)(B)(ii)." (526 U.S. 434, 458).

BAPA creates a statutory exception to the absolute priority rule applicable in individual Chapter 11 cases. If an individual Chapter 11 debtor commits all disposable income into the plan for at least five years, then the plan is subject to cramdown over the objection of unsecured creditors. This makes an individual Chapter 11 consistent with the similar requirement applicable in Chapter 13 cases.[52]

A plan may be confirmed over the objection of a class of interest holders under two circumstances. First, if the affected interest holders are paid any redemption prices to which they may be entitled, the plan may be confirmed over their objection. Second, if no junior interest holder retains

50. Case v. Los Angeles Lumber Prods., 308 U.S. 106 (1939).
51. Norwest Bank Worthin v. Ahlers, 484 U.S. 999 (1988). A debate has raged in the case law ever since. It is beyond the scope of this text to more completely analyze this issue. Readers facing a problem in this area should familiarize themselves with the most recent decisions from their area.
52. 11 U.S.C. §1129(b)(2)(B)(ii). 11 U.S.C. §1129(a)(15) discussed above. See chapter 23, supra.

any interest in the estate, the plan may be confirmed over rejection by a dissenting class.[53] In essence, the same principles apply to the cramdown of an affected class of interest holders that apply to the cramdown of unsecured claims — payment in full of the interest's value or application of the absolute priority rule to interest holders. Obviously, this provision will only be problematic in a proceeding involving multiple classes of shareholders that will receive dividends; it is not problematic in most common situations.

There may only be one confirmed plan in existence at any given time. If the court is faced with two competing plans, each of which has been accepted by the creditors, the court shall consider the preference of the creditors and interest holders in determining which plan to confirm.[54]

H. EFFECT OF CONFIRMATION AND CHAPTER 11 DISCHARGE

A confirmed Chapter 11 plan acts as a new contract between the debtor and *all* of its creditors.[55] Thus, any creditor that violates the plan will be in breach of this new contract. Confirmation also revests the debtor with all property of the estate free and clear of all liens and interests except as provided for by the plan.[56] Confirmation of a plan also acts to discharge all debts that arose before the date of confirmation except as provided in the plan.[57]

A Chapter 11 discharge is virtually identical to a Chapter 7 discharge except that all Chapter 11 debtors receive a discharge, including corporate and partnership debtors. Debts that are nondischargeable under Section 523 are, however, also nondischargeable through a Chapter 11, unlike the somewhat more potent effect of a Chapter 13 discharge.[58] A discharge under Chapter 11 is the only way in which a corporation or partnership may receive a discharge under the Bankruptcy Code.

In certain instances, a Chapter 11 debtor will not be entitled to a discharge under Chapter 11. A debtor liquidating its assets through a Chapter 11 plan that does not plan to continue in business and would not be entitled to a Chapter 7 discharge if the proceeding were a Chapter 7 will not be discharged by the confirmation of a Chapter 11 plan.[59] Thus, a corporate or partnership debtor with a liquidating Chapter 11 plan will not

53. 11 U.S.C. §1129(b)(2)(C).
54. 11 U.S.C. §1129(c).
55. 11 U.S.C. §1141(a).
56. 11 U.S.C. §1141(b)(c).
57. 11 U.S.C. §1141(d)(1).
58. 11 U.S.C. §1141(d)(2).
59. 11 U.S.C. §1141(d)(3).

receive a discharge from an unpaid obligation because a corporation or partnership is not entitled to a Chapter 7 discharge.[60] On the other hand, if the debtor is an individual and liquidates all nonexempt assets to pay creditors a dividend through a Chapter 11 plan, the individual will be entitled to a discharge because an individual may receive a Chapter 7 discharge. Under BAPA, an individual Chapter 11 debtor does not receive a discharge until all payments under the plan have been completed.[61] A confirmed plan may be revoked by motion made within 180 days after confirmation if the confirmation has been fraudulently obtained.[62]

As a final bit of practical advice, when a plan proposes to pay creditors over a period of time, the creditors should insist upon provisions in the plan requiring regular reporting on the debtor's postconfirmation plan performance. In this manner the creditors will know if the plan is being performed or if action should be taken to enforce the debtor's compliance with the plan up to and including revocation of confirmation and conversion of the proceeding to a Chapter 7.

Summary

A basic outline of the Chapter 11 plan confirmation process, as to both documents and deadlines, has already been provided in chapter 25 supra. This chapter explores this process in more detail.

The first step in the process is to file with the court a reorganization plan (Plan of Reorganization) and a disclosure statement. The disclosure statement is a history of the debtor and an analysis of the debtor's reorganization plan. The basic contents of a disclosure statement are outlined in the checklist accompanying this chapter.

Before creditors may be given an opportunity to vote for or against the plan, the court must approve the contents of the disclosure statement at a disclosure statement hearing. This hearing requires 25 days' notice to creditors. The court will approve the disclosure statement and authorize the plan proponent to solicit ballots to the creditor body if the disclosure statement is found to contain "adequate information" to enable creditors to make an informed decision when voting on the plan. In an electing small business case, the court may conditionally approve a disclosure statement and combine the disclosure and confirmation hearings.

---

60. 11 U.S.C. §727(a)(1). See chapter 13 supra regarding entitlement to a Chapter 7 discharge.
61. 11 U.S.C. §1141(d)(5).
62. 11 U.S.C. §1144.

Section 1126 of the Bankruptcy Code regulates the voting on a Chapter 11 plan. Each impaired class of creditors or interest holders is permitted to vote. A class of claims accepts a plan if a majority in number and two-thirds in dollar amount of those class members voting approve the plan. A class of interest holders accepts a plan if two-thirds in amount or percentage of those class members voting approve the plan. Special provisions permit the court, in some circumstances, to consider ballots obtained by the plan proponent in connection with a prefiling composition agreement (sometimes known as a "prepackaged bankruptcy"). A vote found to have been obtained in bad faith may be disallowed. An unimpaired class is conclusively deemed to accept the plan. Conversely, an impaired class that will receive no dividend is presumed to have rejected the plan. The results of the balloting are filed with the court in a report prepared pursuant to Federal Rule of Bankruptcy Procedure 3018.

The final step in the Chapter 11 confirmation process is the confirmation hearing held pursuant to Bankruptcy Code Section 1128. This hearing also requires 25 days' notice to creditors. The ballots are sent to creditors with a notice of the confirmation hearing along with the other documents described in checklist 25.2 in chapter 25 supra.

At the confirmation hearing, the court must make 16 findings to confirm a plan. These 16 findings are contained in Section 1129(a) and are outlined in the checklist accompanying this chapter. Many of these findings will not be problematic in most cases. The issues of feasibility and cramdown are commonly the most problematic.

The analysis performed to determine a Chapter 11 plan's feasibility is similar to that described in connection with a Chapter 13 plan, particularly where a Chapter 11 plan offers to make payments to creditors over a period of time from the surplus revenues of an operating business. If the plan involves a different methodology, such as a sale of assets or refinancing loan, the court, in ruling upon the plan's feasibility, will need to determine the debtor's ability to conclude any sale or refinancing.

The issue of a Chapter 11 cramdown will only arise if an impaired class rejects the plan and the court can make all other findings that permit confirmation. For a plan to prevail in a Chapter 11 cramdown, the court must find that the plan is "fair and equitable" and does not "discriminate unfairly" against a rejecting class. Whether a plan is "fair and equitable" as to a rejecting class will vary depending upon the rejecting class's status as secured, unsecured, or equity security holders. The common thread among these provisions is that if the class is being paid in full or if no junior classes will receive a dividend, then a cramdown may succeed and the plan can be confirmed over the objection of a rejecting class. In an individual Chapter 11 case, the plan is also subject to cramdown if the debtor pays all disposable income into the plan for at least five years. The checklist accompanying this chapter outlines the various cramdown provisions of Bankruptcy Code Section 1129(b)(2). This provision is one of the most complex in the Bankruptcy Code.

As in Chapter 13, a Chapter 11 plan may be modified before or after confirmation. In addition, confirmation can be revoked if it has been fraudulently obtained.

Confirmation of a Chapter 11 plan results in a discharge of the debtor pursuant to Bankruptcy Code Section 1141. Corporations and partnerships may obtain a Chapter 11 discharge. This is the only way in which a partnership or corporation may receive a discharge in the bankruptcy system.

KEY TERMS

absolute priority rule
disclosure statement
feasibility requirement
liquidation analysis
prepackaged bankruptcy
pro forma
substantially consummated

Chapter 26 Checklist

26.1 DISCLOSURE STATEMENT CONTENTS

26.1.1 Debtor's Prepetition History

26.1.2 Disclosure of Prepetition Debt and Assets

26.1.3 Disclosure of Future Income Projections

26.1.4 Disclosure of Any Sale or Refinancing Details

26.1.5 Disclosure of Any Other Plan Performance Method

26.1.6 Describe Reorganization Plan

1. Identify classes
2. Identify performance method

26.1.7 Disclose Liquidation Analysis

26.1.8 Disclose Postconfirmation Management and Compensation

26.1.9 Disclose Any Pending Litigation and Evaluation of Success

26.1.10 Disclose Insider Transactions

26.1.11 Disclose Tax Consequences of Plan, if Any

26.2 FINDINGS REQUIRED TO CONFIRM CHAPTER 11 PLAN

		Authority
26.2.1	Plan Complies with Bankruptcy Code	11 U.S.C. §1129(a)(1)
26.2.2	Plan Proponent Complies with Bankruptcy Code	11 U.S.C. §1129(a)(2)
26.2.3	Plan Is Proposed in Good Faith	11 U.S.C. §1129(a)(3)
26.2.4	Issuing Securities Broker Fees Reasonable and Approved	11 U.S.C. §1129(a)(4)
26.2.5	Approval of Postconfirmation Insiders	11 U.S.C. §1129(a)(5)
26.2.6	Any Rate Changes Subject to Regulation Are Approved	11 U.S.C. §1129(a)(6)
26.2.7	Each Impaired Claim Accepts the Plan or Receives a Dividend Not Less Than Would Be Received in a Chapter 7	11 U.S.C. §1129(a)(7)
26.2.8	Each Class Accepts or Is Unimpaired	11 U.S.C. §1129(a)(8)
26.2.9	The Following are Paid on the Effective Date of the Plan, Unless Claimant Otherwise Agrees	
	1. Administrative claims	11 U.S.C. §1129(a)(9)(A)
	2. Nontax priority claims	11 U.S.C. §1129(a)(9)(B)
	3. Priority tax claims may be paid over five years from date of the order for relief	11 U.S.C. §1129(a)(9)(C)
26.2.10	At Least One Impaired Class Accepts	11 U.S.C. §1129(a)(10)

		Authority
26.2.11	The Plan Is Feasible	11 U.S.C. §1129(a)(11)
26.2.12	All Court and United States Trustee Fees Are Paid	11 U.S.C. §1129(a)(12)
26.2.13	Employee Benefits Preserved	11 U.S.C. §1129(a)(13)
26.2.14	Postpetition Domestic Support Obligations Current	11 U.S.C. §1129(a)(14)
26.2.15	Five-Year plan for individual debtors	11 U.S.C. §1129(a)(15)
26.2.16	All transfers of property in accordance with local law	11 U.S.C. §1129(a)(16)

26.3 CHAPTER 11 CRAMDOWN OUTLINE

26.3.1	May Only Occur if All Findings in 26.2 Except 26.2.8 Can Be Made by the Court	11 U.S.C. §1129(b)(1)
26.3.2	The Plan Is Fair and Equitable and Does Not Unfairly Discriminate Against a Rejecting Class	11 U.S.C. §1129(b)(1)
26.3.3	A Plan Is Fair and Equitable to a Class of Secured Claims if	
	1. The class retains liens and is paid the full amount of secured claim over the life of the plan	11 U.S.C. §1129(b)(2)(A)(i)
	2. The claim is paid in full by sale, *or*	11 U.S.C. §1129(b)(2)(A)(ii)
	3. The claim receives "indubitable equivalent"	11 U.S.C. §1129(b)(2)(A)(iii)
26.3.4	A Plan is Fair and Equitable to a Class of Unsecured Claims if Either	
	1. The class will be paid in full over the life of the plan, *or*	11 U.S.C. §1129(b)(2)(B)(i)

	Authority
2. No junior class will retain an interest in the estate	11 U.S.C. §1129(b)(2)(B)(ii)
26.3.5 A Plan Is Fair and Equitable to a Class of Interest Holders if Either	
1. The interests are retained or paid in full, *or*	11 U.S.C. §1129(b)(2)(C)(i)
2. No junior class will retain an interest in the estate	11 U.S.C. §1129(b)(2)(C)(ii)

DISCUSSION QUESTIONS

1. What is a disclosure statement? What is its purpose? What essential information should be included in a disclosure statement?
2. Which creditors may vote to accept or reject a Chapter 11 reorganization plan?
3. When is a class of creditors conclusively presumed to have accepted a plan? To have rejected a plan?
4. How does a class of claims accept a plan? How does a class of interests accept a plan?
5. What findings must the court make to confirm a Chapter 11 reorganization plan?
6. How may a plan proponent obtain a cramdown of a Chapter 11 reorganization plan?
7. How may a Chapter 11 plan be modified?
8. What is the scope of a Chapter 11 discharge?

27

Chapter 12: Reorganization Proceedings

A. PURPOSES OF CHAPTER 12

Throughout the 1980s, family farmers were faced with serious economic problems. Many farmers were forced to seek voluntary protection under the Bankruptcy Code to obtain debt relief and protect their family farms. (Recall that a farmer may not be the subject of an involuntary proceeding.)[1] The Bankruptcy Code of 1978, as enacted, did not contain sufficient protection for the unique economic predicament of family farmers. This resulted primarily from the recognition that a family farmer is simultaneously a wage earner and the operator of an increasingly sophisticated business.

Prior to the enactment of Chapter 12, a fundamental problem faced by many farmers seeking bankruptcy relief was the choice of proceeding. Many family farmers cannot afford the costs of a Chapter 11 proceeding. The expeditious and relatively inexpensive procedures of Chapter 13 are more consistent with an economically pressed farmer's budget. However, because many farmers owe more than $922,975 in secured debt they do not qualify to file a Chapter 13.[2] As a result, farmers have had no alternative but to seek the more complex and expensive Chapter 11 proceeding if a family farm is to be preserved.

However, once a farmer becomes a Chapter 11 debtor-in-possession, the farmer's frustrations are just beginning. A secured creditor can move for

---

1. 11 U.S.C. §303(a). See chapter 4 supra.
2. 11 U.S.C. §109(c). See chapters 5 and 23 supra.

relief from the automatic stay on the grounds that there is no equity in the property. The debtor-in-possession farmer can defend by asserting that the property is necessary for an effective reorganization. The court invariably orders adequate protection payments to maintain the automatic stay in effect. If the debtor cannot afford the payments, then the stay will be relieved and the undesired foreclosure becomes inevitable.[3]

The problem was even more severe when a bank or cooperative had a lien on crop proceeds. Such a lien can prevent the family from receiving even the necessities of life due to the lienholder's rights in cash collateral, as described in chapter 18 supra.

To counteract each of the above problems, Congress enacted Chapter 12 on an experimental basis in 1986. Chapter 12 was enacted on a temporary basis from 1986 to July 1, 2000 and has remained almost continuously in effect by statutory extension. The 2005 legislation makes Chapter 12 permanent. Additionally, the legislation expands the scope of Chapter 12 to a **family fisherman**.

Chapter 12 is essentially a hybrid of Chapters 11 and 13. There are provisions in Chapter 12 that are virtually identical to the corresponding provisions in the other reorganization proceedings. There are also a few provisions unique to Chapter 12. Chapter 12 seeks to provide a family farmer with the benefits of a Chapter 13, the flexibility and control of a Chapter 11, and a partial abrogation of the sometimes harsh effects of the "adequate protection" requirement in the special circumstances of a family farm. In short, Chapter 12 gives a beleaguered family farmer a fighting chance to resolve economic problems and retain the family farm.

B. WHO MAY FILE CHAPTER 12

Only a **family farmer** with regular income may be a Chapter 12 debtor.[4] A family farmer with regular income is a family farmer who can afford to make payments under a Chapter 12 plan.[5] Not all family farmers are farmers or families. The term *family farmer* is defined in 11 U.S.C. §101(18). When the Chapter 12 debtor is an individual or individual and spouse, the debtor will qualify for Chapter 12 relief if four conditions are met. First, the proposed debtor must be engaged in a "farming operation." The Code does not define this term but, fortunately, an ample body of case law defining *farm* has developed from interpretation of the earlier Bankruptcy Act

3. 11 U.S.C. §362. See chapter 12 supra.
4. 11 U.S.C. §109(f).
5. 11 U.S.C. §101(19).

provisions preventing the filing of involuntary bankruptcies against farmers. Generally, a farming operation is one in which primarily crops or herds are raised for purposes of ultimate sale. Hence, a gold mine with a small garden will not be a farming operation. A sheep ranch that discovers gold on the property will likely be a farming operation.

Second, the proposed debtor's total debt must not exceed $3,237,000. Third, no less than 50 percent of the undisputed liquidated debt must arise from the farming operation, exclusive of the debtor's residence unless it is also the farm. Finally, more than 50 percent of the proposed debtor's and the debtor's spouse's gross income for the year preceding the filing must be derived from the farming operation.[6] For example, Perry Mason, who visits his farm on weekends but earns only 10 percent of his income from the farm, will not qualify as a family farmer.

A corporation or partnership may also qualify for Chapter 12 relief. There are six requirements for qualification. First, the entity must be a farming operation as described above. Second, more than 50 percent of the stock or equity must belong to members of the same family. Thus, where the Hatfields and McCoys are equal partners, the partnership may not qualify because no single family owns a majority of the stock.

Third, more than 80 percent of the assets must relate to the farming operation. Fourth, the total debt may not exceed $3,237,000. Fifth, at least 80 percent of the total undisputed liquidated debt must be related to the farming operation, exclusive of a dwelling house that is not related to the farm. Finally, if the debtor is a corporation, it must be privately held.[7] If all these requirements are satisfied, Green Acres, Inc., may file a Chapter 12 proceeding.

A **family fisherman** is an individual whose debts do not exceed $1,500,000 and 80 percent of which are related to commercial fishing operations, excluding debt on the debtor's personal residence, and from which more than 50 percent of the debtor's income in the year preceding the filing has been earned. A corporation may also qualify as a family fisherman if more than 50 percent of the stock is held by family members, debts do not exceed $1,500,000, and more than 80 percent of the assets and debts are related to the fishing operation.[8]

6. 11 U.S.C. §101(18)(A). The dollar amounts are subject to adjustment for inflation pursuant to 11 U.S.C. §104(b). The amounts shown will apply until April 1, 2007.
7. 11 U.S.C. §101(18)(B). The dollar amounts are subject to adjustment for inflation pursuant to 11 U.S.C. §104(b). The amounts shown will apply until April 1, 2007.
8. 11 U.S.C. §101(19A). This amount is also subject to triannual inflation adjustment pursuant to 11 U.S.C. §104(b).

C. COMPARISON TO CHAPTERS 11 AND 13

In examining the general provisions of Chapter 12, it becomes readily apparent that Chapter 12 is no more than a hybrid of Chapters 11 and 13. Many elements of Chapter 12 are borrowed from those proceedings, though there are a few elements that are not present in one of the other reorganization proceedings.

There are three basic similarities of Chapter 12 to Chapter 13. First, Chapter 12 imposes an automatic stay in favor of codebtors that is identical to the provision contained in Chapter 13.[9] Second, as in Chapter 13, the debtor's postpetition earnings are property of the estate.[10] Third, a Chapter 12 may be dismissed for many of the identical reasons for which a Chapter 13 may be dismissed or converted.[11] A proceeding may also be dismissed if it appears there is no reasonable likelihood of rehabilitation.[12] However, only the debtor may convert a proceeding from a Chapter 12 to a Chapter 7.[13] This is consistent with the principle that an involuntary proceeding may not be commenced against a farmer.[14]

There are two general similarities between Chapter 12 and Chapter 11. First, a Chapter 12 debtor has duties and powers that are somewhat analogous to those of a Chapter 11 debtor-in-possession.[15] This is so notwithstanding the additional fact that there is also a trustee appointed in every Chapter 12 proceeding. Second, a Chapter 12 debtor-in-possession may be removed for causes identical to the related Chapter 11 provision. A Chapter 12 debtor-in-possession may not, however, be removed from possession on the ground that removal is in the best interests of creditors.[16]

D. UNIQUE CHAPTER 12 FEATURES

There are three general features of Chapter 12 that are unique to it. The first of these is the existence of a trustee even though the debtor is the equivalent of a debtor-in-possession.[17] A given district may have a standing Chapter 12 trustee whose duties are analogous to those of a Chapter 13

9. 11 U.S.C. §1201; 11 U.S.C. §1301. See chapter 23 supra.
10. 11 U.S.C. §1207; 11 U.S.C. §1306. See chapter 23 supra.
11. 11 U.S.C. §1208; 11 U.S.C. §§1307(a)(1)-(8). See chapter 23 supra.
12. 11 U.S.C. §1208(c)(9).
13. 11 U.S.C. §1208(a).
14. 11 U.S.C. §303(a). See chapter 4 supra.
15. 11 U.S.C. §1203; 11 U.S.C. §1107. See chapter 24 supra.
16. 11 U.S.C. §1204; 11 U.S.C. §1104(a)(1). See chapter 10 supra.
17. 11 U.S.C. §1202.

standing trustee.[18] To the extent that the trustee is not a standing trustee, the trustee's duties are somewhat the same as that of a Chapter 11 trustee with the additional duty that a Chapter 12 trustee has the responsibilities of receiving and disbursing the debtor's Chapter 12 plan payments and that the debtor commences making timely payments under a confirmed Chapter 12 plan. If the debtor owes domestic support obligations, the trustee must also provide notice to the claimholder in a manner identical to a Chapter 7 trustee.[19]

A second unique feature of Chapter 12 is a special definition of *adequate protection* applicable only in Chapter 12. Section 361, regarding adequate protection, does not apply in Chapter 12. This ameliorates the harsh results that were being meted out to farmers in Chapter 11 and Chapter 13 proceedings prior to Chapter 12's enactment. Section 1205(b) retains the traditional adequate protection methods of periodic payments and additional or replacement collateral, but adds two additional modes of adequate protection. First, customary rent in the community where the property is located may constitute adequate protection. Presumably, this sum might be less than the payments that would be required to service debt on a trust deed or mortgage secured by the debtor's real property. Second, the court has specifically been granted broad equitable discretion to formulate an adequate protection order in Chapter 12.[20] This is supposed to give a family farmer or fisherman a fighting chance.

The final unique feature of Chapter 12 permits a sale free and clear of liens if the property sold is farmland, farm equipment, or property used to carry out a commercial fishing operation. This is in addition to the five methods for obtaining approval of a sale free and clear of liens under Section 363(f).[21] For example, Ma and Pa Kettle, Chapter 12 debtors, want to sell their farm for less than the amount of all liens and encumbrances upon it. Unless the affected lienholders consent or are to be paid in full from the proceeds, the sale would not be permitted in a Chapter 11 or Chapter 7 sale free and clear of liens. However, because Chapter 12 specifically permits a sale free and clear of liens of farmland or farm equipment, the sale may take place over the lienholders' objections even though an affected claim will not necessarily be paid in full from the proceeds of the sale.

18. 11 U.S.C. §1202(a). See chapter 10 supra.
19. 11 U.S.C. §1202(b), (c); 11 U.S.C. §1226(c). See chapters 10 and 23, supra.
20. 11 U.S.C. §1205(b)(4).
21. 11 U.S.C. §1206; 11 U.S.C. §363(f). See chapter 18 supra.

E. CHAPTER 12 PLANS AND DISCHARGE

With surprisingly few exceptions, the provisions of Chapter 12 relating to the contents and confirmation of a plan are virtually identical to the related provisions contained in Chapter 13. This is consistent with congressional intent to provide the speed and reduced expense of a Chapter 13 proceeding to family farmers who would otherwise be required to file more complex and expensive Chapter 11 proceedings.

A Chapter 12 plan must be filed within 90 days of commencing the proceeding unless the court extends the period upon finding an extension substantially justified.[22] This is substantially longer than the 15-day period permitted under Chapter 13 but less than the exclusivity period provided to Chapter 11 debtors. Unlike Chapter 11, however, the Chapter 12 plan filing deadline is a mandatory deadline.[23]

Section 1222 is identical to Section 1322, describing the mandatory and permissive elements of a Chapter 12 plan.[24] The one difference from Chapter 13 is that a Chapter 12 plan may modify the rights of a secured claimant secured by the debtor's principal residence. Recall that this is not permitted in Chapter 13.[25] A Chapter 12 plan is subject to the same performance limits (no longer than five years), and on the identical grounds previously described for Chapter 13 proceedings.[26] A Chapter 12 plan may be modified prior to confirmation in a manner identical to a Chapter 13 plan.[27]

A Chapter 12 confirmation hearing is to be given expedited treatment. The confirmation hearing shall be concluded no longer than 45 days after the plan is filed. A party in interest may object.[28] Except for the expedited treatment accorded the hearing date, this provision is identical to the similar provision in Chapter 13.[29] Note that no disclosure statement is required, nor do creditors vote on the plan. This is identical to Chapter 13.

The standards for confirmation of a Chapter 12 plan are almost identical to the confirmation standards for a Chapter 13 plan.[30] The provisions for the making of Chapter 12 plan payments are essentially identical to the sister provision in Chapter 13. The standards for achieving cramdown of a Chapter 12 plan are identical to the Chapter 13 cramdown provisions. The one difference is that there is no mandatory length for a Chapter 12 plan.

22. 11 U.S.C. §1221.
23. See chapters 23 and 25 supra.
24. 11 U.S.C. §1222; 11 U.S.C. §1322.
25. 11 U.S.C. §1222(b)(2); 11 U.S.C. §1322(b)(2). See chapter 23 supra.
26. 11 U.S.C. §1222(c); 11 U.S.C. §1322(c). See chapter 23 supra.
27. 11 U.S.C. §1223; 11 U.S.C. §1323. See chapter 23 supra.
28. 11 U.S.C. §1224.
29. 11 U.S.C. §1324. See chapter 23 supra.
30. 11 U.S.C. §1225; 11 U.S.C. §1325. See chapter 23 supra.

Instead, the plan may be crammed down on unsecured claimants if the debtor pays all disposable surplus income into the plan for at least three years. (This is identical to Section 1325 prior to the 2005 legislation).[31]

The effect of confirmation of a Chapter 12 plan is identical to the effect of confirmation in Chapter 11 and Chapter 13 proceedings. The confirmed plan has the status of a binding contract between the debtor and all creditors, those in agreement with and those opposed to the plan. Thus, as with the other reorganization proceedings, a Chapter 12 plan is no more than a judicially approved composition agreement.[32]

On the other hand, a Chapter 12 discharge is analogous to a Chapter 11 discharge and lacks the effect of a Chapter 13 discharge.[33] However, a Chapter 12 debtor may receive an early discharge under the same terms and conditions as a Chapter 13 debtor.[34] Finally, a Chapter 12 plan may be modified after confirmation under the same terms and conditions as a Chapter 13 plan.[35]

Summary

Chapter 12, commonly known as a family farmer reorganization, was enacted into the Bankruptcy Code in 1986 in an effort to provide viable bankruptcy relief to family farmers. Prior to the enactment of Chapter 12, many family farmers failed in bankruptcy reorganizations for three basic reasons. First, many family farmers could not afford the expense of a Chapter 11 proceeding. Second, many family farmers lacked the ability to provide secured creditors with proper forms of adequate protection, as described in Chapter 12 of this text. Third, many family farmers possessed debt in excess of the permissible Chapter 13 amounts. Chapter 12 has been enacted to neutralize these problems and, as a result, to provide family farmers with a viable form of bankruptcy relief. The 2005 legislation expands Chapter 12 to family fishermen.

A family farmer may be an individual, corporation, or partnership. In the latter two instances, more than 50 percent of the ownership must belong to the same family. A qualified family farmer's debt may not exceed $3,237,000. A family fisherman may also be an individual, corporation, or partnership, in a manner similar to farmers, except that the debt limit is $1,500,000.

31. 11 U.S.C. §1225; 11 U.S.C. §1325. See chapter 23 supra.
32. 11 U.S.C. §1227; 11 U.S.C. §1141(a); 11 U.S.C. §1327(a). See chapters 23 and 26 supra.
33. 11 U.S.C. §1228; 11 U.S.C. §1141. See chapter 26 supra.
34. 11 U.S.C. §1228(b); 11 U.S.C. §1328(b). See chapter 23 supra.
35. 11 U.S.C. §1229; 11 U.S.C. §1329. See chapter 23 supra.

Chapter 12 is a hybrid of Chapters 11 and 13. The speed and brevity of the Chapter 13 confirmation process are combined with the debtor-in-possession provisions of Chapter 11.

A Chapter 12 debtor has rights similar to a Chapter 11 debtor-in-possession. However, a trustee will always be appointed in a Chapter 12. The functions of a Chapter 12 trustee are similar to those of a Chapter 13 trustee.

Additional methods of providing adequate protection to secured creditors are available to Chapter 12 debtors. Periodic payments, replacement of additional collateral, customary rent in the community, or any equitable order granted by the court may constitute adequate protection.

The elements of a Chapter 11 plan and the findings required for confirmation are identical to Chapter 13, but with three exceptions. See the checklist to chapter 23 for further description. First, a Chapter 12 plan may be filed within 90 days of filing the proceeding. Second, a Chapter 12 confirmation hearing must take place within 45 days of filing the plan. Finally, a Chapter 12 plan, unlike a Chapter 13 plan, may modify the rights of secured creditors of the debtor's residence.

KEY TERM

family farmer **family fisherman**

DISCUSSION QUESTIONS

1. Why was Chapter 12 enacted? What is a family farmer for purposes of Chapter 12?
2. What provisions of Chapter 12 are similar to those of Chapter 13?
3. What provisions of Chapter 12 are similar to those of Chapter 11?
4. What features of Chapter 12 are unique to Chapter 12 proceedings?
5. What elements must be included in a Chapter 12 plan? What elements may be included in a Chapter 12 plan?
6. How is a Chapter 12 plan confirmed? What findings must the court make to confirm a Chapter 12 plan? How can a Chapter 12 plan achieve a cramdown?
7. How may a Chapter 12 plan be modified?
8. What is the effect of a Chapter 12 discharge?

PART VI

Review

28

Introduction to Courts and Jurisdiction

A. BANKRUPTCY AND FEDERAL JUDGES

Article III of the United States Constitution creates the federal court system and **federal judges**.[1] Federal judges are distinguishable from other judicial officers by the constitutional requirement that federal judges be provided with two basic protections to ensure their independence: lifetime tenure during good behavior and that their salary shall not be subject to reduction during their term of office.[2] The Constitution provides these protections to federal judges to keep an independent judiciary free of interference by the executive or legislative branches of the federal government. A federal judge cannot be relieved of duty by the president for deciding an issue against the president's wishes. Congress may not act to reduce a serving federal judge's salary because it dislikes the judge's decisions. These constitutional protections prevent the president or Congress from using tenure or salary as leverage to produce the results they desire rather than the results required by the Constitution or laws of the United States.

Prior to 1979, when the Bankruptcy Code went into effect, Bankruptcy Judges did not exist; until 1973 the individuals who administered the bankruptcy system were called referees. Bankruptcy referees were roughly analogous to federal magistrates. They had little judicial power, except as it pertained to the Bankruptcy Act. In 1973, bankruptcy referees received the title of Bankruptcy Judges.

One of the most complex areas of practice under the Bankruptcy Act was determining whether an issue was within the jurisdiction of the

1. U.S. Const. art. III.
2. U.S. Const. art. III, §1.

Bankruptcy Court. Generally, if the matter was "summary" in nature, involving specific application of a provision contained in the Bankruptcy Act, such as a preference action, its resolution would be within the court's jurisdiction. Otherwise, the matter was considered "plenary" and not within the Bankruptcy Court's jurisdiction.

When Congress reformed the bankruptcy laws in 1978, it attempted to do away with the jurisdictional complexities that had been created by statute and case law. The 1978 statute gave the newly created Bankruptcy Judges jurisdiction to deal with any matter whatsoever having any relationship to a bankruptcy estate.[3] This was, in essence, a grant of full plenary jurisdiction to Bankruptcy Judges. This broad grant of jurisdiction made Bankruptcy Judges equivalent to full federal judges except that their jurisdiction was limited to matters involving bankruptcy proceedings.

However, the Bankruptcy Judges created by the 1978 Bankruptcy Reform Act were not given the lifetime tenure or the salary protection of full federal judges. Instead, Bankruptcy Judges were given 14-year terms and their salary could be subject to reduction while in office. The Bankruptcy Judges were created by Congress pursuant to article 1, section 8, of the Constitution, which gives Congress the right to enact bankruptcy laws. Bankruptcy Judges were not created by article III.[4]

In 1982, in Northern Pipeline Construction v. Marathon Pipeline Company, the Supreme Court reviewed the constitutionality of the Bankruptcy Court system enacted with the Code.[5] In this case, the debtor, Northern Pipeline Construction, filed an adversary proceeding in the Bankruptcy Court to collect an account receivable due from Marathon Pipeline on a turnover theory pursuant to Section 542. In state court, this action would have been a simple debt collection suit not based upon a preference or a fraudulent conveyance or any other subject even remotely involving the Bankruptcy Code. Marathon Pipeline argued that the Bankruptcy Courts were unconstitutional because Bankruptcy Judges were not given the protections provided federal judges under article III of the Constitution and therefore they had no jurisdiction to rule upon matters unrelated to the Bankruptcy Code. In its opinion, the Supreme Court thoroughly analyzed these constitutional issues and ruled that the Bankruptcy Judge and Bankruptcy Court system enacted in 1978 was unconstitutional.

At the time of this ruling, in June 1982, the United States was in the middle of a recession. Thus, at the height of a recession the Supreme Court held the Bankruptcy Courts unconstitutional! The Supreme Court, out of necessity, did something it rarely does: It suspended the effect of its

3. 28 U.S.C. §1471, Pub. L. No. 95-598, 92 Stat. 2549 (1978).
4. U.S. Const. art. I, §8.
5. 458 U.S. 50 (1982).

decision for three months to give Congress an opportunity to enact new legislation that would be constitutional. In September 1982, when this grace period expired without congressional action, the Supreme Court suspended the effect of the decision again, this time until December 24, 1982.

Congress did not act by the deadline. The Office of the Administrative Courts of the United States came to the rescue and adopted what became called the "Reference Rule."[6] The Reference Rule decreed that all bankruptcy cases would now be under the jurisdiction of the district courts and, hence, the Bankruptcy Judges would be article III judges. Next, the district courts appointed all Bankruptcy Judges as special masters to administer bankruptcy cases and referred (hence "Reference Rule") all bankruptcy cases to them unless a party in interest objected, in which case the district court would retain the matter. In other words, a rule was adopted that resulted in no practical change of the then-existing system. The Bankruptcy Courts functioned under the Reference Rule from December 24, 1982, until the remedial Bankruptcy Amendments and Federal Judgeship Act (BAFJA) went into effect in October 1984.[7]

B. ACTIVITY WITHIN A BANKRUPTCY

To understand Congress's solution to the problem, it is important to review the various levels of a bankruptcy proceeding. First, there is the overall proceeding. This is the type of Chapter proceeding filed: 7, 9, 11, 12, or 13. It should now be obvious that, unlike traditional litigation, a multitude of activities will take place within a bankruptcy proceeding, for the simple reason that all of a debtor's financial affairs are subject to the scrutiny and control of the court. In contrast, a traditional piece of litigation will normally examine only one event or transaction in a vacuum without regard to the parties' other financial affairs.

Within a bankruptcy proceeding, matters will be brought before a Bankruptcy Judge by one of two methods: motion or adversary proceeding. For example, a sale will generally take place by way of a motion.[8] On the other hand, an action to avoid a preference takes place by way of an adversary proceeding.[9] Adversary proceedings may also arise that will not

6. 1 Bkr. L. Ed. (LCP BW) Sec 2:144 at 389 (1985).
7. Bankruptcy Amendments and Federal Judgeship Act of 1984 (BAFJA), Pub. L. No. 98-353 (July 10, 1984).
8. See chapters 12 and 18 supra.
9. See chapters 12 and 16 supra.

involve application of the Bankruptcy Code. For example, the collection of an account receivable, while theoretically a turnover complaint, is nothing more than a simple breach of contract dispute involving no application of bankruptcy law to determine the amount due.[10] All of these factors have been taken into account in Congress's solution to the problem.

C. BAFJA

In 1984, the BAFJA statute resolved the constitutional issue by enacting into law the essence of the Reference Rule. The process thus established is summarized in the nearby flowchart. Initially, the district courts have original and exclusive jurisdiction over bankruptcies, but Congress may elect to make the jurisdiction nonexclusive. Congress has done this in enacting Bankruptcy Courts into law.[11] This means that a federal district court or federal Bankruptcy Court may hear a bankruptcy proceeding.

The nonexclusive grant of jurisdiction to the Bankruptcy Court is set forth in 28 U.S.C. §157. The essence of this provision is the former Reference Rule. The specific portions of Section 157 that incorporate what was known as the Reference Rule are subsections (c) and (d). Under present law, all bankruptcy proceedings and motions or adversary proceedings occurring within them are referred to Bankruptcy Judges, but any party in interest may request withdrawal of the reference at any time and have the matter referred back to the district court (the article III judge) for disposition. When the reference is withdrawn, the matter may not be heard by the Bankruptcy Court at all unless all parties in the matter consent or the district court determines in its discretion to retain jurisdiction with the Bankruptcy Court. Further, any Bankruptcy Judge's rulings can be subject to the further approval of a District Judge.[12]

To distinguish the matters within a bankruptcy proceeding that the Bankruptcy Court may hear, Congress has eliminated the concepts of "summary" and "plenary," which created much confusion and litigation in practice under the Bankruptcy Act. In their place is the designation of "core" and "noncore" proceedings and the phrases "arising under" or "related to" defining adversary matters within a bankruptcy proceeding.[13]

Bankruptcy Judges now have jurisdiction to hear all **cases** under Title 11. *Case* under Title 11 means the proceeding itself, such as a Chapter 7, a

---

10. See chapter 14 supra.
11. 28 U.S.C. §1334.
12. 28 U.S.C. §§157(a)(c), (d).
13. 28 U.S.C. §157(b); 28 U.S.C. §1334.

BANKRUPTCY JURISDICTION

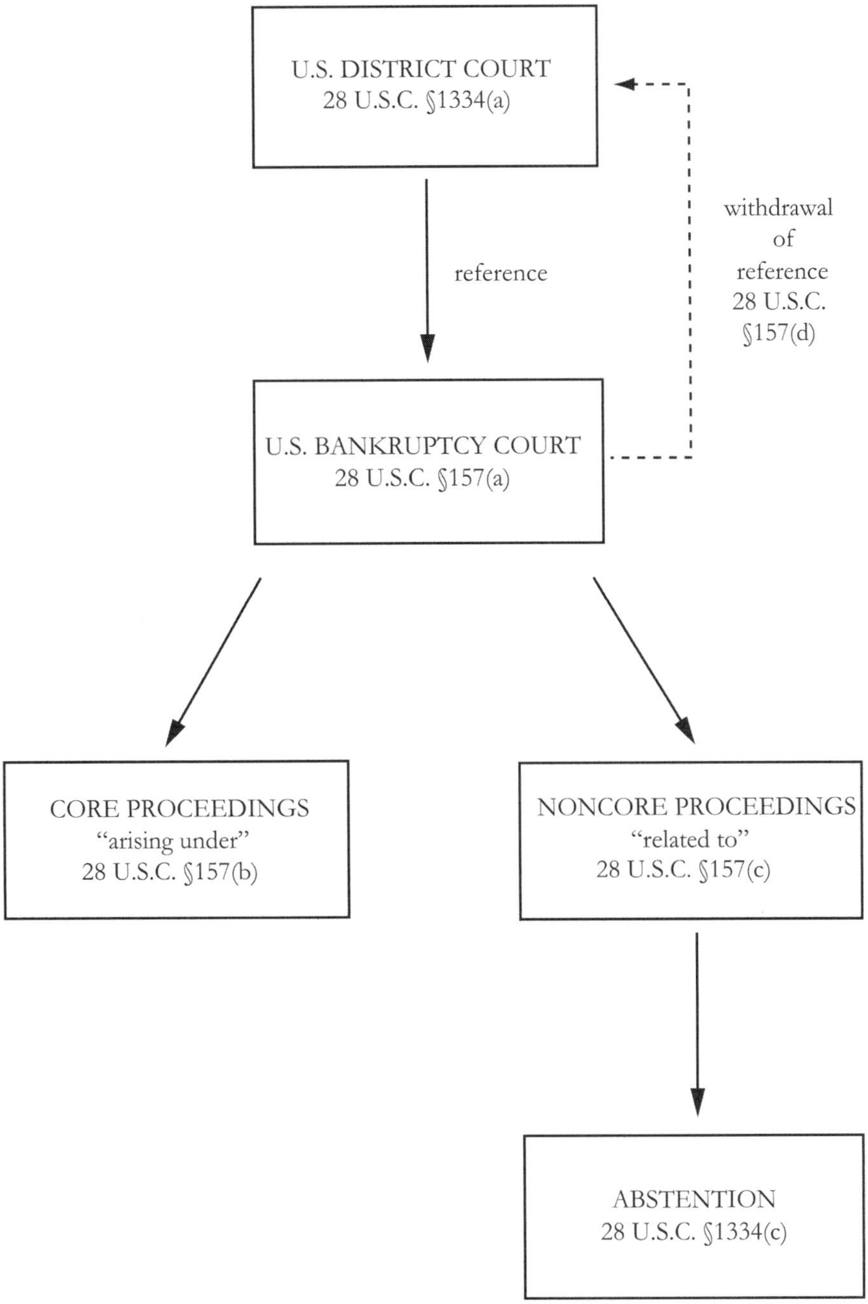

Chapter 13, or a Chapter 11 proceeding. Bankruptcy Judges may also hear all core proceedings arising within the proceeding and matters "related to" the bankruptcy proceeding.[14]

D. CORE AND NONCORE PROCEEDINGS

Generally, **core proceedings** "arising under" the Bankruptcy Code are those matters that arise by way of motion or adversary proceeding and involve the specific application of one or more provisions of the Bankruptcy Code for their resolution. The matters identified in 28 U.S.C. §157(b)(2) as core proceedings are items that are generally the subject matter of specific Bankruptcy Code sections. For example, objections to claims, relief from stay motions, motions to assume or reject executory contracts, objections to exemptions, objections to the dischargeability of debts or to the debtor's discharge, preferences, and other uses of the trustee's avoiding powers are all defined as *core proceedings*.[15] The resolution of these issues normally requires the application of specific Bankruptcy Code provisions.

On the other hand, a matter "related to" a bankruptcy proceeding is a matter that would arise for a debtor whether or not the particular bankruptcy proceeding exists. For example, the debt collection suit filed in *Marathon Pipeline* supra is such a matter. Matters such as these are generally considered **noncore proceedings**. The Bankruptcy Court may hear noncore matters.[16] However, if a party objects to the Bankruptcy Court's hearing of a noncore matter, the Bankruptcy Court must determine whether the matter is a core or noncore proceeding. If the matter is noncore, the Bankruptcy Court must either refer the case to the district court or abstain from further hearing the matter.[17] Personal injury and wrongful death claims are specifically designated as noncore.[18] The practical effect of these provisions is to have a personal injury suit or complex commercial litigation tried in a court other than the Bankruptcy Court in appropriate circumstances.

28 U.S.C. §1334(c) permits the Bankruptcy Court or district court to abstain from hearing a particular matter. If a matter is "related to" the bankruptcy proceeding but would not be heard in the federal court system absent

14. 28 U.S.C. §157(b)(1).
15. 28 U.S.C. §157(b)(2).
16. 28 U.S.C. §157(b)(1).
17. 28 U.S.C. §§157(b)(3), (b)(4), (c), (d).
18. 28 U.S.C. §157(b)(5).

the fact that one of the parties is a debtor in a bankruptcy proceeding, then the Bankruptcy Court or district court may abstain from hearing the matter and will defer to local jurisdiction.[19] A decision to abstain is not reviewable by appeal or otherwise.[20] For example, a trustee seeks to litigate a breach of contract suit in Bankruptcy Court. The defendant moves the court to abstain on the grounds that the claim is noncore and has no independent source of federal jurisdiction. The Bankruptcy Court agrees. This decision may not be appealed.

The various circuits within the federal judicial system have been given the power to appoint Bankruptcy Judges in each district. Bankruptcy Judges are appointed by the circuits for 14-year terms.[21]

E. REMOVAL AND APPEALS

It is possible to remove pending actions from the state court system to the Bankruptcy Court pursuant to 28 U.S.C. §1452. The procedure for removal is contained in Federal Rule of Bankruptcy Procedure 9027.[22] Many times when there is pending litigation at the time a bankruptcy proceeding is filed, the debtor or a creditor will seek to remove the litigation from state court to the Bankruptcy Court. If removal occurs and there is no objection, the Bankruptcy Court will then hear the case.

Appeals from the rulings of a Bankruptcy Court may be made to either the district court in the district to where the Bankruptcy Court is located, to the Bankruptcy Appellate Panel (BAP) of the Bankruptcy Court's particular circuit, or directly to the Court of Appeals for a given circuit.[23] A BAP may be created within a given federal judicial circuit. This panel will be comprised of three Bankruptcy Judges from districts within the circuit. The 1994 Bankruptcy Reform Act makes the establishment of BAPs mandatory unless the judicial council for a particular circuit finds insufficient resources or the likelihood that undue delay would result from establishment of a panel.[24] The BAP will hear all appeals unless the appellant elects, when filing the appeal, or the

19. 28 U.S.C. §1334(c)(2).
20. 28 U.S.C. §1334(c)(2).
21. U.S.C. §§151, 152.
22. 28 U.S.C. §1452; Bankruptcy Rule 9027.
23. 28 U.S.C. §158(a).
24. The First and Ninth Circuits have BAP panels. The Second, Third, Fourth, Fifth, Seventh and Eleventh Circuits do not. The Sixth, Eighth and Tenth Circuits have BAP panels for limited districts within each circuit.

BANKRUPTCY APPEALS

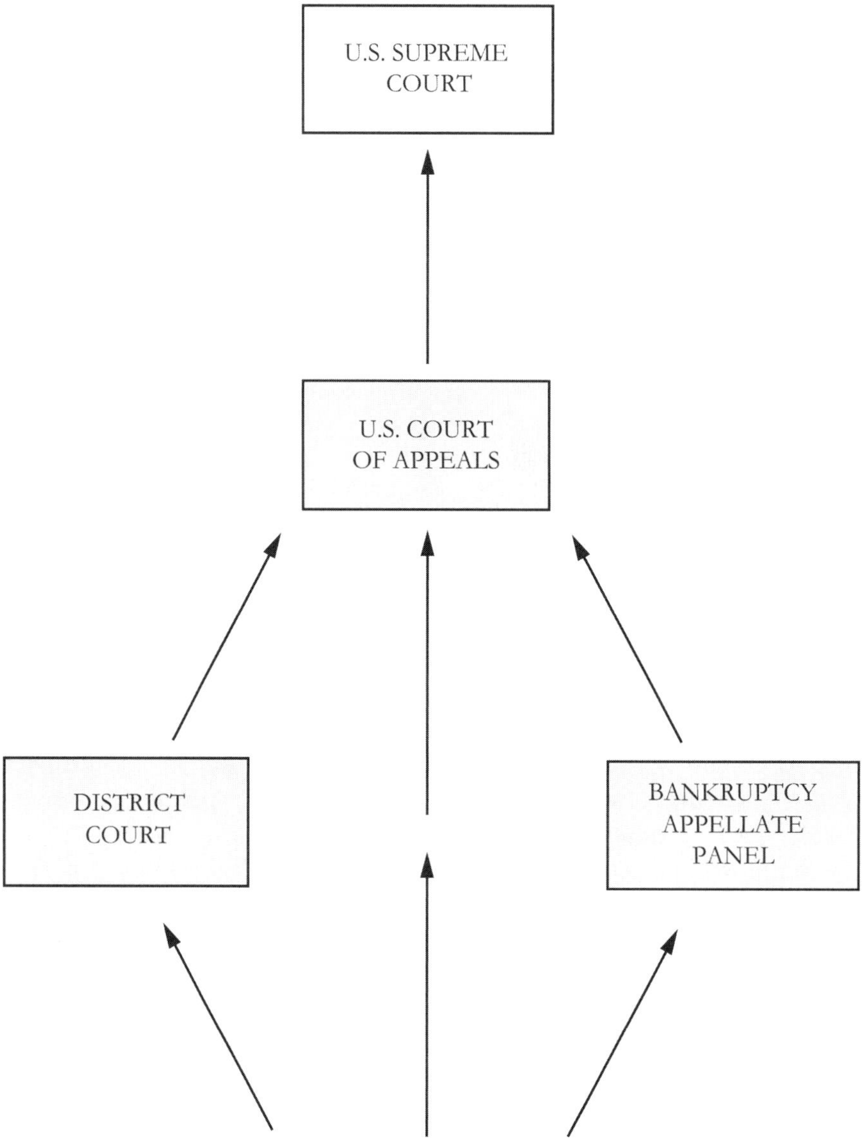

appellee elects within 30 days after service of the appeal, to have the appeal heard by the district court. In some limited instances, an appeal may be made directly to the circuit if the lower court so certifies.[25] Part 8 of the Federal Rules of Bankruptcy Procedure governs appeals. Otherwise, appeals of bankruptcy matters are similar to other federal judicial appeals, including applicability of the Federal Rules of Appellate Procedure. See the nearby flowchart.

F. JURY TRIALS

In Granfinanceria, S.A. v. Norberg, the Supreme Court explored the right to a jury trial in adversary proceedings before the Bankruptcy Court.[26] In this case, Norberg, a trustee, sued Granfinanceria to avoid fraudulent transfers. Granfinanceria requested a jury trial. The lower courts held that because suits to avoid fraudulent transfers were not triable by jury under common law and because an action to avoid a fraudulent transfer is a core proceeding, no right to a jury trial existed. The Supreme Court disagreed and reversed.

The Supreme Court held, in essence, that any action to recover money is an action at law for which a Seventh Amendment constitutional right to trial by jury exists. Notwithstanding this decision, the occurrence of a jury trial in the Bankruptcy Court is extremely rare. The 1994 Bankruptcy Reform Act permits the Bankruptcy Court to conduct jury trials if designated to do so by the district court and with the express consent of all parties.[27] Local rules should be consulted to ascertain the procedure in a particular district.

Summary

Federal law confers jurisdiction to hear bankruptcy proceedings on all federal district and Bankruptcy Courts. In some situations, a party may seek removal of a bankruptcy proceeding from a Bankruptcy Court to a federal district court. Normally, however, virtually all bankruptcy proceedings are presided over by the Bankruptcy Courts.

A Bankruptcy Court will always hear core matters. A core matter is any issue whose resolution requires specific application of a Bankruptcy Code

25. 28 U.S.C. §158.
26. 492 U.S. 33 (1989).
27. 28 U.S.C §157(e).

provision. A claim objection, an action to avoid a preference, or a motion for relief from the automatic stay are examples of core proceedings.

On the other hand, a matter arising before the Bankruptcy Court that does not require application of a specific Bankruptcy Code provision for its resolution is known as a noncore matter. A party may request the Bankruptcy Court to abstain from hearing a noncore matter. A decision by the court to abstain is not reviewable by appeal or otherwise. A personal injury action is a good example of a noncore matter.

KEY TERMS

cases
core proceedings
federal judges
noncore proceedings

DISCUSSION QUESTIONS

1. What factors distinguish a federal District Judge from a federal Bankruptcy Judge?
2. What is the so-called Reference Rule?
3. What is the difference between a core and noncore proceeding? Identify the following as core or noncore proceedings: motion for relief from stay; breach of contract claim; preference complaint; objection to claim of exemption; personal injury claim.
4. Describe the higher courts to which a bankruptcy ruling may be appealed.

29

Statements and Schedules Tutorial

A. INTRODUCTION

Approximately 95 percent of all bankruptcy proceedings filed are consumer Chapter 7 or Chapter 13 proceedings. In these cases, the practitioner's most important task is to prepare the data required to be in the Statement of Financial Affairs and Schedules of Assets and Liabilities, commonly known as the Statements and Schedules. Performing this task well will make the debtor's trip through the bankruptcy system as smooth and uneventful as possible. Proper preparation will also minimize the trustee's effort to administer the case. In an asset proceeding, performing this task well will help maximize the estate's recovery because the schedules will serve as an easy reference guide for the trustee as to the location and value of any assets.[1] Where the debtor's major goal is to satisfy nondischargeable tax claims, well-produced schedules will aid in achieving this result. Paralegals will frequently participate in this process. In a practice emphasizing bankruptcy law, a paralegal will spend a significant amount of time assisting in this preparation.

It is important, when representing creditors, to carefully read the Statements and Schedules. Because these documents will comprise the initial evidence that allows creditors or the trustee to determine the existence of assets available for liquidation and distribution, potential objections to an individual debtor's discharge, or the feasibility of a successful

1. See chapter 11 supra.

reorganization, understanding their contents is an important lesson to learn. This chapter is an exercise in learning to prepare and read Statements and Schedules. This chapter also serves as a review of the Bankruptcy Code and as a final illustration of the Bankruptcy Code's functioning as a system.

The first form analyzed is the Schedules.[2] The second form analyzed is the Statement of Financial Affairs.[3] This document is used by all Chapter 7, 11, and 13 debtors.

There follows a statement of facts concerning two hypothetical joint debtors. Then each form is analyzed, item by item, on the basis of the fact scenario.

Note: This material does not account for any necessary changes to the Schedules that may be required for compliance with needs based bankruptcy. Chapter 5 above contains examples that describe and work through the formula. Appendix One contains a simple worksheet. The forms disk contains proposed interim forms (forms 5.3 to 5.7).

It is also not known to what extent counsel's duty of reasonable investigation as set forth in Section 707(b)(4) may alter the preparation of Schedules. The text reflects custom and practice from throughout the country immediately prior to the 2005 legislation.

Finally, note that the Pittz' annual income is $42,000. This amount is less than the median family income for a family of four in most, if not all, states. The Pittz' would not need to comply with needs based bankruptcy.

B. BRAD AND JENN PITTZ FACT MEMO

Brad and Jenn Pittz want to file Chapter 7 without delay. Circuit City is threatening to attach their computer, and Toyota Credit is threatening to repossess their Pathfinder. Only an immediate Chapter 7 filing will prevent a loss of the car to the repossessor.

Brad and Jenn have lived at 1066 Conqueror Road in the town of Hendrix in this district for the past year. Prior to this they lived for six months at 55 Fer-Sure Terrace in Berkeley, California, and for six months before that at 45 Coldfish Lane in Frosty Falls.

Brad has been employed by Hecko-Techno, Inc., for two years as a salesman. He receives an annual salary of $30,000. Jenn is currently employed as an assistant manager at the Tea Jamboree and receives a salary of $12,000 per year. She has been working for the Tea Jamboree for

2. Official Form 6.
3. Official Form 7.

one year. For one year before that, she was in a partnership with Nancy Cook. The name of the partnership was Top O' the Mornin' Irish Tea Co. Top O' the Mornin' went out of business for lack of sales, and all assets were liquidated.

The Pittz's have three bank accounts: checking and savings accounts at the People's Bank and an IRA account at the Bank of America. The checking account has an average balance of $500. They have savings of $1,000 and a balance of $2,000 in the IRA. The Pittz do not have a safe deposit box.

No creditors have attached any assets of the Pittz's as of the present time. Brad and Jenn hold no property in trust for any third party. No third party holds property in trust for them.

The following suits terminated in the past year: Symphonic Sounds v. Pittz (judgment for plaintiff) and Dr. Laventhol v. Pittz (judgment for plaintiff). The following suit is still pending: Williams-Sonoma v. Pittz. Each suit is for debt collection. The Pittz's dispute the amount due Williams-Sonoma.

Within the past six months, Jenn has transferred title to an empty lot in Santa Cruz to some old friends, Ozzie and Harriet Oddborn, for no consideration. The lot is valued at $10,000.

The Pittz have maintained their own personal records and have kept copies of their tax returns.

The Pittz have seen no attorneys in the past year other than our firm. They will be paying us a $600 fee for the present Chapter 7.

The Pittz's owe $5,000 in income taxes to the IRS for 2002. They are not entitled to any tax refunds at the present time. They have not received any tax refunds in the past two years.

The Pittz's do not own their own home. They owe their landlord, Mr. Katchup, rent for three months at $800 per month. They have a month-to-month lease. They live in their home with their twin 15-year-old sons, Bill and Ted. They have cosigned a $7,500 student loan for their daughter Missy, who is an honors student at the University of Relativity where she is double-majoring in Quantum Physics and Barn Dancing. They owe Toyota Credit $25,000 secured by the 2003 Pathfinder. The vehicle is worth $20,000. All their furniture is secured to Futura Finance Company, to whom the Pittz's owe $10,000. The furniture is worth $5,000. The debt was not incurred to purchase the furniture. The computer is worth $1,500.

The Pittz's have the following unsecured debts:

Circuit City	$5,000
Symphonic Sounds	3,000
Dr. Laventhol	500
MasterCard	3,000
Visa	3,000
American Express Green Card	5,000

American Express Gold Card	5,000
Macy's	300
Wal-Mart	1,500
Nordstrom's	1,500
Neiman Marcus	3,000
Saks Fifth Avenue	2,000
Magic Carpet	4,500

The Pittz have personal wardrobes collectively worth $4,000 at liquidation value. Brad also has a collection of Jerry Garcia ties worth $1,000. They each own a pair of custom WarpSpeed rollerblades, worth $400 a pair. They have no assets other than described. All assets and liabilities are jointly owned or owed. No debts are in dispute except as noted above. They will claim exemptions pursuant to 11 U.S.C. §522 (d).

Brad's gross monthly income is $2,500; Jenn's gross monthly income is $1,000. They have provided us with the following approximate monthly expenses:

Rent	$800
Utilities (gas and electric)	75
Telephone	50
Cable TV	75
Food	600
Clothing	100
Laundry	30
Transportation	200
Entertainment	200
Insurance —	
Auto	150
Health	200
Renter's	20
Car payment	350
Internet network fees	15

C. SCHEDULES

Official Form 6 is entitled the Schedules of Assets and Liabilities. Together, the Statement of Financial Affairs and Schedules of Assets and Liabilities are commonly known as the Statements and Schedules. Collectively, the Schedules form an accrual basis form of a financial statement. Debts not paid are in fact accrued debts within generally accepted accounting definitions. In the Schedules, liabilities are listed according to the distribution scheme described in chapters 21 and 22 supra. Assets are segregated between real property, personal property, and other property. The debtor's claim of exemptions are also included in the Schedules. The Schedules will also disclose any executory contracts or leases, codebtors, and the debtor's monthly income and expenses.

(Official Form 1) (12/03)

FORM B1 **United States Bankruptcy Court Eastern District of Pennsylvania**	**Voluntary Petition**
Name of Debtor (if individual, enter Last, First, Middle): PITTZ, BRAD	Name of Joint Debtor (Spouse) (Last, First, Middle): PITTZ, JENN
All Other Names used by the Debtor in the last 6 years (include married, maiden, and trade names): None	All Other Names used by the Joint Debtor in the last 6 years (include married, maiden, and trade names): fdba TOP O' THE MORNIN' IRISH TEA CO.

Description:

All names by which either debtor has been known or has conducted business during the prior six years should be listed in the caption if any creditor would recognize the debtor only by the alias. This is important because creditors need to know all possible names that an account may be listed under for the creditor notice to have meaning. For example, a creditor of Top O' the Mornin' Irish Tea Co. may not recognize the names Brad or Jenn Pittz. It would be acceptable to have just "Brad and Jenn Pittz" as the caption, but it would be most accurate and informative to note Jenn's prior business name, Top O' the Mornin' (fdba). A creditor may know who Top O' the Mornin' is but not who Jenn is.

A spouse's maiden or prior married name need not be included unless any of the debts listed are in the spouse's maiden or prior married name.

If a debtor has aliases that creditors have used for billing purposes, such as a business name like Top O' the Mornin', then the name should be designated in the caption. A nickname need not be included unless it is the name creditors may use in rendering billings.

SCHEDULE A - REAL PROPERTY

DESCRIPTION AND LOCATION OF PROPERTY	NATURE OF DEBTOR'S INTEREST IN PROPERTY	HUSBAND, WIFE, JOINT OR COMMUNITY	CURRENT MARKET VALUE OF DEBTOR'S INTEREST IN PROPERTY WITHOUT DEDUCTING ANY SECURED CLAIM OR EXEMPTION	AMOUNT OF SECURED CLAIM
NONE				
	Total ▶		$ 0.00	

(Report also on Summary of Schedules)

Description:

Schedules A through C itemize all property of the debtors and contain their claim of exemptions. Schedule A is an itemization of real property. All ownership interests in real estate must be disclosed so the trustee will be able to ascertain all potential property of the estate.[4] In a typical consumer proceeding where the debtors are renting, the name and address of the rental are not described in this Schedule. The lease will be disclosed in Schedule G — Executory Contracts and Unexpired Leases infra.

4. See chapters 11 and 14 supra.

SCHEDULE B - PERSONAL PROPERTY

TYPE OF PROPERTY	NONE	DESCRIPTION AND LOCATION OF PROPERTY	HUSBAND, WIFE, JOINT OR COMMUNITY	CURRENT MARKET VALUE OF DEBTOR'S INTEREST IN PROPERTY WITH-OUT DEDUCTING ANY SECURED CLAIM OR EXEMPTION
1. Cash on hand.	X			
2. Checking, savings or other financial accounts, certificates of deposit, or shares in banks, savings and loan, thrift, building and loan, and homestead associations, or credit unions, brokerage houses, or cooperatives.		SAVINGS - PEOPLE'S BANK PEOPLE'S BANK	J	1,000.00
		DEBTOR CASH ON HAND AND ANY OTHER PROPERTY UP TO THE LIMITS OF THE EXEMPTION Debtor's Residence	J	10.00
		CHECKING - PEOPLE'S BANK Debtor's Residence	J	500.00
3. Security deposits with public utilities, telephone companies, landlords, and others.	X			
4. Household goods and furnishings, including audio, video, and computer equipment.		HOUSEHOLD GOODS DEBTOR'S RESIDENCE- NO ITEM EXCEEDS $475 IN VALUE	J	5,000.00
5. Books. Pictures and other art objects, antiques, stamp, coin, record, tape, compact disc, and other collections or collectibles.		COLECTION OF JERRY GARCIA TIES Debtor's Residence	J	1,000.00
6. Wearing apparel.		WEARING APPAREL - NO ITEM EXCEEDS $475 IN VALUE Debtor's Residence	J	5,000.00
8. Firearms and sports, photographic, and other hobby equipment.		WARPSPEED ROLLER BLADES - 2 PAIR Debtor's Residence	J	800.00
11. Interests in IRA, ERISA, Keogh, or other pension or profit sharing plans. Itemize.		IRA - BANK OF AMERICA BANK OF AMERICA	J	2,000.00
23. Automobiles, trucks, trailers, and other vehicles and accessories.		2003 TOYOTA PATHFINDER ($25,000 OWED) Debtor's Residence	J	20,000.00
				Total 35,310.00

Description:

Schedule B is an itemization of personal property of all kinds. Only those items that most commonly appear in a consumer proceeding appear in the fact memo and in that portion of Schedule B shown. This is why the numbers are not consecutive. See form 4.3 on the forms disk for the complete Schedule B.

Cash on hand is the first item. Most debtors usually have a very small amount of cash on hand or "pocket money." "None" or "nominal" are common responses. The location, such as "debtor residence," should also be disclosed. Note that the new form contains a column for "None." It should be used where applicable. No item should be left blank.

The next item identifies funds on deposit. Bank balances are described here. In addition, the name and address of the depository bank and the account number should also be disclosed. This information was previously disclosed in the Statement of Affairs. It will now be disclosed only in the Schedules.

Item B-4 identifies household goods, supplies, and furnishings. Simply provide the total value at liquidation prices. It is also a good idea to provide the additional legend "no item exceeds $475 in value" and to list any exceptions. This legend may affect exemptions under federal law. Recall also that "each item" specifically means each item.[5] The computer should be separately listed because it exceeds $475 in value. Note that the form is in error because it has failed to account for the value of the computer. The same description and comments apply equally to Schedule B-4 and B-6 regarding the debtor's household goods and wardrobe. Note that there is no Schedule B-3 item described in the fact memo. The "None" column has been checked.

Item B-11 identifies any IRA or pension accounts. There are no other entries for the Pittz's Schedule B. Even so, the "None" column should be checked for all other items so there will not be a question raised as to the existence of any assets in any of the other categories.

Item B-23 describes vehicles. It is also a good idea to note, as shown, the amount of any lien upon the vehicle. This will help the trustee easily determine the existence or lack of equity in the vehicle.

Finally, note that all assets have been identified as being jointly owned by the Pittz's.

---

5. See chapter 9 supra.

SCHEDULE C - PROPERTY CLAIMED AS EXEMPT

Debtor elects the exemption to which debtor is entitled under

(Check one box)

☑ 11 U.S.C. §522(b)(1) Exemptions provided in 11 U.S.C. §522(d). Note: These exemptions are available only in certain states.

☐ 11 U.S.C. §522(b)(2) Exemptions available under applicable nonbankruptcy federal laws, state or local law where the debtor's domicile has been located for the 180 days immediately preceding the filing of the petition, or for a longer portion of the 180-day period than in any other place, and the debtor's interest as a tenant by the entirety or joint tenant to the extent the interest is exempt from process under applicable nonbankruptcy law.

DESCRIPTION OF PROPERTY	SPECIFY LAW PROVIDING EACH EXEMPTION	VALUE OF CLAIMED EXEMPTION	CURRENT MARKET VALUE OF PROPERTY WITHOUT DEDUCTING EXEMPTIONS
SAVINGS - PEOPLE'S BANK	(Husb)11 U.S.C. 522(d)(5)	1,000.00	1,000.00
DEBTOR CASH ON HAND AND ANY OTHER PROPERTY UP TO THE LIMITS OF THE EXEMPTION	(Husb)11 U.S.C. 522(d)(5)	10.00	10.00
CHECKING - PEOPLE'S BANK	(Husb)11 U.S.C. 522(d)(5)	500.00	500.00
HOUSEHOLD GOODS	(Husb)11 U.S.C. 522(d)(3)	5,000.00	5,000.00
COLECTION OF JERRY GARCIA TIES	(Husb)11 U.S.C. 522(d)(5)	1,000.00	1,000.00
WEARING APPAREL - NO ITEM EXCEEDS $475 IN VALUE	(Husb)11 U.S.C. 522(d)(3) (Wife)11 U.S.C. 522(d)(3)	4,000.00 1,000.00	5,000.00
WARPSPEED ROLLER BLADES - 2 PAIR	(Husb)11 U.S.C. 522(d)(5)	800.00	800.00
IRA - BANK OF AMERICA	(Husb)11 U.S.C. 522(d)(5)	2,000.00	2,000.00
2003 TOYOTA PATHFINDER ($25,000 OWED)	(Husb)11 U.S.C. 522(d)(2)	0.00	20,000.00

Description:

Schedule C is the debtor's claim of exemptions. Each exemption should be itemized and the statute that the debtor selects should be identified with particularity, whether the debtors select state exemptions or the federal exemptions, where applicable. Note the prefatory box at the top of the form. The most probable effective selection for the Pittz's is shown.[6] Claim

6. It may appear that the exemption limit for household goods, furnishings, and wearing apparel of $9,850 has been exceeded, inasmuch as the value of these assets is $10,000 (11 U.S.C. §522(d)(3)). However, recall that each joint debtor may make a claim of exemption, effectively doubling all the dollar amounts (11 U.S.C. §522(m)) in a state that has not opted out of the federal exemption scheme. See chapter 9 supra.

the maximum statutory amount exempt for each asset subject to an exemption even if there is no apparent equity in the asset. This will relieve the necessity of later making an amendment should an issue as to value arise.

Also, note that a disclosure of an asset's market value must be disclosed alongside the exemption. Recall that there is $25,000 owed on the vehicle and this lack of equity does not appear on *this* sheet although it appears in Schedules B and D, respectively. This also applies to the personal property secured to Futura Finance Co.

SCHEDULE D - CREDITORS HOLDING SECURED CLAIMS

State the name, mailing address, including zip code and last four digits of any account number of all entities holding claims secured by property of the debtor as of the date of filing of the petition. The complete account number of any account the debtor has with the creditor is useful to the trustee and the creditor and may be provided if the debtor chooses to do so. List creditors holding all types of secured interests such as judgment liens, garnishments, statutory liens, mortgages, deeds of trust, and other security interests. List creditors in alphabetical order to the extent practicable. If all secured creditors will not fit on this page, use the continuation sheet provided.

If any entity other than a spouse in a joint case may be jointly liable on a claim, place an "X" in the column labeled "Codebtor," include the entity on the appropriate schedule of creditors, and complete Schedule H - Codebtors. If a joint petition is filed, state whether husband, wife, both of them, or the marital community may be liable on each claim by placing an "H", "W", "J", or "C" in the column labeled "Husband, Wife, Joint, or Community." If the claim is contingent, place an "X" in the column labeled "Contingent." If the claim is unliquidated, place an "X" in the column labeled "Unliquidated." If the claim is disputed, place an "X" in the column labeled "Disputed." (You may need to place an "X" in more than one of these three columns.)

Report the total of all claims listed on this schedule in the box labeled "Total" on the last sheet of the completed schedule. Report this total also on the Summary of Schedules.

☐ Check this box if debtor has no creditors holding secured claims to report on this Schedule D.

CREDITOR'S NAME, MAILING ADDRESS INCLUDING ZIP CODE, AND ACCOUNT NUMBER (See instructions above.)	CODEBTOR	HUSBAND, WIFE, JOINT OR COMMUNITY	DATE CLAIM WAS INCURRED, NATURE OF LIEN, AND DESCRIPTION AND MARKET VALUE OF PROPERTY SUBJECT TO LIEN	CONTINGENT	UNLIQUIDATED	DISPUTED	AMOUNT OF CLAIM WITHOUT DEDUCTING VALUE OF COLLATERAL	UNSECURED PORTION, IF ANY
ACCOUNT NO.								5,000.00
FUTURA FINANCE CO.		J					10,000.00	
			VALUE $ 5,000.00					
ACCOUNT NO.								5,000.00
TOYOTA CREDIT		J					25,000.00	
			VALUE $ 20,000.00					

Subtotal ➤ (Total of this page)	$ 35,000.00
Total ➤ (Use only on last page)	$ 35,000.00

(Report total also on Summary of Schedules)

Description:

Schedule D itemizes all secured claims. List the creditors' names and addresses alphabetically. Also list any account numbers that the debtor provides. (These have not been provided in the example.) Frequently, correspondence will be received from creditors requesting account numbers. If these numbers are included in the Schedules it will be helpful. Describe the collateral as succinctly as possible, as shown in the example, and when the creditor acquired the security interest. List the market value of the collateral as shown. Finally, identify the amount of each secured creditor's claim. From this data there can be estimated the existence or lack of any equity in the collateral for the benefit of the debtors or unsecured creditors. Identifying the date when a security interest was acquired will help identify the security interest as a potential preference or as a nonpurchase money lien in consumer goods that may be avoided under Section

522 (f)(2).[7] (Yes, the Pittz's may want to consider such a motion with respect to Futura Finance Company on the facts provided.) Finally, note that the joint nature of the debts must also be disclosed.

SCHEDULE E - CREDITORS HOLDING UNSECURED PRIORITY CLAIMS

Taxes & Debts to Governments

TYPE OF PRIORITY

CREDITOR'S NAME, MAILING ADDRESS INCLUDING ZIP CODE, AND ACCOUNT NUMBER (See instructions above.)	CODEBTOR	HUSBAND, WIFE, JOINT ORCOMMUNITY	DATE CLAIM WAS INCURRED AND CONSIDERATION FOR CLAIM	CONTINGENT	UNLIQUIDATED	DISPUTED	AMOUNT OF CLAIM	AMOUNT ENTITLED TO PRIORITY
ACCOUNT NO. IRS		J	Consideration: 2002 INCOME TAXES				5,000.00	5,000.00

Subtotal ➤ (Total of this page)	$	5,000.00
Total ➤ (Use only on last page of the completed Schedule E.)	$	5,000.00

(Report total also on Summary of Schedules)

Description:

Schedule E is an itemization of Section 507 priority claims, listed in the order of priority designated in Section 507(a).[8] The claim of the IRS is the only priority claim in the example. In this Schedule, as in all of the Schedules, it is more important to place all potential creditors on the list so they receive notice. Exactness as to the amount is secondary. Often a debtor may not be certain about the exact amount due a particular creditor. When in doubt, insert the debtor's best estimate. A dischargeable debt will remain dischargeable even if an incorrect amount is listed in the Schedules but the creditor has received notice of the proceeding. However, a dischargeable debt may become nondischargeable if it is not listed in the Schedules.[9]

---

7. See chapters 9 and 16 supra.
8. See chapters 21 and 22 supra.
9. 11 U.S.C. §523(a)(3). See chapter 13 supra.

SCHEDULE F - CREDITORS HOLDING UNSECURED NONPRIORITY CLAIMS

State the name, mailing address, including zip code, and last four digits of any account number, of all entities holding unsecured claims without priority against the debtor or the property of the debtor, as of the date of filing of the petition. The complete account number of any account the debtor has with the creditor is useful to the trustee and the creditor and may be provided if the debtor chooses to do so. Do not include claims listed in Schedules D and E. If all creditors will not fit on this page, use the continuation sheet provided.

If any entity other than a spouse in a joint case may be jointly liable on a claim, place an "X" in the column labeled "Codebtor," include the entity on the appropriate schedule of creditors, and complete Schedule H - Codebtors. If a joint petition is filed, state whether husband, wife, both of them, or the marital community maybe liable on each claim by placing an "H," "W," "J," or "C" in the column labeled "Husband, Wife, Joint, or Community."

If the claim is contingent, place an "X" in the column labeled "Contingent." If the claim is unliquidated, place an "X" in the column labeled "Unliquidated." If the claim is disputed, place an "X" in the column labeled "Disputed." (You may need to place an "X" in more than one of these three columns.)

Report total of all claims listed on this schedule in the box labeled "Total" on the last sheet of the completed schedule. Report this total also on the Summary of Schedules.

☐ Check this box if debtor has no creditors holding unsecured claims to report on this Schedule F.

CREDITOR'S NAME, MAILING ADDRESS INCLUDING ZIP CODE, AND ACCOUNT NUMBER (See instructions above.)	CODEBTOR	HUSBAND, WIFE, JOINT OR COMMUNITY	DATE CLAIM WAS INCURRED AND CONSIDERATION FOR CLAIM. IF CLAIM IS SUBJECT TO SETOFF, SO STATE.	CONTINGENT	UNLIQUIDATED	DISPUTED	AMOUNT OF CLAIM
ACCOUNT NO. AMERICAN EXPRESS - GOLD CARD		J					5,000.00
ACCOUNT NO. AMERICAN EXPRESS - GREEN CARD		J					5,000.00
ACCOUNT NO. CIRCUIT CITY		J					5,000.00
ACCOUNT NO. DR. LAVENTHOL		J					500.00

3 continuation sheets attached

Subtotal ➤ (Total of this page) $ 15,500.00

SCHEDULE F- CREDITORS HOLDING UNSECURED NONPRIORITY CLAIMS

(Continuation Sheet)

CREDITOR'S NAME, MAILING ADDRESS INCLUDING ZIP CODE, AND ACCOUNT NUMBER (See instructions above.)	CODEBTOR	HUSBAND, WIFE, JOINT ORCOMMUNITY	DATE CLAIM WAS INCURRED AND CONSIDERATION FOR CLAIM. IF CLAIM IS SUBJECT TO SETOFF,	CONTINGENT	UNLIQUIDATED	DISPUTED	AMOUNT OF CLAIM
ACCOUNT NO. MACY'S		J					300.00
ACCOUNT NO. MAGIC CARPET		J					4,500.00
ACCOUNT NO. MASTERCARD		J					3,000.00
ACCOUNT NO. MR. KATCHUP		J					2,400.00
ACCOUNT NO. NEIMAN MARCUS		J					3,000.00

Sheet no. 1 of 3 continuation sheets attached to Schedule of Creditors

Subtotal ➤ (Total of this page) $ 13,200.00

SCHEDULE F- CREDITORS HOLDING UNSECURED NONPRIORITY CLAIMS

(Continuation Sheet)

CREDITOR'S NAME, MAILING ADDRESS INCLUDING ZIP CODE, AND ACCOUNT NUMBER (See instructions above.)	CODEBTOR	HUSBAND, WIFE, JOINT ORCOMMUNITY	DATE CLAIM WAS INCURRED AND CONSIDERATION FOR CLAIM. IF CLAIM IS SUBJECT TO SETOFF,	CONTINGENT	UNLIQUIDATED	DISPUTED	AMOUNT OF CLAIM
ACCOUNT NO. NORDSTROM'S		J					1,500.00
ACCOUNT NO. SAKS FIFTH AVENUE		J					2,000.00
ACCOUNT NO. SYMPHONIC SOUNDS		J					3,000.00
ACCOUNT NO. UNIVERSITY OF RELATIVITY	X	J					7,500.00
ACCOUNT NO. VISA		J					3,000.00

Sheet no. 2 of 3 continuation sheets attached to Schedule of Creditors — Subtotal ➤ (Total of this page) $ 17,000.00

SCHEDULE F- CREDITORS HOLDING UNSECURED NONPRIORITY CLAIMS

(Continuation Sheet)

CREDITOR'S NAME, MAILING ADDRESS INCLUDING ZIP CODE, AND ACCOUNT NUMBER (See instructions above.)	CODEBTOR	HUSBAND, WIFE, JOINT ORCOMMUNITY	DATE CLAIM WAS INCURRED AND CONSIDERATION FOR CLAIM. IF CLAIM IS SUBJECT TO SETOFF,	CONTINGENT	UNLIQUIDATED	DISPUTED	AMOUNT OF CLAIM
ACCOUNT NO. WAL - MART		J					1,500.00
ACCOUNT NO. WILLIAMS - SONOMA		J					Unknown

Sheet no. 3 of 3 continuation sheets attached to Schedule of Creditors

Subtotal ➤ (Total of this page)	$	1,500.00
Total ➤ (Use only on last page of the completed Schedule F.)	$	47,200.00

Description:

Schedule F is an itemization of unsecured claims or creditors. Schedule F is normally the longest Schedule to complete. As with secured claims, it is always best to list the claims alphabetically and to include any account numbers that exist. There are a couple of commonly occurring errors that require further description. A careful review of the fact pattern will reveal that Mr. Katchup and Williams-Sonoma are not listed on the specific list of creditors in the memo although they appear in the memo. When a debtor has described a lawsuit or overdue rent, the debtor may inadvertently omit these debts from any list of creditors provided to the practitioner. However, these creditors are also unsecured creditors and should be included in Schedule F. Omitting these debts from a creditor's list is a frequent error, but one that can affect the debtor's discharge.[10]

The middle column should be completed to identify the year in which the debts were incurred or became past due. A one-word description such as "goods" or "services" will normally be sufficient to identify the consideration. This information has not been included in the fact memo for this example. It would have to be obtained before these Schedules can be completed.

Note also the identification of all debts as joint obligations of the Pittz's. Finally, regarding the Williams-Sonoma debt, note that it is disclosed as disputed.

10. 11 U.S.C. §523(a)(3). See chapter 13 supra.

SCHEDULE G - EXECUTORY CONTRACTS AND UNEXPIRED LEASES

Describe all executory contracts of any nature and all unexpired leases of real or personal property. Include any timeshare interests.

State nature of debtor's interest in contract, i.e., "Purchaser," "Agent," etc. State whether debtor is the lessor or lessee of a lease.

Provide the names and complete mailing addresses of all other parties to each lease or contract described.

NOTE: A party listed on this schedule will not receive notice of the filing of this case unless the party is also scheduled in the appropriate schedule of creditors.

☐ Check this box if debtor has no executory contracts or unexpired leases.

NAME AND MAILING ADDRESS, INCLUDING ZIP CODE OF OTHER PARTIES TO LEASE OR CONTRACT	DESCRIPTION OF CONTRACT OR LEASE AND NATURE OF DEBTOR'S INTEREST. STATE WHETHER LEASE IS FOR NONRESIDENTIAL REAL PROPERTY. STATE CONTRACT NUMBER OF ANY GOVERNMENT CONTRACT
MR. KATCHUP, LANDLORD	MONTH TO MONTH LEASE FOR RESIDENTIAL REAL PROPERTY LOCATED AT 1066 CONQU

Description:

Any executory contract or unexpired lease is disclosed in Schedule G. Be specific enough in describing the asset so as to help enable the trustee to determine the effect of the contract or lease as an asset or liability of the estate.[11] Also note that the nondebtor party to the contract or lease is also a creditor who needs to be scheduled appropriately on Schedules D, E, or F supra.

SCHEDULE H - CODEBTORS

Provide the information requested concerning any person or entity, other than a spouse in a joint case, that is also liable on any debts listed by debtor in the schedules of creditors. Include all guarantors and co-signers. In community property states, a married debtor not filing a joint case should report the name and address of the nondebtor spouse on this schedule. Include all names used by the nondebtor spouse during the six years immediately preceding the commencement of this case.

☐ Check this box if debtor has no codebtors.

NAME AND ADDRESS OF CODEBTOR	NAME AND ADDRESS OF CREDITOR
MISSY PITTZ	UNIVERSITY OF RELATIVITY

Description:

The existence of any codebtor of any debt is described in Schedule H. Note also that in Schedule F, supra, unsecured claims, the column denoting the existence of a codebtor has been checked.

11. See chapter 19 supra.

SCHEDULE I - CURRENT INCOME OF INDIVIDUAL DEBTOR(S)

The column labeled "Spouse" must be completed in all cases filed by joint debtors and by a married debtor in a chapter 12 or 13 case whether or not a joint petition is filed, unless the spouses are separated and a joint petition is not filed.

Debtor's Marital Status:	DEPENDENTS OF DEBTOR AND SPOUSE	
	RELATIONSHIP	AGE
Married	SON	15
	SON	15
	DAUGHTER	19

Employment:	DEBTOR	SPOUSE
Occupation	SALESMAN	ASSISTANT MANAGER
Name of Employer	HECKNO-TECHNO, INC.	TEA JAMBOREE
How long employed	2 YEARS	1 YEAR
Address of Employer	134 PU-CPU BLVD.	6996 KARMA STREET
	GATESVILLE CA	CAMMAMILE CA

Income: (Estimate of average monthly income)	DEBTOR	SPOUSE
Current monthly gross wages, salary, and commissions (pro rate if not paid monthly.)	$ 2,500.00	$ 1,000.00
Estimated monthly overtime	$ 0.00	$ 0.00
SUBTOTAL	$ 2,500.00	$ 1,000.00
LESS PAYROLL DEDUCTIONS		
a. Payroll taxes and social security	$ 0.00	$ 0.00
b. Insurance	$ 0.00	$ 0.00
c. Union Dues	$ 0.00	$ 0.00
d. Other (Specify:)	$ 0.00	$ 0.00
SUBTOTAL OF PAYROLL DEDUCTIONS	$ 0.00	$ 0.00
TOTAL NET MONTHLY TAKE HOME PAY	$ 2,500.00	$ 1,000.00
Regular income from operation of business or profession or farm (attach detailed statement)	$ 0.00	$ 0.00
Income from real property	$ 0.00	$ 0.00
Interest and dividends	$ 0.00	$ 0.00
Alimony, maintenance or support payments payable to the debtor for the debtor's use or that of dependents listed above.	$ 0.00	$ 0.00
Social security or other government assistance (Specify)	$ 0.00	$ 0.00
Pension or retirement income	$ 0.00	$ 0.00
Other monthly income (Specify)	$ 0.00	$ 0.00
	$ 0.00	$ 0.00
TOTAL MONTHLY INCOME	$ 2,500.00	$ 1,000.00

TOTAL COMBINED MONTHLY INCOME $ 3,500.00

Description:

Schedule I discloses the existence and number of the debtors' dependents and the debtors' monthly income. Only the facts given in the memo are shown in the illustration. Reference to form 4.2 on the forms disk will reveal that information regarding any deductions from the Pittz's gross pay, such as for taxes, will also need to be obtained and disclosed. The information regarding dependents will aid the creditors and trustee in determining the reasonableness of the expenses disclosed in Schedule J infra.

SCHEDULE J - CURRENT EXPENDITURES OF INDIVIDUAL DEBTORS

Complete this schedule by estimating the average monthly expenses of the debtor and the debtor's family. Pro rate any payments made bi-weekly, quarterly, semi-annually, or annually to show monthly rate.

☐ Check this box if a joint petition is filed and debtor's spouse maintains a separate household. Complete a separate schedule of expenditures labeled "Spouse."

Rent or home mortgage payment (include lot rented for mobile home)	$ 800.00
Are real estate taxes included? Yes ____ No ✓	
Is property insurance included? Yes ____ No ✓	
Utilities Electricity and heating fuel	$ 75.00
Water and sewer	$ 0.00
Telephone	$ 50.00
Other ____	$ 0.00
Home maintenance (Repairs and upkeep)	$ 0.00
Food	$ 600.00
Clothing	$ 100.00
Laundry and dry cleaning	$ 30.00
Medical and dental expenses	$ 0.00
Transportation (not including car payments)	$ 200.00
Recreation, clubs and entertainment, newspapers, magazines, etc.	$ 200.00
Charitable contributions	$ 0.00
Insurance (not deducted from wages or included in home mortgage payments)	
Homeowner's or renter's	$ 20.00
Life	$ 0.00
Health	$ 200.00
Auto	$ 150.00
Other ____	$ 0.00
Taxes (not deducted from wages or included in home mortgage payments)	
(Specify) ____	$ 0.00
Installment payments (In chapter 12 and 13 cases, do not list payments to be included in the plan)	
Auto	$ 350.00
Other ____	$ 0.00
Other ____	$ 0.00
Alimony, maintenance, and support paid to others	$ 0.00
Payments for support of additional dependents not living at your home	$ 0.00
Regular expenses from operation of business, profession, or farm (attach detailed statement)	$ 0.00
Other INTERNET FEES	$ 15.00
TOTAL MONTHLY EXPENSES (Report also on Summary of Schedules)	$ 2,790.00

(FOR CHAPTER 12 AND 13 DEBTORS ONLY)
Provide the information requested below, including whether plan payments are to be made bi-weekly, monthly, annually, or at some other regular interval.

A. Total projected monthly income	$ N.A.
B. Total projected monthly expenses	$ N.A.
C. Excess income (A minus B)	$ N.A.
D. Total amount to be paid into plan each N.A. (interval)	$ N.A.

Description:

The debtors' typical monthly expenses are disclosed in this Schedule. As in the other Schedules illustrated, only the data contained in the fact memo has been shown. Form 4.2 on the forms disk discloses additional categories. As with all other Schedules, it is helpful to enter zero for those categories in which the debtor incurs no monthly expense. In an individual Chapter 7, the information in Schedules I and J will help permit the trustee to determine whether or not an abuse of Chapter 7 exists pursuant to needs based bankruptcy (see chapter 5, supra).[12] Remember, the forms shown do not reflect the changes in them that will be required to comply with needs based bankruptcy. In a Chapter 13, the data will help determine the feasibility of a Chapter 13 plan.[13]

D. STATEMENT OF FINANCIAL AFFAIRS

1. Income from employment or operation of business

None ☐

State the gross amount of income the debtor has received from employment, trade, or profession, or from operation of the debtor's business from the beginning of this calendar year to the date this case was commenced. State also the gross amounts received during the two years immediately preceding this calendar year. (A debtor that maintains, or has maintained, financial records on the basis of a fiscal rather than a calendar year may report fiscal year income. Identify the beginning and ending dates of the debtor's fiscal year) If a joint petition is filed, state income for each spouse separately. (Married debtors filing under chapter 12 or chapter 13 must state income of both spouses whether or not a joint petition is filed, unless the spouses are separated and a joint petition is not filed.)

	AMOUNT	SOURCE (if more than one)
2003(H)	$30,000.00	2004 WAGES FROM HECKNO-TECHNO, INC.
2002(H)	$30,000.00	2003 WAGES FROM HECKNO-TECHNO, INC.
2003(W)	$12,000.00	2003-4 WAGES FROM TEA - JAMBOREE
2002(W)	NOMINAL	TOP 'O THE MORNIN' IRISH TEA CO.
2002(W)	UNKNOWN	2003 WAGES FROM TOP 'O THE MORNIN' IRISH TEA CO.

Description:

This item discloses the debtors' income for each of the past two years from employment or trade. "Preceding years" is commonly understood to mean tax years. For instance, in 2004, income for calendar years 2003 and 2002 would be described.

---

12. See chapters 5 and 7, supra. See also forms 5.2-5.7 in the Forms Disk.
13. See chapter 23 supra.

2. Income other than from employment or operation of business

None ☒ State the amount of income received by the debtor other than from employment, trade, profession, or operation of the debtor's business during the two years immediately preceding the commencement of this case. Give particulars. If a joint petition is filed, state income for each spouse separately. (Married debtors filing under chapter 12 or chapter 13 must state income for each spouse whether or not a joint petition is filed, unless the spouses are separated and a joint petition is not filed.)

AMOUNT	SOURCE

Description:

Income earned from sources other than employment should be disclosed here. Interest or dividend income and spousal or child support would be disclosed here.

---

3. Payments to Creditors

None ☒ a. List all payments on loans, installment purchases of goods or services, and other debts, aggregating more than $600 to any creditor, made within 90 days immediately preceding the commencement of this case. (Married debtors filing under chapter 12 or chapter 13 must include payments by either or both spouses whether or not a joint petition is filed, unless the spouses are separated and a joint petition is not filed.)

NAME AND ADDRESS OF CREDITOR	DATES OF PAYMENTS	AMOUNT PAID	AMOUNT STILL OWING

None ☒ b. List all payments made within one year immediately preceding the commencement of this case to or for the benefit of creditors, who are or were insiders. (Married debtors filing under chapter 12 or chapter 13 must include payments by either or both spouses whether or not a joint petition is filed, unless the spouses are separated and a joint petition is not filed.)

NAME AND ADDRESS OF CREDITOR AND RELATIONSHIP TO DEBTOR	DATES OF PAYMENTS	AMOUNT PAID	AMOUNT STILL OWING

Description:

This requires debtors to disclose loan repayments made during the 90 days prior to filing or, in the case of insiders, payments made during the past year. This inquiry reveals the potential existence of preferences or sometimes a fraudulent transfer. Recall that, in a consumer proceeding, up to $600 of preferences are essentially permitted, which is why the question is concerned with payments greater than $600. In the example there are no such transfers.[14] Hence, "None" has been checked. Remember, every question should be answered, even when the answer is "None."

---

14. See chapters 16 and 17 supra.

4. Suits and administrative proceedings, executions, garnishments and attachments

None ☐ a. List all suits and administrative proceedings to which the debtor is or was a party within one year immediately preceding the filing of this bankruptcy case. (Married debtors filing under chapter 12 or chapter 13 must include information concerning either or both spouses whether or not a joint petition is filed, unless the spouses are separated and a joint petition is not filed.)

CAPTION OF SUIT AND CASE NUMBER	NATURE OF PROCEEDING	COURT OR AGENCY AND LOCATION	STATUS OR DISPOSITION
DR. LAVENTHOL V. PITTZ 03-0002	DEBT COLLECTION		JUDGEMENT
SYMPHONIC SOUNDS V. PITTZ	DEBT COLLECTION		JUDGEMENT
WILLIAMS - SONOMA V. PITTZ	DEBT COLLECTION		PENDING

None ☒ b. Describe all property that has been attached, garnished or seized under any legal or equitable process within one year immediately preceding the commencement of this case. (Married debtors filing under chapter 12 or chapter 13 must include information concerning property of either or both spouses whether or not a joint petition is filed, unless the spouses are separated and a joint petition is not filed.)

NAME AND ADDRESS OF PERSON FOR WHOSE BENEFIT PROPERTY WAS SEIZED	DATE OF SEIZURE	DESCRIPTION AND VALUE OF PROPERTY

Description:

Item 4 requires disclosure of all legal actions involving the debtors that have occurred during the preceding year. Item 4a asks the debtor to disclose all lawsuits pending within one year prior to the bankruptcy filing in which the debtor is a party. In the example, all suits are included in 4a. When answering this inquiry, disclose the case number and the court where the litigation is or was pending. To this extent, the example here is incomplete.

Note that this question does not ask merely for those cases in which a debtor may be the defendant. All lawsuits that are pending in which the debtor is a *party* when a bankruptcy petition is filed must be disclosed. If the debtor is or has been a plaintiff in a lawsuit, this must also be included in the response. The suit will be an asset of the estate unless it can be exempted.[15]

Also remember that a plaintiff in any lawsuit pending against the debtor is also a creditor of the debtor. Often, lawsuits pending against a debtor will be described in the Statement of Affairs but the same information will not appear on the list of creditors included in the Schedules. Remember, when

15. See chapter 14 supra.

a creditor is suing a debtor, the creditor must be listed on the Schedules if the debtor is to successfully seek and obtain a discharge of the obligation sued upon.[16]

Item 4b asks for the disclosure of any property that has been seized by legal process within the four months prior to the bankruptcy filing. In this example there is no such activity. If, however, a judgment creditor has a wage garnishment or some other type of judgment execution outstanding on a debtor, this action would be described here.

---

5. Repossessions, foreclosures and returns

None ☒ List all property that has been repossessed by a creditor, sold at a foreclosure sale, transferred through a deed in lieu of foreclosure or returned to the seller, within one year immediately preceding the commencement of this case. (Married debtors filing under chapter 12 or chapter 13 must include information concerning property of either or both spouses whether or not a joint petition is filed, unless the spouses are separated and a joint petition is not filed.)

NAME AND ADDRESS OF CREDITOR OR SELLER	DATE OF REPOSESSION, FORECLOSURE SALE, TRANSFER OR RETURN	DESCRIPTION AND VALUE OF PROPERTY

Description:

Any voluntary or involuntary return of or repossession of secured collateral should be identified here. These transactions could be preferential or fraudulent.[17]

---

16. 11 U.S.C. §523(a)(3). See chapter 13 supra.
17. See chapters 16 and 17 supra.

6. Assignments and Receiverships

None ☒ a. Describe any assignment of property for the benefit of creditors made within 120 days immediately preceding the commencement of this case. (Married debtors filing under chapter 12 or chapter 13 must include any assignment by either or both spouses whether or not a joint petition is filed, unless the spouses are separated and a joint petition is not filed.)

NAME AND ADDRESS OF ASSIGNEE	DATE OF ASSIGNMENT	TERMS OF ASSIGNMENT OR SETTLEMENT

None ☒ b. List all property which has been in the hands of a custodian, receiver, or court-appointed official within one year immediately preceding the commencement of this case. (Married debtors filing under chapter 12 or chapter 13 must include information concerning property of either or both spouses whether or not a joint petition is filed, unless the spouses are separated and a joint petition is not filed.)

NAME AND ADDRESS OF CUSTODIAN	NAME AND LOCATION OF COURT CASE TITLE & NUMBER	DATE OF ORDER	DESCRIPTION AND VALUE OF PROPERTY

Description:

Item 6a requires a debtor to identify the existence of any third-party custodian of estate property so the estate assets may be properly turned over to the trustee or debtor-in-possession.[18] Item 6b requires the same disclosure if the debtor has effectuated an assignment for the benefit of creditors.[19]

18. See chapter 14 supra.
19. See chapter 3 supra.

7. Gifts

None ☒ List all gifts or charitable contributions made within one year immediately preceding the commencement of this case, except ordinary and usual gifts to family members aggregating less than $200 in value per individual family member and charitable contributions aggregating less than $100 per recipient. (Married debtors filing under chapter 12 or chapter 13 must include gifts or contributions by either or both spouses whether or not a joint petition is filed, unless the spouses are separated and a joint petition is not filed.)

NAME AND ADDRESS OF PERSON OR ORGANIZATION	RELATIONSHIP TO DEBTOR, IF ANY	DATE OF GIFT	DESCRIPTION AND VALUE OF GIFT

Description:

This item discloses evidence that may lead to the discovery of fraudulent transfers made by the giving of extraordinary gifts.[20] As noted, any extraordinary gifts or contributions should be disclosed. In the fact memo there do not appear to be any, but because the information is not specifically included in the memo, this item would have to be double-checked before the document is filed.

8. Losses

None ☒ List all losses from fire, theft, other casualty or gambling within one year immediately preceding the commencement of this case or since the commencement of this case. (Married debtors filing under chapter 12 or chapter 13 must include losses by either or both spouses whether or not a joint petition is filed, unless the spouses are separated and a joint petition is not filed.)

DESCRIPTION AND VALUE OF PROPERTY	DESCRIPTION OF CIRCUMSTANCES, AND, IF LOSS WAS COVERED IN WHOLE OR IN PART BY INSURANCE, GIVE PARTICULARS	DATE OF LOSS

Description:

This item requires disclosure of any losses sustained by the debtors from fire, theft, or gambling during the year preceding the petition's filing. The reason for this disclosure is first to ascertain the existence of "calamity" losses, which might be a cause of the bankruptcy. Second, a fire or theft loss may involve an insurance claim. If unpaid when the bankruptcy proceeding is filed, the insurance claim may be an asset of the estate.[21] In the example, this data has not been provided. It should be ascertained and completed before filing. Every item must have a completed response. "Unknown" is not a responsive answer to an inquiry that calls for a "yes" or "no" answer. If there is a "yes" response, provide all pertinent data as shown in the responses to the other items.

20. See chapter 17 supra.
21. See chapter 14 supra.

9. Payments related to debt counseling or bankruptcy

None ☐ List all payments made or property transferred by or on behalf of the debtor to any persons, including attorneys, for consultation concerning debt consolidation, relief under the bankruptcy law or preparation of a petition in bankruptcy within one year immediately preceding the commencement of this case.

NAME AND ADDRESS OF PAYEE	DATE OF PAYMENT, NAME OF PAYOR IF OTHER THAN DEBTOR	AMOUNT OF MONEY OR DESCRIPTION AND VALUE OF PROPERTY
YOUR FIRM		$1,000.00

Description:

Item 9 requires disclosure of payments to attorneys over the past year for legal services pertaining to debt relief. The purpose of these disclosures is to help ensure that the attorneys working on the case do not receive excessive compensation or are not themselves the transferee of a fraudulent transfer.[22] The fee paid in connection with the bankruptcy ought to be disclosed here.

This question is a significant departure from question 15 of the superseded form, which required disclosure of *all* attorneys' fees paid and all attorneys consulted in reference to any and all matters in the year prior to the filing.

---

22. See chapters 7 and 17 supra.

10. Other transfers

None ☐ List all other property, other than property transferred in the ordinary course of the business or financial affairs of the debtor, transferred either absolutely or as security within one year immediately preceding the commencement of this case. (Married debtors filing under chapter 12 or chapter 13 must include transfers by either or both spouses whether or not a joint petition is filed, unless the spouses are separated and a joint petition is not filed.)

NAME AND ADDRESS OF TRANSFEREE, RELATIONSHIP TO DEBTOR	DATE	DESCRIBE PROPERTY TRANSFERRED AND VALUE RECEIVED
OZZIE AND HARRIET ODDBORN Relationship: NONE	PAST 6 MONTHS	VACANT LOT SANTA CRUZ $10,000.00

Description:

Any transfer of property must be disclosed here unless disclosed elsewhere in the form. This evidence may lead to the discovery of fraudulent transfers or preferences made by the granting of a security interest or other transfer of property.[23] All pertinent details, including purpose, identity of transferee, value, and the date of transfer should be concisely disclosed as shown in the example. A practitioner should obtain a copy of any closing statement so it may be made promptly available to a trustee upon the trustee's request.

11. Closed financial accounts

None ☒ List all financial accounts and instruments held in the name of the debtor or for the benefit of the debtor which were closed, sold, or otherwise transferred within one year immediately preceding the commencement of this case. Include checking, savings, or other financial accounts, certificates of deposit, or other instruments; shares and share accounts held in banks, credit unions, pension funds, cooperatives, associations, brokerage houses and other financial institutions. (Married debtors filing under chapter 12 or chapter 13 must include information concerning accounts or instruments held by either or both spouses whether or not a joint petition is filed, unless the spouses are separated and a joint petition is not filed.)

NAME AND ADDRESS OF INSTITUTION	TYPE OF ACCOUNT, LAST FOUR DIGITS OF ACCOUNT NUMBER, AND AMOUNT OF FINAL BALANCE	AMOUNT AND DATE OF SALE OR CLOSING

Description:

This item requires disclosure of all bank accounts closed by the debtor in the year prior to the filing. This question represents a significant departure from older forms, which required disclosure of information for open accounts as well. Data concerning open accounts will now be disclosed in Schedule B. For any account for which disclosure must be made, itemize

23. See chapters 16 and 17 supra.

the name of the bank, its address, the account number, the type of account (such as checking or savings), and identify the signatories.

---

12. Safe deposit boxes

None ☒ List each safe deposit or other box or depository in which the debtor has or had securities, cash, or other valuables within one year immediately preceding the commencement of this case. (Married debtors filing under chapter 12 or chapter 13 must include boxes or depositories of either or both spouses whether or not a joint petition is filed, unless the spouses are separated and a joint petition is not filed.)

NAME AND ADDRESS OF BANK OR OTHER DEPOSITORY	NAMES AND ADDRESSES OF THOSE WITH ACCESS TO BOX OR DEPOSITORY	DESCRIPTION OF CONTENTS	DATE OF TRANSFER OR SURRENDER, IF ANY

Description:

If the debtors have a safe-deposit box, disclose the requested data. Otherwise, check the box "None."

---

13. Setoffs

None ☒ List all setoffs made by any creditor, including a bank, against a debt or deposit of the debtor within 90 days preceding the commencement of this case. (Married debtors filing under chapter 12 or chapter 13 must include information concerning either or both spouses whether or not a joint petition is filed, unless the spouses are separated and a joint petition is not filed.)

NAME AND ADDRESS OF CREDITOR	DATE OF SETOFF	AMOUNT OF SETOFF

Description:

This item requires disclosure of setoffs made during the year preceding the bankruptcy. A setoff might constitute a preference.[24]

---

24. See chapters 16 and 20 supra.

14. Property held for another person

None ☒ List all property owned by another person that the debtor holds or controls.

NAME AND ADDRESS OF OWNER	DESCRIPTION AND VALUE OF PROPERTY	LOCATION OF PROPERTY

Description:

This item simply requests disclosure of any assets held by the debtor on behalf of a third party. In this example there is no such activity.

15. Prior address of debtor

None ☐ If the debtor has moved within the two years immediately preceding the commencement of this case, list all premises which the debtor occupied during that period and vacated prior to the commencement of this case. If a joint petition is filed, report also any separate address of either spouse.

ADDRESS	NAME USED	DATES OF OCCUPANCY
1066 CONQUEROR ROAD HENDRIX CA	BRAD AND JENN PITTZ	DECEMBER 2003 - PRESENT
55 FER SURE TERRACE BERKELY CA	BRAD AND JENN PITTZ	JUNE 2002- DECEMBER 2003
45 COLDFISH LANE FROSTY FALLS MN	BRAD AND JENN PITTZ	DECEMBER 2001- JUNE 2002

Description:

Item 15 requires the debtor to list all residence addresses for the two years prior to the proceeding's filing. Any earlier addresses are irrelevant. It is always easiest to read the information by listing the most current residence first and proceeding backwards chronologically. It is not usually required to recall exact addresses. An approximate address will generally suffice if the exact information cannot be recalled. Many debtors may not be able to recall all of their exact street addresses. Finally, if joint debtors have different addresses for portions of the period, the response should distinguish which debtor lived at which address and for what period.

16. Spouses and Former Spouses

None

☒ If the debtor resides or resided in a community property state, commonwealth, or territory (including Alaska, Arizona, California, Idaho, Louisiana, Nevada, New Mexico, Puerto Rico, Texas, Washington, or Wisconsin) within the six-year period immediately preceding the commencement of the case, identify the name of the debtor's spouse and of any former spouse who resides or resided with the debtor in the community property state.

NAME

Description:

Item 16 requires the debtor to disclose the identity of any existing or former spouse if the debtor has lived in a community property jurisdiction in the 6 years preceding filing of the bankruptcy. The affected states are delineated on the form. The reason for this disclosure is that a present or former spouse in a community property jurisdiction could have a joint interest in estate property affecting the trustee's rights. See chapters 15 and 18 supra.

17. Environmental Sites

For the purpose of this question, the following definitions apply:

"Environmental Law" means any federal, state, or local statute or regulation regulating pollution, contamination, releases of hazardous or toxic substances, wastes or material into the air, land, soil, surface water, groundwater, or other medium, including, but not limited to, statutes or regulations regulating the cleanup of these substances, wastes, or material.

"Site" means any location, facility, or property as defined under any Environmental Law, whether or not presently or formerly owned or operated by the debtor, including, but not limited to, disposal sites.

"Hazardous Material" means anything defined as a hazardous waste, hazardous substance, toxic substance, hazardous material, pollutant, or contaminant or similar term under an Environmental Law

None ☒ a. List the name and address of every site for which the debtor has received notice in writing by a governmental unit that it may be liable or potentially liable under or in violation of an Environmental Law. Indicate the governmental unit, the date of the notice, and, if known, the Environmental Law:

SITE NAME AND ADDRESS	NAME AND ADDRESS OF GOVERNMENTAL UNIT	DATE OF NOTICE	ENVIRONMENTAL LAW

b. List the name and address of every site for which the debtor provided notice to a governmental unit of a release of Hazardous Material. Indicate the governmental unit to which the notice was sent and the date of the notice.

None ☒

SITE NAME AND ADDRESS	NAME AND ADDRESS OF GOVERNMENTAL UNIT	DATE OF NOTICE	ENVIRONMENTAL LAW

c. List all judicial or administrative proceedings, including settlements or orders, under any Environmental Law with respect to which the debtor is or was a party. Indicate the name and address of the governmental unit that is or was a party to the proceeding, and the docket number.

None ☒

NAME AND ADDRESS OF GOVERNMENTAL UNIT	DOCKET NUMBER	STATUS OR DISPOSITION

Description:

This item asks the debtor to disclose any environmental issues that may affect estate property. This question is required in all cases. The purpose of this question is to bring any environmental issues to the specific attention of the trustee and creditors.

18. Nature, location and name of business

None ☐ a. If the debtor is an individual, list the names, addresses, taxpayer identification numbers, nature of the businesses, and beginning and ending dates of all businesses in which the debtor was an officer, director, partner, or managing executive of a corporation, partnership, sole proprietorship, or was a self-employed professional within the six years immediately preceding the commencement of this case, or in which the debtor owned 5 percent or more of the voting or equity securities within the six years immediately preceding the commencement of this case.

If the debtor is a partnership, list the names, addresses, taxpayer identification numbers, nature of the businesses, and beginning and ending dates of all businesses in which the debtor was a partner or owned 5 percent or more of the voting or equity securities, within the six years immediately preceding the commencement of this case.

If the debtor is a corporation, list the names, addresses, taxpayer identification numbers, nature of the businesses, and beginning and ending dates of all businesses in which the debtor was a partner or owned 5 percent or more of the voting or equity securities within the six years immediately preceding the commencement of this case.

NAME	TAXPAYER I.D. NO. (EIN)	ADDRESS	NATURE OF BUSINESS	BEGINNING AND ENDING DATES
TOP 'O THE MORNIN' IRISH TEA CO.		CLOSED	SALES PARTNERSHIP WITH NANCY COOK	2003 - 2004

b. Identify any business listed in response to subdivision a., above, that is "single asset real estate" as defined in 11 U.S.C. § 101.

None ☒

NAME	ADDRESS

Description:

This item asks a debtor to identify any business ventures in which the debtor has been involved in the two years prior to filing. Any affirmative response should include a brief description that will explain to the trustee and creditors all pertinent facts. The most pertinent facts are the name of the business, its length of operation, how its assets were disposed of (closure, sale, or otherwise), and whether the debtor's interest retains any value. Sometimes a debtor may have been involved in more than one business over the preceding two years. Each should be described in this manner. Thoroughness here will save time at the creditors meeting.[25] The response in the example, although only two sentences in length, provides the most critical data that the trustee and creditors initially need to know. Part "b" of the question will not apply in a consumer Chapter 7 case.

25. See chapters 7 and 11 supra.

19. Books, record and financial statements

None ☒ a. List all bookkeepers and accountants who within the six years immediately preceding the filing of this bankruptcy case kept or supervised the keeping of books of account and records of the debtor.

NAME AND ADDRESS DATES SERVICES RENDERED

None ☒ b. List all firms or individuals who within the two years immediately preceding the filing of this bankruptcy case have audited the books of account and records, or prepared a financial statement of the debtor.

NAME ADDRESS DATES SERVICES RENDERED

None ☐ c. List all firms or individuals who at the time of the commencement of this case were in possession of the books of account and records of the debtor. If any of the books of account and records are not available, explain.

NAME	ADDRESS
BRAD AND JENN PITTZ	1066 CONQUEROR ROAD HENDRIX PA

None ☒ d. List all financial institutions, creditors and other parties, including mercantile and trade agencies, to whom a financial statement was issued within the two years immediately preceding the commencement of this case by the debtor.

NAME AND ADDRESS DATE ISSUED

Description:

Recall that under Section 727, a trustee may object to a debtor's discharge for failure to keep books and records commensurate with the debtor's affairs.[26] Item 17 discloses whether the possibility of such an objection may exist in the proceeding. Further, a trustee may request to examine any such records to investigate the existence of assets, including any avoidable transactions.[27]

Never leave the response to any question unanswered or blank. When this happens, the trustee will invariably ask the same question at the meeting of creditors. This can be avoided by properly responding in the first place.

Items 19 through 25 are not used unless the debtor has been engaged in business. In the example, item 21 of the form will disclose the identity of partner Nancy Cook. Items 22 and 23, by implication only, will suggest that the business has been terminated. See form 4.3 on the forms disk.

26. See chapter 13 supra.
27. See chapters 10 and 15 supra.

Summary

It is important in learning the bankruptcy system to know how to effectively prepare and read the most important documents filed at the inception of any bankruptcy proceeding, the Statement of Financial Affairs and Schedules of Assets and Liabilities. These documents are commonly known as the Statements and Schedules. Effective preparation of these documents by the paralegal will expedite an estate's administration. Knowing how to read these documents effectively will permit a creditor's representative to ascertain the potential for a dividend to the creditor or a potential objection to the debtor's discharge.

In effectively preparing the Statements and Schedules, all questions should be answered even when the answer is a simple "no" or "none." All information required to be provided should be provided in as concise a form as possible. It is good practice to identify creditors' account numbers if applicable. Although this bit of information is not required, it will greatly ease the administration of an estate.

In effectively reading the Statements and Schedules, the paralegal should focus on identifying the existence and value of nonexempt assets to determine the potential for unsecured creditors to receive a dividend.

To ensure compliance with the requirements of BAPA, the paralegal will also want to make sure that there is sufficient detail in the file to corroborate the debtor's current monthly income, debts, and asset. Copies of the debtor's most recent pay stubs, for example, should be in the file. A copy of a bill from each creditor, including payoff amounts to secured creditors, and/or a copy of a current credit report should be obtained from the debtor. Copies of all relevant tax returns that a trustee may request should also be obtained. As practice under the 2005 legislation evolves, these requirements may be added to.

DISCUSSION QUESTIONS

1. What purposes do the Statements and Schedules serve?
2. What are the concerns of a debtor in effective preparation of the Statements and Schedules?
3. What are the concerns of a trustee or creditor in effective review of the Statements and Schedules?

30

Researching Bankruptcy Issues

A. TRADITIONAL METHODS

It is impossible for any member of the legal profession to know all the law: There is simply too much law to know. As a result, the ability to conduct efficient, accurate, and speedy research is a fundamental skill for anyone involved in the legal profession. Knowing where to look for the answer to a question is a paramount concern. No study of the bankruptcy system can be complete without providing a useful method for researching bankruptcy issues. Fortunately, because the Bankruptcy Code is designed to be a selfcontained system, an effective methodology for approaching the research of a bankruptcy issue is relatively easy to formulate. The sources described below, used in the order of their description, should produce an answer to even the most complex issue at a minimum of time and effort.

The primary source for answering all bankruptcy questions is the Bankruptcy Code.[1] Most basic bankruptcy questions can be answered correctly simply by finding the right Code section.

The Code is well indexed, and by following the systems approach of this text any practitioner should generally have an easy time establishing a reference point in the Code to commence researching an issue.

It is also important to note a critical difference in statutory research versus research of other sources. Each word of a statute, and often each punctuation mark, has meaning and significance. Each word must be understood to comprehend the full meaning of any Code provision. Careful reading is thus the most useful tool in conducting effective research of this sort. At the end of each Code section there is a text normally entitled

1. U.S.C., Title 11.

"Historical and Revision Notes." The Historical and Revision Notes contain a capsule description of the legislative history of a particular Code section, including the section's derivation from any predecessor section in the Bankruptcy Act. Leading court decisions that interpreted any predecessor Bankruptcy Act section are often referred to in these notes. The analysis will discuss the rationale of any cases cited and attempt to indicate if the Code is intended to follow or modify the prior law. The analysis is helpful in interpreting the meaning of a particular provision. The Historical and Revision Notes are a first valuable secondary source of finding answers to bankruptcy questions. Because these notes are included in many published editions of the Bankruptcy Code, one does not need a second volume to locate them.

The Bankruptcy Code defines the collective rules regulating the collection and distribution of assets to creditors in a bankruptcy proceeding. The Code directs what may or may not be done in a bankruptcy proceeding. However, the Code often does not direct how to implement or use a Code provision within the bankruptcy system. To direct the implementation of a Code provision in the bankruptcy system, the Administrator of the United States Courts, in conjunction with the United States Supreme Court, has formulated the "Rules of Practice and Procedure in Bankruptcy," commonly known as the Federal Rules of Bankruptcy Procedure. The Federal Rules of Bankruptcy Procedure direct the method of doing things in a bankruptcy proceeding: What information is required in a form? What should the form look like? How is a motion filed and when? How is a creditor claim filed? And so forth. Many basic questions of actual practice that are not contained in the Code are answered by the Federal Rules of Bankruptcy Procedure. The rules should never be overlooked when seeking the answer to a bankruptcy question, particularly a "how to" question.[2]

Appended to the Federal Rules of Bankruptcy Procedure is a group of forms called "Official and Procedural Bankruptcy Forms." The Official Forms provide guidance as to the contents and appearance of a particular document.

In addition to the Federal Rules of Bankruptcy Procedure, each Bankruptcy Court has the power to formulate its own local rules as long as they are not inconsistent with the Code or Bankruptcy Rules. Many Bankruptcy Courts have devised their own local rules; some Bankruptcy Courts have not. Local rules vary from district to district and can sometimes be the source of answering a practice or procedure question. In addition to local Bankruptcy Court rules, each federal District Court has its own local rules. These also may sometimes help in answering a procedural question. The guidelines of any applicable United States Trustee office will also prove helpful.[3]

2. 28 U.S.C. §2075. Federal Rules of Bankruptcy Procedure.
3. See chapter 10 supra.

The Bankruptcy Courts are a part of the federal court system. The Federal Rules of Civil Procedure and the Federal Rules of Evidence apply in bankruptcy proceedings.

There are several reporter systems that publish only bankruptcy cases. Cases decided by Bankruptcy Courts, district courts, courts of appeal, and the Supreme Court that relate solely to bankruptcy and bankruptcy-related issues are contained within these reporter systems. The largest reporter system is called the Bankruptcy Reporter and is published by West Publishing Company. Another reporter system is called Bankruptcy Court Decisions (BCD), which is published by CRR Publishing Company. Many of the cases reported in BCD are also included in the Bankruptcy Reporter, but sometimes a case will appear in one system and not in the other. It is acceptable to cite from either set of reporters when writing a brief for a Bankruptcy Court. Sometimes the BCD will release a case before it appears in the Bankruptcy Reporter and vice versa. Collier also publishes a reporter system called Collier Bankruptcy Cases. Many of these reporter systems have also been incorporated into computer research databases such as Lexis-Nexis or Westlaw.

In addition, there are simplified methods of conducting bankruptcy research into secondary treatises. The bankruptcy system has its own separate treatises. The most commonly used and cited treatise on bankruptcy is Collier on Bankruptcy.[4] Collier's is a seven-volume work, well organized so that a chapter number in Collier's corresponds to the same numbered Bankruptcy Code section. Thus, Chapter 521 in Collier's corresponds precisely to Section 521 of the Bankruptcy Code. If you want to find the answer to an issue involving exemptions, which is Section 522 of the Bankruptcy Code, you simply look in Chapter 522 of Collier's. There are several other major treatises, but Collier's is cited in court opinions more frequently than any other major work.[5] The publishers of Collier's also publish a major set of practice forms and guides entitled the Collier Bankruptcy Practice Guide. The Guide contains detailed practice tools and sample pleading forms, among other things.

Often a bankruptcy issue will be determined in reliance upon existing nonbankruptcy state or federal law. In these situations, one will have to make use of traditional research sources and methods outside the bankruptcy system.

The above are the primary sources of researching a bankruptcy issue, starting with the Code and continuing to the reporter systems. With this relatively small nucleus of materials reviewed in the order described in the checklist accompanying this chapter, most bankruptcy questions can be answered effectively, efficiently, and rapidly.

---

4. Collier on Bankruptcy (15th ed. rev. 2003) (hereafter Collier's).
5. E.g., Cowans, Cowans Bankruptcy Law & Practice (1987 ed.).

B. THE INTERNET

The evolution of the Internet through the 1990s, and continuing into the present, has transformed accessibility to both legal and factual information to assist in conducting legal research or in investigating facts. The availability of online computer research facilities such as Westlaw or Lexis-Nexis make legal source materials more accessible but do not necessarily make the task of finding applicable case law any easier unless the researcher knows to search under an appropriate word, phrase, or statute.

To this extent, the above methodology can also be used in computer research. First input the precise Code section or Rule that is the subject of your inquiry. Then narrow your search by selecting an appropriate word or phrase in the universe of cases you have located by Code section. For example, assume that you need to research an issue of the effect of oral misrepresentations in dischargeability litigation (see chapter 13 supra). A word search combining the phrase "oral misrepresentation" and the word "dischargeability" appearing in the same paragraph will be likely to produce a myriad of potentially relevant cases.

Each of the two major computer research services (Lexis-Nexis or Westlaw) has its own unique advantages. Westlaw makes use of the West Key system that any person who has had a course in legal research will be familiar with. Lexis-Nexis permits the user to search by a specific period of time (such as last week) that effectively allows the user to review the most current decided cases on a given subject.

In addition to enhancing legal research, the Internet explosion adds an array of bankruptcy research access tools to the fingertips of any person with online access. Many professional bankruptcy organizations have their own Web sites, the most notable being that for the American Bankruptcy Institute (www.abiworld.org). This site will give you daily news and report important case and legislative developments. The Federal Judiciary Home Page (www.uscourts.gov) will allow you to access any Bankruptcy Court that has created its own Web site. You can find your local court and place it on your Favorites menu.

Federal Rule of Bankruptcy Procedure 9036 authorizes local rules to permit electronic transmission of notices and documents. Some Bankruptcy Courts already permit electronic filing of petitions, a practice that will become commonplace in the near future.

As of mid 2004, all bankruptcy courts are being gradually incorporated into what is known as the Electronic Case Filing (ECF) system. Under ECF, all pleadings are filed with the bankruptcy court online. All documents filed with a court that has adopted ECF are accessible to attorneys who enroll in the ECF system. Parties in interest may register to receive notices of all pleadings filed in a particular case, making service of process virtually instantaneous.

Use of the internet will be important to comply with the requirements of needs based bankruptcy or means testing (see chapter 5 supra) and other filing requirements imposed by the 2005 legislation. With respect to needs based bankruptcy, the internet is essential to remain current with the official state median family income and for the various IRS expense standards applied in computing the formula. Current links necessary for means testing compliance are located at www.usdoj.gov/ust. Additionally, as counsel's duty of reasonable investigation required by Section 707(b)(4) evolves, the internet provides rapid access to a debtor's current credit report and sites that provide valuation data for used vehicles (e.g. NADA.com, for example).

Chapter 30 Checklist

30.1 BANKRUPTCY RESEARCH CHECKLIST

- 30.1.1 Bankruptcy Code
- 30.1.2 Historical and Revision Notes
- 30.1.3 Federal Rules of Bankruptcy Procedure
- 30.1.4 Local Rules, Including United States Trustee Guidelines
- 30.1.5 Federal Rules of Civil Procedure, Federal Rules of Evidence
- 30.1.6 Bankruptcy Reporter Systems
- 30.1.7 Bankruptcy Treatises

DISCUSSION QUESTIONS

1. What are the basic resources to utilize in researching a bankruptcy issue?
2. Describe the role that computers can play in conducting bankruptcy research.

Appendix 1

Needs Based Bankruptcy

The 2005 BAPA legislation enacts into law the new concept of needs based bankruptcy or means testing (see chapter 5 supra). The essence of the concept is that if a debtor's **current monthly income** is greater than the **applicable state median income** for a household of the debtor's size, and if the debtor has disposable monthly income sufficient to repay at least 25% of general unsecured debt over a 60 month period with minimum monthly payments of $100 ($6,000), or if a debtor can pay $10,000 or more over 60 months without regard to the percentage repaid, then a Chapter 7 petition is presumed to be an abuse and is subject to dismissal unless the debtor can show special circumstances, or voluntarily converts the case to a Chapter 13. This determination is made according to a formula set forth in Section 707(b)(2) of the Code. The formula utilizes data extrinsic to the Bankruptcy Code, such as expense data used by the Internal Revenue Service in working out repayment plans for the payment of delinquent taxes and Census Bureau data on state median family income.

The purpose of this appendix is to provide a simple worksheet to aid in performing the needs based bankruptcy analysis for individual debtors and to provide as much of the extrinsic data as is possible to assist in performing the analysis. Various versions of official form 22, the means testing form, are on the Forms Disk. This worksheet may be helpful before the new forms become available. The data provided on national family median income and IRS Collection Standards have been obtained from their respective internet websites. For the IRS Collection Standards, the internet address is *www.irs.ustreas.gov*. As of mid-2005, on the IRS Home Page, hit Individuals. On the Individuals page, hit the entry for Collection Financial Standards. For state family median income data, hit *www.census.gov*. At the Census Bureau home page, hit People and then hit State Family Income. It is also highly likely that all or most bankruptcy courts will post the links to this data on their websites. Links may also be found at www.usdoj.gov\ust. The Forms Disk also contains links.

This worksheet is not an Official Form. It is presented to help the reader gain a basic understanding of how the needs based bankruptcy calculations are performed.

Needs Based Bankruptcy Worksheet

(11 U.S.C. §521(a)(1)(B)(ii); §707(b)(2))

1.	**Current monthly household income (11 U.S.C. §101(10A))**	
	Debtor (wages):	____________
	Debtor (non-wages):	____________
	Joint Debtor (wages):	____________
	Joint Debtor (non-wages):	____________
	Other:	____________
	Total:	____________
2.	**Deductions (11 U.S.C. §707(b)(2)(A))**	
	IRS Expense Allowances	____________
	Expenses and fees (10% of projected plan payment)	____________
	Private School Tuition	____________
	Secured debt payments (average over 60 months)	____________
	Priority Claims	____________
	Total:	____________
3.	**Total 1 minus Total 2**	____________

If 3 is $100 or more and will result in a dividend of at least 25% to unsecured creditor, or if the debtor can pay $10,000 or more over 60 months without regard to the percentage of dividend, then a presumption of abuse exists and the case is subject to dismissal or voluntary conversion to Chapter 13. If the Debtor's income is greater than the national median family income for a family of similar size, then any party in interest may bring a motion to dismiss for abuse of Chapter 7. If the debtor's family income is equal to or less than the state median family income for a family of similar size, then the motion may not be brought at all.

Comments

Income

Separate line items are included for wage and non-wage income because the trustee will require evidence of every income source, such as pay stubs for the 60 days preceding the filing (see chapter 4 supra and 11 U.S.C. §521(a)(1)(B)(iv)). Non-wage income includes unemployment compensation, pension or annuity income, payments of alimony or support. Other income includes income contributed from any other household member for payment of monthly household expenses (see 11 U.S.C. §101(10A) and chapter 6 supra). Social security benefits are excluded from the definition of current monthly income as are certain war crimes reparations.

The amounts scheduled are to be the average received from the income source for the six months prior to the filing of the petition. For example, if a debtor receives $1,000 for three months, divide the total by six, for an average of $500. See the examples at chapter 5G supra.

Deductions

Estimated administrative expenses and attorney fees are defined as 10% of all payments to be made under a Chapter 13 plan as set forth in 11 U.S.C. §707(b)(2)(A)(ii)(III). For example, in a minimum situation, requiring $100 per month for 60 months, $10 per month would be deducted under this line item.

Monthly expenses are calculated as per the Internal Revenue Service Collection Financial Standards for individuals. There are three separate lists provided for by these standards: National Standards for Allowable Living Expenses; Housing and Utilities Allowable Living Expenses which are broken down by County; and, Allowable Living Expenses for Transportation which are broken down by metropolitan areas. The statute (11 U.S.C. §707(b)(2)(A)(ii)) permits the deduction of actual expenses for the care and support of an elderly, chronically disabled or ill household or immediate family member.

Private school tuition of up to $1,500 per year per child under the age of 18 may be deducted. This amounts to a deduction of up to $125 per month per child.

Secured Debt payments is the debtor's average monthly contractually due secured debt payments for 60 months as per 11 U.S.C. §707(b)(2)(A)(iii). For example, a debtor has 36 months remaining on a secured car loan as of the filing date. The monthly payments are $300. The average of this amount for 60 months is $180 ($300 × 36 = $10,800/60 = $180).

Priority Claims are any debts entitled to priority pursuant to 11 U.S.C. §507(a) (see chapter 21, supra) and that are required to be paid in a Chapter 13 (see chapter 23, supra). The amounts to be paid are averaged over a 60-month period exactly as secured debt payments above.

Appendix 2

Noticed Motions and Ex Parte Applications

Common Ex Parte Applications

Application	*Code Section or FRBP*
Payments to trustees	§§1225, 1325
Joint Administration	FRBP 1015
Debtor requested conversion	§§706(a), 1112(a), 1208(a), 1307(a)
Debtor requested dismissal	§§1208(b), 1307(b)
Approval of examiner or trustee	§1104; FRBP 2007.1
Extensions of time	FRBP 9006b
Rule 2004 examinations	FRBP 2004
Deferral of entry of discharge	FRBP 4004(c)
Reopening a closed case	§350(b)
Conditional approval of disclosure statement	§1125; FRBP 3017.1

Common Noticed Motions

Motion	*Code Section or FRBP*
Dismissal of Chapter 7 as abuse	§707(b)
Compensation of professionals	§§326, 330, 331, FRBP 2016
Enforcement of bankruptcy petition preparer rules	§110

Motion	*Code Section or FRBP*
Dismissal in best interests of creditors	§305
Motion to avoid lien	§522(f)
Objection to claim of exemptions	§522(c); FRBP 4003(d)
Appointment of trustee in involuntary case	§303(g); FRBP 2001
Motion to appoint trustee or examiner	§1104
Motion for relief from the automatic stay	§362(d); FRBP 4001
Turnover from debtor	§542; FRBP 7001(1)
Sales of property of $2,500 or more and when there is no co-owner	§363; FRBP 6004
Motion to use cash collateral	§363(c)
Motion to sell property free and clear of liens	§363(f); FRBP 6004(c)
Motion to assume or reject executory contract or unexpired lease	§365; FRBP 6006
Motion to compel abandonment	§554; FRBP 6007
Objection to claim	§502; FRBP 3007
Payment of administrative expenses	§503(a)
Valuation hearing	§506
Motion to dismiss/convert	§1112, 1307
Approval of insider compensation in Chapter 11 cases	FRBP 9014(a)
Extend or reduce exclusivity	§1121
Chapter 11 confirmation hearing	§1128

Note: A noticed motion must normally be served on all creditors, the trustee, and the United States Trustee, except for motions for relief from the automatic stay, which generally require service only upon the debtor, trustee, and any other party with an interest in any property subject to the motion (such as a junior mortgage). An ex parte application is normally served only upon the trustee and the United States Trustee and any party that has requested notice. In all situations, readers should consult any applicable local rules.

Appendix 3

Documents and Deadlines

Document	Authority
Petition	Official Form 1
Filing Fee	FRBP 1006
List of Creditors	FRBP 1007(a)(1) §521(a)(1)(A)
Statement of SSN	Official Form 21; FRBP 1007(f)
Credit counseling certificate	521(b)
List of 20 Largest Unsecured Claims — Chapter 11	FRBP 1007(d)
Corporate Debtor — Exhibit A	Official Form IX
Bankruptcy Petition Preparer/ Statement of Compensation	§110(h)

Document	Authority
Prepetition credit counseling	§109(h)
Debt relief agency disclosures/ signed contract	§§526-528

Document	Authority
Statement of Financial Affairs	§521(a)(1)(B), FRBP 1007(7)
Schedules of assets and liabilities	§521(a)(1)(B), FRBP 1007(b)
Schedule of current income and expenses	§707(b)(2)(c)
Certificate of debt relief disclosures and payments received within 60 days	§521(a) (1)
Statement of Compensation	§329; FRBP 2016
Plan Chapter 13	FRBP 3015

Document	Authority
Statement of Intention	§521(a)(2)
1st Plan Payment — Ch. 13	§1326(a)
DIP Bank Accounts — Ch. 11	§345
Retain Professionals. Pay Insiders — Ch. 11	§327
Commence Operating Reports — Ch. 11	FRBP 2015(a)

Time (Days) (approx.)	Event	Authority
0 A	Petition Filed	11 U.S.C. §301
10 B	Interim Trustee	11 U.S.C. §701
15 C	Notice to Creditors	11 U.S.C. §341 FRBP 2002, 2003
30		
40 D	Creditor Meeting	11 U.S.C. §341(a)
70 E	Objections to Exemptions	FRBP 4003 (30 days after "D")
90		
100 F	Objection to Discharge/ Dischargeability	FRBP 4004, 4007 (60 days after "D")
150 G	Discharge/ Reaffirmation	11 U.S.C. §524 FRBP 4004 Personal Financial Management Course 11 U.S.C. §727(a)(11)

Glossary

This glossary has been designed to accomplish two goals. The first is to define basic bankruptcy terms in as succinct a manner as possible. The second is to treat the glossary as a mini-index. At the end of each definition one or more numbers will appear in parentheses. The numbers correspond to the chapter or chapters of the text that contain the primary discussion of the term or phrase defined. Terms defined elsewhere in this glossary are italicized at their first mention within other definitions.

abandonment—the act of a *trustee* to remove from *property of the estate* assets that are burdensome or of inconsequential value to the estate. An asset with no *equity* or a meritless personal injury claim are common examples. Abandonment is governed by Section 554 of the Bankruptcy Code. (20)

absolute priority rule—prohibition against *confirmation* of a Chapter 11 *reorganization plan* if junior classes will receive dividends or retain interests and one or more senior classes has rejected the plan. (26)

accrual accounting—an accounting method that measures all financial transactions of an entity. A *debt* owed is an accrued expense. An account receivable is accrued income. (24)

adequate assurance—the providing of *adequate protection* to a nondebtor party to an *executory contract* subject to Bankruptcy Code Section 365. A *trustee* or *debtor-in-possession* assuming an executory contract must provide the nondebtor party to the contract with adequate assurance of future performance. An assignee of an executory contract must also provide adequate assurance of future performance. Providing adequate assurance includes curing existing defaults and convincing the creditor and the court that future performance will be rendered by the *debtor*. (19)

adequate protection—methods of protecting a *creditor's* interest in *property of the estate* during pendency of the *automatic stay*. The making of periodic payments or the providing of additional or replacement *collateral* are methods of adequate protection. Section 361 statutorily defines *adequate protection*. (12)

administrative expenses— generally, all expenses incurred by a bankruptcy *estate* after a bankruptcy filing. Trustee's fees, auctioneer fees, attorneys' fees, and postpetition rent are common Chapter 7 administrative expenses. (21)

adversary proceeding— a separate lawsuit filed in connection with a *bankruptcy proceeding*. For example, an action to set aside a *preference* is commenced as an adversary proceeding. A contested motion will be treated as an adversary proceeding pursuant to Federal Rule of Bankruptcy Procedure 9014. (12)

affiliate— a nondebtor entity owning or controlling 20 percent or more interest in a *debtor* or a debtor entity owning or controlling 20 percent or more interest in a nondebtor entity. Section 101(2) of the Bankruptcy Code defines *affiliate*. (6)

"after notice and a hearing"— a phrase statutorily defined in Section 102(1) of the Bankruptcy Code. Use of this or a similar phrase in any Bankruptcy Code provision triggers the notice requirements of Section 102(1), as placed into practice by Federal Rules of Bankruptcy Procedure 2002 and 9006. Generally, 23-day notice by mail to all *creditors* and *parties in interest* is necessary to properly accomplish many bankruptcy procedures. (5)

allowed claim— a *claim* entitled to receive a dividend from a bankruptcy *estate*. (21)

antecedent debt— a debt incurred or existing before the making of a transfer. (16)

Anti-Assignment Act— a federal statute, 41 U.S.C. §15, that prohibits the assignment of a federal government contract except upon the government's consent. (19)

Applicable Committment Period—the required length of time for a Chapter 13 repayment plan, dependent upon whether or not the debtor's income is higher or lower than the state median family income. If equal to or higher, the period is five years. If lower, the period is three years. (23)

assignment for the benefit of creditors— the assignment of assets to a third party, in trust, to sell the assets and apply the proceeds to the payment of *creditor* claims. (3)

assisted person—any person whose debts are primarily consumer debts and whose non-exempt assets are less than $150,000 pursuant to 11 U.S.C. §101(3). Assisted persons are entitled to written retainer agreements and prepetition written disclosures from *Debt Relief Agencies* pursuant to 11 U.S.C. §§527 and 528. (4, 6)

automatic stay— a statutory bar to the conducting of any collection activity by *creditors* after a bankruptcy petition has been filed. All litigation involving the *debtor* as a defendant is stayed. Foreclosures and repossessions are stayed. A creditor may seek relief from the stay in some situations. The automatic stay is one of the three major elements of debtor relief provided by the Bankruptcy Code and is the subject of Bankruptcy Code Section 362. (12)

avoidable preference— a prepetition transfer of *estate property* in full or partial payment of an antecedent *debt*, subject to the *trustee's avoiding powers*. Avoidable preferences are the subject of Bankruptcy Code Section 547. (16)

avoiding powers— the ability of a *trustee* to set aside certain pre- or postfiling transactions that might otherwise be valid under nonbankruptcy law. *Preferences*, *fraudulent transfers*, and the ability to set aside unauthorized postpetition transfers are the most common of the trustee's avoiding powers. (15)

Bankruptcy Act— the name of the bankruptcy laws in effect in the United States between 1898 and September 30, 1979. (1)

bankruptcy alternatives— assignments for the benefits of creditors, bulk sales, and composition agreements. (3)

bankruptcy assistance—goods or services provided to an *assisted person* for the purpose of providing advice, counsel, document preparation, or court appearance in a bankruptcy proceeding. (4, 6)

Bankruptcy Code— the name of the bankruptcy laws in effect in the United States since October 1, 1979. (1, 2)

bankruptcy petition preparer— a person other than an attorney or an attorney's employee who prepares for compensation a document for filing with the Bankruptcy Court. An unsupervised paralegal may be a bankruptcy petition preparer. Bankruptcy petition preparers are the subject of Bankruptcy Code Section 110. (7)

bankruptcy proceeding— A bankruptcy case filed pursuant to a particular Chapter of the Bankruptcy Code. Bankruptcy proceedings are Chapter 7 *liquidations* and the various *reorganization* proceedings provided for by Chapters 9, 11, 12, and 13. (2)

bankruptcy systems— the methods developed by societies to resolve the effects of financial crisis between *debtors* and *creditors*. (1)

bulk sale— a nonbankruptcy notice procedure affording *creditors* an opportunity to file *claims* when all or substantially all the assets of a *debtor* are sold at one time or to limited buyers. Bulk sales are the subject of Article 6 of the Uniform Commercial Code. (3)

capital asset— an asset used to operate a business, such as equipment or fixtures. (18)

cash accounting— an accounting method that measures the cash transactions (income and expenses) of an entity. (24)

cash collateral— cash, or its equivalent, in which a secured *creditor* may have an interest. Section 363(c) of the Bankruptcy Code restricts the use of cash collateral absent court approval. (18)

Chapter— a specific statutory division of the *Bankruptcy Code*. Three Chapters contain general rules applicable in all *bankruptcy proceedings* (1, 3, 5). The remaining five Chapters comprise the specific types of bankruptcy proceedings (7, 9, 11, 12, 13). (2)

Chapter 7 — a *bankruptcy proceeding* in which a *debtor* seeks to have nonexempt assets *liquidated* for the payment of dividends to *creditors*. Chapter 7 is the most common bankruptcy proceeding. (2, 4, 7)

Chapter 11— a *reorganization* proceeding available to any *debtor* qualified to be a Chapter 7 debtor. Chapter 11 is the most complex, time-consuming, and expensive of all *bankruptcy proceedings*. The goal of a Chapter 11 *debtor-in-possession* is to obtain confirmation of a *reorganization plan*, a judicially approved *composition agreement*. (1, 2, 24-26)

Chapter 13— a *reorganization* proceeding available for individuals with regular income whose unsecured debt is less than $307,675 and whose secured debt is less than $922,975. Chapter 13 is the most commonly filed reorganization proceeding. (23)

claim— a right to payment of any kind or a right to performance that may be compensated by damages. Section 101(4) of the Bankruptcy Code defines *claim*. (6)

claims bar date— a deadline set in a *bankruptcy proceeding* for *creditors* to file *claims*. A claim not filed before expiration of a claims bar date is subordinated to all timely filed claims. (21, 22)

claims docket— an itemized summary of *creditor claims* filed in a *bankruptcy proceeding*. (22)

collateral— an interest in property or other rights held by a secured *creditor* to secure repayment of a *debt*. For example, real property is normally collateral for a mortgage or deed of trust. (12, 21)

community claim— a *claim* enforceable against community property under nonbankruptcy law. Section 101(6) of the Bankruptcy Code defines *community claim*. (6)

Complaint to Avoid Discharge— an *adversary proceeding* initiated by a *trustee* to entirely avoid a *debtor's discharge*. (13)

Complaint to Avoid Dischargeability of a Debt— an *adversary proceeding* initiated by a *creditor* or *debtor* to determine the dischargeability of a specific *debt* pursuant to Bankruptcy Code Section 523(c).

A creditor must initiate such a complaint within 60 days of the date first set for the creditors meeting. A debtor may initiate such a complaint at any time. (13)

composition agreement— an agreement between a *debtor* and multiple *creditors* for the repayment of *debt.* The various *reorganization proceedings* of the Bankruptcy Code (Chapters 9, 11, 12, and 13) are judicially approved composition agreements. (1, 3)

confirmation— the act of obtaining court approval of a *reorganization plan* in the reorganization proceedings of Chapters 9, 11, 12, or 13. A confirmed reorganization plan creates a new binding contract between the *debtor* and all *creditors.* (1, 23-27)

confirmation packet— a group of documents, including a *Plan of Reorganization* and a *Disclosure Statement,* that are sent to creditors when authorized to solicit votes for or against a Chapter 11 plan. (25, 26)

consideration— the element of exchange in any contract. (16)

consolidation— a merger, by court order, of two or more related bankruptcy proceedings. Other than a husband and wife, who may file a *joint case*, consolidation is the only way in which multiple debtors may have their bankruptcy proceedings administered as if they were one debtor. Consolidation is the subject of Federal Rule of Bankruptcy Procedure 1015. (4)

consumer no asset bankruptcy— a Chapter 7 *bankruptcy proceeding* for an individual in which there are normally no assets available for distribution to *creditors.* A consumer no asset bankruptcy is the most common and simplest of all bankruptcy proceedings. (7)

contemporaneous exchange— the presence of consideration in the transfer of property from a debtor to a creditor. (16)

contested matter— an opposed motion. A contested matter is treated as an *adversary proceeding* pursuant to Federal Rule of Bankruptcy Procedure 9014. A contested matter is resolved by way of an *evidentiary hearing.* (12)

convenience class— a group of unsecured *claims* treated as a class for administrative convenience in a Chapter 11 *reorganization plan.* A convenience class may receive treatment that the Bankruptcy Code would otherwise prohibit. (25)

conversion— the act of converting a bankruptcy proceeding from one chapter to another. A typical scenario is a failed reorganization proceeding converted to a liquidation. (8, 23)

core proceeding— a matter arising before a Bankruptcy Court that involves the specific application of a Bankruptcy Code provision for its resolution. Bankruptcy Judges have jurisdiction over core proceedings, as described in 28 U.S.C. §157. For example, an action to *avoid* a *preference* is a core proceeding. (28)

cramdown— the act of obtaining *confirmation* of a *reorganization plan* over the objection of *creditors*. Different tests or procedures may be utilized to effectuate a cramdown on either secured or unsecured creditors. (23, 26, 27)

credit counseling agency—an agency approved by the *United States Trustee* pursuant to 11 U.S.C. §111, to provide prepetition credit counseling to consumer *debtors*. (4)

creditor— an entity with a *claim* arising before the filing of a bankruptcy petition. Section 101(9) of the Bankruptcy Code defines *creditor*. An entity that a *debt* is owed to is a creditor. (1, 6)

creditors meeting— see *meeting of creditors*.

current monthly income—the monthly income of a consumer *debtor* generally determined by the average of income received from all sources in the six months preceding the filing of a bankruptcy petition, as described in 11 U.S.C. §101(10A). *Current monthly income* is a key element in determining whether or not a consumer debtor is abusing Chapter 7 pursuant to *needs based bankruptcy*. (5)

custodian— a third party appointed to administer a *debtor's* assets in a nonbankruptcy context. A court-appointed receiver or assignee for the benefit of *creditors* are examples of custodians. This term distinguishes bankruptcy *trustees* from nonbankruptcy *fiduciaries*. Section 101(10) of the Bankruptcy Code defines *custodian*. (6)

debt— a liability upon a *claim*. Section 101(11) of the Bankruptcy Code defines *debt*. (6)

debt collection—the process of collecting a debt. (1)

debt relief agency—a bankruptcy attorney or *bankruptcy petition preparer* and any person providing bankruptcy assistance to *assisted persons* for money or other valuable consideration pursuant to 11 U.S.C. §101(12A). *Debt Relief Agencies* are subject to written retainer and disclosure requirements of 11 U.S.C. §§527 and 528. (4)

debtor— an entity that owes a *debt*. The entity filing a *voluntary bankruptcy* proceeding or against whom an order for relief is entered in an *involuntary bankruptcy* is known as the debtor. (1, 6)

debtor-in-possession— the *fiduciary* entity created by a *debtor* filing a Chapter 11 *reorganization* proceeding. (10)

debtor relief— what an individual filing personal bankruptcy seeks: a discharge, exemptions, and the benefits of the automatic stay. (1, 7)

disallowed claim— a *claim* not entitled to receive a dividend from a bankruptcy *estate*. (21)

discharge— legal relief from *debt* provided for by Section 524 of the Bankruptcy Code. The discharge is one of the three elements of *debtor* relief provided for in the Bankruptcy Code, the other two being *exemptions* and the *automatic stay*. In certain defined instances a debtor may not be entitled to a discharge. (1, 7, 13)

dischargeable debt— a *debt* subject to a *debtor's discharge*. The discharge relieves a debtor from legal liability for the debt. (7, 13)

Disclosure Statement— a document filed in a Chapter 11 proceeding that describes a *debtor-in-possession's reorganization plan*, its effect upon the *creditors*, the ability of the plan to be performed, and a comparison of the reorganization plan's repayment proposal to the results likely to be obtained in a Chapter 7 proceeding for the same debtor. The creditors of a Chapter 11 debtor-in-possession may not vote for or against the reorganization plan until the court approves the contents of the *Disclosure Statement* at a Disclosure Statement hearing. (25, 26)

disinterested person— The subject of Bankruptcy Code Section 101(14). A person who is not creditor, equity security holder, insider, or who does not have an interest materially adverse to an estate. Only disinterested persons may be employed by a bankruptcy estate or debtor-in-possession. (7, 24)

dismissal— the act of terminating a *bankruptcy proceeding*, the general effect of which is to restore the parties to their rights and liabilities as they existed prior to the bankruptcy filing. (8)

disposable income— all income not necessary for the maintenance or support of the debtor or a dependent of the debtor. (23)

domestic support obligation—obligations for alimony, support, or maintenance, regardless of when incurred. (6)

due process— notice and an opportunity to be heard. (5)

effective date of plan— a specific date upon which performance of a Chapter 11 plan begins. This date may be a specific date upon which a defined event occurs, such as an order of *confirmation* becoming final. (25)

Electronic Case Filing (ECF)— The name for online filing of documents with the bankruptcy court and accessibility thereto. A related system know as "Pacer" affords access to review of online court records. (30)

equity— the value in an asset over and above that of any *liens* or encumbrances, such as equity in a home or motor vehicle. This is sometimes also known as an equity cushion. (9, 21)

equity security holder— an entity owning an interest in a *debtor*. The shareholders of a corporate debtor are its equity security holders. The partners of a partnership are its equity security holders. Section 101(16) of the Bankruptcy Code defines *equity security holder*. (6)

estate— the *debtor's* property owned at the time of the bankruptcy filing. The estate is created by the filing of a *bankruptcy proceeding*. The estate is administered by the *trustee*. (14)

evidentiary hearing— a hearing held to take sworn testimony to permit a Bankruptcy Court to make a decision in a *contested matter* that is not a separate *adversary proceeding*. An evidentiary hearing is similar to a trial in a nonbankruptcy environment. A "trial" on a contested motion for relief from the *automatic stay* is properly called an *evidentiary hearing*. (12)

examiner—an individual appointed in a Chapter 11 proceeding to conduct an independent investigation of some or all of a *debtor's* financial affairs. (10)

exclusivity period— a period of time in a Chapter 11 proceeding when only the *debtor-in-possession* may file a *reorganization plan*. This period, as provided for in Section 1121 of the Bankruptcy Code, is the first 120 days from the entry of an order for relief. In *small business* cases, the period is 180 days. This period can be extended. The period terminates upon the appointment of a *trustee*. (25)

executory contract— contracts for which performance remains due to some extent on both sides. Franchise or license agreements are common executory contracts. Executory contracts are the subject of Bankruptcy Code Section 365. An executory contract may be assumed or rejected. (19)

exemptions— statutorily defined property that an individual *debtor* may protect from administration by a bankruptcy *estate*. Exempt property is not available for *liquidation* to pay a dividend to *creditors*; a debtor may keep exempt property. Exemptions are a primary element of debtor relief. (1, 9)

ex parte— an application made to the court without notice or with limited notice to limited parties. Ex parte applications are specifically permitted for various ministerial functions. In other circumstances, a legitimate extraordinary circumstance must exist for the court to consider ex parte relief. (5)

family farmer— a *debtor* meeting the filing qualifications for a Chapter 12 proceeding. A family farmer may be an individual, corporate, or partnership debtor. In the latter two instances, more than 50 percent of the ownership must belong to members of the same family. A qualified family farmer's total *debt* may not exceed $2,237,000 Section 101(17) of the Bankruptcy Code defines *family farmer*. (27)

family fisherman—a *debtor* meeting the qualifications for a Chapter 12 proceeding. A family fisherman may be individual, corporate, or partnership. In the latter two instances, at least 50 percent of the ownership must belong to the same family. A qualified family fisherman's total *debt* may not exceed $1,500,000 and at least 80 percent must be related to the fishing operation. (27)

feasibility requirement— finding that the Bankruptcy Court must make to permit confirmation of a Chapter 11 reorganization plan. (26)

federal exemptions— *exemptions* permitted under federal law, specifically, Section 522(d) of the Bankruptcy Code. (9)

federal judges— judges appointed to the federal bench pursuant to U.S. Const., art. III, §2. (28)

Federal Rules of Bankruptcy Procedure—national rules promulgated to govern practice in all *bankruptcy proceedings.* (4, 30)

fiduciary— an entity that holds assets in trust for another. A bankruptcy *trustee* is a fiduciary. (10)

first-day order— common name of orders entered within the first day or two of a large corporate Chapter 11 filing. (4, 24)

floating lien— a line of credit from a bank, financial institution, or other lender secured by the existing and after-acquired inventory, equipment, and proceeds of a *debtor's* business. (16)

fraudulent transfer— a *transfer* made by a *debtor* with an intent to hinder, delay, or defraud *creditors*. A transfer without reasonable or fair consideration made while a debtor is *insolvent* or that renders a debtor insolvent will also be fraudulent. Fraudulent transfers are the subject of Bankruptcy Code Section 548. Fraudulent transfers are one of the *trustee's avoiding powers*. (17)

fresh cash rule — portion of a debt incurred by use of a false written financial statement. (13)

fresh start— the phrase most frequently used colloquially to describe the basic elements of *debtor* relief: *discharge*, *exemptions*, and the *automatic stay*. (1, 2)

gap claim— a *claim* arising during the period of time between the filing of an involuntary petition and the entry of an order for relief. (4, 21)

gap period— the common term for the period of time between the filing of an involuntary petition and the entry of an order for relief. (4, 21)

health care business—a business that provides health care services. Special rules apply for a trustee's disposition of health care business records and for the placement of patients in alternative facilities. The court will appoint an *ombudsman* to speak for the best interests of the patients unless the court can find that such an appointment is not necessary. (10, 20)

homestead — an *exemption* permitted in an individual *debtor's* place of residence. Section 522(d)(1) of the Bankruptcy Code provides a federal homestead exemption. State law also provides homestead exemptions. (9)

impaired claim — a claim not paid according to its terms on the effective date of a Chapter 11 plan. For example, unsecured *creditors* who are to be paid over an extended period of time are impaired. An impaired class of claims is entitled to vote to accept or reject a Chapter 11 *reorganization plan.* (25)

insider — generally, an entity in control of a *debtor* or a debtor's relatives. The definition of an insider will vary depending upon the debtor's identity as an individual, partnership, or corporation. Section 101(30) of the Bankruptcy Code defines *insider.* (6)

insolvent — an entity is generally insolvent when its liabilities exceed its assets. Section 101(31) of the Bankruptcy Code defines *insolvency.* (6)

intellectual property — patents, copyrights, and trademarks. (19)

interim trustee — the *trustee* appointed by the *United States Trustee* to administer a bankruptcy *estate* prior to the *meeting of creditors* called for by Section 341(a) of the Bankruptcy Code. The interim trustee will become the permanent trustee unless the creditors elect a different trustee at the meeting of creditors. (7)

inventory — any form of personal property that a debtor uses to produce revenue. (16)

involuntary bankruptcy — a *bankruptcy proceeding* initiated by one or more *creditors* (or general partners of a partnership) by filing a petition seeking the entry of an order for relief, a judgment that the *debtor* is bankrupt. Also known as an involuntary petition. Section 303 of the Bankruptcy Code governs involuntary petitions. (4)

ipso facto clause — a clause in a contract defining insolvency or a bankruptcy filing as an act of default. These clauses generally are not enforceable in *bankruptcy proceedings.* (14, 19)

joint case — a *bankruptcy proceeding* involving an individual and the individual's spouse. (4)

judicial lien —a *lien* arising by virtue of a court order or judgment. A judicial lien may be a prejudgment writ of attachment or a postjudgment writ of execution. Section 101(32) of the Bankruptcy Code defines *judicial lien.* (6)

lien — a right to property to secure repayment of a *debt* or the performance of an obligation. A lien may be a *judicial*, consensual, or *statutory lien.* Section 101(33) of the Bankruptcy Code defines *lien.* (6)

liquidation — the sale of an *estate's* assets to repay *creditors.* A Chapter 7 bankruptcy is a *liquidation* proceeding. (1, 23)

liquidation analysis — portion of a *Disclosure Statement* comparing a *reorganization plan* to the results likely to be obtained if the case were a *Chapter 7.* (26)

liquidation value — the value to be obtained from a forced sale of assets. (9)

mandatory provision — a provision in a *reorganization plan* required by the Bankruptcy Code. (23, 25)

market value — the value of an asset, real or personal, sold in the ordinary course of business according to commercially reasonable terms. (9)

means test—see *needs based bankruptcy*.

median family income—the most current figures provided by the Bureau of the Census as set forth in 11 U.S.C. §101(39A). The amount of median family income determines whether or not a debtor is subject to *needs based bankruptcy* analysis. (5)

meeting of creditors — a mandatory hearing, held within 40 days after the entry of an order for relief in any Chapter proceeding. At the meeting of creditors, the *trustee* and *creditors* may examine the *debtor* regarding the assets and liabilities of the bankruptcy *estate*. Section 341(a) of the Bankruptcy Code mandates the meeting of creditors. (7)

motion for relief from the automatic stay — a motion made by a *creditor*, pursuant to 11 U.S.C. §362(d), to be freed from the effect of the *automatic stay*. (12)

needs based bankruptcy—also known as "means testing." Title given to formula contained in 11 U.S.C. §707(b)(2) to determine whether or not a consumer debtor is presumed to be abusing the bankruptcy system by filing a Chapter 7. Abuse is presumed when a debtor's *current monthly income* exceeds the state *median family income* and the debtor can repay unsecured creditors at least $100 per month over 60 months and a dividend of at least 25%, or can repay unsecured creditors at least $10,000 over 60 months without regard to the percentage repaid. Where abuse is presumed, the case will be dismissed unless the debtor consents to conversion to Chapter 13. (5, Appendix 1)

new value — the providing of new consideration in a transaction between a *debtor* and *creditor*. An *avoidable preference* will generally not exist where a transaction occurs for new value. This definition is unique to avoidable preferences. (16)

noncapital asset — an asset not used to operate a business. For example, inventory is generally a noncapital asset. (18)

noncore proceedings — matters that are related to a bankruptcy proceeding but that do not require specific application of a Bankruptcy Code provision for the matter's resolution. (28)

nondischargeable debt — a *debt* not subject to a *debtor's discharge*, a debtor is not relieved from legal liability for the affected debt. Some types of nondischargeable debts require the filing of a Complaint to Determine Dischargeability of Debt for the debt to become nondischargeable. Nondischargeable debts are described in Bankruptcy Code Section 523(a). (13)

nonpurchase money security interest — a security interest in collateral where the purpose of the loan is other than to purchase the collateral. (9)

nonresidential lease — a real property lease obtained for purposes other than to reside in the leased premises. The lease of a store is a common nonresidential real property lease. (14)

notice and a hearing — Bankruptcy Code phrase, which triggers some form of due process, such as a noticed motion, notice of intent, or exparte application. (5)

notice of intent — the common method of providing notice to *creditors*, when required, to properly accomplish a bankruptcy procedure. This procedure is also sometimes known as a "notice of intended action." Generally, 23 days' notice by mail upon all creditors and *parties in interest* is necessary to properly accomplish many bankruptcy procedures. (5)

noticed motion — a motion brought by a party in interest seeking a ruling from the Bankruptcy Court. (5)

Official Creditors Committee — entity created in a Chapter 11 proceeding to act on the collective behalf of unsecured *creditors*. (10)

ombudsman—an independent person who may be appointed to serve the best interests of patients in the bankruptcy of a *health care business*. An *ombudsman* may also be appointed to report to the court on the protection of *personally identifiable information* in the sale of customer lists. (10, 20)

operating reports — a regular report of a Chapter 11 *debtor-in-possession's* postpetition financial activity. Local rules will normally require the filing of monthly reports. (24)

Order for Relief — a statutory term of art, which signifies that a debtor has obtained bankruptcy relief. (4)

ordinary course of business — generally, normal everyday business transactions. (18, 20)

party in interest — a party with a stake in the outcome of a *bankruptcy proceeding*. The *debtor*, *creditors*, *trustee*, *United States Trustee*, and *equity security holders* are all parties in interest. (2, 10)

permissive provision — a provision in a reorganization that is not mandatory. (23, 25)

person — any kind of entity, individual, corporate, or partnership, except a governmental unit. Section 101(35) of the Bankruptcy Code defines *person* for purposes of the Bankruptcy Code. (6)

personally identifiable information—information that may generally be used to contact or locate an individual, such as name and address, social security number, date of birth, and other similar information. (6)

petitioning creditors — creditors initiating an involuntary petition against a debtor. (4)

plan — a Chapter 13 plan (23)

Plan of Reorganization — common title of a Chapter 11 *reorganization plan*. (25)

postpetition transaction — a *transfer* of *estate property* after a bankruptcy filing that is made without court approval or is not otherwise authorized by the Bankruptcy Code. An unauthorized postpetition transaction may be *avoided* by a bankruptcy *trustee*. Postpetition transactions are the subject of Bankruptcy Code Section 549. (17)

preference — a *transfer* of property or an interest in property to a *creditor*, on the eve of bankruptcy, in full or partial satisfaction of *debt* to the exclusion of other creditors. A preference meeting certain defined conditions will be avoidable by a bankruptcy *trustee*. (16)

prepackaged bankruptcy — an effort at a composition agreement, which nonetheless ends up in Bankruptcy Court. (26)

prepetition credit counseling—counseling that a debtor must receive from a *credit counseling agency* as a prerequisite to seeking individual bankruptcy relief. (4)

priority claim — a *claim* given priority over other unsecured claims. Section 507(a) of the Bankruptcy Code describes priority claims. Tax claims and certain wage claims are common priority claims. (21)

professional —an attorney, accountant, auctioneer, appraiser, and the like. A professional rendering services to a bankruptcy *estate* must be approved by the court for the services to be compensable. The fees of a professional rendering services to a bankruptcy estate are subject to court approval by way of a fee application as described in Bankruptcy Code Sections 330 and 331. (7).

pro forma — a financial forecast of future performance over a period of time. Pro formas are frequently used in Chapter 11 plan practice. (26)

proof of claim — the filing of a formal written *claim* by a *creditor* in a *bankruptcy proceeding*. A proof of claim must always be filed in a Chapter 7 proceeding for a claim to be entitled to receive a dividend. It is always wise to file a proof of claim on behalf of a creditor. (21)

property of the estate—property subject to administration by a bankruptcy trustee for the distribution of dividends to *creditors*. (14)

proponent—the *party in interest* proposing a specific *reorganization plan* in a Chapter 11 proceeding. Also known as a *plan proponent.* (25)

pro rata—a distribution to *creditors* within a given class on a proportional basis. (3, 22)

purchase money security interest—a security interest in collateral when the purpose of the loan is to purchase the collateral. (9)

reaffirmation—a *debtor's* agreement to remain legally liable for repayment of a *debt* otherwise *dischargeable* in a *bankruptcy proceeding*. For a debt to be legally reaffirmed, strict compliance with the provisions of Bankruptcy Code Section 524 is required. (7)

receivable—a right to payment, whether or not such right has been earned by performance. (16)

redemption—a right given a Chapter 7 consumer *debtor* to pay a lump sum to a secured *creditor* in an amount equal to the value of any *collateral.* A valuation hearing may be necessary to determine the adequacy of the redemption amount. Section 722 of the Bankruptcy Code permits redemption. (21)

regular income—income sufficient and stable enough to support performance of a Chapter 13 plan by an individual. Regular income is not limited to wages or salary. Pension, social security, and commissission income may all constitute regular income for Chapter 13 purposes. (5)

reorganization—a *bankruptcy proceeding* where a *debtor* seeks *confirmation* of a plan that will repay *creditors* while permitting the debtor to retain assets or continue in business. The proceedings permitted by Chapters 9, 11, 12, and 13 of the Bankruptcy Code are reorganization proceedings. (1, 23)

reorganization plan—a repayment plan prepared according to the requirements of Chapter 11 of the Bankruptcy Code. (25)

residential real property—real property in which a *debtor* resides. (19)

Rule 2004 examination—an extended examination of any *person* pursuant to Federal Rule of Bankruptcy Procedure 2004 regarding one or more aspects of a *debtor's* financial affairs. A Rule 2004 examination is similar to a deposition in nonbankruptcy proceedings. (7)

sale free and clear of liens—a sale held pursuant to 11 U.S.C. §363(f). Such a sale seeks court approval to sell liened property over the objection of any lienholder. (18)

Schedules of Assets and Liabilities—a fundamental bankruptcy pleading consisting of a prioritized and itemized list of a *debtor's* assets (property) and liabilities (*debt*). (4, 29)

secured creditor — a creditor with collateral that may satisfy part or all of the creditor's *allowed claim.* (21)

security — commercial documents used to evidence an ownership interest in an entity, among other things. Section 101(43) of the Bankruptcy Code defines *security*. (6)

security agreement — an agreement creating a security interest. A *security interest* is a consensual *lien* created by agreement. Section 101(44) of the Bankruptcy Code defines *security agreement.* (6)

serial filing or serial bankruptcy— a debtor who files a second (or third) bankruptcy proceeding after dismissal of one or more prior proceedings. (5)(12)

setoff — the common law right of a *creditor* to balance mutual *debts* with a *debtor*. (17)

single asset real estate — real property that generates substantially all the gross income of a *debtor* and on which no substantial business is conducted other than operation of the property and activities thereto, not including *residential real property* with three or fewer units. Single asset real estate is the subject of Bankruptcy Code Section 101(51B). (6, 12)

small business debtor — a Chapter 11 debtor with liquidated debts not in excess of $2 million who elects treatment as a small business debtor, excluding a *debtor* whose primary activity is owning and operating real estate. Small business debtors are the subject of Bankruptcy Code Section 101(51C). (10, 24)

solvent estate — an *estate* capable of paying all claims in full and returning assets to the *debtor*. (22)

spendthrift trust — a trust containing a clause precluding invasion of the trust assets to satisfy the debts of a beneficiary. (14)

stacking — individual joint debtors claiming state and federal exemptions. (9)

Statement of Financial Affairs — a fundamental bankruptcy pleading consisting of a questionnaire concerning a *debtor's* financial affairs. (4, 23, 29)

Statement of Intention — a notice to be given, within 30 days after a filing, to the holders of collateral security the repayment of consumer debt. The debtor must advise any affected creditor of the debtor's intention regarding the collateral. The debtor may reaffirm the contact, redeem or return the collateral, or avoid the lien under specific defined circumstances. (21)

Statements and Schedules — common name of the Statement of Financial Affairs and Schedules of Assets and Liabilities filed by any *debtor* within the *bankruptcy system*. These pleadings will be the most important initial pleadings in any *bankruptcy proceeding*. (4, 29)

statutory lien — a *lien* created by operation of law other than a court order. A state law mechanic's lien is a *statutory lien*. Section 101(47) of the Bankruptcy Code defines *statutory lien*. (6)

strip off/strip down—ability to avoid the unsecured portion of an otherwise secured debt in some circumstances in Chapter 13 cases. (21, 23)

strong arm clause—the trustee's rights as a super-creditor, which are contained in the Bankrukptcy Code Section 544. (15)

subordination—the relegation of a *claim* to a lesser status than it is otherwise entitled to under the Bankruptcy Code. A *creditor* may consent to subordination or the court may order subordination for equitable reasons. Subordination is the subject of Section 510. (21)

substantially consummated—the taking of an irrevocable act in performance of a Chapter 11 Plan, such as closing escrow or repaying a substantial portion of a dividend. (26)

substantially contemporaneous—an exchange taking place in the normal course of business. (16)

30/30/30 rule—time periods within which a *motion for relief from the automatic stay* must be resolved, as described in Bankruptcy Code Section 362(e). (12)

transfer—any means that may be devised of to dispose of property or an interest in property. This is an intentionally broad definition. Section 101(50) of the Bankruptcy Code defines *transfer*. (6)

trustee—a *fiduciary* appointed by the *United States Trustee* to administer a bankruptcy *estate*. (7, 10)

turnover—the right of a bankruptcy *trustee* under 11 U.S.C. §542 to recover property of an *estate* in the possession of the *debtor* or other third party. A trustee generally obtains a turnover by filing a turnover complaint. (14)

undersecured creditor—a secured creditor whose collateral is worth less than the total amount of its allowed claim. (21)

unimpaired claim—a *claim* paid according to its terms on the effective date of a Chapter 11 *reorganization plan*. For example, if a *debtor-inpossession* pays all unsecured claims in full on the effective date of a plan, the claims are unimpaired. An unimpaired class of claims will be deemed to have accepted a Chapter 11 plan. (25)

United States Trustee—a division of the Department of Justice responsible for monitoring the administration of bankruptcy *estates*. (10)

unlisted debt—a debt not included in a debtor's schedules. (13)

valuation hearing—a hearing held, pursuant to 11 U.S.C. §506, to determine the value of a secured *creditor's collateral*. (21)

venue—the proper Bankruptcy Court (federal district) in which a *bankruptcy proceeding* should be commenced. Generally, venue is where the *debtor* resides or where the debtor business's primary business address or assets are located. Venue may be changed by a motion of a *party in interest.* (4)

voluntary bankruptcy—a *bankruptcy proceeding* initiated by a *debtor* filing a petition for relief. Also known as a voluntary petition. Most bankruptcy proceedings are voluntary. (4)

Table of Cases

Table of Statutes

United States Constitution

Statutes at Large and Public Laws

United States Code

Uniform Commercial Code

Miscellaneous State Statutes

English Statutes

Other

Table of Federal Rules of Bankruptcy Procedure

Local Bankruptcy Rules

Table of Secondary Authorities

Index